SCHUBERT

SCHUBERT

The Music and the Man

BRIAN NEWBOULD

University of California Press

BERKELEY   LOS ANGELES

University of California Press
Berkeley and Los Angeles, California

Published by arrangement with Victor Gollancz

© 1997 by Brian Newbould

Library of Congress Cataloging-in-Publication Data
Newbould, Brian, 1936–
Schubert, the music and the man / Brian Newbould.
p.   cm.
"List of works"; p.
Includes bibliographical references and index.
ISBN 0-520-21065-4 (cloth)
1. Schubert, Franz, 1797–1828—Criticism and
interpretation. I. Title.
ML410.S3N48   1997
780'.92—dc21

[B]   96-49876
                                                         CIP

Picture acknowledgements
Page 1: top, Bildarchiv der Österreichischen
Nationalbibliothek, Wien; bottom, AKG/Erich Lessing. Page 2:
top, AKG/Erich Lessing; middle, Mansell Collection; bottom,
Mary Evans Picture Library. Page 3: top, AKG Photo; middle
and bottom, Bildarchiv der Österreichischen
Nationalbibliothek. Page 4: top left, AKG/ Erich Lessing; top
right, Frau Helene von Ravenstein, Carlsruhe; bottom, Hulton
Getty. Page 5: Bibliotek Jagiellonska, Cracow. Page 6: top,
middle and bottom, AKG/Erich Lessing. Page 7: top left and
right, AKG/Erich Lessing; bottom, Mansell Collection. Page 8:
top, Bildarchiv der Österreichischen Nationalbibliothek;
bottom, Pierpont Morgan Library, New York.

Printed in the United Kingdom
9   8   7   6   5   4   3   2

It was clear that he really did nothing but music – and lived by the way, as it were.

Ferdinand Hiller

Music was the atmosphere in which he lived and breathed, in which his subjectivity unconsciously attained its highest development, and in which his whole being attained a state of ecstasy.

Louis Schlösser

Even with his intimates . . . he was silent and uncommunicative, except in matters which concerned that Divinity to whom he dedicated his short but entire life . . . On the walks which the pupils took together, he mostly kept apart, walking pensively along with lowered eyes and with his hands behind his back, playing with his fingers (as though on keys), completely lost in his own thoughts.

Franz Eckel

The composer and writer Ferdinand Hiller, a pupil of Hummel, visited Schubert in 1827. Louis Schlösser, a violinist and composer who studied with Salieri in Vienna, knew Schubert in his last years. Franz Eckel was a fellow-pupil of Schubert's at the Stadtkonvikt, who later became Director of the Vienna Veterinary Institution.
Otto Erich Deutsch (ed.), *Schubert: Memoirs by his Friends* (London, 1958), pp. 284, 329 and 50.

Contents

Introduction

It may not be entirely coincidental that the unprecedented growth in Schubert research witnessed in the last quarter of the twentieth century came in a period framed by two anniversaries. In the early 1970s the imminence of the 150th anniversary of the composer's death (1978) stimulated preparations which, particularly but not only in the Vienna libraries, led to a re-examination of the documentary inheritance, the re-evaluation of old documents and discovery of new ones, and the production of new or updated listings. The publication of the second edition of Deutsch's Catalogue of the composer's works was one significant outcome. The next twenty-year period saw a proliferation of research on several fronts – archival, papyrological, graphological, biographical and iconographical, to identify some characteristic strands (performance practice must be added too). At the same time, those analysts of music who are driven by an absorption in analytical methodology and, more lately, by a concern with gender issues have lighted upon the Schubert oeuvre with relish. Through all of this period, the dominant format of research or analytical findings was the academic article, the scholarly edition, the realization of a sketch.

Much of this material was slow to penetrate the consciousness of Schubertians who were not also musicologists, for reasons which were sometimes understandable. A different market was served by the flow of coffee-table productions and biographies, in which the music (with few exceptions) took second place. A rapprochement between the two media – the short, close scholarly study and the readable catch-all exposition – remained a largely neglected aim, except in the compact context of the occasional programme note and record liner note. In these circumstances it takes some temerity to pursue that path between the covers of a hefty 'critical biography' which attempts to revive the fortunes of a genre conventionally addressed to a wide readership.

But the present work is not intended to fit the traditional mould of critical biography, which in the case of a prolific composer contents itself with a sentence or two on even a major work, and a meagre ration of music examples. The supply of biographical fact about Schubert is relatively small when set against the vastness of his life's work – roughly one thousand works squeezed out of an active composing existence of a mere eighteen years if we admit the earliest juvenilia of a fourteen-year-old into the canon. And it is the musical product, with its enduring power to enhance the times we distant generations spend on earth, that gives his life its interest to us. If, in that sense, the music dwarfs the man, let that be reflected in the title, subject-focus and interior proportions of this study.

No writer at this stage in the affairs of Schubert can but owe an enormous debt of gratitude to those who have gone before, and none went before with such a combination of industry, patience and wisdom as Otto Erich Deutsch, on whose foundation so much has been and will be built. Deutsch was concerned principally, of course, to sort, list and interpret documents, to locate musical sources, and to attempt a chronological catalogue of all the works. He provides the biographical bones, and the starting point for a study of the music. For models in the study of Schubert's music one looks elsewhere. One attempt to come to grips with the whole corpus of his music remains a guiding beacon to the latter-day venturer, despite the fact that it is half a century out of date – a half-century that has changed our knowledge of all areas of Schubert's extensive repertory. The fact that so much of the symposium (*Schubert*) edited by Gerald Abraham and published in 1946 can be read with pleasure today is a tribute to the philosophy that inspired it as well as to the insight of those who wrote it. A single-author assault on similar objectives, with biography interwoven, is no doubt a foolhardy undertaking, but it is hoped that it will offer something to the keen listener, the student, and the professional musician wishing to compare thoughts with those of one who has enjoyed a hands-on relationship with Schubert's music for twenty years as well as being an enthralled listener for more than forty.

Since the 1920s, when the musical *Das Dreimäderlhaus* hit the stage (reaching the English-speaking world as *Lilac Time* or, in the USA, *Blossom Time*), the notion of Schubert as a podgy, love-lorn Bohemian *Schwammerl* (mushroom) who scribbled *gemütlich* tunes on the back of menus in idle moments has never been quite eradicated. Popular misconceptions have a way of lingering; moreover, the time-gap between scholarly revelation and public awareness is long (witness the number of published references to the 'Great' C major Symphony during the 1980s and 1990s as having been composed in 1828, long after that date had been discredited on several counts in the 1970s). Schubert did have his loves, he was five foot tall, and he could compose at speed if 'composing' means putting pen to paper (though we cannot know how much of the composing was done mentally before pen and paper were taken). But what went for the dances and the shorter, simpler songs (even for the 'Trout' Quintet) did not hold for the greatest instrumental works, or even for some of the finest of the songs. The idea of the composer plucking melodies out of the air, relying on instinct more than well-honed craft, in contradistinction to Beethoven's way of dripping perspiration into sketchbooks as he sculpted this and that detail to perfection with a fine chisel, dies hard.

Many Schubert songs exist in two or more versions, and not only because when he 're-composed' a song from memory for a friend who asked for a copy of a recent product his memory played tricks (not surprisingly in view of the volume of music he had probably composed in the intervening days or hours). Sometimes second versions incorporate inspired, deliberately bidden second thoughts. Many well-known works were the result of extensive sketching. Even when he composed a symphony directly into score, as with the 'Great' C major, the autograph shows layers of addition and correction made over many months. The third movement of the 'Tenth' Symphony, with its contrapuntal ingenuities, required careful testing of possibilities before even a first two-stave continuity draft could be begun. In his 'Wanderer' Fantasy Schubert generates a mirror image of one passage as the basis of a later passage – a calculated device the likes of which will probably not be found in the scores of Beethoven himself. And if he was incapable of the painstaking work associated with Beethoven, how did he create, in one of his operas (*Die Zauberharfe* – The Magic Harp), the only true, orchestral palindrome in the whole of nineteenth-century music, in which nineteen bars of music are repeated with not only melody and rhythm but harmony too reversed?

The analytical discovery of such remarkable features as these in Schubert's scores, in the last quarter of the twentieth century, owes nothing to Schenkerian analysis nor to the other specialist techniques which have attracted a following during this period. There is still much to be said about Schubert's music which depends on honest-to-goodness musicianship and powers of observation, in which regard the 'methods' are a distraction rather than a help. Readers who regard Schenker-graphs as indispensable to any commentary on music need read no further. There will, however, be demands placed on the reader's understanding or tolerance from time to time by the author's refusal to overlook the fact that, if Schubertians were asked what characteristics of Schubert's music most appeal to them, many would include harmony and key-relations in their answer. These are the most difficult aspects of music to talk or write about without resorting to technical language. It is hoped that an acceptable solution has been the relegation of any prolonged commentary on harmonic matters to a chapter concerned with technicalities alone (Chapter 23; see page 389), and the inclusion of a glossary (page 444) to help those less experienced in the time-saving jargon to appreciate the occasional technical references elsewhere in the book.

Two issues concerning Schubert the man have come to the fore and been debated at length in recent years – the cause of his death and the question of his sexual orientation. Did he die of syphilis or of some other ailment? Was he gay? The evidence will be reviewed at the appropriate places. Since no one has yet demonstrated that there is an identifiably gay way of proportioning a sonata movement, structuring a cadence, arguing a fugue or handling a symphony orchestra, the question of sexuality would seem to have little bearing on our consideration of Schubert's music, although it could have affected his choice of song texts in some instances. Claims to the contrary will have to overcome a widespread, deep-seated scepticism among those who doubt whether earlier generations of Schubert-lovers – should it now be proved that Schubert was homosexual – will have taken with them to the grave a false appreciation of his music.

The aims of this study are, first, to share a lifelong love of the best products of Schubert's unique genius; second, to offer a conspectus of the composer's output, in which ghetto treatment of the genres is minimized so that the songs and sonatas, for example, are seen as one outcome of the same overarching musical impulse that gave rise to the symphonies, masses, chamber music, operas and dances; and third, to take account of recent developments in Schubert scholarship which may permanently change or enhance our experience of his sublime art in time to come. The second of these aims is paramount. Schubert did not regard himself as a song-composer who also wrote sonatas, or a symphonist who tried his hand at masses, dances and quartets. He saw himself as a composer, and was a devoted, workaholic example of the species, combining the relish and wonder of an amateur with the discipline and technical rigour of a professional. He was prolific to a fault, moving comfortably and quickly between the genres and leaving yesterday's effort unfinished if he had reached an impasse or a new venture enticed him away. Accounts of his strict working regime, with long mornings given to composing, are credible: yet, although he clearly found time to develop his strong literary interests, to enjoy the company of friends, to take country walks, to attend concerts and operas, and to frequent inns and coffee-houses, it is unthinkable in the light of his productivity that during or between those activities he was not in effect extending his working day by mentally continuing his morning's brief or conceiving what would be committed to paper at the next opportunity.

No writer is an island, and I cannot begin to count my debts to friends near and far, amateur and professional, living and late. Certain preparatory tasks would have been much harder to accomplish without the New Schubert Edition (alas, still uncompleted), John Reed's compendious *Schubert Song Companion*, Graham Johnson's comprehensive song recordings for Hyperion, or the many fine performers on whom we depend to keep the repertory alive, and many of whom make their own contribution –

not necessarily consciously – to Schubert scholarship. The translations of song-texts used are taken with kind permission from Richard Wigmore's estimable volume (*Schubert: The Complete Song Texts*, Gollancz, 1988). Richard Wigmore himself, as my editor, has taken a constructive and valued interest in the book's progress, showing particular forbearance in its closing stages. I am greatly indebted to Katrina Whone and Elizabeth Dobson who, for the publisher, brought so much skill and commitment to bear on the task of bringing the project through to publication. Thanks are also due to colleagues in the University of Hull, for funding research in Vienna and facilitating study leave in times of acute pressure on British university staff, and to my students for accepting some disruption caused by my recurring absenteeism. My wife, Ann, and daughter, Fiona, showed philosophic resilience as my study consumed me and a rainforest for days at a time over a period of years: to them, and to all who have tasted what it is that draws the human soul into communion with Schubert, the following chapters are dedicated.

1

1797–1813

Vienna was something of a racial melting-pot at the end of the eighteenth century. It was home not only to immigrants from the outer reaches of the Empire it dominated, including territories formerly and/or latterly Hungarian or Czechoslovakian, but also to Italians, Germans, Croatians, Poles, Greeks, Turks and others – 40,000 of them (about a fifth of the total population).[1] The 'Viennese Classical style' was even more dependent on immigrant endeavour than was the city which lent it its name. It was established by composers who were not Viennese by birth; and it was polyglot in origin. Haydn came to Vienna from Rohrau, near the Hungarian border, and absorbed some local colour from his employment close to where the respective parts of the Austro-Hungarian Empire met; Mozart's birthplace was Salzburg, two days to the west by stagecoach, but there was a strong Italian ingredient in his musical make-up, and his travels enabled him – or his chosen operatic libretti required him – to assimilate elements of alien cultures, from France, Czechoslovakia (as it was to become), Turkey and elsewhere; and Beethoven brought with him from the Rhineland a North German training and outlook. Even the attendant figures we now regard as lesser lights in the music of the imperial capital were anything but indigenous. Gluck was born in Bavaria and spent his childhood near Prague, Hummel hailed from Bratislava, Krommer spent his youth around his native Brno, the Bavarian Franz Lachner (Schubert's friend and drinking companion) left Munich for Vienna at the age of twenty, Koželuh was born near Prague and moved to Vienna at the age of thirty-one, and Salieri spent his first sixteen years in his native Italy – not that any of these composers contributed significantly to the formation of the Viennese Classical style.

It was fortunate that all these composers converged on Vienna, for the richness of the city's thus implanted culture was to be a boon to the only proponent of the Viennese Classical style who was truly Viennese. But even he, Franz Schubert, was only of the first generation of Schuberts to be born there. And because his earliest masterpieces entailed the union of musical and literary art, as well as for other possible reasons, some would hesitate to align him with Viennese Classical objectives at all. There is abundant cause to override such hesitation, as will be seen later.

Schubert's father had come to Vienna only in 1783. Franz Theodor
Florian Schubert (1763–1830) was the schoolteacher son of a Moravian
peasant farmer, and he came to Vienna in the footsteps of his elder brother
Carl (1755–1804), who was already established as headmaster of the Car-
melite School in the suburb of Leopoldstadt (in which the Prater now
lies). Franz Theodor took up the appointment of assistant to Carl early in
1784. In the same year he met Elisabeth Vietz (1766–1812), whose father
Johann Franz Vietz, a locksmith and gunmaker, had emigrated to Vienna
two years previously from Zuckmantel in north-eastern Silesia. Johann
Franz, a sick fugitive who had served a prison sentence for financial mal-
practice, died within hours of reaching Vienna, leaving Elisabeth and her
sister Marie and brother Felix to make their own way in the world. The
two sisters entered domestic service while Felix became a weaver. The
three of them (their mother was also dead) settled in Lichtental, where
there was a flourishing weaving trade.

Franz Theodor and Elisabeth married in January 1785, in the parish
church at Lichtental, and only two months later the first of their children,
Ignaz, was born. Elisabeth Schubert, like any good Catholic mother of the
time, would labour oft, but for little ultimate return. There were to be
fourteen births, but nine of the children died in infancy. Ignaz was one
of the lucky ones, along with Ferdinand (b. 1794), Carl (1795), Franz
Peter (1797) and Maria Theresia (1801).

Franz Peter was born on 31 January and baptized into the Catholic faith
the following day. His father was by now well established as a teacher in
the Himmelpfortgrund district, in the parish of Lichtental, teaching and
living in a building called the Red Crayfish (Zum roten Krebsen), which
is now 54 Nussdorferstrasse. The Schuberts occupied a one-room apartment on the first floor, comprising a small kitchen with open fire leading
off a larger room. Access to the apartment was by a covered walkway
having one side open to the elements, and it was no more than ordinary
maternal prudence that planned the January birth in the heated kitchen
recess.

In this cramped setting our composer first saw the light of day, such as
it would have been at 1.30 p.m. on a January afternoon. The conditions
were not necessarily worse than they were for most of the city's quarter
of a million inhabitants. An English musician, Edward Holmes, visited
Vienna in 1827 and described it as 'a small city, thickly inhabited; its walls
enclose more men and buildings than can be found in the same space in
any other capital I have visited'. He admired the Graben, the broad central
street close to St Stephen's Cathedral, but deplored the 'detestable stench'
of some of the narrower ones.[2] In the Himmelpfortgrund alone, 3000
people lived in 86 houses on 9 streets. They were accustomed to the

hazards of life – overcrowding, lack of sanitation, the prevalence of irre-
mediable diseases, poor healthcare in general; and they knew the hazards
of birth – new babies had a less than even chance of survival. Franz was
to reach manhood unscathed, and would perhaps have matched his brother
Ferdinand's lifespan of 65 years, if not his sister's remarkable 77, had he
not fallen victim to the hazards which Vienna put in the path even of
adults.

It should be remembered that the composer's parents were not merely
immigrants, but were both natives of that part of the Austro-Hungarian
Empire that was subsequently to become Czechoslovakia. A later composer
who idolized Schubert and absorbed certain influences from him was
Dvořák, and it is tempting to think that, for all that the cosmopolitan
musical environment and repertory of Vienna helped shape Schubert's
style, there were in his musical personality also hereditary strands from the
more northerly culture, which Dvořák intuitively recognized as familial in
a national sense.

Franz Theodor's school flourished, thanks to hard work and a growing
clientele, and he was soon in a position to take out a mortgage on a house
at 3 Säulengasse nearby. These larger, two-storey premises, with central
courtyard, housed both the school (on the ground floor) and the Schuberts'
living quarters above. The family moved in during the autumn of 1801,
and it was here that the young Franz grew up, leaving to take up residence
at the City Seminary in 1808 but returning from time to time until the
year 1818, when his father was offered a teaching post in the Rossau district
and took up residence there.

In the Säulengasse house (Zum schwarzen Rössel – the Black Horse),
Franz Theodor's school roll steadily grew, reaching 40 in 1804 and 300 in
1805. His son Franz became a pupil there himself in 1803, and it is reported
that he outshone his fellow pupils. He will have had a thorough grounding
in the basic schoolroom skills, for his father was the well-educated product
of the Brno Gymnasium (grammar school) who evidently ran a disciplined
establishment, while an education act passed in 1805 required teachers to
teach by the book and insist on rote learning.[3] Musical education was more
a matter for family and friends. Brother Ignaz, twelve years Franz's senior,
gave him his first piano lessons; but, as Ignaz later revealed, '. . . after only
a few months, he told me he had no further use for my teaching and
would continue on his own.'[4] In fact Franz soon attained a standard beyond
Ignaz's reach.

When Schubert had been in his father's school for a year and had reached
the age of seven, he was sent for an audition with Anton Salieri. It seems
probable that it was the young boy's father who arranged the meeting,
although no evidence survives. Franz Theodor, noting his son's exceptional
musical promise, and perhaps having consulted Holzer, choirmaster at the

Schuberts' local parish church, may well have decided to seek advice from a leading figure in musical education. Salieri (1750–1825), the conductor, teacher and composer, was one of the most influential musicians in Vienna, an Italian immigrant who had risen to the position of Hofkapellmeister (Court Music Director). He had come to Vienna in 1776 and gained a foothold in the city's musical life through the good offices of Leopold Gassmann. Winning the patronage of the Emperor Joseph II, who was well disposed towards Italians, he enjoyed several operatic successes in the city. When the boy Schubert was sent to him he was already in his fifties, not regarded highly as a composer by the cognoscenti but respected for his power and position.

Salieri interviewed Schubert and was duly impressed.[5] He placed the boy, whom he described as a mezzo-soprano, sixth in a list of nine singers who were examined on 28 September 1804 and found fit to sing for services in the Court Chapel.

When Schubert was eight, his father gave him his first violin lessons. By this time the local parish church at Lichtental, where his parents had been married, had also begun to impinge on his musical development. The organist and choirmaster, Michael Holzer, had already witnessed the young boy's promise, and took him on for lessons in singing, organ, figured bass and counterpoint. Holzer (1772–1826) had, like Beethoven, studied counterpoint with Albrechtsberger (1736–1809), and clearly had the musical competence as well as the kindly disposition to be of timely help in advancing the young composer's talents on fronts which were beyond the scope of the family circle. Schubert's brother Ferdinand later recalled that Holzer had often told him, with tears in his eyes, that he had never before had such a pupil: 'For,' he said, 'whenever I wished to impart something new to him, he always knew it already. I often looked at him in silent wonder.'[6] Anton Holzapfel, who was to be a fellow student of Schubert at the Stadtkonvikt, described Holzer in his 1858 memoirs as 'a bibulous but competent contrapuntist'.[7] Schubert will soon have developed an awareness of Holzer's limitations in the face of the great challenges of the non-ecclesiastical musical forms, but he was to dedicate his Mass in C to him and retain a lifelong affection for his memory.

According to Ferdinand, Schubert was already composing songs, string quartets and piano pieces.[8] To talent was thus added a motivation to compose, and, given that Salieri had already approved him as a prospective chorister, it was appropriate that he should be entered into the competition to fill vacancies in the Court Chapel Choir announced in the *Wiener Zeitung* in 1808.[9] Success in the audition would confer a bouquet of benefits on Franz and his family. He would have a place in a leading choral establishment and be involved in regular choral singing to a high standard. To a young musician who had already demonstrated his innate musicality, this would offer an ideal opportunity to develop his 'inner ear' and sharpen his powers of aural perception generally. He would also be given a free place in the I & R Stadtkonvikt (Imperial and Royal Seminary), which would provide the best general and musical education available in Vienna, until his voice broke. And, thanks to the school's dynamic programme of instrumental ensemble rehearsal (orchestral and chamber), he would come into daily contact with the works of Haydn, Mozart and Beethoven – the greatest boon possible to anyone destined to become a composer at this time.

Schubert duly gained admission, donned his new school uniform of dark brown cut-away coat, gilt epaulette on the left shoulder, polished buttons, short breeches and three-cornered hat, moved into living quarters in the school in early November, and began five years of hard-working collegiate life from which he would emerge at the age of sixteen well prepared to make his way in the world, and, if such was his destiny, to do so as a musician. The Seminary was not a specialist school in the sense that every pupil was expected, or likely, to enter the music profession. Schubert made an early and lasting friendship with a law student, Josef von Spaun, who recognized his fellow-pupil's special musical talent and later wrote about these early Stadtkonvikt days with Schubert in his memoirs.

The Stadtkonvikt was run by Piarist monks, whose order was founded in the seventeenth century to educate the poor. Its director was one Dr Innocenz Lang, a theologian who was regarded as severe and rather gloomy by the boys but loved music and appears to have been remarkably encouraging to pupils and staff in their musical pursuits. Soon after his arrival at the school, Schubert was given a place among the second violins of the school orchestra. The conductor was Wenzel Ruzicka (1785–1823), viola player in the Burgtheater and court organist, and a student was appointed to deputize for him when necessary. Spaun, nine years older than Schubert, was Ruzicka's deputy, as well as leader of the second violins. Spaun noted the spirit, commitment and rhythmic accuracy with which the quiet and serious bespectacled youngster performed, standing behind him and playing from the same copy.[10] His young charge quickly memorized a part, and immediately noticed any slips in other parts. Each evening a complete symphony and several overtures would be tackled, and 'the young orchestra's forces sufficed for the successful performance of Haydn's, Mozart's and Beethoven's masterpieces'.[11]

Already Schubert showed discrimination in his musical tastes. According to Spaun again, Mozart's Symphony No. 40 in G minor and Beethoven's Second Symphony made the deepest impression, and Schubert 'even shortly before his death . . . spoke of how greatly these compositions had moved and touched his youthful soul'.[12] Soon, when he began composing himself, this discrimination was coupled with a determination to select his

own models and media for composition, which was to bring him into
conflict with Salieri. Salieri tried to channel him into opera composition,
using Italian models for practice, and was apparently unable to comprehend
Schubert's enthusiasm for Beethoven or his interest in the writings of
Goethe and Schiller as potential song material. If Schubert soon found
there was little left for him to learn from Salieri (who seems to have ceased
to be his tutor after about 1816) we who hear Salieri's works today may
well feel the experience corroborates Schubert's judgement. If ever a
composer was ignited by a divine spark, it was not Salieri.

There is no doubt that the works of Haydn, Mozart and Beethoven
stimulated the young Schubert's own invention without, at this stage,
appearing to inhibit him. For a student having an urge to compose at this
time, various circumstances combined to liberate creativity. The basis of
the current musical language was a *lingua franca* that any educated
Kapellmeister could manipulate to serviceable, workaday purpose. This
common musical tongue was based on an orderly system of tonality providing an ever-present reference point against which harmonically conceived
melody achieved clarity, coherence, and musical meaning. It was a formula
characterized by simplicity (to those who were blessed with the key to
unlock its secrets) and potency. At the same time these fundamental 'Classical' principles of utterance seemed themselves to suggest ways of structuring
music that could be applied to a range of emerging or revalidated musical
media. The symphony, string quartet, keyboard sonata, piano trio and duo
sonata were all, to some extent, the product of a common method and
impulse. The same principles could bring an up-to-date transparency to
song, mass and miniature. Of course, each composer spoke the language
with an individual inflection, but the underlying *modus parlandi* had such
a logic and energy of its own that one could speak it – like one's native
verbal language – as 'second nature'. This condition enabled Mozart to
compose a quite elaborate piece while playing billiards and hold it intact
in his head for days before writing it down. Schubert enjoyed something
of the same naturalness in his command of the language, which facilitated
his well-known fluency, speed of composition, and phenomenal productivity.

If one compares a Stamitz symphony with, say, the opening chorus of
the *St Matthew Passion* or the six-part ricercar from the *Musical Offering* one
may well conclude that the transition from Baroque to Classical entailed a
radical harmonic simplification. Later, the 'high' Classical composers added
some harmonic enrichment of their own, so that while with middle-period
Beethoven one admires the skill of harmonic timing and planning which
had become of the essence in Classical thinking, one also relishes the
harmonic audacity which leads him to unprecedented dissonance or richness, or to awe-inspiring juxtapositions of key. In this respect Schubert

was born at exactly the right moment: with his ready ear for harmonic colour and venturesome modulation, he was to diversify still more the scope of Classical thought, to the extent that – with our hindsight – we see in his more vivid flights of fancy the seeds of heart-on-sleeve Romanticism.

A range of media beckoned him when he first put pen to paper. It might be supposed that he would take his first steps as a composer in the medium of song, not just because he was to become the most prolific and accomplished song-composer of all time, but because this genre offers the learner the assurance of a ready-made form as a fallback, providing a useful halfway house to the more daunting challenge of constructing something out of nothing. But, interestingly enough, of the sixty or so works composed or begun up to the end of 1812, only eight were Lieder. Most were for string quartet or orchestra, with three church works and an incomplete opera, all involving orchestra too. These were the unmistakable early signs of an ambition to write instrumental music. The singer who knows no other part of Duparc's output than the songs, or the pianist who knows no Chopin except the piano music, will not necessarily have a distorted view of the composer concerned. But those who approach Schubert from a similar special-interest position – whether practical (as singer, pianist, violinist or church musician) or aesthetic (as literary buff, or student of drama, social history, or gender politics) – have to resist the tendency to appropriate him for their own purposes, to know him in so far as he serves their own specialist ends. Schubert wrote music, choosing this medium or that as an unavoidable step on the path to realizing his overriding goal. To know the true Schubert we have to follow his free-ranging aspirations, seeking out the immortal gems wherever they may lodge.

A few months after Schubert entered the Stadtkonvikt, Napoleon brought his French army to the gates of Vienna and laid siege to the city. The Emperor Franz, aware for some time of the looming threat, had already fled. The attack began at 9 o'clock on the evening of 12 May and buildings were soon ablaze. A howitzer shell landed in front of the Stadtkonvikt and another penetrated the roof and came to rest in a room on the first floor. For Schubert the consequences of the siege were probably as demoralizing as the bombardment itself was terrifying. The Court Chapel was closed, and the nightly orchestral rehearsals were suspended. Senior students had enrolled in the Austrian army in anticipation of Napoleon's attack, but an imperial edict soon demanded their resignation and return to study. The work of the second semester thus continued with some of the focal musical activities curtailed; moreover, to add to what must already have been a frustrating deprivation for Schubert, Spaun reached school-leaving age at the end of the same semester. Schubert's sorry state is reflected in the remark he made to Spaun (as Spaun later recalled) when the senior law student bade farewell in September: 'Lucky you! You are about to escape from this prison. I am so sorry you are leaving'.[13] Spaun was the only boy with whom the composer had struck up a real friendship, and although this friendship was not lost for ever, the immediate outlook for the young pupil left behind must have seemed bleak.

None the less, Schubert's end-of-year reports were good. He was found to be a serious-minded and industrious pupil, and he received special mention for 'exemplary application to the art of music'[14] as a Court Chapel chorister. And when the new school year began in November, the French occupation ended and normal musical activities were quickly resumed. By the end of this, Schubert's second year at the Stadtkonvikt, a report went to Hofmusikgraf Kufstein (the imperial court's director of musical education) requesting that 'special attention should be paid to the musical education of Franz Schubert, since he shows so excellent a talent for the art of music'.[15] In the orchestra, he had now graduated to first violin, and when Ruzicka was absent was called upon to direct the orchestra from the violin. At times when the wind players were not available for rehearsal, the string players met to play quartets – Schubert's own early efforts as well as the established repertoire.

Spaun soon took a government post and was able to visit Schubert at the Stadtkonvikt and take him out to concerts and the theatre in the school holidays. Having gained his first experience of opera in this way, Schubert set about writing one of his own, taking Kotzebue's *Der Spiegelritter* (The Looking-glass Knight) as his libretto. He came near to completing the first act of what would have been a three-act Singspiel. An interest in music for the stage was to stay with him throughout his career, but many projects remained unfinished and most of them lay unperformed.

The cost of wars with France had left the Austrian state bankrupt. The Stadtkonvikt was evidently not well heated, nor the pupils particularly well fed. Schubert was as likely to ask his brothers as his father for extra pocket money with which to ease his Spartan existence. 'You know from experience,' he wrote to one of them, 'that we all like to eat a roll or a few apples sometimes, the more so if after a middling lunch one may not look for a miserable evening meal for eight and a half hours.'[16] Despite such rigours, music flowed from him in increasing diversity during the years 1811 and 1812: overtures, songs, the first string quartets (complete surviving ones, that is), church music, part-songs – and fugues. Clearly counterpoint formed a major part of his studies and current interest, especially from the middle of 1812. At this time (in June to be precise) he was required to take private lessons from Salieri in composition, and Salieri placed counterpoint and fugue high on the agenda, along with the setting of Italian texts (some exercises in which have survived).

Two more personal turns of events date from this year. Schubert's mother died in May. At the age of forty-five she had succumbed to what the death certificate recorded as '*Nerven Fieber*', a common blanket diagnosis of the day implying symptoms of fever and delirium without identifying the cause or source, although a typhoid infection was a strong possibility. Two months later, the march of adolescence robbed Schubert of his boy's singing voice, and of his place in the Chapel Choir. The precise date of this eventuality is known, for he was singing the alto part of a mass by Peter Winter, and he wrote into the copy (which has been preserved) 'Schubert, Franz, crowed for the last time, 26 July 1812'.[17]

During his fifth year at the Stadtkonvikt, Schubert's knowledge of opera was enhanced both by study of scores with Salieri and by visits to the opera-house with Spaun. By the end of 1812 he had seen on stage at least six operas: Weigl's *Das Waisenhaus* and *Die Schweizer Familie*, Mozart's *Die Zauberflöte*, Cherubini's *Medea*, Boieldieu's *Jean de Paris*, and Isouard's *Cendrillon*. To these was added, in January 1813, Gluck's *Iphigénie en Tauride*. According to Spaun, who accompanied him to the Kärntnertor Theatre, Schubert 'was totally beside himself over the effect of this magnificent music and asserted that there could be nothing more beautiful in the world'.[18] It is surprising, in view of this reaction, that there is so little evidence of Gluck's musical ideas affecting Schubert's own later scores. Usually, when he was strongly attracted to a piece, he could not suppress its direct influence (in melodic shapes, for instance) on his own music, as was the case with Mozart's Symphony No. 40 and Beethoven's Second Symphony. There was, perhaps, enough of a style-gap between Gluck (who had one foot in the Baroque world) and Schubert for the latter to be able to admire Gluck's product 'from afar', without assimilating more than its generalized qualities (purity, simplicity, naturalness, poise) within his own music. It is probable that he saw other operas, while no complete list is available of the ones he studied with Salieri. That he knew Mozart's *Figaro*, for example, is unmistakably implied by a fragment for string quartet dated 9 September 1812 (Fig. 2, page 29), although it is quite possible that he had merely played its overture at the Stadtkonvikt and the tune beginning at its eighth bar had stayed with him. His attendance at Gluck's *Iphigénie* had another consequence: he enjoyed performances by Anna Milder (Iphigénie) and Johann Michael Vogl (Orestes), both of whom were to be of some importance to his later career, the former as dedicatee (now Anna Milder-Hauptmann) of *Suleika II* and *Der Hirt auf dem Felsen* (The Shepherd on the Rock), and the latter as an influential friend and champion of his songs.

So prolific was Schubert in 1813, as the academic year wore on, that one wonders how he managed to give proper attention to his school subjects too. He apparently did not, and received warnings that his standard was slipping in Latin, and later in mathematics. It is not clear how far his father, who had re-married in April, was involved in discussions about the boy's progress and future at this stage. (The marriage, to thirty-year-old Anna Kleyenbock, was a happy one and Schubert enjoyed good relations with his stepmother, who bore fifty-year-old Franz Theodor five more children, one of whom died in his first year.) But in October the education authorities offered Schubert an endowment for further study only on the condition that he worked to bring his weaker subjects up to standard during the recess and achieved a high grade in a special examination – 'since singing and music are but a subsidiary matter, while good morals and diligence in study are of prime importance and an indispensable duty for all those who wish to enjoy the advantages of an endowment'.[19] Schubert, now sixteen, had other views as to what was important and what subsidiary. If the demands of school subjects were already in conflict with his urge to compose, he could not see the situation improving in the months ahead. The poet Mayrhofer, who was to become acquainted with Schubert the following year, later wrote in his memoirs that '[Schubert] was confronted with the alternatives of giving up either music or the endowment'.[20] The outcome was that Schubert declined the endowment and withdrew from the Stadtkonvikt. There is no evidence that the decision was his father's rather than his own, nor that his father resisted and imposed conditions. While Schubert's subsequent enrolment at the Imperial Normalhauptschule (Normal High School) to train as a primary school teacher might have been the result of parental pressure, it could equally have been the consequence of fraternal example, since both Ignaz and Ferdinand, like the father himself, had taken such training. Schubert obviously realized that he would need an income of sorts, which his musical talents at this stage could not produce, and in such circumstances it is perhaps only natural for a youngster who sees no beckoning alternatives to be drawn to an occupation already known intimately to him as a feature of his early home life. In any event, Schubert's relations with his former teachers and fellow-pupils remained cordial, and he continued to attend musical events at the Stadtkonvikt after he left.[21] Even eighteen months after his departure he felt impelled to dedicate his newly completed Second Symphony to its director, Dr Innocenz Lang.

First Steps in Composition

There was perhaps no safer route by which an under-age Classical composer might venture into instrumental composition than by writing a fantasia. The accumulated tradition of fantasy-writing suggested formal prerequisites that were minimal and conveniently elastic. The piece would fall into as many sections, of any length, as the composer saw fit. A work of this description is the first of Schubert's efforts to have survived. The Fantasy in G for piano duet (D.1) is a twenty-minute piece in twenty-three sections, sometimes suggesting earlier composers of fantasies (Bach, Mozart), and passing with butterfly nonchalance from Adagio to Allegretto or Andante to Vivace, though with some attempt at thematic unification. It is prophetic of later Schubert on two counts: it is the first of a series of works for four hands at one piano, some later examples of which are among his finest products; and it inaugurates a whole chain of experiments with multipartite one-movement form which include ballads for voice and piano as well as further keyboard fantasies for two or four hands.

Written mostly in April and finished on 1 May 1810, the Fantasy in G merits special attention not only because it demonstrates a grasp of compositional principles which is phenomenal in a thirteen-year-old, but also for the seeds it contains of some of his later exploits and style traits. First, one has to admire the sheer fecundity of the piece, its fearlessness of invention, and the tireless industry it represents. There is a teeming flow of ideas and keys, not checked by too much thought of how they square with traditional norms of coherent large-scale structure. The piece runs to 1195 bars: the shortest of the 23 sections amounts to 2 bars, the longest to 232. Second, there is already a glimmer of recognition of the fact that extended movements need to be held together by unifying threads of some sort if they are not to fall apart. But it is only a glimmer. Cross-references between sections are confined to the following: the theme of section 1 (Adagio) is the theme of section 9 (March and trio); the theme of section 8 (Presto) is the theme of section 23 (finale); there are strong resemblances between sections 16, 19, 21 and 22; all the themes referred to above have the one common bond of a 'feminine' melodic cadence falling by a third from strong to weak.

The musical language has as its basis the *lingua franca* of early and middle Classicism, a synthesis of those elements of practice common to most if not all of the hundreds of composers at work in the period 1760–1810. But there are passages that Haydn and Mozart would not have disowned. Moments of Mozartian *buffa* or Rossinian effervescence rub shoulders with Bachian sequences; and in such surroundings there sits rather oddly a passage which peers self-consciously into the future (section 18, Fig. 1). The chromatic polyphony in quartet-texture in the first four bars was probably suggested by the opening of Mozart's 'Dissonance' Quartet, as were the parallel rising passing notes (G and E) in the fourth bar. What Fig. 1 as a whole lacks, of course, is Mozart's sureness of phrase, a certainty in the shaping of successive spans to make a convincing paragraph, while there are places where the part-writing does not quite measure up to the acknowledged good practice of the day. But the itch to explore is encouraging, and was to stay with Schubert, intermittently, to his last weeks. The melodrama *Die Zauberharfe* of 1820 is an extreme case of this thirst for experiment. In fact the somewhat quixotic progress of the Fantasy in G as a whole, with its many changes of tempo – sometimes rhetorically if not dramatically conceived – and the impression easily received that it has a programmatic background, already seems to point to Schubert's potential as a composer of melodramas.

Fig. 1

A youngster so inventive, committed, and intrepid with it at this tender age could hardly fail to become a composer by inclination. Whether the happy-go-lucky stance on large-scale architecture and the technical insecurity would stand in his way would depend on discipline (imposed by external influence or by self-learning and self-realization, no matter which) and on his instinctive selection of the right models. There was already a response to Mozart's example, which augured well as he now ventured quickly into other fields. Call to mind the first entry of the wind in Mozart's *Figaro* Overture and you have the germ of a piece for string quartet (D.3, see Fig. 2) which he began soon, possibly in 1812, did not finish, but liked enough to recast and complete as a piano piece later in the year (D.29). Debts to Mozart were to surface throughout Schubert's oeuvre, and they would not always be so undigested (or actionable, as we might feel, bound as we are by modern intellectual property law). In fact, Schubert's occasional overt homage to others did nobody harm, did him some good in helping him to find himself, and was hardly a matter for reproach in a composer who was to conceive more musical ideas of his own in a short career than many did in an extended lifetime.

Fig. 2

One last point about the Fantasy in G: it is of interest that Schubert chose to write for four hands at one piano in this, his first listed work. True, it was a medium he was to make his own, but its choice at this stage requires further explanation. It was, of course, something of a catch-all combination, in that, having acquired credentials as a serious medium at the hands of Mozart, it became a favourite domestic pastime, and already by Schubert's time the beneficiary of numerous arrangements of works first conceived for other media. It was not only the popularity of duets that might have prompted this early show of compositional interest. It was in some ways a less demanding and more promising keyboard medium, to the inexperienced composer, than the two-hand alternative, for it offered something like an orchestral compass and density and lacked the restrictive demand for economy with notes which the two-hand format imposed. Certainly the Fantasy shows signs of Schubert's exploiting the utilitarian advantages of having twenty fingers to deploy over the then five- to six-octave range of the piano, but it is also sensitive to the idiomatic needs of the duet specification. The primo player does not steal all the tunes while the secondo merely accompanies. The secondo sustains the first Adagio, and some of the following Andante, unaided, and there are numerous obbligato contributions from the secondo as well as alternations between the two players.

From 1810 and 1811 there survive fragments for bass voice and piano, string quartet, solo piano, orchestra, and piano duet, as well as a few complete Lieder and some minuets for wind instruments (some finished, some not). The unfinished orchestral efforts include an overture and a symphony – genres which Schubert was exposed to on a daily basis as a violinist in his school orchestra. The scores bear no indication as to whether they were school exercises or self-initiated out-of-hours endeavours. One may hear traces of Haydn as well as Mozart in many of these efforts. Beethoven enters the picture in the Symphony in D begun in 1811 (the surviving fragment D.2B may be all that was written of this). After the slow introduction, the nineteen bars of Allegro are clearly modelled on the opening Allegro of Beethoven's Second Symphony, which Spaun declared to be one of Schubert's favourites.[1] Perhaps even Schubert's choice of key was derived from that same model.

For his first complete surviving song, *Hagars Klage* (Hagar's Lament), Schubert took Zumsteeg's setting of the same Schucking text (based on Genesis 21) as his model. The copy on which the first edition was based is inscribed: 'Schubert's first song composition, written in the Konvikt at the age of fourteen, 30 March 1811.' Schubert's piano opening takes Zumsteeg's initial descent through four notes as its thematic substance, and echoes Zumsteeg's cadences too, all in the same key of C minor. But where Zumsteeg has the voice enter conventionally – after a formal caesura – over solid tonic harmony, Schubert's voice enters in the middle of a musical phrase, which is already on the way to G minor. After five lines of text, when Zumsteeg has passed through F minor to A flat major, Schubert has chosen a more wayward path, through G minor to B flat minor, thence through E flat minor to D flat major. Thus Schubert's predilection for vivid harmonic and tonal colouring leaves its mark early on his music. Like Zumsteeg, he sets the longish poem as a series of sections in contrasting tempi and keys.

In some of these early works, including *Hagars Klage* and the Fantasy in G, Schubert began and ended in different keys. This was almost certainly not a calculated device like Nielsen's 'progressive tonality'. It occurs less in the later works, but survives longer in songs than in instrumental works. It would happen in a string quartet, but not in a symphony. Obviously it can be put down to the inexperience of a fledgeling composer who, typifying youthful expression in speech as in music, blurted out what he had to say without having a clear view of long-term goals and design. These more long-term concerns with tonality and the larger structure became instinctive to him as time passed, to the extent that we can say with assurance that Schubert would not have held, any more than enlightened posterity would, that the two movements of the 'Unfinished' Symphony, in two different keys, could be regarded as 'complete'.

Three months after *Hagars Klage*, Schubert wrote an Overture in C minor for string quintet which uses the opening bars of that song note for note. (The scoring, incidentally, is for Mozart's combination with two violas, not Schubert's own later preference with two cellos.) The following month (July 1811) he arranged this Overture for string quartet. And two months later still, he composed another Fantasy for piano duet (in G minor, D.9), this time using not only the *Hagars Klage* opening for its slow introduction, but also basing the following Allegro on the fourth section (Geschwind) of the song. These, then, are the earliest instances of Schubert's recycling song material for instrumental purposes, and there is no evidence that he wanted to identify the origin of the material to the reader of his manuscript, nor that he saw the particular 'programmatic' association of the original as being relevant in the new compositional context.

Some of the earliest surviving works and fragments were the products of Schubert's pupillage of Salieri. There were projects involving the setting of Italian words, for example, none of them of special musical distinction, although the composer's 'rhythmic vocabulary' in word-setting was probably enriched by the discovery of rhythms to which the Italian language readily lends itself. And there were exercises in counterpoint. For the most part the techniques involved here were fugue and canon, but exercises in species counterpoint (based on sixteenth-century style) were also worked, and separate attention was paid to imitation, as required in fugal answers. The canons were more successful than the fugues: a canonic Sanctus (D.56, April 1813) is a particularly ingenious example.[2] The fugues show Schubert coming to grips with the basics of contrapuntal interplay, but tend to suffer from sprawling subjects, prolix working out, and a thirst for harmonic exploration which isn't always reconcilable with the imperatives of contrapuntal discipline. The boy Schubert's difficulty in finding the best 'answer' to a fugue subject is similar to that often experienced by modern music students rather more advanced in years. He was obviously keen to let his growing contrapuntal skill affect his real compositions in genres not based on strict counterpoint. A fragment of a Mass in F (D.24E, probably 1812) shows him adapting sequential clichés learned by way of a Fugue in C (D.24A) to serve a Gloria, and using his knowledge of species counterpoint in the opening of a Credo, while the strong rhythmic thrust of the three-part counterpoint which opens the song *Verklärung* (Transfiguration) of May 1813 is that song's most striking feature.

In these early years of composing, Schubert gradually gained confidence in a variety of media, including partsongs and piano duets – although he showed no interest yet in the piano sonata. The means through which he gained experience of large-scale instrumental form, and sonata-type schemes in particular, was by writing string quartets. He completed seven quartets before he completed a symphony, and nine quartets before his first piano sonata. In no medium is the difference in technique and inspiration between his earliest effort and his last greater than it is between his first and last string quartets. The String Quartet in mixed keys (D.18) has to carry that unorthodox title because it begins in C minor, proceeds to a Presto in G minor, and closes with a slow movement and finale in B flat major. This scheme of keys has neither tradition nor any particular logic to explain it. Moreover, the tonal path plotted within movements seems to owe more to whim than to any directional overview, and the self–consciously contrapuntal passages contain gaucheries to which posterity should turn a benign if not deaf ear.

Hilmar gives 1809 as a possible date. The difference in competence between this and other quartets makes that possibility credible. It is only natural to put the bizarre tonal practices found in D.18, like the gaffes in part–writing, down to inexperience. But if this implies that Schubert had failed to observe the traditions of key-choice for the individual movements of multi-movement works by, say, Haydn and Mozart, a word of caution is called for – and not only because he had been playing their works for some time by now. Long after he had accepted the principle of a mono-tonal 'frame' for multi-movement works, he still preferred on occasion to set a minuet or scherzo in a key other than the title-key. This he did even in the G major String Quartet of 1826. By that time, the practice was clearly a matter of artistic choice, not inadvertence; and it seems a perverse habit, when it is borne in mind that examples before Schubert were rare, and seemingly confined to Beethoven, whose Seventh Symphony provides an example. Was Schubert departing from convention with considered gains in view? It is clear that overall unity and cohesion is served by casting outer movements in the same key, as Schubert later appreciated. But there is no compelling reason why a minuet or scherzo should adopt the 'frame–key' rather than align itself with the traditional tonal function of a slow movement – which is to occupy some neighbouring, contrasting tonal terrain – and Brahms, for one, was happy to follow Schubert's example.

There is nothing tentative, nothing tongue-tied, about these early flights of creativity. The 'nice idea but short wind' syndrome which can bedevil a young composer is totally absent. For the time being at least, once Schubert begins a piece he appears unstoppable. This very characteristic may indeed help to explain his later abandonment of works begun: he was so fluent in these early works that he saw this facility as natural and came to expect that nothing would stem the flow of creation, and if it did he circumvented the obstacle by beginning another piece. It is worth noting, too, that he achieved this early fluency without dependence on words to unlock his invention and guide its direction. This embryonic command of the art of non-referential, free composition marked him out as potential champion and master of the instrumental media.

Blessed with such ease of invention in the formative years, it is no surprise that Schubert was to produce more notes per day than some authors produce words per month. Whence this tripping volubility? Schubert, at the Stadtkonvikt and in Lichtental parish church, was regularly performing the current musical repertory. A good ear and quick powers of observation will have enabled him to assimilate the principles of musical construction without being formally taught. What especially enabled him to capitalize on these aptitudes was the fact that he was born when he was. He benefited from the nature of the musical language at this time. It is significant that the *lingua franca* formulated in Classical times – with its built-in disposition to clarity, its transparent background of regular phrase-structure, and its orderly basis in a hierarchic system of keys – has remained a 'fallback' common tongue through later periods, in hymns, football chants, community singing, to some extent modern musicals, and a whole range of popular forms of music. While some music students of our time may dispute the fact, it is palpably true that a musician – given the basic talents of musicianship – may speak this *lingua franca* more easily than any other 'historic' idiom. (That is not to say that the result will be great music.) It is hard to believe that many twentieth-century composers have been able to compose in finished detail works which they then hold in their heads for three days before writing them down, as Mozart is reputed to have done. Schubert was born into this period in which musical parlance could be practised and perfected by usage at an early age. Even the relatively taxing demands of composing for orchestra held no fears for him. He was able to compose his first six symphonies directly into score, sometimes without need for any revision; and although the pioneering Eighth and 'Tenth' Symphonies had to be begun in the more provisional form of piano sketches, even in the Ninth – the 'Great' C major – Schubert maintained his confident youthful practice, writing directly into full score and thus building the work steadily, block by block, until its more than fifty-minute span was complete. In this, his greatest (finished) symphonic masterpiece, he subsequently had to make some revisions, but the fundamental substance of the score did not have to be disturbed.

1813–1815

In November 1813 Schubert began his ten-month course of study at the Normalhauptschule. He had returned to the family home in the school-house on the Säulengasse, where he was to live for three years. He travelled from there to the college in Annagasse in the inner city six days a week, but perhaps found the work less demanding than at the Stadtkonvikt. At any rate he continued to compose prolifically, to take lessons with Salieri twice a week, to sing in the choir at the Lichtental church, and to meet old friends at the Stadtkonvikt.

For some time quartet practices, involving his father and brothers Ignaz and Ferdinand, had been a feature of his home life in the Säulengasse schoolrooms. The ensemble grew in size as friends joined in, until in 1814 it was capable of playing arrangements of Haydn symphonies. Vocal music was also performed, with guests who included Albert Stadler and Anton Holzapfel, two old friends from the Stadtkonvikt. When the instrumental ensemble was too large for the Säulengasse house, an offer from a city merchant, Franz Frischling, to hold the meetings in his house was accepted. By now it was possible to include Schubert's orchestral works, a facility which – in the almost total absence of any opportunity for public perform-ance of his music – must have been a godsend to the composer. Schubert's was not the only private musical group active in the city. Raphael Kiese-wetter, Ignaz Franz von Mosel and Ignaz Sonnleithner were among others who hosted private concerts. All were known to Schubert, who may well have been involved in their activities on any number of (unrecorded) occasions as participant or composer or both. The scope of such organiza-tions ranged from songs and piano pieces to oratorio and opera. Sonn-leithner's brother Josef had played a leading part in founding the Philharmonic Society (Gesellschaft der Österreichischen Musikfreunde) in 1812–13, with the purpose of arranging annual oratorio performances and other concerts, and Ignaz and his son Leopold were at the centre of musical evenings held at their house from 1817 onwards. A more comprehensive account of burgeoning amateur activity in Vienna in the early years of the century is given in Hanslick's history of Viennese concert life, according to which a visitor to the city in 1808 had witnessed 'countless so-called "private academies" – music in distinguished houses. No nameday or birthday takes place without music-making. Every young lady must learn to sing and play the piano whether or not she is talented, first because it is the fashion and secondly because it is the most agreeable way to appear in society.'

The parish church at Lichtental was another important focus of musical endeavour for Schubert. Week-by-week details of his involvement at the church in these early years were evidently not recorded, but the grand public performance of his Mass in F in October 1814 – a work written to mark the centenary of the church and involving the musical personalities who regularly contributed to the church's music – would probably not have come about had the ground not been prepared by Schubert's participation on an ongoing basis in the preceding months. The Mass in F was Schubert's first complete mass, but he had already written several smaller church works, including three settings of the Kyrie and one of the Sanctus, and it is quite possible that these had been performed, in private situations if not in the church.

That Schubert was a man of devout religious feeling is evident from his writings. In a letter to his father and stepmother, written in late July, 1825, while he was on a recuperative holiday in Upper Austria, he tells them that people 'wondered greatly at my piety, which I expressed in a hymn to the Holy Virgin [Ave Maria, D.839] and which, it appears, grips every soul and turns it to devotion. I think this is due to the fact that I have never forced devotion in myself and never compose hymns or prayers of that kind unless it overcomes me unawares; but then it is usually the right and true devotion.'[1] At the same time, whatever his convictions amounted to, he was evidently unable to align them with the tenets of the institutionalized church. This much is an almost inevitable conclusion to be drawn from his free editing of the mass text, in various of his settings. A regular feature of this editorial licence is the omission of the words 'Et in unam sanctam catholicam et apostolicam Ecclesiam'. Had he not consistently omitted these words, from all his six settings, one might put the matter down to carelessness or suppose that he called the text to mind (from his regular singing of it) without checking it and his memory failed him. Equally, it could be imagined that by 'thinning out' the text of the Credo Schubert was hoping to reduce the disparity between the syllabic treatment that was desirable and traditional in a movement with a long text and the necessarily melismatic treatment of, for example, the Kyrie. There does remain a possibility that he found these words musically unpromising, not because of their connotation but because of their implied rhythm or the length of the verbal phrase as a whole; and that aesthetic objection to a particular section of text would then explain why his rejection of it was invariable. There are, on the other hand, phrases elsewhere

in the Credo (and the Gloria, for that matter) that a composer might find
somewhat intractable musically and feel tempted to omit; but Schubert
omitted no other passage consistently. The line concerned is, of course,
an article of the creed; and in this connection it is relevant to refer to an
invitation Schubert received from a friend, Ferdinand Walcher, in 1827,
which began with the words 'Credo in unum Deum!' (set to the notes of
the Gregorian intonation) followed by 'You do not, I well know; but you
will believe this – that Tietze is going to sing your *Nachthelle* [Night's
Brightness] at the Little Society [i.e. Philharmonic Society] this evening.'[2]
This seems a clear enough suggestion that Walcher knew that Schubert
did not swallow the creed hook, line and sinker, and although it may be
wondered if documents from the last three years of Schubert's life are sure
reflections of his outlook in 1814, the fact that his first mass makes the
textual omission in question, as does the last one (the E flat of 1828)
and all those between, rather points to an unchanging viewpoint in
this respect on Schubert's part. Be that as it may, the music of the Mass
in F surely embodies piety and devotion, as generalized but recognizable
characteristics.

Schubert worked on this setting from mid-May to mid-July, directed
the rehearsals, and conducted the performance in October.[3] Michael
Holzer, the choirmaster, was probably instrumental in arranging for the
commission, and probably took part in the performance in some capacity.
Schubert's brother Ferdinand was at the organ, and the well-known leader
of the Court Opera Orchestra, Josef Mayseder, was invited to lead the
orchestra, a full complement including trombones but excluding flutes.
Civic dignitaries were present, as was Salieri who, according to Kreissle,
embraced Schubert saying 'Franz, du bist mein Schüler, der mir noch viele
Ehre machen wird' (Franz, you are my pupil, and you will bring me yet
more honour).[4] Six vocal soloists were required, the first soprano part
being taken by Therese Grob, the first and most ardent love of his life.
The Grob family lived close to the Schuberts and had known each other
for some time, through their attendance at the church and participation
in its music. Therese, two years younger than the seventeen-year-old
composer, was a member of the church choir, and was said to possess a
particularly pleasing high soprano voice.

The clearest testimony of Schubert's love for Therese was contained in
a letter he sent to Anton Holzapfel early the following year (1815), which
was subsequently lost by the addressee. The alleged facts – and there is no
reason to doubt them – were referred to in some notes written by Holzapfel
in 1858 and now kept in the Wiener Stadtbibliothek. Holzapfel wrote:
'When Dr Eckel says that F. Sch. was usually sparing of words and not
very communicative, I must certainly agree with this, especially in contrast
to the generally rather noisy way in which young people carry on, and,

in this connection, it might have been characteristic that F. S. did not tell me about his affection for Therese Grob by word of mouth, which he could have done very easily in private, but in a long, enthusiastic letter, unfortunately since lost . . .' Holzapfel replied to Schubert in dissuasive terms, and said in the 1858 note that he still had in his possession a draft of that reply, although that too is now lost. He described her as 'not by any means a beauty, but well shaped, fairly buxom, with a fresh, childlike little round face and a fine soprano voice extending to D in alt'.[5] Another description of her was offered by Anselm Hüttenbrenner in a biographical note of 1854:

> During a walk which I took with Schubert into the country, I asked him if he had never been in love. As he was so cold and unforthcoming towards the fair sex at parties, I was almost inclined to think he had a complete aversion for them. 'Oh no!' he said, 'I loved someone very dearly and she loved me too. She was a schoolmaster's daughter, somewhat younger than myself and in a Mass, which I composed, she sang the soprano solos most beautifully and with deep feeling. She was not exactly pretty and her face had pock-marks; but she had a heart, a heart of gold. For three years she hoped I would marry her; but I could not find a position which would have provided for us both. She then bowed to her parents' wishes and married someone else, which hurt me very much. I still love her and there has been no one else since who has appealed to me as much or more than she. She was just not meant for me.[6]

While Hüttenbrenner's witness always has to be treated cautiously, since he was writing of one who had died more than a quarter of a century before, and prefaced some of his later remarks (1858) with a caveat to the effect that his memory was unsure on certain matters about which he had been specifically asked, the above is not in conflict with other accounts and no compelling grounds have been advanced for distrusting it. A debate by late twentieth-century writers concerning the possibility that Schubert was prevented by one of Metternich's marriage laws from marrying, on account of his financial prospects, must be regarded as unresolved, pending further research.[7] It would, in any event, not have taken a legal prohibition to stand in the way of his marrying if he could not see himself in any case as able to support a wife (as Hüttenbrenner's recollection implies) or if Therese's family persuaded her that she must look for better prospects elsewhere. According to Hüttenbrenner's later note, Therese 'could not marry Schubert because he was too young at that time and without money or position. Then, against her inclination, she is said to have submitted to her father's wishes and married someone else who was able to provide for her.' There is an apparent flaw in this statement, in that Therese's father was already dead when Schubert first paid her attention. On the other hand, he was right about Therese's marrying someone else, for she gave her hand to Johann Bergmann, a master baker, in 1820. The widowed Therese Grob senior, who managed a silk factory near Lichtental church established by her late husband, was probably sufficiently versed in matters of financial survival to have given her daughter the kind of advice her father might otherwise have offered.

The Mass in F, as performed in the Lichtental church in 1814, made a lasting impression on those who attended, several of whom referred enthusiastically to the event in much later writings. It shows a remarkable awareness, for a seventeen-year-old, of the qualities and habits peculiar to the Viennese Classical mass, a genre which acquired its own phraseology and dynamic in the hands of Haydn, Mozart and Beethoven, whose Mass in C was one of Schubert's favourite works.[8] One thinks of the sonata and its siblings (quartet, symphony, trio) as representing the core of Classical thinking, and quite rightly. The mass, not immune to sonata influence, derived its individuality from the characteristic structure of its text and the distribution of thought, sentiment and image within that structure, while the piano concerto, another 'non-core' genre but one more extensively reflective of sonata practice, owed its essence to the presence of the keyboard and the need to construct a scenario in which keyboard and orchestral action and colour could interact to mutual advantage. Listening to a mass or piano concerto of the period, one is at once captivated by a unique, genre-specific atmosphere. Schubert lacked the will or the time or the nature to work his way fully into the world of the concerto, but his successful first venture in mass composition sparked off a lifelong interest in the form. It was not simply that the Mass in F had brought him his first public performance, pointing to the possibility that here was a commodity that might bring him further performance opportunities and public recognition. He had a genuine love of the recent musical inheritance of the church; and in any case his motivation as a composer came as much from an inner compulsion to write music as from an urge to be performed.

Soon after beginning work on the mass in May (1814), Schubert saw the final version of Beethoven's *Fidelio* at the Kärntnertor Theatre. On 16 June he presumably witnessed the homecoming of Emperor Franz I, a cause of public celebration to which Schubert's father contributed by placing a placard outside the house bearing a patriotic poem and a Latin chronogram.[9] The Emperor was returning from Paris, where the allies had crushed the French and toppled Napoleon, who took himself off to Elba at the end of April. The Viennese populace was jubilant, hoping no doubt that the economic stringencies of the past few years (including a devaluation in 1811) would give way to a period of growth and prosperity. In truth there was more bitter economic medicine to come, as the costs of war remained a burden, to which would be added the bill for the extravagant Congress of Vienna in 1815. In mid–1814, however, optimism was in the air, and Schubert himself shared in it, marking the allied victory in Paris by setting for bass voice and piano a specially written text by J. C. Mikan entitled *Die Befreier Europas in Paris* (The Liberators of Europe in Paris) – 'Sie sind in Paris! . . . Nun ist uns der Friede gewiss!' (They are in Paris! . . . Now we are assured of peace).

Vienna's problems, however, had internal as well as external causes. The repressive regime of Metternich excited resentment especially among the liberal youth, and student riots became a feature of city life. The riots spread to the Stadtkonvikt later in the year, and one Johann Senn had his endowment withdrawn after trying to free a fellow-student from prison. Senn's sympathizers apparently included Schubert, and both were to have a brush with the police a few years later (see pages 167–8). But Schubert's principal social concerns and friends were as much artistic as political. A 'Schubert circle' was already in being, in that old friends from the Stadtkonvikt – including Spaun and Josef Kenner – had kept in close touch and forged an enduring social bond. It was the arrival of Mayrhofer on the Schubert scene in December which was to establish the circle as an identifiable, semi-official group. Before then, Schubert completed his teacher training course at the college in August, passing his final examination with especially good marks for all aspects of German (writing, grammar, pronunciation, spelling and reading) and for arithmetic, but a bad mark for religion. In the same month his father applied for a teaching post at the so-called 'Scottish Monastery' (which had been founded, in fact, for the use of Irish Benedictines) but failed to gain it, whereupon he engaged the newly qualified Franz as his sixth assistant at the flourishing Säulengasse school, with special responsibility for the youngest pupils. According to Kreissle, Franz was a strict teacher, somewhat irascible, and ready to exert discipline with a slap on the head.

The break between graduation and employment was conveniently timed to give Schubert the opportunity to see to final preparations for the performance of the Mass in F, which he conducted on 16 October. He also used the time to compose the String Quartet in B flat (D.112), which occupied a nine-day period in October, and several songs, including *Gretchen am Spinnrade* (Gretchen at the Spinning-wheel) – the first of his Goethe settings and an important landmark along the high road towards the creation of the 'Schubertian Lied'. He also worked on revisions to the three-act Singspiel completed in May, *Des Teufels Lustschloss* (The Devil's Pleasure-palace), having the second version ready by October.

Schubert had discovered *Faust* in the second half of 1814, and *Gretchen am Spinnrade* was the first of six Goethe settings to be composed in the last quarter of the year. In December, a text by Johann Mayrhofer caught his imagination. Mayrhofer (1787–1836) was an old friend of Spaun, who gave Schubert the poem concerned – *Am See* (By the Lake). When Schubert had set the poem (D.124), Spaun introduced him to the poet. Mayrhofer was a member of the Vienna branch of a 'circle of friends' which had been established in Linz in 1811. Such circles, whose members were intellectuals and aesthetes, usually well educated but often preferring a dilettante existence, were centred on artistic pursuits but propounded ideals of friendship and self-improvement. It was probably Schubert's meeting with Mayrhofer that led to the composer's becoming a member of his circle, hereinafter called the 'Bildung Circle' following the suggestion of Elizabeth Norman McKay.[10] *Bildung* (self-improvement and education) was one of its concerns, and for a time it issued a yearbook entitled *Beyträge zur Bildung für Jünglinge* (Contributions towards the Education of Young Men). One of the circle's objectives was to support young artists, which could be done by offering encouragement or opportunity.[11] The opportunities presented to Schubert by membership of the circle were, in the first place, literary. The study of literature was one of its prime activities, and such study would bring obvious benefits to a composer whose range of musical interests included the setting of literary texts. As some members were poets themselves, a more immediate and direct source of texts offered itself. Thus Schubert was exposed to a wealth of contemporary German writing, by members or by others whose work was read at meetings, as well as to worthwhile literature of the past. Schubert's hunger for German texts in the years ahead had a marked impact on his musical output, and suggests that he must have found Salieri's teaching, with its emphasis on Italian word setting, frustratingly narrow.

The year 1815 has been called Schubert's *annus mirabilis*. This hardly overstates the case. His output in this year can be summarized as: four Singspiele, a symphony and a half, a string quartet, nine works for solo piano, eight or nine church works involving orchestra (from the 109-bar Offertory (D.181) to the Mass in G major, D.167), some two dozen partsongs mostly with piano accompaniment, and about 140 songs. It is worth analysing the rate of productivity more closely and extrapolating an illustration that will be readily understood by anyone who has dabbled in composition, has played music if only for private pleasure, or simply knows a few works by Schubert. Schubert composed about 21,850 bars of music in this one year, of which 11,072 involved an orchestra. (It will be appreciated that orchestration adds an extra layer to the conceptual process of composing as well as adding significantly to the time needed to write out a score.) Averaged out over the calendar year of 52 weeks, this amounts to an output of 420 bars a week, of which 213 bars involve an orchestra.[12] This would mean that Schubert produced, in each week of 1815, the equivalent of: the slow movement of the Third Symphony; the Gloria of the Mass in G; the slow movement of the E major Piano Sonata, D.157; the partsong *Trinklied* (Drinking Song) for TTBB and piano, D.267; *Erster Verlust* (First Loss); *Heidenröslein* (The Wild Rose); *Sehnsucht* (Longing), D.310.[13]

Given that this illustration permits of no weekends off and not even a single day's holiday throughout the year, it would be remarkable enough if Schubert were a full-time composer. But he was employed throughout the year as a teacher in his father's primary school. Taking all these factors into account, and the fact that Schubert maintained social contacts with old students of the Stadtkonvikt and with the Bildung Circle, had twice-weekly lessons with Salieri, went to concerts and opera performances, undertook some private teaching, attended the regular orchestral rehearsals at Frischling's, and presumably enjoyed moments of relaxation and exercise, his productivity was phenomenal. Some of the works produced were of exceptional quality for their vintage, examples being *Erster Verlust*, *Erlkönig* (The Erl-King), and the finale of the Third Symphony. But critical considerations apart, the sheer industry sustained over a long period bespeaks an astonishing fluency, speed of working, and intensity of motivation. If a true composer is one who can seldom escape the compulsion to compose, Schubert was possibly the truest composer of all time.

It can only be guessed how extensive was the repertory of works composed by Schubert which, through loss or destruction of the sole manuscript source, failed to reach the public domain and are unknown to posterity. Sometimes the Schubert documents refer to works of which no trace has subsequently been found. These works were entered by Deutsch in his catalogue of the composer's works with the comment '*verschollen*' (lost without trace). A symphony of 1825 was so entered – the work generally referred to as the 'Gastein Symphony'. This symphony was mentioned in letters and reminiscences by Schwind, Ottenwalt, Spaun and Bauernfeld, as well as by Schubert himself. In the 1970s it was finally established that the symphony concerned was in fact the 'Great' C major, which was found to have been composed in 1825 and not 1828 as tradition had had it. (A symphony in E major purporting to date from 1825 which was issued on compact disc in the 1990s has no connection with the 'Gastein Symphony': it is a fake).[14] More colourful is the alleged history of a work of 1815, the three-act Singspiel *Claudine von Villa Bella*. According to Kreissle, the reason for the survival of only the first act is that the manuscript of the second and third acts was passed to Josef Hüttenbrenner, whose servant used it to light the fire while his master was absent in 1848.

Two new friends entered Schubert's life in 1815. Anselm Hüttenbrenner of Graz was a young law student who came to Vienna in 1815 to study composition with Salieri. Franz von Schober was another law student, born in Sweden, who came to Vienna in the autumn of the same year to further his legal studies. Both became friends of Schubert and influential members, in their different ways, of the expanding Bildung Circle.

4

The Composer of Lieder

Although vocal forms flourished in a variety of contexts in Baroque Germany and Austria, the birth of a true, idiomatic German song genre had to await the abandonment of the continuo and the emergence of the piano. Pre-1800 examples, even by C. P. E. Bach, Haydn and Mozart, tend to pale beside those composers' grander exploits in other media, although their respective *Bitten* (Pleading), *O Tuneful Voice* and *Abendempfindung* (Evening Reflections) are fine early pointers to the potential of the genre. Beethoven's songs do not deserve total neglect, least of all his epoch-making *An die ferne Geliebte* (To the Distant Beloved) of 1816, the first song-cycle of any importance. However, Schubert's true predecessors in song-composition were not giants but a handful of writers celebrated by posterity's sleuthing historians for little other than their trend-setting Lieder.

One such man was Johann Friedrich Reichardt (1752–1814), prolific German writer of well over a thousand songs. In Reichardt's oeuvre one can see how gradual was that liberating of the song-composer's imagination that was one outcome of the dissolution of Baroque thought. (The continuo was only one part of the Baroque baggage that had outlived its purpose: old principles of form, scoring and continuity went into decline, while the eclipsing of modal residues as the force of tonal harmony asserted itself with growing strength and clarity pointed the way to new imperatives and new opportunities in the marshalling of musical ideas.) Reichardt relied overmuch on the doubling of the vocal line in the pianist's right hand, neglected the value of rhythmic variety in an often too-persistent fidelity to one pattern without the benefit of compensating linear or harmonic inspiration, and tended to be imprisoned by tonality rather than emancipated by it. Yet he was au fait with the harmonic adventures of the late eighteenth century, as *Des Mädchens Klage* (The Maiden's Lament) demonstrates, while his *Amalia* anticipates Schubert's melodic boldness, supple phrase structures and ease of travel between keys a third apart.[1]

That Reichardt provided something specific for Schubert to build on is evident from a comparison of certain settings of the same text by the two composers. In *Trost in Tränen* (Consolation in Tears), for example, Schubert's key-scheme, down to the change from major to minor, is Reichardt's, as is the strophic plan, with two stanzas of verse to a strophe, although Schubert amplifies the structure beyond Reichardt's model. There are sometimes rhythmic or melodic affinities between other common settings by the two composers, such as *Heidenröslein* and *Rastlose Liebe* (Endless love). Restraint is called for in evaluating these affinities, since a particular set of words may carry a narrow range of rhythmic possibilities, while even the melodic options can be circumscribed. But in cases like the close of the Goethe *Ganymed* Schubert's debt to Reichardt, whether knowing or involuntary, is inescapable.[2]

Another influential precursor of Schubert was Carl Friedrich Zelter (1758–1832), who was much favoured by Goethe – probably because most of his settings are strophic, the style simple, the musical imagination held in firm check. Zelter at his best displays a fine ear, and if Schubert knew his *Sehnsucht* (which is likely, as he set the same text, 'Nur wer die Sehnsucht kennt weiss' – Only he who knows longing) he would surely have appreciated its textural economy – almost Mozartian – and the disposition of lines, venturesome and poetic, in the shapely piano postlude. Both Reichardt, who was a friend of Goethe, and Zelter won that poet's admiration. Indeed any composer who would set his verses in a simple strophic manner with the music decidedly in second place would presumably have had his approval. It has to be added that many ordinary listeners shared Goethe's resistance to any urge to place music on an equal footing with words in song settings. As late as 1827 the critic of the Munich *Allgemeine Musik-Zeitung* is found insisting that 'the accompaniment . . . should remain altogether subsidiary in a true song'.[3]

A different kind of influence on Schubert was exerted by Johann Rudolph Zumsteeg (1760–1802), a German composer of Singspiele and over three hundred songs. Zumsteeg specialized in extended ballads, and these were standard fare at the Konvikt in Schubert's time. Schubert's very first song, *Hagars Klage* (D.5 of 1811), is clearly indebted to Zumsteeg's setting of the same text, and his dependence on Zumsteeg's models may be seen in several of the early ballad-like works, such as the *Leichenfantasie*, and persists in songs up to the year 1816, *Die Erwartung* (Expectation) and *Ritter Toggenburg* (The Knight of Toggenburg) being examples from that year. Zumsteeg's ballads, with their rambling alternations of recitative and arioso, show him blithely unaware of the inescapable fact that music cannot serve words unless it also serves itself: there must be a minimal attention to matters of unity and continuity on a musical level, and there must be a degree of interesting musical incident to engage the ear. Even Schubert took some time to resolve the structural problem posed by the ballad, although he had no difficulty in outshining his mentors in musical interest from an early age.

Schubert knew the repertoire of these other composers from performances and from published copies. He learned the art of song-writing, as he learned symphonic composition, partly by copying out the scores of other composers. His copy of Reichardt's *Monolog der Iphigenia* survives from 1815, for example, although there may well be other copies – of Reichardt and others – which have not survived. He did not gain supremacy as a song-composer (in posterity's eyes rather than those of the contemporary world) in his first year or two of 'apprenticeship', but had arguably lodged a claim to such distinction before the end of 1814, with *Gretchen am Spinnrade*, and had certainly established a mastery of a range of generic types of song by the end of 1815, by which time *Erlkönig* was written. Although songs from this period onwards became fairly widely disseminated in the 1820s, through performances and publication, their pre-eminence was not unanimously acknowledged. The critic of the Leipzig *Allgemeine Musikalische Zeitung*, writing in 1828, thought that Schubert's *Erlkönig* matched neither Reichardt's nor Zelter's.[4] Perhaps Mendelssohn, who played the piano part in the performance being reviewed, had a better appreciation of its virtues.

Why was it that Schubert achieved greatness in song before he mastered the instrumental forms? First, the relative nature of the two kinds of musical product must be considered. Composing a song is a reactive task, composing an instrumental piece a proactive one. In that sense the instrumental project taxes creativity the more, whether it's an undertaking large or small. A necessary part of what a composer has to do is impose a limitation on himself. The possibilities facing a musical creator are immense, until the first notes are penned. Thereafter the range of options narrows, for in the succession of one thought by another, coherent continuity is demanded. Composers welcome the narrowing of options, the proliferation of limitations, which makes their task more manageable. The hardest part of a piece, accordingly, is the beginning, because there are as yet no limitations. Limitations are created by the context set up in the opening bars. However, the adoption of a verbal text creates a context before a note of music is written down or conceived. The range of options is limited at the outset by the need to relate musical invention to a verbal *fait accompli*.

Second, there is the question of cultural geography. Schubert had a negligible tradition of Austrian song-writing to build on, and virtually no tradition of Austrian poetry to feed on. At the same time, the traditions of German poetry and song were becoming known in Vienna, and the association of Haydn, Mozart and Beethoven with the city will have been something of a catalyst in this regard. There was an Austrian tradition waiting to be established, and young Austrian writers there to begin. Perhaps Schubert saw himself – having the rare distinction of being a Viennese-born composer – as being well placed to light a torch. His strong interest and developing taste in literature, furthered by apt friendships as he grew to manhood, provided a further stimulus.

And third, Schubert did not have such towering models to daunt him in song composition as he did in the other principal media. To match Mozart and Beethoven in instrumental music would require more sustained effort than to outshine Reichardt and Zumsteeg in Lieder. At the same time, he nurtured a talent in instrumental writing which would provide valuable cross-fertilization, while his precursors in the song field had no such broad success to enhance their creative base. Zelter produced little but songs, and neither Reichardt nor Zumsteeg excelled in other musical arenas.

It goes without saying that Schubert's potential in Lieder would have gone unrealized if there had not been a fund of literature in his native tongue on which to draw for song texts. The poems taken by Schubert, not all written with musical setting in view, were for the most part ideal material for such use, displaying structures, imagery and sentiments which could not only be portrayed comfortably in musical terms but would find apt echoes in the increasing richness and expressiveness of the musical language in the early decades of the nineteenth century. A profoundly sentient being with technical facility at an impressionable age was the ideal agent to effect a fusion of German 'Romantic' verse and the musical idiom of the day. The extraordinary productivity of 1815 clinched Schubert's commitment to and success in this task. Although the Viennese interest in song grew at this time, with many collections of Lieder being published there in the second and third decades of the century especially,[5] and song-writers coming to the fore in neighbouring lands (like Tomášek in Bohemia[6]), the volume, breadth and depth of Schubert's oeuvre was to remain without peer in his day or since.

The myth that Schubert was indiscriminating in his choice of texts for songs dies hard. He turned to no poet more frequently than Germany's greatest, Goethe. Before his first Goethe venture, *Gretchen am Spinnrade*, most of his teenage settings were of Schiller, highly regarded in his day. And in his last months he 'discovered' an auspicious new talent, setting six of Heine's poems in quick succession. Some other of his poets were of lower rank. Müller is hardly a great lyric poet read the world over: the *Winterreise* (Winter Journey) the world knows is essentially Schubert's. Still less esteem attaches to Schober, although he enabled his friend to compose those twin masterpieces, *An die Musik* (To Music) and *Trost im Liede* (Consolation in Song). Schubert could make better songs of lesser poems than a Reichardt or Zelter could make of Goethe's. Above all, he chose what he did because he had a voracious and versatile appetite, and if there was something in a poem that fired a response, that was good enough reason for adopting it, whether its author was an unknown hopeful or one of the great and the good.

He would probably have gravitated to Goethe sooner had not Salieri been so keen to school him in the setting of Italian text and had he been less driven by an urge to set large-scale dramatic scenas and ballads. His first song, *Hagars Klage*, was a scena, and he returned to the genre several times in the early years, often favouring examples with two or more vocal protagonists. As in the extended keyboard fantasies he also undertook at this early stage, it proved a tall order to sustain inspiration over a large, multi-sectional canvas, just as it was not easy to reconcile the demands of the passing moment with the need to bind the whole together convincingly with unifying threads. These scenas are, however, often characterized by strong ideas, confidently expressed, even if they fail as compelling wholes. *Hektors Abschied* (Hector's Farewell) (1815), for example, would need special pleading as an entity, but Andromache's opening question is set to music impressive enough for Schubert to have later borrowed its harmonic structure in the same key to launch the Fantasy in F minor for piano duet of his last year.

The ballads presented similar problems of unity and consistency, yet they were more than the exercises of a raw and voluble note-spinner. It may be that at a particular juncture Schubert's response quickens and a haunting turn of phrase emerges. Or he may try a one-off strategy far ahead of its time. Or he will display a subtlety in circumventing a textual problem that is worthy of a seasoned artist of mature years. *Der Taucher* (The Diver) is one of his earliest dramatic ballads, almost a one-act opera for solo male voice and piano. It lasts nearly half an hour, which is not much less than his shorter one-act operas. It is not the most horrific of the texts set by Schubert, but it portrays the menace of the sea more fearsomely than any other of his song-texts; indeed the marine and sub-marine terrors rather upstage the less than convincing human characters in this chilling nightmare. The diver is twice challenged to retrieve the king's golden goblet from the depths. The prize for success is to keep the goblet. This is duly accomplished, whereupon at a second challenge the king offers as reward his daughter's hand in marriage.

The song fails to achieve the effect many other Schubert Lieder attain in a fraction of the time with a fraction of the notes. None the less, Schubert uses the resources appropriate to this kind of text fluently – fast scales, oscillations, fiery arpeggios, stark octaves, vivid harmonic effects. He also touches on all twelve keys, each appearing in both minor and major mode. There are unusual harmonic adventures, particularly at the point where the diver is hurled around by the raging torrent, unable to resist it. What is especially remarkable here, though, is that Schubert inserted, in his second version, before the last (twenty-seventh) verse of the poem, an astonishing pre-*Grimes* sea-interlude, in part ferocious and in part reflecting in pre-*Tristan* gestures the poignant plight of the princess who has watched the hero plunge into the maelstrom. (The grief-laden appoggiaturas are marked 'compatiente' – compassionate – in the final version and 'bedauernd' – sorrowful – in a sketch.)

Even when a ballad is only half the length of *Der Taucher*, Schubert's patchwork method of setting incurs risks of disunity. But in a case like *Minona* (1815) the problem can be overstated. Friedrich Bertrand was a little-known poet, whose naïveté appealed to the young Schubert in two instances, the other being *Adelwold und Emma*. It is quite possible that *Minona* was never performed until it was recorded in the last quarter of the twentieth century.[7] Or, if Schubert did hear it sung, the generations between him and us had no such opportunity. Harsh judgements were meanwhile made on the evidence of the printed page.

The ballad concerns a hunting excursion by Minona's lover, Edgar. One of Edgar's dogs returns to Minona with news she must discern from its body language. She has already had a premonition of Edgar's death. She now finds him, slain by her own father in an act of vengeance. She withdraws the fatal arrow and sinks it into her breast. There are many beautiful and many touching moments in Schubert's setting. But is there cohesion enough? In its eleven-minute course there are twenty-five changes of tempo, six changes of time-signature, four of key-signature, and ten fermatas. These statistics imply a daunting threat to cohesion and continuity. Moreover, the thematic cross-referencing between sections is minimal: there are simply five bars of reprise, at the end, of an idea introduced in mid-course, and two other short recollections of earlier material, in a song of 240 bars. Yet the song makes a considerable impact, and in the end the tiny quantity of palpable unifying factors, coupled with the framing of a roving key-scheme by an opening and close in A minor, exerts a strong influence. Beyond that, it is Schubert's sensitivity to Bertrand's poem at every turn that offsets the musical risks implicit in his approach by focusing on the poetic unity of the text and allowing that to override a musical disunity which in the case of a textless piece would be unthinkable. Despite all odds, the song works.

At one particularly emotive point at the centre of the ballad the piano usurps a vocal role. The first five of the ballad's twelve stanzas set the scene and convey Minona's love for Edgar and her foreboding (she imagines the huntsman's clothes covered with blood). Now comes the line 'Wohl minnen die Toten uns nimmer!' (For the dead never love us!), set to music which Graham Johnson rightly regards as the heart of the work (Fig. 3), this being the passage which is brought back later to conclude the song. After the fifth stanza Schubert inserts a piercingly beautiful piano interlude, marked 'Klagend' (lamenting) (Fig. 4). At its close the singer enters with

Fig. 3

Fig. 4

'So klagt sie' (Thus she laments). The interlude is, then, a kind of a summative lament, encapsulating and intensifying the foreboding touched on in the first five stanzas. Thus the piano assumes a role which, in the dramatic context of a ballad, one might well expect the singer to take. Johnson, incidentally, is clearly wrong to interpret this interlude as the dog's music, depicting the creature's whining, panting and fretfulness. The poem's reference to the dog *follows* the words 'So klagt sie' and is marked in the score by a change of time–signature and tempo. The retrospective reference of the interlude is clinched when it is observed that it is a variant of the earlier Fig. 3.

A particularly subtle instance of the piano's having a vocal function occurs in another of the 1815 ballads, *Der Sänger* (The Singer), a Goethe setting described aptly by Richard Capell as a 'ballad of idealized mediaevalism'.[8] The king and his knights hear singing outside the gates, and send a page to invite the minstrel to sing inside the hall. The minstrel enters and sings. When offered a golden chain in reward, he declines, saying that the singing of the song is reward enough, but asks for a cup of the best wine. John Reed, following Capell, finds fault with Schubert's treatment of this poem: '. . . the centre point of the story – the minstrel's song – is missing, and without it it is difficult to sustain the tension of the opening'.[9] This is not quite fair to Schubert, for in fact the minstrel's song is there. The third of the six verses begins:

> The minstrel closed his eyes
> And sang in resonant tones;
> Resolutely the knights looked on,
> While the fair ladies looked down into their laps.
> The king, well pleased with the song,
> Sent for a gold chain . . .

Clearly, in Goethe's verse the minstrel's song begins after line 2 and is over before line 5. Lines 3 and 4 describe events simultaneous with the singing of the song. What Schubert does is to present a complete closed-form piece in D major between lines 2 and 5. But, as the singer of Schubert's song must narrate lines 3 and 4 while the minstrel's song proceeds, he cannot sing the minstrel's song at the same time. So Schubert gives the minstrel's song to the piano. As it is instrumental, song becomes sonata. What the piano plays is a sonata movement, in sonata form, but the most compressed sonata form imaginable, with only two or three bars serving as second subject in the sense that they appear in the exposition in the dominant key and in the recapitulation in the tonic, and with no development but merely a few bars of dominant preparation for the return. It is towards the end of the exposition of this sonata movement that the voice delivers lines 3 and 4. The voice part here is an adornment of the sonata texture and not essential to it; remove the vocal line and the 'sonata' remains unaffected.

The minstrel recognizes the nobility and splendour of the hall and its occupants and sings in dignified, courtly fashion. His song (that is, his 'sonata') has courtly overtones, adopting the style of early Classical galanterie, perhaps Haydn. Thus it can support the sung lines 3 and 4, referring to the knights and ladies present, without incongruity. And thus it can serve another purpose in Schubert's song, at a point where a dual reference to the minstrel's song and to royal company and ambience is needed. Goethe opens with the words of the king: 'What do I hear outside

the gate? ... Let that song echo in our ears throughout the hall!' Thus
the music with which Schubert begins is a preview of his 'sonata' (a
curtailed version of its exposition). As Reed says, this beginning is 'court
music': it is that, but it is also the minstrel's song, which is what the king
is meant to be hearing at that point.

From this structural consideration others follow. The minstrel's 'sonata'
is a sonata in D and is therefore in D on both occasions. As tonal contrast
between its two appearances and after the second one, Schubert places
verses 2 and 5 – both the remarks of the minstrel – in F major. The music
of verse 2, in which the minstrel greets the king, knights and ladies, is
even more courtly and formal and un-Schubertian than the rest. The last
verse, in which the minstrel savours the 'draught of sweet refreshment'
and expresses appreciation of it, demands a glow of its own, which comes
from a new (B flat) tonality and a tendency to lyrical expansiveness which
at last unites courtly vestiges with Schubert's own composing voice. The
composer, having so far distanced himself in a depiction of 'idealized
mediaevalism', has established that stance by now, and allows himself to
come closer to the minstrel, perhaps drawn by the epoch-bridging lure of
a good vintage.

Some of the ballads have been considered in some detail since they are so
little known, are now recorded, and do show Schubert grappling with
large-scale design and finding ingenious solutions to dilemmas posed by
his texts. But these hefty songs are not what come to mind when one
muses on the quintessence of the Lied genre. Brevity and economy are
more characteristic than epic vastness; the intimacy of chamber music is
an important touchstone; an eloquent interplay between the differing but
complementary roles of voice and piano is essential, the voice often express-
ively melodious, the piano filling out detail which – even when ostensibly
pictorial – sharpens or enriches the psychological dimension; and inflections
of harmonic and key colour, in which the piano's part is necessarily paramount, are perhaps the least dispensable element of the genre's Romantic
heartbeat.

Schubert developed a flair for this 'other' Lied – with its demand to set
a scene or atmosphere in a few deft strokes and to portray sentiment or
drama without stage, spectacle or cast-list – within the first few years
of song-writing endeavour. A mastery of miniaturism was the essential
requirement, and he met it several times over in the year 1815. Nowhere
in this year's prodigious output do so few notes say so much so tellingly
as in *Erster Verlust*. For all that Schubert was too young at eighteen to
share the nostalgia of Goethe's lament for the lost happiness of his earlier
days, this is a gem of a song. It has the classic simplicity and conciseness
of the true Lied, yet it adumbrates the Romantic eloquence of a Brahms

or a Strauss, for all its Mozartian economy. Had Schubert composed it thirteen or even ten years later, he might have identified more closely with its message, but one wonders if he would have written a better song.

There are specifics galore to admire here: the natural fluidity with which phrase follows phrase, the subdivision of the song into four unequal spans of 5+4+7+6 yet resulting in a perfect balance: the easy way in which several different kinds of texture succeed each other, with no hint of disruption: the way in which a few notes of piano countermelody emerge above the voice – a stunted but poignant stab of oboe or clarinet colour to illuminate the word 'Wunde' (wound): the subtle matching of music to the irregular rhyme scheme, so that only 'Klage' (line 6) has the same figure as 'Tage' (line 1). But somehow less scrutable, as though under divine control, is Schubert's sophisticated deployment of the song's two main keys and his handling of Goethe's potentially problematic reprise.

For Schubert, the loss is symbolized by F minor, the happiness by A flat major. The miracle is that the eighteen-year-old knows how to imply A flat major and draw on its associated colours long before he cadences in that key. 'Ah, who will bring back . . .' indicates loss and is supported by an F minor chord; '. . . those fair days' recollects happiness, and Schubert steps outside F minor at once (in the second bar of the song!) to a chord of A flat which is, however, not properly bedded down on its root, because it is too early to remain there. He returns to F minor briefly but then veers back to cadence fully in A flat at the end of line 4. The miracle is that when, at the end of the poem, Goethe restates lines 1 and 4 only, Schubert is able to tack the music of line 1 to the music of line 4 accordingly. This, of course, leads him back to A flat again. The voice finishes in that key, secure in its nostalgia ('Ah, who will bring back those fair days, that sweet time?'). It is then for the piano to pull back to the home F minor, and back to the poet's hapless present – which it does in a tiny postlude which crams a world of remorse into a mere five notes, clinching the poetic conception and the musical structure with an intensity all the more direct for its concentration. Even Schubert himself would rarely quite match the perfect *multum in parvo* miniaturism represented by *Erster Verlust*.

That song, in itself, would have stood as a good day's work. But Schubert produced two more on the same 5 July 1815, and they both merit quick examination, for different reasons. *Wandrers Nachtlied* (Wayfarer's Night Song) is another short Goethe verse, and the poet's insistence on simplicity in song settings would have been well satisfied by it, although it was in fact one of the songs which brought no response from Goethe when Schubert sent them to him. Eight lines of poetry prompt eleven bars of song. Not surprisingly, something of the quality of *Erster Verlust* resides here: at least, in its short space the poem moves from an initial invocation, through a declaration of world-weariness, to a prayer for inner peace, and

Schubert is able to mirror these changes in the stance of the poet with a gradually evolving texture. The song is another interesting study in compression, although it has to be said that Loewe's setting of the poem, written thirteen years after Schubert's, is not inferior. We learn from this that the Muse does not bestow her best gifts with indefinite generosity, even when called upon within a space of hours. The poetic thought, or its realization in words, either lights a spark or it does not. Some commentators have seen Schubert's change of tempo for Goethe's last couplet ('somewhat faster') as an obstacle to the song's success. It is there, presumably, because there is a slowing of the harmonic rhythm (rate of chord change) after this point. It can have a dislocating effect, for which reason it is best that the change is so slight as to be scarcely perceptible.

All the songs discussed above are through-composed. The third of the songs composed on 5 July 1815 may be taken as a prototype of another strain that runs through Schubert's oeuvre – the strophic song. *Der Fischer* (The Fisherman) typifies the strophic principle: each stanza is set to the same music, and that music is robustly tuneful with clear-cut phrase-structures and a regular piano figuration running through. There would usually be short piano interludes between the verses, and a piano prelude. ('Prelude' and 'postlude' are misnomers for these outer extremities of a Lied, since the terms imply something that lies outside the main business or essential structure of the song, which is not the case. The 'prelude' may indeed constitute the first exposition of the musical material of the first verse that follows it, or may present expository matter to which the vocal verses will only ultimately refer, as in *Im Frühling* (In Spring). Like the term 'accompanist', 'prelude' and 'postlude' tend to downgrade functions which are of at least equal importance. Musicians prefer 'pianist' to 'accompanist', but no snappy alternative to the other two terms has been devised: so we live with the misnomers and must always see through them.) This is the strophic formula that would serve, the following month, for the famous *Heidenröslein*, and, later still, for the still more famous *Die Forelle* (The Trout).

There are drawbacks to strophic form, which will be examined in Chapter 10. At the same time, there is one broad category of text to which it is well suited, while there can also be peculiarities of an individual poem that suggest it. Broadly, any poem in folk style invites strophic treatment, especially if the stanzas maintain an unflagging rhythmic momentum and there is a clear narrative thread running through from beginning to end. The narrative may encompass a variety of incidents, including surprising ones, but these can have their effect in the regularly reiterative context of strophic form as they can in the similarly reiterative context of regularly constructed folk poetry. Goethe often adopted a *Volkston* (folk style) and evidently expected a composer to match it. *Der Fischer* is a prototypical example, and if it fails to drive as convincingly to its close as other examples, that is not because it is strophic but because the feminine cadence (strong beat to weak) with which Schubert closes the last line of each stanza after all the other lines have ended with a masculine cadence (weak beat to strong) sounds awkward and pushes the postlude forward into a smaller space than it naturally needs.

Schubert had ignored the strophic form during his earliest years of song–writing, preferring to plot his own path through forms which in some ways lay closer to instrumental schemes (like that of the through–composed fantasy, which was one of his early instrumental interests). But by 1815 he had found the measure and worked with the gains of strophic design, and he was soon finding poems for which the form was tailor-made and identifying other cases where the principle could be adapted to special needs.

In Schubert's *Wiegenlied* (Lullaby) of 1816 the mother rocks her child to sleep in three short verses which could hardly not be set strophically. This, Schubert's simplest, most childlike song, is innocent of all chords except two, between which the cradle rocks securely. Not even the allusion to the cradle as a grave in the middle stanza encourages Schubert to do anything which might disturb the hypnotic motion (he does not even turn to the minor for this verse). The only deviation he allows himself is to vary slightly the rhythm and force of his two harmonies. The melody is likewise circumscribed, being 'about' the homely linear motion 5–4–3–2–1 (the descending half-scale to the keynote). The way this line is gradually forged, varied, partly reversed and finally restored gives the clue to its charismatic simplicity. Schubert was not averse to loosening rigid strophic observance when the need arose. Did he withhold the minor from his second verse because the mother's errant thoughts must not affect the child, whose lullaby must be heard to continue with soothing sameness? Or is it that Schubert, his mind brought to bear on his maker, was already capable of viewing death with the optimistic fortitude of his later years?

Goethe would not have been too happy with Schubert's setting (D.325, 1815) of the first of the *Harfenspieler* (Harper's Songs) from *Wilhelm Meister*. Not only does the composer disregard the poet's intention that the song should be accompanied by a harp and should mix recitative and arioso, but he also ignores the poet's grouping of his sixteen lines into two stanzas of eight lines each, preferring a strophic division of 10+6, so that the opening music returns at the third line of the second stanza. Beyond that, he varies a good half of the strophe on the second time through, and adds two repetitions of the last line of the poem. The result is an asymmetry usually obtained by the through-composed method, yet a closely integrated design nevertheless. This is a poignant song about loneliness; and whatever

Goethe might have said, the repetitions of the last line allow Schubert to forge a single long phrase which extracts maximum anguish from harmony and line on its way to its cadence. The little piano coda floats swaying parallel sixths over pedal harmony in a way strongly reminiscent of the slow movement of Beethoven's third 'Rasumovsky' Quartet.

The 1814 song *Andenken* (Remembrance), to a text by one of Schubert's favourite poets in these early years, Friedrich von Matthisson, is a gentle, innocent love-song in folk style, a strophic setting of four stanzas. The stanzas are short, and Schubert dares to extend the fourth one so that it occupies almost as much space as the other three together fill. Such confident youthful assertiveness on his part is usually justified. But no less interesting in this song is the neat recall of the first two notes of the piano prelude (which are not literally replicated in the body of the song) as the singer's final utterance. The song's end is thus in its beginning, the beginning in its end (Fig. 5). Is it coincidence that in a notable case where Brahms achieves the same neat circular unity (the slow movement of his Clarinet Quintet) he does so with the same fall from fifth to major third?

Fig. 5

The genealogical link between Matthisson's poem and Goethe's *Nähe des Geliebten* (Nearness of the Beloved), which Schubert set in the following year, has been explored by Walter Frisch, who shows that an imitation of the Matthisson by one Frederike Brun was set by Zelter, whose version came to Goethe's notice.[10] Goethe then wrote a poem of his own, based on the same theme and employing a similar structural device. That device is a recurring form of words at the beginning of each stanza. *Nähe des Geliebten*, in Schubert's fine strophic setting, has been characterized by Graham Johnson as a litany.[11] A litany is a series of petitions. Here each stanza begins 'Ich _____ dein (dich/dir), wenn . . .' (but not 'wenn' in stanza 4). Moreover, each stanza has the same unusual structure which lends itself naturally to a musical realization in three-bar phrases. A through-composed setting would have been perverse, in this light; also, as Johnson points out, it would not have served so well Goethe's depiction of the lover's constancy.

There are two particularly remarkable things. The melody begins at its highest point, and falls by an octave in the course of each stanza. This reflects the point that the first words of each stanza are in effect the climax of that stanza, bearing a direct reference to the loved one: 'I think of you, when . . .', 'I hear you, when . . .', 'I see you, when . . .', 'I am with you . . .'. The second point follows on from this. A climax stands little

chance of being heard as a climax in music if it is not prepared. It is largely
the aggregate effect of what goes on in the music before it that generates
the climax. So Schubert had to precede the first stanza with a piano
introduction, one that somehow brought force to the voice entry yet did
not dwarf the song itself by indulging in too thoroughgoing (and long)
climax-building. Schubert hits unerringly upon the right solution. He
approaches his key obliquely, and somewhat tortuously, but with accom-
panimental matter only, so leaving the stage empty for the entry of the
voice. It is only when the voice appears that a bright, warm G flat major
materializes. Hence the heightened impact of the first words. It was presumably to allow this first phrase to fall away from its first downbeat like a
firework from the sky that Schubert decided, when reconsidering his first
version of the song, to push the next first beat further ahead by rewriting
his 6/8 song in 12/8 time. The idiosyncratic Schubertian chord by which
G flat major is gained for the entry of the voice will receive attention in
Chapter 23.

Already Schubert showed a predilection for certain poetic themes, as
did the early Romantic poets themselves. Love and nature are foremost –
especially the joy and pain of young love, and the interplay of human
states and manifestations of nature. Songs with titles such as *Calm Sea* and
To the Moon are never the simple nature pictures these titles might imply:
the human spirit – its hopes or its fears – are always palpably present. The
sea in Goethe's *Meeres Stille* may be, on the face of it, calm. Schubert's
music (D.216) is pianissimo throughout, and the piano does nothing but
spread one chord in each bar – an unmeasured spread, tending to banish
all ictus from the first beats and create a floating becalmed stillness. Under-
neath this calm, however, is the sailor's unease: 'bekümmert' is Goethe's
word for it, and the silence of the scene is a 'Todesstille' (silence of death),
which is 'fürchterlich' (dreadful, terrible). All the sailor seeks, perhaps, is
a breeze. Schubert qualifies his 'Sehr langsam' with 'angstlich', and after
establishing a secure C major in four chords moves off to spend three-
quarters of the song in other keys, or in a kind of limbo from which
various remote keys are momentarily glimpsed. The modulations are far-
reaching and the final return to C major magical, setting the seal on this
ultra-calm seascape, whose tranquillity is however skin-deep: the voice
finally freezes on one note as though to perpetuate the underlying fears of
the sailor. The simplest of Lieder can strike deep if, like this, they depict
both the natural world and man's inner thoughts with the same penstrokes.

In *An den Mond* (the Hölty setting, D.193, again from 1815) the moon
is the agent of the poet's nostalgia and despair, for this is the lament of a
forsaken lover. The outer two of the four verses are united with a rolling
triplet pattern recalling Beethoven's 'Moonlight' Sonata. The middle two,
in which memories of the beloved come to the surface, form a distinct

strophic-song-within-a-strophic-song, in the relative major of the song's framing F minor. 'Fantasies and dreamlike images' in the third line of the first verse occasions a haunting melodic phrase anchored to heart-tugging harmonies. When this returns to support the third line of the fourth verse ('Weep down through the hazy clouds'), with an anguished melisma on the word 'weine' ('Und weine durch den Wolkenflor'), one wonders whether the musical idea originated in response to the fourth verse rather than the first. There can, in any case, be no doubt that Schubert at this young age was becoming a skilled strategist in the perception and exploitation of the relationship between poetic structure and musical design. The question we cannot answer – but it is less important anyway – is whether this awareness was, in individual instances, conscious or subconscious on his part.

The extent to which Schubert, in his eighteenth year, had developed this control of an aspect of song-writing in which art and craft meet shows itself nowhere more dazzlingly than in *Erlkönig*. *Erlkönig* is, of course, a dramatic ballad, this time by the greatest of Schubert's poets, Goethe. It is the seventeenth of Schubert's ballad settings, but only the second to words by Goethe (*Der Sänger* had been the first). A poem exuding such mystery, suspense and excitement, and driving relentlessly forward on waves of juvenile fear and paternal anxiety – both approaching panic – was bound to encourage Schubert to draw upon the more dramatic elements of his musical vocabulary. *Erlkönig* is a highly charged, graphic portrayal of a nightmare tale, missing no opportunity to point up its passing details yet maintaining a galloping momentum from start to finish.

Schubert gives the voice a commanding presence, investing its part with a sturdy power that asserts itself against the unflagging energy assigned to the piano. Even so, a special degree of responsibility is entrusted to the piano. Its triplets persist throughout, except for the last three bars of the 148-bar song, while the voice part never adopts them. Furthermore, the voice enters after the piano has departed from the song's harmonic starting-point and drops out before it has reached its harmonic destination, as was to happen on a much bigger canvas twenty-five years later in Schumann's *Dichterliebe*. The delaying of the first vocal entry so that it comes *in medias res* has programmatic point: the question 'Who rides so late through the night and wind?' rightly comes when the music has already begun on its journey. As regards the triplets, it is an interesting feature of the song that while Schubert gave it a time-signature C (four crotchet beats a bar, each subdivisible into two quavers), he could have given the piano part a 12/8 time-signature (four dotted crotchet beats, each subdivisible into three quavers). Only for four bars would this not work, although localized indications could have circumvented that problem.

The confidence with which Schubert writes for the voice in *Erlkönig* is, then, matched by his assured exploitation of the pianist's technique. At the same time the song serves to make the point, early in Schubert's career, that it is the integration of the two, towards a single expressive goal, that is the hallmark of a true Lieder-composer. But in performance the 'instrument' – whether piano or voice is meant by this – is an extension of the performer. To what extent are singers and pianists different kinds of musician, responding to the written music by different sets of interpretative criteria? And did Schubert allow for any such differences? He clearly had some practical know-how in both singing and piano-playing. He was known to sing his songs to friends, the newly composed *Winterreise* being the best-known instance, but there is no evidence of any public soloistic urge. He was content to accompany notable singers inside and outside his circle. David P. Schroeder has nevertheless put forward the view that 'Schubert thought like a singer and calls for gestures in instrumental writing that can be understood only in vocal terms'.[12] This proposition raises a number of awkward questions. For instance, Schroeder continues his thinking along these lines: Schubert is sparing with his expression marks in the voice parts of his songs; this is because singers knew instinctively what to do, whereas pianists did not (this being attributable not to superior intelligence or musicality so much as to the nature of the instrument); Schubert gives instructions to the pianist which will encourage the performance of certain gestures in a way that is fundamentally vocal; when similar marks appear in non-vocal music, they still have a vocal significance.

This is an interesting idea that merits further research. Was Schubert more sparing with performance markings in vocal parts than other composers of his own and preceding generations were? Was an indication in the piano part to serve for both performers, just as 'frame dynamics' were an invariable short-cut in Schubert's notation of orchestral scores, allowing him to write one set of indications to cover an entire orchestral section, or indeed the whole orchestra? (Schubert's manuscripts abound with time-saving devices.) Did the schoolboy's long experience as a string player, through daily orchestra practices and frequent chamber music meetings, go for nothing in determining his approach to instrumental writing? Schroeder notes that the wedge – by which he denotes Schubert's familiar accent marking which looks like a shortened hairpin decrescendo sign – was regarded by Gerald Moore not necessarily as a dynamic accent (as it is conventionally used and understood) but sometimes as an invitation to make a slight prolongation on the chord or note on which it appeared. Schroeder seems to endorse this interpretation. Much depends on the meaning of 'slight', and whether the prolongation is compensated for in the manner of rubato. Sonnleithner, whom Schroeder quotes, appears to give a warning on the composer's behalf against this kind of licence, stressing the need for 'the strictest observation of the tempo'; he recalls that 'Schubert always indicated exactly where he wanted or permitted a ritardando, an accelerando or any kind of freer delivery. But where he did not indicate this, he would not tolerate the slightest arbitrariness or the least deviation in tempo.'[13]

What Moore proposed – which could be called an 'agogic accent' – has for long been seen as the likely connotation of some of Schubert's wedges, in the chamber music especially. But the solution was arrived at by a different route from Moore's — by concluding that a dynamic accent was inappropriate for the context (the context sometimes being over-accented already) and intuiting an alternative meaning. Despite Sonnleithner, this interpretation of the 'short wedge' sometimes makes excellent sense, and Schroeder's suggestion that the sign can sometimes indicate that the note concerned is to be approached with a slight delay is also an appealing one, although the case for this being an effect which is necessarily vocal in derivation cannot be regarded as unassailable. Still, the potential for inter-generic research, which seeks to find instructive links between the Schubert repertories for different performance media, is surely not exhausted.

Erlkönig impresses on other fronts too. Its harmonic imagination will occasion comment elsewhere in this study, as will its way of grafting strophic elements on to a through-composed form. The song's ending is unique. A memorable event in *Gretchen am Spinnrade* had been the sudden arrest, in mid-song, of the fluid figuration that otherwise runs right through, encapsulating the motion of the spinning-wheel and the constant yearning of Gretchen: she remembers her beloved's kiss in a moment of rapture that stills everything. In *Erlkönig* any such arrest is postponed till the very last line – 'In his arms the child lay dead.' Goethe's placing of the words 'war tot' (lay dead) at the end of the line is an invitation to the composer to hive them off, separated from 'das Kind' (the child) by a pregnant caesura. Schubert's masterstroke is to adopt the manner of recitative, elevating one of the most mannered, cliché-ridden devices in the whole of music to the highest level by using it with such economy and point to drive a harrowing tale to its stark conclusion with a few frank, declamatory gestures punctuated by bleak, peremptory cadence chords. If Schubert had lived only to his nineteenth birthday, this and a handful of other Lieder would already have marked him out as a song–writer not merely of exceptional promise but of impressive accomplishment.

～ 5 ～

1815–1818

At the end of 1815 the orchestral meetings which had taken place at Frischling's house were transferred to the house of Otto Hatwig on the Schottenhof, where they flourished. This development is perhaps reflected in the fact that Schubert gave less attention to opera and more to orchestral and instrumental ensemble music in 1816. In much of this music the tendency to look back beyond Beethoven, to the late eighteenth-century world of Haydn and Mozart, is pointedly present. In April Schubert finished his first minor-key symphony, No.4 in C minor, which despite its 'Tragic' title suggestive of C minor Beethoven is a nineteenth-century throwback to an eighteenth-century genre – the *Sturm und Drang* symphony. The Fifth Symphony that followed in September–October espouses early Classical manners even more wholeheartedly, using reduced pre-Beethoven orchestral forces and making exhilarating capital out of ideas that pulsate with Mozartian *esprit* and Schubertian magic but turn a blind eye to Beethoven's example. The Overture in B flat of September sounds like a trial run for the symphony, while the Adagio and Rondo Concertante for piano quartet (Schubert's sole gift to that ensemble) brims over with the *joie de vivre* of a Mozart piano concerto. Earlier in the year came a spate of works highlighting the violin. The so-called Concerto in D and Rondo in A again take their inspiration from years before 1800, while the three works published under the title 'Sonatina for violin and piano', which are properly sonatas (D.384 in D, D.385 in A minor, and D.408 in G minor), are intimately scaled heirs to the Mozart sonata tradition.

Was Schubert, then, going through a conscious back-to-Mozart phase? A diary entry from 13 June 1816 points that way:

As from afar the magic notes of Mozart's music still gently haunt me . . . Thus does our soul retain these fair impressions, which no time, no circumstances can efface, and they lighten our existence. They show us in the darkness of this life a bright, clear, lovely distance, for which we hope with confidence. O Mozart, immortal Mozart, how many, oh how endlessly many such comforting perceptions of a brighter and better life hast thou brought to our souls![1]

Schubert had been listening to a Mozart string quintet. We are not told which, but it may well have been the G minor, which left its mark on Schubert's March in G minor (No. 2 of D.819) for piano duet. Three days later, in a further diary entry describing a party celebrating Salieri's fifty years in Vienna, Schubert turned on Beethoven, blaming the 'eccentricity' (*Bizarrerie*) which 'is due almost wholly to one of our greatest German artists; that eccentricity which joins and confuses the tragic with the comic, the agreeable with the repulsive, heroism with howlings and the holiest with harlequinades . . .'.[2] Such criticisms of Beethoven are, of course, quite uncharacteristic of Schubert, and it is quite likely that he, mindful of some recent press remonstrations against the more recent Beethoven (the word *bizarr* had been used by a Leipzig critic), had been temporarily infected with the deference to Salieri that had characterized the celebratory event. Indeed, Schubert goes on to contrast Beethoven with that paragon of purity, Gluck, who was Salieri's idol. Nevertheless, when the two diary entries are taken together they do tend to reflect a trend in the compositions of 1816 – a clinging to the ideals of an earlier Viennese Classicism, which decidedly suited his still youthful purpose but would have to be superseded in the years ahead if a constructive path forwards to a fruitful maturity was to be found. It was in the period 1818–21 that this quest beyond current horizons was to be broached, not without some tribulation.

Alongside these instrumental preoccupations, Schubert continued to consume and set German literature, producing about a hundred songs in the year. The meetings of the Bildung Circle, and private contacts with its members, stimulated much of this activity. His friend Albert Stadler, reminiscing in 1858 about the composer's contribution to German song, recalled that 'Spaun, Holzapfel, I and anyone else who was interested diligently supplied him with subjects for this, and ransacked the lyric and epic poets for as many as we could lay hold of. He seldom rejected anything we chose.'[3] He turned his attention to several authors new to him, often setting several of their texts in succession: Stolberg, Salis-Seewis, Schlegel, Uz, Mayrhofer and Claudius. He returned to poets 'discovered' in 1815, Hölty, Klopstock and Ossian. And from time to time he came back to Schiller and Goethe. There is no doubt that the early Goethe settings are among the greatest of all his songs. Perhaps recognizing this, Spaun spearheaded a campaign to publish eight volumes of the songs, arranged according to poet, with the Goethe settings to date occupying the first two volumes; moreover, he wrote to Goethe on 17 April 1816 sending the first volume as a specimen and asking if the whole series might be dedicated to Goethe. Goethe declined to answer. Deutsch suggested that the letter may have been disregarded because Spaun's uncle 'had turned from a profound Goethean scholar into a malicious opponent of the poet'.[4] Perhaps Spaun's somewhat undiplomatic statement, in his letter, that the seventh and eighth volumes would contain songs from Ossian, 'these last excelling all the others', touched a raw Goethean nerve. It was, however, characteristic of Goethe, who thought a song should be not a work of art in its own right so much as a simple, strophic 'frame' for the poem, to ignore such approaches. (In 1825 Schubert himself sent him three settings asking for permission to dedicate them to Goethe, who again failed to reply.)

Composing was, for Schubert, an all-consuming passion – or, at least, he would have liked it to be so. One has no difficulty in believing that he found the daily round of primary teaching an intrusive chore. Why, in April, he applied for a teaching post at Laibach (now Ljubljana) is uncertain. Was it the much higher salary, and the promise of a fair amount of spare time to compose that tempted him? Or was he hoping that, with a well-paid job in the offing, he might yet succeed in surmounting the barriers to marriage with Therese Grob? The matter was decided for him, much later in the year (September), when he was notified that the job had gone to someone else. It is the fact that he then did not resume duties in his father's school, but became a freelance composer, that raises the question as to his motives in trying for the Laibach post.

Aside from the principal strands of the Schubert legacy – sonatas, symphonies, songs, and kindred works – there was a steady production of one-off *pièces d'occasion*, minor 'social' pieces (such as those for male voices), and other works which stand outside the mainstream forms and media. An 1816 *pièce d'occasion* was the cantata *Prometheus*, written in honour of Professor Heinrich Josef Watteroth. Watteroth (b.1756), Professor of Law and Political Science at the University of Vienna, was a freethinking radical, liked by his students but not by the state authorities, who counted among his pupils several of the Bildung Circle, including Spaun, Stadler, Mayrhofer, Schober, Sonnleithner and Schlechta. Living as a tenant in Watteroth's house was one Josef Witteczek (1787–1859), who was a music–lover like Watteroth himself, and became an important collector of Schubert's works. Spaun lived in Witteczek's apartments for a while, and invited Schubert to move in for a few weeks in the middle of 1816. It was presumably at this time that Schubert was drawn into a plan hatched by some of Watteroth's law students, to celebrate his nameday with a serenade concert. Schubert was commissioned to write a cantata for the occasion, to a text by Philipp Draxler, one of the law students. (Prometheus, the revolutionary hero, would have been an apt choice of subject in the eyes of his students.) The concert was to be given in the garden of Watteroth's house, but bad weather on the nameday forced postponement until 24 July, when Schubert conducted the première. After his death all trace of the work disappeared, but it was reported to be an impressive piece, lasting three-quarters of an hour and including recitatives, three choruses and a duet, with orchestral accompaniment. Schlechta wrote an appreciative poem about it for the *Wiener Allgemeine Theaterzeitung*, and a second private performance was given in 1819.[5] *Prometheus* also marked a turning point, in this year in which Schubert would burn his salary-earning boats: he received a fee of a hundred florins for it. 'Today I composed for money for the first time,' he proudly wrote in his diary. Another outcome important for the future was the presence at the performance of Leopold Sonnleithner, a pupil of Watteroth, who now introduced himself to Schubert and was to become an influential friend and champion of the composer.

In 1816 there was, as in most years, a batch of short settings for male voices. Stadler, in his reminiscence, threw light on the genesis of some of this year's products. He and Spaun would attend the Sunday afternoon service in the university church, which 'always lasted a good half hour. If Schubert was with us, we shut him up in the "Kamerate" during this interval, gave him a few scraps of manuscript paper, and any volume of poems which happened to be at hand, so that he could while away the time. When we returned from church there was usually something finished and this he gladly let me have.'[6] Stadler added that he still possessed the autographs of works which came about in this way, citing *Der Geistertanz* (D.494, for TTBBB), *Widerschein* (properly *Widerhall*, D.428, for TTB), *Andenken* (D.423, for TTB) and *Erinnerungen* (D.424, for TTB). (These works have all survived, while others mentioned by Stadler are lost but are duly listed in the Deutsch catalogue.)

Schubert's first attempt at grand opera dates from this year. *Die Bürgschaft* (The Pledge: author unknown, after Schiller) took its story from classical sources. With its emphasis on the power of friendship it was, as Elizabeth Norman McKay has pointed out, very much in line with the ideals of the Bildung Circle.[7] Schubert abandoned the opera after completing two acts and beginning the third. Perhaps, despite his admiration for Gluck, he found classical subjects unrewarding for operatic purposes, since his only other classical operas – *Adrast* and *Sakuntala* – are also fragments. Or it could be that he undertook it in half-hearted response to pressure from Bildung members. On musical grounds, few tears need to be shed over its incompleteness.

'Blissful moments brighten this dark life,' wrote Schubert in his diary on 8 September 1816. Perhaps he was infected by the melancholy of Mayrhofer, whom he visited the previous day, after Mayrhofer had written to Schober to say: 'Schubert and several friends are to come to me today, and the fogs of the present time, which is somewhat leaden, shall be lifted by his melodies.' If, as a reading of surviving documents suggests is possible, he had just heard that his application for the post at Laibach had been unsuccessful, this could explain his gloom, and the reference in the same diary entry to the obstacles to marriage. Did his failure to gain the Laibach position effectively dash for all time any residual hopes of winning Therese Grob's hand? Was he contemplating a new unsalaried existence with apprehension? Were the tightening bonds of Metternich's police state demoralizing even one who had the constant spiritual reward of his art? The truth may be an amalgam of these and other factors. It may be significant that in November Schubert copied out seventeen songs for Therese and presented them to her as a souvenir, and that this collection, in a specially bound volume, was retained by her, and subsequently by her family, until the second half of the twentieth century.

It may have been Franz Schober, who had come to Vienna at the end of the previous year, who persuaded Schubert to abandon schoolteaching. At any rate, he wrote to Schubert's nephew Heinrich, in 1876, about his 'dear, never-to-be-forgotten, boyhood friend Franz Schubert', saying: 'I shall always retain the eternally uplifting feeling of having freed this immortal master from the constraint of school, and of having led him on his predestined path of independent, spiritual creation . . .'.[8] It was probably Schober, too, who prevailed upon his mother to take in Schubert as a non–paying lodger in the second half of 1816. Schober himself left for Sweden in June. Schubert was probably already installed with his mother and younger sister when he returned towards the end of the year. He was to stay there until the following August.

The connection with his father's school was not the only association that came to an end in 1816. In December he ceased his regular studies with Salieri, impatient with his tutor's insistence that he should abandon his interest in the 'barbarous German language'.[9] The two eventualities combine to mark the symbolic end of his apprenticeship as a composer. From now on he is a trained, full-time composer. Just as this is an end, so it is a beginning. Gaining one's professional freedom is one thing: sustaining it and justifying it is another.

Franz Schober, in whose house Schubert was now living, stood rather apart from other members of the Bildung Circle. A year or so older than Schubert, he was born in Sweden of a Viennese mother and a father of Saxon extraction who managed a castle estate near Malmö. He had come to the city of his mother's birth to study law, but preferred a dilettante lifestyle. His home in Vienna, where he lived in reputed luxury, was the focus of many a social gathering. But although he was a pillar of the Bildung Circle, his outlook differed from the high-minded, morally virtuous intellectuality which was their pledged ethos, while his indolence was at odds with the Circle's exhortations to activity, typified by Ottenwalt's words in the second issue of the *Beyträge* which Mayrhofer edited: 'Only activity makes man fresh and happy, only activity is life; doing nothing is the true death of the soul.'[10] Schober was a work-shy hedonist, notable for sensual rather than intellectual pursuits, who settled in no employment. Following his legal training, he tried his hand at landscape-painting, poetry, and acting, while long after Schubert's death he joined the staff of noble families and even became Liszt's secretary. And he was a womanizer. Bauernfeld's 'The Outcasts', a skit on the 'Schubert Circle' read at Schober's on New Year's Eve, 1826, depicts Schober as Pantaloon, lying in bed and smoking a very long pipe. When Harlequin announces that he's finding it hard not to fall in love with Columbine, Pantaloon replies: 'Fall in love? And why just that? Can you not have some other relationship with her? Must I recall my own example to you?' He then discusses her inadequate physical attributes. Later, Pantaloon makes a long speech, the short message of which is: 'I see the true significance of life in repose.'[11] How far Schubert was influenced by Schober's moral philosophy is debatable. Only a few months after moving in with him, he turned two of his poems into songs which are among his greatest, in their simple perfection (*Trost im Liede*, D.546, and *An die Musik*, D.547). Both poems celebrate the solace of music in ways which obviously had a direct emotive appeal to Schubert. Four years later Schubert was to collaborate with Schober as librettist in his opera *Alfonso und Estrella*, and the two men remained good friends until Schubert's death. It has to be considered whether the fact that Schubert's compositional activity was reduced by a third in 1817 and much more severely diminished in the years after that is due wholly to causes unconnected with Schober. The composer's contracting of syphilis in 1822 demands consideration in the same light.

Schubert was, after all, an impressionable young man, constantly open to the suggestions of friends even in the artistic sphere which was central to his life (the selection of texts to set, for example). But these sources of personal influence were, at least, diverse. Three other people prominent on the Schubert scene in 1817 are worth mentioning. First, there was Mayrhofer, not the most cheerful of friends (his inveterate melancholy and hypochondria eventually got the better of him and he committed suicide in 1836). A gloomy intellectual, who saw the ideal world as other than this one, he was – within the Bildung Circle – an upright antidote to the possibly destabilizing influence of Schober. But his role as a poet was arguably more important to Schubert's development than his role as a would-be human mentor. The poems he offered Schubert to set in the first half of 1817 led the composer down new imaginative paths, and Schubert was ready to be so led, realizing whatever darker undertones Mayrhofer embedded in a particular verse, but not fearing to invent motives, figurations or structural devices to impose a musical agenda that would meet the poet halfway. Goethe would not have approved; but no criticism by Mayrhofer of Schubert's treatment of his verse has come down to us – not even when the composer abridged a poem as in *Erlafsee* (Lake

Erlaf) (November) or added a final reprise of the first verse as in *Fahrt zum Hades* (Journey to Hades) (January) – and in an obituary recollection the poet made the generous admission that 'I wrote poetry, he composed what I had written, much of which owes its existence, its development and its popularity to his melodies.'[12] Thus, in *Der Schiffer* (The Boatman) (month uncertain), Schubert stakes all on the boatman's resolute challenging of wild nature – 'O celestial joy, to defy the storm with a manly heart!' – with a rollicking figuration that pounds through a subtly modified strophic form: in *Erlafsee*, Mayrhofer's sole allusion to human sorrow in a serene picture of the lake – 'I am so happy, and yet so sad, by the calm waters of Lake Erlaf' – becomes a mere dissonant nuance (at 'so weh' – so sad) amid barcarolle-like tranquillity: and in *Auf der Donau* (On the Danube) (April), as peace gives way to ghostly stirrings and the poet reflects that 'the works of man all perish' whereas 'waves, like time, threaten doom', a conventional enough opening figure compatible with the gliding of the boat soon twists unpredictably, disintegrates, and returns in a remote, darker and tenser key. The circling coda anticipates some haunting later ones, such as that in *Der Wegweiser* (The Signpost) in *Winterreise*, and in the threefold 'Untergang' (doom), Schubert seems to have the etymological derivation of the word in mind (*unter*: beneath; *Gang*: a going) – and perhaps its alternative connotation (sinking) – as he draws out a chromatic descent in the piano that seems to prophesy late Verdi, and takes the bass voice down to the new depths of the low keynote.

Vogl would have relished that ending, and probably did: for Johann Michael Vogl, who, unlike Mayrhofer, was making his first appearance on the Schubert scene in 1817, was a distinguished baritone – lately a leading opera singer at the Kärntnertor Theatre. Schubert had been impressed by his Orestes in *Iphigénie en Tauride*, and may well have remembered him as Pizarro in the second version of *Fidelio* (1814). When Schober introduced Schubert to him in February or March, his tall, commanding presence must have dwarfed the diminutive composer – not much more than five feet and known as 'Schwammerl' to his friends. Prevailed upon by Schober to try out there and then some of Schubert's most recent songs, Vogl found in them 'fine ideas' and 'something special', and thereafter gave many a performance of Schubert's songs.[13]

A third person of some importance for Schubert at this time crossed paths with him in the summer of this year. Josef Hüttenbrenner, younger brother of Anselm, visited Vienna and met Schubert. He was something of a composer himself, but became an ardent admirer of Schubert's work, telling his brother Heinrich in a letter of 1819 'Schubert will really shine as a new Orion in the musical heavens'.[14] As for Josef's older brother, Anselm, Schubert had already befriended him on his arrival in Vienna in 1815, and they met two or three times a week. In a later reminiscence,

Anselm offered a cameo of Schubert at this time:

Schubert's outward appearance was anything but striking or prepossessing. He was short of stature, with a full, round face, and was rather stout. His forehead was very beautifully domed. Because of his short sight he always wore spectacles, which he did not take off even during sleep. Dress was a thing in which he took no interest whatever; consequently he disliked going into smart society, for which he had to take more trouble with his clothes. As a result many a party anxiously awaited his appearance and would have been only too glad to overlook any negligence in his dress; sometimes, however, he simply could not bring himself to change his everyday coat for a black frock coat; he disliked bowing and scraping, and listening to flattering talk about himself he found downright nauseating.[15]

The solo piano had already become a prime focus of attention a few months earlier. The 1817 products include an A minor Sonata (the first of the three in that key, D.537), notable for the fire and poetry of its first movement; the rather more retrospectively Classical Sonata in A flat (D.557); the E minor Sonata (D.566); the amiable D flat sonata (D.567) which Schubert later transposed to E flat (see D.568); a substantial fragment of the first movement of a Sonata in F sharp minor (D.571), which points forwards to the expansive, ruminating manner of some of the late instrumental works;[16] and the imposing B major Sonata (D.575) which is probably the *ne plus ultra* of Schubert's sonata composition up to this time. Schubert also extended the interest he had shown in the violin in the previous year, adding a Polonaise in B flat for violin and orchestra (D.580) and the Sonata in A (sometimes called Duo) for violin and piano (D.574).

Some sixty songs came from Schubert's pen in 1817, including the only one for which he wrote his own text. *Abschied von einem Freunde* (D.578) is a touching farewell to his friend Schober on his departure from Vienna in August. A charmingly simple strophic song which could have been conceived and written down within an hour or so on 24 August, it has a gentle wistfulness at once conveyed by the epigrammatic piano 'prelude', which Schubert recalled in starker form but in the same B minor key in *Irrlicht* in *Winterreise* ten years later. As in that later song, Schubert moves early to the relative major, here at the words 'Du lieber Freund!' (dear friend!) – a modulation which Graham Johnson aptly finds 'as tender as an embrace'.[17]

In October Schubert began work on his Sixth Symphony, turning aside in November to compose two works now known under the title Overture in the Italian Style – in D (D.590) and in C (D.591). It is not insignificant that the genesis of the overtures is intertwined with that of the symphony. At the end of 1816 the Italian Opera Company had made its first visit to

Vienna, bringing with it Rossini's *Tancredi* and *L'inganno felice*. The visit sparked off a rage for Rossini among the Viennese public that was to last for several years and result in regular visits from the Italian company. Schubert himself admired aspects of Rossini's style and technique, specific traces of which may be found in both the overtures, although it was not Schubert who added to them their title 'in the Italian Style'. The symphony likewise nods in Rossini's direction, although the debt naturally shows itself less transparently than it must in an overture. Here it is a matter of the cut of the themes, the weave of the fabric, whereas in the overtures there are structural characteristics too. This readiness to absorb alien idioms, which might or might not have an enduring effect on his own style, spilled over into other works in the 1817–18 period. In the *German Requiem* of August 1818, for example, a work conceived for performance at the Imperial Orphanage, Schubert was content to suppress his usual impulses for sacred settings and adopt the simple chordal style (for SATB and organ only) of a popular church music tradition. More interesting is the 'Grazer Fantasy' for solo piano. Discovered only in the 1960s, among a collection of music in the possession of Josef Hüttenbrenner, this piece assumes with relish the styles of other composers (living or yet to come!) in a quite fascinating way. The treatment of the fantasy form and the stylistic klepto-mania point to a date within this period.

In December Schubert's father finally succeeded in bettering his position, when he was offered the headship of a school in the Rossau district, not far from Lichtental but closer to the city. The accommodation was more spacious, and Schubert moved with the family and resumed some teaching duties. But the later reminiscences of friends indicate that he remained dissatisfied and frustrated with schoolteaching, and as the graph of his productivity plummets in the first months of 1818 we can only guess that life placed more obstacles in his path than the improved circumstances of his family could compensate for.

As Schubert approached and passed his twenty-first birthday, in the early months of 1818, the circumstances of his life and of his art seemed to join ranks in creating a vicious circle of despair. Teaching duties became more irksome than ever. Relations between son and father were becoming strained. Inspirational problems seemed to dog his progress in composition – problems perhaps brought about by the trials of daily life but in turn exacerbating them. As he continued and finished (in February) the Sixth Symphony, he must have realized that he was here marking time, paying homage to Rossini in a way which would not carry him forwards in a fruitful new direction, building productively on a Beethovenian model in the Scherzo but then failing abysmally to sustain that level of invention in the Trio, glimpsing visions of a new symphonic future in the finale yet constrained by an inability to achieve any real dynamic or deck out the rather patchwork construction with ideas of true Schubertian magic.

Another work, dating from January, suggests a similar impasse. The Rondo in D for piano duet (D.608), although someone (perhaps Diabelli?) gave the piece a charismatic subtitle ('Notre amitié est invariable' – 'Our friendship is unchanging'), rises only here and there above workaday invention, and the one or two experimental passages turn out to be cul-de-sacs. That is all there was to show for the first three months of the year, but for a single song and a short partsong. Even some small compensations – in February the first publication of one of his songs (*Erlafsee*) and in March a public performance of one of his Italian-style overtures – seemed not to lift his spirits significantly. Then came a particularly personal blow in March when his application for membership of the Gesellschaft der Musikfreunde was turned down. The Gesellschaft was a society of amateurs, later known as the Musikverein, which already ran an established series of choral and orchestral concerts and was planning a new series of recitals of domestic music. Schubert wished to gain admission as an accompanist, although he would have hoped to have works of his own performed, but he was rejected ostensibly on the grounds that he was not an 'amateur', despite the fact that there were already professional musicians among the membership. Whatever the true reasons for his being spurned – it only needed one or two members of the committee to query his social standing or bring into question his political stance — they were to disappear three years later, when admission was granted. But Schubert could not have foreseen that later change of wind as he nursed his present disappointment at this depressing time.

Schubert could always find solace in the company of his friends. In the first half of 1818 he enjoyed convivial evenings with Anselm Hüttenbrenner, who later recalled that Schubert drank Bavarian beer at the Zur schwarze Kätze (Black Cat) in the Annastrasse or the Zur Schnecke (Snail) in the Petersplatz, smoking a great deal at the same time. When they had more money they drank wine, and, if they were feeling rich, punch. On 21 February Anselm had received some bottles of Hungarian red wine (Szekszard) as a gift, and invited Schubert in. They drained the wine to the last drop (Anselm does not say how many bottles), after which Schubert sat down at his friend's desk and 'composed the wonderfully lovely song *Die Forelle*'. Having done so he wrote a note in the margin of the manuscript paper to Anselm's brother Josef, offering, as a token of friendship, a song he had just written at Anselm's 'at 12 o'clock at night'. The story throws an informative light on the nature and status of the autographs of Schubert's songs. Many of the songs exist in several versions. When he penned a further version, it may have been because he wished to improve the song. But this is not always the case. Anselm was in error in implying that

Schubert had 'composed' *Die Forelle* that February evening: the song had been composed in 1817. The song was simply being written out from memory for a friend. It is not surprising that sometimes the successive versions of the same song show minor differences: it would be a tall order to recall every little detail of one of last year's works, when last year's works totalled about ninety. Rather, it was a feat of musicianship to reproduce the music with even near-exactitude, and a further sign that Schubert spoke the language of music with the naturalness of conversation.

In May, Schubert's only recorded foray into composition was an attempt at another symphony. It is likely that, aware that he was approaching a critical stage in his development as a composer, he felt he should review the method of symphonic composition that had produced the Sixth. The first six symphonies had been composed directly into score.[18] New, more experimental symphonic visions would demand a more careful preparation: setting them out first in 'piano score', on two staves, would enable him to fix passing detail fairly fully in a minimum of time and move forwards speedily enough to preserve an effective ongoing overview of the unfolding structure. In the present case, Schubert got no further than about one-third of the way into a first movement and finale. As yet he could not unlock that new symphonic thinking to which he must have hoped he would soon discover the key. The finale, though, is so attractive that when he breaks off tantalizingly in mid-flow and never resumes, it must be because the first movement (and therefore the symphony), rather than the finale, is irredeemable.

In the middle of the year some relief from the woes of this *annus catastrophicus* was promised when Schubert received an invitation to tutor the two young daughters of Count Johann Karl Esterhazy of Galanta at his summer estate at Zseliz. Schubert's name had been suggested to the count by Johann Karl Unger, Professor in the History of Law at the Theresian Academy in Vienna and a close friend of the Count. Schubert was later to set one of Unger's poems (*Die Nachtigall* - The Nightingale) as a male-voice quartet (D.724). Zseliz, now Zeliezovce in Slovakia, was at that time in Hungary – a small market town more than a hundred miles from Vienna, where the Esterhazys' summer residence stood in extensive grounds, a one-storey Baroque palace with a central courtyard.[19] Schubert, having never ventured far outside his native city, took himself off on what would have been a two-day journey by stage-coach.

Schubert's brief at this country retreat was to teach piano and singing to the two young Countesses, Marie (aged 16) and Karoline (12), and provide musical entertainment for the family and their guests. Board and lodging were provided, and a salary of about seventy-five florins a month. Schubert's letters to Vienna, not all of which have survived, indicate that he liked teaching the Countesses, got on well with the numerous palace staff, and had time to enjoy the rural surroundings. 'Thank God I live at last,' he wrote to his friends Spaun, Schober, Mayrhofer and Senn on 3 August, 'and it was high time, otherwise I should have become nothing but a thwarted musician.'[20]

As the summer wore on, his letters volunteered more detailed information about his circumstances. On 8 September he described the palace and its staff, with a series of thumbnail sketches. The inspector, his son and his wife; the steward; the doctor ('really accomplished, ails like an old lady at the age of twenty-four. Very unnatural'); the surgeon; the magistrate; the Count's companion; the cook; the lady's maid; the chambermaid ('very pretty and often my companion'); the nurse; the manager; the two grooms; the Count himself ('rather rough'); the Countess ('haughty but more sensitive'); the little Countesses ('nice children').[21] Whether the chambermaid, Pepi Pockelhofer, was more than Schubert's 'companion' is a matter for speculation. Count Esterhazy's friend Karl von Schönstein, who met Schubert at Zseliz and became a champion of his music, did refer in an 1857 memoir to Schubert's love affair with a maidservant while at Zseliz.[22] The younger of the Count's two daughters, Karoline, seems to have made a more lasting impression on Schubert, as becomes evident from later events.

A letter sent to Schubert on 12 October by his brother Ignaz, who was still living and working in the father's schoolhouse, contained reminders of the domestic travails Schubert had been glad to leave behind when he left for Zseliz. 'You happy creature! How enviable is your lot! You live in a sweet, golden freedom . . . You will be surprised when I tell you that it has got to such a pitch in our house that they no longer even dare to laugh when I tell them a funny yarn about superstition in the Scripture class. You may thus easily imagine that in these circumstances I am often seized by a secret anger, and that I am acquainted with liberty only by name. You see, you are now free of all these things . . .'[23] The letter points to a clear division in religious attitude between the freethinking Ignaz and his strictly Catholic father, implying quite clearly that Franz's outlook was closer to that of Ignaz. Ignaz describes a religious occasion in slightly irreverent terms, remonstrates about 'dunderheaded bigwigs' (*dummköpfigen Bonzen*) – some of whom may be inferred to be church authorities – and quotes from a poem by Gottfried August Burger:

Beneide nicht das Bonzenheer	Nay, envy not the massive skulls
Um seine dicken Köpfe,	Of consequential people,
Die meisten sind ja hohl und leer	For most of them as hollow are
Wie ihre Kirchturmknöpfe.	As knobs upon a steeple.

He then adds a cautious postscript: 'If you should wish to write to Papa and me at the same time, do not touch upon any religious matters.'[24]

Schubert heeded the postscript, omitting the father from the addressees of his reply, in which he compliments Ignaz: 'Your implacable hatred of the whole tribe of bigwigs does you credit.' But Franz's experiences at Zseliz are no better: 'But you have no conception what a gang the priesthood is here: bigoted as mucky old cattle, stupid as arch-donkeys and boorish as bisons. You may hear sermons here to which our most venerated Pater Nepomucene can't hold a candle.'[25]

As Schubert had become familiar with life at Zseliz he had also become more critical, and not only of the clergy. Members of the household had their shortcomings too: 'Not a soul here has any feeling for true art, or at most the countess now and again (unless I am wrong)' (8 September).[26] As time wore on, reminders from home of the irritations of city life and of the family problems in Rossau did little to quell Schubert's growing homesickness. By the end of October he was admitting to his siblings: 'My longing for Vienna grows daily.'[27] In the third week of November, when the Esterhazys had completed their period of summer residence in Zseliz, Schubert returned to Vienna with them. But he was not to live with his family in Rossau. It had been arranged, probably with his father's agreement, that he would stay with his friend Mayrhofer on the Wipplingerstrasse. For the time being, he probably had some savings from his Zseliz salary, but other sources of income soon came his way. According to Schönstein, the young countesses continued their lessons with him during the winter. And there was a commission from the Kärntnertor Theatre to write the music for a one-acter, to a libretto by Georg von Hofmann. *Die Zwillingsbrüder* (The Twin Brothers) was not exactly the kind of libretto he would have chosen to set, but even a trivial farce might enable him to win the confidence of theatre managements in Vienna and make a name as an opera composer.

Thus a year which began unpromisingly brought two auspicious surprises – a paid change of scene which provided some much-needed money and the tonic of a kind of holiday away from it all, and a chance to develop a career in opera, with some hope of staying solvent thereby. And both surprises helped to rekindle the creative spark which had been all but extinguished. Zseliz provided the stimulus to compose a succession of works for four hands (including the Sonata in B flat, D.617, the Variations on a French Song, D.624, and the *Marches Militaires*, D.733); and the Kärntnertor commission re-awakened the shelved interest in theatrical ventures so effectively that the completed score of *Die Zwillingsbrüder* was ready by 19 January 1819.

The Early Symphonies

Let us imagine that we are music–loving citizens of Vienna, born in the middle of the eighteenth century and well connected enough to be savouring all that the city's musical life has to offer, in private as well as public events. The year is 1797. Excited by the new direction music has been taking since the eclipse of 'continuo thinking', as it offers a direct appeal yet seems to contain much more than can be fully absorbed at a single hearing, we are taking stock of the current state of the art. In particular, we thrill to what composers are doing in the medium of the orchestra – a body which is proving such a suitable vehicle for a kind of music still full of youth and promise, called 'sinfonia'. We have been lucky enough to hear not only the efforts of Stamitz, Wranitzky, Koželuh, Vanhal, Boccherini, Pleyel and Gyrowetz, but also the late Mozart, whose last four symphonies are especially far-reaching, and the recent creations of Haydn, whose symphonies written for England tell us with equal compulsion that the symphony as a genre has well and truly reached maturity. We are unaware that a boy has just been born in a suburb of our own city who is to contribute significantly to the stock of symphonies. Nor would it occur to us that a young man from Bonn in his twenties who has been composing sonatas and chamber works will one day become a noted symphonist. We are not concerned so much with looking forward as with enjoying what we have already, a corpus of outstanding works by our towering contemporaries Haydn and Mozart.

This, then, was the situation into which Schubert was born. And those works by Haydn and Mozart were his inheritance too – a precious legacy indeed since the challenge to write symphonic music himself was one of the first to fire him as a composer. It is true that, by the time he first recognized and met the challenge – just fourteen years into his life as far as we know – the immigrant from Bonn had already composed six symphonies. Imposing as these six were, they did not upstage the great works of Haydn and Mozart which were the staple repertory of young Schubert's school orchestra and which were to become the most influential models for his own early symphonies. As the Beethoven symphonies became known, they too had a powerful effect on Schubert, although for the most part he beat a path of his own forwards from the Haydn–Mozart legacy.

One could of course point out that by the time Schubert wrote his Symphony No. 1 in D (in October 1813), Beethoven's Seventh was only two months off its first public performance, and the two works are rather different in stature. But one might equally then observe that Schubert was twenty-eight when he embarked upon his Ninth Symphony, and when Beethoven was twenty-eight he had not yet produced a first. Beside Beethoven's nine, then, Schubert's symphonies up to and including the 'Great' C major were all juvenilia. The distinction is a critical one. Schubert chose to undergo a working apprenticeship as a symphonist in his teens, while Beethoven found other outlets for his creativity until his thirtieth birthday approached. The symphonic cycles of the two men therefore sit in quite different biographical contexts.

In outward appearance, the symphony had already acquired a regular format when Schubert came to interest himself in it. It was a four-movement work of close to half an hour's duration, with two fast outer movements in sonata form (sometimes rondo in the case of the finale) enclosing a slow movement and a minuet and trio. Beethoven had speeded up the minuet to create a scherzo genre, but Schubert showed an early preference for the minuet, which had strong roots in his native Viennese culture. The outer movements were in the same key, providing a tonal frame, while the slow movement exploited the contrast of some closely related key. The minuet, which had infiltrated the original three-movement genre in the 1740s, was in some ways an ill-fitting addition to the symphony. Its provenance as a dance suited it better to membership of the suite than the symphony (or sonata or string quartet, for that matter), where its particular set of structural conventions promised to constrain the composer more than the relatively free and roomy formal traditions of the other movements. Yet its 'alien' character became a virtue in skilled hands, and the history of the minuet/scherzo as a symphonic component becomes a matter of special fascination thereby. Schubert as a young man largely ignored the innovations of Beethoven in this form, tending to work within Haydn–Mozart conventions in the first five symphonies at least.

Other almost obligatory requirements of the now standard format were that the minuet or scherzo should be in the symphony's 'frame-key', although it might appear more logical to treat it like the other inner movement, assigning it a contrasting key. Perhaps the association of the minuet with the suite, in which all movements were in the same key, was an influential factor. In later Classical symphonies, the treatment of the minuet or scherzo as part of the frame, as far as key was concerned, was reinforced by its treatment as part of the frame in its orchestration: instruments which, used in the first and last movements, dropped out for the slow movement, tended to be reinstated for the third movement. Also standard – once Beethoven in his first two symphonies had cemented Haydn's practice in his last few – was the make-up of the orchestra, which comprised four woodwind pairs, two each of horns and trumpets, a pair of drums, and strings.

Schubert's First Symphony accepted this *status quo*, but two years or so before that he had attempted a symphony which, oddly enough, included trombones. Oddly, despite the fact that by 1811 Beethoven had incorporated trombones in three symphonic movements, for the early Schubert orchestral style is one in which trombones simply have no place. When he next introduced trombones, in the unfinished Seventh Symphony in E of 1821, there was every musical justification for doing so. But in this fragment of a Symphony in D (D.2B) written ten years earlier, when he was fourteen, the trombones have nothing special to contribute. Nor is the youngster sure how to notate their part. How far Schubert got with the composition of this work is uncertain, but only thirty bars of full score survive – a complete slow introduction and little more than the first theme of an Allegro. The fact that the Allegro is modelled on that of Beethoven's Second, which has no trombones, makes it all the more surprising that Schubert included the instruments. Perhaps he was merely obeying one of those headstrong impulses that impel the young to run before they can walk.

Trombones apart, Schubert shows a precocious grasp of orchestral writing, especially as he was composing directly into score.[1] He also demonstrates a sure command of harmonic principles. The Symphony No. 1 in D, following in 1813, consolidates those virtues. This is a big-limbed work in which the sixteen-year-old does not fear to come to grips with the symphonic timescale and orchestral panoply that Haydn had worked with in his sixties. The very presence of a slow introduction evokes the Haydn of the 'London' Symphonies too. But this Adagio is more than the traditional preface to the first movement proper. Schubert recalls it later, when the Allegro vivace has run more than half its course, to prepare for the recapitulation; and to avoid giving the effect of slowing the Allegro to permit this reprise of the introduction, he rewrites it with note-values of double length. Thus continuity of tempo within the Allegro is preserved, while there is an allusion to (and illusion of) something like the original Adagio. This device would be taken a stage further in the 'Great' C major Symphony. Louis Spohr had already used the same strategy in the Concert Overture (Op. 12) of 1806 and the Violin Concerto (Op. 62) of 1810.

The Allegro vivace itself displays an abundance of boyish energy. After a short transition that is not actually shorter than in some later Schubert movements but sounds less convincing, the second subject pays unmistakable homage to Beethoven's 'Prometheus' tune, which Schubert could have known from the finale of the 'Eroica' Symphony. It is a delightful idea, whatever its derivation; but when Schubert proceeds to make it the basis for a long peroration to the exposition, one questions his sense of proportion. So did he, for he subsequently deleted part of this section, the cut being clearly explained in the Eulenberg score and in the New Schubert Edition. Even then, he goes on to make this theme the subject of the entire development section, although it must be said that when it is presented in A minor early on, the new second half of the strain contains a heart-warming Schubertian nudge towards C major and characteristic swing back to the pathos of A minor that is poignantly prophetic of glories to come in much later works (Fig. 6).

Fig. 6

The extended woodwind lead into the recapitulation, with its sequences methodically unfurling over a dominant pedal, recalls Mozart's G minor Symphony (No. 40), which Spaun tells us was Schubert's favourite among all Mozart's symphonies.[2] The prolonged celebration of the power of the Classical orchestra with which this movement ends sees Schubert, in boyish exuberance, taking the first trumpet to an altitude not uncommon in late Baroque music but decidedly rare in Classical usage. It was a means of exhilaration he chose to avoid in later scores.

There is a way of listening to music – for those with artistic curiosity – which pays dividends where especially arresting incidents in a score are concerned. It might be called 'recreative listening'. One stops at a point of particular mystery, difficulty or beauty (ideally when going over the music again mentally after a hearing of it) and asks, 'Is there something more obvious the composer might have done here?' Set beside the answer, the incident in the actual score may be seen in a beneficial new light. The opening of the slow movement of Schubert's First Symphony presents a simple example, in the fourth bar, which marks the end of its first phrase. What might Schubert more obviously have done here? He might have introduced a new texture at the fifth bar, with the new phrase: but he introduces it at the fourth bar, where a new pattern is born in the middle strings while the first violins complete their first phrase.

The effect is a delight of the simplest kind, and it is Mozartian. In the slow movement of the 'Prague' Symphony, Mozart introduces a new string figuration at the eighth bar, rather than the ninth. But there is another, perhaps more concrete, connection with Mozart's No. 38. Schubert's first theme has much in common with Mozart's (in the slow movement), and it is more than a matter of the same key, time and tempo, and the same tonic pedal persisting in the bass. But Schubert pointedly avoids Mozart's most distinctive element, the chromatically upward-curling group of short notes at the end of the first phrase (Fig. 7a). In fact, that element is only temporarily suppressed; for how does Schubert conclude his movement but with that same chromatic group (Fig. 7b)? By calling the third note E flat rather than D sharp, is the youngster salving his conscience? He need do no such thing, of course, for such homage to one great composer by another is touching, and building on good models is a fair way for a teenage composer to learn. In any case, Schubert uses his model as a means of self-discovery, as there is more of Schubert than of Mozart in this charming movement.

Fig. 7 a   b

The following minuet, restoring the frame-key and orchestration, combines dignity and grace in a manner which recalls many a late Haydn third movement. Schubert is content to stay in D major for the trio, hardly leaving that key for more than a moment during its homely course. Instead, variety is achieved by doubling the melodic line of the violins with different woodwind colours in turn, using four permutations in all. The opening of the finale is another unmistakable example of Schubert's looking back beyond Beethoven to his early Classical roots, but when the full orchestra enters with the 'afterstatement' the tonal tactics used by Beethoven at the beginning of the first Allegro in his First Symphony are clearly invoked. After repeated cadences and a caesura, which might be thought to herald a second subject, Schubert seems to start the movement again. Thus there is a double statement of the first subject, and it may be because of this that Schubert later decides not to repeat the exposition, although he ends the exposition by moving back from the second-subject key (the dominant) to the tonic as though he is intending to repeat. Another reason for not repeating might be the extensive use already made, throughout the exposition, of a little upbeat figure (two slurred quavers preceded by a grace-note) that both adorns the first subject and initiates the second. The second subject itself is a winsome variant of that of the first movement (and therefore of Beethoven's 'Prometheus' theme again), but it would be idle to suppose that Schubert had any cyclic intention.

In these early symphonies Schubert seems intuitively aware of what might be regarded as a problem in the conventions associated with a recapitulation. Tradition has it that both the first and second subjects should here be recalled in the tonic key. Thus a long span of music (the recapitulation was more than a third of the movement in early Classical practice, where developments are rather short) was tied to the home key. For a composer with Schubert's developed taste for the colour of key-shifts the observance of this convention would probably have necessitated an irksome degree of self-denial. There was no cause for such restraint, and he found three ways of building tonal contrast into symphonic recapitulations. Two of these, the use of an excursion in the coda and the placing of the first or second subject in a key other than the tonic, were to be implemented in later symphonies. In the finale of the First Symphony a unique scheme is possible. At the beginning of the movement there had been a double presentation of the first subject. In the recapitulation Schubert retains this feature, but casts the second presentation in D minor, moving to B flat major for the 'afterstatement'. Thus D major can be restored for the second subject with fresh impact.

Schubert took twice as long to compose the first movement of the Second Symphony as he was to spend on the whole of the Third. There was nothing else to divert his attention during these sixteen days, except the Goethe setting, *Szene aus 'Faust'* (Scenes from 'Faust'). He tried something more ambitious, less orthodox, than in either the First or Third, and it probably cost him more effort and more pause for thought, although the autograph score offers no definitive indication of this. The symphony, in B flat major, begins with an imposing enough slow introduction, with its pointed chordal rhythm in the wind set against flowing cascades of short notes in massed upper strings, but there is no attempt this time to restate this material in the course of the first movement proper, an Allegro vivace with a certain nervy excitement that exceeds that of Beethoven's *Prometheus* Overture, which was surely at the back of Schubert's mind when he wrote it.

The afterstatement is this time a forceful, fully scored version of the same theme, rather than a different one as in the First Symphony, and it is extended into one of those exhilarating passages in which Schubert pits an emphatic wind rhythm against tireless quavers in the violins. Repeated cadences and a caesura may be heard as preparation for a second subject, unless one knows the First Symphony. This time, instead of going back to the beginning, Schubert leads off in a close minor key, makes more relaxed play with the violin quavers, and veers to the unusual key of the subdominant (E flat major) for his second subject. The more spacious tread of this second subject is an illusion, produced by its preference for longer notes. But a bunch of quavers which occasionally punctuates it in the bass reminds us of that livelier activity that has run through almost non-stop from the beginning of the movement.

The quavers soon reassert themselves, running non-stop once more and dominating, until a mighty dissonance of Beethovenian power draws the music to emphatically repeated cadences which might be thought to close the exposition. But there is more to come, for Schubert is here giving birth to the concept of the three-key exposition, and the key of E flat is now to be supplanted by F major, the dominant. This scheme was to become a model for Schubert's later three-key expositions, in which the third key is always the orthodox second-subject key, the dominant. But Schubert courts controversy in this instance by beginning this third and final block of the exposition with a reprise of his first subject, a potentially confusing strategy since the ear may try to hear it as a repeat of the exposition, despite the fact that the key is now F major, not B flat major. Schubert avoided doing this in his later three-key expositions. We should perhaps hear the third block, in this instance, as an enlarged codetta – but more literally retrospective than usual.

The first subject is debarred from the development, which reinstates the continuous quavers and sets against them a three-note figure heard for the first time in the last bars of the exposition. It is a neat way of forging continuity at this point, and one whose virtues were known to Mozart. Indeed this figure exerts its influence right up to the end of the development – one of Schubert's most successful early spans of contrapuntal writing. When the recapitulation is reached, it begins in E flat major, the subdominant – a deviation from tradition which Mozart too had ventured in, for example, the Piano Sonata in F major, K.545. Mosco Carner's *faux pas* in claiming that this permitted Schubert to generate his recapitulation by simply transposing his exposition wholesale without making any adjustment to the transition has been exposed elsewhere.[3] It might be crediting the seventeen-year-old composer with more foresight or tactical concern than he possessed to say that he brought the first subject back in a key other than the tonic because the third block of the exposition, which had begun with a further statement of this first subject, would naturally be recapitulated in the tonic, so that the subject would in any case be 'resolved' to that key. Schubert adds a short but suitably conclusive coda to this long and energetic first movement.

The only instance of variation form in a Schubert symphony follows in the Andante. Why was Schubert a less devoted writer of sets of variations than Haydn or Mozart or Beethoven? Perhaps it was because a composer with such a marked flair for travel between contrasted keys felt unduly constrained by a form which afforded little scope for the exercise of that skill, in that earlier Classical practice decreed that all the variations should defer to the same tonic. He did in fact relax the 'rule' in this E flat set, but only to place the fourth of the five variations in the relative minor, C minor. Schubert seems to have conceived this movement as a short, gentle interlude after the relentless energy and tensions of the first movement, the use of a 'modular' form also presenting the ear with a different kind of structural perspective from that of a more than full-blown sonata form. Drama is confined to that fourth minor-key variation, which points forwards perhaps to the 'Tragic' Symphony (No. 4 in C minor), but more immediately to the opening of the minuet, with which it shares a strong identity of sound, thanks to similar scoring and harmony in the same key.

The minuet itself, since it is C minor and not B flat, shares with those of three other Schubert symphonies (Nos. 4, 5 and 7) the unorthodoxy of being cast in a key other than the title-key of the symphony. The first symphony to exhibit this unusual characteristic had been Beethoven's Seventh, but before that Beethoven had ventured an out-of-key minuet or scherzo in chamber works. Although the third movement of the Piano Trio in E flat, Op. 70, No. 2 (1808), is not headed 'minuet', it is virtually a minuet in metre, character and form, and is in A flat major. The second movement of the String Quartet in E flat, Op. 74 (1809), is a scherzo (so–called by Beethoven) in C minor. Schubert's minuet in the Second Symphony has an earnestly resolute rhythm and would not be out of place in the 'Tragic' Symphony: indeed, it is in the conventionally 'correct' key for that role, while the actual minuet of the C minor 'Tragic' is in an 'errant' E flat major. Schubert's trio is in E flat (Fig. 8a), is a variant of the flute's 'descant' at the beginning of the minuet (Fig. 8b), and also bears a close relationship to the theme of the second movement's variations (Fig. 8c).

Fig. 8

The 'finale problem' with which nineteenth-century symphonists are supposed to have wrestled should not have troubled the young Schubert, taking his cue from late eighteenth-century models. The finales of the Second and Third Symphonies are both aptly conceived and finely executed examples. That to No. 2 trips along, Presto vivace, each limb of its infectious little tune set in motion by a zippy dactylic rhythm. The contributions of the woodwind to this tune are witty and exhilarating, adding to the general effervescence, though the latent energy is held in check for the time being at a pianissimo level. A forte supervenes, in Haydnesque manner, and Schubert proceeds to shape a big-boned exposition by just the same processes as obtained in the first movement – second subject in the subdominant followed by restatement of the first subject in the dominant. The dactyls take over in the development, being absent for not a single bar. Judicious use of dissonance – especially naked minor seconds – help to propel the music, and the canny orchestral scoring is a delight. Yet, although this is seemingly spontaneous composition that takes its message direct to the heart, the closely knit thematic working is fascinating to the analyst.[4] Where, in the first movement, Schubert had enriched the otherwise stay-at-home tonality of a recapitulation by recalling the first subject in the subdominant, in the finale it is the second subject that evades the tonic, being in the relative minor.

Twice, as symphony succeeds symphony in Schubert's teenage years, a sense of retrenchment is felt. It is most evident when the Fifth follows the Fourth, but the Third also abandons lines of development pursued in the Second. There are no three-key expositions here, no lengthy codettas, no outer movements stretched by such expansionist thinking. Schubert's watchwords are Mozart's – economy, restraint, finesse. All is sunlit under a clear blue sky, as though all shadows are to be suppressed and reserved for the following symphony. Subtlety is not absent, however; nor is innovation. The Adagio maestoso introduction may appear unrelated to the Allegro con brio it prefaces, as was the case in the Second Symphony: but there is a common thread binding them together internally. The violins' threefold answer to the woodwind, at the beginning of the Adagio, is progressively extended until it becomes Fig. 9a. Following the soft first theme of the Allegro, which is not unlike its counterpart in the 'Great' C major, the forte afterstatement adopts this very idea, extending it in a manner which calls to mind the first movement of Mozart's Symphony No. 40 in G minor, a favourite of Schubert's (Fig. 9b). Significantly, it is the forte afterstatement in the Mozart that is referred to. Fig. 9b contains,

Fig. 9 a

b

in its third bar, the seed of the second subject that soon follows: and, since the other prime element in the second subject is the dotted rhythm which impels the first subject, there is an unusual degree of thematic integration. But the integration goes even further than that, since the movement ends with a coda which is based on the afterstatement but now fills its built-in short silences with a woodwind falling-third figure which earlier punctuated the component gestures of the first subject, but can also be traced back to the slow introduction.

In all this Schubert obviously relishes the particular sonority obtainable from the standard Classical orchestra when it is working in D major. Choice of key certainly has an effect on orchestral sound in this period, partly because it affects the number of resonant 'open' strings that may be brought into play, tends to invite use of certain parts of the woodwind compass more than others (and there are timbral differences between the various notes and tessituras within a woodwind instrument's range), but no less importantly affects the way in which the limited capabilities of the brass instruments will help determine the overall sound. The gaps in the scale of horns and trumpets – notes which they were unable to obtain before the days of valves – have a far less noticeable impact on scoring in 'low' keys such as D major.[5] D major has this and other positive advantages, enjoyed especially by Haydn in the 'Clock' and 'London' (No. 104) Symphonies and by Mozart in the 'Haffner' and 'Prague'. But, since Schubert's first known symphonic effort (D.2B) owes a thematic debt to Beethoven's Second, and like that work is in D major, it was perhaps through the Beethoven that he first came to recognize the working advantages of the key.

The second movement of the Third Symphony is a short Allegretto in ternary form, exquisitely detailed but not seeking to develop its material beyond what is required simply to shape each theme into a coherent thematic statement. The first theme is in binary form, and the repeat of the first section indicated in some old editions is not Schubert's instruction, since the repeat of that section is already written out by Schubert so that the flute can be added to the violins. The central episode, in the subdominant, comprises a sixteen-bar melody in the clarinet, a varied repetition, and a short (but not passionless) link back to the first theme. Accented upbeats resound through the minuet, lending a touch of Beethovenian perversity to an otherwise rather Haydnesque conception. The trio, retaining the D major key of the minuet, presents its theme in oboe and bassoon, yoked together in near-parallel. Where one might expect a change of woodwind timbre for its second section, Schubert interestingly persists with the double-reed pair, letting them play out their cloudless thoughts to the very end.

Such generous soloistic favours are no part of the finale, however, for this is a tour de force of ensemble scoring and of sustained high spirits, in which mixed colours predominate and a sense of corporate endeavour carries all before. A breathless tarantella with the finale of Mozart's No. 34 in C as its nearest precedent, it scurries, darts and scintillates its way through a sonata form that sounds wholly natural and convincing despite the oddity of a recapitulation beginning in the dominant. In the coda, Schubert discovers another way of breaking out of the all-tonic syndrome that makes itself felt as a recapitulation progresses (though not so acutely here, since the first theme was recapitulated in the dominant): he embarks on an excursion – learned no doubt from that which exalts the coda of the first movement of Beethoven's Second – which touches on distant keys and displays its harmonic conception so proudly that it almost loses sight of the thematic references which sparked it off. In its blend of sheer elan, technical certainty and flawless continuity this finale is a matchless jewel among the treasures of Schubert's youth.

Schubert's first symphony in a minor key owes less to the example of Beethoven's Fifth – a 'conflict symphony' in which C major ultimately triumphs over C minor – than to the eighteenth-century *Sturm und Drang* symphony. This observation is not intended as an apology for the Symphony No. 4 in C minor, for such a stirring work hardly needs an apology; but a better understanding results if the aspirations of a young schoolboy marvelling at the wonders of late Haydn and Mozart and keen to mine the same seam are kept in mind. (Although that work Schubert particularly admired, Mozart's Symphony No. 40 in G minor, is not usually classified as a *Sturm und Drang* symphony, it is perhaps the most distinguished product of that lineage.) Similarly, the title 'Tragic' which the composer appended as an afterthought some time after the work was completed must not be allowed to raise false expectations. The wide-eyed apprentice's intent was surely neither Beethovenian nor Shakespearean.

The inspiration for the slow introduction may well have been cosmic, though. Traces of Haydn's *Representation of Chaos* Prelude may be discerned deeply buried inside its opening bars, although this is not so much a *Creation* as a re-creation. By the tenth bar Schubert has traversed to the opposite side of the tonal universe, G flat major. The Allegro vivace contains some remarkable tonal exploration too. Although the agitated little first theme seems to point to sources in early Beethoven, the more songful second subject (in A flat major) is in Schubert's most personal lyrical vein. The contrast between the two ideas is not total, for the first subject – a coiled spring of a theme – generates a nervous tension and propulsive energy that is not dissipated even with the arrival of the second subject, which shares with the first an anxious syncopation across the middle of the bar ('x' in Fig. 10). It is immediately after the announcement, and varied repetition, of this second subject that Schubert weighs tonal anchor and moves – by three eight-bar sequential blocks – through the keys of E major and C major back to A flat major again, three plunges down a major third in direct succession. It so happens that (by accident or design?) the horns and trumpets can find notes to play in all these three keys. (Schubert uses four horns, two of them in C and two in E flat, for technical reasons to do with the choice of a minor key for the movement.) But in any case modulations by a third were to become a favourite weapon in his tonal arsenal, and in this respect the present circular, symmetrical tour could be seen as a manifesto.

Fig. 10

Schubert finally reaches C major, capping the process with an invigorating coda. Beethoven, like Mozart, would normally conclude a minor-key first movement in the minor, postponing any major-key resolution until the other end of the symphony (or quartet, or whatever). A more easy-come, easy-go approach to the major-minor antithesis was characteristic of the young Schubert, although he could exploit it with supreme expressive and tactical purpose, and often did. Both the middle movements of the 'Tragic' are then cast in close major keys. The A flat Andante, solemn but affecting, alternates the Romantic warmth of its main sections with the sharper melodic profiles, uneasy pulsations and more volatile texture of the two episodes that come between. The use of E flat major for the minuet of a 'tragic' symphony is doubly perverse. When it is recalled that the title was a later addition, this E flat major remains only singly perverse – and that because of the convention that the key of a symphony was the key of its minuet. In the event, the perverse slurring and searching chromaticism of the theme could almost persuade the ear that some of the expressive properties of the minor are present. In the trio in the same key, Schubert allows himself more variety of instrumental colour than in its counterpart in the previous symphony, with the confiding tone of the strings supplanting the woodwinds for the mysterious probings in its quasi-development.

C minor is resumed for the finale, whose first theme shapes itself in one large paragraph. When the afterstatement follows, it begins – surprisingly enough – softly, although it quickly rises to fortissimo. What distinguishes it is the continuous quavers in the violins, set off by a pointed 'heightened vamp' rhythm in the other instruments – a source of energy in Schubert that never fails to exhilarate. With the arrival of the second subject, in A flat as in the first movement, the quavers patter on in the middle strings while the tune is presented in mosaic-like pieces that almost anticipate

Schoenberg's *Klangfarbenmelodie* (melody of tone colours): two notes in the violins, two in the clarinet, two in the violins – each pair emotively shaped as a sigh. This is one of the teenager's happiest inspirations, as is the development, where fragments of the first theme fall through distant keys in a piano cycle, then rise through more in a forte cycle. When the recapitulation begins in C major, this is not a hard-won resolution, since the opening span of the first theme has been heard in several major keys already in the development. But it is still a joy to hear the whole of the large first paragraph now freshly coloured by conversion to the major. Schubert adds no coda at the end of the movement, preferring the simple affirmation of three unison Cs.

The justly popular Symphony No. 5 in B flat opens with a strategy perhaps suggested by the 'Tragic', finished five months earlier. The finale of the C minor Symphony had begun with a four-bar in-tempo preface. The Fifth adopts the in-tempo preface as a substitute for a slow introduction, doing so in the most winsome way. But there the affinity between the two works stops. The 'Tragic' was a minor-key work using Schubert's largest symphonic orchestra so far (four horns instead of the usual two): the Fifth is in the sunniest B flat major and uses the smallest ensemble to date, excluding clarinets, trumpets, drums, and the second flute. Moreover, whereas the four-bar preface in the previous finale returned just once – turned major – to herald the recapitulation, in the Fifth the preface becomes a substantive ingredient, being the basis of nearly one third of the development.

   This is a 'chamber symphony', wearing its nostalgia for pre-Beethoven symphonism on its sleeve, as it were. The debt of its first theme – a wonderful amalgam of vitality and elegance – to Mozart's Symphony No. 40 will be evident to the listener who sings mentally from Mozart's twenty-eighth bar, then compares Schubert's theme in rather slower motion than Schubert intended. ('Theme' here means more than 'tune': Schubert adopts Mozart's bass line and harmony.) Schubert's way of building (possibly subconsciously, who knows?) upon ideas already 'in the air' is instructive, the results often a far-reaching, sublime re-creation. This first movement is in a compact, transparent sonata form, Mozartian in the sense that melody reigns supreme and one could sing it through from beginning to end, never at a loss to locate a leading line. But it is not as compact as Hans Gal asserted, for the recapitulation is not 'a transposed but otherwise completely identical repetition of the exposition'.[6] Schubert in fact adds, just before the end, sixteen bars of brand-new invention which gloriously crown the movement.

   Having expanded the form of the slow movement of the Third Symphony (ABA) to ABABA in the slow movement of the Fourth, Schubert retains this scheme in the Andante con moto of the Fifth. The eloquent A melody in E flat is perhaps the sort of theme Haydn might have composed if he had still been alive and writing symphonies, much as one thinks of its as Schubertian. The B theme is less formal, more conversational, and the short modulatory link to C flat for it (to G flat the second time round) epitomizes the kind of heart-easing key-shift for which Schubert is famed. Memories of Mozart lurk close to the surface of the minuet, where passing echoes of the minuet of No. 40 are unmistakable. At the same time, the minuet itself recasts in triple time (Fig. 11b) a theme from an opera which Schubert had completed just four months previously, *Des Teufels Lustschloss* (the quartet, No. 5, given as Fig. 11a), while the trio (Fig. 11d) is an adaptation of Robert's Lied, No. 2 of the same opera (Fig. 11c). One of the wonders of the minuet is the transformation of the virile opening theme into a flowing cantabile in the second section, where an intimate dialogue evolves between violins and lower strings, the addition of a few notes of oboe above the 'answer' being a sublime thought.

Fig. 11

If the ultimate reason for Mozart's supremacy in the affections of posterity is his easy blend of lightness of touch and depth of feeling, then the finale of Schubert's Fifth could not aspire higher. The intimacy of the slender string quartet medium is never far away, even though the weight of a small orchestra brings shades of emphasis beyond the reach of a quartet. There are even specific reminders of a chromatic dialogue in Mozart's K.387 in G major (finale) in Schubert's development. If this movement had been the sole survivor of all Schubert's works, its only source were an unauthenticated copy and we were unaware of the existence of a composer called Schubert, modern musicology would have had little hesitation in ascribing it to Mozart. Its close without a coda but with simply a transposed version of the same material that closed the exposition is the final reminder that Schubert's sights were firmly focused on the heady heyday of the early Classical symphony.

The Sixth Symphony is a meeting point of manifold influences – a symphony quite different in bearing from the Fifth or its predecessors yet giving no certain pointers to the way in which the genre would develop as Schubert reached symphonic manhood. The opening slow introduction is broadly in line with, say, Mozart's aspirations in that to the 'Prague' Symphony. The Allegro, at first indebted to Haydn's 'Military' Symphony (No. 100), pays homage to Rossini in its turn of phrase, its orchestral treatment and the general directness of its language. This is the first of Schubert's symphonic movements to have a coda faster than the main body of the movement, a device to serve him again in the 'Great' C major. There are dissonances in this coda that surely betray familiarity with Beethoven's *Leonora* Overture No. 3.

The slow movement combines Rossinian prettiness with Haydnesque grace, sounding more earnestly Schubertian in the throbbing triplets which dominate its contrasting episode and bring tough dissonances to offset the otherwise harmonically bland atmosphere. What follows, however, is probably the most overt evocation of a Beethoven scherzo that Schubert ever wrote. In fact, it so enlarges the conventional binary scheme that it stands midway between the earlier Beethoven scherzi and the full-blown sonata-form scherzo of the Ninth. In character, though, it owes most to the scherzo of Beethoven's First (or rather, the minuet, as Beethoven called it – although Schubert evidently regarded it as a scherzo). Whether or not Schubert realized it, his theme unites the contour of the finale tune of Mozart's Piano Concerto in F major, K.459, with the rhythm of Beethoven's tune in the 'minuet' just referred to. It is a characterful idea, and Schubert's later treatment of it is so original as to repay detailed study with a score. It is a pity, then, that the attempt to write a trio in strong contrast – at a slower tempo and with drawn-out rhythm as in Beethoven's Fourth and Seventh Symphonies – did not produce something more absorbing than the crumbs of melody over to-and-fro harmonies that Schubert extends to inordinate lengths. Whatever its intrinsic weakness, however, it is possible to see in this trio the seeds of the highly individual and successful trio of the 'Great' C major Symphony.

There are further premonitions of the 'Great' in the finale, whether in the cut of a rhythm, the presentation of an idea in parallel thirds, or the multiplication of tiny cells. The structure of the movement is not so much prophetic as eclectic. The initial patchwork progress puts one in mind of Schubert's familiar episodic form for slow movements. At the same time, some kind of sonata form is a possible interpretation, especially if the Schubertian three-key exposition can be regarded as expandable to at least a five-key exposition. Nearer the mark, perhaps, is the overture form preferred by Schubert, this often having little or no development and so resembling the Rossini norm. Rossini, closing an exposition in the dominant key, likes to repeat its closing chord adding a flat seventh to create a home dominant seventh, thence moving straight back to the tonic for a recapitulation. The *Tancredi* Overture illustrates the pattern clearly, and the same procedure is there for all to hear as exposition leads to recapitulation in this finale.

Why does Schubert specifically ask for three bars' rest after the last chord of the Sixth Symphony? Is he wanting the players to remain still? Or an audience to delay its reaction? The real reason is more intrinsically related to the music just heard. The tendency of the music of this time to imply larger bars than those actually written in the score, the actual bars grouping themselves in twos or fours which possess an accentual hierarchy in the same way as beats within a single bar do, sometimes becomes so pronounced that the composer feels it proper to recognize it in his notation. Just as a composer always fills any superfluous part of his last bar with rests, to make up the value of the whole bar, so Schubert here is making up the value of his 'larger bar', which is a group of four bars: the last chord of the work falls on the first bar (beat) of this larger bar. Four-bar groupings become an especially influential metrical unit in the finale of the 'Great' C major Symphony.

The adoption of overture habits in a symphony is a timely reminder that the overture was an important arena for the practice of large-scale orchestral architecture in Schubert's case. In addition to his overtures to stage works he wrote eight concert overtures in the years up to 1819, all except one surviving complete. Several of these overtures predate the First Symphony and show Schubert apparently improvising his structures without regard for and probably without knowledge of conventional key-schemes. The Overture in D, D.4 (*Der Teufel als Hydraulicus*), never leaves its home key in 327 bars of music. Another Overture in D (D.12) has its entire exposition in the tonic, including what we would call the second group if it were in any other key. Schubert is so obsessed with his first theme, which is obviously indebted to Mozart's in the 'Prague' Symphony, that he announces it six times in the exposition alone, always in D major. Perversely, he goes to the dominant for the second group in the recapitulation. The overture to *Die Spiegelritter* (D.11) shows undue reluctance to leave its tonic, and uncertainty in eventually doing so, while the Overture in D, D.26, repeats the bizarre key-scheme of D.12. All these overtures were composed in 1812, when Schubert was fifteen. But he had extended his grasp of tonal planning by the time he wrote the two Overtures 'in the Italian Style' in 1817. For the symphonic historian it is interesting that the trial-and-error adventures of the very young composer in large-scale instrumental form were carried out for the most part in media other than the symphony (in the less challenging context of the overture and less labour-intensive one of the string quartet). For this reason Schubert's early symphonies represent some of the most assured and rewarding invention of his apprenticeship.

The Early Piano Music

Schubert was no virtuoso pianist, but, if we accept the witness of his friends, a thoughtful, sensitive, absorbed one. 'A beautiful touch, a quiet hand, clear, neat playing, full of insight and feeling. He still belonged to the old school of good pianoforte players, whose fingers had not yet begun to attack the poor keys like birds of prey.' Thus wrote his school friend Stadler.[1] Gahy noted his 'clear, fluent playing, the individual conception, the manner of performance, sometimes delicate and sometimes full of fire and energy'.[2] Hiller considered that his playing, 'in spite of not inconsiderable fluency, was very far from being that of a master'; yet his performance of songs with Vogl was 'a revelation'.[3] According to Anselm Hüttenbrenner, 'Schubert was not an elegant pianist but he was a safe and very fluent one'.[4] Schubert's brother Ferdinand recalled that a musician who heard the composer play his own late sonatas exclaimed: 'Schubert, I almost admire your playing even more than your compositions!'[5] For Louis Schlösser, Schubert's playing was like improvisation. 'How spontaneous it sounded! How his eyes shone. I listened to the sounds with indescribable excitement.' But he could not compete as a virtuoso: 'With Schubert, the expression of the emotions of the world within him obviously far outweighed his technical development.'[6]

As a composer, his relationship with the piano was an enduring and complex one. Essentially rooted in Classical practice, his use of the instrument became so diversified and idiosyncratic that with hindsight it is possible to trace certain strands of Romantic thought back into his oeuvre. Despite the volume of piano compositions he produced (and it is not irrelevant to consider, along with the repertory for piano alone, a tally of over six hundred songs making use of the instrument) he was not a specialist piano composer in the sense that Chopin was, nor one whose piano idiom tends to underlie his other works, as in Schumann's case. The piano was but one medium of a rounded composer who wrote as idiomatically for orchestra or string quartet or a vocal ensemble as he did for the piano. His lifelong commitment to the sonata was inherited from his Classical forebears. His later cultivation of the short piano piece points the way to a later Romantic obsession. It is tempting to see his interest in the fantasy genre as a symptom of a quest for Romantic freedom of expression, and his song accompaniments – at times vividly evocative of the extra-musical images of their text – as a palpable fulfilment of one of Romanticism's urges. But fantasy and song were both avenues explored by Schubert's precursors and older contemporaries, and his preoccupation with ways of imposing clear design principles on the *carte blanche* of the fantasy (for instance by building in elements of sonata architecture) appear to temper any trend towards Romantic libertarianism with a concern to extend Classical control.

His very first piano fantasy at once shows him paying homage to a Classical model. The Fantasy in C minor, probably composed in 1811, begins with a Largo which contains unmistakable echoes of Mozart's C minor Fantasy. The following Andantino, in E major, is still more transparently based on the B flat major Andantino from the same Mozart source: Schubert adopts the opening almost literally, but brings forward by one beat Mozart's first sequence of the initial idea, in the same way as Mozart brings forward his second sequence in the second bar. Schubert constructs from this material a six-bar strain, cadencing into a repetition of itself. This repetition, like Mozart's, is at the lower octave. Schubert, however, builds a set of four variations on this idea before, like Mozart again, he brings back his slow opening to round the piece off.

Variation form, with which Schubert sought to structure this early fantasy, was a centuries-old form which the Classical composers made their own, reaffirming its intrinsic unities of key and length (all variations having the same keynote and number of bars) but then gradually allowing themselves enrichments within this rigid frame and, eventually, some relaxation of the frame rigidity itself. Schubert soon turned to the Variation genre. A month after including a set of variations as slow movement of his Second Symphony, he wrote his first free-standing set, the Ten Variations in F major for piano. He never found variation form as liberating as Beethoven did, and in this set the invention is characteristically constrained by the protocol of the form. But he does allow himself one little liberty: while in most of the variations he preserves the refreshingly irregular phrase-structure of the theme (4+5, 7+5), in Variation 2 the 7-bar phrase is reduced to 6 and in Variation 3 the first 5-bar phrase is extended to 6 by stretching its harmonic limbs.

Six years later, in the Thirteen Variations on a theme of Anselm Hüttenbrenner, there is appreciably greater freedom in departing from the details of the model, while still no danger of the model's being lost sight of. The theme, from Hüttenbrenner's First String Quartet, is obviously modelled on that of the slow movement of Beethoven's Seventh Symphony. Schubert loved that symphony, but never used the slow movement theme as a model as overtly as Hüttenbrenner does here. Perhaps he felt easier about

making use of it at one remove, as it were, through the medium of
Hüttenbrenner. Even the bare fifth at the final cadence of Hüttenbrenner's
first section (something of a rarity in late Classical and early Romantic
music of the Austro-German composers) seems to echo the bare fifth of
Beethoven's third bar. The ninth variation (Fig. 12b) has a Schumannesque
beauty, and its comparison with Hüttenbrenner's theme (first section)
(Fig. 12a) shows how far Schubert now feels able to go in reinterpreting
a model. The first phrase of melody is derived from the inner part of the
model, and the second freely extends this newly minted idea, while the
conversion from A minor to A major opens up C sharp minor as an
alternative midway destination to C major. It is hard to agree with Maurice
Brown that the Hüttenbrenner set is less interesting than the earlier F
major set, and equally hard to reconcile his view of 'academic contrivances'
as 'the nursery apparatus of composition'[7] with his regret that the Hüttenbrenner Variations lack the 'variety and interest which scholastic devices
could have given to these variations'.[8]

Fig. 12

Among the early piano works are several single movements which have
been supposed to belong to otherwise incomplete sonatas. Not so explained

are two independent scherzi (D.593). The first, in B flat, makes an attractive concert piece, with its debonair skips, pecking staccato, and airy-textured *joie de vivre*. The reprise in the second section is finely engineered, and the sparing fortissimo gestures are well judged to clinch the structure. The lower-pitched legato of the trio provides an ideal foil. Altogether, this handsomely wrought '*moment musical*' needs no sonata context to set it off. The second scherzo, in D flat, seems less at ease with itself. In its second section it settles disarmingly for the key of E and for a texture close to that of the previous scherzo, but the return to D flat is uncomfortable and the bravura which Schubert finds necessary to add in order to clinch this homecoming sounds overdone in relation to the nature of the piece. The lovely A flat major trio is not lost to us if the scherzo is not performed, since Schubert had already used it in the E flat Sonata, D.568.

There are at least two good reasons why Schubert's unfinished pieces may be of interest: they may illuminate the composer's self-critical judgement, or they may contain fascinating things which one may wish to rescue or which throw light on other works. Another free-standing piece, the unfinished Adagio in G (D.178) of 1815, is worth a glance for the second reason. Bland as it is, it includes in its second version a middle section which tries out some of the wilder harmonic adventures of the sort found in later works such as the G major String Quartet. At one point we are reminded of Domenico Scarlatti when Schubert gets hold of a little motive and works it somewhat persistently through harmonies that change minutely (in that the bass may merely slip a semitone) but radically (since the harmonic upshot may be far-reaching). The same piece serves to illustrate one of the textual problems which editors of Schubert's works encounter. In composing he obviously moved his pen fast to keep up with his teeming invention, and was not always careful to mark up his scores fully, let alone edit them. Incomplete or inconsistent dynamic or phrasing indications are more of a problem with Schubert than with most composers, as are omitted accidentals. But sometimes even a false note escapes his notice. At the twenty-second bar of this piece (first version), for example, a D natural on the first beat is in conflict with a D sharp on the second beat in another part. This cross-relation is not typical of Schubert's harmonic style, and either it was an aberration which he would have edited out if he had allowed himself time, or it may be that he simply forgot to add a sharp before the first D natural. The error has survived both complete editions of Schubert's works without comment.

One of the most fascinating of the early piano works outside the sonatas is a Fantasy in C for piano discovered in the 1960s in the collection of manuscripts which had been in the possession of Josef Hüttenbrenner of Graz. The manuscript is in a copyist's hand, but the title page, written by Hüttenbrenner, states that the work is Schubert's. The question of its authenticity was thoroughly debated by Walther Dürr in his preface to his edition for the Neue Schubert-Ausgabe.[9] The piece has since been entitled the *Grazer Fantasie* and catalogued as D.605A.

In its outward structure this substantial work resembles the fantasies of Schubert's youth rather than the two later keyboard examples, the 'Wanderer' and the F minor Fantasy for piano duet. There is no attempt to implant sonata characteristics. Outer sections in C major, Moderato con espressione, frame a succession of inner sections, including, in second place, an Alla polacca in F sharp major. What is truly remarkable about the piece, though, is its musical style. While it does not make anything like the virtuoso demands of the 'Wanderer' Fantasy, it tends towards the outwardly pianistic manner of the pianist-composers of the first half of the nineteenth century, whether in its brilliant passagework or in its more poetic sentiments. Hummel and Weber are the models cited by Dürr, but in several places the idiosyncrasies of Chopin are strikingly anticipated.

The quietly undulating left-hand pattern which begins the piece evokes the opening of Chopin's D flat Nocturne or Liszt's third Consolation. The little fioriture with which Chopin embellishes many a gentle cantilena are much in evidence here too. The twisting ascent with which Schubert extends his 'polonaise' (Fig. 13a) shows the composer conceiving a pianistic idea along disconcertingly similar lines to Chopin in his Fantasy Impromptu (Fig. 13b) and the Impromptu in A flat, Op. 29, No. 1 (Fig. 13c), both transposed here to make comparison easier.

Fig. 13   a

One may hear more Liszt (bars 174–8) and even the finale of Brahms's First Symphony (bars 237–42) in these astonishingly prophetic pages; yet, the more closely one listens, the more one recognizes Schubertian fingerprints, which back up the more extra-musical arguments for the work's authenticity adduced by Dürr. The haunting theme which turns up in the middle of the fantasy inhabits the world of the intimate Schubert impromptu more certainly than it would have been within the imaginative scope of a Hummel or a Weber.[10] Indeed the second contender for authorship of the work whose claim Dürr finds himself having to argue against is not one of these, but Anselm Hüttenbrenner, Josef's brother and, like Schubert, a pupil of Salieri. Dürr in fact proposes the idea that Schubert deliberately set out to write in an adopted style, a reason for his dating the work in 1817–18, when Schubert also pretended to transalpine manners in two Overtures in the Italian Style (D.590 and D.591). The observation that the fantasy inherits an earlier formal prototype rather than attempting the later sonata-fantasy synthesis tends to support this conclusion.

However strong Schubert's allegiance to the fantasy was (particularly when writing for four hands at one piano), it was the sonata among all the two-hand piano genres that claimed his major effort throughout his career. There are seventeen more or less complete sonatas, representing an almost unbroken chain of activity from 1815 to 1828, but for a three-year silence in 1820–2. This level of productivity is broadly similar to that of Beethoven, who issued thirty-two sonatas over a period of twenty-seven years. While Schubert was less radical than Beethoven in re-interpreting the concept of sonata during his career, it is worth reflecting that if Beethoven had died at the age of thirty-one the 'Moonlight' and 'Pastoral' would have been his last, and fifteen sonatas would have remained unwritten.

Schubert's first surviving attempt in the field is a Sonata in E major (D.157). It was presumably intended as a standard-format four-movement work, but only three movements exist; there is no trace of a finale. By this time Schubert had created some immortal songs. He aspired to greatness as an instrumental composer, but greatness in that field was harder won. It is an interesting exercise to count the immortal song composers who have also excelled as instrumental composers. This first sonata is a work of fresh, competent invention, with some unorthodoxies that already point forward to the composer's individual mature style. If Schubert failed to embark on a finale (which is not certain), it could have been because he was less convinced by his first movement than by the middle movements, and outer movements traditionally share common problems. The first movement has a tendency to set up patterns to become models for repetition or sequence which are on the long side, and somewhat plain, with the result that as they are processed the invention seems too thinly spread, the material too cumbersome. There are some outrageously far-reaching modulations that titillate but do not wholly convince, such as the move from B major to F major in four bars at the beginning of the development.

The slow movement is a pure rondo whose two episodes sport some game metrical effects, producing interesting phrase-structures. In its first return the rondo theme is varied in an unusual way: it is simplified rather than elaborated. In distilling this simplified version (Fig. 14) did Schubert create the seed for a symphony? Did he consciously plunder his unfinished sonata for the starting point of his Seventh Symphony (in E, D.729)?

Fig. 14

The scherzo, which Schubert conservatively calls a minuet, is a colourful
and convincing movement. The fleeting implications of numerous keys,
near and distant, in the first seventeen bars of the second section are but
one of its virtues. The trio's restless crotchets in G major look forward to
those of a later trio, in the D major Sonata, D.850, where they serve
altogether more daring ends. For all that, this trio is not to be devalued
as a 'superseded model'. Deftly coloured with by no means ordinary detail,
it takes its worthy place in the eighteen-year-old composer's first sonata
scherzo – an effort as impressive in its way as the first symphonic scherzo
of the thirty-year-old Beethoven had been.

Some six or seven months later came a Sonata in C (D.279) which
begins as Mozart might have begun a sonata but comes to resemble more
and more those early and middle Beethoven sonatas that are inclined to
virtuosity, notably the C major, Op. 2, No. 3, and the 'Waldstein', as its
exposition proceeds. At the beginning of the development Schubert ventures a quite extraordinary harmonic experiment, to be discussed elsewhere
(page 399). This is Schubert's first movement in sonata form to begin its
recapitulation in the subdominant, a procedure which may be put down
to innocence rather than thrift on Schubert's part, whatever notable commentators may have inferred (see Chapter 23, pages 394–5). To prepare
for this recapitulation, Schubert recalls to active service the music used for
the transition; and in the coda the eighteen-year-old composer expects the
pianist to play in the right hand rapid semiquaver part-scales in octaves, a
feature which again may have come from the 'Waldstein' Sonata, although
the glissando which Beethoven evidently intended (finale, bars 465–9) is
impossible because Schubert's scale turns a corner, while there is no chance
of the left hand helping out (as some latter-day pianists permit in the
'Waldstein') since the left hand is already engaged at this point.[11]

The slow movement is a simple ternary design with a central episode
in which Schubert catches the occasional echo of the slow introduction
to his treasured Beethoven Symphony No. 2. The memory of his other
sinfonia grata, Mozart's G minor (No. 40), seems to impel the minuet, which
is in A minor. In the year after this sonata, the theme of Mozart's minuet,
and its chromatic passages, would affect Schubert's Fifth Symphony. The
Mozart features recognizable this time are the cadence which closes both
Mozart's sections (heard at Schubert's eighth bar), the transference of the
theme to the bass at the beginning of the second section, and the passages

of counterpoint, with syncopations prominent. The unassuming little trio in A major has much charm, and anticipates that of the last sonata, the B flat, in preparing for the reprise in the second section by re-establishing the pattern of the opening almost exactly in the previous bars, so that a minuscule adjustment to the pattern is needed to let the actual reprise materialize. There is an alternative trio in F major which has one or two distinctive touches.

An unfinished Allegretto in C minor (D.346) was written on paper of the same type as D.279. The date given for it in the Deutsch catalogue (D2) is a speculative one of 1816, and it is possible that it may have been written in the previous year as finale to the C major Sonata. Its themes are rondo-like but the form is nearer to sonata form. The Haydnesque opening, in 'quartet texture', shows a deft lightness of touch, while the galumphing first episode sounds like Schubert's answer to the equivalent episode in Mozart's *Rondo alla Turca* (Sonata in A, K.331).

The five movements listed in D2 under D.459 and D.459A were taken by Ferguson to comprise one single complete Sonata in E major (1816), although it is not certain what Schubert's intention was. The first (posthumous) edition bore the title *Fünf Klavierstücke*. The lost autograph was rediscovered in 1930, but although it is headed 'Sonate' it comprises only the first movement and part of the second. The inclusion of the remaining three *Klavierstücke* within the sonata would be consistent with Schubert's practice in that they are a slow movement, a scherzo, and a potential finale, while the keys are C major, A major and E major respectively; but it would be inconsistent as it results in a five-movement sonata with two scherzi. If Schubert did decide that a second scherzo was desirable, there can be little doubt that he would have seen this as feasible only if the total number of movements were increased to five. Accordingly, it is worthwhile to establish whether there could have been reasons for adding a second scherzo.

The opening Allegro moderato is one of Schubert's most compact sonata-form first movements. The material is attractively varied and none the worse for two unobtrusive distant echoes of Beethoven's First Symphony (Beethoven's very first bars at bars 43–4, and bars 42–6 of Beethoven's slow movement at bars 25–9), but it also flows in cogent continuity. Once more Schubert begins his recapitulation in the subdominant. The second movement is in 3/4 time and is marked 'Allegro', but it is not headed 'Scherzo'. One cannot play its first eight-bar strain, however, and feel it was intended as anything other than a scherzo. There is no repeat-mark at the eighth bar, for the simple reason that Schubert wishes to vary the repeat, so must write it out. It is not clear at what point he decided this was not to be a conventional scherzo. After the varied repeat there is some development of the theme (consistent with normal practice

in a second section of scherzo), but this eventually cadences in the dominant, where there is a caesura (covered by a single line of quavers in the
right hand), and a second subject (Fig. 15b) based on 'x' in the first theme
(Fig. 15a) then runs for a further forty-two bars, duly closing, still in the
dominant, with a drawn-out cadence. A four-bar single-line link leads to
a double bar with repeat-marks. Thus the scherzo has become a movement
in sonata form, the point reached so far being the end of the exposition.
Instead of the repetition of binary modules, as in a conventional scherzo,
the whole section of ninety-seven bars is repeated.

Fig. 15

Did Schubert realize, as his second subject flowed on and on, that he
was bursting his binary bonds and a decision to follow sonata form was
now inevitable? Or had he decided this at the end of the written-out
repeat of the first section? Or had he planned the structure even before
he set pen to paper? The likelihood is that the decision was made no
later than the beginning of the 'second section'. It is even possible that a
sonata-form scherzo had been envisaged from the start, in which case
Schubert could have been taking his cue from Beethoven's String Quartet
in C minor, Op. 18, No. 4. There, Beethoven follows his first movement
with a movement in triple time and actually marked 'Scherzoso' which
turns out to be in sonata form. Moreover, he follows this in turn with a
movement headed 'Menuetto' which is as much a scherzo as a minuet. If,
then, the presence of two scherzi among Schubert's five movements appears
to be a reason for discarding the notion that they make a sonata, it need
not be. Schubert follows his exposition with a development, and a recapitulation in which a revised transition enables the second subject to appear
in the tonic.

The compact Adagio in C major, in an abridged sonata form, has a
transition-theme recalling the eighteenth-century *Empfindsamer Stil* (literally, 'sentimental style') and containing, moreover, a double echo of

Mozart. When it first appears, after the opening thematic paragraph in C major, the way in which it leads off from C major into C minor, with a rising arpeggio upbeat to a high accented dominant, is reminiscent of a similar procedure at the same juncture in the slow movement of the 'Jupiter' Symphony (bars 18–19). When this theme returns in the recapitulation in A minor, it is the opening of Mozart's Sonata in that key (K.310) that is brought to mind.

The 'Scherzo con trio' is an Allegro, but Schubert marks his trio 'Piu tardo'. Here is an instructive case (the Sixth Symphony being another) of Schubert indicating that a trio should be at a slower tempo, in the light of which one should hesitate to adopt a slower tempo for a trio if there is no such indication. This trio is noteworthy for the fact that the reprise usually incorporated into the second section, and thus repeated when that section is repeated, is omitted from the second section, but is written out to follow the repeat of that section, so that it is heard only once. Schubert extends it to form a bridge back to the scherzo.

The unusual marking 'Allegro patetico' is given to the finale, and it is an unusual movement. First, it makes a thematic feature of quintuplet semiquavers (Beethoven had used them as a development tool in the first movement of his 'Appassionata' Sonata, but never used them as part of a theme). Second, the proportions of the exposition are bizarre, with the first group more than three times as long as the second. Third, the piano writing becomes technically quite taxing in the development and coda in a way which suggests the influence of those pianist-composers such as Hummel, Kalkbrenner, Field and Moscheles. And finally, the last cadence of the exposition requires some hand-crossing that is very rare in Schubert.

The Sonata in A minor (D.537) is the first of three in that key. Composed in 1817, it has a fine first movement, a patchy finale, and a slow movement of no great interest except that Schubert later improved its theme and used it for the rondo finale of the late A major Sonata, D.959. It is partly the quality of material that sets the first movement apart. Combining fire with poetry, it has an abundance of imaginative detail, and an impetus that never fades, even in the twenty bars tapering from pianissimo to triple piano that comprise the codetta and first segment of development. The codetta, incidentally, is a variant of the second subject, over the same tonic pedal F, and its last bar (characterized by a falling appoggiatura) is the source of the whole development, which includes, after a trenchant, energetic fortissimo passage, a lyrical theme – ostensibly new but still germinating from the appoggiatura – in remote A flat major. This movement presents a further instalment in Schubert's love-affair with the subdominant recapitulation. Was it because he thought highly of his development (with justification) that he called for the repeat of the entire development and recapitulation? It is, in any case, a unique instance of such repetition in these early sonatas, there being only one case in the later sonatas (in the 'Little' A major, D.664). After the repeat, a wonderfully terse coda closes the movement.

Each of the remaining two movements brings some modest formal innovation. The slow movement is a rondo with two unrelated episodes (therefore, an 'old' rondo) in which the first return of the rondo theme is not in the 'textbook' key of the tonic, but a semitone higher (F major instead of E major). And the finale is in an abridged sonata form, but in this instance there is not even a short link to replace the development: Schubert goes directly from the end of the exposition into the recapitulation, which begins in the dominant (compare the finale of the Third Symphony). Two points of detail, one backward-looking and one forward-looking, invite comment. Do we hear a distant echo of Beethoven's *Leonora* No. 3 Overture (bars 577–83) at bars 119–26 and 290–7? And the leisurely winding down to the last suddenly loud chord adumbrates the spacious ways of Schubert's very final group of sonatas.

What comes to us as the Sonata in A flat (1817) may or may not be a complete sonata. The third of the three movements is an Allegro in sonata form, not a 'normal finale' according to Ferguson, although he doesn't say why.[12] In fact it is an admirable little finale, within the circumscribed world which it – with the rest of the sonata – inhabits. And its form is that of the finale of D.664 in A major, but on a reduced scale. More of a problem is that this finale is in E flat, like the slow movement, while the first movement is in A flat. Schubert did tend to begin and end works in different keys in his early days (his first string quartet is an example), although this was not what one would expect from him in 1817, and the autograph is dated by the composer. Could it be, hasty worker that he was, that when a musical idea came to him in a particular key he would start to set it down without reference to the key of the multi-movement work he was writing? At this stage in his career, mono-tonality was perhaps not so *de rigueur* that he couldn't let the work stand. It is doubtful, however, if he would have let such a conception stand from about 1819–20 on.

The first movement is a tightly constructed and rather tight-lipped sonata form, immaculately put together in a middle-Mozart style, even having moments of Mozartian genius as when the one-bar closing theme is at once repeated with one note raised. There is little here that is Schubertian. The theme of the slow movement has something in common with the second subject of the slow movement of Mozart's E flat Symphony (No. 39). The finale, with its fourteen-note anacrusis, is a delightful mixture of Mozartian and Haydnesque ingredients, and is also an early Classical throwback in that, without transition, the first group ends *on* the dominant and the second subject immediately begins *in* that key; or rather almost immediately, because here Schubert adds a one-bar 'curtain' after the caesura, as though in hasty belated compensation for the lack of transition. The second subject itself has a tuneful bonhomie that makes one want to whistle it.

Of the Sonata in E minor (D.566) of 1817 two complete movements exist. A third movement is included in D2 despite the fact that it is in A flat major. The question of its possible belonging to D.566 has been discussed by Maurice Brown.[13] The Moderato in E minor and Allegretto in E major are both in sonata form and similarly paced. Both show Schubert at a stage where he can't quite make sonata form work for him. The developments are unsatisfactory: in the first movement, Schubert tries at this point to create a climax (indeed he rises to the only fortissimo in the sonata), but the last two-thirds of the development, containing this climax, have little thematic relevance to the movement – there is no sense of inevitability. The development of the second movement is perfunctory, and nearly half of it is dominant preparation for the return. Both movements contain one enchanting idea. In the first, it is the second idea which, with its trilled second beat, looks forward to later sonatas and closes in a delightful cadence-idea which Schubert lets us hear four times and takes up at the beginning of the development in a remote key after a pointed silence (a lesson learned from Haydn perhaps) whereupon a further four modulating statements are heard. In the second, the second theme of the second group has real Schubertian charm, and something of the glistening gem-like miniaturism of certain Mozart closing themes. The A flat scherzo is unremarkable.

Later in 1817 Schubert wrote a Sonata in D flat, possibly an unprecedented key for a sonata of any kind. A transposed version of this work in E flat also exists. It was for long assumed that the E flat version was made in the same year as the D flat, 1817. Martin Chusid[14] has marshalled evidence to suggest that a dating of 1825–6 is more likely for the E flat version, and John Reed has added further valuable support for this view.[15] Why should Schubert transpose a work originally written in the key of D flat? It was for long assumed that his second thoughts found D flat an unsaleable key for a piano sonata. The possibility that the slow movement would sound better in a key other than C sharp minor was another factor raised. Perhaps, though, the reason has to do with the tessitura of the first movement. Could it be that the last two dozen bars were found to lie uncomfortably low in relation to their density of texture, impairing their harmonic clarity?

The E flat version is in fact not just a transposition, but a revision too. Schubert's enlargement of the development section of the first movement may itself argue for the later date of revision, as he was writing considerably longer developments in the piano sonatas of the 1820s. Certainly the proportions of the original D flat version, with a second group of 70 bars compared with a development of only 28 bars, would have been, from Schubert's 1820s perspective, unbalanced. Even so, in the E flat revision, that proportion was not adjusted beyond 71:48. The themes are of the sort Mozart might have used in a string quartet or piano sonata; indeed the triadic first one is a distant cousin of that which opens the B flat Piano Sonata, K.570. After the second there is a fetching modulation to D flat (in the E flat version), where a derivative of the second subject appears in the bass under a right-hand accompaniment, followed soon by a move to C minor, where the same derivative now sings out in the right hand above its accompaniment. Such sharing out of roles adds to the length of a second group. This 'multiplying favours, multiplying minutes' syndrome is one that caused Mozart's string quintets (with an extra player to keep happy) to outlast his string quartets. It has its effect, too, on Schubert's Octet.

A detailed comparison of the two versions of all the movements, which space forbids here, is instructive. It is as though Schubert, on returning to the sonata later, treated it as a sketch which he was now filling out. At the recapitulation of the first movement, for example, he 'shadows' the first theme by letting the right hand follow the left a half-beat later, instead of playing the same line simultaneously an octave above the left. Perhaps Schubert was aware of the difficulty of finding one uniform tempo which would suit all the ideas in the movement, for this change mitigates the sudden reduction in fast-note activity after the end of the development. One incidental detail worth noting is best appreciated with reference to the D flat version: Schubert anticipates at one point a left-hand pattern to appear four years later in Beethoven's A flat major Sonata, Op. 110. Where this first appears, in the exposition of the first movement (Fig. 16a), the key too is Beethoven's (Fig. 16b). The notes, which incorporate a tonic A flat pedal as well as the diminished seventh on the leading-note, are the same in each case, except that Schubert's twelve are grouped in three fours and Beethoven's in two sixes, producing different accentuation. As Schubert's work remained unpublished, this interesting similarity of thought is presumably coincidental.

Fig. 16   a   b

The two versions of the Andante molto (an ambiguous marking which presumably means slower than andante since there is a familiar alternative term — andantino — if faster than andante is intended) are in C sharp minor (first version) and G minor (second version). Interestingly enough, Schubert first sketched the movement in D minor. When transposing and revising, Schubert added a minuet and trio — a delightful, perfectly proportioned miniature on an intimate scale, Mozartian in its note-thrift, Schubertian in its graceful charm. The trio has supremely natural five-bar phrases, and periodically rejoices in that Schubertian habit (often found in his keyboard dances) of lifting an inner harmony note out so that it lies above the melody, as a momentary descant.

The finale is one of those gently flowing movements in which Schubert cannot bring himself to close the exposition. But the player or listener who perseveres (for the piece does not divulge its pleasures straight off) and soldiers on through the place where Schubert seems to lose his way will be rewarded. There is, for one thing, a truly wonderful interplay of lines — not too complex — in the extensive second group, where Schubert adds five bars not present in the D flat version of the sonata, these being a restatement in the final second-subject key (B flat) of five bars previously heard in a diversionary key of D flat. And there is an attractive development, all the better for having been worked for. This development replaces the shorter one in the D flat version, though the smooth, long descent into the recapitulation is a happy thought Schubert preserved from that earlier version. When the development begins, one fancies one hears a variation come adrift from the B flat Impromptu (D.935/3), but the slower harmonic rhythm and aerated texture is a particularly welcome contrast here, and further relief comes with the ensuing 'cello tune', an elaboration though it be of the first theme. The first theme of this finale contains a peculiarly rich discord in its first bar (Fig. 17a), and as a parting shot in his coda Schubert provocatively shifts this idea into the 'wrong' half of the bar, creating a changed accentual effect, then follows the original discord with a new version of it (a double appoggiatura in supertonic seventh harmony instead of dominant seventh harmony) (Fig. 17b). That, in essence, is all Schubert is concerned to do in the coda of this amiable, unpretentious finale.

Fig. 17 a   *Allegro moderato*   b

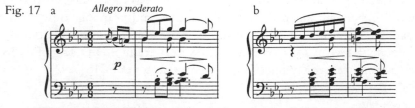

One of the most innovatory sonata movements of 1817 is a fragmentary Allegro moderato in F sharp minor (D.571). An Andante, D.604, and a scherzo and unfinished finale (D.570) are usually taken to go with this first movement, making up an incomplete four-movement Sonata in F sharp minor, thus: Allegro moderato (D.571) breaking off at end of development; Andante (D.604) complete; Scherzo: Allegro vivace (D.570) complete; Allegro (D.570) breaking off at end of development.

What is so enterprising in the first movement is its texture in relation to its structure. There is an almost continuous flow of quavers; in fact, the flow is continuous from bar 44 to the end of the development (end of sketch) at bar 143. Yet the movement is in sonata form. Sonata form was traditionally viewed as a dramatic form, thriving on oppositions, contrasts, rhetorical gestures. This usually implied variety of rhythm, figuration, harmonic rhythm, phrase span, texture, dynamics. The seminal example of a movement which contradicts this norm – being an essentially monotextural sonata form – was the first movement of Beethoven's 'Moonlight' Sonata. Here, the near-unity of texture brings with it a reduction in the other kinds of variety referred to above. Another landmark example in this connection is Beethoven's third-period Sonata in A, Op. 101. Although the first movement is not so rigorously mono-textural as the first movement of the 'Moonlight', there is a marked tendency to non-articulation of the phases and junctions of sonata form by means of the continuity of textural elements, coupled with a similarly marked tendency to compression. The result is that the sonata-form basis of the movement is usually overlooked.

Schubert's movement embodies a stance halfway between these two models. The musical thought is expansive, not compressed. While there is a fair degree of textural consistency, the rhythmic and dynamic unity are more conspicuous still. The initial rolling left-hand figuration is unvaried for the first twenty-seven bars, where it gives way (for the transition) to a tendency towards continuous quavers (shared between the parts). At bar 44 the transformation is complete, with continuous quavers established for good. In the whole fragment of 143 bars, only 10 bars are marked forte. The rest is pianissimo (117 bars) but for 16 bars of piano. There is just enough variety of texture to articulate the form, at least to point up the close of the exposition. Thus a ruminant, rhapsodic, relaxed air prevails. This is a piece of unusual poetic beauty for its period, standing apart from other Schubert instrumental pieces of its time and pointing ahead to the expansive, ruminating manner of some of the later instrumental works. There are a few passages of exquisite lyrical counterpoint (e.g. Fig. 18) such as one occasionally finds in the works/sketches of 1817–21.

Fig. 18

Of the movements with which this one is customarily associated, the second is a short movement in abridged sonata form, with a beautifully wrought second group in the subdominant. It is not altogether surprising that in a finale in F sharp minor Schubert should take in A major on the way to a second subject in C sharp minor: that he should interpose, between the sections in A major and C sharp minor, a passage in F major, is. He makes the transition from F major to C sharp minor in six volatile bars. Once he reaches C sharp minor, he abandons the prevailing semi-quavers, and writes continuous triplets from here right through to the end of the development. In this respect the movement has an obvious kinship with the first movement of this supposed 'sonata' (D.571), a kinship which would tend to support the attribution of the two movements to the same multi-movement scheme.

None of these early sonatas has a more imposing opening than the Sonata in B major. Seldom in Schubert does triadic material combine with dotted rhythm to such powerful effect. But the real promise shows itself a few bars later, where the upward–springing leap which began the movement is stretched and twisted out of key, quickly reaching the threshold of G major. In this new key the allegiance to gesture more than to theme is maintained. A new idea circles around in ostinato fashion, producing a series of one-bar modules, the one being the same as its forerunner but with the counterpoint inverted (Fig. 19), as though for the time being a

Fig. 19

lyrical seed is encased within a prism which turns to reflect the light off its different facets. The Romantic, almost self-indulgent upbeat harmony is in sharp contrast to the tough, forceful opening just heard. What follows is no less striking, for G is only the second key, not of a three-key exposition but of a four-key one. The development then resumes the first theme, builds new dramas from its steep melodic plunges, and adds some challenging harmonic shocks. Keys fly past (D major, F major, A flat major), bringing the music full circle back to B in so short a time that it would be premature to embark on recapitulation at this point, if recapitulation means reintroducing the opening material. In any case, Schubert has presumably already decided that his recapitulation will begin in E, not B (see above). So he uses B here as a step on the way to E. The purpose of beginning the recapitulation in the subdominant is that the idiosyncratic and complex key-chain of the exposition (B–G–E–F sharp) can be preserved for further hearing, being literally transposed as E–C–A–B in the recapitulation.

The slow movement is a simple, pensive movement in ternary form with an extraordinary ending. There are three beats to the bar, but at the close Schubert in effect writes four-beat bars, maintaining this illusion (or is it reality?) through the last six bars and doing nothing to restore triple metre to the listener's mind before the movement ends. Likewise the minuet and trio seem unremarkable, until at the end of its first section a little cadence-idea struts in and Schubert at once begins his second section by setting this in the Brucknerian distance of B flat major. What follows is a marvel of epigrammatic wit. Based on nothing but the cadence-idea, it imitates and varies it with rare economy and point, pretending to make a new little paragraph out of it, and finally twisting it back towards the home key, before it gives way to the returning first theme. This alone earns the sonata its immortality, although it is a pity Schubert could not match such fecund invention in his trio section.

A Haydnesque playfulness impels the finale. One of Schubert's witticisms merits special attention. In most music of the Classical period, the bars (as written) are grouped in pairs (as far as the ear is concerned). The exposition of this finale, typically, consists entirely of pairs of bars. A strong bar is followed by a weak bar, just as a strong beat may be followed by a weak beat. When, as his cadence-theme, Schubert introduces Fig. 20a, the quavers are on the weak bar and the low note on the strong bar (see prosody signs on the figure). The sole concern of the development section is to re-interpret this idea, by (among other things) re-siting it in relation to the bar-groupings: the quavers now fall in the strong bar (Fig. 20b). The distinction is clear when the passage is heard in context. Schubert had done something similar in September of the previous year in the finale of his Fifth Symphony.[16]

Fig. 20

The casualties of the critical years 1818–22 included three unfinished piano sonatas. Of the Sonata in C (D.613) there are fragments of the first and last movements, while an Adagio in E bearing the same date (April 1818) is sometimes taken to be the intended slow movement. The first movement begins in the Mozart tradition and has a Rossinian second

subject in E flat before the expected move to G major. The development
lacks distinction, as does most of the exposition, except for the strange
modulation from A flat to E, made still stranger by the triplets which
appear from nowhere, just before the end of the fragment. The finale's
style is congruous with that of the first movement, except that the second
subject this time sounds more prophetic of Verdi than redolent of Rossini.
After its E major has given way to G major, Schubert curiously supports
a descending chromatic scale with a second part in four-note modules
which suggest the dominant and tonic harmony of, respectively, G major,
E flat major, and B major (Fig. 21). These keys are, of course, symmetrically
related, each being a major third distant from both the others; and Schubert
is thus compressing into a tiny space a larger-scale structure tried during
the exposition of the first movement of his Fourth Symphony, where the
keys of A flat major, E major and C major succeed each other at eight-bar
intervals. The sequential pattern produced in Fig. 21 implies a kind of
hemiola, hemiola being a triple-time concept which is valid in 6/8 time
if one bar is thought of as two of 3/8. This adds further interest to the
passage, which is repeated three bars later in inverted counterpoint. The
succession of keys G–E flat–B is, of course, not commonplace, and would
seem less strange if the progressions were fully harmonized. The Adagio
in E is a compact sonata form which, after a plain opening which contains
an echo or two of the slow movement theme of Beethoven's Piano Concerto No. 2 in B flat, sprouts an abundance of florid elaborations of a type
far from routine.

Fig. 21

The most interesting of this group of unfinished works is the Sonata in
F minor. It is likely that the Adagio in D flat (D.505) was intended as its
slow movement, in which case only the first movement is unfinished,
although part of the finale's recapitulation is sketched as a single line, which
needs to be – and by analogy can easily be – filled out. The Allegro
has a strong, elemental opening, evoking the atmosphere of a Bruckner
symphony. The theme soon returns, now harmonized, with due minor-key
Angst, but quickly moves to the relative major – as happened in the
earlier minor-key movements from piano sonatas. This is another of those
movements, too, where a faster figuration set up early in the second group
persists right through to the end of the exposition, then through the
development to the recapitulation (with only two bars' intermission). The

movement breaks off at the end of the development, though the last three notes penned here were presumably not to have been a statement of the opening theme in F major, but an allusion to it on the dominant of B flat minor. There is many a glimpse of the later Schubert, in the figuration and the assimilation of thematic snatches within it. The way in which, in the development, the first theme is extended into new territory looks forward to the last great B flat Sonata.

There are times when a harmonic strategy forms the very crux of what Schubert is doing in his music, and if we want to say what is going on there is really nothing else to talk about but that. In this movement, for example, he makes a point of exploring the ambiguities of the augmented triad. Sometimes Schubert's harmony is so surprising that an editor suspects he has not notated what he intended. Howard Ferguson, in his fine edition of the sonatas for the Associated Board, replaces Schubert's chord in bar 109 with a quite different one. The chord he suggests is not more credible than what Schubert wrote, nor can it realistically be claimed that what Schubert wrote could have been mistakenly written in place of the chord Ferguson thinks he intended.

The Adagio is a compact ternary piece (placed third by Sviatoslav Richter). The middle section begins with sonorities which anticipate the equivalent section in the slow movement of the last B flat Sonata. The tonal scheme is the same, too: there, A major in the context of C sharp minor; here A major in the context of D flat major (C sharp = D flat). After that, Schubert's thinking in this middle section shows extraordinary freedom. The scherzo is one of the most interesting and ambitious of Schubert's finest pre-1820 movements. At the outset the ear is teased by a long-held note, and may well fail to construe correctly the relationship of the following shorter notes to the underlying pulse. Instead of repeating this section as it is, Schubert writes out his repeat, filling in all the phrases with regular quaver movement – and so giving the ear a yardstick against which to measure and 'place' these longer note-values. The quavers form an added descant, which obliges Schubert to compress into the pianist's left hand his original chordal theme. This produces some unusual stretches and densities, and clearly the breaking of chords to facilitate performance would be quite out of place here. The harmony at one point, just before it is 'straightened out' in the closing cadence of the section, has a post-Wagnerian air-of-another-planet quality about it.

The second section is launched with a gesture inspired, one fancies, by late Beethoven. Then a new idea is given a double presentation, as the first idea had been: first, with 'holes' on the first beat, then with the holes filled in by quavers. When the quavers are subsequently transferred to the right hand, and the tune to the left, there follow some harmonic distortions (or perversities of harmonic rhythm) which perpetuate the late-Beethoven atmosphere. The reprise poses for Schubert the question as to whether the first or second statement of the first theme should be recalled, with quavers absent or present. The comprehensive compromise is chosen: the first phrase appears without quavers, which are then added for the second and third phrases. The trio provides a textural contrast, but by letting the spirit of harmonic adventure overflow into it Schubert cements its association with the scherzo.

Premonitions of Chopin have been discovered in the virtuoso outburst which begins the finale. Schubert, in turn, had perhaps been touched by the stormy energies of two Beethoven sonata movements, the finale of the 'Appassionata' and the first movement of Op. 111. In any case, this is Schubert's best finale to date, in the piano sonatas. He does not become obsessed by one figuration or rhythm for too long: there is continual interchange between a number of sharply differentiated ideas – the stormy torrent of semiquavers at the start, the measured dignity of the following chordal theme, the triplets which accompany the second hearing of this idea, the grandeur of the second theme's varied re-statement at the close of the exposition. A strong momentum and intensity of expression run through from beginning to end. And this must also be one of Schubert's shortest finales, which only enhances its power.

The Sonata in C sharp minor (D.655) consists of a fragment of a first movement only, of statistical rather than musical interest, in that the proportions of its three-key exposition are unusual. The second group, in E major then A flat major, is more than four times the length of the first. There are a few bars of particular beauty or polish (bars 36, 42–3, 47–58), but Schubert is found wrestling with a particular problem: having set up a figuration for a theme, he has difficulties adapting this to the changing harmonic situations that arise during the course of the theme, and some of the solutions are awkward. The closing theme resembles the closing theme from the second movement of Mozart's String Quintet in G minor.

It is easily forgotten that while Schubert, in these early and middle years, was so frequently opting to face the challenges of large-scale design and enjoy the opportunities it offered, he was at the same time turning out keyboard dances aplenty, usually in a simple and terse binary form with themes of no special distinction and chords to be found in the first chapter or two of an elementary harmony book. There were exceptions. The undoubted melodic charms of some of the Ländler and Deutsche were celebrated in *Lilac Time*, and, once lodged in the mind, stayed there. It was mainly in the later period that harmonic enterprise spilled over into this modest, social genre, with transcendental results.

The Early Chamber Music

It is not certain when Schubert's family string quartet first played together, but its existence is certain to have been one of the stimuli responsible for the proliferation of quartets issuing from the young composer's pen in his first seven or eight years of creativity. A prime stimulus, too, will have been his growing awareness of the imposing quartet legacy of his forebears, whether he heard them inside the home or in other venues, or simply studied them in score. What does become clear from an examination of this youthful oeuvre is that Schubert found early success more elusive in the quartet medium than in the symphony. There is no work of such charm, polish, ear-catching tunefulness and finely proportioned construction among the early quartets as the Fifth Symphony, a judgement not wholly explained by the fact that the production of symphonies lagged some two years behind the outflow of string quartets. But it was in the quartets that Schubert first made his sustained attack on the problems of large–scale instrumental composition.

And problems they were, for the young Schubert. True, in the half-century before he entered the field the quartet had been born, nurtured and brought rapidly to maturity. Whatever the wonders that lurk among string quartets of the later nineteenth century, there is no doubt that the 'Rasumovsky' Quartets written by Beethoven some three years before Schubert's first known efforts clinch the genre's astonishingly fast rise from infancy to full-grown adulthood. But in the string quartet of all media, what had been achieved by forerunners was not the automatic inheritance of successors. The three composers in whose hands the quartet had emerged to become one of the prime arenas for Classical thought were, by historical accident, the greatest contemporary (or at least overlapping) threesome of all time. The string quartet was a medium of extraordinarily expressive potential to a composer schooled in its rigours, able to deploy its slender resources to unerring purpose. That – which might be called the textural challenge so long as that implies that the test is not only of inventing a suitable texture but is as much of sustaining, varying and developing texture effectively over long spans – was Schubert's first problem.

The second was to marshal the melodic, harmonic and tonal resources of late Classical style skilfully enough to generate larger designs that were valid, whether in traditional or non-conventional terms. Schubert's first essay, the Quartet in mixed keys (D.18), was little more than a limbering-up in the medium, a testing of the water. Ignoring the closed key-scheme (beginning and ending in the same key) of tradition, it follows its own structural path – except in the minuet – in an arbitrary manner which does not compel. He would write several quartets before he was to gain any real command of quartet texture and long-term thinking.

A year or two later, the first movement of the D major Quartet (D.94) follows the convention of having two sections, the first of which is repeated, but in the first section Schubert never leaves the home key (but for an idea in D minor which never returns later). As though to compensate, after a short development he begins a recapitulation in C major, the key of the flattened leading-note. If this happened in late Beethoven we would admire the 'third-period daring'. In early Schubert it is a combination of inexperience and of a try-anything approach to key-structure which was to stay with him – not always to negative effect – in some of his later exploits. The recapitulation, nearly twice as long as the exposition, mixes restatement with new derivatives of old ideas in an ear-baffling hotchpotch which hardly justifies its longwindedness.

The attractive slow movement introduces an early dramatic touch – two loud chords which cause a pleasing irregularity in the phrase-structure – but its unenterprising tonal plan of two outer sections in the tonic framing a central one in the dominant gives little foretaste of the more vivid key-colouring to come in later slow movements. The minuet is a stunted throwback to Haydn models and the key-relationship of its trio (B flat) to the minuet itself (D) is Haydnesque too. Of the finale, which gropes towards rondo form, it can only be said that Schubert picks up various gestures from various Haydn periods and fails to make a coherent synthesis of them.

Schubert takes an appreciable step forwards in the C major Quartet (D.32). Now, at the age of fifteen, he ventures a key-scheme that moves uncertainly towards the 'three-key exposition' which was to become a distinctive and effective principle in some later first movements. For now, after a second subject in the unorthodox subdominant, he does not move directly to the dominant (which was to become the usual third key) but returns quickly to the tonic, spends considerable time there, and veers to the dominant only at the eleventh hour for a short codetta. There is then no trace of the second subject in the recapitulation. Yet the freshness of invention, the sharp-etched ideas, the crisp textures and the freedom from longueurs all conspire to make this an exhilarating movement in its own terms. The 'Presto' marking, unusual for a first movement, reflects boyish exuberance. The 'Allegro vivace' of another C major movement in 6/8 time, the finale of Mozart's Symphony No. 34, K.338, would have sufficed.

The slow movement is a compact, well-wrought Andante in 6/8 time, like the first movement. In fact this work is unusual if not unique among four-movement works in having all its movements in triple time (the last two) or with the beats divisible by three. It is a welcome trait of the minuet, then, that it periodically challenges the triple pulse with a stamping hemiola which suggests the spirit and physicality of the Czech furiant. The trio appears also as the last of a set of keyboard dances probably dating from the same year, the *Zwölf Wiener Deutsche*, D.128.

The finale is the most ambitious of the movements, and the most promising. On the one hand, it ventures neo-Baroque counterpoint – even the theme (presented unison at the outset) is a free paraphrase of a melodic type epitomized in the subject of Bach's 'Wedge' Fugue: on the other, it adopts Classical practice more convincingly than the first movement, turning sonata form to individual account, with a strong hundred-bar development. The contrapuntal passages are as impressive as the more divertimento-like ones are engaging, and the development includes some incidents which are unmistakably driven by Schubert's memory of Beethoven's sonata-form scherzo in the first 'Rasumovsky' Quartet, yet sound compellingly integral to Schubert's fresh argument. The one unorthodoxy, smacking of inexperience rather than genius, is the move back to the tonic some way short of the close of the exposition, equivalent in effect to an extended group of 'first-time bars' which are, however, not so indicated, and are therefore to be played the second time as well.

In the first movement of the B flat Quartet, D.36, Schubert is seen paying homage to Haydn's 'Fifths' Quartet in D minor, Op. 76, No. 2. It is not so much the first theme itself that is indebted, although the interval of a fifth does dominate it, as the treatment of it in canon with a quick counterpoint set against it, notably at the beginning of the development, but elsewhere as well. The counterpoint is dutiful rather than inspired, but the main defect of the movement is the tendency of its first-group material to segment itself into two-bar modules. A striking instrumental effect occurs in mid-development, when the running semiquavers that have been put to contrapuntal use become a circling ostinato-like *moto perpetuo* in the viola, to which the first violin is added in unison, then the second violin likewise in unison, then the cello an octave below. The accretion of tone, as the single line is progressively reinforced, was clearly the objective here, and Schubert had surely taken his cue from the similar passage towards the close of Beethoven's *Leonora* No. 3 Overture.

Like many of the influences at work in these early quartets, that Beethoven is an orchestral model. Schubert was writing orchestral works alongside these quartets, although not all attempts have survived, and the distinction between orchestral and chamber style is not always a certain one. In the B flat Quartet it is mainly in the finale that Schubert goes beyond the usual limits of chamber style, in passages where the four instruments – in far-flung textures covering a huge range – toil away at fortissimo volume (and in one instance triple forte). The theme of this Allegretto finale, coincidentally, testifies to the composer's early interest in irregular phrase-structures, but this seven-bar example is not too well engineered.

The finale is a rondo, although not announced as such. It is a full sonata rondo, except that there is hardly a central episode or development at all; it qualifies as a sonata rondo by its inclusion of a second group. Before the finale is a minuet in an unorthodox D major, which has an over-extended first section. And before that comes the most successful movement, an Andante in the key of the work, B flat major, in which fragmented utter-ances are made to hold together in broader lyrical spans, with debts due to both Haydn and Mozart. Darker sonorities collude with the tints of distant keys (including C flat major and minor) to make the middle section prophetic of more exploratory and dramatic episodes in the slow move-ments of the mature quartets.

Schubert had so much to say in the quartet medium, and could say it at such speed, that he could afford to build up experience by producing a large number of 'exercise' quartets in his teens: there would still be time and inspiration to spare when mastery had been achieved. The C major Quartet (D.46) was, typically, written in five days. If Schubert had Mozart's 'Dissonance' Quartet (also in C) in mind when he began the Adagio introduction, he was not concerned with the subtlety of detail and plan in that Mozart model but had simply absorbed the idea of chromatic solemnity before a bursting forth in C major. Schubert's Allegro has real vitality. More than that, when the first theme has momentarily exhausted itself, Schubert reinstates the chromatic line of the Adagio as counter-melody, in the faster tempo of course. Then, at the end of the exposition, he brings it back not just as a line but in its original polyphonically woven texture (again, without reverting to adagio tempo). The development then uses this chromatic idea in a manner more reminiscent of the finale of Mozart's Quartet in G major (K.387). All this is achieved in a concise, clearly designed movement which does, however, have a formal peculiarity. The exposition never really leaves C major behind. Only fifteen bars of it have the appearance of being in G (which is not the same as actually being in G) and they are recapitulated in C twenty-eight bars from the end of the movement. To what extent this was conscious formal experiment, or nonchalant, come-what-may, intuitive extemporization, we may only guess. Conscious without question was the omission of the first eight bars of the first subject at the point of recapitulation.

The Andante con moto slow movement has a seven-bar theme which is only given an eighth bar when it is recalled at the very end of the movement. One would say that this movement is Haydnesque (indeed Einstein did) were it not that the theme bears more than a passing resemblance to the second subject of the Andante slow movement (same key, G major, and same triple time) of Mozart's Sonata in D for piano duet (K.381), a theme which is itself of irregular length, spanning six bars, but expanded to seven on repetition.

B flat major is the extraordinary key of the minuet, which echoes the spirit of early Beethoven scherzi. The key-relationship between this and the trio (B flat major—C major) is not merely extraordinary but may well be unique in the whole history of the minuet/scherzo, but Schubert makes it work with the help of succinct linking bars fore and aft. The finale has a buzz and sparkle of its own, although there is something in Einstein's suggestion that it anticipates the 'rollicking informality' of the finale of the C major String Quintet despite the difference of tempo.[1] And who would argue with Einstein's less contentious *bon mot* that Schubert here 'sits in that paradise to which others longingly aspire'?[2] The theme has the same contained boyish ebullience that was to surface again in the first allegro theme of the overture we now know as *Rosamunde* (originally that to *Die Zauberharfe*). The second subject, incidentally, begins with a seven-bar strain, like the theme of the slow movement.

The two movements which are all we have of a Quartet in B flat of 1813 (D.68) present two peculiarities of key-planning. In the finale, which is a sonata-rondo after Haydn but with Mozartian touches, the second subject is recapitulated in the supertonic major. Theorists writing more than ten years earlier had noted the tradition of recapitulating second subjects in the tonic, and so resolving elements which had first appeared in an alien tonal area.[3] It is not clear whether Schubert had fully observed standard practice and understood the principle that underlay it. Perhaps his invention sometimes led him in a particular (and unconventional) direction and he saw no reason to backtrack so as to take a path to a more traditional sequel. The other idiosyncrasy is that in the first movement the second subject begins in the tonic and modulates to the dominant during its course. Were his thoughts with Mozart's String Quintet in G minor? Did he consciously adopt this unorthodox strategy, not thinking of any connection with a unique Mozart precedent? Or did he simply follow the dictates of compositional caprice, having no thought for what was 'usual' or 'conventional'? Whatever the answer, such deviations from fundamental norms hardly touch the works of Schubert's later years at all, presumably because either his observation of normal practice sharpened and widened or he came to appreciate and value more highly the principles on which that practice was founded. Such enigmas aside, it would be hard to hear the climactic dominant minor ninth a few bars from the end of Schubert's first movement without the climactic throes of Beethoven's *Leonora* No. 3 Overture being summoned to mind.

Already, by the age of sixteen, Schubert had developed a flair for 'quartet thinking' and none of the quartets of this time lacks passages which captivate the ear by their well-conceived texture. He was still equipping himself, however, with the technique Haydn and Mozart had striven to acquire with industry and persistence, and did not yet have the assurance or courage to step significantly beyond them. The D major Quartet, D.74, is in fact more affected by echoes of Mozart than any other of this series of quartets composed before the First Symphony. The layout of the theme of the first movement looks back to the two D major Quartets of Mozart. In the coda of this movement there is no mistaking the paraphrase of a resounding gesture from the coda of the *Magic Flute* Overture. And the second movement seems to bow to the slow movement of the 'Prague' Symphony, if a little less tangibly than the slow movement of the First Symphony was to in a few weeks' time. New, in Schubert's first-movement treatment, is a feature inherited from early Mozart, but also evident in so late a work as the *Figaro* Overture. His transition to the second subject is a non-transition. He jumps into the dominant as he leaps the caesura between first and second groups. He then compensates for having had no real transition by taking time to 'dig the dominant key in' during his second group. At the same time this second group, partially functioning as a delayed transition, acts also as a premature development, concerned largely with the anapaest rhythm which the first violin hurls, forte, into the cadence which closes the soft first theme (an imaginative touch).

Although written close upon the heels of the B flat and D major Quartets, the Quartet in E flat marks a distinct advance in its handling of quartet texture and form. The first movement, still reliant on the Haydn–Mozart tradition for its thematic types, has varied, aerated textures and finds Schubert setting out on a planned, orderly transition which, though dependent on longish sequential limbs, leads securely to the dominant for a second subject that is simple and characterful, enlivened by the syncopation in its second bar. The development is short, but Schubert is clearly on his way to marshalling the ingredients of a concise and effective sonata form with success.

All the movements of this work are in E flat, an unusual feature which places a special onus on the composer's ability to individualize them. The extreme tempo contrast between the middle movements (Adagio, unusual for Schubert, and Prestissimo, also rare) is one way of achieving this, while their brevity shortens the time–scale over which this contrast operates. The Adagio maintains a quiet serenity over its compact, sonata-form span, while the Prestissimo adds a dash of hectic Beethovenian roughness to a Haydn-inspired conception. Another unusual feature is the incorporation, in the scherzo, of a trio which must obviously move at a less fast pace, without any difference of tempo being indicated. It could have been in the light of experience in the performance of this quartet that Schubert subsequently took care to mark a tempo distinction between a minuet/scherzo and trio if he wanted one.

The finale again crisply articulates its sonata form, with a bustling first subject and the most fetching of all the second subjects in these early quartets. Curiously dismissed by Einstein and ignored by Westrup, the E flat Quartet is arguably the finest of all the pre-1820 quartets. Its succinctness (it is shorter than the foregoing D major Quartet, for example) probably contributes to its success. There is no justification for playing the slow movement before the scherzo, as happens in some performances.

The quartet movement in C minor written in 1814 must be distinguished from the Quartettsatz in C minor of 1820. The 1814 piece is a fragment: a moving first attempt to begin a quartet in a minor key, it starts and stops too often, stopping for all time when the recapitulation is reached. But when Schubert returned to the medium later the same year, in a Quartet in B flat (D.112) he brought something new to it, especially in the outer movements. Does the first violin begin the first theme at the beginning of the quartet (Fig. 22), or is this a leisurely anacrusis in which the viola joins at the fourth bar, on the way to the first theme at the seventh bar?

Fig. 22

In fact, as later use shows, both elements are equally thematic, but the ambivalence adds a dimension to the traditional Classical opening. The expansive spotlighting of solo lines seems to hark back to the late ('Prussian') quartets of Mozart. The next idea, pairs of loud chords separated by silence or softer utterances (Fig. 23), alludes elsewhere: the second 'Rasumovsky' Quartet of Beethoven may have been seminal in this regard, while Brahms – an avid student of Schubert's music – may in turn owe events in the first movement of his C minor String Quartet to this Schubert model. A little later, the haunted atmosphere of *Erlkönig* darkens the scene. All this is part of a rich first group, in which may be found the seeds of a comparable richness in the opening pages of the late D minor and G major Quartets. The movement follows an orthodox sonata form, with a short development in which every major key touched upon is followed by its minor form.

Fig. 23

The finale is a unique discovery of part of the soul of the string quartet: light, fleet, involving the players now in brilliant repartee, now in common, self-negating purpose, it offers scintillating confirmation that the composer has by now assimilated the true spirit of chamber music, and revels in the fact. Einstein's statement that all the themes of the scherzo of the 'Great' C major Symphony are already present cannot quite be substantiated, but the anticipations of that work are arresting. And does this finale give a further cue to Brahms? The use of plucked notes to reinforce certain pitches among chains of running short notes was to become an exhilarating source of colour in the finale of Brahms's G major String Sextet.

The slow movement and minuet are more modest, the latter doing little more than a youngish Haydn and Mozart – pooling their ideas – might have thought of doing. The Andante sostenuto is a compact sonata form without development with unusual key-relationships and a broadly lyrical second theme that one could call song-like were it not so instrumentally conceived. After a final reprise of the first theme Schubert closes with a six-bar coda which brings unexpected drama and the movement's only fortissimo. Twice, hammered-out octave-unisons in sextuplet rhythm, recalling the moment of recapitulation in Haydn's 'Chaos' Prelude in *The Creation*, highlight the note A flat (the 'Neapolitan') before the tonic reassuringly eases its way back.

Imagine the rhythm of the first eight bars of the finale of Beethoven's G major Quartet, Op. 18, No. 2, allied to the harmonic structure of the first eight bars of the finale of Mozart's G minor Symphony (No. 40), and you have – give or take the odd detail – the opening of Schubert's String Quartet in G minor, which occupied him for eight days in the spring of 1815. There are other debts to the Mozart G minor and to works by Beethoven. The minuet has an obvious kinship with Mozart's, although the trio in B flat is more like a transcription of a keyboard dance of Schubert's own than anything by Mozart. And the earnest contrapuntal impulses behind Mozart's development sections in the outer movements of the symphony come to mind when Schubert, late in the exposition of his first movement, forces second subject material into close, stretto-like imitations against a running viola part. Schubert's finale theme, indebted to Haydn on the face of it, has a 'secret' affinity with another quartet of Beethoven's Op. 18 set (No. 4 in C minor), as may be tested by removing Schubert's first eight-bar melodic strain (first violin) and using his under-lying parts to support the first eight bars of Beethoven's finale – suitably transposed of course. But Schubert's way of plucking nuclear principles from the repertoire all around him in his teenage years and using them as deep models or foundation stones on which his own invention will blossom seldom causes the commentator to invoke the term 'derivative' in its denigratory meaning, since it is part of a positive, learning, and properly creative process.

There are, in any event, Schubertian things here that represent the first stirrings of inclinations that were to come to fruition in later works. Schubert discovers for the first time, in his first movement, the short transition. And in the finale, when the first violin eventually gets going with continu-ous semiquavers, Schubert sets up a four-bar rhythmic pattern in the lower instruments which is then repeated four times in succession, as he would do, for example, in the outer movements of the Fourth Symphony, where massed violins would take the semiquavers and the wind section would lend its weight to the supporting rhythm. Finales in Schubert, however they may begin, often develop a tendency during their course to move in four-bar blocks, which is why so many of his works, especially among the early quartets, end with a silent bar: Schubert had to satisfy himself in notation that the last bar of a four-bar group was present, even if it was silent.

The first movement defies convention by beginning its recapitulation in the relative major. And in the slow movement, which is in sonata form with a few linking bars instead of development, Schubert uses a subdominant recapitulation for the first time (*his* first time; Mozart, for one, had done it). This does save labour, in that the recapitulation can reproduce the exposition a fifth lower, but the effect is aesthetically satisfactory in movements like this one where the exposition is not repeated. In any event, to round the movement off, the first theme is aptly brought back in the tonic. The finale's libertarian approach to what follows what enables us to regard it as either an irregular rondo or an irregular example of sonata form.

The Quartet in E major (1816) is the last of the series of teenage quartets, after which there was a four-year gap before the next quartet attempt – the unfinished work in C minor. It makes more demands on its players than the previous quartets: Schubert was clearly reaching out beyond the limitations of domestic music-making, well as he knew them, and giving his expanding visions full rein, in a way which implicitly requires the professional performance for which his later quartets were in fact written. Perhaps he was not fully aware of his demands. His tempo marking for the slow movement, Andante, is misconceived: the sextuplet decorations in the first violin ensure that a larghetto tempo will be pragmatically taken, if not a largo.

To his first movement Schubert attaches the (for him) novel marking Allegro con fuoco. Even so, and despite the superficially challenging initial forte gesture with its accents, octave leaps, and fiercely jagged rhythm, it is a rather bland affair. If the second subject does, as Einstein suggests, bear some resemblance to the opening of Mozart's Symphony No. 40 in G minor, it is given an Italian lightness, frivolity even, far removed from Mozart's *Innigkeit*. This movement, like the work as a whole, is of interest as a part of Schubert's self-education in quartet writing, if its intrinsic musical value is not such as to have earned it a secure place in the repertoire. At times the composer flexes his creative muscles in big textures (on the scale of Beethoven's 'Rasumovsky' rather than Op. 18 textures) with a bold confidence that would stand him in good stead in the three last quartets.

In the A major slow movement, Schubert approaches his coda (which takes up the first theme back in A major) from D flat major. The oblique way in which he moves from the one key to the other, without the help of dominants, simply involves a double pivot: the notes D flat and F flat (when D flat major is turned minor) are, differently named, the third and fifth of A major, and Schubert swings across on them with gracious ease (Fig. 24). Such moves, short-circuiting the 'straight line' approach involving dominants, have their analogy on the chessboard in the surreptitious crab-like motion of the knight.

Fig. 24

At the end of this movement, by the way, Schubert curiously recycles the last two bars of his previous quartet slow movement (of the G minor Quartet composed a year before) in the first violin. The descending leaps through compound intervals are distinctive (Fig. 25).

Fig. 25

The 'Menuetto' remains solidly a minuet, despite Schubert's slightly optimistic Allegro vivace, but the trio is arguably the most innovative part of the work. It sets a smooth legato theme against a patter of staccato quavers, usually in two parts only but often with octave-doubling. It eschews the conventional binary form, though, preferring a through-composed design in which traces of the binary convention are not really present at all. The theme comes round, in its own key of C major (the minuet was in E major), several times, each time cancelling some modulatory implication in what preceded it, and one is reminded of the obsessively circling progress (not to mention unremitting counterpoint) of the trio in Beethoven's second 'Rasumovsky' Quartet, although the asperity of Beethoven's linear interplay is not part of Schubert's inheritance. That supposed Beethoven model appears to be, at least, the only available precedent in the works of the Classical composers of a trio which is not in binary form.

'Rondo', Schubert proudly announces at the head of his finale. There is a hint of Mozart's E flat Symphony (No. 39) in the theme, although Mozart's finale is not a rondo. A rondo has its first theme returning several times in the tonic key. Schubert's theme ('A' in Fig. 26) returns three times in other keys, and only once in the tonic, at the very end. But the whole cycle of ABA-development at the beginning of the movement is reproduced a fifth lower later, in the manner of a subdominant recapitulation in sonata form. (There are tiny but interesting differences of detail between this 'exposition' and 'recapitulation'.)

Fig. 26

	A	B	A	dev. of A	A	B	A	dev. of A	A	coda
keys	E	B	G		A	E	C		E	E

exposition?   recapitulation?

Schubert's observation of rondo practice may have been incomplete, but his finale is not ineffective in its own terms. It is interesting that his fascination with the idea of subdominant recapitulation extends outside the confines of sonata form.

Between these early quartets and the mature examples beginning four years later, the strings-only medium to which Schubert transferred his interest was the string trio. A few months after the E major Quartet he began a String Trio in B flat (D.471), getting only as far as he did with the Quartettsatz (D.703) four years later: he finished the first movement and penned thirty-nine bars of a slow movement. This is no pioneering work; indeed its roots lie in earlier stylistic soil than do those of the E major Quartet. Rather, it is a valuable exercise in the more stringent discipline (compared with quartet-writing) of handling a spare medium which is notoriously intractable, whether in composition or performance. As such it succeeds brilliantly, in its complete first movement, which combines economy of texture with clarity of thought, re-enacting early Classical ideals in a most amiable way. The spirit of Mozart hovers everywhere: even the four-note idea which that composer runs into the final cadence of his 'Dissonance' Quartet turns up at Schubert's close, although here it is underpinned by enterprising cadential harmony (involving an augmented sixth on the flattened second degree of the scale) which points ahead to similar junctures in the first movement of the late B flat Piano Trio and the finale of the even later String Quintet (Fig. 27). The discarded slow movement fragment, incidentally, was to provide a melodic/harmonic cell for the trio section of that same B flat Piano Trio and for a theme in the E flat Piano Trio too (bar 140 of the first movement).

Fig. 27

Haydn replaces Mozart as Schubert's mentor in another String Trio in B flat (D.581) which was begun – and this time finished – in the following year. Its first movement is one of the composer's shortest, with a second subject (if one can call it that) so closely related to the first that Haydn's monothematic model comes to mind. An ornate gathering of short notes as upbeat in the violin's second bar spawns a plethora of florid neo-galanterie which, curiously enough, has something in common with that of Richard Strauss's Oboe Concerto. A Haydnesque blend of wit, surprise and ornament distinguishes the slow movement, but the minuet perhaps owes more to Mozartian suavity, and the scoring of the trio section as a viola melody with trim chordal accompaniment recalls its counterpart in Mozart's Divertimento for string trio (K.563). The finale sets out as a modest little rondo but the second of the intervening episodes gives room to plucky escapades which are brought to heel – ready for a final return of the rondo theme – with a teasing humour again borrowed from Haydn. The succession of tempi in the four movements of this work – allegro moderato, andante, allegretto, allegretto – is a reminder that speed is not a pre-requisite for vitality.

Schubert combined piano with strings for the first time in 1812, with a one-movement Piano Trio in B flat (D.28) which already shows a good ear for the particular colour of the ensemble, and does so with somewhat Mozartian material, but gives little hint of what expressive depth he was to discover in the medium when he returned to it some fifteen years later. Meanwhile, he gave attention to other combinations, producing four works for violin and piano, one for piano quartet, and one for a group we might call 'piano quintet' were it not that that designation is reserved for works using what was to become the standard line-up of string quartet plus piano, which is not what Schubert opts for in his 'Trout' Quintet.

The four works for violin and piano are all sonatas, although the first three were published as 'sonatinas' and the fourth as 'Duo in A major'. It would not be untrue to say that the first three are not works of the stature of Beethoven's or Brahms's violin sonatas, but neither Beethoven nor Brahms – as far as we know – tried writing violin sonatas at the age of 19: Beethoven was 28 and Brahms 45 when they broached the medium. More to the point, it should be said that the promise of these early examples makes it a matter for regret that Schubert did not write violin sonatas in his last ten years. In fact, he totally ignored the duo-sonata genre (piano and one other instrument) throughout his musical adulthood, with the exception of that curiosity, the 'Arpeggione' Sonata.

All three sonatas are compact works with movements of traditional generic type, broadly eighteenth-century in scale and outlook. The second and third run to four movements, having a minuet which the first lacks. Initially, the three-movement Sonata in D major (D.384) shows its affinity to Mozart through the obvious likeness of its first theme to that of Mozart's E minor Violin Sonata, also presented in bare octaves (Fig. 28).

Fig. 28

But a generalized Mozart model invades the whole fabric of this first movement, which is tuneful, compact, and economical with notes to the last. Yet the inspiration is fresh, not derivative: the dialogues between violin and the pianist's left hand, for example, are pure Schubert, anticipating those in the minuet of the Fifth Symphony six months later. After a gentle slow movement with a songful middle section in the minor, the finale alternates its shapely rondo tune with episodes in which the prevailing simple, crisp textures are leavened by an injection of contrapuntal fibre. Although this work holds its own with young players to the almost total exclusion of the two minor-key sonatas that follow, there are more strikingly individual features in those other two, as so often happens when Schubert works within a minor-key framework.

The Sonata in A minor (D.385) begins with a theme whose soft, measured cantabile strides display their *alter ego* when the violin takes them

Fig. 29 a

up forte, each note accented. Schubert was sufficiently enthralled by his
second subject (Fig. 29a) to remember it when he worked on the second
number for *Die Zauberglöckchen* (The Magic Bells) a few years later
(Fig. 29b). In his three-key expositions, the third key is normally the conventional second-subject key (the dominant, or, in the case of minor-key
movements, the relative major), but in the present movement Schubert,
having reached the relative major as second key (Fig. 29a), goes on to F
major as his unorthodox third key, there to present another well-
characterized theme with rapid repeated triplets in the piano. Melody
reaches into every corner of these sonatas – another echo of a Mozartian
impulse. Even when the finale of the A minor Sonata is, in mid-course,
robustly contrapuntal, it remains infectiously tuneful. The G minor Sonata
(D.408) shares the virtues of its two predecessors, as well as the unusual
exposition key-structure of the A minor Sonata. In both the outer movements Schubert accompanies one of the themes with a rapid alternation
between two chord-notes, imparting by this means an exhilarating vivacity.

The tuneful extraversion that runs right into the final cadence of the G
minor work spills over, a year later, into the Sonata (Duo) in A major.
But now there is a degree more abandon, more virtuosity. Not that the

earlier three sonatas are to be eclipsed; for while the A major would be no less popular than the 'Arpeggione' Sonata were it as inviting to the transcribers, it does not add significantly to Schubert's achievement. If he had begun it a year or two later and if it had required as much labour in completing it as an orchestral work, he might well have set it aside in an unfinished state – perhaps after his game attempt at ambivalent phrase-structure in the trio of the scherzo (which is the second movement) had turned out to be not wholly convincing.

One can count the piano quartets in the standard repertory on the fingers of two hands. Compared with the piano trio and piano quintet the medium has been shunned by composers. There is some justification for this. Three string players are a crowd, if the intimate, all-involving democracy of the piano trio is to be emulated; but three is too few if the piano quintet's facility to have the piano offset by a self-sufficient group – the string quartet – is sought. Which critic was it who said that the string group in a piano quartet can sound like 'an understaffed pit band'? Schubert lived close enough to the two scintillating models bequeathed by Mozart, both of which prove that the medium is gloriously viable, to be blind to the problems. Inheriting Mozart's urge to explore the ensemble, he also inherited – and magnified – the tendency of Mozart to treat the ensemble in concerto-like fashion.

The work in which Schubert tested the water was the Adagio and Rondo Concertante in F major, a single movement comprising a slow introduction and a large-scale rondo. His critics have tended to give the work short shrift. One can understand string players sometimes forgetting they are taking a role in chamber music rather than in a pit band, but they are of course the servants of the composer, whose target is the ear of the listener, and it must be said that the listener tends to be more captivated by the youthful effervescence of the piece than worried by the distribution of favours to the participants. The Adagio is imposing and colourful, intro-ducing at times the delightful effect – familiar from later piano quartets and quintets and from Schubert's own 'Trout' Quintet – of a high melodic piano part given out by the two hands an octave apart above a carpet of string sound. After its opening flourishes, the theme at the sixth bar is an ornamented homage to that of the slow movement of Mozart's Clarinet Concerto. The rondo itself, despite its size, lacks a central episode. In its ABAB structure, A is the rondo theme and B the second group of themes in the dominant key; but the second B transposes the first B down a fifth to the tonic, as would a recapitulation in sonata form. Since, additionally, there is no final return of A, as would be proper to a rondo, this is not a rondo at all, but what the textbooks call an abridged sonata form with no development, such as one finds in some early opera overtures and instru-mental slow movements. The length of the piece stems from the fact that

the B section, the second subject group, is four times as long as the A
section. While the style is rooted in the late eighteenth century, there is
a wonderfully innovative modulation directly from F minor to E major –
from old tonic chord to new tonic chord by means of a pivotal A flat
(renamed G sharp): the moment magically coincides with the first lyrically
melodious entry of the violin (Fig. 30). Both B sections culminate, in
concerto fashion, with a technically demanding bravura section complete
with supertonic trill, followed by a closing tutti which seems to take us
back to the jubilant close of 'The heavens are telling' in Haydn's *Creation*.

Fig. 30

According to Schubert's beloved Therese Grob, the Adagio and Rondo
was written for her brother, Heinrich Grob, who was a pianist.[4] This might
explain the importance Schubert attached to the keyboard's role. The
remaining piano-and-strings work to be considered, the 'Trout' Quintet,
likewise owes its origin to social circumstance: it was commissioned by
Sylvester Paumgartner, wealthy amateur cellist at Steyr. There are signs of
hasty composition. In the first movement, the recapitulation is a transposed
repetition of the exposition, with two sections omitted and other adjust-
ments only where compass dictates. The following slow movement consists
of sixty bars of music heard twice: the succession of keys in the first sixty

(F, F sharp minor, D, G) is transposed up a minor third for the second sixty (A flat, A minor, F) and one connecting bar is then inserted to enable the passage in G to return in F to close the movement. The finale is a Schubertian derivative of binary form: there are two sections of equal length, the first moving from A to D, the second being a rerun of the same music transposed up a fifth, to lead from E to A. If Schubert's curious instruction to repeat the first section (though not the second) is observed, the same music is then heard three times.

The sparkling scherzo is offset by a self-effacing trio, and the Andante variations in D major on *Die Forelle*, in which the song's leaping accompaniment figure is reserved till the final Allegretto, offer pleasantries which make as few demands on the listener as they did on the composer, until the more enterprising fifth variation – unconventionally stepping aside to B flat major – is reached. As a whole the work shows that Schubert could toss off an attractive *pièce d'occasion* without undue effort. It all sits comfortably within the divertimento genre, not aspiring to transcend it as some Mozart examples do (the two Serenades for wind octet, for instance.) The presence of the double bass, rather than a second cello, and the peculiarities of the piano writing, lend the work a certain individuality, but it is not surprising that Schubert's next quintet was a more homogeneous all-string one, closer to Mozart's favourite among the larger chamber ensembles. It was to be in the piano trio, eventually, that he would find his ideal piano-and-strings medium.

The Early Church Music

A study of Schubert's music for the church soon brings us up against a problem that has much teased musicologists – the nature of his religious convictions. The documentary and musical sources towards which one would naturally look yield a number of clues, but these tend to point in irreconcilable directions. Different documentary references point to differing conclusions, while the musical features which might support one or other of those conclusions are compatible with either, depending on one's interpretation of them. That Schubert gave thought to the role of faith in human existence is evident from some notes made in his 1824 diary: 'It is with faith that man first enters the world. It comes long before reason and knowledge; for to understand something one must first believe something.' 'Reason,' he goes on, 'is nothing other than analysed faith.'[1] From such thought-provoking yet question-raising comments no explicit personal credo can be erected by posterity, which brings us to the evidence, such as it is, of the music itself.

We have already seen (Chapter 3, pages 35–6) that Schubert consistently omitted the words '[Credo] in unam sanctam catholicam et apostolicam Ecclesiam' from his settings of the mass. However, one must also take account of the further fact that he omitted various other parts of the mass text in some instances, but these not consistently. In the G major Mass the words 'Qui sedes ad dexteram Patris' are missing from the Gloria, while later in the same movement, after 'Quoniam tu solus sanctus, tu solus altissimus, tu solus Dominus' (in that order), the words 'Jesu Christe' do not appear. In the Credo of the same work the omission of 'Et expecto resurrectionem' leaves the nonsense statement 'Confiteor unum baptisma in remissionem peccatorum . . . mortuorum' (I confess one baptism for the remission of the sins of the dead). In the Credo of the B flat Mass, the words 'consubstantialem Patri' do not appear, while 'suscipe deprecationem nostram' is missing from the Gloria of the Mass in C major. The unpredictability of these omissions, of which the above list is far from complete, does not suggest that they are deliberately made on grounds of religious conviction. If they are made for other reasons, can we be certain that the expunging of 'Et in unam sanctam catholicam et apostolicam Ecclesiam' is deliberate, simply because it is the only consistent omission? And if it was deliberate, was Schubert withholding his ultimate commitment to the deity or was he simply expressing a lack of sympathy with the established church and its personnel? Reinhard Van Hoorickx has detailed all these excisions and many more, debated the issues arising, and drawn conclusions. Among these conclusions, he affirms that it is possible that the omission of 'Et in unam sanctam . . .' was deliberate, though this is not proved; and that many omissions were probably the result of carelessness or absent-mindedness.[2]

To the points emerging in Van Hoorickx's discussion may be added a few further observations. Schubert composed fast, often without care for less essential details (such as dynamic indications, slurs and ties, or consistency of notation as between an exposition and a recapitulation). Could it be that for him the text of a mass was among the less essential details? The mass text was, unlike the poems Schubert set as Lieder, always 'there'; it had been part of his daily furniture since youth, and he thought he knew it by heart. But it was in an alien tongue, and despite what was presumably a good education in the classics he may well have had an imperfect grasp of its vocabulary and syntax. Knowing that he could always check details later, if he remembered or had time to do so, he could well have made assumptions at certain points in mid-composition where the Muse was favouring him and the musical invention was 'taking over'. Moreover, in the Vienna of a generation before Schubert's, an archiepiscopal edict had imposed limitations on the length of a mass, with the result that even in Mozart the text of the Credo is not always complete. During his Salzburg period Mozart had been subject to a limitation of three quarters of an hour for a mass, and told Padre Martini in a letter dated 4 September 1776 that 'a special study is required for this sort of composition'.[3] It was necessary, then, for any setting to consume a large amount of text in a short space of time. The masses of Mozart and his contemporaries were Schubert's inheritance. It would be natural enough for him to follow precedent, and in any case the liberal atmosphere prevailing among the current church authorities in Vienna meant that there was no bar to the performance of his textually corrupt settings. Reinhard Van Hoorickx reminds us that omissions and alterations to the text were commonplace in mass settings through most of the nineteenth century. It should also be borne in mind that there is an element of musical convenience in omitting some of the text of the Gloria and Credo. The text of the Kyrie comprises four words, or, with the repetition hallowed by tradition, six. The Credo has 162, and the Gloria 84. Any seasoned listener to Classical masses knows that in the Gloria and Credo a composer tends to compromise his style through the need to accommodate a positive deluge of syllables. In the usual up-tempo scramble (as it may sometimes appear) through this proliferating Latin, was

there not an invitation to the composing subconscious to put out of mind
the bits that fell by the wayside?

Schubert's treatment of texts, then, provides no definitive clue to his
religious outlook. In view of some remarks in his letters which suggest he
was sometimes impatient with the ways of the clergy and was ready to
share his views with his brothers, we should be inclined to conclude that,
if Schubert was making a point by discarding a regular part of the Credo
text, he was dissociating himself from the all-worldly rather than the
Almighty. In an age when humanism had its adherents, the thought that
Schubert shared some of that movement's outlook is also hard to resist.
The synthesis suggested by Frank Ruppert is, then, appealing:

> Franz Schubert was a Christian humanist, the product of a synthesis
> of messianic Judaism and the Platonic vision of life as an ascent to
> divine perfection. For Schubert man's upward thrust towards human
> dignity is realized in union with the young Messiah who reveals his
> true identity in passing through death to fullness of life. Life, joy,
> peace, and freedom are ultimate victors in the struggle with death,
> victors whose triumph is definitively realized beyond death.[4]

Whatever one's understanding of Schubert's beliefs, he must have been
inclined to produce music for the church in his early years because he was
a regular participant in worship and music at his local parish church, where
opportunities existed ready-made for a young composer to test his efforts.
His early training in composition by the Lichtental organist, Michael
Holzer, will naturally have been conducive to any interest in church composition. The earliest surviving efforts are fragments of a Gloria and Credo
of a Mass in F, probably from 1812. In June of that year he composed the
first of his several settings of the *Salve Regina*. Then in the same September
he completed a Kyrie in D minor which owes something to Mozart's
Requiem in the same key. The heading 'Missa' indicates that this was to
be part of a complete mass, the remainder of which was not composed or
is lost. Three other complete settings of the Kyrie followed between 1812
and 1814, the year of the first Mass in F. Of this total of four, three demand
an orchestra, and two call also for soloists. Exceptionally the Kyrie in B
flat is for SATB choir only, without orchestra. It is a succinct setting,
rather high-pitched, in which a central 'Christe' in G minor is followed
by a complete reprise of the opening 'Kyrie'. The most imposing of these
essays is another Kyrie in D minor, from 1813, again part of a projected
'Missa' according to the autograph. The character is earnest but ceremonial,
and the mass style of Haydn and Mozart is brought to mind. Indeed, the
initial octave drop of the choir within a single bar in triple time for
the first appearance of the word 'Kyrie' recalls the opening of Haydn's
Harmoniemesse, while the lively rhythms which cut through the middle

texture in wind and timpani are part of the familiar stock of enlivening, binding rhythms in the Classical mass. Another typical device, the sequence, plays its part, although not every sequence is obvious in build or direction. The 'Christe' spotlights the solo voices in the usual way.

Schubert had recourse to the mass text just once more before the Mass in F. The Sanctus in B flat stands rather apart from these other ventures, however, since it probably came into being as a scholastic exercise rather than as music for liturgical use. It is a three-part canon, for three equal voices, with no instrumental support whatever. But it is an ingenious canon, for it sets the 'Sanctus' itself in a stately triple time (andante con moto) but the 'Pleni sunt coeli' in duple time at allegro tempo. Clearly, as the second voice enters when the first has already sung six bars, and the third voice joins in a further six bars after that, the two tempi run concurrently. Schubert accordingly plans that three bars of allegro should fill the time taken by one bar of andante. The effect is that, although the pulse never changes, the amount of activity increases by degrees: Schubert achieves by clever canonic means what composers of masses usually do by freer means, that is, to follow a stately 'Sanctus' with a more active (and aptly so) treatment of the 'Pleni sunt coeli'. The three voices then unite in a non-canonic, all but homophonic 'Hosanna', which sounds duly assertive in consequence. A comparison between the text of this Sanctus and the standard text for this movement as it was to appear, for example, in the imminent Mass in F, is revealing.

Mass in F	*Sanctus in B flat*
Sanctus, sanctus, sanctus,	Sanctus, sanctus, sanctus,
Dominus Deus Sabaoth,	Deus Sabaoth,
Pleni sunt coeli et terra gloria tua.	Pleni sunt coeli et terra.
Hosanna in excelsis.	Osanna in excelsis Deo.

The omission of 'Dominus' and 'gloria tua' is of interest, in relation to the question (already discussed) of textual omissions in the masses themselves. Schubert probably carried the text in his head and forgot the 'Dominus', or found the extra word a musical embarrassment. Something similar may have happened at 'gloria tua'. Could the fact that he had treated the text in this rather cavalier fashion here have set a pattern in his way of working that was responsible in part for his later free approach to the words of the mass?

The Mass in F is the first in a line of six masses completed by Schubert. It can hardly hold its own against the mature last two settings, and there are perhaps not many who would claim for it equality of status with the intervening masses, especially the G major. But if we picture the scene at Lichtental parish church where a group of choral singers, instrumentalists

and solo singers unfolded to the virgin ears of a sizeable audience the first
extended, concerted church work of a local seventeen-year-old, it is not
difficult to enjoy a retrospective share of the excitement of that occasion.
The gentle Kyrie has a simple grace, its effective choral writing coloured
by washes of warm string sound. The merest chromatic inflection in the
harmony has its effect in this purified diatonic ambience. Flecks of woodwind or horn timbre give passing enrichment. Little accents and crescendi
make their point, despite their restraint. It is perhaps significant that the
first soloist to enter, early in the 'Kyrie' section, is the soprano, in the
person of Therese Grob.

In contrast, the Gloria bursts in, Allegro vivace and in a bright C
major (Schubert was later persuaded to add a cautionary 'moderato' to that
tempo indication). Trumpets and trombones, absent from the Kyrie,
now add their brilliance and their sheen. To the choral solidity of the
choir is added the activity of the strings, in charged syncopations, fast
running quavers, or, later, quasi-tremolando. New ideas succeed the old
– a flowing Andante for the 'Gratias' (in which Therese leads a trio of
soloists), a sombre D minor Adagio for the 'Domine Deus' which touchingly enshrines the memory of the opening of Mozart's *Requiem* in the
same key, a strongly rhythmic 'Quoniam', and a fast fugue for the final
'Cum Sancto Spiritu'. This may not be a fugue to clinch the youngster's
mastery of all that Handel, Haydn and others no less distinguished may
have taught him by example. But it has youthful fire, and while the
hypercritical will detect sequential overkill and the odd creaking joint it
moves by way of the statutory dominant pedal to a decisively climactic
close.

Already, after this fugue has spent itself in a stretto and the closing
gestures of a coda are due, Schubert knows the value of a passage of hushed
awe, in which full-throated diatonic glorification is for a few moments
replaced by vista-opening harmonic audacity. He leads into his 'Amen'
section (consisting in fact of only one 'Amen' followed by several
reaffirmations of the opening words 'Gloria in excelsis Deo') with an
imaginative chord-succession that he was to remember and still find apt
currency in the last and greatest of his completed symphonies, the 'Great'
C major (see Chapter 23, page 398).

Surprises were in store in the Credo for those familiar with earlier
Classical mass settings. This is no barnstorming, resolute confession of
faith, but an intimate avowal, replacing trumpets with horns, coupling an
andantino tempo with soft dynamic levels, and speaking from the heart in
a confiding tone based on melodic restraint and plain block-chordal writing
for the choir. Moreover, there is no change of tempo throughout the
movement: the diversity of textual allusion, sufficient to encourage Haydn
and Mozart to break the movement up into sections each with their own

tempo and possibly time-signature as a matter of habit, is accommodated by Schubert through changes in choral and orchestral texture, articulation, rhythm and colour alone. At 'Deum de Deo' suave string figures give way to a choppier string style, while 'Qui propter' becomes a tenor solo, though these disparate textures are unified by the presence throughout of the initial offbeat wind rhythm. Even at those points where composers have been most inclined to close off a section and begin afresh with new tempo, time, key, scoring, texture and/or material, Schubert extends the existing measured, confessional flow. So the 'Incarnatus' is a continuation of the tenor solo, the 'Crucifixus' admits shorter-term dynamic contrasts while moving to the flat side of the key, and the 'Et resurrexit' becomes an affirmative variation of the opening theme, still leaving the basic pulse undisturbed. There are poetic touches in the orchestration, such as the emergence of a solo horn above low strings just before the 'Et resurrexit', and Schubert is ready to unyoke the cellos from the double basses, to give them independent parts or omit the bass octave (as at the first 'Amen') or allow the basses to pluck what the cellos take with the bow (second 'Amen'). The seventeen-year-old has discovered what a radical effect on texture these variant bass treatments afford, and he leaves us conscious of this in the movement's dying bars, where plucked exchanges between cellos and basses underpin the hushed final cadential chord-circuit of the bowed upper strings.

The Sanctus is remarkably prophetic of what would be Schubert's final setting of this text, in the 1828 Mass in E flat. Soft pulsations in the strings gradually build up to massive, majestic chord-blocks in the choir and wind, a process repeated several times in line with the repetition of the word 'Sanctus'. What is different in the 1828 reincarnation is the harmonic daring. But to those at Lichtental not blessed with foresight, the impact must have been stunning. Then Schubert defies expectations by his treatment of the 'Osanna'. Having set up a new texture for the 'Pleni sunt coeli', without any change of tempo, he simply tacks on 'Osanna in excelsis' as a pendant to each statement of 'Pleni sunt coeli', again producing a single unbroken continuum as in the Credo.

Although those first hearers of the Benedictus may not have realized they were listening to a canon, they will have been more or less aware of its effect. That effect is that the movement is structured as a set of variations.

Fig. 31

S1				A
S2			A	B
T1		A	B	C
T2	A	B	C	D
		Var. 1	Var. 2	Var. 3

Four solo voices (two sopranos, two tenors) take the theme, which can be subdivided into four long segments (shown in Fig. 31 as A, B, C and D). The second tenor begins, the first entering when A is complete. The pattern continues until all voices have entered. But the last to enter (Therese presumably) never gets beyond segment A. This is perfectly satisfying, because A is a long thematic paragraph, devised as a basis for variations. The following entries are variations in that each A has different vocal support (B in the first variation, B and C in the second, B, C and D in the third) and each has a different orchestral accompaniment, varied so as to become progressively lighter to permit the ever more elaborate vocal texture to show through. As a technical compositional exercise this is not as demanding as it might seem, but Schubert carries it off skilfully and – more important – the result is a delightful Benedictus. Falling outside the variation scheme is a two-bar orchestral prelude and four-bar coda, after which Schubert presents – as a last-minute post-coda – his 'Osanna' in a single acclamation by the whole company.

With an Agnus Dei that begins conventionally in the minor and moves to the major with a change of tempo for the 'Dona nobis pacem', Schubert ends this especially accomplished and individual engagement with a sacred text which had for long been and still remained the major challenge for a church composer. Some nine months after its completion and six months after its sensational première, Schubert composed an alternative ending to the Agnus Dei. His first version had closed with a varied reprise of the theme of the opening Kyrie. The revised version replaces this with a zippy but over-extended fugue not entirely unrelated to the Kyrie, its countersubject (upper part of Fig. 32b) being a decoration of the Kyrie theme (Fig. 32a). The close of the fugue is contrived, while the original ending is more of a piece with the rest of the work. That preference happily enables posterity to revive the work as – among other things – a memento of an auspicious occasion.

Fig. 32 a

By the time he made his revision to the last movement of the F major Mass, Schubert had already composed his Mass in G. The fact that it took him six days to write is reflected in both its brevity (it is the shortest of all his masses) and its simplicity, but also in its scoring for an orchestra comprising only strings and organ. (Schubert later added optional parts for trumpets and timpani, but the oboe and bassoon parts were added in the 1840s by his brother Ferdinand.) The Kyrie at once sets the tone with its easy fluency, the almost Mozartian naturalness with which the phrases and cadences go past. There is a straightforward symmetry in the form, the A minor 'Christe' for soprano solo (for Therese Grob again, almost certainly) being flanked by the G major choral 'Kyrie' and its reprise, varied only to allow it to close in the tonic rather than lead to the key of the 'Christe'.

It is in the spirited D major Gloria that one first becomes aware that habits of instrumental structure seem to drive the invention, the text being fitted as best it can. This, at any rate, is not Schubert's most meticulous example of word-setting, although the music forges its own momentum with the help of brilliant rhythms, propulsive sequences and textural variation. This impression is no less marked in the Credo, where the text quickly flits by on the back of long-limbed melodic spans and more sequences. The 'Et incarnatus' does not draw particular attention to itself as this Allegro moderato runs its course, but the 'Crucifixus' is marked by long notes in unison as the orchestra stamps on, now in B minor. There is a turn to bright D major for an 'Et resurrexit' that adapts the opening theme, and a true reprise is made at 'in Spiritum sanctum' which Schubert prefaces with the word 'Credo' (which is implied at this point in any case) to make the point.

The Sanctus is imposing but brief, the 'Osanna' this time being a separate section, fugally initiated, that matches the 'Sanctus' itself exactly in length. For the Benedictus Schubert interestingly revives the scheme which had served him well in the Mass in F. This time the canon involves three soloists only, so that we hear a theme and two variations, the plan of Fig. 31 being shortened as in Fig. 33. Again the orchestral weave beautifully

Fig. 33

S	A	B	C
T		A	B
B			A
		Var. 1	Var. 2

enhances the vocal fabric. as before, there is a short orchestral prelude and coda, but this time the complete original 'Osanna' as heard in the Sanctus follows. Conciseness and expressiveness are reconciled in another neat and compact plan for the Agnus Dei. Instead of picking out the 'Dona nobis pacem' for individual treatment, Schubert honours the structure of the text (Fig. 34) irrespective of nuances in meaning. Accordingly he casts the movement in three segments, using the same music for each but in different keys. The orchestra begins in E minor, with an introduction that marries

Fig. 34

Agnus Dei, qui tollis peccata mundi: miserere nobis.
Agnus Dei, qui tollis peccata mundi: miserere nobis.
Agnus Dei, qui tollis peccata mundi: dona nobis pacem.

acute pathos with the pliancy of prose; but by a series of carefully planned modulations within and between segments, a close is reached in G major, the frame-key of the work. Each line or 'verse' of text is allotted to a vocal soloist, the choir adding a hauntingly simple 'miserere nobis' refrain. Schubert could have given the three 'verses' to the tenor, bass and soprano respectively (all three had been used in the Benedictus, and the keys are now right for their re-use), but he preferred to omit the tenor and give the soprano a double share. Favouritism for Therese?

A few months after the G major work, a Mass in B flat followed. It is another piece in the *missa brevis* mould, after Mozart's short masses; but there are signs that Schubert is trying to move away from the fluent *Gemütlichkeit* and ultra-compact build of the G major, although as yet he is merely groping towards compelling, personal alternatives, without on the whole attaining them. The Kyrie displays a new dignity and power, but the ideas are not in themselves distinguished, except that the beloved solo soprano has some gem-like phrases in the 'Christe' (this work and its successor were probably performed at Lichtental, despite the absence of corroborative records). The vehement plunge to D flat major which marks a 'false' return to the 'Kyrie' is arresting enough, and the passage that follows piles up imitative entries one step above each other in a manner that recalls the Fecit potentiam of Bach's *Magnificat*. After this, Schubert returns to the 'Christe' text before beginning a real reprise of the 'Kyrie'.

The theme which opens the Gloria in orchestral octaves bears a certain resemblance to that which began the C major Piano Sonata two months before. There is a stiffness about it which casts an influence on much of the movement. In part this stems from a problem of tempo caused by the rapid scales and passagework in the violins. No such problems affect the central Adagio, however, which sets the 'Domine Deus' and shows a readiness to let the woodwind colours be heard to advantage. The reprise of the opening at 'Quoniam' suffers from an over-extended treatment of 'Cum Sancto Spiritu' in no fewer than four sets of imitative entries at one bar's distance. The Credo has a strong diatonic theme of narrow ambit, which does loyal service for various lines of the text, often in robust octave-unisons. Both 'Et incarnatus' and 'Crucifixus' conform to tradition as a minor-key Adagio, the first tempo and theme returning for 'Et resurrexit'.

An interpretative problem is posed by the Sanctus and Benedictus, each of which ends with the same 'Osanna' taken within the main tempo of the movement. But these tempi are Adagio maestoso and Andante con moto respectively. In fact the same speed is appropriate to both movements from the outset, so that the instinct to let the 'Osanna' move at the same pace on both occasions is easily satisfied. The lesson here is that some composers (and particularly those always composing in a hurry?) judge their tempo markings in relation to the character and tread of the material, not an absolute and fixed notion of pulse. The Sanctus brings jagged neo-Baroque rhythms at 'Pleni sunt coeli', not characteristic of Schubert but common enough in early Classical masses. The Benedictus is freely composed rather than canonic, and the Agnus Dei adopts a faster tempo at the 'Dona nobis' but extracts more mileage from the slender 6/8 material than it will bear.

Schubert's fourth setting of the mass followed six months or so after the third. He had supposedly been fulfilling a local need with this series of works in the *missa brevis* tradition, and perhaps their frequency also reflects his wish to facilitate encounters with Therese Grob. The Mass in C (1816) marks a slight retrenchment from the forward move into stylistic uncertainty represented by the B flat setting. In some ways it looks back to the G major work, but rather than *gemütlich* simplicity with an emphasis on smooth chordal textures and suave fluency it embodies a more palpable renewal of Haydnesque gesture and Mozartian lightness of touch. At times this seems to bring with it a less personal, intense response to the text. It also involves more open textures, including a number of passages where only the two violin sections – sometimes with the cello-and-bass line (there are no violas) – carry the invention forwards.

From its urbane string-trio opening to its delectable epigrammatic close the Kyrie substitutes for suppliant devotion a bright acceptance that prayers will be answered. The tendency for the vocal soloists to interact more closely and frequently with the choir than in the earlier masses is carried forward into the Gloria, the heart of which (at 'Domine Deus') explores keys remoter by far than any approached in those previous masses. A serpentine, chromatically spiralling sequence in the soft strings leads to the usual reprise at 'Quoniam'. The Credo nicely points the single-minded belief in a single God by presenting the initial 'Credo in unum Deum' as an unaccompanied choral affirmation in unison. Schubert allows himself a more frank symbolism, in a long–standing Renaissance tradition, by giving the choral basses a southward plunge at 'descendit' – a pictorial opportunity to which he had succumbed in the B flat but no previous masses. The slow 'Et incarnatus' brings the contrast of sustained lines and exploratory harmony, and the opening allegro tempo is restored at 'Et resurrexit' with a stirring outburst from the unaccompanied choir.

The solemn Sanctus comprises no more than one slowly unfolding phrase, the ensuing 'Osanna' being unconventionally set as a rather jaunty soprano solo answered by a choral refrain. Then the soprano has the Benedictus to herself, and by now Schubert knows how to play on her vocal instrument with a judicious blend of leaps and steps, long notes and short, with frequent excursions into the top part of the range. Fig. 35 shows how, later in the piece, the character of the opening phrase (Fig. 35a) is quite transformed (in Fig. 35b) by the simple device of raising the first two notes by an octave. The singer moves directly into a reprise of her 'Osanna'.

Fig. 35 a

The Agnus Dei defies convention by being cast in a major key, but Schubert taps an apt expressive vein for this closing prayer by exploiting the pleading quality of suspensions, while the accompanying violin utterances are rich in mild dissonances. Trust in an affirmative answer to the prayer is displayed, as so often, in a fast and joyous 'Dona nobis'. To the end, Schubert maintains the close interaction of solo and choral timbres that distinguishes the whole work.

Long after he had completed the Mass in C, in fact not more than seven weeks before his death in 1828, Schubert made a minor revision to it, composing an alternative, choral setting of the Benedictus to replace that for solo soprano. If he had second thoughts as to the effectiveness of the solo soprano setting, that would be surprising. It would be more likely that he knew of a planned performance for which a suitable soprano was not available, or thought the issuing of an alternative might forestall any such problem. The 1828 replacement, in A minor, is not a wholly superior product, but it is of special interest as it is a well-formed piece in sonata form, and the modest little 'second subject' – heard first in C major and later recapitulated in A major as would be expected in a sonata movement in A minor – has an undeniable charm (Fig. 36). The second limb of the tune, a near-monotone, recalls that of the opening themes of two piano

Fig. 36

sonatas, the C major ('Reliquie', D.840) and the A minor (D.845), which were written within weeks of each other in the middle of 1825. The fact that Schubert troubled to write a substitute movement for an 1816 mass as late as 1828 suggests that he retained an affection for the piece as a whole.

Alongside these full-blown masses, Schubert interested himself in all kinds of shorter religious text during these early years. One, indeed, is hardly shorter at all. It is perhaps not surprising that he should have fancied the opportunities presented by Klopstock's German paraphrase of the *Stabat Mater* poem, for it replaces the poetic poise of the original with rather down-to-earth versification which permits the composer to envisage a series of cameos – arias, choruses, trios, and a duet – of fairly contrasted character. The *Stabat Mater*, D.383, is therefore a short oratorio, running to nearly forty minutes. Klopstock's gory first lines are set in suitably lugubrious style with leaden choral writing and dark orchestration – funereal trombones much in evidence. The following sensitive picture of the grieving Mary is contrasting enough on the face of it, but Schubert's decision to indulge in text-repetition not on a line-by-line basis but by presenting the whole text of a movement twice over, in two complete sequences, is not justified by his treatment of it the second time. This is a recurring defect later in the work. Moreover, stylistic inconsistency (echoes of Haydn, Pergolesi, Beethoven, and a Kapellmeister or two) is harder to accept when inspiration is at a premium and clichés sound like clichés because they are not functional parts of riveting contexts. Sometimes the effect of an ear-catching incident is dissipated: in the ninth movement, for example, Schubert points the word 'Lasten' (burden) with an oppressively inflected chord which he then reintroduces for other, less apt purposes. The final choral fugue has a subject which closes with a dramatic, promising downward leap of a seventh, but the promise goes unfulfilled. The answering voice converts the seventh into a plain octave – by Schubert's interpretation of one of the tacit 'rules' governing fugal answers – and so drains its colour, and after the fugue has followed a path through mechanical sequences and routine episodes which suffer from poor linkage, the final unison return of the subject complete with the original seventh leads to a bald final cadence rather than any arresting new consequences of that seventh.

The disparity between this Klopstock setting and the *Stabat Mater* (D.175) based on the original poem and composed a year earlier (in 1815) is huge. The earlier piece is of only five minutes' duration, uses just four stanzas of the twenty-stanza Latin poem, and is a single movement with a self-evident unity that does not preclude contrast. Although the four verses are set twice over, the reprise contains far-reaching variation which creates new shades of intensity on the way to a climax both powerful and poignant. This is one of the most successful of all the shorter church compositions. One aspect of the use of trombones is worth special attention. Schubert's original intention, as the autograph score makes clear, was to use horns, not trombones. The well-known limitations of the valveless horn, which was all that was available at the time, prevented it from obtaining certain notes at all. The trombone, on the other hand, could produce any note within its overall compass. While Schubert no doubt cherished the sonority of the trombones, which were in any case a traditional fixture of many ecclesiastical scores, the present instance of substitution suggests that he also valued their greater bar-by-bar usefulness. D.175 is in G minor, and it is in minor keys that the shortcomings of the horn are most keenly felt, since the 'harmonic series' on which they are built is a major-key phenomenon.

Schubert composed six settings of the *Tantum ergo*, all with orchestral accompaniment. The two versions dated August 1816 are both in C major. The first is scored for solo soprano, chorus and orchestra, and its theme owes an unmistakable debt to that of the serene slow movement of Mozart's Clarinet Concerto. The second version has the majesty of a typical Schubert 'Sanctus', and indeed the initial harmonic progression of the Sanctus of the C major Mass. Among texts which Schubert set once only were the *Magnificat*, of which he completed a grand version closer in style to the Masses in F and B flat than to those in G and C, and the *Trauermesse* (German Requiem), a set of verses by Schmid. This latter piece, for mixed choir and organ, adopts Schubert's simplest choral style in twelve short movements which require no comment except that there is a hint of cyclic relationships between some of the movements, in that they share distinct phrase-rhythms, and sometimes motivic shapes.

The Virgin Mary, a central figure in the *Stabat Mater* text, dominates another old text which exerted a continuing appeal for Schubert. He bequeathed no fewer than seven settings of the *Salve Regina*, six composed in the period up to 1819 and one in the later period. These pieces were, for the most part, musically unambitious, and of only occasional interest to the Schubert connoisseur. The first, in F (D.27), was probably the first piece written for Therese Grob, and the fifteen-year-old composer thought he would put her through the coloratura hoops Mozart would have imposed on his best and most seasoned singers (Fig. 37). For reasons we

Fig. 37

can only guess, he modified his demands on her in future scores. He was two years older when he wrote his second setting, this time for solo tenor (in B flat, D.106), again with the support of a small orchestra. Here the vocal writing is more unassuming, the invention attractive and assured.

The third version, for solo soprano and strings, was almost certainly another offering to Therese, and this time the over-the-top virtuosity of the first setting is replaced by a warmth and good judgement which place the result on a level with some of the mass movements of the period. Two settings for mixed choir followed, the F major (D.379) to a German version of the text and the B flat (D.386) returning to the Latin source. Neither is of much interest to those who turn to Schubert for revelations of soul and mind. He had a facility for spinning out choral tracts based largely, effectively, and even pleasingly on block chords, but the absence of so much as a string body or keyboard proved a limitation to him which is soon felt by the listener too – in that there are no sound-sources not yoked to the text or not serviced by human breath to link the choral utterances, add more freely moving strands to the texture, or extend the pitch-ambit of the music. The sixth *Salve Regina* (in A, D.676) dates from 1819 and is for soprano and strings. A delicate, radiant warmth suffuses this, the most successful of these early settings, which in its intimate pastel-tinted lyricism anticipates one of the most ambitious, pathfinding projects of the later period, the unfinished *Lazarus*.

The Song-writer's Craft

The influence of Schober on Schubert may not have been entirely beneficial, but we have Schober to thank for two poems in which the composer recognized his own artistic credo. The songs with which Schubert responded glow with a sincerity that strikes deep: two minds meet in a humble, united creative manifesto eulogizing the power of music to transcend worldly ills. The first of these two songs is the better known. In fact, *An die Musik* has become almost an article of faith for Schubert-lovers, an intimate glimpse of the composer in communion with his Muse. It is a noble love-song in which the object of the poet's love is music itself. The poem conjures up images of love, intertwined with references to musical art. Schubert's melody plots its course with devotional certainty, while repeated quavers in the pianist's right hand suggest the lover's constancy. Meanwhile the pianist's left hand, which anticipates the melody's initial contour, continues in affectionate dialogue with the voice. The bass never loses its melodic identity in a song which gains its unity not through any close working of motives but rather by staying true to a simple and single texture and allowing the melody to blossom with spontaneous naturalness. So perfectly formed is the verse, with its little preface and sequel in the piano, that anything other than a repetition of the music for the second verse is not to be considered for a moment, by the composer or the listener. Thus strophic form receives its ultimate justification.

It is not only because we hear the music twice in one performance that this song is easier to know than the other Schober masterpiece of the same vintage, *Trost im Liede*, a through-composed setting of an only slightly longer text. Here, there is less dependence upon uniform texture, and more upon the subtle manipulation of a pliant motive first heard in the piano prelude (Fig. 38), a wonderful epigram which sets the sublime

Fig. 38

spiritual tone in two modest, shapely brushstrokes. If the vocal theme that follows is less riveting as such than the preludial epigram, that is part of the conceptual plan: the epigram is to be the expressive nucleus of the song, and the voice only shares in it at the first mention of song at the fifth line ('Aber durch die Sanges Tor . . .' – But through the portals of song . . .), and again at the very end of the song, which asserts the crux of the Schober–Schubert philosophy: 'Es gehört zu meinem Leben, Dass sich Schmerz und Freude eine' (It is part of my life That pain and joy are mingled). These words are preceded by the line 'That I firmly and devoutly believe:' – and the forward-pointing colon is Schubert's cue to bring back the appoggiatura idea which formed the melodic peak of the opening epigram (marked 'x' in Fig. 38), stated thrice with pregnant, emotive harmony. A final return, in the piano, of the pristine epigram is the inevitable fulfilment of these final lines but also seals the circular unity of this compact, delicate-hued gem.

An assumption has been made above that both the Schober settings discussed represent Schubert's attitude to his art. In the absence of any documentary evidence, other than the song itself, are we justified in making this assertion? It is a question not usually asked in Schubert criticism. Anyone, it may be supposed, can recognize sincerity. But is the sincerity of, say, *An die Musik* the sincerity of a person or a persona? Does the creator adopt a stance for artistic purposes? We rely on instincts, judgement, and knowledge of the creator's other utterances – in or out of works of art – to guide us, and in the above cases there would appear little doubt that the real Schubert is at large. A seasoned Schubertian, coming to *Trost im Liede* for the first time, may already have sensed that a combination of joy and pathos lies at the heart of Schubert's genius. The song then seems to epitomize and so confirm that position. In other cases, caution is wise. The Ganymede legend, as presented by Goethe in *Ganymed*, depicts man amid nature, striving forever forwards and upwards into nature's embrace. It would be tempting to say that Schubert readily accepts the pantheistic view embodied in the text and relishes its erotic implications too. But does an ostensibly wholehearted response to a text necessarily arise from personal conviction rather than from a will to create a compelling work of art? It is true that the composer can choose his text, but he may choose on the basis of his artistic temperament and his perception of his own technical strengths and inclinations rather than on whether it incorporates his own attitudes, values, religious beliefs, sexuality, sexual orientation, or whatever. The least that can be said of Schubert's music for *Ganymed* is that it serves the pictorialism, passion, joy and sensuality of the poem.

At this point it is as well to state and amplify some definitions. A strophic song is one in which the same music is repeated for each verse or stanza of a (stanzaic) poem. A through–composed song has no such scheme of repetition. A stanza (or verse) is a subdivision of a poem: within a poem, the stanzas are usually but not necessarily of the same length. A strophe is a span of music which is subject to repetition or varied repetition: the strophe, if present, may or may not coincide with a stanza. A song may be through-composed whether the poem it sets is stanzaic or not. Likewise, a musical strophe may be created even when a text is non-stanzaic. *Die junge Nonne* (The Young Nun) is a fine example.

The term 'through-composed' is one of the principal basic tools of song analysis. Its use as an opposite to 'strophic' cannot be taken to imply an absence of recurrent material: the difference is that in a through-composed song the recurrences are not structured and timed to coincide with the succession of one poetic stanza by another. Even so, the principle of recurrence is central to Classical practice and deeply rooted. Because recurrences may at times seem to tally with stanzaic divisions, it is sometimes impossible to use the terms 'through-composed' and 'strophic' dogmatically and exclusively. It is possible, for instance, to detect some strophic elements in *Trost im Liede*. These problems of demarcation are familiar to all who seek appropriate technical terms (whose advantage is that they comprise to the initiated a whole information package in a nutshell) when sharing their responses to music.

One of the charms of folksong is that it gathers up a diversity of narrative detail and takes it on board within a plain strophic design. One accepts almost any eventuality in the text's denouement, because the rotational clockwork of the music tells us that 'that's life'. The design aids the narrative flow, brings the words into sharper relief as the tune becomes taken for granted, while the tune itself – soon imprinted on the mind through regular repetition – serves as mnemonic, facilitating recall of the words. These virtues no doubt commend the strophic form to composers of art-songs, Schubert among them; and many a strophic art-song sounds folk-like, for one reason or another. When Tovey ascribed to variation form, when well used, the 'enormous momentum of something that revolves on its axis or moves in an orbit', he could have applied the same metaphor to strophic form.[1]

That pure strophic form is as valid a medium as the most complex through-composed structure is demonstrated by a miniature masterpiece like *Ungeduld* (Impatience) from *Die schöne Müllerin* (The Fair Maid of the Mill), where in four verses the protagonist finds one way after another of expressing his ardent love, each stanza capped by the same refrain-line. Where a poem offers short stanzas, Schubert often enlarges his musical canvas by taking two stanzas as the basis of his strophe. *Ständchen* (Serenade) from *Schwanengesang* (Swan Song), perhaps the most famous of all serenades, sets a five-verse Rellstab poem, consuming two verses in its strophe, one repetition of which takes care of four verses. The fifth verse is then treated as a kind of musical development. A degree more licence is taken in *Fischerweise* (Fisherman's Ditty), in which Schubert discards one verse of Schlechta's seven-verse poem and groups the remaining six into three pairs for strophic purposes. Of special interest here is the fact that he enlarges the strophe still further by repeating the second verse to make what is in effect a little coda or codetta, built into the strophe. Later, when the strophe comes round for the third time, in the fifth and sixth verses, he varies it in certain details. Such variation may, as here, be superficial enough to leave the structure of the strophe unchanged: in particular, it is neither shortened nor lengthened. At other times, more profound change may involve the structure, which may be curtailed or expanded. Examples involving some degree of later change to the model strophe come under the capacious umbrella of 'modified strophic form'. Just as in variation form if the composer were to treat too many features of his theme as variable and not enough as constant the variations would not be heard as variations but as new pieces, so in strophic form an excess of modification could leave the listener hearing the outcome as through-composed. Even so, the scope for modification is immense, and the art of modification is so sophisticated and complex in Schubert's hands that it is surprising that the modified strophic category, which accounts for a huge corpus of his songs, has not been broken down into sub-categories: less surprising, in that the task is a peculiarly teasing one. Schubert grew particularly attached to this structural hybrid, which became a dominant type by the time he composed the great song-cycle *Winterreise* in his penultimate year.

One of Schubert's earliest and most enterprising modified strophic essays is *Schäfers Klagelied* (Shepherd's Lament), composed in 1814. Goethe wrote the poem in recollection of a folksong he had heard; his words fit the remembered melody. Clearly strophic form would be appropriate, and doubtless expected by Goethe, who would therefore have approved Zelter's strictly strophic setting. Schubert modifies the strophic scheme to a palindromic plan. The first and the last verses (1 and 6) are set strophically; verses 2 and 5 also share a (different) strophe; and verses 3 and 4 make a separate central development. One may imagine Schubert, when he took the poem, noting that towards the end of both the second and fifth stanzas one can see the poet's brow darken, as it were. Coupling that with the fact that the last stanza recalls the reference to the here-and-now actuality of the shepherd's life with which the first stanza began, he perhaps then saw the poem's end as a conceptual retrograde of its beginning. If his symmetrical solution seems to bear no pastoral purport, the tendency to a uniform siciliana rhythm helps at least to preserve the folksong atmosphere. There are also marked similarities of rhythm and contour between successive stanzas (including the superficially contrasting stanzas 3 and 4: see Fig. 39). These similarities could be seen as further vestiges of strophic

Fig. 39

thinking. The symmetry, incidentally, has a tonal dimension, in that verses 1 and 6 have their own key (C minor), as do 2 and 5 (E flat major).

Fidelity to a textual programme produces a kind of progressive strophic form in *Der Alpenjäger* (The Alpine Huntsman), D.588 (to Schiller's poem). The huntsman pursues a gazelle to the mountain's highest crags, where the spirit of the mountain challenges him and protects the beast. The poem is in eight stanzas. In the first three, the huntsman's mother urges him to peaceful pursuits; one musical strophe serves these three stanzas. When he sets off to the mountains, a new (fast and more volatile) musical strophe supervenes, serving for four stanzas. But it is in the last couplet of this seventh stanza that the mountain spirit is announced, with the word 'Plötzlich' (suddenly). Here Schubert abandons the strophe to set this couplet and the ensuing eighth stanza to music of its own. Schubert marries his progressive strophic treatment to progressive tonality: the song begins in C major and ends in A major.

Schubert's use of progressive tonality deserves some comment at this point. It is not at all unusual for his early works, especially the longer, through-composed songs of ballad type, to begin and end in different keys. In the case of a work like the early String Quartet, D.18 of 1811, designated as being 'in mixed keys' because it begins in C minor and ends in B flat, we could attribute the 'progressive tonality' to youthful inexperience. After all, the principle of monotonality was already a long-accepted imperative of tonal planning in symphonic and sonata-type movements, and one that Schubert is faithful to in his later instrumental music. But he treated songs differently, especially – but not only – when they were long and multi-sectional. If it can be argued that the 'programme' of *Der Alpenjäger* suggests progressive tonality, then it can be argued that most vocal texts do the same, in that events succeed events, thoughts follow thoughts, or one mood gives way to others, in their course. Long after Schubert had yielded to the monotonal principle in other genres, though, he was still writing songs which have no tonal frame. *Sehnsucht* (D.636, 1821) begins in B minor and closes in E major; *Der Pilgrim* (1823) moves from D major to B minor; and *Vergissmeinnicht* (1823) proceeds from F minor to E major. It could be that in texted music, which referred to something beyond itself, Schubert felt in some circumstances absolved from a convention which was more palpably desirable in absolute, self-referential music.

There is, in any case, a difference between the structural conventions of, say, sonata form – which was an expansion of the strictly monotonal binary form – or rondo – whose central principle is the return of the first key as well as of the first theme — and the tonal 'clean slate' of vocal forms without binding traditions, forms which were being largely created by Schubert as he ventured from text to text. And there do remain, in some specific instances, potential expressive gains from the progressive tonal method. *Auf der Donau* begins in E flat major and ends in F sharp minor. The tranquil scene with which the poem begins (portrayed by Schubert in a serene-textured E flat) is to be gradually transmuted by Mayrhofer's gloomy imagination into a picture of human powerlessness in the face of Nature's dark forces; the images of decay and threats of destruction in the final stanza cannot be overtaken by a homely retrospect of E flat major without distorting this pessimistic vision. *Ganymed*, a through-composed song with a vengeance (despite Goethe's unequal stanzaic scheme), comprises sections that are each discrete thematically and unique in texture. There is a procession through eight keys, but never any tonal backtracking. The forward momentum generated by constant thematic and tonal succession helps provide the musical conditions for the sense of continual aspiration and of man's gradual absorption into Nature to shine through.

The poetic texts Schubert favoured tended to demand more sophisticated word-setting than folk-lyrics do, with more individual treatment of passing words and phrases. This is one reason why strophic form in his hands often needed modification where in folksong it would not. If the form is regarded as a rigid straitjacket, then the same music must do for words which fall at equivalent points in all stanzas, whether or not that music particularly fits them. This is the essential, built-in compromise of strophic form. Examples of modification, sometimes radical, will be given later in this chapter and in Chapter 18. But sometimes it is possible to make such minor modifications to the music in a later verse that one is hardly aware of the modification. In the strophic *Lied der Liebe* (Song of Love), for example, the words 'Es lächelt bald Liebe' (It smiles now love) fall at the same point in the first stanza as the words 'Die Sonne wird sterben' (The sun will die) in the last stanza, so that 'Liebe' and 'sterben' must share the same note (Fig. 40). A lowering of the note D, without change to the

Fig. 40

harmony, is all that is needed. In the same song's fifth verse, a further strophic repetition is replaced by recitative, the better to illuminate the reference to midnight – which, as Schubert well knows, does not need a full twelve bell-chimes if the word itself is present.

Another solution to the familiar strophic problem is found in *Wie Ulfru fischt* (Ulfru Fishing). In the first verse Schubert repeats Mayrhofer's last couplet, thereby (since the form is strophic) committing himself – apparently – to repeating the last couplet in other verses, since all three stanzas are the same length. But no: Schubert finds in the last stanza that a better match of music to poetry will result if the *first* couplet is repeated in this instance. The outcome is that the remaining poetic couplets will all come out of phase with their proper musical counterparts (Fig. 41). Schubert found here that the music for the third couplet of the first stanza, with its move away from F major to G minor, was a more apt complement to the second couplet of stanza 3 than the relatively bland original music for the second couplet would have been, because this second couplet of stanza 3 introduces a sharp contrast ('Storms blow from the icy peaks, Hail and frost destroy') and a modulation is the obvious source of contrast to match.

Fig. 41

Stanza 1, 2	couplet	1	2	3	4	4
	music	1	2	3	4	4 varied
Stanza 3	couplet	1	1	2	3	4
	music	1	2	3	4	4 varied

In his early years Schubert did not always make the best choice between strophic and through-composed treatment. He probably opted for a cantata-like approach to Schiller's *Die Erwartung* in imitation of Zumsteeg's setting. While his succession of arioso sections and linking recitatives is more imaginative than Zumsteeg's, there is no musical interrelationship between the sections, the recitatives do not grow coherently out of the sections they follow or lead into the ones they precede, and there are too many halts – halts at which there is no accrual of momentum to carry one through and help avoid the feeling that the ensuing start is another start from cold. One cannot help thinking that a modified strophic setting would have produced a better song. The text offers clear pointers inviting strophic treatment, and Schubert could have produced a more cohesive and beneficially shorter setting without sacrificing respect for the character of individual stanzas. Schubert was nineteen at the time of its composition. Five years earlier, soon after his fourteenth birthday, he had enthusiastically shown Spaun some songs by Zumsteeg, including *Die Erwartung*. 'He said he could revel in these songs for days on end,' recalled Spaun. 'And to this youthful predilection of his we probably owe the direction Schubert took.' Spaun also claimed that Schubert 'wanted to modernize Zumsteeg's song ·form, which appealed very much to him.'[2] He succeeded in doing so more notably elsewhere than in *Die Erwartung*.

Schubert's *Erlkönig* has already been touched upon, and a closer study of its strophic build will now be worth making. Fig. 42 summarizes Goethe's eight stanzas (left) and Schubert's music for them (right). The poetic design displays elements of symmetry. Two verses of pure narrative provide the frame (1 and 8). Between these are six verses of direct speech, involving the father or the son, or both. Verses 4 and 6 follow a similar pattern: the son intervenes, the father explains. Schubert sets these identically, for the most part, though in different keys. His settings of the outermost narrative verses 1 and 8 involve common material and key, although the vocal line goes its own way in each case. These resemble framing ritornelli. Goethe's verses 3 and 5 represent the father's attempts to soothe and distract the son. Schubert sets them as sister episodes, parented by the same architectural instinct. Thus Schubert employs quasi-strophic strategies to give cohesion and strength to his through-composed plan, as well as to point up expressive threads and parallels in the text. At the same time he responds to local, one-off needs as the drama unfolds; and he imbues the song with a single directional sweep by maintaining a triplet rhythm from beginning to (almost) end and by shaping the key-structure in a single arch anchored in the G minor of the outermost stanzas. Characteristically, the keys include many which are not closely related to G minor: A minor, B minor, C sharp minor, C major, B flat minor. Extreme emotions, macabre atmosphere and restless agitation justify such vivid, if not lurid, tonal colouring. Thus, by realizing the structural implications of Goethe's poem, Schubert allows strophic principles to invade what is otherwise a through-composed scenario. We might refer to a strophically inflected through-composed form.

The piano begins *Erlkönig* with material which will accompany the vocal entry. In a song in which the vocal and keyboard material are largely independent of each other, this is a natural opening. There are other ways of beginning, appropriate to other types of song. The first vocal phrase often provides the basis of the piano 'prelude'. The vast *Minona* opens with a most imposing prelude which seems to herald events of life-and-death gravity, but is never referred to again. In a strophic setting, a prelude is often identical with the interlude between verses, which is in turn based on the close of the vocal verse immediately preceding it, as in *Wie Ulfru fischt*. Thus the relevance of the prelude is only perceived after a complete strophe has been presented. A similar case was *Trost im Liede*, already discussed, except that there the prelude presents the riveting thematic kernel of the piece, to which the voice gravitates only seldom and with

Fig. 42

	Musical	Narrative
1.	First theme opening and closing in G minor	Purely narrative, setting the scene
2	Continues texture with which previous stanza ended; modulating	First exchange between father and son
3	'Episode' within one related major key (B flat); self-contained; new accompaniment figure, still triplet-based; musical stanza compressed by halving duration of last line	Father's first stanza attempting to soothe and distract son
4	Same material as *v.* 6 for first three lines; fourth line veers to cadence in new key (G major)	Son's intervention – 'Father, father, do you not hear . . .'; father offers explanation in rustling leaves
5	'Episode' within one related major key (C); self-contained; new accompaniment figure, still triplet-based, musical stanza expanded by doubling duration of last line (by repetition)	Father's second stanza attempting to soothe and distract son
6	Same material as *v.* 4 for first three lines; fourth line veers to cadence in new key (D minor)	Son's intervention – 'Father, father, can you not see . . .'; father offers explanation in gleaming trees
7	Continues texture with which previous stanza ended; modulating	Last exchange between father and son
8	First theme opening and closing in G minor	Purely narrative, taking the tale to its conclusion

special effect. *Im Frühling*, as will be seen in Chapter 18, makes a feature of its prelude and strophe being unrelated, for which a 'programmatic' explanation will become evident. That Schubert gave careful consideration to the prelude is confirmed by a comparison of the two versions of the early *Romanze* (D.114). His first thought was Fig. 43a. This was amended to Fig. 43b, the descent to the tonic now pre-echoing the close of the voice's first phrase, while the change to the first four notes of the prelude provides a link with the middle section of the song (Fig. 43c).

Fig. 43

Schubert's flair for the invention of accompaniment figures in his songs has long been appreciated. It is tempting to see phenomena referred to in a text as the stimulus for certain kinds of figuration, whether aquatic in *Die Forelle* or equestrian in *Erlkönig*. If there is cause for caution in such attribution of stimulus, it is not because the composer may have had no conscious intention of portraying the play of water or the galloping of horses in his score. It is well known, among composers, that many of the most revealing and apposite observations made about a work by people other than its composer touch upon important features of the piece of which the composer was not aware. The features are still there, contributing to the work's effect, whether they were determined by the (usually highly active) subconscious mind or by wide-awake deliberation. Commentators who, before making an observation on a piece, felt impelled to seek evidence that it arose from conscious thought would not get far either with that enquiry or with their commentary. No; caution is required because, first, the figuration may be more complex than supposed, reflecting two or more textual ingredients, and second, it may owe its existence as much to musical functions it is to perform.

The breathless triplet pattern that begins *Willkommen und Abschied* (Hail and Farewell) may be prompted by either of two allusions in the song's first line, or by both – 'Es schlug mein Herz, geschwind zu Pferde!' (My heart was beating. Quick, to horse!). The lover's heartbeat and the horses' hooves may both be heard behind Schubert's emphatically rhythmic device, just as in *Die Post* (in *Winterreise*) the piano's rolling triplets seem to suggest not only the motion of the horse-drawn mailcoach but also the singer's fervent hope that there is a love-letter for him. To accompany the voice in *Ungeduld* in *Die schöne Müllerin* Schubert was to choose the very same figuration as he did for *Willkommen und Abschied*, but there is not a horse in sight. There is, though, the impatient longing of the lover. A figuration may have less specific import even than that: whatever the particular, tangible images thrown up by a text, it may simply be a device to promote momentum, intensity, restlessness, passion, urgency, inevitability, claustrophobia, or a sense of the onward march of life, or some other generalized condition. Or it may constitute a congenial context for other musical ideas envisaged by the composer.

Tempo is always a relevant factor. When Schubert again takes the *Willkommen and Abschied* figuration for *Des Mädchens Klage* II (D.191), the lament of a girl parted from her lover and imagining herself grieving for the dead, the ardour of love is tempered by pangs of dereliction, bereavement even. If Schubert's 'Langsam' (slow) is duly observed, there is a hint of the funeral march in this C minor outpouring, which shares a little more than its key with the slow movement of Beethoven's 'Eroica' Symphony. This is appropriate, given that the melody – especially in its second bar — pays homage to the Lacrimosa of Mozart's *Requiem*. Fig. 44 shows Schubert's line above Mozart's.

Fig. 44   *(Langsam)*

(Could Schubert also have had in mind a passage in Act 3 Scene 4 of Gluck's *Iphigenia in Tauris*: the C minor duet – same key as the Schubert – between Pylades and Orestes, which he heard in Vienna in 1811?)

Like Mozart, Schubert understood the human voice as he understood instruments, and this understanding deepened with age. Some early songs require a range, agility or sustained use of a high tessitura that suggests youthful optimism rather than realism. Of course, he may have known singers with special attributes who could dispose of the demands of such as his earlier version of *Des Mädchens Klage* (D.6) without fear. In later years he contrived a more manageable virtuosity, like that which enlivens the brilliant close of *Der Hirt auf dem Felsen*. Some songs call for sublime control in simple vocal lines at low volume levels. Others are obviously predicated upon operatic extraversion. The piano writing is similarly variable in its technical demands, always requiring sensitivity, sometimes speed, power and stamina (*Erlkönig*) and sometimes agile panache (*Suleika II*). A vexed question is the matching of song to vocal gender. In many cases the gender of a poem's persona is self-evident; usually the vocal tessitura determines a high or low voice, and sometimes the gender. Most would say that either or both of these indicators must determine the gender of the exponent of any particular song. What was Schubert's view on the matter? None has come to us, in written form or through the memoirs of friends. Nor do the autograph scores specify the voice or gender. But when it is observed that the singer of *Der Hirt auf dem Felsen* is the shepherd himself (the poem being written in the first person), that he says that he longs 'so ardently for her' (nach ihr), and that Schubert composed the piece especially for the voice of Anna Milder-Hauptmann, a Berlin soprano, it becomes clear that the gender of the poetic persona does not necessarily decide the gender of the singer in his view. Let us not look harshly, then, on a singer who commandeers a song for his or her repertoire when the words it sets are explicitly those of the opposite sex. There appears to be less cause for complaint than there is in the case of the singer who commandeers a song written for a different range from his/her own, by transposing it (usually down): Schubert judged the density of chords according to their pitch (since notes need to be more widely spaced apart in the lower regions of the keyboard than in the upper – for reasons well known to harmonists and borne out by the disposition of Nature's 'harmonic series'), and if they are lowered there is bound to be loss of harmonic clarity.

Transposition does in any event fly in the face of the concept of key-colour, which decrees that a key has characteristics peculiar to it. Some critics have set considerable store by Schubert's alleged choice of key for its 'colour'. When songs are grouped according to their key, interesting affinities are duly discerned.[3] Most musicians subscribe to the theory at some time, but suffer bouts of scepticism. How does the concept bear up in the light of the change in pitch since Schubert's day? Are the emotional, spiritual and worldly connotations of particular keys in Schubert, and for that matter in other composers, only there because composers themselves came to associate these connotations with the keys, possibly by habitual observance of a tradition which may have no objective cause or justification? Such issues are not resolved by the knowledge that Schubert in one instance is reported not to have been enthusiastic about the transposition of one of his works. The work in question was *Alfonso und Estrella*, and Anselm Hüttenbrenner recalled in a memoir of 1854 that when Schubert played it to Kapellmeister Kinsky in Graz in 1827 'Kinsky remarked that Schubert imposed too heavy a burden on the orchestra and choruses and asked him if he would agree to some of the numbers, which were written in C sharp major and F sharp major, being transposed down a semitone by the copyist; to which Schubert admittedly agreed but, as it seemed to me, reluctantly'.[4] Other evidence suggests that if a publisher wanted to publish a song for a voice other than the one Schubert conceived it for, he did not object to its transposition. In this connection we have to remember that downward transposition would have had a less adverse effect on the harmonic clarity of a piano part in Schubert's day, in view of the construction and tonal characteristics of Viennese instruments of the time. Hearing the effect on a twentieth-century piano, he would surely have shared the reservations of the sensitive modern musician.

The ease – and effect – with which Schubert slips from minor key into major, or vice versa, has often been noted. In the Classical period the potential of the alternation of major and minor modes on the same tonic was increasingly explored, whether for local expressive effect or as a means of opening up the possibility of easy travel to a new set of closely related keys. This major-minor modal change was part of the vocabulary of Haydn, Mozart and Beethoven, but Schubert made it his own. It is encountered in his music in a great variety of contexts and manifestations. Its aesthetic interpretation requires care. The distinction often drawn between major and minor as reflecting 'happy' and 'sad' states is not entirely without objective foundation, but it is too simplistic to explain Schubert's preference for one or the other at a given moment.

True, Schubert seems to authorize the simplistic view in *Wehmut* (Melancholy), when, at the words 'so wohl und weh' (so happy and sad), nothing happens other than that a D major chord yields to a D minor one (Fig. 45). But at the end of a song in which the beauties of Nature remind the poet of the transience of man's life, when beauty 'vanishes' (entschwindet) it is in a major chord, if only because the following minor

Fig. 45

es wird mir dann so   wohl und weh in

chord gains enhanced effect through being heard as a cancellation of the major (the F sharp—F natural of Fig. 45 is now transferred to the bass). This is no major chord of joy. It is the same harsh, uncompromising tonic major first inversion on which Beethoven a few years later was to begin the recapitulation so cataclysmically in the first movement of his Ninth Symphony, and when Beethoven then lets the F sharp in the bass slip down to F natural, as Schubert does here, one hears that F natural not as a sad opposite to joy but rather as a further dimension of the 'untowardness' (to find a neutral but negative term) already implicit in the F sharp.

In Haydn's *Creation*, well known to Schubert, the famous sudden burst of C major after the C minor Prelude represents light where there was darkness, order where there was chaos. In Schubert's *Gruppe aus dem Tartarus* (Scenes from Hades, D.583) major ostensibly denotes good, where minor and much else denotes evil. (Ostensibly, because Schubert uses the resource with irony here.) Schiller's vision of departed souls writhing in the underworld prompts Schubert to depict Hades and its groaning inmates with two apposite musical ingredients – semitones and tritones. The tritone had a history of evil association, as the medieval '*diabolus in musica*' (devil in music). Dividing the octave into two equal halves, the tritone directly threatened the natural division of the octave into unequal segments, the crucial dominant being located a semitone above the halfway point. Semitones could also work as agents of disruption. If extensively used, they challenge the purity and order of the diatonic scale – which is again more 'natural', measured by the yardstick of the natural 'harmonic series'. These are the materials that direct Schubert's harmonic thinking (and the melodic thinking, such as it is) almost throughout the song.

The frame tonality is C. Creeping semitonal movement spawns a key-structure in semitone-related blocks, C, C sharp, D, and eventually E flat. The creeping bass is resumed, leading to A (a 'devilish' tritone from E flat), and further semitone rises underpin the second verse. The third verse begins in F sharp minor (Graham Johnson's diagnosis of C sharp minor cannot be supported[5]) and rises by further semitone stages, with a peculiarly persistent sequential ascent to portray the anxious souls of hell asking if the end of their tribulations is yet nigh. A long crescendo from F sharp to C (the 'devil in music' again) leads to a fortissimo climax on a C major chord at 'Ewigkeit' (eternity). John Reed refers here to the 'clear light of C major', and superficially the forces of light may seem to have triumphed over those of darkness, or those of good over those of evil.[6] But 'eternity' is eternal damnation, as the close of the song tells beyond doubt. This ironic use of the major – the implying of the opposite of what is meant – was to acquire a potent emotive force in the late song cycle, *Winterreise*. Another kind of major usage, related to the ironic use and again in evidence in *Winterreise*, is the major of resignation or acceptance (of, say, an unhappy lot). An earlier example (from 1817) is *Am Strome* (By the River), in which Mayrhofer's characteristic gloomy poem – seeing a river as an analogue of the joy and sorrow of human existence, flowing to a distant sea but unable to find a home there – is brought to a close with the words 'Finde nicht das Glück auf Erden' (I can find no happiness on earth) in the serene B major in which the song began.

Schubert's mastery of the art of modulation, appreciated in numerous contexts elsewhere in this volume, is as evident in the songs as in other media. The term 'modulation' implies a process, more or less extended, of gradually quitting one key and establishing another. In the large-scale genres of music, such as symphonic and sonata movements, there is space for the modulatory process to operate in leisurely fashion. In the often much more confined space of the song, modulations are often accomplished more quickly. *Wehmut* makes the astonishing move from D minor to a ravishing F sharp major in one bar, to colour the word 'Schönheit' (beauty). When the time gap between keys is closed up in this way, the colour of the particular relationship is intensified. There is no doubt that Schubert relished the extra vividness that results from the compressed modulation encouraged by the small scale of the short song.

Sometimes the modulation is so compressed that there is not really any modulation at all: the two keys are juxtaposed without mediation. Schubert distinguishes between the first two couplets of *Der Flug der Zeit* (The Flight of Time) by presenting the first in the home key of A major and jumping into C major for the second (and back to A for the third) without modulatory process. This strategy is sometimes applied in a strophic song to provide contrast between successive strophes. *Der Musensohn* (The Son of the Muses) alternates strophes in G major and B major, again moving directly from one key to the other without connecting modulation. There is no sense of strain, as the tonic chords of the two keys share a common note, B. Indeed, the concentrated flavour of the key contrast is pure magic, while the song dances blithely on. Here, incidentally, is a clone of the texture associated with pounding horses' hooves in *Willkommen und Abschied*, except that the right hand's offbeat chords are spiced with appoggiatura-dissonances each of which is a little cry of joy (Fig. 46):

Fig. 46

Durch Feld und Wald zu schweifen, mein Liedchen weg zu pfei - fen, so

they make the song. Having discovered instant and near-instant key-juxtaposition as a characteristic boon of Lieder miniaturism, Schubert transferred the benefits to other genres. The tiny transitions found in many later symphonic and other instrumental movements are probably a by-product of experience in song.

The symbolism and expressive purpose of key shifts – or indeed of the absence of them – is illustrated many times over in Schubert's song oeuvre. *Selige Welt* (The Blessed World) is a compact through-composed setting of two four-line stanzas by Schubert's schoolfriend Senn (whom he set on only one other occasion). Most effective in this defiant 'take life as it comes' song is the way in which the possibility that, on life's voyage, there is a blessed isle worth seeking is denied. 'Doch eine ist es nicht' (But no such isle exists): Schubert repeats the line, and three times a key-implication is brusquely cancelled – C flat major, G major and E minor are all denied, and C minor supervenes. Thus hopes of finding an island paradise – each one glimpsed in the mind's eye as a beckoning remote key – are dashed. The key of the song, incidentally, is A flat major, and all this tonal tacking (to pursue the nautical metaphor) is contained within its twenty-one-bar span!

A stay-at-home policy with regard to tonality sometimes has a purpose. The hurdy-gurdy played by *Der Leiermann* (The Hurdy-gurdy Man) in the last song of *Winterreise* is evidently stuck in one key and the icy wintry scene all around gives Schubert good reason to stay frozen into that key. *An die Natur* (To Nature) is a tiny hymn which can best express its childlike piety in pastel shades within the one key, and by reverting to a bygone age of German song (Reichardt's) when the pianist's fingers followed the vocal line and gave simple chordal support. To forget the vivid colours of the larger tonal canvas and attune one's ears to the contained world of this little cameo is to savour all the more its real carol-like warmth and charm.

Suleika I is a larger piece in which Schubert restrains his tonal wanderlust to quite different purpose. Will the east wind bring me news of my love? The thought is elaborated in six verses, which take a pulsating piano figuration as a constant thread, enabling such a head of erotic steam to be built up that the slowing of tempo for the final verse – with the pulsations transmuted into a variant form of pianistic heart-throb – does nothing to lower the temperature. Why did Brahms think this the loveliest song ever written? For one thing, the driving passion is in part a product of a narrow tonal range, for the song is rooted to B minor and its relative major D (which Brahms tended to think of as an extension of the home minor key, anyway) and the emotions surge and writhe as though tonally imprisoned and seeking release. Brahms himself as a composer relished such self-imposed limitations. Only in the fifth verse does Schubert permit himself to go further afield, whereupon C major, A minor, F major, B flat major, and F sharp major are all glimpsed within six bars of each other in a headlong thrust to the song's climax. An analogy with the finale of Brahms's own Fourth Symphony suggests itself, for after being confined to one tonal area for page upon page by his fidelity to the passacaglia's recurring ground bass Brahms throws off the shackles in a liberated coda which plunges headlong into remote keys.

One can understand Brahms falling for the slower final verse of Schubert's setting too. The expansive phrases, pedal-point harmony, sonorous piano texture, and a tendency to stress the second beat in triple time – these were all to become a central part of Brahms's compositional resource. The song has such cumulative power that it need not strive for strophic unification; however, Schubert's music for the third verse is a reprise of that for the first, and the slower last verse adopts phrase-rhythms from the first. The rhythm and texture which prevail in the piano part are, incidentally, indicative of the first movement of the 'Unfinished' Symphony, composed eighteen months later (see Fig. 47, where the two are compared). The key and metre are the same, as is the rhythm of the left hand; also in common is the tremolo effect in the upper parts and the scalic progress of the upper parts in the second half of each bar.

Fig. 47

Musical self-denial, often practised by Brahms, who composed the entire development section of his D minor Violin Sonata (first movement) over a pedal-point, was required of Schubert again in *Thekla: Eine Geisterstimme* (Thekla – A Phantom Voice, D.595). The phantom voice of Thekla's spirit is heard, telling of her reunion with her lover beyond the grave. To portray the voice from another world he denies himself most of the freedoms of this world, as far as a composer is concerned. The technical limitations are severe: texture, dynamics, vocal range, keyboard range, harmonic and tonal options, all are circumscribed to an unusual degree. The range of the voice is confined to an augmented fourth. The same piano texture is retained throughout; of the three parts, the upper one has a range no wider than the voice's, the middle one is an Alberti-like harmonic filling almost entirely pinned between middle C and the octave below, and the bass moves to and fro within a narrow circle like a caged beast. The dynamic level is pianissimo, with slight hairpin crescendi at a few places. The 'Sehr langsam' (very slow) marking is, in a sense, the final check. Thus the illusion of a disembodied, self-contained presence is given, the hushed concentration of a seance conveyed.

In a song of 115 bars, slow at that, there must however be some colour, some contrast, some shaping factors. As for shape, Schubert does allow himself to group Schiller's six verses in pairs, to be set strophically in three musical 'verses'. Within his strophe, he fluctuates every eight bars between C major and C minor, thus widening his expressive range; and the colour of three chromatic chords and a modulation to A flat major is admitted, although all else is plain diatonic triads. The song is a unique experiment, which in its rigorous quest of maximum expressive scope within confined technical parameters no doubt had a composer-building value for Schubert.

Self-imposed limitations stretch the imagination and sharpen the technique. Schubert seemed, even by the age of twenty, to have become the confident, sometimes inspired exponent of a variety of song types, from the tight-reined, disciplined examples just studied to the spreading no-holds-barred ballads, from flowing strophic structures to terse through-composed one-off designs, from essays in homage to respected precursors to unbuttoned celebrations of his own powers. (One precursor in whose direction he sometimes nodded was Gluck, whose *Iphigenia in Tauris* had moved him as a boy. In his own *Iphigenia* of 1817 the purity and restraint of Gluck are certainly present, with results a little stiff and archaic but some beautifully shaped lyrical phrases.) Throughout these years in which he demonstrated such mastery and versatility in song, he pursued his other wide musical interests – in symphony, sonata, and music for the chamber, stage, church, salon and special occasions. He turned from one outlet to another with an ease and frequency that suggested they were all bound by a common creative urge and constitute a unified repertory. The interface between the Lieder and this vast 'other oeuvre' is of constant interest: to know one and not the other is to know a part of Schubert the musician. There is a tendency, to some extent natural, to see the world of Schubert song as something apart from the wider entity of Schubert's music. Singers, of course, do not have access as performers to most of this 'other oeuvre'; song recitals tend to draw a specialist audience; the songs themselves engage the attention of special interest groups, such as Germanists and followers of literature and poetry.

Schubert was not addressing himself to numerous splinter audiences, but to a single, if idealized, body of auditors. The cohesiveness and expressive unity of his multifarious creations indicates as much. It was in the period 1815 to 1820 that he wrote most of the songs which he then saw fit to plunder for the creation of new works in other media. These 'borrowings', it should be remembered, were not in the nature of transcriptions or arrangements: Schubert was not merely bringing the songs to a wider or different audience. He left half of the song behind, in every case: the text was set aside, and the musical material was projected into a new context in which it could germinate according to its own lights to produce new growths. What this tells us is not so much that the songs live on in the new medium, but that Schubert's compositional urges sprang from a central source and the boundaries between the genres into which they were (necessarily) channelled were of no abiding consequence. If we have ears that readily overstep those same boundaries, we stand to gain most from his art.

As for the recycled songs, there is no reason why our excitement at what Schubert was able to make of the adopted material when freed of the text should reduce our appreciation of the original song as a song. *Die Forelle*, *Der Tod und das Mädchen* (Death and the Maiden) (both 1817), and *Die Götter Griechenlands* (The Gods of Greece) (1819) all repay study. *Der Tod und das Mädchen* is, indeed, a particularly bold conception. It is a brief dramatic scene, a dialogue between the maiden and the figure of Death in which both parts are taken by the one singer. In fact, the maiden speaks once only, followed by Death once only. The young maiden, pleading to be left alone by Death, naturally sings faster. Death sings slowly, supported by solemn chords. By beginning the song with some of Death's material at Death's tempo, Schubert forges a simple symmetrical unity, and suggests the presence of Death, which gives point to the maiden's pleading.

One enterprising feature is the unusual relationship between the musical ideas, which affects the concept of 'theme', since that term may imply melody and/or 'main topic'. The characteristic 'theme' of the song is the chordal progression associated with Death. The singer never sings this theme. The maiden's utterance is little more than recitative, heightened by a recurring rhythm as accompaniment. When the chordal theme returns for Death's reply, the singer delivers what is mostly a recitational monotone while the principal melodic interest lies in the middle parts of the harmony. In a real musical sense, Death's vocal line is a dispensable add-on. Schubert demonstrates the completeness of the piano part by adopting it, without the vocal line, in the D minor Quartet. There are plenty of places in Schubert's Lieder where we should talk not of piano accompaniment but of vocal accompaniment. The slow dactylic rhythm of Death's music in this song (sometimes referred to as pavane rhythm) has often been regarded as one of Schubert's favourite symbols of death. There is perhaps some point in this observation, given that the rhythm is prominent in *Wie klag ich's aus* (How shall I lament) (D.744), *Das Wirtshaus* (The Inn) (*Winterreise*), and the last song of *Die schöne Müllerin*. The rhythm does, however, appear in songs which have nothing to do with death, such as *Die Liebe hat gelogen* (Love has lied). And one would wish to hold a red light to any attempt to project deathly associations on to *Rosamunde* Nos. 5 (the famous B flat Entr'acte) or 7 (the *Hirtenchor* – Shepherds' Chorus), or the slow movement of the 'Great' C major Symphony.

Die Götter Griechenlands begins and ends with an evocative, questioning figure in A minor – 'Schöne Welt, wo bist du?' (Fair world, where are you?). The main section, not too distinguished musically, is in an illusory tonic major. At the mention of the 'Feenland der Lieder' (magic land of song) there is an arresting shift to the submediant major. It was Schubert's decision to repeat the first questioning couplet at the end of the song, so returning the music to A minor. In both the framing minor sections, the invention hangs on a tonic chord in second inversion, without a root in the bass to anchor it. The lack of any secure resolution is appropriate to an unanswered, unanswerable, rhetorical question. It was merely this musical question that Schubert later took as the starting point of the third movement of his A minor String Quartet, and one can understand his feeling that it was time the question, insofar as it was a musical one, was answered. The quartet movement, a haunting minuet, does indeed offer an intriguing, inventive answer. The tonic major key is then no longer needed for an answer, illusory or otherwise, but is used for a 'trio' which is pure contrast.

The only question surrounding *Die Forelle* (The Trout) concerns its ending. The song is, of course, an innocent delight in musical terms, with a tune of superior folksy cut and a piano figure that touches in both the darting fish and the clear water which shows it up. But Schubert omitted the final verse, in which the poet Schubart points his moral, recommending young girls to beware young men with rods. And he did not seem to know what to do with the third verse that now served as last. At least, for the first three-quarters of it he departs from his strophe to give a superb vignette of the catching of the trout. But by rejoining his rollicking strophe for the last couplet he neither conveys an inkling of the poet's 'regem Blute' (blood boiling) at the sight of the 'Betrogne' (cheated creature) nor manages any convincing impression of a 'that's life' shrug. In that sense, when he augmented a quintet from the usual four movements to five by inserting a set of variations on the song only two years later in 1819 (perhaps acknowledging the song's meteoric rise up early nineteenth-century Vienna's equivalent of the charts), he left a curious enigma comfortably behind – with the discarded text. At the same time he inaugurated a tradition which was to demonstrate that the bouquets of song and the voiceless media are sufficiently independent to allow old wine a refreshing new life in new bottles.

1818–1822

The period from 1818 to 1822 was to be a critical one for Schubert, in both musical and personal respects. These were the years in which he invested considerable time and creative energy in the quest to make his mark as a composer of opera, a strategy which, if it had succeeded, would have been his best route to financial security, as well as to popular success in his own city. The same period saw him labouring under artistic growing pains. Success, in song-writing at least, had come to him young. Although in other media he had not achieved quite the same éclat, he had been blessed with a youthful facility which had stayed with him through his teenage years. He was poised to graduate from a self-directed apprenticeship – self-directed in that he had aspired to more, learned more, and accomplished more that was worthy outside the study programme Salieri mapped out for him – to a maturity in which far-reaching visions would be backed by expert technique. At the same time, he was beginning to earn public recognition in Vienna, and, gradually, beyond. Yet he foundered, leaving many works unfinished.

Was he too impatient, his aspirations racing ahead of his capacity to satisfy his standards? Did he waste his time on projects that would encourage complacency rather than stretch and stimulate him? Was it that, while other composers suppress their inferior or aborted products, Schubert pressed ahead from one attempt to another, having no thought abut prying eyes that might, then or later, want to inspect every note he wrote? He did not, like Mozart, keep a list of his works, and he had no inkling that one day a Köchel or Deutsch would round up every gem and every wart in some grand compendium. It probably did not enter his head that he should plan for a day when those who survived him would want to compile lists of what works were in their hands or were simply known to exist (as did his brother Ferdinand who outlived him, and those contemporaries who had built up collections of his works, such as Witteczek, Spaun and Dumba). Brahms, who knew about making complete editions of past composers, since he had a hand in preparing Schubert's as well as Couperin's oeuvre for publication, was particular enough to destroy whatever piece or fragment of his own did not adequately represent him. For

Schubert, one guesses that not only was the present audience of more concern than any future one, but that even the present audience was not the motivating factor: the fulfilment to be had from the act of creation itself was of more consequence than what happened to a piece after he had set down his pen.

It is fatally easy to attribute the abandonment of works, half finished, to a composer's self-criticism. In Schubert's case, there are at least two works of which none but the most jaundiced being could plead that the composer was dissatisfied with what he had written: the Quartettsatz in C minor (D.703) and the 'Unfinished' Symphony. In these instances, we then move on to an explanation which is near to being a diametric opposite: what he had written so far was a superior product – so good that he did not feel able to sustain its quality over the rest of the work. That is always a hypothesis to be considered, although it loses some of its appeal when one reflects that if a composer knows that he has begun a work on an exalted level of inspiration the motivation to continue and complete the work must be correspondingly higher. If, however, the works left unfinished include some of middling quality, for which neither of the above reasons could be relevant, there must be some other reason for abandonment, and that reason could be a contributing factor in the other instances too. There are indeed works Schubert failed to finish in this period which are neither would-be masterpieces nor feeble fragments. Works that come to mind are *Lazarus*, *Über allen Zauber Liebe* (Love beyond all magic) (D.682), the E major Symphony (D.729) and the Kyrie in A minor (D.755). There would naturally be some disagreement on that assessment: but it is Schubert's assessment that matters, and one can only say that when more than twenty works are involved, some of these are likely to be in our middle category. We should perhaps be looking, then, for a more generalized explanation (or more than one) which might explain some cases wholly and others in part.

Schubert was a prodigiously prolific composer. If he had written none of his songs, he would still have been a prolific composer. He liked to write for a wide range of media – a variety of chamber ensembles, keyboard, the mass, miscellaneous smaller church genres, various orchestral forms, opera, partsongs, one-off groupings for celebratory or other occasions; all this in addition to songs. He socialized with members of the Bildung Circle and other friends so often that opportunities to compose new works must have presented themselves frequently – whether because friends suggested texts for songs or his discussions with them (many of them being musicians or music-lovers) threw up ideas which might then become self-initiated projects. It is a well-documented fact that he often set one work aside to begin on another. If, when he was halfway through a piano sonata, he spent the evening with friends and one of them showed him a poem that appealed to him, he might well have seen immediate possibilities in it and wanted to set to work on it the following day. Perhaps his eye would then be caught by another poem in the same collection, or it may be that he realized he hadn't much time left to prepare a new piece for a name-day. There could be any number and type of distractions from the piece in progress. In many cases he would go back to the original piece and finish it. In some cases he would return to it, add more to it, and put it to one side again. He did not always give himself the luxury of removing himself from society to work uninterruptedly on a major project, as he did in late 1821 for *Alfonso und Estrella*. Sometimes the gap between putting a piece aside and taking it up again was short, sometimes longer. The difference between laying it aside and later resuming it, on the one hand, and laying it aside but never returning to it, on the other, is not so very great. The length of the gap before resumption was possible is of the essence. It becomes harder to think one's way back into a work the longer it has been out of mind. It also inhibits resumption if one's style is changing rapidly or one's outlook is shifting so that one feels the need for different kinds of challenge. These considerations are familiar enough to composers. Schubert's style was in a state of flux especially in the period 1818–22. Because his compositional interests were so diverse and his rate of production so fast it is not altogether surprising, when the above points are taken into account, that some works were left unfinished. The pattern of circumstances was such that a high risk of dereliction was built in.

There is another circumstance, well known to composers, which is relevant here. One can reach a point, in composing a piece, where the invention stalls – temporarily, one hopes. One cannot think which way to move forward, for the time being. That may be a good reason for ceasing work until tomorrow. When tomorrow comes, one begins by re-living the piece as far as it has gone – that is, one listens through mentally. The hope is that the momentum re-activated in the early stages of the piece will this time carry one through the stalling point. If it doesn't, one tries again. The problem is now that, the more one saturates oneself in the early stages of the piece, so as to feel one's way back into the ideas from which – in some way or other – the continuation must grow, the more one becomes used to the piece with its arrest at the stalling point, and this merely adds to the difficulty of winning through. The stalling point becomes fixed and immovable, like a corroded screw.

Some of Schubert's unfinished works were operas. Here two additional elements come into play. The likelihood of performance seemed to matter more to him than in the case of other kinds of work, so that marketability was possibly more of a yardstick as he proceeded with a work for the stage. And if he aborted through dissatisfaction, it could have been towards the libretto as much as the music that his dissatisfaction was directed – although it has to be said that he was somewhat uncritical of libretti (the poor quality of Schober's *Alfonso und Estrella*, for example, did not prevent him from completing his score of that work). There was no difficulty, evidently, in completing *Die Zwillingsbrüder* – perhaps because he chose to stay stylistically within defined limits and in any case he was working to a commission which would yield a fee and probably lead to other commissions.

Having finished *Die Zwillingsbrüder* in January 1819, Schubert was expecting the première to follow in the same year. In fact he had to wait until June 1820. This was not an easy time for a composer of German opera seeking a hearing in Vienna. The taste for Italian opera, boosted by the success of Rossini on his visits in recent seasons, was something theatre managers had to defer to. In the field of German opera, the slighter works of Weigl had a following (even the young Schubert had enjoyed them). Schubert's prospects might have been better if Weigl had not also been conductor of the court theatres. He vented his annoyance in a letter to Anselm Hüttenbrenner on 19 May: 'In spite of Vogl it is difficult to outwit such *canaille* as Weigl, Treitschke, etc. That is why instead of my operetta they give other rot, enough to make your hair stand on end.'[1] Vogl had been instrumental in securing the commission for *Die Zwillingsbrüder*. Treitschke was producer and librettist at the Kärntnertor Theatre.

When eventually Schubert's one-acter appeared, it had a mixed reception. 'Schubert's friends made a lot of noise while the opposition hissed – at the close there was a fuss until Vogl appeared and said: "Schubert is not present; I thank you in his name." ' The fact that Schubert was indeed present, up in the gallery with Anselm, but was roughly dressed and declined Anselm's offer to borrow his tailcoat so as to take a call, may well have gone unnoticed by the audience, but Vogl was clearly aware of the situation he was covering, and he and Schubert's other friends who were trying to further his career must have been embarrassed by his refusal to do the courteous thing and acknowledge applause. In any event, composer and friends were happy enough to celebrate in a wine bar near St Stephen's Cathedral with cheap Hungarian wine.[2] The opera ran for six performances, which was above average at this time.

Schubert received 500 florins for this work. Of this, 150 florins had been paid on account back in July 1819, with 30 florins for copying out the parts. These advances were some compensation for the disappointment he was suffering in 1819; and there were others. In January there had been a second performance of the cantata *Prometheus* at the house of the Sonnleithners, with an orchestral reduction on the piano. The court opera tenor Jäger sang his setting of Goethe's *Schäfers Klagelied* at a public concert in February. In February too he completed the Overture in E minor, and in the first five months of the year he set a dozen or so songs, to texts by Schlegel, Schiller, Silbert, Grillparzer (whom he probably met at the January performance of *Prometheus*), Mayrhofer and Novalis. Then came a summer holiday with Vogl.

Vogl had been born in Steyr and had many friends there. It was at the house of one of them, a lawyer named Dr Albert Schellmann, that Vogl and Schubert stayed. 'The country is heavenly,' wrote Schubert; and as he was permitted to have the domestic piano moved into his room there was opportunity to compose as well as enjoy the surroundings, meet friends, and make music.[3] A leading part in the arrangement of musical activities was played by Sylvester Paumgartner, an amateur musical enthusiast and competent cellist, whose large house in the main square of Steyr was the focus of music-making for all keen amateurs in the town. Those taking part included Josef von Koller, a merchant in whose house Vogl and Schubert took their meals, and his elder daughter Josefine, of whom Schubert said that she 'is very pretty, plays the pianoforte well and is going to sing several of my songs'.[4] Before he left at the end of the holiday Schubert presented to Josefine a new piano sonata, which may have been the A major, D.664. One of the old friends he met up with was Albert Stadler, a fellow-pupil at the Stadtkonvikt who was now working as a barrister in Steyr. To mark Vogl's fifty-first birthday on 10 August Stadler wrote a eulogistic poem which Schubert set for STB and piano. 'Quite a success,' Schubert told Mayrhofer when he wrote to him a few days later from Linz, where he spent some time meeting other old friends, including Spaun and Josef Kenner.

There is some doubt in musicological minds as to what Schubert may have composed during this happy eight-week break, in addition to the (not very long) birthday cantata for Vogl. There are two works which could have been written at this time, and the fact that they were not specifically mentioned in letters or reminiscences has little bearing on the issue, since most of the major works were never referred to in the documents of Schubert's life. There is, in any case, reference to 'a piano sonata', and the A major is music of such wide-eyed youthful contentment that one could imagine it being a response to both the mountain scenery of Upper Austria and a 'very pretty' dedicatee. The 'Trout' Quintet bears a dedication to Paumgartner, who requested it, but it has been suggested that it could have been associated with either Schubert's 1819 visit to Steyr or his return visit in 1825. Those who prefer the earlier year tend to assume it was written after Schubert's return to Vienna in the autumn of 1819. Certain structural features of the work tend to support this earlier dating, but there seems no reason for ascribing it to the autumn rather than the summer in Steyr. The set of parts which is the sole surviving primary source, since the score was lost, was written out by Stadler. Like the A major Piano Sonata, the 'Trout' Quintet presents a sound-image and sense of well-being not wholly characteristic of earlier Schubert: it seems to breathe pure mountain air. It is not hard to believe that the two works, both in bright A major, could have resulted directly from the stimulus of new surroundings.

When Schubert returned to Vienna in mid-September he began a winter schedule which was busy and productive enough without us having to suppose that the 'Trout' Quintet must have been a part of it. Two overtures for piano duet (in G minor, D.668, and in F minor/major, D.675) and seven songs were finished before the end of 1819. (He composed no new songs at Steyr, but performed many with Vogl.) More substantial, though, were the works he began. In November he started work on the Mass in A flat, one of his two finest and most substantial settings, but it took three years of intermittent work to bring this to a definitive form. And he tried another opera. This time he took a libretto more likely to satisfy him, in that it was based on a serious Classical subject which might have rekindled his early enthusiasm for Gluck, and was written by Mayrhofer. Why, having begun *Adrast* so auspiciously, inventing by far his most promising operatic music to date, he should have abandoned it is not known. No surviving document from Schubert's lifetime makes reference to the work by name. In an obituary notice by Leopold Sonnleithner it was simply listed as an unfinished work.[5] But it was a substantial fragment, amounting to something like fifty minutes of music, and it probably occupied him into the early weeks of 1820. *Adrast* stands in stark contrast to the A major music of the Steyr holiday – or to the music of Rossini's *Otello* which Schubert so extolled in a letter to Anselm Hüttenbrenner the previous May ('You cannot deny him extraordinary genius. The orchestration is often highly original, and the vocal parts also . . .').[6] Perhaps, indeed, both Mayrhofer and Schubert saw the work as a positive antidote to Rossini, a new kind of German opera indebted, if at all, to Gluck, with a touching homage to Beethoven's 'Archduke' Trio in one number.

The abandonment of *Adrast* may well be connected with the composition history of the next major work. It has long been supposed, reasonably enough, that the 'Easter Cantata' *Lazarus* was intended for performance at Easter 1820. The fact that it was not performed at this or any later Easter suggests that it was never finished (only two of the three 'acts' have survived). That might have been due to a lack of commitment or confidence, since Schubert was trying to do something new in this hybrid opus. Equally, it may simply have been that time was too short: he began the work in February, and if he had only until Easter to see it through, then as the work progressed and its innovative thrust became clear it is likely that the challenge of suitably crowning this pathfinding project will have increasingly daunted the young composer.

A visit to the police station about mid-March will not have helped

matters. Schubert was drinking at the lodgings of his old friend Johann
Senn in the early hours, when the police paid an unannounced visit and
took both Senn and Schubert, and their friend Josef von Streinsberg, in
for questioning. Senn had for long been viewed with suspicion by the
police, since his involvement in student politics at the Stadtkonvikt; the
Bildung Circle had been known for some years as a potentially seditious
organization; and the assassination of the dramatist Kotzebue (politically
in sympathy with the government) by a radical student in 1819 had made
the state authorities more militant than ever in pursuing their repressive
measures. Senn, who had spoken contemptuously to the police, was incar-
cerated for fourteen months without trial, before being deported to the
Tyrol. Schubert was released, presumably with warnings, and mentioned
in the police report as 'the school assistant from the Rossau' (he was in
fact no longer that, but had perhaps hoped to gain respectability by an
innocuous stretching of the truth).

Once Easter had passed, Schubert may well have returned to the Mass
in A flat for a while. But soon another operatic opportunity came his way.
A new work was wanted for a benefit production at the Theater an der
Wien, and Leopold Sonnleithner was asked for advice as to who should
compose it. A magic opera to a text by Georg von Hofmann was wanted.
Schubert was recommended, received the commission in April, and had
Die Zauberharfe ready for production on 19 August.[7] Intent on furthering
his operatic career, Schubert seems to have given the middle months of
the year over to this new stage project almost exclusively – only the Six
Ecossaises in A flat had to compete with it for attention in the months
April to August.

Sonnleithner recalls in his 1857 memoir that *Die Zauberharfe* 'was ready
in a few weeks'.[8] Only recently has this been questioned. Even Reed
accepts Sonnleithner's statement as gospel.[9] Yet, apart from the fact that
Schubert 'cleared his desk' of other projects for five months, and was
known to be aspiring to operatic success at this time, there are other reasons
for doubting Sonnleithner's memory: the opera was a vast undertaking,
running to 2775 bars plus some additional sketches, and it finds Schubert
once more seeking out a 'new style' appropriate to a new kind of challenge.
It draws from him, for example, harmonic imagination of a special sort,
as part of the fund of resources needed for combining spoken text with
orchestral music. The fact that he contributed to the score a palindrome that
is arguably the most complex technical feat undertaken by any composer
in the nineteenth century further confirms the work's status as a major
undertaking of demanding character.[10]

Die Zauberharfe enjoyed eight performances between 19 August and 12
October. The critics dismissed Hofmann's contribution as trivial and were
divided on the quality of Schubert's score. One of them, at least, recognized

that Schubert was here extending himself: 'In that the young composer here tried his hand at a higher species for the first time, it is only fair to do full justice to his praiseworthy endeavour to remain original . . .'[11] Another took a balanced view of the score's mixed success: 'True, there is the music – and real music! Many good ideas, forceful passages, cleverly managed harmonic pieces, insight and understanding; but also inequalities in abundance, commonplaces side by side with originalities, a mixture of light and far-fetched, valuable and frivolous things.'[12] This is a fair critique, and although Schubert might have hoped for a more wholehearted acceptance of what he had attempted there was nothing here to deter him from future undertakings, especially as he was unlikely to be asked to work on another Hofmann magic play. He had, at least, received a commission, fulfilled it, and had his work both performed and noticed.

There was, in fact, little delay before Schubert embarked on his next operatic venture. In this same October he was at work on *Sakuntala*, an opera with spoken dialogue on an oriental theme. The libretto, by J. P. Neumann, was based on a fifth-century Sanskrit poem by way of intermediate translations – from Sanskrit to English by Sir William Jones, and from English to German by Georg Forster, whose version Neumann then adapted. What impulse led Schubert to take on *Sakuntala* remains a mystery. There is no record of any commission, and it may be that he simply wanted to build on his progress in opera but veer away from Hofmann and magic at the same time. Perhaps the complexity of Neumann's play, combined with its relative inaction, overwhelmed Schubert soon after he had begun work, for he got as far as writing mere sketches of parts of two acts. Brahms saw fit to exclude these sketches from the first complete edition, but they survive (without the libretto, which is lost) in the Vienna City Library.

Outside his composing, 1820 had been a year of social change for Schubert. The orchestral rehearsals which had moved from Otto Hatwig's house to Pettenkofer's in 1819 were dispossessed of their home in 1820 when Pettenkofer won a lottery and decided to retire. This closed off a valuable medium for the performance of Schubert's orchestral music. Although Ignaz Sonnleithner ran a series of fortnightly private concerts at his house, and some of Schubert's music had an airing there, it was mostly smaller-scale works, especially songs, that were involved. Even so, from the end of 1820 the Sonnleithner household was the background to a useful publishing venture which helped to disseminate the songs. Following an impressive performance of *Erlkönig* given at a Sonnleithner concert in December by an amateur tenor called Gymnich, Leopold Sonnleithner and Josef Hüttenbrenner joined with others to publish some of the songs privately. *Erlkönig* was included, and at one of the subsequent Sonnleithner concerts almost a hundred copies of it were sold. Twenty songs had been thus published by the end of 1821. This year also saw an increase in the number of performances in Vienna, at the Gesellschaft der Musikfreunde especially. Again, it was mainly smaller-scale works that were given.

Towards the end of 1820 Schubert moved out of the lodgings he had shared with Mayrhofer, the two of them having one dark, long room between them. Holzapfel suspected that personal difficulties between the two men were to blame: '. . . their continued living together foundered on their day-to-day relations, perhaps on small differences of opinion regarding money matters, in which Sch. may well have often been to blame'.[13] Perhaps, too, the composer found it hard to reconcile Mayrhofer's acceptance of the position of book censor with his own radical sympathies, suggested by his long association with Senn and his circle. In any event, Schubert had earnings from his operatic commissions (*Zwillingsbrüder* and *Zauberharfe*) to sustain him, and he chose to live independently for the time being, in a house further along the Wipplingerstrasse. It may be that the move had to do with Josef Hüttenbrenner as well as the Schubert–Mayrhofer relationship itself. Hüttenbrenner, tireless admirer of Schubert's music, had moved into an apartment in the same building as Mayrhofer and Schubert, an arrangement which allowed Schubert to use his services as a sort of secretary, taking various day-to-day responsibilities off his shoulders. But Schubert became irritated by Hüttenbrenner's fawning attention and began to treat him rudely. He may have seen a move out of the building as a convenient way of terminating this soured working arrangement.

Schubert had retained contact with Schober, particularly at Atzenbrugg in the summer. He had interrupted his work on *Die Zauberharfe* to attend for the first time the house party which took place on the Atzenbrugg estate some way outside Vienna, owned by Klosterneuburg Monastery. The 'Atzenbrugg feasts', in which Schober and Kupelwieser played a leading part, were gatherings of invited friends at which intellectual games leavened by country excursions were the order of the day. These were occasions for carefree informality, captured in famous watercolours by Kupelwieser himself. As for Schober, long absent from Vienna, he was to return to the city at the end of the year, and his life would be closely intertwined with Schubert's in the following two years – 1821–2.

The end of 1820 was a crossroads in several respects: Schubert extricated himself from shared accommodation with Mayrhofer (with Josef Hüttenbrenner under the same roof); Schober returned to Vienna; Therese Grob married Johann Bergmann, a master baker, so dashing any hopes Schubert might yet have harboured of marriage with her; and the composer began a work which represents the first sign of his compositional coming of age as an instrumental composer. The String Quartet in C minor (D.703) was not Schubert's first quartet in a minor key. The Quartet in G minor was,

like the Fourth Symphony in C minor, a late teenage piece: not fully
self-revealing, it owed not a little to *Sturm und Drang* Mozart. But the C
minor was the first quartet in which he set himself a challenge similar to
that which drew from Beethoven the 'Rasumovsky' Quartets: its starting
point was an up-to-date recognition of the scope of the medium as it now
was, along with the confidence to give imagination its head unconstrained
by the defined limits of early Classical quartet style as assimilated through
a self-imposed 'apprenticeship' with Haydn and Mozart. Yet, after a first
movement which creates with unerring mastery a personal re-interpretation
of sonata form, Schubert set down his pen after about forty bars of the
Andante second movement. It is one of the great mysteries of these years
of fast maturing that even when he produced music of such miraculous
certainty as the Quartettsatz (as the solitary first movement of this quartet is
always called) or the 'Unfinished' Symphony his recognition of its supreme
quality (for he surely did recognize it) did not compel him through to its
final completion.

Whatever kept Schubert from completing this work, and however insidi-
ous the musical and personal hang–ups which dogged his path in the next
two years, the seam of gold, once struck, was not to stay beyond his reach
entirely until the crisis of transition was over – and gave way to another,
life-threatening one. Only three months later, for example, in March 1821,
he was able to produce 'the loveliest song that has ever been written', as
Brahms called the exquisite *Suleika I*. A little masterpiece of a less marketable sort, also from March of this year, is the Variation in C minor that
was Schubert's contribution to the set of fifty variations by as many
composers (one apiece) which Diabelli commissioned, the theme being a
trifling but well-structured waltz of his own. Let our admiration for the
towering set of thirty-three variations with which Beethoven responded
(after a due interval of three years) not blind us to the characteristic merits
of the thirty-two-bar miniature with which Schubert responded at once,
before any other of those invited. As a re-exploration in the minor of
Diabelli's innocent C major model it could not be surpassed by any
composer, dead, deaf or alive.

In the larger projects, though, he continued to stumble. In the two
symphonies attempted but left unfinished in 1821, was he over-reaching
himself, later realizing that he could not ultimately reach the beckoning
new horizons he had pointed to in his sketches? Or did lack of time, and/
or the pressure of other 'priorities', delay completion until his thinking
had moved on so far that resumption was not to be contemplated? The
first of these two efforts, known as D.708a and conceivably begun in late
1820, comprises four fragments in piano score whose tonal wanderlust
could not have been satisfactorily reconciled with the limitations of brass
and drums in Schubert's day. The second, now known as No. 7 in E,

D.729, was begun in August, Schubert composing directly into orchestral score. Here Schubert wrote something in every bar of all four movements, charting in the process some notable structural experiments; there was nothing that would have posed impossible obstacles to completion, whether in the orchestration or the 'filling out', and one is tempted to conclude that a prior appointment to work on an opera with Schober in September spelt the sidelining and ultimate abandonment of this particular symphonic project. Indeed, the two men seem to have left Vienna in *early* September in order to visit Atzenbrugg en route to their ultimate destination.[14]

The opera was *Alfonso und Estrella*, and Schober, who was to write the libretto, had arranged to take Schubert to St Pölten, about thirty-five miles to the west of Vienna, so that they could work on the venture alongside each other. The Bishop of St Pölten, who lived in nearby Ochsenburg Castle, was a relative of Schober's, and gave them accommodation in the castle for part of their stay, also hosting some musical evenings. By day, Schober and Schubert worked on the opera, the idea being that Schober would work ahead of Schubert, progressively passing him material to set. Even if the two conferred about the overall shape of the work in advance, this was foolishly trusting of Schubert, especially as Schober had no track record as a dramatist. Perhaps Schubert's willingness was a sign of the influential hold Schober had over him, and of Schubert's determination to pursue any opportunities for opera composition that presented themselves. There was no glut of good librettists in Vienna, and in any case Schubert had not shown himself inclined to vet his intending collaborators: in his wish to succeed in matching music to drama, he showed more ambition than discrimination. Still, the fact that Schubert was wholehearted in his response to Schober's writing brought its compensations: for although the opera is irredeemable as drama – having an unsatisfactory balance of constituents (e.g. aria, duet, chorus) and singers (one female principal role) and a preponderance of static scenes – it has decided musical assets. That most cliché-ridden of operatic procedures, the recitative, which had been so slow to develop into a musically satisfying component of opera now becomes – in the accompanied recitatives of *Alfonso und Estrella* – imbued with up-to-date colour and expression, developing a trend initiated by Mozart in his accompanied examples. And there is no doubt that this is harmonically the most enterprising of all operas to date.

Schubert began to write the score of Act I on 20 September, finishing it on 16 October. Two days later he began Act II, but he and Schober returned to Vienna before the second act was finished. On 3 November they saw Weber's *Der Freischütz*, brought to Vienna in a cut version after its huge success in Berlin in June, and the next day a new production of *Fidelio*. Towards the end of the year the Italian impresario Domenico Barbaja took over the lease of the Kärntnertor Theatre and the Theater an der Wien, and, wishing to encourage the development of German opera, invited both Weber and Schubert to submit scores for consideration for the 1822/3 season. Schubert and Schober were encouraged by this to resume work on *Alfonso* and complete it, which they did by February 1822. The score was sent off to Barbaja, but months passed and there was no response. Meanwhile, Barbaja presided over a long run of Rossini at the Kärntnertor. Eventually Schubert asked for the score to be returned so that he could send it elsewhere. Over the following years he tried to interest other operatic centres in the work (including Berlin, Dresden and Graz), but in vain. It is possible that the theatre management had taken into account the view of Vogl, who saw the score and thought the opera unstageable. Schubert himself, like Schober, was convinced of the work's quality. But when Schober was an old man he recognized the failings of his libretto, describing it in 1876 as 'such a miserable, still-born, bungling piece of work that even so great a genius as Schubert was not able to bring it to life'.[15]

Schubert had at least enjoyed a minor operatic success in June of 1821, when he was invited to write two extra numbers for a production of Hérold's comic opera *Das Zauberglöckchen* (originally *La Clochette*) at the Kärntnertor Theatre. Spaun reported that the authorship of the extra numbers was not revealed to the audience, who nevertheless responded more warmly to their charms than to the music of Hérold. There were eight performances.[16] On other fronts Schubert's reputation was steadily growing. It was in this year that the Gesellschaft der Musikfreunde finally agreed to admit him as a member, and his works were included in no fewer than eight concerts. Although these works were songs and partsongs, and Schubert may well have hoped for more substantial instrumental pieces to gain a hearing, they at least helped to establish his name among the citizenry. Later in the year his E minor Overture, written two years previously, was performed by the Gesellschaft in the Redoutensaal on the same day that his song *Der Wanderer* (D.489) was given in a concert arranged by the Dilettanten Gesellschaft (Society of Amateurs).

A sure sign that he saw his Muse as being in the ascendant, and accordingly his earlier works as not truly representative of him, is a letter he sent to an enquirer who wanted to perform one of Schubert's orchestral works (which Schubert himself was to choose). 'Since I actually have nothing for full orchestra which I could send out into the world with a clear conscience, and there are so many pieces by great masters, as for instance Beethoven's Overture to *Prometheus*, *Egmont*, *Coriolanus*, etc. etc. etc., I must very cordially ask your pardon for not being able to oblige you on this occasion, seeing that it would be much to my disadvantage to appear with a mediocre work.'[17] As composers would ordinarily be happy to have performed any earlier work (if it was of the quality of, say, Schubert's

Second, Third or Fifth Symphony), Schubert's response seems to betray a lack of confidence in himself. To some extent it might; but at the same time it suggests that he had set himself high standards and knew that one day those standards would be within his grasp. The aspiration to find a new, mature voice in the instrumental media was at no time more evident than in the critical middle years from 1818 to 1822.

A more private celebration of his art was that which took place among friends from time to time – an occasion which came to be called a 'Schubertiad', in that all the music was by Schubert, who would play a central part in the performances. The first recorded Schubertiad took place on 26 January 1821 at Schober's.[18] His friendship with the latter remained at the heart of Schubert's social life. They were both present at another 'Atzenbrugg feast' in July, and when they returned to Vienna after their sojourn at St Pölten in the autumn Schubert moved into the Schober family home. Among other friends, there were some significant comings and goings. Schubert's dear friend Josef Spaun left Vienna in June, to take up a post in Linz. And in the following January (1822) Schubert attended a party at which he met for the first time Eduard von Bauernfeld, a young writer who would soon become a close friend. At the same party he renewed acquaintance with Moritz von Schwind, a painter who developed a lifelong appreciation of Schubert's genius.

Schober, like Schubert, missed Spaun. He would also have liked to see more of Kupelwieser, who towards the end of 1821 was spending much time at Belvedere Palace, working on a copy of Correggio's *Jupiter and Io*. Indeed on 4 November Schober wrote to Spaun telling him how much he was missing him and Kupelwieser, and that the evenings at the Hungarian Crown inn were now 'utterly desolate', with several of the friends now absorbed in gambling.[19] A year later, in December 1822, Schubert was to write to Spaun asking for news, 'so as to mitigate somewhat the gaping void your absence will always make for me.'[20] Unless intervening letters have been lost, however, this was Schubert's first letter to Spaun for thirteen months. Other friendships seemed to cool off too during 1822; and there is no surviving record of any contact between Schubert and members of his family. There is, however, ample evidence that Schober was now a regular companion and influence. It was perhaps about now that the Bildung Circle ceased to exist in its original form as an offshoot of the Linz Circle sharing its proclaimed moral and philosophic ideals. Schober became the focal point, and the emphasis at meetings was on reading, as Schubert told Spaun in his December letter ('We hold readings at Schober's three times a week as well as a Schubertiad').[21]

The last half of 1822 was the most critical period of Schubert's life, both artistically and personally. He was to emerge, through the 'Unfinished' Symphony, one of the most eloquent instrumental tone-poets of all time;

and, probably in an attempt to escape from the harsher realities of life, he sank to a lifestyle which triggered the onset of an illness which would almost inevitably be terminal. It is the greatest irony of Schubert's life story that these two happenings should coincide. Artistic immortality and temporal mortality could hardly be more cruelly juxtaposed.

What, then, were the realities that might have weighed heavily with Schubert in 1822, before the fateful occurrences took place? He was anxiously waiting for news that *Alfonso und Estrella*, in which he placed so much confidence, would be accepted for production, and despaired increasingly as the year progressed. He suffered financial problems. 'I need money,' he wrote to Josef Hüttenbrenner.[22] As Leopold Sonnleithner tells us, Schubert did not manage his own finances well, and even after he had received payments from publishers (which, as Otto Biba has established, were quite generous by current Viennese standards[23]) was quickly in debt: 'We had the first twelve works engraved at our own expense and sold on commission at Anton Diabelli's. From the abundant proceeds we paid Schubert's debts, namely his rent, his shoemaker's and tailor's accounts and his debts at the tavern and the coffee-house, and handed over to him, in addition, a considerable sum in cash; unfortunately some guardianship, such as this, was necessary, for he had no idea of domestic economy and was often led by his tavern friends (mostly painters or poets and only a few musicians) into useless expenditure from which the others benefited more than he did himself.'[24] Sonnleithner confirms the point elsewhere, saying that Schubert, 'who lacked all sense of money matters, was always in difficulties'.[25] Indeed, it was in the course of 1822, and despite payments he had received, that he felt he had to succumb to Diabelli's opportunist offer to buy out with a lump sum the composer's copyright on all the works of his he had already published on a commission basis. His friends doubted the wisdom of his compliance with Diabelli's ploy, but Diabelli will have done well for himself out of the deal.

There are several references to Schubert's pipe-smoking and excessive intake of alcohol in the friends' memoirs. Anselm Hüttenbrenner reports that when the composer was sharing accommodation with Mayrhofer (1818–20) he 'used to sit down at his writing desk every morning at 6 o'clock and compose straight through until 1 o'clock in the afternoon. Meanwhile many a pipe was smoked.' After lunch he had black coffee at a coffee-house and 'smoked for an hour or two'.[26] Schubert's fondness for drinking into the early hours was noted by his friends in 1820 and 1821, and references to excessive drinking multiply after this time. Sonnleithner recalled how Schubert loved to spend the evening at an inn, 'and on such occasions midnight often passed unnoticed and pleasure was indulged to excess'. 'Unfortunately I must confess that I saw him in a drunken state several times,' adds Sonnleithner, who then remembers a suburban party which he (Sonnleithner) left at 2 o'clock in the morning. 'Schubert remained still longer and the next day I learnt that he had to sleep there as he was incapable of going home. This happened in a house where he had not long been known and where he had only been introduced a short time previously.'[27]

Nicotine and alcohol abuse were to become a more recurrent and probably health-sapping feature of Schubert's later years, when they were perhaps increasingly prompted by his undoubted knowledge that a young syphilitic had relatively little chance of avoiding an early death. But clearly these habits had already taken hold earlier. Many of the references to antisocial, irritable, moody or vulgar behaviour in his friends' later recollections are not specific as to date, but there are suggestions that this tendency was also present by 1822. Elizabeth McKay, noting that Schubert confessed to extremes of mood as early as 1816 ('Blissful moments brighten this dark life; up there these blissful moments become continual joy, and happier ones still will turn into visions of yet happier worlds, and so on.'[28]), has posited a case of cyclothymia. She gives the medical definition of cyclothymia as a mild form of manic depression characterized by pronounced changes of 'mood, behaviour, thinking, sleep, and energy levels'.[29] In adults, periods of depression, hypomania (mild mania), and complete normality alternate, the latter lasting no more than two months. The condition is likely to become more severe with the passing of years, and may develop into full-blown manic depression. Any form of manic depression is genetic, and McKay finds evidence of a manic-depressive tendency in members of Schubert's family. She lists symptoms including 'dark moods manifested by apathy, lethargy, pessimism, self-deprecation and irritability'; also, 'uninhibited people-seeking'. There are, in the case of an artist, 'periods of high productivity'. The patient's 'thinking is fast as he moves rapidly from one topic to another' – might this have relevance for the abandonment of works unfinished? Whether rightly or not, McKay sees the prodigal spending of money and indulgence in unrestrained sexual activities as fitting well 'into the cyclothymic pattern of irresponsibility in personal affairs'. And she attributes to the combination of cyclothymia, nicotine and alcohol abuse and syphilis the later continuing deterioration of Schubert's mental health – 'a vicious circle of cause and effect'.[30]

These attributions demand wider and deeper scrutiny than a critical biography can give them, but they potentially enrich our understanding of a man whose life-documentation comprises an ill-assorted and far from complete set of jigsaw pieces. To return to the more certain facts of 1822, we have to note that, while other old friendships waned and new ones began, the lives of Schubert and Schober remained closely intertwined. Schober was inclined to a life of luxury and idleness. His spacious Viennese home was bedecked with Turkish upholstery, Arabian carpets, and Persian pipes.[31] He was later to become a friend of Liszt. As witnesses attested, he played a dominating role in Schubert's affairs. Whether there was a homosexual relationship is unknown and probably unknowable. There was, in any case, evidence of heterosexual urges on both sides. Some of the circle of friends deplored the influence of Schober upon the composer in 1822. Although the letter Spaun's brother Anton wrote to his wife on 20 July is not entirely explicit in its references, neither Schober nor Schubert emerge from it with honour: 'To me Vogl is extremely pleasing. He told me his whole relationship to Schubert with the utmost frankness, and unfortunately I am quite unable to excuse the latter. Vogl is very much embittered against Schober, for whose sake Schubert behaved most ungratefully towards Vogl and who makes the fullest use of Schubert in order to extricate himself from financial embarrassments and to defray the expenditure which has already exhausted the greater part of his mother's fortune.'[32] Josef von Spaun himself had already written to Schober on 5 March complaining that Schubert was faltering in his friendship: 'It cuts me to the soul that Schubert has ceased to sound for me (does not stay in contact with me).'[33]

Some personalities are not fully known or understood, even to their friends. The distance of time which is the latter-day biographer's handicap may not be the only distance that hinders access to the human subject. Much of what people say goes unrecorded and unremembered. The nuances with which they say it are lost for ever. Some thoughts may never be uttered at all. Vicissitudinous thinkers present their own problems to out-of-reach posterity. It is clear that opposed forces were at work within Schubert. Closeted with himself and his work and consumed by a world of the imagination for much of the day, he found release in the more physical pleasures later. Racked by health fears in later years, he yet retained an acute sense of joy in those things that pleased him. It may be that the self-discipline he mustered for his composing routine was offset by an excess of indiscipline in other spheres. This view accords with that of some of his friends who witnessed two sides to his nature. One may likewise see two sides, if not more, in his artistic personality. There is a wild capriciousness in certain places in his music – the last of the Four Impromptus, D.935, or the second movement of the last A major Piano Sonata – that seems at first sight to square oddly with the more Classical orderliness of, say, the 'Great' C major Symphony, the B flat Piano Trio, or the 'Trout' Quintet. The rigours of contrapuntal machination in his last symphonic attempt (the 'Tenth') or in parts of the 'Wanderer' Fantasy, like the meticulously worked out palindrome in *Die Zauberharfe*, imply another outlook again.

These are circumstances that seem to invite posthumous inferences of mental disorder. Yet all these manifestations of artistic diversity are united by a firm sense of control. The urge to break free from conventional patterns of compositional behaviour is checked by a will to lock such outbursts into a framework which is rational by more traditional standards. Was there in Schubert's worldly life a similar tendency to venture extremes of experimental, Bohemian, and sometimes antisocial behaviour that was held in check by an overarching, objective self-perception and control? The attribution of mental illness to Schubert hardly appears an inevitable solution to an impenetrable mystery, and requires more substantiation than is available, or perhaps than ever could be available.

Another debate opened up towards the end of the twentieth century has been the question of Schubert's sexual orientation. Maynard Solomon presented a view of Schubert as a homosexual, by interpreting a variety of contemporary documents in this light. He explored statements by the composer's friends about his attitude to women, the ramifications of his failure to marry Therese Grob, the existence of a male homosexual subculture in Vienna at this time; and he proceeded to identify what he saw as coded terms in the writings of the Schubert community ('griechische', Greek or homosexual, 'Fasanen', pheasants or pretty things, 'Rinden', rinds, barks or condoms). Bauernfeld's statement (in 1826) that Schubert 'is out of sorts (he needs "young peacocks", like Benvenuto Cellini)' is taken by Solomon as an allusion to Cellini's erotic attachments to young men, explained by Solomon's supposition as to 'the meaning of "peacocks" in homosexual argot: they are beautiful boys in extravagant or feminine dress'. Hunting peacocks and other wild birds 'is Cellini's euphemism for his forays in quest of youthful sexual partners'.[34]

Solomon's article was countered by Rita Steblin, who found cause to contradict his view of Schubert's feelings for the women in his life, posited legal reasons for his not marrying Therese, contended that the coded references could 'all be explained in a straightforward manner', and that peacocks were eaten as a cure for illness (in Cellini's case – as in Schubert's – for syphilis, caught from a woman).[35] Steblin's response headed an issue of *19th-Century Music* given over exclusively to Schubert's sexuality. While the wider reaction to all this has in some instances been fiercely partisan, there is no reason not to keep an open mind. It remains hard to accept an absence of heterosexual sentiments and appetites on Schubert's part, but it is possible there were bisexual tendencies. Proof either way is elusive, and while the issue will echo through the columns of publications academic and commercial for some time to come, we can take some comfort from the certainty that the Schubert inheritance, which is what prompts our interest in the man in the first place, will remain almost wholly impervious to the debate.

The most forthright condemnation of Schober's influence, and of Schubert's weak submission to it, comes from Schubert's old friend from

Stadtkonvikt days, Josef Kenner, who refrains from mentioning Schober by name:

> Schubert's genius subsequently attracted, among other friends, the heart of a seductively amiable and brilliant young man, endowed with the noblest talents, whose extraordinary gifts would have been so worthy of a moral foundation and would have richly repaid a stricter schooling than the one he unfortunately had. But shunning so much effort as unworthy of genius and summarily rejecting such fetters as a form of prejudice and restriction, while at the same time arguing with brilliant and ingratiatingly persuasive power, this scintillating individuality, as I was told later, won a lasting and pernicious influence over Schubert's honest susceptibility. If this was not apparent in his work it was all the more so in his life. Anyone who knew Schubert knows how he was made of two natures, foreign to each other, how powerfully the craving for pleasure dragged his soul down to the slough of moral degradation, and how highly he valued the utterances of friends he respected, and so will find his surrender to the false prophet, who embellished sensuality in such a flattering manner, all the more understandable. But more hardened characters than he were seduced, for longer or shorter periods, by the devilish attraction of associating with that apparently warm but inwardly merely vain being into worshipping him as an idol.
>
> This intimation seemed to me indispensable for the biographer's grasp of the subject, for it concerns an episode in Schubert's life which only too probably caused his premature death and certainly hastened it.[36]

There being no extant evidence with which to repudiate a statement which has the ring of sincerity about it despite its partial reliance on hearsay ('as I was told later') – indeed it sounds like a sober and earnest plea that posterity should get it right – one is inclined to give Kenner's testimony some credence. There is no indication as to whether the act which brought on Schubert's illness was a homosexual or heterosexual one. There is known to have been a flourishing trade in (female) prostitution in Vienna at this time,[37] and Schober himself was a known womanizer, a 'favourite with women'[38] who was reported as having an 'affair with a woman' in 1827[39] and whom Bauernfeld depicted in a parodistic play (*The Outcasts*) for a New Year's Eve party in 1825 as disposed to recommend enjoying relations with the opposite sex without falling in love and to assess women according to their bodily features and proportions.[40]

Three particular documents of 1822 have attracted attention as possibly throwing light on Schubert's personal situation, although they all remain enigmatic in their import. One, dated 3 July, and written in pencil by

Schubert himself, is headed 'My Dream. Franz Schubert.' It depicts relationships within a family (not recognizably Schubert's family), includes two graveside scenes, and is expressed in romanticized, somewhat incoherent and dreamlike prose.[41] John Reed has put forward the suggestion that it could have been a relic of some party game.[42] Schubert apparently attended an 'Atzenbrugg feast' again this July, although there is no specific reference to the occasion or its precise date in the documents. More recently, Elizabeth McKay, who believes some of Schubert's pipe-smoking may have involved opium, has seen this short tract as an attempt to capture the essence of an opium-induced dream-state.[43] Both are credible explanations and, in that either could explain why the writing is in pencil (the writer is away from home, at Atzenbrugg or in a café where smoking takes place) and why the manner of expression is not Schubert's customary style, to be preferred to attempts to look for speculative psychoanalytical interpretations.

The second document is a double-sided single sheet addressed to Albert Schellmann, a barrister in whose house Schubert had stayed in Steyr.[44] Dated 28 November, by which time Schubert may already have been infected with syphilis, it reproduces a couplet wrongly attributed to Martin Luther on one side:

> Who loves not wine, maidens and song,
> Remains a fool his whole life long.
>
> Martin Luther.

For eternal remembrance.   Franz Schubert.

and, on the other, the last verse of Goethe's *Beherzigung* (Heeding):

> One thing will not do for all.
> Let each live in his tradition,
> Each consider his own mission,
> And who stands, beware a fall.
>
> Goethe.

For remembrance.

(In the first passage, 'maidens' is a misquotation, and should be 'women' – '*Weib*' as in Johann Strauss's '*Wein, Weib, Gesang*'.) Is Schubert simply proclaiming his current hedonistic outlook? Or does Goethe's last cautionary line now carry the endorsement of experience, expressed with mock-nonchalance through the words of another because Schubert could not bring himself to speak directly of his plight in words of his own? If that last explanation is near the mark, then we may be right to see further concealed clues of similar significance in our third document, a letter Schubert wrote to his long–neglected friend Spaun nine days later. 'Now I have told you all the news that I could of me and my music.' Was there, then, some news that he could not tell? 'I'd be quite well if the wretched business of the opera were not so exasperating.' As Elizabeth McKay points out, in all previous correspondence Schubert had used the term '*recht*' to qualify the state of his health: '*recht gut*', '*recht gesund*', or '*recht wohl*'. But now, instead of 'very well', he is only '*ziemlich gut*' – 'quite well'.[45]

The music of this critical autumn appears to show Schubert revelling in his newly extended powers and applying them to a variety of musical purposes. When he set aside the B minor Symphony in November, he must have proceeded with little respite to the 'Wanderer' Fantasy, which was finished in that same month. In a sense the two works are opposites. One is a private document couched in a grand public medium – a symphony sprung from an intimate, poetic impulse, whose most apocalyptic climaxes can be traced back to that underlying source; and the other is a grand public statement which stretches the domestic medium of two hands at one keyboard beyond the limits of extravert virtuosity previously observed. In one the composer makes cautious progress (sketching in piano score, which he did not do in the previous symphony) towards a structural goal which he never attains, while in the other he forges a daringly new structural unity which one could believe was clearly mapped out from the start. Few pairs of works so close in chronology reveal such disparate characters.

In September he had completed his Mass in A flat, a work of which he thought highly, and before the end of the year he seems to have found time to produce a rich little miscellany of settings of Goethe and Collin as well as of his friends Schober, Senn and Bruchmann (although some small residual doubts as to chronology remain). *Der Musensohn* rollicks from beginning to end with a breezy, exhilarating drive, *Wehmut* is a classic Schubertian intermingling of joy and sadness, *Selige Welt* demonstrates how – for Schubert at this time – extreme tonal fluidity can be made to work within a compact frame, and in *Der Zwerg* (The Dwarf) the combination of dramatic vividness and tireless impetus that had impelled *Erlkönig* bears flavoursome new fruit.

Did Schubert realize that he had now found himself, had fully served his apprenticeship and had developed the imaginative resource as well as the technique to create masterpieces that would be ranked among the greatest of musical art? The flattering Josef Hüttenbrenner may have gone too far too soon when he told the publisher Peters of Leipzig in August that Schubert was 'a second Beethoven'. But from late 1822, on, as work succeeds work, the idea of Schubert facing Beethoven with equanimity across a pantheon of 'great composers' becomes so comfortable that its rightness is not to be questioned. What was happening to Schubert's name in early nineteenth-century Vienna has little to do with this assessment. Some of his songs were now published in his own city, several of his works had been performed at the Gesellschaft, a mechanical clock at the Hungarian Crown played a Schubert song; but if Vienna fancied it knew its Schubert, that was patently not the case. The number of Viennese who knew more than a few of the songs, and perhaps the odd partsong, an early mass, and even an operatic number or two, must have been very small. A dozen or so amateur musicians might recall the early symphonies they had played. But there was nothing here on which to base any assessment of the composer. That could only begin in the late nineteenth century, the process subsequently being much refined by the historical and supranational perspective that the twentieth century could, progressively, give to it.

The work which, for posterity, seals Schubert's claim to immortality is the 'Unfinished' Symphony. Schubert's own attitude to the work was ambivalent, to say the least. He wrote it for no occasion, for no commissioner, for no individual or organization, but from the lifelong inner compulsion to write symphonies. Having abandoned it, he kept it until the following year. Then, in April, the Styrian Music Society in Graz, which knew nothing of the symphony, awarded Schubert its Diploma of Honour. And later that year Schubert gave it to Josef Hüttenbrenner (who had brought the diploma to Schubert) 'out of gratitude for the Diploma of Honour'.[46] In all this time he appears to have mentioned the work to nobody. Not even the letter to Spaun of December 1822, which refers to *Der Musensohn* and other recent Goethe settings as well as to the 'Wanderer' Fantasy, makes any mention of a recent symphony.[47] John Reed explains this secrecy as a result of Schubert's 'anxiety to establish himself as a worthy successor to Beethoven', implying that if he had won through to a cathartic finale to crown a complete symphony he might then have shown the same active concern to promote a performance of it as he did the 'Great' C major Symphony.[48] There is no evidence that Schubert saw the situation in that light, and the fact that he let the half-finished symphony out of his clutches, sending it to Hüttenbrenner, suggests that he would have been happy to have it performed in that state. Multi-movement works were often dismembered, and individual movements performed, at concerts in Schubert's time. It is possible that Schubert's decision to let the manuscript go merely reflects his apparent unconcern as to the whereabouts or safe keeping of his autographs. It is known, for example, that at one stage more than a hundred of his songs were out of his sight, in the hands of various friends. The real mystery, though, arises from the fact that the completed first two movements of the symphony are of such higher stature than anything he had previously composed. Their genesis must have excited him, surely, and a composer who would sometimes refer to works not yet composed (for instance, the planned '*Grosse Symphonie*' that would materialize as the 'Great' C major) would surely wish to talk about one on which such dazzling progress had been made. There is another explanation for his not doing so. His friends were not interested in symphonies: works with literary associations, and domestic genres, yes; but there is no evidence in the documents of any real interest on the part of Schubert's circle in his endeavours in what the composer himself regarded as one of the 'higher forms'[49] of music. We must remember that the symphony was a test of musical sophistication and dedication on the part of a listener. At the same time, Schubert may well have hoped that he could complete the work at an early date. If it is accepted that only the sketched scherzo was incomplete, and that he had already finished the finale and was holding it in piano score,[50] then it is possible that all that stood in the way of completion of the whole symphony was the composition of the remainder of the scherzo and the scoring of the finale. That outcome became less likely after he decided, at the end of 1823, to use the finale as a number in his incidental music for *Rosamunde*, whereupon he took out the piano draft and scored it. This solution differs from Reed's in one essential respect: it assumes that Schubert was happy with his projected finale, and only used it later for another purpose because he was so short of time to put together the *Rosamunde* music that he had to recycle earlier material in order to meet his deadline. Schubert was not, according to this solution, waiting to clone a new finale on Beethoven's example, nor to anticipate by half a century or more some Tchaikovskian or Mahlerian solution to the 'finale problem'. The 'original finale', which later became an Entr'acte for *Rosamunde*, is, after all, a credible finale for the 'Unfinished', although it takes some time for listeners who have been brought up on the 'Unfinished' as a two-movement work to hear it that way. It is a full, eventful movement in sonata form, breaking new expressive ground and evoking an atmosphere comparable to and compatible with that of the first two movements. Reed's description of it as fitting 'more readily into the regular sectional pattern of ballet music' would be much more aptly applied to the finale of the Sixth Symphony.

The first documentary allusion to Schubert's illness is found in a letter dated 28 February 1823, in which he explains that 'the state of my health still prevents me from leaving the house'.[51] The implication is that he had been ill for some time. Although the illness can therefore only be dated with certainty from 1823, two aspects of Schubert's life in the previous December leave open the possibility that he may already have become infected, and known as much, before the turn of the year. There is no documentary record of his attending any social events in December; and in December or shortly before he suddenly moved back into the parental home in Rossau (from where the letter to Spaun dated 7 December was sent). Returning to the father's house could have permitted him to live a more private life while he came to terms with his condition. Elizabeth McKay even raises the possibility that he was already infected in November, the month of the 'Wanderer' Fantasy. Citing Anthony Storr's description of 'manic defence', a condition in which 'a man reverses and denies his depression . . . triumphantly proclaims his ability to overcome every obstacle' and 'omnipotently claims complete self-confidence',[52] she notes that this quality distinguishes the fantasy from other works of Schubert, and suggests that the work might have been a mechanism of manic defence upon discovery of the alarming damage his hedonistic lifestyle had wrought.[53] If the crisis did indeed fall that early, then the Goethe songs of December, including *Der Musensohn* (displaying again the ebullience of manic defence?), could be seen as the first in a line of works, spanning the remaining six years, which seem to gain some of their intensity (be it inherent, or imagined on our part) from the composer's stark realization that his existence was under threat.

Music for the Theatre

As Tovey once observed, all Schubert's works are early works. In no context are we more aware of this fact than when considering and assessing his contribution to civilization's stock of operas. He lacked nothing in interest and assiduity, having set about composing an opera at least eighteen times and completed eight in all; but he was a victim of both the prevailing situation in theatrical Vienna and his own propensity and fast-maturing flair for Lieder. On stage, the here and now is in immediate focus; on the recital platform, it is witnessed through a filter. Schubert's aptitude for portraying action at one remove in song was well-nigh natural, but the realization of action in a live, raw form on the operatic stage – with all the demands on musical invention and control of timing that this entails – presented a challenge which he was less well equipped to meet. Of course, Mozart had ventured into opera at a similarly youthful age. Mozart's operas, like his letters, show him to be a keen observer of human character – an attribute with which Schubert was perhaps not quite so obviously endowed. The distinction should not be exaggerated, however: if Mozart had had operatic opportunities denied him after the age of twenty-six – at which age Schubert produced his last complete opera (*Fierabras*) – he would have reached his stage climax with *Il Seraglio* and never given the world *The Impresario*, *Figaro*, *Don Giovanni*, *Così fan tutte*, *La clemenza di Tito* or *Die Zauberflöte*. It was to a considerable extent a matter of opportunity.

There were two court theatres in Vienna, both owned by the Emperor, both subsidized by him and managed under his scrutiny. By the time Schubert ventured into opera, one of these, the Burgtheater, which had housed the premieres of *Seraglio*, *Figaro* and *Così*, had ceased to include opera in its programmes and was reserved for straight drama. The other, the Kärntnertortheater, had been since the same time (1810) devoted to opera and ballet, but it was in financial difficulty and standards of perform-ance were slipping. The Congress of Vienna brought many foreign visitors to the city, and the Kärntnertor offered, along with *Figaro* and Beethoven's *Fidelio*, many lighter works and translations of French pieces. From 1816 Rossini's operas made their appearance, and as these caught the popular

Viennese imagination the number of performances grew in a Rossini crescendo, as did the local acclaim by press and public alike. Soon after Barbaja's appointment as director in 1821 the Rossini trickle had become a veritable flood, and local composers could only struggle in the face of Italian domination.[1]

Three other adverse forces came into play. Metternich, Foreign Secretary since 1809, maintained strict censorship laws, designed to eliminate any threat of subversion or challenge to imperial authority by liberal thinkers. He kept a tight rein on the court theatres, leading Weber to exclaim '*Der Freischütz*! Ach Gott!' following the première of his opera in November 1821, in which the parts of Samiel and the Hermit were excised and the Wolf's Glen was replaced by a large hollow oak tree in which Max and Kaspar fashioned their magic arrows, to be fired by a crossbow.[2] Schubert was in the audience – but his librettists already knew the threat Metternich posed to their artistic freedom. Second, there was the simple fact that the Viennese public seemed not to want German opera, or at least to give it only lukewarm support. The lighter works of such locals – or Vienna-domiciled composers – as Weigl, Schenk and Gyrowetz were another matter. And third, there was a dearth of competent librettists in Vienna.

In addition to the court theatres, there were three suburban theatres, the Leopoldstädter-theater, the Josefstädter-theater and the Theater an der Wien. The first of these was Vienna's *Volkstheater*, the second largely reflected current public taste and suffered various financial and managerial problems, and the third, although it offered a broad mix of repertoire, went into financial and artistic decline in the 1820s. In all, the scope for a composer of German opera in Vienna in the late 1820s was bleak.[3]

Schubert began his operatic career, wisely enough, by choosing a librettist well versed in current theatrical taste, with a string of popular successes behind him, and a libretto with something of a track record, having been set by five other composers already. August von Kotzebue's *Der Spiegelritter* was a three-act magic play which Schubert saw as a suitable text for a Singspiel, with spoken dialogue interspersed between musical numbers, but when he had nearly completed the first act he abandoned the enterprise. The music, dated 1811–12, shows the fourteen-year-old's grasp of the basic principles of scoring for voices and small orchestra, but does not compel attention. Much more interesting is his second encounter with a Kotzebue libretto, which followed in 1813–14.

Des Teufels Lustschloss had likewise been set by other composers, including Reichardt. In the castle of the title, Oswald is put through all manner of trials by his father-in-law, to test his character and worthiness. He comes through his ordeals and is reunited with his Luitgarde in a peremptory happy ending. The scenic requirements of the play are extravagant in the extreme, a fact which no doubt militated against there being any stage production in Schubert's day. But it was probably these same 'magic' and spectacular elements (including statues which come to life, devices which rise from the earth, a near-execution, attempted seduction by the Amazon, ghosts, vanishing tricks, floods and thunderstorms) that stirred Schubert's musical imagination and inclined him to take the project on. At any rate, he exerts his powers of invention and of orchestration most vividly at the more colourful and improbable moments in this over-the-top scenario.

The opera consists of ensembles (mostly duets), a few arias, occasional recitative, a few choruses, and two melodramas. There is also an example of the Lied, a genre Schubert occasionally introduced into his later operas; but it seems to have suggested itself to him only when a portion of text seemed ripe for strophic treatment. To put it another way, if he ever puts a through-composed Lied in an opera, it masquerades under the title of 'aria'. There is, it has to be said, a certain amount of feeble invention, and there are moments when Schubert's enterprise in scoring teeters on the brink of absurdity. But if we consider his technical achievement in the light of his age (he was seventeen), and his venturesome spirit in the light of the models that were available to him, we have to raise two cheers. There is nothing in these pages to support any case for Schubert as a musician with a fine theatrical sense, especially if Mozart is to be a yardstick. But there are many things to enhance his standing as a musician, and to stand him in good stead as a composer destined to excel in instrumental media.

The extremes to which Schubert was prepared to go when his Romantic sensibilities were aroused in a context where expressive gestures may aptly be writ large (that is, the theatre) are well illustrated by the end of Act I and beginning of Act II. The first act ends with the statues becoming statuesque once more and the Amazon returning to the grave. The chorus sings, 'It is done, it is becoming night. The voices are quiet. The spirits climb down in the dark grave.' All is reduced to a quiescent bare C in octaves, threatened only by a chromatic surge in the violins. As the chorus fades ('es werde Nacht!' – it will be night!) the chromatic surge is transferred to the cellos and basses (now pianissimo), is repeated, is further repeated in augmentation (as crotchets), and further in double augmentation (minims), while the other strings sustain the C. It is a daring way of tapering an operatic act into silence, the action vanishing into the blackness of night but with the chromatic murmurings implying menaces to come.

Night continues at the rise of the curtain on Act II, where Robert lies on the ground in the darkness. The orchestral opening is fragmentary, spectral; the passage shown in Fig. 48, with its dislocated texture of five minimal utterances from five instrument-groups, would surely be attributed to the decade of *Der Freischütz* and the Fantastic Symphony at the very earliest – if we didn't know it to come from the seventeen-year-old Schubert in 1814.

Fig. 48

There are, not surprisingly, echoes of Mozart in Schubert's early operas, but none so nonchalant as the adoption of an episodic idea from Mozart's Rondo, K.494 (Fig. 49a), as the starting point of Act III of *Des Teufels Lustschloss* (Fig. 49b). Schubert finds developmental possibilities in the idea that Mozart did not. But more interesting is the threat this 'borrowing' poses to our instinctive notion that the bonding of music to the 'textual programme' in vocal works is crucial, and close – if not absolute.

Fig. 49   a

For the second Singspiel he was to complete Schubert turned to the promising young poet Theodor Körner, killed in battle at the age of twenty-two. *Der vierjährige Posten* (The Four-year Sentry Duty), which Schubert completed in twelve days in 1815, is typically light-hearted and improbable. When a regiment leaves its village quarters, Duval gets accidentally left behind, while on sentry duty: he marries locally and leads the life of a farmer. When, four years later, he hears that his old regiment is returning to the village, he fears he will be shot for desertion. The villagers hatch a plot to save him, and all ends happily. The music is spirited and agreeable. After a pastoral opening chorus, for example, Duval and his wife Kathe rejoice in their love in a well-contrived duet whose theme anticipates that of the finale of the Fifth Symphony. When the regiment is about to re-enter the village, a quartet of the young couple, a magistrate and another farmer sings a round (misleadingly called a canon by Einstein among others) in which each asks in turn 'Wie soll er (ich) der Gefahr entspringen?' (How shall he (I) escape the danger?). A round, which is a discipline less demanding of its composer than a true canon, is here an effective way of allowing the four characters to share their common anxieties.

Schubert's old friend at the Stadtkonvikt, Albert Stadler, wrote the libretto of *Fernando*, another one-act Singspiel probably put together in a few days in the summer of 1815. Both plot and music are more serious in tone than in the previous Singspiele, although there is nothing here to indicate that the composer was to produce *Erlkönig* in four months' time. Eleonora (the reminiscence of Leonora and Beethoven's *Fidelio* is probably intentional) seeks and finds her lost husband, being finally reunited with him in a love duet. After a few bars of Largo, an Allegro agitato/D minor soundalike of the D.2B Symphony, the D.2A Overture and, in turn, Beethoven's Second Symphony announces a Pyrenean stormscape, with taut syncopations in the strings, terse figures flashing by in the woodwind, and the menacing chromaticisms of *Sturm und Drang*. As one might except, the eighteen-year-old's storm music makes use of diminished sevenths against conflicting pedals, Neapolitan sixths, forzato accents, sudden unisons; but there is a freshness in the dramatic effect. Indeed, the opening scene is arguably the best part of the opera. Eleonora's twelve-year-old son, having lost his mother in the storm, sings an affecting prayer for protection, in the guise of a lament in G minor accompanied by wind only. His father Fernando appears and sings an aria in which three trombones pretend they are three bassoons (trombones come more readily in threes than bassoons do). The finale begins with an Adagio maestoso that sounds like the beginning of a Haydn mass, and the jolly Allegro that follows does little to negate the illusion, despite the piccolo (a rarity in Schubert). No doubt the absence of a chorus helps to give this work a more intimate emotional focus than its precursors.

Now in full spate in this summer of 1815, Schubert continued in July with yet another Singspiel, *Claudine von Villa Bella*, of which only one act survives. It displays a lightness of touch that ultimately produces a bland effect, there being little in the way of imaginative phrase-structure or resourceful harmonic invention or notable orchestration to arrest the ear. There is an overture, which like the others to these stage works is discussed elsewhere in this volume, after which the first number, for three solo voices and orchestra, has the first violins playing continuous quavers for 90 per cent of its course — an extreme example of Schubert's almost obsessive fondness for quavers in the violins as a means of giving them something distinctive which avoids simply doubling the vocal parts in voices-and-instruments media.

The last of the 1815 Singspiele, begun in November and probably finished early in 1816, is to a text by Mayrhofer. For all that Mayrhofer provided Schubert with some fine song-texts, his diffuse *Die Freunde von Salamanka* (The Friends from Salamanca) was little more than practice-fodder for the tireless young aspirant to success as an opera composer: indeed he seems to have had the critical good judgement to destroy it, so that the spoken dialogue of the Singspiel is lost for all time. The plot was easily reconstructed, nevertheless, by Einstein and others. It is a celebration of friendship and love, from a male perspective, but involving a trio of eligible sopranos: the doctrines of the Bildung Circle, of which Mayrhofer was a key member, are brought to mind. Matches are made, through a series of alarms and excursions, and significantly it is the three male friends (with whom the first scene of the opera was concerned) who point the moral at the close: 'Freundschaft und Liebe wollen wir preisen' (Let us praise friendship and love).

The C major overture, using the sonorities of that key much as Beethoven's First Symphony had done, falls into two-bar groupings from beginning to end, with never any ambiguity nor any real overlaps of phrases. This is a decided weakness, and it is reflected in a certain stiffness that runs through most of the opera score. A somewhat inhibited deference to Haydn and Mozart – but not to their inspired departures from regular phrasing – obscures the true Schubertian voice. There is an over–dependence on one-bar figurations that tire, and on ritually formal cadences. The introduction to Act II, called *Weinlese* (grape harvest), celebrates the grape with picturesque orchestration and vivid material. A duet for Diego and Xilo enjoys enterprising and slightly grotesque scoring, with high horn parts. Laura's final-scene aria combines human warmth and real musical interest, but ends with the usual stiff, routine cadences.

One particular value of the work is that it provided, in the duet for Laura and Diego (No. 17), the theme for the variations in the fourth movement of the Octet of 1824, D.803. Olivia's melody in her duet of reconciliation with Alonso ('Der Strom der Entzuckungen theilet' in No. 14) seems to anticipate that of Schumann's 'Am leuchtenden Sommer-morgen' in *Dichterliebe* (No. 12). Schumann had access to much of Schubert's manuscript material after the latter's death, but it would probably be wrong to read into this resemblance more than confirmation that the two composers shared a certain common ground inspirationally.

Five days after completing his 'Tragic' Symphony (No. 4 in C minor), Schubert began his first opera on a classical theme – *Die Bürgschaft*. The libretto is of unknown authorship but was probably based on a ballad of the same name by Schiller. Schubert completed two acts and began a third before abandoning the work. For whatever reason, he could not muster a sympathetic response to the project, although he had obviously under-taken it in the belief that the plot – about sedition against the tyranny of the King of Syracuse and the tests of loyalty and friendship arising therefrom – offered some promise. He goes through ordinary modulations in a routine way, depends unimaginatively on workaday sequences, employs too much plain repetition of plain ideas in the choruses, and relies heavily on near-automatic use of the augmented sixth chord for conventional purposes. Clearly he has some idea that the spirit of Gluck is guiding him, but he is unable to convert the influence into something alive and productive. One could say that it is surprising he did not give up sooner. But that response ignores the nature of his composing urge and of his thirst for experience. Where another composer might well call a halt in frustration, Schubert, undoubtedly one of the most fluent and fast-working purveyors of notes in the history of music, counted the cost of continuation more cheaply and saw in it the opportunity to exercise his technique of musical construction (in the widest sense) within a large-scale and 'real' context. It is arguable that we owe it to his youthful energy and – let's be honest – his not invariably engaged powers of self-criticism that he was able to retain his fluency while sharpening his technique to produce such a spate of masterpieces in the last few years of his life.

Schubert returned once more to the Singspiel medium, completing *Die Zwillingsbrüder* in January 1819. This time the libretto was adapted from a French comedy (*Les deux Valentins*) by Georg von Hofmann, who was on the staff of the Kärntnertor Theatre, and the finished piece ran for six performances at the theatre, commencing 14 June 1820. Schubert headed the score 'Posse in einem Aufzuge' (Farce in one act), which caused needless problems as the critics found it too serious for a farce. Treat the epithet with imagination and indulgence, as one does 'Tragic' in the case of the Fourth Symphony, and the problem disappears.

When the village mayor's daughter, Lieschen, was born, a young neigh-bour called Spiess offered to be her godfather and bank a handsome dowry for her on condition that she should become his wife if he returned in eighteen years' time. The opera takes place on her eighteenth birthday, and as far as Lieschen is concerned this is the day on which – as Spiess is surely not going to return – she can become engaged to her lover Anton. After an opening chorus in which the villagers celebrate the auspicious dawn with a melody which Schubert was later to transform into the second subject of his 'Tenth' Symphony (see page 386), the mayor tells Lieschen and Anton of this 'contract'. After making the contract, Spiess had gone to France to look for his brother who joined the Foreign Legion there. Franz Spiess duly returns, saying he did not find his brother in France; but, unknown to him, brother Friedrich Spiess turns up too. Franz and Friedrich are identical twins, and the rest of the libretto neatly intertwines

the ramifications of mistaken identity with the anxieties and hopes of
Lieschen and Anton.

In none of Schubert's operas is the spirit of Mozart more in evidence.
That is not to say that Schubert is in material debt to Mozart. While No. 3,
a tender aria in which Lieschen contrasts her new womanhood with her
now-past childhood, is Mozartian in tone and bearing, it is particularly in
the ensembles that the debts are evident. When Franz Spiess returns, a
quartet (No. 5) projects the reactions of himself, the mayor, Lieschen and
Anton in delicious *buffo* style, with pithy utterances and a deft lightness of
touch in the orchestration. It is over in a flash, much of it impelled by
rolling little neo-Baroque sequences which seem to say to us 'the plot's
engaged in gear now and there's no turning back'. Finer still is the trio
(No. 8) in which Franz claims Lieschen and asks Anton to leave. A sizeable
extract is given in Fig. 50 so that the reader may appreciate how the
composer deploys quickfire exchanges and contrasts to build a vibrant
ensemble in which well-aerated orchestral textures allow the voices to
show through. Even in Schubert's later operas, there is no comparable
instance of the models of Mozart, arch-composer of ensembles, directing
his pen to such exhilarating effect.

Fig. 50

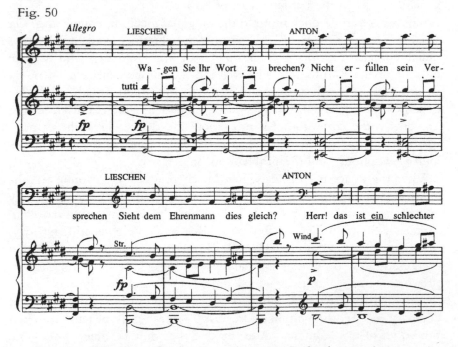

(LIESCHEN: You dare to break your word? ANTON: To break a promise,
LIESCHEN: Is this the same honourable man? ANTON: that's a dirty trick, sir!
FRANZ: Quiet! Yours is the dirty trick. Who made any promise? Who gave his
word? Break it up, Lieschen; give way, you young devil, away with you!
ANTON: You won't separate me from Lieschen. See, I'm not afraid!)

There is another well-wrought ensemble, the quintet (No. 9), placed just before the denouement, which is achieved through the medium of spoken dialogue; and a short closing chorus celebrates the union of Lieschen and Anton and the reunion of the happy brothers. The chorus does not have time to build up a head of steam, and in any case the steam has gone out of the situation by this time. A more satisfying close might have been effected by running the quintet and chorus together into an ensemble finale. In that case, the intervening dialogue could have been set as a further, central ensemble section leading from quintet to chorus; or, it could probably have worked well as a section of melodrama. *Die Zwillingsbrüder* is worth an occasional revival, preferably without the gimmick of the original Vienna production, when Schubert's friend Michael Vogl took the parts of both twin brothers – raising an acute problem near the end, where both brothers are on stage simultaneously.

Of all Schubert's fragmentary operas, *Adrast* is the most promising. Probably begun in the autumn of the same year (1819), it amounts to a mere eight numbers, with sketches of four more. Its qualities are musical ones. They cannot be dramatic ones, since it is not possible to deduce much about the plot or, therefore, Schubert's handling of his dramatic material. Einstein and Reed give short accounts of the presumed story, in conflict with each other as to whom Adrastus has killed. Mayrhofer presumably took Herodotus as the source of his (lost) libretto. A few examples of Schubert's innovative musical visions must suffice. When Krösus (King Croesus) dreams that his son is being taken from him, the quixotic irregularity of the phrasing prophesies Berlioz while the fiery, athletic bass anticipates Dvořák (Fig. 51). The harmonic dislocation after the silent pause is radical; yet the Andante phrase combines pathos with economy of notes

as Mozart would have done it, especially when subtle nuances are added
at the soft varied echo in the strings.

Fig. 51

(What a dream! That my son, noble, warmly loved, should be snatched from
me for all time by early death. Ye gods, let this not happen!)

In the ensemble (No. 3) between Krösus and the male chorus of Mysians,
the stalking of a boar occasions a lean, strangely spaced texture over a
tramping bass, while harmonies as remotely related as F sharp major, B

flat major and E major are drawn into disorienting proximity to depict
the boar's trail of destruction (Fig. 52).

Fig. 52

(What your servants have sown, he [the boar] destroys fast, with a wild passion.)

The harmonic character of Krösus's recitative and aria (No. 5) is again
more in line with the habits of Berlioz than Austro-German thinking.
Adrastus's aria (No. 6) is a murky experiment in low string scoring. Incidentally one wonders if Brahms saw the beginning of No. 2 before beginning
his Alto Rhapsody; and there is no doubt that the lovely theme of the
recitative of No. 7 is a tribute (even if unconsciously) to Beethoven's
'Archduke' Trio. It may be pointed out that the resemblance between the
Schubert (Fig. 53a) and the Beethoven (Fig. 53b) lasts for only three notes,
until it is recalled that Schubert's two-quaver variant of the fourth note
was precisely Beethoven's idea at his recapitulation.

Fig. 53 a   b

If *Adrast* were complete, and all were of the same quality as what survives,
Schubertians would have something to celebrate. And if the result were
stageworthy, that would be a bonus indeed.

Like *Adrast*, the next operatic project put in Schubert's path stimulated
him to further innovation. He was commissioned by the Theater an der

Wien to write the music for a three-act *Zauberspiel mit Musik* (magic play with music). The text was by Georg von Hofmann, who also wrote the libretto for *Die Zwillingsbrüder*. Schubert completed his task and the result was duly performed at the Theater an der Wien. *Die Zauberharfe* is usually referred to as a 'melodrama'. Melodrama is, essentially, a kind of texture, in which words are spoken against an orchestral background. Melodramatic movements would sometimes be included in operas or other stage works which were otherwise made up of conventionally sung numbers. *Die Zauberharfe* is known as a melodrama because the dependence on melodrama is unusually extensive: six numbers out of thirteen are melodramas. Unfortunately this opera is now no more accessible to posterity than Schubert's unfinished operas are. The libretto is lost, and without the lengthy connecting dialogue a clear picture of the plot is unattainable.[4] Some of the text of the melodramas is also missing, and what remains is of feeble quality and makes poor sense. This is especially unfortunate, because, in the melodramas at least, Schubert responded to the passing images with relish, the music having a singular blend of vividness and abandon.

Why did Schubert find such stimulus in melodrama? There are perhaps two contributing reasons. But first, it may be useful to draw a distinction between melodrama and Schoenbergian Sprechgesang. In Sprechgesang the rhythm of the voice part is notated, as in sung music: pitches are also indicated, and the voice is expected to touch each pitch before moving freely away from it. In melodrama neither rhythm nor pitch is specified, although a rhythmic coincidence at barlines may be implied. The words are freely spoken, either while the orchestra is playing or in gaps between orchestral utterances. The removal of the obligation to create a melodic line to fit the words was a liberating condition, and that was one element of melodrama's appeal to Schubert, freeing up his orchestral imagination. The orchestra became at the same time an accompaniment and the leading (because sole) musical force.

The other was the special approach to continuity made possible when words were assigned to be spoken during orchestral silences. These silences give time for the ear to register the last musical sound before the silence, retain it during the spoken passage, and build up an expectation of what would follow it. For a composer with an exploratory sense of harmonic progression and key-relationship this presented an obvious invitation. Fig. 54 shows a typical passage, where a C minor cadence is followed by a shock C sharp, a quasi-dominant of F sharp; and a similar step to D ensues after the next vocal utterance. Schubert does not merely respond to such opportunities: his already acute sensitivity to harmonic and tonal effect seems to be heightened by the context, enlivening his writing elsewhere, and not only at these points of linkage. The vertical combination of notes at bar 6 of Fig. 54 is a case in point: the harmony is in itself unusual, but the doubling of the D two octaves down, adjacent to the bass C sharp, creates a bizarre clash rare, if not unique, in a Classical score. (One hesitates to use the epithet 'Classical', for if Schubert's music anywhere attracts the epithet 'Romantic' on purely linguistic grounds, it is here in these melodramas.)

Fig. 54

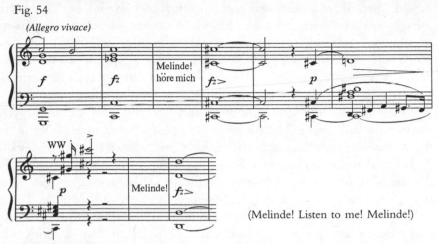

(Melinde! Listen to me! Melinde!)

One could fill a chapter with such instances – and more arresting ones – of harmonic bravado. But mention must be made of two other extraordinary features of *Die Zauberharfe*. At the end of melodrama No. 12 the minstrel Palmerin plays his magic harp to exorcize the demoniac powers of the fire devil Sutur. Hearing a series of diminished sevenths in harp arpeggios which could come out of the Symphonie Fantastique, Sutur asks 'Welche Töne! Welcher Klang?' (What sounds?). The answer follows at once, and it is a voiceless Italian aria which one could swear was conceived by Verdi on a good day. At its close, Sutur feels his powers dying: he sinks to the ground, woodwinds tumble down the octave, and the piece is concluded by a wonderfully textured 'dying' coda.

Then there is the palindrome. Within the long third movement of the opera Schubert embeds a passage of nineteen bars which, more than three hundred bars later, return in retrograde. This is a true palindrome, in which not only melodic lines and rhythms but harmonies too are heard in reverse. This palindrome has been reproduced and analysed in detail elsewhere.[5] Fig. 55 shows the melodic line only of the first six bars of the original and the last six of the retrograde.

Fig. 55

The purpose of the palindrome is obscure, but it may refer to Sutur and be a 'demonic symbol – a product of intellectual manipulations, the wilful reversal of values, as in the "black mass" . . ."[6] Whatever its bearing on the plot, it is a remarkable technical feat, the likes of which have been found in no other score of the nineteenth century.

The Overture to *Die Zauberharfe* is well known, since Schubert later re-used it as an overture for *Rosamunde*, having first tried and rejected the overture to *Alfonso und Estrella* for that purpose. The chords which begin the overture also frame the palindrome in No. 3, while the overture's main Allegro is recycled after the retrograde panel of the palindrome has been heard. To give a palindromic reversal, as it were, of Maurice Brown's view, this opera contains much of note, and it is an exhilarating experience to turn the pages of the score.[7]

Sakuntala, which occupied Schubert intermittently from October 1820 into the spring of 1821, was abandoned in such a sketchy form that it can never be usefully completed.[8] The cast list is long, the plot – as far as it can be deduced – convoluted. There is a fine vengeance aria for bass voice (No. 2) which would have pleased Sullivan and, if he saw the sketch, might have been a stimulus for *Ruddigore*. This, and a promising quintet, taken along with all Schubert's other operatic achievements to date, suggests that he now had some chance of making operatic history in the way Weber was to do when *Der Freischütz* reached the stage in Berlin a few weeks after *Sakuntala* was laid aside.

Further evidence of his prowess came when he met an invitation to compose two additional numbers for the Vienna première of Hérold's operetta *La Clochette*, given under the title *Daz Zauberglöckchen* on 20 June 1821. The critics rightly praised his duet and extended aria, but it is doubtful whether the audience assembled for Hérold's undemanding frivolity appreciated the fine quality of Schubert's items. He could hardly have written a more shapely tune in the opening Allegro if he had been composing an opera of his own.

After an Andante in which Schubert remembers a theme he had written in his A minor Violin Sonata, D.385, an Allegro molto in E minor leads into a final section in E major which begins with the same 'sprung' accompaniment he was to use for the finale of the Seventh Symphony in the same key. New harmonic tensions based on a 'kaleidoscopic' treatment of diminished sevenths to be developed further in *Alfonso und Estrella* and *Fierabras*, giving a fleeting impression of touching on one physically close but technically remote key after another, crown this most imposing aria.

The time was ripe for Schubert to tackle – and complete – a grand opera on a worthy subject which involved real characters displaying genuine emotions in credible situations. The Singspiele and the experiments in melodrama, the fairies, magicians, demons, and extravagant stage effects, all had served their purpose, stimulating, liberating and exercising his inventive powers. Friend Schober's libretto for *Alfonso und Estrella* provided a partial answer to the need. Schober's plot harks back to times of medieval chivalry, with a touch of up-to-date romantic nostalgia. Froila (eighth-century Spanish King of Leon, incorrectly named as Troila in printed versions of the opera[9]) has been usurped as King of Leon by Mauregato, and now lives in exile in a valley beyond the mountain. Froila's son, Alfonso, falls in love with Mauregato's daughter, Estrella. An insurrection led by Mauregato's army chief, Adolfo, dislodges Mauregato and places Estrella in danger. Alfonso saves Estrella, the two kings are reconciled, and the succession passes to Alfonso, who marries Estrella. The story in essence is not intractable as opera material, but the absence of spoken dialogue throws the onus of furthering the drama entirely on to the composed continuum, and here Schober fails Schubert by providing too many dramatically static spans of text, too much lyrically reflective material, and Schubert enjoys the lyrical opportunities without doing enough to compensate for the relative lack of dramatic thrust. The preponderance of arias and duets is one facet of the problem. Much of the music is in itself rewarding, but perhaps not enough to justify even concert performances of the whole opera, beyond the obligatory one or two in a lifetime.

Early in the first act, after a Ländler-like chorus ('Versammelt euch, Brüder'), a soprano detaches herself from the chorus to offer gifts to King Froila and Alfonso. This charming aria becomes a duet when a choral tenor joins in for a second verse, and a trio with the addition of the King himself, each addition adding a luxuriance to the verse, which is already enriched by the frisson of twos-against-threes in the orchestra. (That frisson is lost if the tempo is too fast.[10]) When Froila and Alfonso express their mutual love in a duet, Schubert calls on the clarinet – as so often in these middle-period works – initially to touch in an implied countermelody, which is then drawn into warm unison with the voice. In accompanied recitatives Schubert makes effective use of tiny motives which fulfil a variety of emotive or atmosphere-generating purposes as they are transferred to other parts of the texture. When Alfonso bemoans a ruling which confines him to the valley of exile, the accompanying motive leans heavily on the sixth of the minor scale, with a poignancy Verdi was to exploit by the same means in the 'Willow Song' of *Otello* (Fig. 56a). When this motive is transferred to the bass, as Froila gently confirms the decree, the harmonic and textural 're-interpretation' produces a wonderful change of hue (Fig. 56b). A similarly evocative use of terse motives and highly coloured harmonies enlivens the recitative in which the rebel Adolfo confronts Estrella, to begin pressing his attentions on her. The tremolando pulsations that highlight a variety of pointed side-step harmonies bring an apt touch

Fig. 56 a   *Allegro ma non troppo*

b

of tension to this new scene. Recitative had remained a cliché-ridden genre throughout and beyond the Baroque period, despite Bach's expressive innovations. The clichés were not only cadential: there were melodic and rhythmic formulae in abundance, and frequently a rough or not too particular approach to harmony. Mozart could not altogether escape his inheritance – and in any case the roughness is often part of the raciness which is his objective. But already he brought to recitative at times a new intensity, expressive point and musical finesse. Schubert added a degree of enrichment, as many instances in *Alfonso* testify. Certainly, the melodic and rhythmic conformity lives on, but a colouristic dimension is added by harmonic and textural means.

How many 'themes' did Schubert create during his career? One thousand works; several hundred of these having a number of movements; often several themes per movement, whether it is a symphonic movement, an operatic number, or an extended song of, say, ballad type; perhaps upwards of two thousand themes in all? Is it surprising, then, that he sometimes repeats himself? There is no dramatic reason for Estrella, expressing her love for Alfonso towards the end of Act II, to do so with a melody (Fig. 57b) closely resembling that with which Alfonso in Act I yearns to escape the confines of the valley of exile (Fig. 57a), each theme supported by rocking semiquavers in a middle part.

Fig. 57 a   *Larghetto*

b   *Andantino*

Perhaps the most striking feature of this opera is the widening of harmonic resource, building on the new harmonic visions which the genre of melodrama had encouraged in *Die Zauberharfe*. The spirit of enterprise is aptly supreme at dramatic highspots, as when Mauregato the usurper finally repents and offers Froila back the stolen crown (Fig. 58). Weber and Berlioz play a well-known part in the liberation of the diminished seventh chord as a multi-exit harmonic roundabout a quarter of the way into the nineteenth century, but Schubert's explorations of it were not less venturesome.

Fig. 58

(MAUREGATO: Woe is me! His ghost! Let go! Have mercy! How your look tortures me! Cease! See the golden crown – here, have it back!)

There is an apt foretaste of these adventures in the overture, which appropriately has rather more than the cursory development section usual in Schubert's opera overtures. Schubert subsequently purloined the overture for use in *Rosamunde*, and it seems that he had it in mind to compose a new one for *Alfonso*. There is no evidence that he ever did so – or that he would have objected to posterity's re-instating the original. Schubert later adopted the *Zauberharfe* overture for *Rosamunde*, having second thoughts as to the suitability of the *Alfonso* overture. Liszt directed the belated first performance of the opera *Alfonso und Estrella* in 1854, at Weimar.

Schubert returned to the Singspiel medium in 1823 and wrote what is undoubtedly his best example of the genre. To what is the success of *Die Verschworenen* (The Conspirators) owed? Firstly, to the libretto by Castelli, who adapts the *Lysistrata* of Aristophanes, using Vienna and the Crusades as the peg on which to hang the tale of the absentee warrior-husbands and their rebellious neglected wives. This formula draws from him some witty dialogue and effective texts for musical numbers with the emphasis on ensembles and choral participation. Secondly and equally, Schubert's score is highly accomplished and well suited to its purpose. It is true that he does not here plumb the depths of his instrumental music from 1824 to 1828; nor is there a single number to match the excellence of the best items in *Fierabras*, composed a year later. On the other hand, this last Singspiel is somehow more consistent and homogeneous than that imminent grand opera, and its fusion of tenderness and gentle wit is achieved without any inflation of the piece into something it was never intended to be. One admires particularly Schubert's knack of varying the pace, character and scale of the movements, or sections within movements, which helps to keep the dramatic momentum alive throughout, with no needless hold-ups in the drama while the composer works through some favourite musical routine. Only in the finale, when the denouement is complete in any case, is there some sense of spinning out the material with neither dramatic nor musical justification.

Schubert dispels formalism from the outset, by introducing the voices for the first duet before the opening orchestral strain has run its course, and by referring back to that orchestral strain only about fifty bars into the piece. Perhaps the gem of the opera is Helene's Romanze, a short strophic Lied in F minor in which she longs for the return of her husband from battle. Apart from its beautiful scoring for strings with the added colours of clarinets and bassoons now and then, this has a clarinet obbligato. It is another of those memorable instances – ultimately to culminate in 'The Shepherd on the Rock' – where Schubert used the most flexible and wide-ranged of the woodwind instruments in duet with the soprano voice.

Most affecting is the final postlude or ritornello with which the clarinet
lays Helene's song to rest, for it takes the 'Picardy' cadence at the end of
Helene's strophe, F major supplanting F minor, and deflects to F major's
subdominant, B flat major, bringing a quite new and appealing harmonic
colour which would not have been accessible earlier from an F minor
starting-point (Fig. 59).

Fig. 59

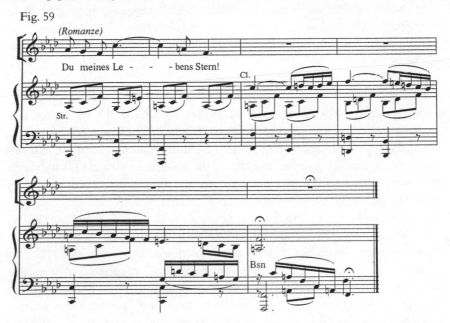

When the Countess, addressing her fellow wives (in No. 7), is exhorting
them to stand firm and implement their threat of feigned frigidity towards
their husbands, and simultaneously the Count, knowing of the wives' plot
and having steered the husbands into a counterplot of anticipating their
wives' frigidity by greeting them with complete indifference, exhorts his
comrades to pursue their design (Fig. 60), canon fits the situation like a

Fig. 60

(Be all strength and courage! Don't weaken! Stick to your guns and all will
be well! Tie things up well and truly – love grows through resistance!)

glove. The Count and Countess can use the same words of exhortation
and sing the same melodic line, some slight deviation from canonic strictness keeping the two conspiracies distinct. It is a masterly application of
canonic technique, wearing its learning lightly.

In the month after completing *Die Verschworenen* Schubert began *Rüdiger*,
abandoned it after writing two fragments which amount to about three
hundred bars and are of no special interest, and set to work on the three
acts of *Fierabras*. The title is strangely chosen, as Fierabras misses being a
focal character for two reasons: his love for the Princess Emma being
rejected, he finishes up at the last curtain with honour but without a mate,
while Emma is united with Eginhard, and Roland with Florinda; he appears
relatively little on stage, and is absent for the whole of Act II. The two
pairs of lovers steal the show, their fortunes being interwoven with the
politicking that is the aftermath of the battle between the Moors and
the victorious Frankish army. The weave is in fact denser than Leopold
Kupelwieser had the skill to display effectively in an opera libretto. The
complexities, often of the sort that have to be conveyed through inter-
personal exchanges and reactions, occur largely outside the 'set pieces'. It
is strange that Schubert should have opted to use spoken dialogue, perhaps
under pressure from Kupelwieser or more likely Barbaja, since he had
begun to make accompanied recitative such a flexible, expressive medium
in *Alfonso und Estrella*. There are some recitatives (in addition to spoken
dialogue), and a few passages of melodrama, and there is some compensation in a twenty-minute finale to Act I, which does advance the plot
somewhat but includes some unnecessary dramatic hold-ups; yet much of
the 'action' still takes place when the music is silent, and through a lack
of vision for which both librettist and composer must be chided *Fierabras*
turns out to be not quite the glorious climax to Schubert's operatic career
which might have materialized at this time if circumstances had been
different.

It does, however, contain some fine music, and three outstanding numbers may be singled out for special comment. The finale to Act I begins with a duet in which Eginhard serenades Emma with his lute, lamenting the fact that as soon as he has declared his love for Emma he must part from her. The orchestral introduction is on a par with Schubert's best chamber music. One thinks of his chamber music, indeed, because of the intimacy and pathos and the depth of feeling. The pizzicato of the strings clearly stands for the plucked lute, but it is the added colour of wind instruments, and the bowed first violins, that makes this song so affecting. It is another instance of the clarinet coming to the fore in Schubert's operas.

Emma responds, reciprocating Eginhard's love, and she does so by subtly modifying Eginhard's A minor strophe in A major. (The first lines, given with bass line only, may be compared in Fig. 61.) The plangent appoggiatura G natural in Eginhard's second bar (Fig. 61a) suggests both the intensity of his love and the uncertainty as to how Emma will respond. The radiance of the F sharp with which Emma replaces it is as decisive a response as one could ask for. It is part of a sublime re-composition of the melody – rather than simple transliteration – in the major.

Fig. 61

In Act II Florinda expresses to her companion Maragond her love for Roland, in a duet which is a perfect wedding of line, harmony, texture and colour. 'Weit über Glanz und Erdenschimmer' (Far above the glitter and gleam of earth), she sings, 'Ragt meiner Wünsche hohes Ziel' (Towers the lofty goal of my desire). The setting of those first words boldly and aptly strains convention by not turning back after rising an octave within its first six notes (Fig. 62). Always the surging emotion, the sense of rapture, is kept within the bounds of an intimate lyricism. The duetting of the two voices later in this piece is prophetic of 'The Shepherd on the Rock', in which the clarinet is Schubert's second soprano. And the duet ends with a potent last tug at the heartstrings by means of a chord which was one of Tchaikovsky's expressive favourites.

Fig. 62

Weit   ü-ber Glanz   und   Er - den - schimmer

Later in Act II, Florinda's 'Die Brust, gebeugt von Sorgen', in which she resolves to rescue the imprisoned Roland, is without doubt one of Schubert's finest operatic conceptions. At the same time it is one of the most conventional: it is an aria. Moreover, it is in a long tradition of furioso arias, though the combination of rage, resolution, fire, and anguish is new, and new for Schubert too; he stretches himself to produce a piece of extraordinary passion and fizz. The ingredients are simple. For most of the time the strings are in two parts only, the violins massed in a ferment of quavers, the lower instruments in implacable crotchets; the wind instruments provide continuity, emphasis and weight where needed. Propelled by these tireless currents, the singer has no hyperactive, virtuoso part, but motion in consistently longer notes (minims) which allows a sizzling tempo to be maintained while the voice can register its temper on every note. Instrumental interludes are minimal; the effect is of breathless, relentless activity from first note to last. But there is a fine rhetorical touch, where quavers cease in favour of a defiant, more measured gesture, the essence of which is its fourfold reiteration. It first appears towards the end of the first musical 'stanza', reinforcing the climactic line 'dein Segensgruss ist Blut!' (your benediction is of blood) (Fig. 63). A remote B flat major chord dramatically underpins the word 'Blut'.

Fig. 63

The fourfold gesture here is a preparation for the more overwhelming one later, at the end of the middle section, which culminates in the word 'Tod'. So cataclysmic an outcome of all the pent-up energy of the rest of the piece is this fourfold shaking of the fist that Schubert cannot allow it to be heard only this once: it returns at the final 'Blut'. It should be remembered that this figure, a slurred front-accented descent from minor third to tonic, was first occasioned by 'Tod'. There is, perhaps, no more evocative note for 'Death' than the minor third within a falling phrase; no note of the minor scale conveys 'minorism' more than the third. The classic instance is the setting of 'O Tod' in Brahms's *Four Serious Songs*. Schubert abandons all accompaniment for his 'Tod' figure here, and presents it naked, with the weight of almost the whole orchestra behind it.

One is reminded of the four 'hammer-strokes' late in the finale of the 'Great' C major Symphony.

The overture, incidentally, is notable for its opening string tremolo, perhaps more arresting even than the examples in the Octet (D.803) and the G major String Quartet. The crescendo on the second chord, which strictly speaking covers ninety-six quickfire reiterations of the chord, has an extraordinary depth, and the third chord – at which the fortissimo is reached – is the remote minor version of the Neapolitan sixth, used in several Schubert works at emotive junctures but never so early in a piece.

It is an irony that Schubert's best-known work for the theatre was a set of pieces scrambled together at great speed as incidental music for a play by an inexperienced authoress that would be badly mauled by the critics. Such was *Rosamunde, Fürstin von Zypern* (Rosamunde, Princess of Cyprus). 'Empty, tedious, unnatural' was one critical reaction after the first perform-ance on 20 December 1823.[11] The plot of Wilhelmina von Chézy's play, such as it was, was reproduced in detail in the *Theaterzeitung* of 30 December 1823.[12] No purpose would be served by recounting the story here, except to note that the play was billed as a 'Grand Romantic Drama in Four Acts' and incorporated many of the elements that were fashionable in the more extravagant entertainments of the day. Schubert's music, charmingly simple for the most part, requires little comment either.

Current thinking accepts that Schubert had only a short time to put together his ten items, though not necessarily the mere five days suggested in one account. It was evidently for this reason that he borrowed extensively from his existing compositions, and in two instances derived two numbers from the same (new) material. The overture was taken from *Alfonso und Estrella*. The D major Entr'acte (No. 3) is an orchestral version of the Chorus of Spirits (No. 5). The Ballet Music in B minor (No. 2) is based on the Entr'acte in B minor (No. 1). In the Entr'acte in B flat (No. 6), the B flat minor episode is based on the song *Der Leidende* (The Sufferer) of 1816. The framing major-key sections of this movement share their theme with the slow movement of the A minor String Quartet. It remains a possibility that the quartet version was conceived first, even if the quartet as a whole was written in the early months of 1824, since there is no reason to disagree with the view expressed by Gerald Abraham and Maurice Brown that Schubert is much more likely to have amplified a quartet texture by adding winds than stripped down a string-and-wind texture and found that a viable four-part core remained.[13] Given such a high incidence of recycling, the often-expressed view that the big B minor Entr'acte (No. 1) began life as the finale of the B minor Symphony gains a touch extra credence (see pages 379–80). This Entr'acte, in full sonata form with development, displays harmonic audacities – in addition to its structural sophistication – which place it beyond the 'charmingly simple' epithet which holds for the remainder of the *Rosamunde* music. It is not certain whether it was Schubert himself who subsequently assigned the *Zauberharfe* Overture to *Rosamunde*, but that is the piece which has been known as the 'Overture, *Rosamunde*' for well over a century.

Extensive as the sketches for the two-act *Der Graf von Gleichen* are, they are insufficient either to give posterity an idea as to whether Schubert could have made a successful opera of the venture, or to enable a later hand to bring them to a useful completion. But they do reveal some musical ideas that are not without interest, including a recitative for the Count himself (No. 2) which looks to Wagner in its questingly chromatic orchestral polyphony, and a *buffo* trio (No. 3) from which Schubert subsequently appropriated material for part of the first movement of the symphony he sketched in his dying weeks.[14] The student of Schubert, hopeful that he could have combined his mastery of instrumental writing with his understanding of solo voices (through the Lieder) and massed voices (through the masses and like works) to create an enduring stageworthy opera, must then harbour a number of regrets: that no operatic project came to fruition in the last five years of his life; that no experienced and gifted librettist was on hand during his short stay on earth to work on a grand opera with him in true partnership; that he had such little opportunity to see his operatic endeavours put to the test in the theatre, since he could have learned from that even more than he could by witnessing the performance of his non-operatic works; and that he could not survive to enjoy a maturity in years which in itself was more likely to put success in opera within his grasp.

13

1822–1825

For all of the last six years, Schubert's life was affected in one way or another by the illness which first struck him at the beginning of 1823 if not late the previous year. Physically, it was a story of severe pain and socially embarrassing visible symptoms, interspersed with periods of remission; artistically, of expressions of acute anguish mingled with paeans of joy, sometimes in the selfsame work; socially, of withdrawal, to home or hospital, alternating with returns to something like the former pattern of contacts with society.

Syphilis was a familiar disease in Vienna in the early part of the nineteenth century; particular doctors became known as specialists in its treatment, and treatises about it were published. Thus the typical course followed by the disease through its primary, secondary and tertiary stages at this time in its history is documented. How this pattern is to be reconciled with the activities of Schubert's life – and the written exchanges between members of the Schubert circle – as recorded in the surviving documents was one concern of the pathfinding research undertaken by Eric Sams and published by him in 1980.[1] Such details need only be referred to in summary form here. The first manifestation, we are told, would be a genital chancre and swollen lymph nodes in the groin, appearing about a month after infection. It was a highly infective condition and sufferers were advised to stay at home. The likely period for such quarantine in Schubert's case is put by Sams at mid-January (after he had appeared at a January Schubertiad) to mid-February. These symptoms would be followed within two months by 'fever, malaise, and a generalized rash of pinkish circular spots, 5–10 mm in diameter, with a characteristic coppery sheen, on chest, back, abdomen and upper thighs'.[2]

Schubert would have reached this stage by mid-April. By now well known in certain Viennese circles, frequently invited to social events involving literature and/or music, and largely dependent on others for accommodation and for guidance in business matters, he could not have made a secret of his ill-health for long, although its precise nature he may well have kept to himself for some time. His feelings would then be expected to come out in private contexts, and that may help to explain a poem he wrote on 8 May 1823, although its meaning is fairly explicit in any case. Entitled *Mein Gebet* (My Prayer), it is given here in its original language, with Eric Blom's free verse translation which allows the reader to savour something of the poetic atmosphere of the original.

Tiefer Sehnsucht heil'ges Bangen	With a holy zeal I yearn
Will in schön're Welten langen;	Life in fairer worlds to learn;
Möchte füllen dunklen Raum	Would this gloomy earth might seem
Mit allmächt'gem Liebestraum.	Filled with love's almighty dream.
Grosser Vater! reich' dem Sohne,	Sorrow's child, almighty Lord,
Tiefer Schmerzen nun zum Lohne,	Grant Thy bounty for reward.
Endlich als Erlösungsmahl	For redemption from above
Deiner Liebe ew'gen Strahl.	Send a ray of endless love.
Sieh, vernichtet liegt im Staube,	See, abased in dust and mire,
Unerhörtem Gram zum Raube,	Scorched by agonizing fire,
Meines Lebens Martergang	I in torture go my way,
Nahend ew'gem Untergang.	Nearing doom's destructive day.
Tödt' es und mich selber tödte,	Take my life, my flesh and blood,
Sturz' nun Alles in die Lethe,	Plunge it all in Lethe's flood,
Und ein reines kräft'ges Sein	To a purer, stronger state
Lass', o Grösser, dann gedeih'n.	Deign me, Great One, to translate.

Frz. Schubert.[3]   Frz. Schubert.[4]

Schubert was a creative artist, who expressed himself usually in music, sometimes in poetry. The fact that he now gave vent to his emotions in an artistic medium, bringing him no doubt some sense of release but at the same time a modicum of aesthetic fulfilment, is significant, and points to the prospects for his musical creativity. The ingredients to be found in the poem could be expected to find their way into his forthcoming music: awareness of present and continuing pain, on the one hand; and, on the other, faith in an omnipotent superior being, hope for redemption, and love — the love that 'will lead you to your goal'. Faith, hope and love: Kuffner's poem of that title — *Glaube, Hoffnung und Liebe* — would be among the last he was to set, three months before his death. 'Lest anything should darken your skies,' urges Kuffner in his final couplet, 'Have faith, hope and love!' We do not know when Kuffner (b. 1780?) penned his poem, but, as a Viennese court official and musician, he would probably be known personally to Schubert. Perhaps the latter already knew the poem in 1823.

Hospital treatment might be needed in the next two-month period, after which there would be an eruption of 'dome-shaped dull-red papules about the size of a pea' (here Sams quotes R. Scott[5]) on the face, scalp and palms, as well as the trunk and limbs. According to the Sams hypothesis, there might have been cause for hospitalization in April and/or May, while the papular eruption would have occurred not later than mid-July. Various friends reported that Schubert spent some time in hospital this summer. Reed doubts whether this would have happened in May, when his compositional productivity held steady, and prefers to posit a June/July date.[6] Since Reed proposed thus, however, evidence has come to light which seems to suggest that an invitation from Bruchmann addressed to Schober on 30 April 1823 to take Schubert for a few weeks to the summer residence of Bruchmanns senior at Hütteldorf was accepted, and that Schubert spent some time at Hütteldorf (a village just west of Vienna) with Schober and Josef Kupelwieser. Four silhouettes have come to light in a private collection in Vienna, one of them depicting Schubert with the caption 'Der Compositeur Herr Franz Schubert als er allhier in Hütteldorf verweilte' (The composer Franz Schubert when he stayed here in Hütteldorf).[7] Although the silhouettes are undated, there is no documentary support for a visit to Hütteldorf at any other time in Schubert's life. The Bruchmanns themselves were to occupy the Hütteldorf house, called Mutwille (Caprice), for the summer, and the invitation to Schober asked, 'Is there to be a Schubertiad in the Caprice on 13 May?'[8] There is no reason to suppose that Schubert could not have continued composing there, in May, but it is somewhat harder to believe that he could have done so while in hospital, given the hospital conditions of the time. In any event, both visits – to Hütteldorf and hospital – must have been completed in time for the summer trip to Steyr and Linz, on which Schubert set off with Vogl on 25 July. There was also the last visit to Atzenbrugg to be fitted into that period, although that will have been a mere three-day weekend.

While at Steyr, Schubert remained ill and kept in touch with Dr Schäffer, who had been treating him. Doblhoff visited Steyr and found Schubert 'seriously ill' there.[9] Beethoven's nephew Karl wrote in his uncle's conversation book in August, 'They greatly praise Schubert, but it is said that he hides himself.'[10] Schubert was evidently well enough to perform some of his songs with Vogl for the Hartmann family in Linz on 28 July. Thereafter, the two of them spent most of August in Steyr, returning to Linz for a more extended stay later in the month. Both musicians were there invested with honorary membership of the Linz Musical Society, and there were several musical evenings at which both performed. On the way back to Vienna, where they arrived in the middle of September, Vogl took Schubert to Kremsmunster, where Vogl and several of Schubert's other friends had been educated at the Seminary.

How Schubert saw his state of health during this holiday can be deduced from a letter to Schober, written from Steyr on 14 August: 'I correspond busily with Schäffer and am fairly well (*ziemlich wohl*). Whether I shall ever quite recover I am inclined to doubt.'[11] Back in Vienna, he stayed with Josef Huber, but suffered further symptoms of secondary syphilis. Schwind wrote to Schober on 9 November to say that on 6 November, the day before Kupelwieser left for a long stay in Rome, the friends attended 'a kind of bacchanal at the Crown, where we all dined, except Schubert, who was laid up that day'.[12] A new eruption of papular rash required head-shaving, probably undertaken in hospital, and a strict diet was recommended by Dr Josef Bernhardt, who was now treating him. By the end of the year both Schubert and his doctor were agreed that there was a general improvement, and Schwind was able to report to Schober that 'Schubert is better, and it will not be long before he goes about with his own hair again, which had to be shorn owing to the rash. He wears a very cosy wig.'[13]

It is clear from this summary that Schubert suffered bouts of deep despair and depression in 1823, but enjoyed periods of respite from physical discomfort, was able to benefit from trips outside the city, and managed to sustain his social activities at a reduced level. One of the best tonics for a compulsive composer who finds himself in this situation would be the salvaging of as much opportunity as possible for composing. In fact, his productivity this year was comparable to that of the immediately preceding years. He had still not been sufficiently deterred by past operatic disappointments to abandon his ambition to succeed in this field, but 1823 was to be the last year dominated by such attempts. Between March and October he completed two works, quite dissimilar in scale and in kind, which in their differing ways represent the highest point he was to reach in his quest for success in opera.

Schubert knew well Weigl's lightweight operetta *Die Schweizerfamilie*, based on a libretto by Ignaz Castelli. In February Castelli published a new libretto for a comic Singspiel, with a challenge in his preface to complaining composers who sought German libretti: 'The German composers' complaint is usually this: "Indeed, we should gladly set operas to music, if only you would supply us with the books!" Here is one, gentlemen! . . . Let's do something for true German opera, gentlemen!'[14] *Die Verschworenen* was a well-wrought little comedy, playing off scheming woman against warring man to fine theatrical effect. Schubert needed only the months of March and April to complete his attractive score, which has seen more stage performances than any of his operas. He clearly hoped the Kärntnertor Theatre would take the work up, but this never happened. The censors thought they smelt political provocation in the play's title, though this would not have been a reason for rejection. The name was changed to *Der häusliche Krieg* (Domestic Warfare), a private performance was given after Schubert's death with piano accompaniment (1830), and a concert performance was given under Herbeck in 1861. Hanslick recorded that this performance was attended by Castelli himself, now in his eighties, who had been unaware of the work's existence and was overwhelmed by it.[15] The work was staged for the first time later that year, in Frankfurt and Vienna.

The success of *Die Verschworenen* lies in its stageworthiness. *Fierabras*, the altogether more ambitious undertaking which occupied Schubert from May to October, when health and holidays permitted, raises many more questions in the theatre.[16] It must stand high in the Schubert ratings not because its three sizeable acts add up to appreciably more than the sum of their parts, but because it is more ambitious musically than its immediate precursor, more thoroughly reflective of where Schubert's musical imagination had taken him by 1823, and contains at least two numbers which, if they were components of a more marketable entity, would enjoy parity of esteem with some of the finest of the composer's later works.

The librettist was Josef Kupelwieser, who was at this time secretary to the management of the Kärntnertor Theatre, and, since the theatre's director Barbaja had on a previous occasion asked Schubert for a German opera, Schubert might reasonably have judged the prospects of performance at the Kärntnertor to be good. In the early stages he worked fast. The first act was finished by the end of May, possibly at or shortly after the visit to Hütteldorf, where the librettist was a fellow-guest. The second act was complete by 5 June. Two days later the third act was begun, but this was not completed until 26 September, and the overture on 2 October. Schubert sent the score off to the Kärntnertor, but learned in November that it would not be performed. There is no reason to doubt his surmise as to the reasons, expressed in a letter to Schober on 30 November: 'Kupelwieser has suddenly left the theatre. Weber's *Euryanthe* turned out wretchedly and its bad reception was quite justified, in my opinion. These circumstances, and a new split between Palffy and Barbaja, leave me scarcely any hope for my opera.'[17] Kupelwieser, the important link between Schubert and the directorate, had probably left because several leading German singers had been sacked and replaced with Italians. The failure of *Euryanthe*, itself a German heroic-romantic opera, would obviously deter the management from taking on another of the same type. As the Viennese public were readier to support Italian than German opera, Barbaja, who had commissioned *Euryanthe* so was willing to encourage German opera, had reason for giving increased attention to works from his native Italy. Of course, if he had used Italian singers in *Euryanthe*, that might not have helped Weber's chances of success. Schubert, for his part, had problems with Weber's opera itself, rather than its performance: asked by Weber, with whom he was by now good friends, 'Well, how did you like my opera?' he replied that while he liked some of it, it contained too little melody for him and he liked *Der Freischütz* very much better. Weber, according to Spaun, was thoroughly offended by this remark, and, having earlier promised to get *Alfonso und Estrella* performed in Berlin under his direction, never mentioned the idea again.

With this last failure to dispirit him, Schubert abandoned opera composition for the time being, and never again invested time in composing for the Kärntnertor Theatre. He is thought to have considered three other operatic subjects in later years: in one of these instances – *Der Graf von Gleichen* – he began work, composed nearly three thousand bars in piano sketch, but failed to finish. There were, however, still two lesser ventures from 1823 to be mentioned.

Back in May he had sketched two numbers of an untitled opera now known as *Rüdiger* after the name of its hero. The libretto is thought to have been written by Ignaz von Mosel, who held out hopes of a performance in Dresden. When, later in the month, the libretto of *Fierabras* arrived, Schubert transferred his attention to that. It is probable that the latter fired his imagination more than the former, which is lost. Then, towards the end of the year, the eccentric Dresden-born poetess Wilhelmina von Chézy provided Schubert with a play, seemingly at Josef Kupelwieser's request, to which he would write incidental music. Elizabeth McKay suggests that Schubert may not have begun work on *Rosamunde* until the beginning of December, basing this suggestion on the fact that he did not mention the project in a letter to Schober on 30 November in which he mentioned his two recent operas.[18] This would have given him less than three weeks to complete his score for the first performance on 20 December, but this time-scale is easily reconcilable with the known facts about the score, for it involved the recycling of a considerable amount of pre-existent music. Schubert was, moreover, preoccupied with *Die schöne Müllerin* in October and November, and, as has been noted, hospital treatment including head-shaving was probably required at this time too. (There are several documentary indications that the song-cycle was composed partly in hospital.[19])

It is not known in what circumstances Schubert came across the poems of the young Prussian poet Wilhelm Müller, who was three years his senior. In 1827 his cycle *Winterreise* was to inspire one of Schubert's greatest works. Now, in late 1823, *Die schöne Müllerin* caught his imagination and impelled him to compose his first song-cycle, a work which, at its best, is on a level with his finest inspirations in these middle years. *Die schöne Müllerin* is, in both its poetic and musical manifestations, a less ambitious work than *Winterreise*. Its theme of thwarted love is essentially the same, but it moves with relatively explicit narrative progression from initial promise, through disillusion, to tragedy. The folk-like character purposefully built into some of Müller's poems is reflected in a higher proportion of strophic settings than Schubert saw fit in the later cycle, and some have seen this as a disadvantage: but a strophic song which pulsates with the urgency and inventive charm of *Ungeduld* is a winner in any context.

There remain two keyboard works of 1823 which, although they represent genres to which Schubert turned frequently (the sonata and the
dance-set), both contain something uniquely and valuably Schubertian.
The A minor Sonata, D.784, offers vistas which invite explanation outside
the parameters of traditional keyboard writing. The measure and sound of
the vast first movement are awesome in their newness: innovations of
texture and timing take their place within a compelling vision. Embedded
here, moreover, are important seeds of the exalted spaciousness of some
notable late Schubert. Just as few would say that the Third Symphony
is Brahms's greatest but most would concede that it is essential to our
understanding of the true Brahms, so it is with the self-revealing second
of Schubert's three piano sonatas in A minor. But this newly discovered
world of Schubert's was evidently too much of a commercial risk for
Diabelli, who declined to publish the work.

No less negligible, despite its unpretentious format, is a humble set of
keyboard dances published as *Zwölf Ländler* and now catalogued as *Zwölf
Deutsche*, D.790. It should not surprise us that these date from May, the
month in which Schubert penned his prayer for peace and salvation in
the face of his encroaching disease. At the heart of this set lie the most
transcendental dances Schubert ever wrote under an overt dance title. The
B minor (No. 5) is an intense, inward-looking miniature beyond compare
in the Schubert oeuvre.

1824

Hindsight tells us that, as he moved through his upper twenties, each
passing year was critical to Schubert, in the sense that each would turn
out to represent a considerable proportion of his adult life. Time stands
still for no one; least of all, for one who knows his days may be numbered
but has the potential to achieve so much. A question that is inevitably
raised in the mind of any serious student of the composer's life and work
concerns Schubert's own attitude to his current life expectancy: did he, as
an artist, devise a strategy (consciously or subconsciously) for coping with
the shortening odds of survival? Did a Schubert who knew he might be
mortally ill compose faster than a healthy Schubert would have done?
More intensely? With sharpened intellectual and emotional perceptions?
With an urgency that would raise the level of inspiration, telescoping
decades of development into five years? That the quality of imagination
was changed is a possibility harder to resist than that he turned out works in
even greater profusion, for the fact is that he had always been astonishingly

productive. The huddle of masterpieces in the months just before his death will cause us to re-open the question, though.

In the course of 1824 there was appreciable change on most fronts, not only artistic. Schubert changed course compositionally, his health declined further, and socially things were not what they had been. His own aware-ness of time and change was perhaps symbolically acute when he returned to Zseliz for a long stay in the summer. His letters from Zseliz, few as the surviving ones are, are not nearly so communicative about his impressions of the place and its people as his letters during the first visit in 1818 had been. The youthful excitement, the interest in personalities, had faded. 'Now I sit here alone in the depth of the Hungarian country,' he wrote to Schober in September, 'whither I unfortunately let myself be enticed a second time, without having a single person with whom I could speak a sensible word.' Wretched in his surroundings, he was also missing his friends. 'I want to exclaim with Goethe: "Who only will bring me back an hour of that sweet time?"'[20]

Even back in Vienna, friends had been missed. Schober went to Breslau the previous year and would not be back until 1825. Kupelwieser was on his way to Rome. Just as earlier he had had to acclimatize himself to the departure from Vienna of Spaun, Stadler, Kenner, and other good friends from his schooldays, finding compensation in Schober and Kupelwieser, he was now grieving the absence of those two. But there was again some compensation. Bruchmann remained a good friend, still in the city, and a firm friendship was already developing with Schwind. By March, Schwind was telling Schober that he went to see Schubert nearly every evening.[21] That Schubert welcomed his company is evident from his letter to Kupel-wieser later the same month: 'Thus, joyless and friendless, I should pass my days, did not Schwind visit me now and again and turn on me a ray of those sweet days of the past.'[22] Schwind was a leading German painter who was also something of a writer and was steeped in music. Schubert seemed to depend more and more on such friendships. The reading circle which Schober used to preside over, and which the painter Ludwig Mohn had hosted during the winter since Schober's departure to Breslau, ceased to appeal to Schubert, and in any case folded up after the first quarter of 1824, as the March letter to Kupelwieser intimated: 'Our society (reading circle), as you probably know already, has done itself to death owing to a reinforcement of that rough chorus of beer-drinkers and sausage-eaters, for its dissolution is due in a couple of days, though I had hardly visited it myself since your departure.'[23]

Unhappy though he professed himself to be at Zseliz, Schubert enjoyed two beneficial social contacts while there. Baron Karl von Schönstein, the civil servant and baritone Schubert knew from his previous visit to Zseliz, who was to move Liszt to tears with his performance of *Die schöne Müllerin* in 1838, was present there again for a few weeks and joined in some music-making. And Countess Karoline, the younger of the Esterhazy daughters, now eighteen, was this time the recipient not only of musical coaching but of a special kind of affection. The later reminiscences of Schönstein himself refer to a 'poetic flame which sprang up in his heart' for Karoline. 'This flame continued to burn until his death. Karoline had the greatest regard for him and for his talent but she did not return this love; perhaps she had no idea of the degree to which it existed. I say the *degree*, for *that* he loved her must surely have been clear to her from a remark of Schubert's – his only declaration in words. Once, namely, when she reproached Schubert in fun for having dedicated no composition to her, he replied "What is the point? Everything is dedicated to you any-way." '[24] The nearest Schubert himself came to disclosing this affection in writing was in a letter to Schwind, sent from Zseliz in August, when Schubert was already looking forward to returning to Vienna. 'I often long damnably for Vienna, in spite of the certain attractive star.'[25] Of course, Schubert's words here are not explicit; and in turning to Bauernfeld as the third person appearing to corroborate the story, we have to bear in mind that Bauernfeld was, on occasion, unreliable.[26] According to Bauernfeld, Schubert was 'head over heels in love with one of his pupils, a young Countess Esterhazy, to whom he also dedicated one of his most beautiful piano pieces, the Fantasy in F minor for piano duet. In addition to his lessons there, he also visited the Count's home, from time to time, under the aegis of his patron, the singer Vogl . . . On such occasions Schubert was quite content to take a back seat, to remain quietly by the side of his adored pupil, and to thrust love's arrow ever deeper into his heart.'[27] The writer may have been unreliable at times, but was not always so. Indeed, in one instance Bauernfeld was the only one of Schubert's friends to have advised posterity of the existence of one of the composer's works (his 'last symphony' of 1828 – that is, the sketched 'Tenth' Symphony in D, D.936a).[28] Bauernfeld was right about the dedication of the F minor Fantasy to Karoline, and his description of Schubert's behaviour on his subsequent visits to the Count's home (in Vienna) does not have the ring of a fabrica-tion.[29] Nor, for that matter, does Schönstein's above account of Schubert's feelings.

Whether, at this juncture in his life, Schubert's new feelings for Karoline brought him more joy than sadness is a matter for speculation. It was recognized by those aware of them that the difference of social standing between the two people would have made it virtually impossible for any amatory relationship to develop, even if Karoline's own feelings were not as neutral as Schönstein maintains. In his diseased state, if she had been aware of his inclination and responded, he would anyway have found a deep irony in the possibility of a fulfilled and enduring partnership opening up after he had robbed himself of the capacity to pursue such an option. Daily contact with Karoline, then, would have stirred ambivalent emotions. But the presence of Schönstein for part of the summer must have raised Schubert's spirits. Indeed, Schubert's reportage on his Zseliz sojourn was not all gloom. There are some indications that, intermittently at least, he had come to terms with his situation and was enjoying what his 'working holiday' offered.

In any event, a degree of apparent emotional instability is only to be expected when all Schubert's current circumstances are taken into account. He had, in the first few months of the year, suffered more syphilitic symptoms and endured further treatment. After a fairly untroubled January, on the last day of which he celebrated his birthday with friends at the Hungarian Crown, at some time in February he was recommended new treatment by Dr Bernhardt, with whom he had been in constant touch. Confined to his lodgings (in Huber's house), he was prescribed a strict diet of cutlets one day followed on the next by panada – a dish prepared from flour, water, breadcrumbs and milk. Generous quantities of tea were to be drunk and frequent baths to be taken. The diet was still in force in early March, when some improvement was noted, but by the end of the month he was fighting severe symptoms associated with secondary syphilis. The expected 'lesions of the mouth and throat'[30] affected his voice ('Schubertiads are hardly mentioned any more; Schubert himself cannot sing'[31]); he still suffered from aching bones.[32] A letter to Kupelwieser on the last day of March begins with Schubert welcoming 'an opportunity' to 'wholly pour out my soul to someone'. He goes on:

I feel myself to be the most unhappy and wretched creature in the world. Imagine a man whose health will never be right again, and who in sheer despair over this ever makes things worse and worse, instead of better; imagine a man, I say, whose most brilliant hopes have perished, to whom the felicity of love and friendship have nothing to offer but pain, at best, whom enthusiasm (at least of the stimulating kind) for all things beautiful threatens to forsake, and I ask you, is he not a miserable, unhappy being? 'My peace is gone, my heart is sore, I shall find it never and nevermore,' I may well sing every day now, for each night, on retiring to bed, I hope I may not wake again, and each morning but recalls yesterday's grief.[33]

By mid-April, Schwind was reporting to Schober that Schubert had pains in his left arm and could not play the piano at all.[34] Such deep-rooted despair, which sees no joy in the present and no hope for the future, was not going to be purged by a mere change of scene, although the duties of supervision involved at Zseliz would require its regular suppression. The continuing bouts of depression at Zseliz were only to be expected, despite the fact that there are no reports of recurrent physical symptoms during these months. The minutiae of a person's inner torment can never be comprehensively recorded; but a glimpse into Schubert's racked mind even late during the Zseliz stay is afforded by Schönstein's reminiscence of him being 'seized with the notion that he had taken poison'. 'This delusion overcame him to such an extent that in Zseliz . . . he no longer had a moment's peace and on the evening before my return to Vienna . . . he besought me to take him with me. So we travelled together and arrived safe and sound in Vienna and perfectly well. That was at the beginning of September; Schubert ought not to have left Zseliz until November, *with* the Esterhazy family.'[35]

Schubert jotted down some random thoughts in a notebook during March, the most trying month of the year for him. 'There is no one who understands the pain or the joy of others! We always imagine we are coming together, and we always merely go side by side.' Is this merely, as Deutsch suggests, an allusion to some particular estrangement?[36] Or is it a starkly realistic confrontation of the acute isolation that one in Schubert's position senses? In the light of that isolation, words noted two days later seem to offer solace: 'O imagination! thou greatest treasure of man, thou inexhaustible wellspring from which artists as well as savants drink! O remain with us still, by however few thou art acknowledged and revered, to preserve us from that so-called enlightenment, that hideous skeleton without flesh and blood!' The life of the mind can offer escape from the tribulations of the spirit? Is this a hint of positivism, brought into sharper focus with the following: 'Pain sharpens the understanding and strengthens the mind; whereas joy seldom troubles about the former and softens the latter or makes it frivolous'? Schubert is surely talking about his music, or at least about things that are reflected in his music: imagination, under-standing, strengthened mind. Indeed, another of these cursory comments seems to clarify: 'What I produce is due to my understanding of music and to my sorrows.'[37] We are not only being told that great art is born of adversity. This is Schubert treasuring his faculty to compose, worshipping imagination and pleading for it not to desert him, revelling in the creative powers that are enhanced by his current plight. We have only to see what music was being produced by him in this very same month of March to know that he had every reason to be heartened at what the Muse had bestowed and prayerful that his envisioning powers would remain intact. For this was the month that saw the completion of the A minor String Quartet and the composition of the D minor Quartet, works which, as inspired fulfilments of ambitious designs, stand unsurpassed in his oeuvre to date.

If a fertile imagination is our yardstick – and a readiness to take on special challenges – this year of despair brought forth, in addition to those masterpieces of a demanding chamber-music genre, an abundance of supporting riches. It was presumably coincidental that Schubert attended an historic Beethoven concert on 7 May, before his departure for Zseliz on 25 May. Beethoven was, above all, a towering instrumental genius; and it was to the cause of instrumental music that Schubert himself renewed his dedication – in no uncertain terms – in 1824. Putting his failed operatic exploits behind him, he invested his energy wholeheartedly in various instrumental projects, incidentally producing the smallest annual bouquet of songs in his whole composing career. As it happened, the concern of the Beethoven concert was largely choral; it brought the première of the 'Choral' Symphony, and of part of the *Missa Solemnis*. Schubert remembered the 'joy' theme from Beethoven's choral finale to the symphony a year later when he set about another symphony of his own. But he never entertained hopes of admitting voices into a symphony, in either his next one or the last one he sketched in his dying weeks. Although his response to the new Beethoven works is not on record, he must have been awestruck. But this was not the sort of awe that would inhibit or even affect significantly his own composing plans. He picked a path of his own, in 1824, through instrumental media hardly touched, if at all, by the older composer. And 'older' is a consideration, perhaps one in Schubert's own reaction: he was witnessing the latest music of a composer twice his own age. He could have pondered the fact that he had just produced two impressive, mature string quartets at an age at which Beethoven had published none. How might he envisage what he could produce when *he* was fifty-four? Would it not have pained him anyway to project his fancy into a future that far distant, when only five weeks ago he had intimated to Kupelwieser clearly enough that he knew his years were numbered? Whatever the Beethoven concert did for him, he had already launched his manifesto, as it were, in that letter to Kupelwieser. 'I seem once again to have composed two operas for nothing,' he wrote. 'Of songs I have not written many new ones, but I have tried my hand at several instrumental works, for I wrote two quartets . . . and an octet, and I want to write another quartet, in fact I intend to pave my way towards grand symphony in that manner.'[38]

Schubert had begun picking his own path in January with the Introduction and Variations on *Trockne Blumen*. The form was not, of course, un-Beethovenian, but this was a set for flute and piano – a medium much neglected by leading composers in the first half of the nineteenth century – and it was based on one of Schubert's own songs, from *Die schöne Müllerin*. As so often, a musical idea beckoned Schubert to develop it beyond the limitations imposed on it by the song for which it was conceived. Its singularity in the late Classical/early Romantic repertoire has guaranteed this work a place in the affections of flautists. The absence of the flute, like the presence of a double bass, is a clue to the divertimento provenance of the Octet. Schematically, the Octet owes something to Beethoven's Septet, retaining the wind group of clarinet, horn and bassoon, adding a second violin to complete a full string-quartet ensemble in addition to the double bass, and preserving Beethoven's six-movement plan. But whereas the Septet was one of Beethoven's ways of getting into stride for his First Symphony, the Octet is a glorious synthesis of relaxed tunefulness, lyrical warmth, poetic depth, and pin-dropping, visionary moments – all exquisitely shaped with the fluency of a composer who long since graduated from apprenticeship to mastery.

The listener to the Octet does not easily hold it in mind that its composer was fasting and 'under house arrest', soon to be wishing that when he went to bed at night it would be for the last time. But then, just as Beethoven in his deafness was not deprived of what he had learned during his hearing years, so Schubert in adversity was not robbed of the memory of all life's earlier experiences. Music may reflect reality, but the composer's voice is a 'persona' too, which may act out ideals, fancies, fears, hopes, reveries, constructs, conceits, nostalgia. The Octet was finished on 1 March, thirty days before the Kupelwieser letter. Miraculously, the A minor Quartet was also finished in early March, and the D minor followed before the end of the month. While the concentration of masterworks in this short space of time is phenomenal, the two string quartets both seem, for much of their time, to echo the words of Gretchen (from the song *Gretchen am Spinnrade*) which Schubert was about to recall to Kupelwieser – 'My peace is gone, my heart is sore, I shall find it never and nevermore.'

A handful of Mayrhofer songs produced in March echoes the deep spirituality of the String Quartets in A minor and D minor more than the relaxed *Gemütlichkeit* of the Octet. Two of them have very special qualities. *Abendstern* (Evening Star) is a succinct modified-strophic setting of a two-stanza text in which the evening star symbolizes the poet's solitude. There is a subtle touch when, after the first couplet, the piano introduces quicker rhythms in an inner part, and the voice takes that idea up in its next line. Of the infinitesimal – and so all the more telling – modifications in the second strophe, the omission of the piano interlude is the most significant. The stillness of the star is conveyed by a bass line which is more often static – with poignant harmonic consequences – than mobile. *Auflösung* (Dissolution) sets another Mayrhofer poem, embracing death: the poet invites the world to dissolve to the sound of ethereal singing. The rapt concentration of the poetic vision, like eternity itself, becomes in the music an absorption in the tonic chord of G major, which, after a sideslip pointing to another key, returns and reasserts its tonic meaning by sheer obsessive (but hushed) force. The same function is subcontracted to the tonic of A flat major, the 'Neapolitan' key, in the middle of the song. Rarely did

Schubert bend musical resources with such daring unorthodoxy to illuminate a poetic viewpoint.

When Schubert reached Zseliz towards the end of May one of the first things he did was to begin a set of variations for piano duet. Beethoven wrote little for four hands at one piano, and nothing that ranks high in his output. It was rather a Mozartian tradition that Schubert was building on when, in the course of the summer, he produced a whole line of works for two pairs of hands at one keyboard, covering a variety of formal genres – variations, sonata, dances, marches, divertissement. But there is little here that reminds one of Mozart in its turn of phrase, unless, in the second of the Six Grand Marches (D.819), we hear the second motive of Mozart's G minor String Quintet underlying Schubert's climactic moment (Fig. 64). (Schubert had taken a borrowed score of all Mozart's string quintets with him to Zseliz). No, these Zseliz works display the mature Schubert parlance in all its richness.

Fig. 64

The Six Grand Marches were dedicated to Dr Josef Bernhardt, for some time now Schubert's physician-in-attendance. The Variations in A flat bear a dedication to one Count Anton Berchtold, and as he was not a known friend of the composer Weekley and Arganbright may well be right that this dedication was financially inspired.[39] As Schubert gave his attention while at Zseliz almost exclusively to piano music, and mostly to duet works, it may be supposed that these pieces – or some of them – would have been played there, either by the two young Countesses or by Schubert with one of them. Some commentators have tried to guess from the relative difficulty of primo and secondo parts which such arrangement may have prevailed in a particular work, but in fact in the more demanding of the works both parts are fairly taxing. What is a little surprising is that none of these works was dedicated to the Countesses or their parents. A formal dedication to Karoline, for whom he had special feelings, might have seemed politically inept, as she was of higher social status and *in statu pupillari*. In those circumstances it would also have been invidious to favour one Countess and not the other. If we believe Schönstein's story of Karoline complaining in jest that nothing has been dedicated to her, we should believe his reported answer that there was no point because everything was dedicated to her anyway. The accolade did come her way eventually (and her sister Marie went without): posterity would judge that she could not have had better cause to feel flattered than by having the Fantasy in F minor of 1828 inscribed with her name.

The longest of these duets from the Zseliz summer is the Sonata in C, D.812. The familiar title 'Grand Duo' was added when the work was published in 1838. Several writers, beginning with Schumann, have seen the Grand Duo as a symphony by intention, and indeed an orchestration by Joachim has enjoyed wide currency without undermining the work's rightful place in the four-hand repertory. Equally apt for its medium is the most un-Beethovenian of all the year's crop of duets, the *Divertissement à l'hongroise*. When Liszt made a solo piano version of this fascinatingly exotic work he would appear to have bestowed his approval on it as a convincing Hungarian artefact (he even orchestrated the middle movement). Liszt was always ready to appropriate other composers' music for his own two-hand purposes, and it was not his habit to choose works which were ill-suited to their original medium. True as it is that for the main sections of his rondo finale Schubert had used a pre-existing piece for piano solo, the Hungarian Melody in B minor, D.817 (dated 2 September at Zseliz), Liszt's act of transcription probably carried no implication that Schubert employed one pianist more than was necessary. Schubert may have completed the divertissement after his return to Vienna.

One compositional by-product of the summer's music-making at Zseliz deserves mention. The information comes from Schönstein, who tells that the entire company explored with delight such works as Haydn's *Creation* and *The Seasons*, his partsongs, and Mozart's *Requiem*. The Count sang bass, his wife and Karoline contralto, Marie soprano. Schönstein completed the quartet as a high baritone. Karoline's voice was 'charming but weak and so, when there was general music-making, she occupied herself solely with accompanying, at which she excelled'. Schönstein continues:

One morning in September 1824 ... Countess Esterhàzy invited *Meister* Schubert during breakfast, which we all took together, to set to music for our four voices a poem of which she was particularly fond; it was ... *Gebet*. Schubert read it, smiled inwardly, as he usually did when something appealed to him, took the book and retired forthwith, in order to compose. In the evening *of the same day* we were already trying through the finished song at the piano from the manuscript. Schubert accompanied it himself. If our joy and delight over the master's splendid work were already great that evening, these feelings were still further enhanced the next evening, when it was possible to perform the splendid song with greater assurance and certainty from the vocal parts, which had now been written out by Schubert himself, the whole thereby gaining in intelligibility.[40]

Schönstein describes Schubert as a 'heaven-inspired clairvoyant who, as it were, simply shook his most glorious things out of his sleeve'. That much can be corroborated from other sources, in relation to other works: an early string quartet movement was proudly announced by Schubert himself as the product of four and a half hours' work. But *Gebet*, which sets a poem by Friedrich de la Motte Fouqué, is no teenage exercise and no ordinary partsong. Comprising ten stanzas, four of which are allotted in succession to each of the four vocal participants, it culminates in a triple-time section of considerable beauty and ingenuity. One can understand Schubert being thus stirred, in his present situation, by verses like this:

> Whatever you plan for me,
> Lord, I stand ready.
> Whether for the gift of devoted love
> Or for valiant battle.

The first instrumental work of the year had involved the flute, by design. At least one late twentieth-century flautist has now commandeered the last work of 1824, because its musical ideas have proved more enduring than the instrument for which it was originally written, the now obsolete arpeggione. The arpeggione, known also as bowed guitar and violoncello guitar, began its short life around 1814, the invention of one J. G. Stauffer. The first edition (1871) of Schubert's Sonata in A minor (headed by Schubert 'Arpeggione') included a cello part as alternative to that of the arpeggione. With a freer transcription, violists and even violinists have been able to play the work. This is not, on the whole, music to plumb the depths, but the gently lyrical slow movement is attractive, and the opening movement – for all its concessions to gentle virtuosity and lightness of touch – has a pensive theme which embodies not too distant echoes of other A minor music of the same year, the String Quartet in that key and the Mayrhofer setting *Abendstern*.

1825

Since his return from Zseliz Schubert had once more lived in the parental home in Rossau. For the next year or so the only report suggesting any acute health problem comes from his first biographer Kreissle, who had it on the authority of several of the friends that the song *Der Einsame* (The Solitary) was written in hospital. As the song, catalogued in the Witteczek–Spaun collection as belonging to 1825, was sung by Vogl at one of Sophie Muller's musical evenings on 7 March 1825, and 'Schubert's movements in February are accounted for in some detail', John Reed reasonably assumes that – if all these sources of information are reliable – part of January was spent in hospital.[41] (The composer appears to have been absent from the first of a new series of Schubertiads at Witteczek's house on 29 January.) Whatever treatment may have been required at this time, he evidently recovered well enough for his condition not to be of concern to his friends in the remainder of 1825. After his visit to Ottenwalt in Linz in July, the latter was able to write to Spaun that 'Schubert looks so well and strong, is so comfortably bright and so genially communicative that one cannot fail to be sincerely delighted about it.'[42]

This year saw further changes in the pattern of friendships. Schwind remained a good friend and frequent visitor, and introduced Schubert to Anna Hönig, with whom he was in love. In February both Schwind and Schubert visited Bauernfeld, who read to them and played duets with Schubert, before they retired to the inn and coffee-house. Bauernfeld recorded the visit in his diary, noting that he had previously been 'only distantly acquainted' with Schubert.[43] From now on they were to be close friends, forming, with Schwind, a congenial threesome to replace the old Schober–Kupelwieser–Schubert triangle. In the same month Schubert, with Vogl, paid his first visit to Sophie Muller, 22-year-old juvenile lead and singer at the Burgtheater, who lived with her widowed father in Hietzing. They lunched together, and Vogl sang some of Schubert's Schiller songs.[44] According to Anselm Hüttenbrenner, Sophie herself sang Schubert's songs 'most movingly'.[45] Over the following weeks, the visits to the Muller household multiplied, sometimes occurring on successive days. And after Vogl had left for his summer holiday, Schubert visited the house alone on 20 April, accompanying Sophie in songs of his own, including *Der Einsame*, *Die böse Farbe* (The Hateful Colour) (from *Die schöne Müllerin*) and *Drang in die Ferne* (Longing to Escape). Whether there were any romantic feelings on either side, now or later, is not recorded.

In February Schubert moved to the house next door to Schwind, beside the Karlskirche. Another resident not far distant from here was the painter Wilhelm August Rieder, already a friend of Schubert's, who occupied the house in which Gluck died, in the Wieden suburb. Schubert became a frequent visitor, not only for friendship's sake. In none of his various city homes had he possessed a piano, always relying on friends' hospitality and instruments for opportunities to play (except when he was living in his father's house in Rossau). Rieder had a good piano, made by the Vienna firm of Anton Walter, and welcomed Schubert to make use of it whenever

Franz Theodor Florian Schubert, father of the composer, a Moravian schoolteacher who took a post in Vienna some thirteen years before Franz was born. This is a detail from a portrait by his second son, Carl.

Of the composer's three elder brothers, Ferdinand, here depicted in later life, enjoyed the closest relationship with Franz. A composer and teacher himself, he plagiarized his younger brother's music, both after his death and even – with Franz's apparent knowledge – in his lifetime.

Schubert's Wohnhaus

Opposite top: Excursion of the Schubertians from Atzenbrugg. Schubert is shown with the painter at the rear. *Centre*: A party game at Atzenbrugg, where Schubert and many of his friends were guests of the Schober family. Among those shown here are (clockwise from bottom left) Schubert, Mayrhofer, Schober, Kupelwieser and Jenger. (Watercolours by Leopold Kupelwieser from 1820–1.)

Opposite below: Zseliz Castle in Hungary, where Schubert spent two summers as music tutor to the daughters of Count Johann Esterhazy. (Watercolour by H. Probost, 1909.)

Above left: Franz von Schober, a close friend of Schubert, whose occupations after Schubert's death included acting as secretary to Liszt. (Detail from a portrait by Kupelwieser, 1822.)

Above right: Schwind's cartoon from 1862 depicts Franz Lachner, Schwind himself, Eduard Bauernfeld and Schubert serenading. *Below*: 'A Schubert-evening at Josef von Spaun's', also by Schwind, shows Schubert at the piano with his singer-friend Michael Vogl next to him, and other friends gathered round.

The town of Gmunden on Lake Traun, where Schubert worked on his 'Great' C major Symphony in the summer of 1825.

The autograph of *Liebesbotschaft* (Love's Message), to a poem by Rellstab, which formed the first song in the collection of Rellstab and Heine settings published as *Schwanengesang* by Haslinger in the year after Schubert's death.

he was not wishing to be quiet. An anonymous memoir of 1897 tells how the two men agreed 'on a sign which would indicate to him [Schubert] when he was welcome and when he was not. Rieder['s] ... windows overlooked the street [Wiedner Hauptstrasse]. If, at a certain window, the curtains were drawn back, this meant that Schubert could come up; if they were drawn to, it indicated that the master of the house wished to be quiet. Schubert could now very often be seen as he made his way there with hurried steps, pushed his spectacles up on to his forehead and looked at the window, on which so much depended; his face lit up with joy if he saw the favourable sign; he went sadly away if it denied him entrance to Rieder's apartment.'[46] The piano is now in the city's Kunsthistorisches Museum, and may be seen in the oil portrait of Schubert made by Rieder in 1875. Better known is the three–quarter length water-colour portrait he made in this very year (1825), shortly before Schubert left for Upper Austria in May.

Relations with Franz von Bruchmann had been cool for some time, but early in 1825 a particular bubble of contention burst. An affair between Schober and Bruchmann's sister Justina had been carried on for many months in secret. Justina's parents had been kept in the dark, probably because they would not have taken kindly to their daughter's association with an influential idler of dubious moral credentials. Bruchmann, who knew about the affair and considered Schober an unsuitable partner for his sister, now decided to bring it out into the open and demand that Schober break it off. This action was to drive a wedge between segments of the circle. Schwind, who had acted as go-between in the early stages of the affair, sided with Schober, as did Schubert. Rieder seems to have been of similar mind, though he was not as openly hostile to Bruchmann as the others were. Two who took sides with Bruchmann were Michael Eichholzer, painter and colleague of Schwind (whom he could not bear), and Rudolf Smetana, who had his eye on Justina himself and subsequently married her.

Schober, who had been in Breslau for nearly two years, returned to Vienna in July, and the summer also saw the return of Kupelwieser from Italy. But by this time Schubert had long left for an extended visit to Upper Austria. As on the 1819 trip, Vogl was Schubert's companion, and there would be many reunions with old friends en route, and many a musical party. Vogl having gone on ahead, Schubert left on 20 May for Steyr, where he caught up with his friend. They then visited Linz, St Florian and Steyregg, and on 6 June reached Gmunden, where they stayed for six weeks. There were further visits to Linz and Steyr, and trips to Kremsmunster and Salzburg. On 10 August or thereabouts they came to Gastein, for a stay of about two and a half weeks. In September they spent more time in Gmunden and Steyr, moving on again to Linz and Steyregg. Vogl then went on to Italy, and Schubert arrived back in Vienna on his own on 6 October.

As well as meetings with friends, there were visits to castles and monasteries, excursions into the mountains, Schubertiads, and periods set aside for composing. The long stay at Gmunden allowed time – and the majestic, peaceful scenery perhaps gave inspiration – for work on the 'grand symphony' he had signposted as a distant target in his letter to Kupelwieser of March 1824. Anton Ottenwalt, Spaun's brother-in-law, with whom he stayed in Linz immediately after the Gmunden stay, reported to Spaun on 19 July that Schubert 'had worked at a symphony at Gmunden'.[47] The 'Great' C major continued to take shape at Gastein, and no doubt grew in the mind, if not on paper, between times too. Although the symphony was by no means completed by the end of the four-and-a-half-month tour, there can be little doubt that a number of factors – remission of illness, mountain air, magnificent scenery – coincided to provide the initial stimulus for a work which, in its exhilarating mix of vitality, warmth and sheer energy, was not to be surpassed. To Roger Norrington we are indebted for a *bon mot* which neatly characterizes the work: it was Schubert's '*Sommerreise*, his joyful alternative to the *Winterreise*'.[48]

Another of those positive factors, or a by-product of it, was confidence; and this must have come in part from the wide acceptance of his music he discovered in the course of these travels. 'I find my compositions everywhere,' he wrote to his father.[49] And when he performed his recent works, including the Walter Scott *Lady of the Lake* songs and the A flat Variations for four hands, they were rapturously received. The sense of a soul both gratified and stimulated is present not only in the symphony, but in a piano sonata Schubert also found time to compose in Gastein: the Sonata in D major (D.850) would at times have the fingers (of Karl Maria von Bocklet, the professional pianist for whom it was written) taking possession of the keyboard with such racy abandon that one could almost believe it was a sketch for another symphony. One senses from an earlier sonata of 1825, the 'Reliquie' in C major written in April, that the wellspring of super-confident invention was already bubbling up even before Schubert set off on his mind-liberating migration. Before it reaches its finale, which never really takes off and so is properly abandoned in midcourse, the 'Reliquie' has shown itself to be a spacious, visionary, epic and daredevil harbinger of the new thinking, even in its not quite finished scherzo. Also innovative, but not in ways that point ahead directly to the summer's works, is the A minor Sonata (D.845), arresting for the high emotional charge and volatility of its opening paragraphs, which oblige Schubert to forge new perspectives on first-movement form.

One fact that emerges clearly from the documents of this protracted summer trip is that Schubert was delighted, moved and awestruck by many of the works of nature and of man that he set eyes on. This was his first visit to Gmunden, 'the environs of which are truly heavenly and deeply moved and benefited me';[50] he admired the 'beautiful situation' of Kremsmunster,[51] the 'splendid avenues' of Salzburg, and its 'wonderful buildings, palaces and churches';[52] he enjoyed the Salzbach Falls and the Waller Lake, 'which spreads its bright, blue-green water to the right of the road' and 'animates this delightful landscape most gloriously';[53] he was overwhelmed by Salzburg Cathedral – 'a heavenly building . . . The interior of the church is . . . in truth perfectly beautiful in every detail. The light, falling through the dome, penetrates into every corner. This extraordinary brightness has a divine effect and might be recommended to all churches';[54] and of the region including Salzburg and Gastein he wrote that 'the country surpasses the wildest imagination'.[55] If it is recalled that Schubert seldom left Vienna in his youth, and in adulthood never travelled outside the Austro-Hungarian empire, this long and wide-ranging exploration of Upper Austria has to be regarded as *the* holiday of his lifetime. Whatever other effects it had on him, it must surely have enhanced his lifelong love of that Romantic poetry that derives much of its imagery from nature's realm.

When one has allowed for an element of familial ragging in his humorous reprimanding of hypochondriac brother Ferdinand in the letter to his father, his words still suggest that all these experiences had filled him with a new joy and fortitude of spirit:

He has doubtless been ill 77 times again, and has thought 9 times that he was going to die, as though dying were the worst that can happen to a man! If only he could once see these heavenly mountains and lakes, the sight of which threatens to crush or engulf us, he would not be so attached to puny human life, nor regard it as otherwise than good fortune to be confided to earth's indescribable power of creating new life.[56]

Has Schubert been so transformed by his experiences that he would sacrifice his own life as part of Nature's process? Or has his holiday been such a tonic that he believes himself cured of disease and it would not occur to him to relate the above words to his own situation?

The impetus Schubert's journeyings had given to the realization of his dreams for a new grand symphony lasted into the autumn. Back in Vienna, he continued work on the 'Great' to the almost total exclusion of other projects. In December he also gave his attention to two Schulze poems, and marked the death (on 1 December) of the Russian Emperor, Alexander I, by writing a *Grande marche funèbre* in C minor, for which the title is not too pretentious. For four hands at one piano, it is a powerful piece, with a trio in A flat which is one of the most daring and technically enterprising of all Schubert's creations.

With Schober and Kupelwieser back in Vienna, one tradition that was reinstated was the New Year's Party at Schober's. For this occasion Bauernfeld wrote a short satirical drama (*The Outcasts*) based on the old *Commedia dell'arte*, in which the members of the circle are clearly recognizable, Schubert as Pierrot, Schwind as Harlequin, and Schober (of Breslau) as Pantaloon (of Przelavtsch), among others. References to pipe-smoking and drinking abound, and Schober is proved more of a gift for the satirist than Schubert, who in any case was absent through illness.[57]

During 1824 and 1825 Schubert's professional and commercial standing were boosted by performances, publications and honours. His continuing success, by these criteria, has to be seen against a number of background factors. First, none of the great composers of the past enjoyed the recognition in their time that posterity would deem to have been their due, with the possible exceptions of Handel and Haydn. This is true, at least, of pre-twentieth-century composers, but the generalization is not intended to include composers of ephemera whose éclat was more immediate and short-lived. One reason, of course, is that the passing of time lends a perspective – and allows the accumulation of an understanding – that a composer's contemporary audiences lack. In Schubert's case, a specific problem was the Viennese musical establishment. It is true that Vienna had been a prime focal point of Western musical endeavour for many decades before Schubert entered upon the scene; true, too, that Mozart had done well for himself in the city as well as on his travels far outside it. But Mozart was a star performer and had a tireless publicity machine behind him (his father): he came to Vienna with fame as a child prodigy to build upon, and enjoyed the privilege of mind-stretching travel throughout his life. Schubert was a suburban nonentity who had to fight his own battles. His father gave what encouragement he could, and later his circle of friends helped his cause, but only to a limited extent. They facilitated his entry into private homes, the arena for most of the city's musical activity, and themselves provided a ready and appreciative audience for his music. But it was only a fraction of his music that the friends knew, or – for the most part – were interested in. Their predilections were essentially literary and social. Songs were their staple fare; they also heard occasional pieces, celebrating a name-day or whatever, and sometimes partsongs, and danced to Schubert's improvisations. But the Schubert of the symphonies, the string quartets, the piano sonatas, and other heavyweight genres, bypassed them, although there was some widening of repertoire in the Schubertiads of later years. Schubert valued his friends, and resigned himself to the fact that a large part of his creative persona remained unknown to them. This did not deter him from concentrating, in 1824 and 1825

notably, on those genres which interested him but were less likely to
interest the friends. It was an artistic and personal necessity for him to
realize his ambitions in the 'highest art forms' (as he called them), which
always beckoned him. But the global view of Schubert, the recognition
of him as an all-media composer in the Haydn–Mozart–Beethoven line,
only began to emerge in his last years, and then incompletely.

It was through the musical salons, notably those run by Otto Hatwig,
that Schubert was able to find a hearing for his symphonies. Otto Biba
has expressed the view that all the first six symphonies were performed in
this context, with the possible exception of the Fourth.[58] But these salons
ceased to operate before Schubert finished another symphony, and when
he finished the 'Great' C major in 1826 it was to the Gesellschaft der
Musikfreunde that he turned for performance. The Gesellschaft was the
largest of Vienna's private musical organizations, giving frequent public
concerts which provided a platform for living composers. Already, by
1824–5, Schubert had had many of his partsongs performed at these concerts. But the Gesellschaft was blinkered by considerations of politics,
personality and taste. Schubert's application for membership in March 1818
had been turned down, for reasons not explicitly stated. Biba suggests as
a reason that his unconventional determination to live by composition
alone was viewed as 'anti-bourgeois and irresponsible'.[59] Perhaps a corollary
of self-employment, the lack of formal credentials, counted against him
too. But he did become a member in 1821; and now, in the summer of
1825 while he was in Upper Austria, he had the honour of being elected
a deputy member of the representative body, which had some influence
on the content of Gesellschaft concert programmes. He was to become a
full member in 1827. By now the Gesellschaft ran two series of concerts,
one orchestral, the other of Lieder, polyphonic vocal music, and chamber
works (called *Musikalische Abendunterhaltungen*). Biba's archival research
shows that, from 1825 until his death, Schubert was the second most
popular composer in the *Abendunterhaltungen*.[60] We might imagine that
Beethoven, or perhaps Mozart, occupied the first place. But that is to
underestimate the Italian craze sweeping Vienna. It was Rossini who dominated the programmes. The same syndrome had, of course, helped to
scupper Schubert's operatic hopes. Those works of his that were included
in Gesellschaft concerts had always tended to be songs and partsongs.

One of the most useful allies a composer could have, apart from sympathetic holders of high positions (which Schubert lacked in the operatic field),
was the performer. Vogl had helped enormously to disseminate Schubert's
songs. In his later years, Schubert turned more and more to professional
performers to further his cause. The offer of help from the Berlin soprano,
Anna Milder-Hauptmann, which came in two letters dated December
1824 and March 1825, probably came too late. She wished to secure a

performance for a Schubert opera in Berlin, but when he sent *Alfonso und Estrella* she found that unsuited to the Berlin taste. It could have been that she did not care for the part of Estrella or did not find it substantial enough, for in her second letter she suggested what sort of opera Schubert *should* write: it would have a principal part for the soprano – 'a queen, a mother or a peasant woman' – and would involve only two other principals, both male.[61] Much has changed since Schubert's day, but opera singers perhaps not so much. Schubert was by now too demoralized by his failure to secure a foothold on the opera stage to bite the Milder bait, but he did write *Der Hirt auf dem Felsen* for her shortly before his death. Instrumentalists he found more accommodating, less prescriptive. The Schuppanzigh Quartet performed his A minor Quartet in the same month that it was completed, March 1824, and Ignaz Schuppanzigh subsequently premièred three more of Schubert's works. Important later chamber works were written for and performed by leading professionals.

The dissemination of church compositions followed its own uncertain pattern. Since many churches in Vienna have in their possession well-used material dating from Schubert's time, published or in manuscript, it may be supposed that his masses and shorter pieces enjoyed wide currency.[62] One genre much slower to penetrate the market was the piano sonata. There was no such thing as the piano recital, although occasionally a short piano piece would be included in a musical evening or Schubertiad. If sonatas were to be taken up, this would happen in the home; in other words, their dissemination depended on publication. It was only with the A minor Sonata, D.845, and the D major, D.850, both of 1825, that Schubert began to secure publication.

Publication was, of course, the desirable outcome for music of all types, vocal and instrumental, sacred and secular, especially for a composer who was attempting to live by composition alone. Performance, in Schubert's time, provided no income for the composer; publication, however, could be modestly lucrative, for the composer and more especially for the publisher. The preferred method was that the publisher would buy the copyright, once and for all, with an initial fee. Apart from the financial return, publication was a form of recognition, conferring a status which itself probably stimulated sales. In Schubert's case, the take-up by publishers was patchy. Since Cappi and Diabelli took up *Erlkönig* in 1821, it had been the songs that had most attracted publishers. Later, piano duets proved attractive too, and eventually Schubert persuaded Diabelli to publish some shorter church works and the Mass in C, D.452 – the only mass to be published in his lifetime. Occasionally an instrumental work other than a piano duet would appear, but the large majority of instrumental works went unpublished until after his death. The income Schubert received from publication was by no means negligible. For the seven songs of *The*

Lady of the Lake Artaria paid him 200 florins in October 1826. His father earned 240 florins a year as a teacher. In the first two years in which he benefited from publication (1821–2), the twenty songs of Opp. 1–7, the duet Variations on a French Song (Op. 10), three partsongs (Op. 11) and the three *Gesänge des Harfners* (Op. 12) brought in a total of about 2000 florins – five years' income for a minor civil servant. Additionally Schubert received sums from members of the nobility to whom he dedicated works, including 200 florins from Reichsgraf Moritz von Fries for *Gretchen am Spinnrade* (Op. 2).[63] At this rate he would have been able to pay his way in life thereafter, settle some of his earlier debts, and pay for his holidays, if only he had been a careful manager of his affairs. But, as Leopold Sonnleithner relates, he was neither thrifty nor well organized in these matters. It was left to his friends to apply his income to the settling of his debts, while some of his drinking companions encouraged him to spend in ways which would serve his own ends less than those of others.[64] With the means to monitor his financial position thus taken out of his hands to some extent, the scope for prudent saving and financial planning must have been reduced accordingly. These were, of course, hazards over and above those which any artist dependent on irregular and unpredictable income has to face.

— 14 —

Four Hands at One Piano

Composers of instrumental music, when giving birth to a new musical idea, do not always have a clear perception as to the specific instrumental medium in which that idea should be best expressed. An idea may be viable in several alternative media, which is why there are cases of composers creating or sanctioning two or more different versions of the same work, like Beethoven's own arrangement for string quartet of one of his piano sonatas of Op. 14, or Brahms's transcription for piano quintet of a work which had two previous incarnations. The piano duet combination, of four hands at one piano, has proved such an accommodating and adaptable one that it has come to fulfil a significant utilitarian role over the centuries. In the days before recording, when orchestral concerts were much less common than they are now, orchestral works were arranged for piano duet so that they could be explored directly in the home. Composers, in their turn, sometimes used the medium as a convenient one (or provisional one, in some cases) for a new work which would later be transcribed for some other medium. The utility value of the piano duet is easily explained by the observation that twenty fingers were available to cover a compass as wide as any other combination, including an orchestra, could embrace.

Schubert, like Mozart before him, was less seduced by the utilitarian appeal than by the intrinsic virtues of the four-hand ensemble. It is true that he made duet arrangements of some of his own overtures, such as the two 'in the Italian style' and *Alfonso und Estrella*. But his first exploits in the medium were a series of three fantasies especially devised for two players at one keyboard, and from this point he proceeded to create a substantial repertory of true duets – over eight hours' worth of music in fact – which was added to regularly throughout his career and includes a handful of undoubted masterpieces. There was never any sign of Schubert viewing these works as provisional manifestations of something destined for another medium, despite (misguided) attempts by some to see, for example, the Grand Duo as a 'symphony by intention'.

After the Fantasy in G (D.1) discussed elsewhere (see pages 27–9), two other works of the same type soon followed. The Fantasy in G minor

(D.9) is a less ambitious affair than its rambling forerunner. In two sections, it begins with a slow introduction based on Schubert's own first song, *Hagars Klage*, and an Allegro which is affected by the Kyrie of Mozart's *Requiem* but also contains an experimental passage of sliding diminished sevenths, the sort of thing one finds much later in works such as *Die Zauberharfe*. The Fantasy in C minor (D.48) prefers the Mozartian model, with a few sections in contrasting tempi. Although Schubert uses chromatic ingredients which had yielded memorable results in Mozart, he seems unable here to make anything truly unforgettable of them. The slower episodes have a certain charm, there is an attractive use of fast repeated notes in the first Allegro, the central developmental Allegro has a still more imaginative gleam to it (ten minutes into the piece), and the final fugue is competent and more than Kapellmeister-ish – which is as much as we should expect from a sixteen-year-old. The close looks forward in one respect to that of the G major String Quartet, where Schubert suddenly brings in a jaunty tum-ti-tum-ti-tum-ti-tum rhythm for his last cadence, although this rhythm has had no part in the piece.

The sojourn in Zseliz in the summer of 1818 stimulated a renewed interest in piano duets and a desire to try forms other than the fantasy. It was not until Schubert's final year that a successor to the spate of early fantasies appeared. Among the forms Schubert essayed in the early days of duet composition was the overture. He had already completed at least seven orchestral overtures when, in 1819, he wrote an Overture in G minor followed by a more interesting one in F major/minor. The second of these, comprising a slow introduction and an Allegro in the abridged sonata form common enough for overtures, finds Schubert indulging in some teasing metrical displacements, of which the spirited wrong-footing in Fig. 65 is a pleasing instance.

Fig. 65

When the polonaise spread across Europe in the 1790s, Beethoven showed some interest in it (in the finale of his Triple Concerto, for example), and Schubert adopted it in the duet medium. The Four Polonaises (D.599) and Six Polonaises (D.824) date from 1818 and 1826 respectively. These are not works of any great distinction. For one thing, Schubert seems at times to have found the bars of the polonaise too long. In D.824, No. 5 for example, he does not quite know how to fill the fourth or eighth bar, after he has cadenced on to the first beat. But sometimes in the course of the trio sections he is determined to startle and delight the ear. In the trio of D.599, No. 2 for example, a daring elision deposes the first chord of the apocryphal bar 'x', the following chord being brought forward (as in Schubert's actual bar 'y') (Fig. 66). The unusual sequences in the trio of D.824, No. 4 are beguiling, and the beautifully textured forays into canon in the second half are especially captivating as the polonaise genre is not particularly hospitable to contrapuntal device.

Fig. 66

None of the duet forms won over Schubert more frequently than the march. Clearly the fullness of sound obtainable when four opened-out hands are disposed over the keyboard can be a boon in lending gravitas to the solid tread of martial rhythm, but from Schubert the results were sometimes unremarkable. The *Trois Marches Héroiques* can be regarded as limbering-up exercises, of no special interest except that the chromatic slides used as links between sections in two instances in No. 2 are prophetic of later practice. More aptly named are the *Trois Marches Militaires*. The military march was for Schubert a stereotyped affair, with the martial dactyl as mainspring of the principal section, and a trio in the subdominant key more smoothly melodious but still jaunty rather than lyrical. Posterity did right to single out No. 1 for occasional airings, although the duet original, if judiciously played, is more fetching than the more generally known arrangements.

The Six Grand Marches of 1824 are another matter. The second march, in G minor, makes a virtue of its repetitious rhythm, building to a fine climax at which the impact of Mozart's String Quintet in G minor on Schubert is evident (see Fig. 64, page 223). Although the third march, in B minor, sounds quixotic rather than grand, it has an air of purpose, the second section aspiring to a drama that is almost symphonic. The trio seems to anticipate that of Mendelssohn's Wedding March. The long No. 5 in E flat minor, orchestrated by Liszt as 'Funeral March', makes much of the contrast between octave-writing, with occasional sevenths, melting into fully harmonized cadences. In the trio, the insertion of a soft G major chord when the music is on the way to a B flat cadence is a moment to be savoured (Fig. 67).

Fig. 67

In the marches, as in the polonaises, the trios often contain more interest, perhaps because the composer senses that it is time for harmonic colour and rhythmic or textural variety.

Echoes of Beethoven's funeral marches and pre-echoes of Bruckner are to be found in the *Grande Marche Funèbre* in C minor. Two particular incidents demand attention. The first section closes on the dominant (a G minor chord), whereupon the second section plunges fortissimo into a chord of B flat minor. This touch of disorientation (reflecting, perhaps, the havoc-wreaking effect of death or of grief) is exceeded in the trio section. The trio is in A flat major, and Schubert gives the tonic chord of that key unusual emphasis in the first 11 bars, where it holds sway for 34 of the 44 beats. All the more overwhelming, as a result, is the far-reaching harmonic move that follows: the tonic of A flat major gives directly on to the first inversion of E minor (Fig. 68). This *coup de théâtre* uncannily anticipates the first harmonic move in Smetana's autobiographical String Quartet in E minor, after the viola has been presenting its theme over sixteen bars of unchanging tonic harmony. But more revealingly, it echoes

Fig. 68

a song written just a few months before the march, *Fülle der Liebe* (Love's Abundance). Towards the end of the song come the words

Ob auch zerspalten	Although my heart
Mir ist das Herz	Is torn in two

The same chordal change, in the same key, falls on the first two syllables of 'zerspalten' (torn in two), marking the dynamic climax of the song (the only '*fffz*' indication). It would be hard to think of a more dislocating or pained progression with which to symbolize the emotional rent. Was ever the expressive value of harmony, or Schubert's absorption in its power, more tellingly illustrated?

To return to the trio of the funeral march, this is surely one of the most remarkable miniatures in all Schubert. With its regular rhythmic kick in the bar-by-bar figuration, it has the relentless, unstoppable swing of the trio of the 'Great' C major Symphony; the difference is the difference between tragedy and joy. It may be significant that the two works were conceived in the same year. If the piece is reduced to a chart of keys, it will be found that Schubert moves to six keys other than the tonic, but none of these is one of the closely related keys.

The imposing *Grande Marche Héroique* in A minor, written in 1826 for the coronation of Tsar Nicholas I of Russia, takes an extraordinary and unique form, in which two different marches and two different trios alternate in the following pattern: March A, Trio B, March C, Trio D, March C, and a coda in which modules from March A and Trio B alternate. Hardly marches at all in the accepted sense are the Two Characteristic Marches in C, a pair of exhilarating scherzi in 6/8 time which make fine concert pieces. Schubert's last march, rather overshadowed by these impressive examples preceding it, was a *Kindermarsch* in G, written at the request of Marie Pachler of Graz for her seven-year-old son, and first performed by mother and son in 1827.

Another enduring interest of Schubert the piano-duet composer was variation form. There are doubts as to the authenticity of the Introduction and Variations on an Original Theme, D.603, as the autograph is lost and there is no documentary corroboration of its authorship. The theme is closely modelled on that of Beethoven's Variations in A major on a Russian

Dance from the ballet *Das Waldmädchen*, and there are thinly disguised references to Beethoven's 'Pastoral' Symphony in the course of the introduction. This does not rule out Schubert's hand in its creation, and there is a sudden modulation by a third in the fourth variation that leaves the question teasingly open. The final 3/8 romp makes one think of composers other than Schubert, but if the piece was written in the 1817–20 period – when the styles of lesser composers affected him – this again provides no conclusive answer.

The Variations on a French Song are based on *Le bon Chevalier* and comprise eight variations with finale. They make an attractive set, with some harmonic adventures which anticipate those in the next set, the Variations in A flat major of 1824. The A flat Variations are among the happiest of Schubert's four-hand inspirations. They are fairly conventional in form, but always pleasing to the ear. Variations 5 and 7 tend to draw attention to themselves as the most radical deviations from the model (or 'theme'). The fifth variation is in A flat minor, not major, and Schubert avails himself of the different range of related keys opened up by a tonic minor. Thus the first section cadences in C flat major, not C minor; and the final turn to B flat minor before the last home cadence of the model now becomes a turn to B double–flat major (written as A major) – the Neapolitan key, more accessible from a minor starting key.

Variation 7 looks as if it begins in C minor, but is still in A flat major, setting off from the mediant chord, reaching the tonic after two bars, and continuing not to the C minor cadence which closes the first section of the model, but to C major. The harmonic colouring of the whole section is rich and daring; the Purcellian crunch at bar 171, caused by the persistence of the dominant pedal in the top part, is particularly potent (* in Fig. 69). But nothing is more venturesome than the sudden outburst of C major,

Fig. 69

fortissimo. This is a C major not of joy, but of *Angst*; not Haydn's dawn of creation, but a cruel light on harsh reality, with the triple dissonance above the bass F intensifying its painful dazzle. Simplistic mood-equations for minor and major have no relevance here. The final variation renews the virtuoso tendency of earlier variations, in a galloping rhythm familiar through the first movement of Beethoven's Seventh Symphony. It leads seamlessly into the coda, where there are melting last allusions to keys touched on in the previous variations, and a final gathering of momentum to a grand conclusion.

In his last duet variations, on a theme from Hérold's opera *Marie*, was Schubert wanting to take an easy ride on the back of a highly successful product by another composer? As the first two variations pass, without memorable incident, that may be one's conclusion. So far, they add little or nothing to one's knowledge of the theme, and it's only the little codas to each that raise a smile. Then, in Variation 3, Schubert finds a new serenity in the material, and, in No. 4, the harmonic shocks he often leaves till late in a set of variations. The first section is wild indeed; and the second section introduces a new element of virtuosity. No. 5 inhabits a show world of its own, even if there is something in common with the 'Wanderer' Fantasy. From here, virtuosity takes over. In all, this is a scintillating concert piece (in two safe and imaginative pairs of hands), though perhaps not something one should hope to capture on record. The longueurs of the opening seem longer if the live dimension is not there.

There are two independent rondos, one early and one late, but both serenely relaxed in character. The Rondo in D bears the subtitle *Notre amitié est invariable* (Our friendship is constant), which may be a whim of the publisher Diabelli, and could allude to Schubert's acquaintance with Josef von Gahy, with whom he enjoyed a friendly duet partnership. It was for a time considered that a varied form of ending for the piece, which causes the players to finish with their arms crossed, was also Diabelli's, and is itself reflected in, or a reflection of, the subtitle. A rondo in form, it is in metre, tempo and manner a polonaise-minuet hybrid. More compelling is the Rondo in A, which will be reviewed along with other products of Schubert's last year.

The two works of sonata type for piano duet are dissimilar in scale and in aspiration. The Sonata in B flat (D.617), announced as 'Grande Sonate' by Sauer & Leidesdorf, is a modest three-movement work; the Sonata in C, announced as 'Grand Duo' by Diabelli, is a four-movement work of symphonic dimensions, lasting twice as long as the earlier sonata. The first movement of the B flat Sonata anticipates the String Quintet in C (D.956) by having its second subject in the key of the flattened mediant. The single-line chromatic slide down into the new key is also common to both instances. The most memorable parts of the sonata's first movement are the beautiful closing themes, succinct and gracious. After a slow movement moving from D minor to major, the finale approaches its B flat key obliquely by first picking up the closing D major chord of the slow movement but 'explaining' it as a chromaticism within the key of B flat.

With the 'Grand Duo' in 1824, the piano duet became a medium fully equal to the other principal instrumental media – such as the orchestra, string quartet or solo piano – in that it could now sustain a composition of sonata scale and diversity, while a composer essaying such a work was prepared to favour it with his best creative endeavour. It is as true to speak of Schubert's vision in this work as 'symphonic' as it is in the case of the G major String Quartet, the String Quintet in C, or the Piano Sonata in B flat. It does not mean that any of these works was conceived for orchestra; it does mean that the composer seeks to capture the symphony's wealth of incident, range of colour and depth of argument, but within the specifically chosen instrumental framework. When Tovey claims that 'there is not a trace of pianoforte style in the work', he is pretending that piano style, orchestral style, quartet style, and what you will are self-contained phenomena which do not touch, let alone interpenetrate.[1] This is a false view. Does a piano work have to contain some Alberti figuration to prove its pianistic pedigree? If the Grand Duo is orchestral, so – self-evidently – are *Lebensstürme* (Life's Storms), the *Deux Marches Caractéristiques*, the Rondo in A, and several solo piano works too. And if the long-held notes towards the end of the finale (and, by implication, the long one with which it begins) are examples of 'all that the pianoforte can *not* do', one wonders why Tovey did not posit an orchestral provenance for the Piano Sonatas in B flat (opening of finale) and A minor, D.784 (close of first movement), among others.

The first and second movements of the Grand Duo are both expansive movements in sonata form with three-key expositions, the second key in each case being a major third below the tonic. Although the second movement is 'abridged', meaning that it has no development (but a mere seven-bar link between exposition and recapitulation), its size is implicit in its wealth of themes and their leisurely exposition (with an element of development built in). The first movement, in making its initial move away from C major an almost totally unprepared jump into C sharp minor, sets the tonal agenda for the work, which is fearlessly exploratory. The passage from the slow movement in Fig. 70 shows the composer opening up radical new harmonic vistas in each bar, but making only minuscule part-movement to do so. Such sensitivity to fine but decisive harmonic shading is, of course, a hallmark of the mature Schubert.

In third place comes a deft scherzo, with a minor-key trio exhibiting some sublime piano sonorities (*pace* Tovey). Quite unforgettable in the

Fig. 70

scherzo, at the beginning of its second section, is the dialogue in which
bass answers treble with an inversion of its six-note idea, above and below
swinging, bell-like harmonies in the middle. Able to wear learning so
lightly, Schubert yet sought to develop his contrapuntal powers four years
later by taking lessons with Sechter. The finale lacks a three-key exposition,
perhaps because there are already three keys present in that it begins out
of key, its first theme opening in A minor and gravitating – only at some
length – to the home C major. It may be significant that Brahms's Piano
Quintet, whose finale this opening so obviously influenced, was a sonata
for two pianos before it was a quintet.

The second and fourth movements end with magnificent codas which
find new expressive potential in their material and peer into distant corners
of the tonal universe. The coda of the first movement illustrates the high-
level planning – whether conscious or subconscious in origin – which
may determine the pattern of musical events in a Schubert masterpiece.
Fig. 71a shows the first theme; but the conventional (and, by the listener,
subconsciously expected) continuation of the first four bars would have
been as in Fig. 71b. Schubert suppresses this expected continuation – until

Fig. 71

the coda, where 'x' appears in the secondo part and comes to rest on the longest stasis in the whole movement, and 'y' appears after the last forte cadence, and is twice repeated with some variation. The deep sense of homecoming and completeness which these postponed resolutions bring is firm compensation for the rather prolonged and bland ruminations which precede them in this coda.

Two fascinating works labelled 'divertissement' were composed by Schubert soon after his second visit to Zseliz in 1824. The title was perhaps chosen because it would have been immodest to claim sonata status for either work, especially after the implications of 'sonata' had been so ambitiously reaffirmed in the Grand Duo. There is no obvious trace of true divertimento tradition in either work: moreover, there is no other instance of Schubert adopting this particular generic title. The *Divertissement à l'hongroise* is a three-movement work, with two rondos flanking central march-and-trio. Debate will continue as to what ingredients might be Hungarian, and which themes if any he might have picked up at Zseliz. Schönstein, reminiscing in 1857, said that 'The theme . . . is a Hungarian song . . .' which Schubert overheard a Hungarian kitchen-maid singing in Count Esterhazy's kitchen.[2] Maurice Brown was sceptical, questioning whether there was any theme in the work which the kitchen-maid could have sung.[3] Yet the very first tune heard in the piece is just the kind of characterful, slightly modal thing one can imagine her to have sung (see Fig. 72a). While elsewhere in the work it is hard to identify an unquestionably Hungarian accent, there are clear gypsy inflections in the finale (Fig. 72b), and in general an abundance of incidents that are either Hungarian, or deemed by Schubert to be Hungarian, or simply alien. The piece has a whiff of experimentalism: it is as though the composer is deliberately allowing himself (under cover of the Hungarian allusion?) to do things he would probably not normally have ventured.

Fig. 72

The opening rondo has two slightly faster episodes between recurring Andante sections. The following march is not very distinguished, nor noticeably Hungarian. And the finale is a more elaborately worked out realization of the ABABA plan of the first movement, in which – most unusually – each B component is structured like a complete minuet-and-trio or march-and-trio, with a main section in binary form with repeats, a trio in binary form, and a reprise of the main section without repeats.

The three pieces which make up the Divertissement on French Themes are generally thought to belong together, although the first piece was first published separately. As this opening 'Marche brillante et raisonnée' is so rewarding, whereas the second and third pieces have their longueurs, there would appear no objection to programming it separately. 'Raisonnée' means 'worked out': in other words, it is a movement in sonata form, though in march style. But close inspection reveals that it is only sonata form by a thread. True, the key-scheme of sonata form is present, the first theme is well worked out at those places in the movement where one would expect it to be, and there is a real, large and eventful development. But the second subject needs some explaining. It is one of those Schubert themes that repeats itself rhythmically over and over again, yet is endearingly unforgettable. But what of its structure and later use?

It is in a clear binary form, with pronounced formal cadencing as the sections and repeats follow each other. When it returns in the development, Schubert's concern is not really to develop it at all, but just to revel in it once more – or rather twice more, because he gives us it in A flat major, then in B major. And in the recapitulation it returns again without substantive change. Schubert has headed the piece 'Tempo di Marcia'. It is common enough for a composer to warn his performers that a piece should be played 'in the style (or tempo) of a ——'. But in this instance have we here a clue to the piece's origins? Did it begin life as a march with trio? The second subject has, after all, all the characteristics of a trio, and in its presentation in the exposition it follows the same scheme as that of the trio of the second of the *Trois Marches Héroiques* (D.602, No. 2). There is little one can do, or wants to do, with a trio, except repeat it. So it is that even in his development Schubert is content to do just that. The 'reasoning' was applied to this piece, then, after it was already a *marche brillante*.

That peculiarity does not affect this piece's position as one of the most exciting of all sonata movements, partly because of the drive which sweeps the music into the development and then into the recapitulation, and because of the nature of the development itself: initially wild, tough, impetuous, it boasts rivetingly idiosyncratic harmonic moves, builds to hyperactive textures such as that in Fig. 73 which is based on a rare mediant pedal-point, later replaces energetic triplets with even more energetic semiquavers, leads by crescendo to a sudden hush for a rerun of the second

Fig. 73

subject, and finally caps all this drama by festooning the recapitulated first theme with a riot of dotted rhythms, then trills.

The Andantino varié now catalogued as second movement to the foregoing is, for the most part, a rather ordinary variation movement on a severely limited little theme which collapses at least once too often on the tonic chord. Schubert would never have invented a theme like that for variations, and indeed the publisher's heading claims that these are variations *über französische Motive* (on French motifs). 'For the most part' means for three of the four variations. In the fourth, Schubert's choice of major in place of minor unlocks a new harmonic field and, it seems, a new lyrical freedom of expression that is almost Schumannesque. The final Rondo brillante is a big sonata-rondo whose first theme, though in E minor, quaintly spends most of its time in G major. But it is the second idea that spells the movement's downfall, for it spawns a dactylic rhythm which is too relentlessly maintained for the remainder of the rondo.

Three great duet works, of different types, belong to Schubert's last year. The Fantasy in F minor, his last work of this type, is one of the supreme masterpieces of all time in the four-hand medium. Like the 'Wanderer' Fantasy, it is a continuous piece in four sections. Within the frame of first and last sections which share the same material, Schubert ventures as much diversity as in a four-movement sonata. Indeed the Largo second section is a compressed sonata slow movement, on an ABA plan in which B represents a vein of pure Schubertian lyricism to offset the echoes of Baroque grandeur in A's trills and double-dotted rhythms: and the following Allegro vivace is a scherzo complete with trio. The pathos of the outer sections, however, dominates and lends unity to the whole. For although the last section is developmental enough to cast first-section material in new guises, including fugal treatment, it also displays a touching nostalgia for the pristine form of the poignant, songful tune-and-accompaniment thought from which the whole fantasy sprang.

It helps us to appreciate the nature of Schubert's self-appointed formal task in this work if we note that he has compressed into 570 bars what, in a four-movement work proper, fills much more space – in the case of his shortest symphony (the Third) 840 bars. (The longest, the 'Great', runs to 2623 bars.) Only one 'movement' of the fantasy is allowed to spread to dimensions normal for its genre, and that is the scherzo. The first movement dispenses with a second subject, but retains something of the tonal and thematic contrast it would normally bring. The thematic contrast comes with a second theme in the home key of F minor which returns at the end of the movement and is the basis of most of the finale. To provide tonal contrast, there is an early sidestep to A flat major, and a later tonal journey from tonic down to tonic by three jumps of a major third (F minor, D flat minor, A minor, F minor) which replicates an excursion within the exposition of the Fourth Symphony (first movement).

The second movement (in remote F sharp minor, like the scherzo) is especially compact, unfurling its ABA scheme in a mere 13+15+15 bars. The finale is an entirely original structure, probably Schubert's shortest ever at 133 bars, yet fully fit to consummate the overall design of the fantasy. It begins with a reprise of the first 47 bars of the first movement, but at the 48th bar, where Schubert originally introduced a second theme in the tonic, he now adds to that theme a new countersubject, and writes a fugue which dominates the finale, leading only to a short coda. The growth of this fugue shows Schubert to be a finer contrapuntist than he is sometimes given credit for, but equally a masterful composer. The way in which fugal texture is gradually leavened is worth close study. Even though pure four-part counterpoint does not last much beyond the exposition of the fugue, and the countersubject is soon dropped as triplets determine more and more the character and course of the fugue as it builds towards its powerful and sustained climax, the strength of linear thinking stays right up to the last (imperfect) cadence, though by now reduced to triplets in octaves set against chordal blocks. A complete silence is what eventually stems the thrust of this mighty fugue: and the coda, terse but dramatic, is one of Schubert's most telling. The opening theme returns, but the bass soon moves up by a semitone to a G flat which both implants the Neapolitan key-area and reinstates briefly the key of the two middle movements (F sharp minor). A big tutti cadential gesture reactivates the fugue's triplets to drive down to a tonic deep in the bass. But there is an important after-cadence to come: a one-bar crescendo with finely judged dissonances builds to an accented chord of the supertonic seventh, and the progression from here to the tonic is a reversal of the first harmonic progression of the work.

The fact that the two outer movements are both in F minor and the two inner ones both in F sharp minor might seem to suggest that Schubert thought of the outer movements as a frame and the inner ones as a related pair. That inference is borne out by the use of a common chord progression as the underlying foundation of the first themes of both the inner

Fig. 74

movements (Fig. 74). One can hardly object that this is an everyday progression and that its use twice is therefore of no significance, since it is not easy to think of another example in the whole of Schubert's extensive oeuvre. Taken with the strong links between first movement and last already observed, this suggests taut construction which is some artistic feat. Schubert found it easy to spin out long structures, especially in finales, but for him to tighten a design as here, yet leave the listener with the sense of having experienced the diversity of a sonata, is a special accomplishment. The feat would count for less, were it not that the melodic and harmonic invention are consistently of a high expressive order.

One of the most powerful of all these works for piano duet is the Allegro in A minor. Its subtitle, *Lebensstürme*, added by Diabelli when the work was published in 1840, is not inappropriate for such an intense, highly charged piece – a successor to those minor-key *Sturm und Drang* works of the late eighteenth century. Schubert embraces a whole gamut of expression from fiery energy to visionary poetic calm, while maintaining an inexorable momentum from beginning to end. As the piece adopts sonata form, it could have been intended as the first movement of a sonata. In any event, there is an unusual wealth of material, and Schubert expands and develops ideas freely even within the exposition, making it longer than the exposition of any other of his first movements.

Especially notable is the sense of remoteness imparted to the 'second subject' by avoidance of the usual preparatory modulation. Its appearance – a slow-moving theme combining ecclesiastical solemnity with Romantic colour in a way that looks forward to reflective spans in symphonic Bruckner – coincides with a sudden (but hushed) slippage of key by one semitone (to a key unprecedented for a second subject, the major key on the leading-note), smoothed by the secondo player's continuation of a syncopated rhythm whose solo descent to the depths had been the sole signpost to this lull amid life's storms.

The third of these 1828 pieces, the Rondo in A, flows amiably from beginning to end, with a wealth of beautifully turned detail. This work shares certain characteristics with the second movement (finale) of

Beethoven's Piano Sonata in E minor, Op. 90, and there will be some
point in briefly enumerating the common features. Both pieces are
moderate-paced sonata-rondos in 2/4 time with a line of continuous semiquavers threading its way through as middle accompaniment to the first
theme. Both composers arrest this flow only at the transition, and reach a
second subject with contrapuntal pretensions: Beethoven's has the treble
and bass in mirror image, one an inversion of the other, while Schubert's
displays invertible (double) counterpoint. Where Beethoven moves to a
second, less active, theme to complete his second group, Schubert does
likewise, though he extends his theme rather more than Beethoven does
his. Both have a central episode that is as much development as episode,
and in both the keys of C and C sharp are the only ones – or almost the
only ones – touched upon (a point made not less interesting by the fact
that Beethoven's movement is in E major and Schubert's in A). In both
cases the second theme of the second group is the only one developed.
And both movements have an extended coda in which one of the themes
is transferred to an inside tenor part.

These are, of course, schematic similarities, not thematic ones, and this
is not the only instance when Schubert models (subconsciously perhaps,
who knows) by adapting schematic features but avoiding thematic influence. There is, however, in addition a remarkable parallel between the
second sections of the two composers' first themes, at bars 9 to 12 in both
cases (Figs. 75a and 75b). This is not so much a thematic affinity as a

Fig. 75   a

likeness of harmonic plan and phrase-structure. (To clarify the point Beethoven's passage in Fig. 75a has been transposed to Schubert's key.) To many listeners a theme (in the sense of 'tune') may appear to be the dominant feature of a musical idea; but to composers in the Classical period harmonic structures were at least as important, as treatises of the period clearly indicate. The fact that the two passages quoted are rather different from each other melodically is beside the point. The harmonic progression which underpins them may well be unique in each composer's oeuvre, at this point in a theme. If, then, Schubert carried with him in his head these particular harmonic colours from this particular work by Beethoven, is it likely that the other points of similarity between the two works, mentioned above, are coincidental?

Schubert's first theme is wide-ranging in pitch, sounding almost as though it was conceived for a clarinet. The contrasting second theme has only half that pitch-range. It moves almost entirely by step, having a solemn, intimate bearing, and it is five bars long. It is one of those Schubert themes that tend to turn in on themselves in an obsessive manner, but once fixed in the mind by sensitive playing, it haunts. Beyond the themes themselves, there is a wealth of incidental beauties, some florid and some more severe. The stabbing discords with which Schubert peppers the upper repeated triplets at the beginning of the coda must be accounted one of the textural *loci classici* of the piano duet repertoire.

It has been suggested that the Rondo may have been intended as finale to a sonata of which the Allegro in A minor was the first movement. As they share the same keynote, and the Allegro is a substantial piece in sonata form — one of Schubert's finest, indeed — that proposition bears consideration. The 'Allegretto quasi Andantino' marking for the Rondo may seem to argue against its being a finale; on the other hand, the movement is schematically modelled on the rondo of Beethoven's Op. 90 Piano Sonata, and Beethoven's rondo is a finale and moves at a similar pace ('Nicht zu geschwind'). Beethoven suggested a 'programme' for his Op. 90 sonata to its dedicatee, Count Lichnowsky, characterizing its rondo as 'conversation with the beloved'. If Schubert had known that fact, and had lived to offer his own Rondo to a publisher, might he have added a superscription resembling Beethoven's and/or dedicated it to Karoline Esterhazy, to whom the Fantasy in F minor was already inscribed?

It is clear from *Lebensstürme*, the Fantasy in F minor and the Rondo in A that the piano duet provided as fertile a field as ever for Schubert's imagination and that, having built upon Mozart's foundation to create what was now an accredited medium alongside others of his day, he would have cultivated it with further rewarding results if he had been given time to do so.

1826–1827

1826

Judged by the fact that it saw the completion of three outstanding instrumental works, 1826 must be considered a successful year. If performance and publication are the criteria, though, it was not particularly auspicious. Many a Schubert product prized by posterity lay unperformed, and two of the most important works of his oeuvre - both finished in 1826 – were not to be published until well after his death. At least there were contacts with publishers, sometimes initiated by the publisher; and there is some evidence that Schubert's stock was rising, within and beyond Vienna. One approach came from as far afield as Switzerland. The Swiss publisher H. G. Nägeli was planning an anthology of sonatas by various composers in 1826, and in June Schubert received an invitation to contribute. The projected title was imposing (*The Portal of Honour*), but perhaps the fee of 120 florins requested by Schubert was too imposing for Nägeli, for nothing came of these negotiations. The incident serves to show both that Schubert was recognized outside his homeland and that he had acquired – after several years of dealings with publishers – the self-confidence and standing to state his own terms.

Nägeli may have been unsure of the market for full-length works. Another kind of keyboard anthology, more obviously marketable, was regularly produced nearer home by Sauer & Leidesdorf. This Viennese firm liked to publish albums for the Christmas and New Year market – collections of pieces by current composers which would make attractive gifts. At the end of 1823 their album included an *Air russe* he had recently composed, the well-known piece which later became No. 3 of the *Moments Musicaux*, D.780. The 1824 album contained another of his piano pieces, *Plaintes d'un Troubadour*, which would become No. 6 of the *Moments*. These were Schubert's first exemplars of the short piano piece, for which there was a growing public appetite.

Many of Schubert's preoccupations in 1826, however, were on a larger scale. If the 'Great' C major Symphony, which was still on his workbench at the beginning of the year, was in a sense the climax of a planned assault on instrumental genres (by which he would 'pave his way' to the symphony), the completion and despatch of the symphony in the course of 1826 did not mark any appreciable decline in his will to keep instrumental challenges in his sights. Some twenty songs date from 1826 – mostly settings of Seidl, Schlechta, Schulze and Shakespeare; but there were some major chamber and keyboard works too, some of them probably taking shape alongside continuing progress on the 'Great' C major. The D minor String Quartet was rehearsed by the Schuppanzigh Quartet at Lachner's house in late January, and privately performed at Barth's on 1 February. Although Lachner's own account of the rehearsal was not encouraging (since Schuppanzigh is said to have made heavy weather of his part and exclaimed to the composer 'My dear fellow, this is no good, leave it alone; you stick to your songs!'), Schubert did not waver from his intention that the A minor Quartet should be the first of a set of three: there were still new things to be said in a medium in which he had found himself (at the age of 27–29) as surely as Beethoven had in his great threesome, the 'Rasumovsky' Quartets (when he was 36). Indeed, the G major Quartet of June strides boldly into quite new territory, with a daring and aplomb comparable to Beethoven's in the late quartets of his third period. But the result is quite different: Schubert retains the traditional four-movement design, but enters a sound-world of his own from the start, based on a questing approach to quartet texture and an unorthodox deployment of harmonic resources.

There has been a tendency in Schubert criticism to overplay the influence of song on his instrumental works. It is true that in a number of the instrumental works material from Schubert's songs appears. But if the instrumental pieces are counted (the total number of movements is the relevant figure) it will be found that the number which use song material represents not more than 2.5 per cent of the total. But quite apart from that objection, which is a matter of proportion, there is the question of the nature and purpose of the self–borrowing. More often than not, Schubert returns to one of his songs because he relishes the possibilities for musical elaboration or development which were not available to him in the constraining context of the song itself. Seldom can one say with any certainty that Schubert intended the poetic associations of the original material to be revived in the process of borrowing; and, if such revival was his intent, as soon as literal quotation of the song-music stops and development takes over the former associations become attenuated, as the new expressive directions of the moment gain precedence. The G major Quartet does not, like the A minor and D minor Quartets, refer to any existing songs. But John Reed detects echoes of Schubert's Schulze settings ('the tone of melancholy nostalgia' and 'driving rhythms') and pre-echoes of *Winterreise*. Interestingly he does not find in *Winterreise* echoes of the G major Quartet, or in the Schulze settings pre-echoes of the Quartet. There are extremes to which one may go in seeing the songs as the kernel of Schubert's oeuvre: and when Reed says that an instrumental work that has no obvious extra-musical associations must be 'a kind of digression into absolute music', and 'something apart from the main stream of Schubert's work', those extremes have clearly been reached.[1] Schubert spent his whole life sharpening his skills in the composition of absolute music, and this was not a digression. (For this purpose, absolute music may be defined as music which does not borrow material from non-absolute works, makes no explicit reference to real-life situations or anything else outside itself whether or not this involves setting a verbal text, and, even if it had some referential basis in the composer's mind, was issued to the public with any such information suppressed.) To compare the quantity of absolute music produced by Schubert with the quantity of his songs, the only readily available statistics are the number of bars written in each category. The resulting figures may not give a totally fair picture: after all, if one symphony equates in number of bars with, say, 25 songs, it is arguable that the ratio should be modified to reflect the fact that, in writing 25 songs, the composer commits himself to undertaking a new project 25 times, as against once for the symphony. A calculation of Schubert's total output in these categories may be made by anyone who has the Deutsch catalogue and infinite spare time. For now, a sample calculation must suffice, based on two production years of different type. The first is 1815, Schubert's 'song year', and an early one in his career; and the second is a double year from his maturity, 1825–6 – double because the composition of the Ninth Symphony spanned the two years.[2] The sums are as follows:

	songs	absolute music
1815	5985	5555
1825/6	3674	11868
Totals	9659	17423

Even when the reader has modified these figures in the light of the 'commitment' argument above, or any other argument deemed relevant, one could hardly call Schubert's absolute music a digression from his songs.

To a small extent, the self-borrowing between songs and instrumental music in Schubert was a two-way traffic. When something instrumental was borrowed within a song, it was not actual musical material that was borrowed, but a formal principle proper to instrumental music. Thus Der Sänger, a Goethe setting of 1815, contains a miniature sonata in its course,

while one of the 1826 songs, *Im Frühling* (written in March), adopts variation form and interleaves it with strophic song form in a new kind of
variation-Lied.

Examples of Schubert basing a new instrumental work on material plundered from a previous instrumental work, rather than from a song, have
received little attention. The D minor Quartet making use, in its scherzo,
of a dance from the D.790 set was a case in point. Now, in 1826, Schubert
carried this to an extreme: the Piano Sonata in E flat, 'composed' in the
summer, is in fact a transposition and expansion of the Sonata in D flat of
1817. As with his song-borrowings, the composer felt that the original
had potentialities beyond what had previously been realized. He now
enlarged the first movement's development and added a completely new
minuet and trio, among other changes. In a case like this, we may suppose
that the later version supersedes the earlier one; if Schubert had been
Brahms he would have destroyed the original. It was for long assumed
that the (undated) E flat version was made in the same year as the D flat,
but Martin Chusid has marshalled evidence to suggest that 1825/6 is more
likely,[3] and John Reed has subsequently drawn on other facts to make a
convincing case for the summer of 1826.[4]

The other sonata of 1826, the Piano Sonata in G major, is a new work,
completely of its time. In the broadest sense, it calls to mind Beethoven's
second period: expansive and serene, it has a relaxed confidence that may
blind one to the newness of its thinking. Just occasionally another work
in G major written three months previously – the String Quartet – seems
to pierce Schubert's consciousness. When Haslinger had the sonata ready
for issue (early the following year) he offered it not as a 'sonata' but as
'Fantasy, Andante, Minuet and Allegretto', perhaps hoping to convince
would-be purchasers that here was something distinctive. The critic of the
Wiener Zeitschrift für Kunst fell for it hook, line and sinker, perhaps not
noticing that the first movement is in sonata form and the other three
movements are what would be expected in a sonata too. 'The popular and
talented song composer here gives to the musical world a Fantasy', he
boldly announced.[5] The truth was that it was a sonata and he was a practised
and distinguished sonata composer. But no press commentator of that day
would have called Schubert that, because his instrumental music was largely
unknown. In the same month as the sonata (October) Schubert wrote a
special piece for Josef Slawjk, a young violinist who had come to make
his home in Vienna in this same year. Slawjk (Slavik) was obviously a
virtuoso player, and Schubert chose to write a piece demanding great
brilliance and energy: indeed when Artaria published it he announced it
as 'Rondeau brilliant'. It is for violin and piano, was first performed by
Slawjk with Karl Maria von Bocklet, a young pianist in his twenties to
whom Schubert had dedicated his Piano Sonata in D in the previous year.

The Rondo in B minor (D.895) is a fine recital piece which deserves to be better known.

It was in October, too, that the Symphony in C major (the 'Great') was offered to the Gesellschaft der Musikfreunde. Schubert's letter of dedication is a model of its kind: 'Convinced of the Austrian Musical Society's noble intention to support any artistic endeavour as far as possible, I venture, as a native artist, to dedicate to them this, my Symphony, and to commend it most politely to their protection. With all respect, your devoted Frz. Schubert.'[6] By the end of 1825 the work had still been in an incomplete state. Since then, he had made substantial additions to the codas of the first and last movements, recast and added to the trio of the scherzo, and reshaped the Allegro theme of the first movement at all its appearances. In addition to these and other less radical changes, he still had the filling out of much of the orchestration to complete, as well as the general editing of the score.

The Gesellschaft committee acknowledged receipt of the score, sent Schubert a hundred florins as a 'token of obligation', arranged to have the parts copied, but – contrary to long-accepted opinion – did not promise a performance.[7] The parts were ready in the summer of 1827, and the society's Konservatorium orchestra played through the work in Schubert's presence at some time after that. In December 1828, a month after Schubert's death, the work chosen for a memorial concert at the Gesellschaft was the ten-year-old Sixth Symphony – a choice which suggests either that the 'Great' was too difficult for the orchestra to prepare at short notice even when it had already been tried out once, or that the Viennese establishment was more comfortable with Italianate middle Schubert than with the mature, characteristic Schubert. There is evidence that duplicate parts of the 'Great' were made in the 1830s, and the finale was publicly performed in Vienna in 1836.[8] The familiar story of Schumann 'discovering' the work during a visit to Schubert's brother Ferdinand after the composer's death is therefore misleading, although to Schumann this would have appeared to be the case. However that may be, the performance he encouraged Mendelssohn to give at Leipzig in 1839, although not a complete one, came nearer to being a proper première. Later in 1839 (15 December) it was decided that two movements could be given in Vienna, but only with a slice of Italian opera between them (an aria from Donizetti's *Lucia di Lammermoor*).

The events of Schubert's more mundane existence in 1826 are quickly told. Following the death of the court Kapellmeister, Salieri, in 1825, his deputy, Josef Eybler, had been elevated to replace him. In April of 1826 Schubert offered himself to succeed Eybler as second Kapellmeister. It was not until the following January that he heard that a redefining of posts to save money had led to the appointment, not of a second Kapellmeister, but of a court organist, in the person of Josef Weigl, well known and respected as a composer of operetta and a conductor at the Kärntnertor Theatre. Schubert's distress was tempered by his recognition that Weigl was a 'worthy' person for the job.[9] In any event, one wonders if Schubert's reputation as unreliable in keeping appointments would have counted against him.

In the early months of the year, Schubert and Bauernfeld agreed on a subject for a new opera. Schubert, having recovered sufficiently from previous setbacks to contemplate another stage venture, had originally favoured something based on Schulze's *Die bezauberte Rose* (The Enchanted Rose – into which the princess of this Romantic tale was turned), but Bauernfeld persuaded him that *Der Graf von Gleichen*, in which a medieval count on a crusade fell in love with a Saracen princess, Suleika, and brought her home to live in a *ménage à trois* with his wife, offered more dramatic scope. Bauernfeld went to Gmunden in May with Mayrhofer, and had the libretto finished by the end of that month. He asked Schubert to join them in Gmunden so that he could hand over the libretto, but Schubert did not have the wherewithal: 'I have no money at all, and altogether things go very badly for me.' But later in the letter a new cause for urgency showed itself. 'Come to Vienna as soon as possible. As Duport wants an opera from me, but the libretti I have so far set do not please at all, it would be splendid if your libretto were favourably received. Then at least there would be money, if not reputation as well!'[10] Duport was Barbaja's representative at the Kärntnertor Theatre, and here was another chance to make it on the Vienna stage, with the help of a new librettist. If Schubert recognized that a story about bigamy might not go down well with the censors, he will almost certainly have known that a play-with-music version of it had been staged in 1816 without obstacle.[11] As a standby, there was always Anna Milder-Hauptmann waiting to smooth his passage in Berlin – if, presumably, Suleika's was to be a suitably extensive soprano role. The censor duly banned the work in October, but Schubert carried on regardless, sketching substantial portions of the opera in 1827. He then abandoned the project, either because he got wind of the imminent closure of the Kärntnertor Theatre (in October 1828) or because he was worried by unevenness in the libretto. For one whose hopes in this field had been dashed several times before, he would not at this stage have needed much discouragement.

In the letter to Bauernfeld on 10 July Schubert had declared, 'I cannot possibly get to Gmunden or anywhere else, for I have no money at all . . .'[12] But he went somewhere in July, for he spent a part of the month at Währing. As Währing was a suburb of Vienna, little money was needed. And as he stayed at the house of Schober, who now lived at Währing, he was perhaps indulgently treated. Indeed, it may have been *because* he had no money that he was at Währing, since soon after both men returned to Vienna Schubert gave up his apartment in the Wieden district of the city and moved in with Schober. When Bauernfeld returned from Gmunden he did not find happiness all around. 'Schubert ailing . . . Schwind morose, Schober idle, as usual. In myself there's still travel-fever and blood!'[13] Schwind was morose because of the usual ups and downs in his love affair with the barrister's daughter, Anna Hönig, a state of affairs to which the friends were well accustomed. Schober was idle because Schober usually was idle. But why was Schubert *halbkrank* (out of sorts)? For Maynard Solomon, he needed 'peacocks' (young male company) to cheer him up. For Rita Steblin, he was suffering some mild relapse in his syphilis, which the eating of peacocks would cure.[14]

This, anyway, was the scene to which Bauernfeld had returned in August. He did not write that Schubert was penniless, a condition almost as regular as Schober's idleness. It was perhaps to boost his income that Schubert wrote to both Probst and Breitkopf & Härtel in this same month, offering them a mixture of works to publish. Neither approach was to lead anywhere. Probst's reply is probably indicative of a general resistance to Schubert's late instrumental music. 'The public does not yet sufficiently and generally understand the peculiar, often ingenious, but perhaps now and then somewhat curious procedures of your mind's creations.' With songs there was a thread of tangible meaning to cling to – the text: music without words was more demanding of purely musical receptivity and comprehension, and one cannot help wondering if some of Probst's reservations lay behind the Gesellschaft der Musikfreunde's sloth in coming to grips with Schubert's latest and greatest wordless artefact. There is no trace of any reply from Breitkopf; a certain irony may be seen in this, when it is recalled that this company was quick enough to publish the 'Great' once Schumann and Mendelssohn had taken up its cause, and in the last quarter of the century they brought out thirty-nine volumes of Schubert – the first 'complete edition'. One could more readily understand Probst's declared preference for works that were 'agreeable and easily comprehensible'[15] if the composer and publisher were of the twentieth century, when popular taste and composers' inclinations were often separated by a wide chasm. That they were not so separated in Schubert's day is self-evident, and the fact that the Gesellschaft der Musikfreunde promoted more music by living than dead composers merely confirms the point.

The comings, goings and doings of friends and acquaintances were again of some interest in 1826. In February Schubert's father was honoured by the city of Vienna in a decree which mentioned his forty-five years' school service and seventeen years' work for charity. Michael Holzer, choirmaster at the Lichtental church and Schubert's first music teacher, died in April. In the same month, Schubert's old school friend Spaun returned to Vienna, and soon re-established himself as a focal member of the circle. Schober was in financial trouble and had to take a job and move out to Währing, where Schubert visited him. Schwind was preoccupied with the vicissitudes of his amatory affair. There were two marriages: Vogl caused a stir by returning from Italy in April and announcing his engagement to Kunigunde Rosa, daughter of a former custodian of the Belvedere Art Gallery, but no one was surprised when Leopold Kupelwieser married Johanna Lutz in September after a long betrothal. Both men's new loyalties kept them from their regular social contact with Schubert and his friends, but they did appear at Schubertiads, especially at the 'big, big Schubertiad' hosted by Spaun on 15 December.[16] The description is that of Franz von Hartmann, who, a former law student in Vienna, returned to the city in November with his brother Fritz, became a regular member of the current Schubert circle, and kept a diary which records the frequent visits (sometimes daily) to the Green Anchor.[17] Vogl sang on this occasion ('almost thirty splendid songs'), Kupelwieser attended with his wife, and Schubert played duets with Josef von Gahy. It was a large gathering, including Grillparzer, Schober, Schwind, Mayrhofer, Bauernfeld, Schlechta, and many others. After the music there was food and dancing, and the hardier guests went on to the Green Anchor. Schwind's famous drawing of 1868 is thought to be a recollection of this event.

Surviving documents give some indication of the music heard by Schubert in the course of his attendance at public concerts, private performances, and the opera. These records are of interest to students of Schubert's own music, but their value is limited by their incompleteness. We can be sure that Schubert was listening to music in the city on many more occasions than were meticulously chronicled. Moreover, his own music was affected not only by what other music he heard, but that which he read in scores, and his consumption of printed music is even less well documented. There is unmistakable evidence in his music of his being touched by pieces he is not recorded as having heard performed. Where he did not possess scores himself, he could have borrowed, or browsed in the individual Vienna shops in which each publisher set out his wares and in which Schubert certainly met other composers and could well have met Beethoven. Vienna could sometimes offer two concerts on the same day, even at this time. One documented instance was in February of 1826, when Bauernfeld accompanied Schubert to an orchestral concert, including Beethoven's Second Symphony and *Egmont* Overture and the 'Hallelujah Chorus' from Handel's *Messiah*, and afterwards a programme of Haydn, Mozart and Onslow by the Schuppanzigh Quartet.[18] In May, Schubert reported on new productions of *Die Zauberflöte* and *Der Freischütz* to Bauernfeld and Mayrhofer, while they were in Gmunden.

1827

Early in 1827 there were again numerous parties, and frequent visits to the Green Anchor. The Hartmann brothers continued to record these events in their diary, with a list of people attending. Those most often present, apart from themselves, were Schubert, Schober, Spaun and Schwind; sometimes present were Gahy, Bauernfeld, Enderes, Derffel, Mayrhofer, Enk, Hönig, Nágy. From February into the summer, the Castle of Eisenstadt (Zum Schloss Eisenstadt), centrally placed near the Graben, became the favourite haunt. For roughly the same period, Schubert moved in once more with Schober, in his new house on the Tuchlauben.

Beethoven had fallen ill in December with pneumonia. A liver complaint, stomach pains and dropsy followed, and by mid-January there was no hope of recovery.[19] To distract him during this time of suffering early in 1827, Anton Schindler, his friend and factotum, put in front of him a collection of about sixty of Schubert's songs and vocal works, mostly in manuscript. Beethoven 'was amazed at the number of them' but 'utterly astonished when he got to know their content'. He 'simply could not believe that at that time [February 1827] Schubert had already written over five hundred'. According to Schindler, he called out repeatedly, 'Truly, in Schubert there dwells a divine spark!' and prophesied 'that he will still make a great stir in the world'.[20] Although Schindler was not the most reliable of witnesses, there is little reason to doubt the essence of his account, which identifies a few of the songs Beethoven saw (they included *Die junge Nonne* and *Viola*). Beethoven must have known only a tiny proportion of Schubert's oeuvre. His appreciation of what he saw at this late stage suggests that if he had had more than a few weeks to live he might have developed a properly informed admiration of the fellow-composer, such as could not come from a perusal of some of his vocal works. There was almost certainly only one person alive in Schubert's world who could have recognized instantly the value of Schubert's instrumental music, and might have had the power to enlighten the Viennese public and immediately succeeding generations. But on 26 March he was dead. If the two composers had enjoyed a few more years, and had become friends despite the obstacles, they could have benefited enormously from the chance to discuss mutual musical interests and professional minutiae, on a level of erudition and empathy not available to either of them elsewhere. There is no evidence, however, that they were inclined to talk about their art in this way. Whether the opportunity was all that was needed, one can only guess.

Schubert was pleased that Beethoven had enjoyed reading his songs, according to Spaun, who maintained that reports of Schubert visiting the dying composer were false.[21] Schubert was certainly present a few weeks later at Beethoven's funeral, however, where he was one of the torchbearers and witnessed a long and imposing ceremonial, with a fitting oration written by Grillparzer. Afterwards, Fritz von Hartmann joined Schubert, Schober and Schwind at the Castle of Eisenstadt, where they stayed until 1 a.m. 'Needless to say, we talked of nothing but Beethoven, his works and the well-merited honours paid to his memory today.'[22]

Another torchbearer at the funeral was Hummel, a senior German composer more famed by far than Schubert, though barely acknowledged in posterity's hall of fame. Hummel had come to Vienna to talk with Beethoven, bringing with him his sixteen-year-old pupil Ferdinand Hiller. During their stay in the city they were invited to dine at the home of Frau Lászny, the ex-Kärntnertor opera singer to whom Schubert had dedicated his *Divertissement à l'hongroise*. Frau Lászny invited Schubert and Vogl too, and after dinner there began what Hiller later described as 'a unique concert. One song was followed by another – untiring the contributors, untiring the listeners. Schubert had but little technique, Vogl had but little voice, but they both had so much life and feeling, and were so completely absorbed in their performances . . . One thought neither of piano playing nor of singing, it was as though the music needed no material sound, as though the melodies, like visions, revealed themselves to spirtualized ears.' More important for Schubert was the response of Hummel himself, who 'was so deeply moved that tears glistened on his cheeks'.[23] Schubert, in his turn, was sufficiently moved by Hummel's reception of his songs to dedicate his last three piano sonatas to him; but as the sonatas were not published till 1839, and Hummel had meanwhile died in 1837, Artaria dedicated them instead to Schumann.

By now, Schubert enjoyed a good rapport with another publisher, Tobias Haslinger, who first published a set of dances in January (*Valses Nobles*, known to us as *Zwölf Walzer*, D.969), followed that with the G major Piano Sonata in April, and in May issued three Seidl settings. Perhaps on the strength of fresh funds in his coffers as a result, Schubert left the Schober residence in late May and took a two-month holiday at Dornbach, a village to the north–west of Vienna, staying in a guesthouse, the Empress of Austria.[24] Here he set to work on his new Bauernfeld opera, *Der Graf von Gleichen*, with occasional trips into Vienna to renew acquaintances at the Castle of Eisenstadt. It was during this holiday that Schubert was elected to full membership of the committee of the Gesellschaft der Musikfreunde, an honour he duly acknowledged in writing. Dornbach offered pleasant rural surroundings, which he enjoyed on frequent walks, and good local wine, which he probably enjoyed too. At least, Bauernfeld wrote to a friend on 5 June: 'Schubert is staying in Dornbach and drinks there, instead of here.' Bauernfeld suspected that he was depressed, saying that he 'was sensing the inadequacy of our lives'.[25]

Depression can be a largely private condition, and glimpses of the unhappy Schubert provided by Bauernfeld here may be the tip of an iceberg. Likewise not necessarily open to public scrutiny were other aspects of his private life. In these last years, over which his syphilis cast its shadow, there was supposedly an idealized love for Karoline Esterhazy, platonic in practice if not in impulse, on account of her social standing. But were there still sexual appetites to be satisfied, and did Schubert succumb despite the risk of passing on his infection? Again, it is vain to search for neat, documented answers. When Hoffmann von Fallersleben, a Prussian librarian on a visit to Vienna, visits a Heuriger (new-wine tavern) in Grinzing on a Monday night in August, and notes in his diary that 'the old fiddler played Mozart . . . Schubert with his girl we espied from our seat', it is for the reader's own informed understanding and imagination to draw what conclusions it will.

Johann Jenger of Graz, who had moved to Vienna in 1824 to take up a post in the War Office, was a fine pianist who appeared in many concerts in Vienna, sometimes in performances of Schubert's music. He was a friend of Marie Pachler, wife of the Graz barrister Karl Pachler, who was herself an able pianist, highly commended by Beethoven in performances of his works. Marie Pachler kept open house for musicians, and Jengen – knowing that Schubert was anxious to meet her – had tried to arrange a visit to Graz, for Schubert and himself, to be hosted by her. The trip duly materialized in September, and Schubert was warmly received by the Pachler family and fêted in the community. The whole party made an excursion to Wildbach Castle, Schubert was introduced to his friend Anselm Hüttenbrenner's wife and children, and the Styrian Musical Society, which had honoured him some years before, planned a charity concert that would include some of his music. The press announcement of the concert acknowledged 'kind collaboration on the part of an artistic and greatly celebrated composer from the metropolis'.[26] Three items by Schubert were included: the Walter Scott setting *Normans Gesang*, the female chorus *Gott in der Natur*, and *Geist der Liebe* (D.747) for male-voice quartet. It was the usual one-sided display of Schubert's creative art, and it was a pity that Marie Pachler and/or Jenger could not have been involved by playing some of Schubert's keyboard music, to widen the scope of the programme somewhat.

The visitors took four days on the homeward journey, as against one for the outward journey, stopping to see the sights at Fürstenfeld, Hartberg, Friedberg, and Schleinz.[27] On his return to Vienna, Jenger wrote to thank Frau Pachler, 'because both Schubert and I have very seldom spent such glorious days as we did recently at dear Graz . . .'[28] And Schubert expressed similar sentiments in his own letter – 'I spent the happiest days I have had for a long time', adding the hope that he would be able to prove his gratitude 'in an adequate manner'.[29] In the following year he dedicated four songs to her, including the famous *An Silvia*. Schubert had always enjoyed his returns to Vienna no less than his departures therefrom. But on this occasion, as the same letter makes clear, his pleasure to be home sounded less than wholehearted: 'Already it becomes clear to me that I was only too happy at Graz, and I cannot as yet get accustomed to Vienna. True, it is rather large, but then it is empty of cordiality, candour, genuine thought, reasonable words, and especially of intelligent deeds. There is so much confused chatter that one hardly knows whether one is on one's head or one's heels, and one rarely or never achieves any inward contentment.' He may have felt it was a flattering courtesy to his Graz hostess to vilify Vienna, while admiring at Graz 'an artless and sincere way of being together'; but his choice of words does seem to signify a more genuine dejection. And only two weeks later, in a follow-up letter to her, he admitted that 'my usual headaches are assailing me again'.[30] Illness, like depression and sex, is not normally the subject of hour-by-hour confessions, and this one epistolary reference to headaches may point to any number of attacks. The expression 'usual headaches' tells us as much; and, used in a letter to her, it may imply that he suffered headaches while he was her guest in Graz. An apologetic letter he wrote while in Graz, to one Franz Selliers de Moranville, a Graz music-lover with whom he had made an appointment, may be further testimony to these or other symptoms: 'I came to apologize for not having kept my word recently. If you knew how impossible it had been for me to do so, I am sure you would forgive me.'[31]

Headaches were one of the symptoms of secondary syphilis, and their frequency in Schubert earned a mention in one of the obituaries.[32] It may be that this was a recurrent problem during the autumn. Unfortunately Franz von Hartmann ceased to make daily notes of his social activities in his diary during the last three months of the year, simply recording: 'Autumn 1827: Every Wednesday and Saturday evening we got to the ale-house, where Enk, Schober, Schubert and Spaun are to be met.'[33] The occasional absence of one of the party would not necessarily have deterred the writer from using this concise blanket form of words. On 15 October Schubert had to write to Anna Hönig regretting his inability to be present at a party, as he was in no fit state to be with people.[34] It was at some time in the autumn, when Schubert completed *Winterreise*, that he sang the new cycle through to his friends. 'From then on,' recalled Spaun, 'he was a sick man.'[35]

Winterreise was one of the principal compositions of 1827. It was the result of two distinct bursts of creativity, one beginning in February, the other in October. The reason for this is that Schubert had at first come across only the shorter version of Wilhelm Müller's *Die Winterreise*

(Schubert dropped the definite article), and although the extra twelve poems were already published he seemed not to be aware of this until the summer. The poet's projection of the rejected lover's journey through a bleak winter landscape is not an external, narrative account, but an interior, first-person study. While superficial variety is introduced by the poet, through the diversity of images of Nature, for one thing, and by the composer, whose fecund imagination allows him to point up each of Müller's psychological miniatures with its own characterful music, it is not surprising that a mood of prevailing gloom overwhelmed the friends when Schubert sang them the cycle 'in a voice wrought with emotion'. It goes without saying that he was well aware of the special quality of these songs; in inviting his friends to hear them, he had revealed more of his feelings about them than he usually did in talking of his compositions. 'Come to Schober's today, I will sing you a cycle of awe-inspiring songs. I am anxious to know what you will say about them. They have affected me more than has been the case with any other songs.'[36] And when, at the end, Schober said that he liked only *Der Lindenbaum* (The Lime Tree), Schubert replied: 'I like these songs more than all the others and you will get to like them too.'

Commentators who see *Winterreise* as a reflection of Schubert's depression or worsening illness have to be cautioned. A composer composes through a 'persona' who is to some extent free of the day-to-day baggage of the composer's life, suspended above present reality but sharing the composer's accumulated past. How else could Mozart compose two utterly contrasted string quintets in quick succession, or three quite different (last) symphonies in so short a time? As Denis Matthews observed, in explaining how Beethoven could produce his Second Symphony in the same year as his *Heiligenstadt Testament*, the relation between art and life is a subtle affair, 'for the true artist creates out of his total experience'.[37] It need be no surprise, then, that at the same time as Schubert was working on Part II of *Winterreise* he was shaping his Piano Trio in B flat, a bright and ebullient work whose opening theme bounces in without preliminaries, brimful of youthful vigour and freshness.[38] And in November its un-identical twin, the E flat Trio, was begun – a state of the art product of Schubert at the height of his powers, running the gamut of expression from joyful affirmation to rapt meditation. Both trios make considerable demands on the technique and stamina of the professional players for whom they were self-evidently conceived (Bocklet and members of the Schuppanzigh Quartet). It is an 'unbuttoned' Schubert who speaks, sings, confides and dances here, not the 'contained' Schubert who had nothing further from his mind than virtuosity when he followed the trudgings of Müller's world-weary traveller. An extreme of virtuosity was reached in yet another chamber work to be fitted into 1827, the Fantasy in C for violin and piano composed in December. This was another offering to the young virtuoso Josef Slawjk, and returns (not for the last time) to a genre favoured by Schubert in his early days. Its multi-sectional build is enterprising if not entirely convincing: Schubert remained ready to set himself new challenges in these last twelve months of his life. One little irony is that, having taken for one of the sections a five-year-old song, *Sei mir gegrüsst* (I Greet You), and elevated it to a new plane by means of inspired changes in its melodic and harmonic resolution, he proceeds to write variations on it which absorb us less the more pyrotechnical they become.

If the array of chamber works produced in the last three months of 1827 along with the second part of *Winterreise* causes wonderment at Schubert's industry, the addition of the Four Impromptus (D.935) to the authenticated list for December merely adds to the congestion. Two factors may temper our awe. First, none of these works required more than three staves in the writing of its score. With symphonies and opera, the writing of multi-stave scores added appreciably to the time required of the composer. In chamber music, the composer's pen stood more chance of keeping up with the pace of his invention, which was, at best, fast. Second, chronology is usually determined by the composer's dating of his autograph scores. It can never be assumed that the process of composing coincided neatly with the writing of the score. The writing may have been preceded by hours, days, weeks or months of thinking, which did not necessarily involve sketching on paper and was probably not documented.

The D.935 Impromptus were the second of two groups written in 1827. The first group, the Four Impromptus, D.899, dates from the summer, between Schubert's visits to Dornbach and Graz. Schubert seems to have thought of the second set as a kind of Part II, since he numbered them five to eight. But even this was not the total of short piano pieces for 1827. Having already written some separate short pieces a few years earlier, the *Air russe* and *Plaintes d'un Troubadour*, he now added to these four more pieces, the whole set of six being published in July 1828 by Leidesdorf as *Momens Musicals* (by which was meant *Moments Musicaux*). The provenance of the title 'Impromptu' will be discussed in Chapter 20 (pages 341–2). It was Haslinger, not Schubert, who decided to adopt the title which had appeared five years earlier on Voříšek's Op. 7. Schubert will none the less have known Voříšek's short pieces, which may well have provided the stimulus for all these pieces of his own. Like the Bohemian, he tended to favour ternary form, but in Schubert's case this may mean anything from a clear, symmetrical three-part structure with central 'trio' to a more closely woven, less transparent episodical form.

The short Romantic piano piece had, then, already been invented; but it was Schubert who raised it to an art form of the highest order. Mendelssohn was to call his pieces of this type 'Songs without Words'. Although

Schubert's examples do not resemble song-transcriptions, Mendelssohn's title might be superficially apt for most of them, in that they tend towards lyrical simplicity, with appealing, pianistic textures and memorable melodic ideas. Sometimes Schubert appears to go beyond that prescription, as in the first of the D.935 Impromptus, which sounds more like the beginning of a sonata. But that is a short-lived illusion, for these pieces are more concerned with sentiment than argument. Beethoven's 'Bagatelles' are more intellectual, whimsical, succinct; yet even they sometimes affect the more lyrical or dance-like manner of the Schubert miniatures, while Schubert was to come closer to the echt-bagatelle in the last piece of his final year (D.946). There must be many listeners who have come to Schubert through the impromptus. They are excellent ambassadors of his art, displaying a populist facet without compromising his true self.

The Last Year: 1828

At the stroke of twelve, 1828 began with a toast in Malaga. The company was assembled at Schober's as usual: Spaun, Schwind, Bauernfeld, Fritz and Franz von Hartmann, Enk, Gahy, Eduard Rössler (a new boarder in Schober's house), Schober and Schubert. This would be Schubert's last New Year party; and coincidentally, as soon as the toast was done, Bauernfeld read his new poem for the occasion, a ten-verse Goethean rhapsody on the theme of *Ars longa, vita brevis*. 'Es rollen die immer kreisenden Jahre' (the years roll by, constantly circling); and 'der Jüngling muss doch zum Greise werden' (youth must turn to senility, that's sure). The eighth verse focuses on the artist:

> Der Zauber der Rede, der Quell der Gesänge –
> auch er vertrocknet, so göttlich er ist;
> nicht rauschen die Lieder, wie sonst, im Gedränge,
> denn auch dem Sänger ward seine Frist: –
> die Quelle eilet zum Meere wieder,
> der Liedersänger zum Quelle der Lieder.[1]

> The magic of speech, the source of all song –
> That too, divine though it be, will dry up.
> The songs will no longer resound for the assembled company,
> For the singer's time will be up, too: –
> As the stream rushes towards the sea,
> So speeds the bringer of songs to the source of all song.

Whether one takes singer to denote poet, or composer, or indeed singer, the prophecy is safe and the theme is a familiar poetic one. Besides, did anyone go to a New Year party at which someone did not allude to the speedy passing of the years? Bauernfeld did round his poem off with two verses exhorting the company to enjoy the scenery of life on the way to their sure destination, and they all made their way to Bogner's coffee-house at 2 a.m. to continue the festivities.[2]

January was a month of parties, for reading rather than for music, but the concord of New Year was not sustained: Franz Hartmann's diary records an unpleasant disagreement between Spaun and Schober, made up

on the next evening. On 20 January Schubert's Fantasy in C for violin
and piano received its first performance, played by Slawjk and Bocklet:
the critic of the *Sammlung*, like others in the audience, left before the end.
On 15 January Spaun had announced his engagement to Franziska von
Roner, and on 28 January he gave a special celebratory Schubertiad. Schubert was pleased for Spaun, but said he would be sorry to lose him.[3] In
Franziska's honour he arranged for Bocklet, Schuppanzigh and Linke to
come and play the E flat Trio, while Schubert himself joined Bocklet in
the A flat Variations for piano duet. This was also the month in which he
began work on what is arguably the finest of a long line of his fantasies,
the one in F minor for four hands; but there were several additions and
alterations to be made before a final score could be written in April. This
was to be one of those special works in which a supreme melodist with a
well-developed ear for texture and modulatory technique was able to forge
a unique and wholly satisfying structure which bears witness to the distance
he had travelled down the path towards perfection as an instrumental
composer. That so personal and masterly an example of his mature art
should be dedicated to Karoline Esterhazy testifies to the warmth of his
regard for her. Although in one sense she was a 'distant beloved' – because
of the social divide that separated them – she lived in the same city and
the fact that there is no documentary record of their meeting in the last
three years of Schubert's life does not necessarily mean that the flames of
his 'idealized love' were not fanned by her presence at all during that time.

During February two German publishers, Schott of Mainz and Probst
of Leipzig, both approached Schubert asking what works he could offer
them. His reply to Schott is of special interest, reflecting the shift in
aspiration which had led him to rather ignore song composition and con-
centrate on the wordless media – not for any commercial reasons but for
personal fulfilment. He offered the recently finished E flat Trio, two string
quartets, the second set of impromptus, two recent fantasies (presumably
one of these was the F minor, which he would hope to have written up
by the time a reply was received from Schott), and the comic trio *Der
Hochzeitsbraten* (The Wedding Roast).[4] To these he added a list of other
works – operas, a symphony and a mass 'only to acquaint you with my
striving after the highest in art' (*meinem Streben nach dem Höchsten in der
Kunst*).[5] There were, of course, still many songs – including some fine
ones – not yet published, but if Schubert had included these in the list he
might have feared that they would be chosen and the instrumental works
ignored.

The negotiations dragged on through the early summer, and beyond.
Schott eventually offered to take the impromptus and the quintet for male
voices and piano, *Mondenschein* (Moonlight); but Schubert heard in October
that they had decided against accepting the impromptus, being advised by

their Paris agents that they were 'too difficult for trifles'.[6] As Schott had earlier rejected the E flat Trio, Schubert sent that off to Probst in May, and Probst accepted it: but it did not appear in print until October. The May letter to Probst contains some important recommendations for performance: 'The cuts indicated in the last movement are to be most scrupulously observed. Be sure to have it performed for the first time by capable people, and most particularly see to a continual uniformity of tempo at the changes of the time-signature in the last movement. The minuet at a moderate pace and *piano* throughout, the trio, on the other hand, vigorous except where *p* and *pp* are marked.'[7] Most interesting here is the reference to cuts in the last movement, a matter on which the Schubert literature is either silent or inexplicit.[8] It is clearly a fact that Schubert did authorize cuts, either because the players recommended this or because after the performance in March 1828, which was given complete, he himself decided that the finale was too long – possibly in response to comments by the players and/or audience. Sonnleithner, some thirty years later, referred to the tradition of cuts in performance without throwing any light on the circumstances in which they were first mooted: 'Incidentally one cannot deny the fact that the Trio *is too long* and that it has only gained in effect through the cuts which have been tried out in recent times.'[9] A few days before Schubert wrote the letter to Probst, he had had the work rejected by Schott, who said that it was 'probably long' (*wahrscheinlich gross*).[10] He made two cuts in the finale, one of 50 bars and one of 48 bars, reducing its length from 846 bars to 748. The first cut removes blocks of the structure which are in essence reworkings in other keys of blocks already present elsewhere, and while they contain slight variation their absence hardly results in more being lost than gained. The second cut, though, removes a passage which uniquely combines two themes simultaneously.[11]

Also during February, Schubert was making plans for a high-profile public concert of his own music. He judged that his reputation was now sufficiently established for him to emulate Beethoven's venture of May 1824 with a self-promoted event for which he would select the repertoire and artists. He was offered free use of the hall, that of the Musikverein in the Tuchlauben, and planned a mixed programme of vocal works and chamber music, some items being recent ones but some as much as twelve years old but not yet performed. Among the most recent were the songs *Der Kreuzzug* (The Crusade) (November 1827) and *Die Sterne* (The Stars) (January 1828), and the E flat Piano Trio. The first movement of the G major String Quartet was played by the Schuppanzigh Quartet, members of which joined Bocklet in the Trio. Schuppanzigh himself was indisposed. The concert was eventually scheduled for 26 March, which was the first anniversary of Beethoven's death, although Schubert had first intended 21 March. The one work written especially for the concert was the song

Auf dem Strom for tenor, horn and piano, whose even-numbered verses adopt a tune which unmistakably echoes that of the Funeral March of the 'Eroica' Symphony. This dual reference to the death of Beethoven may, as John Reed has pointed out, have been intentional, but if so he kept the matter to himself.[12] Either way, it was very much Schubert's day, the hall was filled to capacity, and Schubert netted proceeds of eight hundred florins.

According to Hüttenbrenner, Handel's *Messiah* was one of Schubert's favourite works.[13] The Handel interest strengthened in 1828, when he acquired scores of the oratorios, according to Sonnleithner,[14] and of the complete works according to Breuning.[15] Hüttenbrenner recalled that when Schubert played Handel's music at the piano 'he sprang up as though electrified and cried: "Oh, the daring of these modulations! Things like that could not occur to the likes of us even in a dream!"'[16] And to Sonnleithner he is reported to have said: 'Now for the first time I see what I lack; but I will study hard with Sechter so that I can make good the omission.'[17] The stated intention to study with Sechter, a renowned Viennese theorist, was to be realized in November, when Schubert worked at exercises in counterpoint which were not specifically Handelian in style or principle. But in March he conceded something to his knowledge of the Baroque composer, extracts from whose works appeared from time to time in concerts in Vienna, by writing a cantata called *Mirjams Siegesgesang* (Miriam's Song of Victory). Schubert admired 'Handel's mighty spirit', said Sonnleithner;[18] it is that spirit, rather than particularities of Handelian style, that one should look for in this rather weak stylistic hybrid, in which the ear is occasionally arrested by truly Schubertian gestures. The piece was written for solo soprano, four-part choir, and piano, but Schubert evidently planned to orchestrate the piano part.

The Fantasy in F minor for four hands was completed and written up in April, and played privately in May – with Lachner's help – to Bauernfeld, whose word for it was '*wunderbare*'.[19] Paganini gave several concerts in Vienna in 1828, and Schubert, who went to one of the earlier ones, took Bauernfeld to hear him on 4 May. Bauernfeld relates that he offered to pay for his ticket, but Schubert would not let him. 'I have stacks of money now – so come on!' The financial arrangements of the current inner circle – Bauernfeld, Schwind and Schubert – are revealingly described by Bauernfeld: 'Whoever was flush at the moment paid for the other, or for the others. Now it happened, from time to time, that two had no money and the third – not a penny! Naturally, among the three of us, it was Schubert who played the part of a Croesus and who, off and on, used to be swimming in money.'[20] Bauernfeld did well that night, for after the concert by the 'diabolically sublime violinist' Schubert stood him drinks at the inn, 'and a bottle more than usual was charged up to enthusiasm'.

And after saying goodnight to Bauernfeld, Schubert moved on to the Snail, where he celebrated with Franz von Hartmann.[21]

A miscellany of keyboard compositions was the product of May. First, there was the set of three piano pieces now known as *Drei Klavierstücke*, D.946. These could well have been called 'Impromptus', but Schubert left them untitled, as he had with previous short pieces, perhaps assuming that his publisher would add appropriate or marketable titles as before. In the event, they were not published until long after his death (1868), and then not by one of his regular firms. Then there were two movements for piano duet, the earnestly impassioned Allegro in A minor to which Diabelli gave the not inapt title *Lebensstürme* when he published it in 1840, and the serene Rondo in A.

The Rondo was Schubert's last work for piano duet, unless one allows an unusual piece written in the following month. On 3 June Schubert set off on a two-day excursion into the countryside south of Vienna with his composer friend, Lachner. They went by coach to Baden, where their host, one Herr Schickh, suggested that the following morning they should go to Heiligenkreuz, to hear the famous organ in the fine Cistercian monastery. Schubert suggested that Lachner and he should each compose a fugue to play there. The fugues were finished at midnight and the party duly drove off at 6 o'clock the next morning. The story comes from Lachner, who says that his Fugue in D minor and Schubert's in E minor were played in the presence of several monks.[22] Whether the piano duet version subsequently published by Diabelli originated from the composer is unknown, and it must be said that on paper it looks unpromising, thanks partly to the lack of dynamic markings. But a perceptive performance which ignores the editorial 'Allegro moderato' indication and adopts a suitably stately pace makes an impressive piece of it; and the extract given in Fig. 76 reminds us that if Schubert had been blessed with Beethoven's lifespan, he would not have lived long enough to see *Tristan und Isolde* but he might have seen *The Flying Dutchman*, *Tannhäuser* and *Lohengrin*.

Fig. 76

On the same day as the Heiligenkreuz visit, a music lecturer at the University of Breslau, J. T. Mosewius, wrote to Schubert complimenting him on *Die schöne Müllerin* and *Winterreise*.[23] And three days after his return to Vienna, a review in the *Wiener Zeitschrift für Kunst* extolled both the 'well-made and beautiful' *Winterreise* (Part I, which had appeared in January) and the Rondeau brilliant for violin and piano.[24] Towards the end of June, Franz Hartmann went with Schubert and others to Grinzing: his diary entry was succinct – 'All four tipsy, more or less, but Schubert especially.'[25] Spaun, commenting on the Kreissle biography of the composer after its appearance in 1864, referred to an occasion at Grinzing when he 'drank rather more than was good for him', but denied that a 'chance occurrence like that' was 'justification for charging him, who as a rule was extremely moderate, with intemperance'. He continued: 'When one considers how he composed every day from early morning until 2 o'clock in the afternoon, at white heat and to the point of exhaustion, one will find it understandable and, indeed, recognize it as forgivable that, after long walks and tired out by the heat of the day, he used to enjoy a glass of wine or beer. But of intemperance there was not a trace in him.'[26]

It was in June that the Mass in E flat was begun. The F major Mass of 1814 and this last setting of 1828 stand – as two disparate triumphs – at opposite ends of Schubert's career. The earlier work brought together many performers known to the seventeen-year-old boy and impressed them and the audience of important personages as the harbinger of an exceptional career as a composer. The E flat Mass marks both the climax and swansong of that career (as far as the composition of masses is concerned), and only fourteen years after its inauguration: it does so in contrasting privacy, though, for none of those present at Lichtental church in 1814 would hear it in Schubert's lifetime. If we compare it with the teenage effort we have to note an enlargement and sharpening of the imagination as well as commensurate development of technique, and this is perhaps most keenly appreciated in that movement in which the two settings spring from the same gestural germ, the Sanctus, for the later version has such an intense visionary quality in its harmonic thinking that knowledgeable music-lovers coming to it late doubt that it could have been written before 1830 at all. But comparison with an earlier mass is only half the story, for Schubert's growth as a man and musician, not just as a 'church composer', is what contributes to the enrichment witnessed here.

Schubert evidently had hopes of visiting Gmunden and Graz again this year. He made an enquiry of a potential host at Gmunden but never followed it up.[27] Various delays prevented Jenger and him from going to stay with the Pachlers in Graz during the summer, but the possibility was kept open until September, when Schubert came to a decision. Meanwhile, work on the Mass in E flat continued into July, and, perhaps as a gesture of solidarity with the Jewish community in Vienna who had suffered harsh deprivations and impositions under Maria Theresa but were now more liberally treated and had opened a new synagogue in the city in 1826, Schubert set the Hebrew text of Psalm 92 for baritone solo, SATB soloists and SATB choir. This work was dedicated to and perhaps commissioned by Salomon Sulzer, cantor at the synagogue, who may well have helped Schubert with the taxing task of setting Hebrew poetry – or 'poetical prose'.[28]

Although August appears a relatively barren month for Schubert, in that the catalogue of his works lists just one song as being completed, he also made a start on some settings of Rellstab and Heine (to be posthumously published as the *Schwanengesang*), and must surely have given some time to the flood of major masterpieces that were to carry a September date but could not have been conceived from first note to last in that short period. Two works bearing the same name date from this time. *Glaube, Hoffnung und Liebe*, a setting of a text by Reil for male-voice quartet, SATB choir and wind band, composed for the dedication service for the recast bell at Holy Trinity church on 2 September, short, regressive in style, and of no great moment, is not to be confused with *Glaube, Hoffnung und Liebe*, a beautiful song which is Schubert's only setting of the poet Christoff Kuffner. Faith, hope and love, the eternal threesome of human spiritual yearning, each have a stanza apiece (set strophically by Schubert), but Kuffner frames these with an introductory four-line verse whose return at the end of the song presents the four lines in a different order, so that the song ends as it began with the injunction to trust, hope and love: *glaube, hoffe, liebe!* Schubert gives these framing verses their own strophic relationship (but reverses the order of the two musical ideas at the return) so that the result is a strophic song within a strophic song.

Schubert's final decision on Graz was communicated to Jenger on 25 September – 'Nothing will come of the journey to Graz this year, as money and weather are wholly unfavourable.'[29] The explanation – money and weather – is a strange one. Does one cite the weather – in early autumn – as a reason for not going away, when one has no way of foreseeing the meteorological morrow? And as for money, Schubert's income for the year, from publications and from his March concert, had actually been well above average. Was he offering Jenger reasons? Or excuses? The real cause of Schubert's reluctance to travel was more likely to have been a deterioration in his health. He had been ill enough in August to consult the court physician, Dr Ernst Rinna, who recommended that he should move into his brother Ferdinand's apartment in the Wieden suburb. Ostensibly Wieden, then outside the city boundary and to the east of the Wien river, would give Schubert the benefit of purer air, but perhaps Rinna also saw an advantage in having a member of his family at hand. On 1 September

Schubert joined Ferdinand in what was then a new and damp building, now known as Kettenbrückengasse 6. The sanitary arrangements in this new part of Wieden were inadequate, even by the then prevailing standards. Without detailed records of changes in the composer's health during August and September it is not possible to verify the reports that he had been plagued by headaches, giddiness and worse. The fact remains that he did receive and take advice from Rinna. On the other hand, whatever symptoms were evident in September, he managed to conduct some sort of social life, and to bring to completion a batch of his finest works – the String Quintet and the last three piano sonatas.

Honest and open though Schubert tended to be with his friends, he may have had reason for keeping his current condition from Jenger. If he had been warned by Rinna that the medical outlook was not good, he perhaps wished to banish such prospects from his own mind – and therefore from his communications with others. Although he had referred to his troubles periodically since their onset in early 1823 or late 1822 (and most particularly in the letter to Kupelwieser in March 1824, which was perhaps the worst moment of realization), for much of the time he suffered, worked and lived without dwelling on his ills. If this was part of a stoic determination to pursue life's goals come what may, that well-tested resolve was surely the key to his continued (if not heightened) productivity in his final autumn, and to his enjoyment of friends' company whenever that was possible. Of course, Rinna will have required his fee; indeed the claim of financial difficulties in the letter of 25 September to Jenger might have been genuine if Schubert suspected that the professional services of physicians were destined to place an increasing burden on his purse.

Two days before he moved to Wieden, Schubert had the Hartmann brothers as drinking companions for the last time, before they returned to Linz. On 5 September he attended the première of Bauernfeld's play *Der Brautwerber* (The Suitor), which was a flop. If he met his friends at inns or coffee-houses in the following weeks, as seems likely, such meetings went unrecorded as the Hartmanns had left Vienna at the end of August. Strangely, in the very letter in which he called off the Graz trip, he responded affirmatively to an invitation from Jenger to a musical party at the home of Dr Ignaz Menz, at which Schönstein would sing. And even stranger is the fact that in early October he went on a three-day walking tour to Eisenstadt in Hungary, to visit Haydn's grave, with Ferdinand and two friends. This excursion could have been recommended by Rinna, who believed in the therapy of exercise, and if, as Deutsch suggests, Rinna also wanted Ferdinand to go with Schubert, this points to a possibility that Rinna had advised against Schubert going to Graz with Jenger.'[30]

It is tempting to refer to the three piano sonatas Schubert now completed as an imposing final trilogy that recalls the genesis of Mozart's last three symphonies in a short period of three months. But in both cases 'trilogy' is a misleading term. Mozart's symphonies are individual works, quite different in character, intended to stand alone and losing nothing by doing so. So with the Schubert sonatas: the C minor is a dynamic, probing and highly original work, not to be dismissed as Beethovenian for all that the flattery of imitation at the outset is so explicit; the A major is a consummation of the lyrical urges never absent for long in earlier sonatas, now given unprecedented space to work themselves out, inside a 'frame' provided by the majestic pillars of the opening returning at the end; and the B flat quietly asserts an elevated, measured, transcendental presence from the start, reflects – from its lofty plane – much of the composer's accumulated musical experience, and assimilates sharp contrasts between movements, yet never sheds the aura of sublimity with which its opening was bathed. There is little doubt that these three masterpieces were taking shape in Schubert's mind at the same time as the String Quintet in C. That being so, one's aesthetic perception that the slow movements of the B flat Sonata and the Quintet flow from the same emotional wellspring – finding expression in similar musical textures – gains biographical reinforcement. The outer movements of the Quintet also share with the first movement of the B flat Sonata an unhurried pulse which easily accommodates a wide range of rhythmic activity, from the statuesque to the hyperactive. But the unique feature of the Quintet is its pioneering of a medium – with two cellos rather than Mozart's two violas – that could be called new, in that Boccherini's two-cello quintets are idiosyncratic creations with a concertante first cello part to show off Boccherini's own cello playing rather than exemplars of a true chamber-music genre.

The other works with whose genesis that of the last chamber works is interleaved are songs – the Rellstab and Heine settings grouped by Haslinger as *Schwanengesang*, to which *Die Taubenpost* (Pigeon Post) (October) was added. There is no reason not to savour these songs individually as self-contained artefacts, the best of them showing that Schubert still had something as questingly original and inspired to say within a time-span of from two to five minutes as in expanded multi-movement forms. The potent atmospherics of *Der Doppelgänger* and *Der Atlas* point forwards to the expressive world of later Romantic generations, *Die Stadt* (The Town) is an impressionistic tone-poem even more ahead of its time, and *Ihr Bild* (Her Picture) could not be surpassed in its application of Mozartian economy of note and gesture to the expression of Romantic heartache.

Der Hirt auf dem Felsen, another product of October, creates a category of its own, having a foot in the chamber-music camp and another in the Lieder camp without belonging wholly to either. The frankly melodious style and the formal alternations of the protagonists seem to point to an earlier date than 1828. Yet Frank Ruppert has seen the song as a final farewell to life, and at the same time a greeting. 'Life is agony. The singer is ready to move on.' In the final section ('Spring will come'), the new and higher life beckons. 'Spring is coming. Yet the spring is death, or at least must be approached through death ... Schubert is ready to wander away!'[31] Given that interpretation, the song stands more credibly in the month before Schubert's own death.

On the last day of October, Schubert dined at the Red Cross, close to the Schubert family home in the Himmelpfortgrund and often used by them. He ate fish, which made him feel ill. While this is often taken to mark the beginning of the final illness, Bauernfeld implies that there had been similar instances before. Commenting on the fact that in early November he 'complained of lack of appetite and had felt unwell', he adds: 'but this happened from time to time and we attached no importance to it.'[32] He recovered from this fish meal sufficiently to hear a requiem by his brother Ferdinand four days later, following this with a three-hour walk with Josef Mayssen. It was on the day after this that he went to Simon Sechter's residence to begin a study of counterpoint, with Josef Lanz as his fellow-pupil. This was to be what we would call a 'refresher course', for Schubert had already proved himself an adroit contrapuntist, as works such as the D minor String Quartet, the 'Wanderer' Fantasy, and the Fantasy in F minor for piano duet demonstrate. The more formal fugal demands traditionally imposed by the mass had been less confidently met by Schubert, it is true, and the study with Sechter seems to have addressed that discipline while also concerning itself with those techniques, such as invertible counterpoint and canon, which are serviceable in any context, not just in the formal fugue.

When Spaun called to let Schubert check a copy he had been asked to make of Psalm 23 (D.706) for a ladies' choral society in Lemberg, Schubert did what was required and is reported to have said: 'There is really nothing the matter with me, only I am so exhausted I feel as if I were going to fall through the bed.'[33] When the second lesson with Sechter was due, on 10 or 11 November, Lanz turned up alone and told Sechter that Schubert was very ill.[34] On 12 November Schubert wrote to Schober: 'I am ill. I have eaten nothing for eleven days and drunk nothing, and I totter feebly and shakily from my chair to bed and back again. Rinna is treating me. If ever I take anything, I bring it up again at once.'[35] In the same letter, Schubert asked Schober to bring more volumes of Fenimore Cooper, other than those he had already read (*The Last of the Mohicans*, *The Spy*, *The Pilot* and *The Pioneers*, all in German translation). Schönstein's account of a supper party he gave for Schubert and friends 'about ten days before [Schubert's] death' and 'several evenings' after the fish supper (therefore, about 6–10 November) may be inaccurate, for he referred to the 'large amount of wine' Schubert drank that evening, whereas in his letter to

Schober on 12 November Schubert said that for eleven days he had drunk nothing.[36]

There is an unconfirmed report that on 14 November Beethoven's String Quartet in C sharp minor was played to the now bedridden Schubert.[37] Rinna fell ill himself, and called in Josef von Vering, who had written books on the treatment of syphilis. On 16 November there was a bedside conference between Vering and Johann Wisgrill, and a new course of treatment was prescribed. Schubert kept a pocket-watch hung on a chair by his bed to ensure that the doses of medicine were taken at the time intervals advised. According to Gerhard von Breuning, Vering's nephew, Vering had already told him on the day he took over the case (16 November at the latest) that he had 'no hope of being able to save Schubert', because of 'advanced disintegration of the blood corpuscles'.[38]

Schubert's thirteen-year-old half-sister Josefa had been helping to nurse him, along with Ferdinand's wife Anna. Other nurses were brought in, on a rota basis. On 17 November, Bauernfeld and Lachner visited Schubert, Bauernfeld to discuss *Der Graf von Gleichen*. That evening Schubert was 'violently and continuously delirious'.[39] Spaun, who visited him during these last days, tells us that when he fell into delirium he 'sang ceaselessly', and when he was lucid he corrected the proofs of the second part of *Winterreise*.[40] On 18 November Schubert had to be restrained in his bed. The next day (19 November) Schubert's devout father wrote to his son Ferdinand, in whose apartment the composer lay, urging fortitude, but by 3 o'clock in the afternoon Schubert was dead.

The death certificate gave the cause of Schubert's death as *Nervenfieber*. This has been taken to indicate one of two conditions, between which later periods would have made a distinction: typhus, or typhoid fever.[41] Deutsch accepted this verdict, attributed the condition to Schubert's obesity, an inclination to alcoholism, and the poor water and sanitary conditions in the Wieden district. More recently this view has been challenged. Eric Sams has demonstrated that the term *Nervenfieber* applied to a distinct condition not covered by typhus ('a louse-born plague of infested jails and slums') or typhoid fever ('a disease of polluted water-supply'). It 'denoted a critical impairment of the higher nervous centres, for example by delirium or stupor'. Sams finds neither Schubert's symptoms nor the treatment prescribed for him to be reconcilable with his being a typhus or typhoid fever victim: but tertiary syphilis would have been a sustainable diagnosis. The 'advanced disintegration [decomposition] of the blood' would have signalled the deteriorative anaemia that characterizes tertiary syphilis.[42] The feeling of being poisoned, which Schubert experienced during his October fish supper and a few years earlier at Zseliz, could have been a product of the insomnia, giddiness and headaches caused by mercury poisoning, mercury being a standard medication administered to syphilis sufferers. D. Kerner considered the cause of death to be brain syphilis – 'the occlusion of a cerebral artery, whether basal or in the *fossa sylvii* region'.[43] 'Among the possible causes of death in the tertiary stage,' writes Sams, 'modern textbooks mention arterial narrowing or occlusion of a major vessel . . . or endarteritis of a main cerebral artery leading to ischaemic stroke.' Fever and brain damage would be evident, and these were 'precisely the syndrome known as *Nervenfieber*'.[44] Since the tertiary stage of syphilis may be reached anything from three to ten years after infection,[45] there is no difficulty in diagnosing the third stage in Schubert's case, five or six years after infection. If this deduction brings us to the truth, there would be no reason to think that Schubert's family or friends would have wished to be more explicit as to the root cause of the problem, since venereal diseases carried a stigma at this time, and for long after.

Dr Robert Kurth observes that *Nervenfieber* would have been used by a physician at the time of Schubert's death not as an etiologic diagnosis but rather a descriptive clinical syndrome with probably diverse causes. This would not be incompatible with the observable features during the terminal events of neurovascular syphilis. Despite the strong case for Schubert's tertiary syphilis, he postulates as an alternative 'a combination of malnutrition, the effects of alcoholism, possible immuno-suppression followed by an acute infectious disease of one type or another'.[46] This latter possibility gains support from Professor Peter Gilroy Bevan, who avers that the advanced stages of syphilis would have triggered an immune deficiency syndrome of the kind associated with modern AIDS.[47]

A contrary view is expressed by Dr Anton Neumayr, who considers it likely that Schubert was cured of syphilis. He holds that the symptoms and treatment documented in Schubert's case are compatible with a diagnosis of typhoid fever. The headaches referred to at Graz in 1827 would have been attributable to long hours of work in poor lighting with glasses which 'did not properly correct for his nearsightedness'. The short-lived pains in the arm in 1824 were probably caused by over-exertion, and the short periods of indisposition in 1825 and 1826 'could have resulted from some completely banal illness'. He states that typhoid fever was endemic (the word 'epidemic' is avoided) in Vienna's outlying communities at the time.[48] Incidentally, Neumayr believes that Schober caught venereal disease at the same time as Schubert, and was cured (he lived into his eighties).[49] Neumayr does not explain why a specialist in syphilis (Josef von Vering) was in attendance during the last week; nor does he refer to Vering's diagnosis of 'advanced disintegration of the blood'. Hans D. Kiemle believes that Schubert died of mercury poisoning and that his brothers Ignaz and Ferdinand and sister Maria Theresia died of the same, the toxin being passed to all of them as embryos from their mother, whose own death, like that of her father, was also attributable to this cause.[50]

Schubert died on a Wednesday. Two days later, on Friday 21 November, a funeral service was held at the parish church of St Joseph, Margareten, where the burial would also have taken place if Ferdinand had not intervened, through a letter written to his father early on the Friday, to convey what he saw as the composer's wishes as to interment. Ferdinand told his father that on the evening before he died, Franz – in a half-conscious state – had said to him: 'I implore you to transfer me to my room, not to leave me here, in this corner under the earth; do I then deserve no place above the earth?' Ferdinand had answered: 'Dear Franz, rest assured, believe your brother Ferdinand, whom you have always trusted, and who loves you so much. You are in the room in which you have always been so far, and lie in your bed!' And Franz is reported to have said: 'No, it is not true: Beethoven does not lie here.'[51] Ferdinand had taken this to indicate a wish to be buried at the Währing cemetery, where Beethoven's body lay. After what must have been a hasty rearrangement, there at Währing, in bad weather, Schubert's remains were duly laid to rest. Schober wrote a special poem to be sung to the music of Schubert's own song *Pax vobiscum* at the service at St Joseph's. Set for choir and wind instruments, it was naturally enough – two days after the loss — a lament for a departed friend, whose giving of roses in life had been reciprocated by Fate with thorns, rather than an attempt to pay homage to his life's work.

Other tributes, from wider perspectives, followed in time – in both printed word and organized celebration. There was a memorial service at the Augustiner church in the heart of Vienna on 23 December, and a monument was raised by subscription in 1830. Grillparzer's famous inscription – 'The art of music here entombed a rich possession, but even fairer hopes' – was but one of a series of expressions in poetry and prose by his friends in the months following Schubert's death. It would be hard to conceive of a more apt epitaph, a masterpiece of poetic truth and compression reminding one of those tiniest gems among Schubert's own songs. Yet Grillparzer could not have known how rich a possession music had lost – not because the judgement of posterity has to be awaited for a true evaluation, but because many of Schubert's most significant works will have been unknown to him. Nor could he have understood, as later generations were to do in a crescendo which has not yet reached its peak, just what fairer hopes were consigned to the soil. Similarly, when Bauernfeld penned three stanzas on the deaths of both Beethoven and Schubert, observing that 'music's glorious reign is over',[52] he could not have known that from the standpoint of distant posterity the close of the third decade of the nineteenth century could indeed be seen to mark the end of a musical dynasty, to which Haydn and Mozart also belong.

The Late Church Music

In the middle years of Schubert's life a number of major projects proved problematical to him. In the case of the Mass in A flat, he spent three years (from 1819 to 1822) at work on it, and even then felt impelled to revise it four years later, in 1826. *Lazarus*, begun in 1820, was never finished at all. There were problems with symphonies, the B minor Symphony being the fourth in a row of symphonic efforts from 1818 to 1822 that were abandoned. And the String Quartet in C minor was set aside early in its slow movement during 1820. One explanation must be that this was a period of transition which caused him some stylistic unease. Schubert's style never developed so rapidly as in the years 1818 to 1822. It was a time of high aspiration, as he tried to move on from a long-practised teenage style and stretch his technique and imagination to realize more probing, personal visions. He seemed to lose patience if he met with obstacles in the progress on a work, and once he had set something aside for even a short time he presumably saw it as yesterday's casualty when he had his sights fixed resolutely on tomorrow's challenge. Miraculously, the Mass in A flat survived this harsh, self-inflicted process of filtration, and it will be appropriate to ask why.

Another element in what was undoubtedly a compound problem lay in the nature of the works undertaken. The first movement of the C minor Quartet, the only one finished, was a movement *sui generis*: listeners who know it well as a stand-alone piece but have never thought to enquire as to its provenance are sometimes surprised to learn that it was in fact conceived as a first movement. The innovatory nature of the first movement of the 'Unfinished' Symphony, in which the cellos and basses lead the ear into uncharted areas of human thought, would pose the same problem as the Quartettsatz: how does one play the game through to a successful conclusion when the goalposts have just been moved, even if one moved them oneself? In the Mass in A flat the *terra firma* of many a juvenile mass was being decisively overstepped, and there may well have been a need for reassurance as the ideas came to him. As for *Lazarus*, here was a new genre for Schubert – in fact in essential respects a new one for a composer of any time: and it stimulated from him invention that not only looked forwards but also looked inwards – into the peculiar expressive world of a text which bears certain pre-echoes of *The Dream of Gerontius*. This was not a recipe for the debonair confidence and momentum that had propelled many a youthful symphony, sonata, quartet, or mass through to its last double-bar.

Lazarus, or *The Feast of the Resurrection*, has been variously called an Easter cantata, a religious drama and an oratorio – a sure sign of its generic waywardness. The poem by A. H. Niemeyer, based on the Gospel according to St John (chapter 11, verses 1–45), is in three 'acts' (*Handlungen*), concerned respectively with the death, burial and resurrection of Lazarus. Schubert completed the first act and much of the second. There is no trace of the remainder and it is almost certain that the work was left unfinished. There are six characters, and the score bears stage directions. It is not easy to visualize a staged performance of *Lazarus*, but the notion of the work as a kind of 'sacred opera' should be allowed to challenge the designation most widely accepted: 'oratorio'. Some of the conventions adopted by Schubert are operatic ones, and there is no doubt that he accepted Niemeyer's appellation of his text as a 'sacred drama' (and drama without action, as Niemeyer wrote in his preface, is not drama at all).

The tradition of applying dramatic principles to a biblical story, to allow performance in church of 'theatrical' music while the theatres were closed in Lent, was of course a long one. But Schubert was not simply transferring techniques of opera construction from the pit to the nave. The divisions between recitative and aria are not always obvious, and an arioso middle ground is the arena for much of the 'action'. Given the novelty of this approach within the context of Viennese Classicism, the death and burial of Lazarus found a ready creative response in Schubert, but perhaps his resurrection did not. Had he, in a burst of innovative zeal, bitten off more than he could chew? The first two acts display a combination of delicacy and radiance unique in Schubert's oeuvre. Einstein justly referred to 'a shimmer of transfiguration',[1] which Maurice Brown attributed in part to a self-denying restriction to diatonic harmony.[2] As a step along the road to music-drama, Einstein dared to claim that Lazarus far surpasses *Tannhäuser* and *Lohengrin*.[3] In it, Schubert also stumbled upon a (for him) individual coloration and atmosphere, as did Elgar confronting a similar subject in *The Dream of Gerontius* eighty years later.

Recitative can in other contexts sound perfunctory or merely convenient, but there is little of that here. If we see the work as a part of operatic history, then it points clearly forwards to the 'through-composed' operas of the later nineteenth century, in which set pieces are hard to find. This structural outcome arises from Schubert's determination to follow implicitly the dramatic unfolding of the text, without imposing formulaic musical strategies upon it. And this same objective drives the bar-by-bar

musical invention, which is pliant, changeable, and impelled by a desire
for dramatic observance and continuity so strong that the ideas seem rather
self-effacing, so that – although one could not say the music is not tuneful
– there is little in the way of themes that one would pick out and carry
home with one after a performance. Not that some expressive details, such
as Fig. 77 from the first act where the dying Lazarus sings 'with feeble
voice' in the garden of a rustic house, do not linger obstinately in the
mind. Indeed Schubert's absorption, and apparent empathy, shows itself
in music which has a purity, grace, and gentle warmth that is largely of
its own, with a turn of phrase that one can say is characteristic of *Lazarus*,
although because of the freedom from formula it is easier to define it as
an idiosyncratic fragrance than to distil it in objective, let alone analytical,
terms.

Fig. 77

Did Schubert abandon this novel undertaking because he could not
conceive how the concept of 'climax' in musical terms could be applied
to his so far arguably amorphous score – as it presumably must in the later
stages? Or because some worldly interruption broke the spell and he could
not find his way back into the delicately flavoured individual world he
had thus far created? Or is Walther Dürr right that Schubert saw death as
perfection, as a goal, as a friend (as in the song *Der Tod und das Mädchen*)
and there was no place for resurrection? 'How can one rise from infinity
and return to imperfection?'[4] The obvious objection to that view would
be that Schubert knew the third act depicted the resurrection of Lazarus
before he began composing. Or perhaps the implied corollary is that Schubert's view of death became more sharply defined as he worked on the

death and burial of Lazarus in the first and second acts. Whatever the explanation, a unique part of Schubert's creative self remains embodied in a musical torso which can never be made complete (for no surrogate hand could square the circle, although Niemeyer's complete text survives) – failing a miraculous rediscovery of lost treasure.

Schubert eventually finished his Mass in A flat just before Beethoven completed his *Missa Solemnis*. The spirituality of the Beethoven, informed by the contrapuntal and rhythmic freedoms of the fifty-year-old's third period, is in contrast to the more Romantic approach of the Schubert, with its sharp harmonic focus and exploitation of key colour. But pointing to the individuality of the Schubert is not a way of excusing him for not producing a monumental, challenging document to match Beethoven's. The Mass in A flat does not yield up its treasure easily, but when it does one is tempted to see it as a provocatively original piece that stands to the Beethoven rather as the G major String Quartet stands to the late Beethoven quartets. Schubert's readiness to put more of himself into it up to seven years after the seed was first sown was not for nothing.

If, when one first hears the Kyrie, one is tempted to dismiss it as an example of soft-centred sweet lyricism which doesn't go far beyond that of the slighter *Salve Regina* in A of 1819, to be discouraged would be a mistake. If, however, the performance is anything short of superb – in this or the later movements – one can only resolve to reserve judgement and wait for the next opportunity. A chorus tenor line which wavers from just intonation, or soloists who only visit the centre of a note en route through a wide vibrato, or orchestral soloists who lack concentration or control for one moment seem to be able to do more damage to this work than any other of Schubert's. Only the ultimate in poise and discipline will do.

Lyrical though the Kyrie is, with touches of mild chromaticism recalling *Lazarus*, it has a certain reserve, its gentle choral phrases interwoven with equally gentle string and wind colour. Schubert follows the convention of allotting the central section, 'Christe eleison', to the vocal soloists, but brings back the soloists to initiate an unusually extended coda which lays to rest both the 'Christe' (solo) and 'Kyrie' (choral) elements.

The Gloria is impelled by a new kind of energy. True, the athletic hyperactivity of the violins is not entirely new in a Schubert Gloria, but the variations in texture coupled with some refreshingly unhackneyed juxtapositions of chords which are perfectly ordinary when viewed as separate entities does generate a special atmosphere. Schubert brings his orchestra up to full strength for this movement, adding a flute, two trumpets and three trombones, and subdivides the lengthy text into four main sections. The initial 'Gloria' section sets off exuberantly in a remote E major, includes an episode for the soloists (at 'Laudamus te'), and is given a circular unity by the ensuing repetition, on Schubert's part, of 'Gloria in excelsis

Deo'. At the change of tempo (to andantino) and key (to A major), first and second violins introduce a setting of 'Gratias agimus' for the soloists. The use of solo voices is traditional here, but Schubert creates a neat three-part structure to this section by assigning 'Domine Deus, Rex coelestis' to the chorus in the minor and forging a kind of development section in which choral interjections are interspersed with the continuing 'Gratias agimus' entries of the soloists in a succession of keys, before the original 'Gratias agimus' theme of the soloists returns.

A new theme in C sharp minor serves as the basis of the third part of the movement (Allegro moderato), encompassing the series of petitions beginning 'Domine Deus, Agnus Dei, qui tollis peccata mundi'. For each of the three petitions, a soloist leads and the choir reinforces the final entreaty, 'miserere nobis'. The temperature cools considerably, until the striking 'Tu solus altissimus', from which point the invention moves on to a new plane – until the final 'Cum Sancto Spiritu' fugue takes off. E major has returned for this fourth section. Inevitably, fugue, because it depends to a perceptible extent on contrapuntal formula however imaginative its composer may be, prompts a smile (or sigh?) of recognition in the listener. Although, like all fugues in Classical masses, this one tends to sound neo-Baroque, what is less obvious here is the tendency for it to retain its narrow thematic focus and sustain a texture and dynamic almost single-mindedly from beginning to end. Schubert is not slave to fugal convention or strictness: he varies the texture and admits gestural variety early on, as though he has just learned lessons from Handel. Nor is the harmonic path at all obvious. The subject is not overworked, and its fresh entries in the later stages have an exciting impact. Perhaps the final stretto is somewhat to formula, but the ending builds to a magnificent climax *sui generis*. One is left in no doubt by this far from routine close to a highly original movement that Schubert believed in fugue as an unsurpassed means of consummating a Gloria. And only for this one movement did he use the device in this convention-defying mass.

As though exploiting contrasting registrations on an organ, Schubert presents the first chord of the Credo in three successive pitch and timbre combinations – for low brass, for higher woodwind and trumpet mix, and for choral voices in a reined-in register expressive of humility. So he imparts to his opening a Brucknerian perspective which lights the movement as a whole. The variety of choral and orchestral groupings, the wonderful surges of colour at 'Et incarnatus', the high-low alternations with divisi choral scoring – these face two ways, pointing to Bruckner's inheritance from the Venetian polychoral style of the Gabrielis. The alert ear will detect a parade of shifting colours, some of a vividness prophetic of Berlioz. There are moments of perverse individuality, and at times a contrapuntal toughness that is quite different from Beethoven's. This blend of ingredients

enriches the slow core of the Credo — the 'Et incarnatus' and 'Crucifixus'
— as never before. Fig. 78 samples the eight-part choral sonority, shows
minor firmly supplanting major at 'Crucifixus', and displays in its last bar
the tortuous, indeed torturous, theme by which is conveyed the pain of
the cross. The whiff of Romanticism often infiltrates late Schubert, but
seldom does he peer beyond old horizons as he does here. When the
arrival of the 'Et resurrexit' has brought a reprise of the opening, newly
enlivened by the tireless motion of the violins, there is even something
approaching Verdian drama at 'vivos et mortuos'. But the movement ends
with the bright, festive C major implicit in its beginning, although not
without piercing shafts of harmonic colour on the way.

Fig. 78

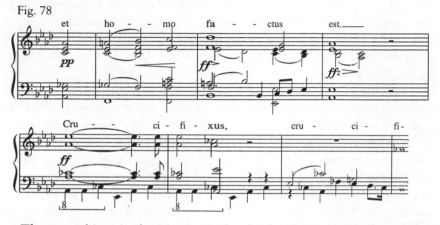

There are things in the Mass in A flat that hardly touch Schubert's other
works at all. It is the kind of piece in which one asks, at each successive
thrill or shock, whether that one is not the most original of all. Is the
boldest invention of all, then, what now follows in the Sanctus? A soft F
major chord is transmuted, by an ambivalent intervening step, into the
awesome, engulfing F sharp minor one with which the choir enters. Twice
again the process is repeated, minor chords of unexpected allegiance suddenly looming from limbo. Something settled and melodious comes only
with the 'Pleni sunt coeli', underpinned by persistent trumpet and drum
rhythms. The tripping 'Osanna' sounds at first like a chorus of shepherd-
esses, but is soon affected by the unique atmosphere of the preceding
movements. The Benedictus offers more that must have stirred Bruckner,
with its modulating sequences over a walking bass, while the threefold
petition of the Agnus Dei allows a threefold hearing of its stream of inspired
melodic and harmonic invention, dramatized by finely judged effects of
crescendo and diminuendo. But the melting modulation which enables it
to cadence in a distant key each time is heard only twice, so that special
preparation for the 'Dona nobis' is possible. As in Haydn's masses and
Beethoven's Mass in C (much loved by Schubert), this last section brings

a musical lightening of the atmosphere, but the cut and dried four-bar regularity of its progress, seeming at first to prepare us too suddenly to re-enter the real, secular world, is soon modified by individual and devotional touches which reflect the character of the opening Kyrie and keep the work true to itself until the last chord fades into silence.

Before his next and last mass, Schubert returned to some texts previously set and explored several new ones. Of the later settings of the *Tantum ergo*, that in D (D.750) is remarkable for the bold way in which it fans out from its initial unison, as though it is in D minor; but the sovereign key is to be D major, and Schubert juxtaposes the two modes more daringly than ever, and with slightly disorienting effect. The close, on the other hand, has a dark richness that calls to mind Tchaikovsky. The *Tantum ergo* in E flat composed in Schubert's last year is an attractive version for soloists, choir and orchestra, in which instrumental colours contribute as much as eloquent vocal phrases to the simple devotional beauty. The *Salve Regina* in C (D.811) presents its text twice over, as do a number of Schubert's shorter church works, but the second presentation is not quite so eventful as the first, especially in its middle section which is less interesting harmonically. Like the better-known setting of Psalm 23, it depends for its effect on immaculate singing with perfect intonation. These slighter works, although they often seem to have cost little creative effort, sometimes divulge points of interest in relation to the major works. The *Hymnus an den heiligen Geist* (Hymn to the Holy Ghost), for example, closes with a cadence which anticipates the close of the trio in the third movement of the String Quintet in C quite unmistakably. For those already familiar with the Schubert mainstream, then, these smaller tributaries offer their delights, prompting many a knowing smile.

The Offertory *Intende voci* was probably the last of such pieces, and like the Mass in E flat and the last *Tantum ergo* in E flat was probably written for the Church of the Holy Trinity at Alsergrund, where Beethoven's funeral had taken place. Scored for solo tenor, choir and orchestra, it does not carry specific echoes of other works so much as it projects the idiomatic Schubert familiar to us into a new medium – a new medium at least in the sense that the oboe is singled out for soloistic treatment, often becoming the tenor's *alter ego*, and there are some wonderful gleams of trombone colour, so that a coda flecked by the merest wisps of oboe and trombone timbre makes a fitting end. Written only a month or so before Schubert's death, it is a happy offering with a spring in its step – especially when the cellos and basses break out in pizzicato. Other pieces are of interest because they reflect the influence of local church personalities. J. P. Neumann, who wrote the libretto for Schubert's opera *Sakuntala*, was one of Vienna's more liberal-minded churchmen, who encouraged the provision of simple music to appeal to the widest possible congregation. The *Deutsche Messe*

(German Mass) which he commissioned from Schubert is a set of eight hymns with epilogue, written in a block-chordal style that one imagines was very much the tune called by the one who paid the piper. A different tune was required for the Jewish synagogue officially inaugurated in the Seitenstettengasse in 1826. Here the moving force was Salomon Sulzer, the warm-hearted cantor who inspired admiration and affection beyond his congregation and indeed outside the city limits, later breaking down even the anti-semitic tendencies of Liszt.[5] Sulzer was renowned as a singer, and sang Schubert's *Der Wanderer* to the composer's warmest approval. The work Schubert wrote for him (possibly to a commission) was a setting of Psalm 92 ('It is a good thing to give thanks unto the Lord'). Schubert wrote for baritone solo, solo SATB quartet and choir; but more significantly, it was the Hebrew text he chose to set. In matters of declamation, according to Elaine Brody, he must have had Sulzer's help, since he treats the non-metrical Hebrew with such skill.[6] Interestingly enough, in coming to terms with the idiosyncrasies of the Hebrew Schubert did not have to compromise his style unduly, as a hearing of his Psalm 92 in German translation demonstrates.

It is not known what prompted Schubert to compose his Mass in E flat in the summer of 1828 less than six months before his death. Nor do external reasons for its composition have to be sought. The inner compulsion to compose accounts for a weighty fraction of the life's work, and a mass was by now as credible an outlet for that urge as was a symphony, a sonata or song. He had shown his commitment to the genre by his extended labours on the Mass in A flat, and through that work had brought the mass into that group of media in which he could reveal his mature creative personality as truly – if in different directions – as in the orchestral, chamber, keyboard and other vocal genres that excited his pen.

Schubert's last mass displays a curious mixture of self-limitation and libertarianism. On the one hand, he curtailed the role of solo voices, chose a far more restricted range of keys for his six movements than he had in the Mass in A flat, dispensed with flutes altogether, and revived the convention of fugal counterpoint at the places in the text from which he had banished it in the previous work. On the other, he allowed himself new textual omissions and restructuring, and gave his wayward harmonic urges their head. As usual, the reference to 'unam sanctam catholicam Ecclesiam' in the Credo is gone. So is 'Patrem omnipotentem', 'genitum, non factum' and 'consubstantialem Patri'. These deviations – whether the result of religious conviction, oversight, or artistic strategy – have caused more problems for ecclesiastical posterity than they probably did in the liberal atmosphere known to Schubert in Biedermeier Vienna. At any rate, they did not stand in the way of a church performance at Holy Trinity in the Viennese suburb of Alsergrund within the year after Schubert's death.

It has to be said from the start that anyone who has been introduced to this work through membership of a choral society which performed it with organ or piano accompaniment is at a singular disadvantage. The choral writing can only 'breathe' through its orchestral setting, which is the core of the work's being as much as anything else is. That truism applies to most music for choir and orchestra, of course, but what is at risk in this mass is exceptional. Parts of the work, including its opening, can sound sentimental, and others can fall flat, if the sonic panoply that was in Schubert's ear is not transmitted to the listener's. Even an E flat chord is something specially vibrant with the mix of orchestral and choral sound he could impart to it.

The Kyrie, which demonstrates the point at every turn, dispenses with the orthodoxy of a 'Christe' section assigned to solo voices in more intimate petition. Rather, the chorus at this point imparts a special urgency to the words, rising to new dynamic and pitch levels. We may even hear 'life's storms' behind the passage, since it is a reincarnation of the distinctive second subject of *Lebensstürme* for piano duet, composed in the month before this Kyrie. It is not long before the throbbing triplets of the 'Christe' subside into the hushed reverence of the 'Kyrie', a varied reprise of which leads to a valedictory coda.

The opening section of the Gloria points, in its harmonic juxtapositions and scoring, to paths along which the mass was to develop in the hands of Bruckner. (The opening of the Credo of the Mass in C seems to have provided the germ.) In these first pages Schubert achieves a notable diversity of character and pace. This can only be an illusion where pace is concerned, since there is no change of tempo: the illusion is effected by variation in the degree of energy implicit in the harmonic rhythm and in the melodic contour, among other things. Thus the earnest fervour of 'Gloria in excelsis Deo', its vitality clinched by the rocketing first entry of the violins, gives way to a serenely solemn 'Adoramus te' and a dance-like 'Gratias agimus tibi'. The tempo then changes at 'Domine Deus, Agnus Dei', within which consistent tempo come further strong contrasts, as the menacing power of 'Domine Deus' – introduced by a chant-like strain in the brass in G minor almost as forbidding as the Dies irae – yields to the soft supplication of 'miserere nobis' in lightly accompanied choral harmony. A climax of some vehemence is reached (with the only triple forte marking in the whole Gloria) before the 'Quoniam' reinstates the opening material of the movement.

The reprise at 'Quoniam' is followed by a long final 'Cum Sancto Spiritu' fugue. Its subject is based on that of Bach's E major Fugue from Book 2 of the 'Forty-eight' (Fig. 79a). But Bach's pithy subject is not half long enough for Schubert's 'Cum Sancto Spiritu in gloria Dei Patris, amen', so Schubert adds a sequence of it and a further extension besides (Fig.

Fig. 79 a

Cum   san - cto   Spi - ri - tu   in   glo - ri - a   De - i

Pa-   tris,   a - - - -   men

79b). It is, accordingly, a long–limbed fugue; and it would be a rare performance in which it were not too long. Some stretches of creeping chromaticism add colour but do nothing to instil purpose. When Schubert later tightens things up in a stretto, the entries are still only following each other at Bach's original distance (Fig. 80a), while the close stretto towards the end of Schubert's fugue (Fig. 80b) exploits compatibilities used by Bach less than a quarter way through his (Fig. 80c).

Fig. 80 a

Schubert later moves things on to a higher imaginative plane in time for an impressive close, but by then many pages have been filled. His problems with fugue were most acute in choral fugues, and particularly in their early middle stages, where the need to accommodate fixed verbal phrases inhibited the free growth of counterpoint. Outside the choral sphere, as the last section of the Fantasy in F minor for piano duet (written earlier in this last year) should remind us, the problems virtually disappeared.

Schubert sets the whole of the Credo up to the 'Et incarnatus' as one section, on one pool of melodic material, with the opening drum roll returning to link its several components. One could not call the opening a robust affirmation of faith: rather, there is a touch of cosy *Gemütlichkeit*. But this is surely an attempt to obviate the all too familiar syndrome of two loud and fast movements meeting each other head-on. Judged as a successor to the Gloria in concert (i.e. non-liturgical) performance, this

Credo begins refreshingly. For the 'Et incarnatus' vocal soloists are introduced for the first time, two tenors and soprano sharing a theme which owes something to one in the slow introduction to Schubert's *Rosamunde* Overture. The three solo voices behave strictly as in a round, and it is hard to resist the thought that Schubert had in mind the similarly round-like precedent of the 'Et incarnatus' of Haydn's *Heiligmesse*. With no change of time or tempo a choral 'Crucifixus' ensues. Unlike the 'Et incarnatus' it speaks to us through harmony more than through melody, and if the debt to the Rex tremendae of Mozart's *Requiem* is coincidental, the coincidence is perhaps a meaningful one. One can see, then, why Schubert alternates the 'Et incarnatus' with the 'Crucifixus' once more, to make more mileage of their effective contrast. As this second 'Crucifixus' subsides, in its final 'sepultus est', nothing but a complete break can clear the way for the reprise of the opening of the movement at 'Et resurrexit'. Another extended fugue follows at 'Et vitam venturi saeculi'. As in the Gloria, Schubert manages an impressive close after over-long stretches without textural relief. On reviewing these two closing fugues in the Mass in E flat, one cannot but conclude that these closes were better contrived in the Mass in A flat (through a better fugue, or no fugue at all) and that it was partly because of dissatisfaction with these choral fugues that Schubert sought advice on counterpoint later in the year from Simon Sechter.

When he came to the Sanctus, would Schubert try to match the harmonic alchemy which distinguished his previous setting of this text, in the Mass in A flat? He does, and he succeeds. Although the present Sanctus has an atmosphere of its own, again remotely related minor chords are the awe–inspiring nodal points. The 'Osanna' is an energetic fugue on a sprightly subject, with long melismas and some rather cloying chromaticisms to clog its flow. In the Benedictus, where a composer has to work hard to create a musical form with minimal clues implicit in the text (since it consists of one short sentence) Schubert forges a rondo-like structure by alternating the soloists' opening melodious strain with a more robust imitative choral passage. When the soloists' strain returns the melody is transferred to the tenor line, where its simple eloquence shows through agreeably.

Arrestingly, but unconventionally, the Agnus Dei begins with a fugal treatment of another Bach subject (the tortuous, claustrophobic one from the C sharp minor Fugue in Book 1 of the 'Forty-eight'). A touch of menace is added by the syncopated bass figure and the horn knells, setting into relief the softer string-accompanied pleas of 'miserere nobis'. The prevailing C minor tonality is swept aside as E flat major is restored for the final 'Dona nobis pacem', introducing a new theme whose initial fourfold repetition of a note is a Schubert fingerprint. As in the Benedictus, Schubert finds a basis for creation of his own design by opposing two contrasting themes. The compound falling thirds of the second theme (Fig. 81) lend themselves to some particularly fruitful developments.

Fig. 81

The eventual return of the dark 'Agnus Dei' motif is a master-stroke: by following this with a resumption of the 'Dona nobis pacem' Schubert is able to conclude the work with the two moods of fear and hope closely intermingled to the last. For all its unevenness, the Mass in E flat offers unique insights into the direction of Schubert's thinking in his final year. Clearly, all his masses taken as a unified chronicle of creative exploration down a single generic track would have provided a formidable bank of experience with which to approach the writing of a further mass had he lived to do so. The self-motivated approach to Sechter might have helped him overcome his fugal uncertainty in this context. But the highlights of his swansong mass, such as the awe–inspiring, probing visions of the Sanctus, remain as legacies for all time of a creative vitality that can excite and enrich the hearts and minds *venturi saeculi* (of the world to come).

The Late Songs

Once Schubert had acquired a taste for setting a truly great poet, he tended to return again and again to that poet over a period of many years. Goethe and Schiller were the notable examples, but Mayrhofer occupied a similar position in Schubert's esteem. The reasons why Schubert turned away from all three a few years before his death (the last Goethe settings came in 1826, the last Schiller and Mayrhofer in 1824) were probably that he had exhausted the stock of their suitable poems known to him, and that his attention was caught by Müller for the extensive *Winterreise* cycle in 1827 and by Heine and Rellstab for the two near-cycles published as the *Schwanengesang* in 1828. While the Goethe—Schiller—Mayrhofer oeuvre still offered him regular sustenance, other poets would come and go. Only Schober, among the lesser writers, motivated his pen over a long period, no doubt on account of their friendship and a shared artistic outlook.

Some of the poets Schubert favoured with short bursts of song composition were, in spite of the generalization, writers of some distinction, and the resulting songs make up in quality for what they lack in quantity. Two notable cases were Rückert and Collin, both of whom captured the composer's interest in the early 1820s, when he was already beginning to make a name for himself as a song-writer but also, significantly, had reached maturity in the main instrumental genres. From now on, when he returned to song from his instrumental exploits there was an added sureness, stemming perhaps from his self-fulfilment outside the field of Lieder (despite the abandoned major works such as the Quartet in C minor, *Lazarus*, and the 'Unfinished' Symphony) as well as from his long-proven prowess within it. Of the Rückert settings, both *Du bist die Ruh* (You are Repose) and *Lachen und Weinen* (Laughter and Tears) are, in their differing ways, models of restraint. *Du bist die Ruh*, aptly called by Richard Capell an 'erotic hymn', seems to express the dedication and fulfilment of love with an almost religious purity. While the beautifully drawn vocal line leads the ear from start to finish, the fact that the economical piano part has a highly pitched bass line — so that there are no sounds below a contralto's range until the last cadence of the strophe — gives an exalted, upward-gazing quality. The third strophe is modified, the modification sparked off by a marvellously subtle change to the second bar. Here the upward gaze takes the soprano to a high A flat, supported by the only crescendo from the prevailing pianissimo and by a thickening and deepening of the piano part that is all the more effective after the previous lightweight texture. After the caesura, allowing a few moments' contemplation, the voice drops an octave to continue the original strophe. *Lachen und Weinen* combines light, tripping textures with a Haydnesque tunefulness that ideally catches the young girl's ups and downs. The major-minor change is guilelessly applied, and neatly inverted in the second strophe.

These are settings that go straight to the heart of the poetry, and it is poignant to think that they were probably composed in late 1822 or early 1823 when Schubert became infected with his deadly disease. The same can be said of the Collin *Nacht und Träume* (Night and Dreams), a serene and Romantic reflection on the interwoven joys of night and dreams. This is one of Schubert's slowest conceptions – if we take into account not merely tempo but also the span of the strains and the duration of the harmonies. Pianissimo throughout, it requires of its singer exceptional control. The design is unique: the eight-line text is not stanzaic, but Schubert nevertheless imposes a 'strophic rhyme', in that he moulds the song in two strophes with matching conclusions but different beginnings. The unusual pattern that results may be seen below, where the numbers represent the lines of the poem and the letters denote the musical phrases assigned to them.

1	2	3	4	5	5	6	7	8	8
A	B	B	C	D	E	F	B	B	C

Another Collin setting of similar date, *Der Zwerg*, is of special importance because Schubert invests it with something of the momentum and working-out of an instrumental first movement, and the vividness of a fast-moving operatic number. Collin's ballad presents a chilling tale (it is almost a horror ballad) of the dwarf resolved to murder his beloved on account of her forsaking him. The thoughts of both of them, the strangulation itself, and the sequel are played out in a setting – on board ship at dusk – which brings an added touch of eeriness to the proceedings. Schubert responds to the inherent dramatic aspects of this scenario most graphically, as though this were an opera and the piano were an orchestra (complete with trombones, surely). Yet he responds not just to the terror and the grotesquerie, but to the pathos in the plight of the helpless girl and that of the manic dwarf.

The illusion of opera is sustained not simply by the colour of both the vocal writing and the piano's 'orchestration' but by the harmonic and tonal freedom of movement. In a great operatic scena, or a multi-partite act finale, virtually unlimited modulatory scope is afforded, such is the size of the canvas and such the tonal liberties composers permitted themselves within it. Schubert, so obviously fired by his subject's musical possibilities, eagerly and determinedly seeks this kind of harmonic and tonal scope even in the humble Lied medium. He does so by maximizing the opportunities for through-composition offered by a nine-stanza design and by allowing the bizarre elements of the story to dictate his tonal scheme. He touches on ten keys outside his framing A minor; yet, whereas one would expect such keys as F major, D minor, E minor, E major, or G major to be involved (according to the purely musical conventions of key-architecture) those keys are avoided and the likes of E flat major, B flat minor, G minor and B minor are given their head. It is as though Schubert is intent that each incident or inflection in the unfolding of the narrative shall be assigned a key or key-relationship appropriate to it and the accommodation of that key or relationship shall be left to his technical resourcefulness. From the first departure (direct to C minor) to the final homecoming (indirect from E flat major) the tonal agenda appears wide open. No doubt the symphonic character of some of the ingredients goes with the tonal volatility to produce this operatic atmosphere. The opening texture resembles that familiar from the 'Unfinished' Symphony and *Suleika I* (see Fig. 47, Chapter 10), though when John Reed writes that the opening of *Der Zwerg* is little more than a transposition of the 'Unfinished' theme into another key he should perhaps have added 'and into another metre', since one has three beats to the bar and the other four.

The four-note motive in the bass (akin to the propulsive cell of Beethoven's Fifth Symphony) is the compact seed of many a later development, such as the plunge of a diminished fifth at the dwarf's mention of his prospective victim's 'early grave', or the theme which gradually emerges – like a kind of second subject – and exerts its supremacy at the height of the drama (Fig. 82).

Fig. 82

The setting is not completely un-strophic: Schubert forges musical connections between verses 1, 2 and 7, while the material which began verse 1 reappears in the second half of verse 9, but now with the fully fledged 'second subject' all-powerful in the bass, challenging the singer's reprise of the opening vocal theme in a newly compressed version. A special technique for assimilating direct speech is illustrated in Fig. 83. The words which introduce but do not form part of the direct speech ('so ruft sie aus') are marked off from the quoted words of the girl, despite there being no rest in the vocal line before or after them, by being given their own rhythm and being excluded from the thematic sense which unifies the words on either side (see markings on figure), thus aiding the singer's urge to make a distinction between them.

Fig. 83

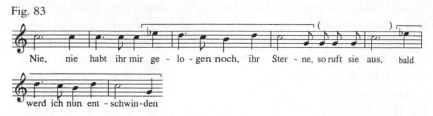

Schubert wrote few ballads in the 1820s: the genre, particularly the extended type, was an early interest of his, but he produced no examples after 1823. *Der Zwerg* stands unrivalled as a compelling successor to *Erlkönig*. There is an abundance of fine Lieder of the shorter type among the works of his later years, even if many of them belong to cycles, but it is a matter for regret that he did not provide a sequel to *Der Zwerg* in, say, the last year of his life.

The song cycle, in the sense of a set of songs united by a common poetic idea and intended to be performed as an entity, was a nineteenth-century phenomenon, a by-product of the rise of the German Lied. The first example of the genre is Beethoven's *An die ferne Geliebte*, which was followed closely by Schubert's two Müller cycles, *Die schöne Müllerin* (1823) and *Winterreise* (1827). In that these same composers, like their early Classical forebears Haydn and Mozart, were habitual composers in the multi-movement instrumental genres (sonata, quartet, symphony) and the multi-movement vocal-and-orchestral genres (mass, opera, cantata), it is not surprising that this tendency to think in terms of successions of movements should eventually be applied to the voice-and-keyboard medium. The surprise is that it took so long. The scena cultivated spasmodically by, for example, Mozart (such as *Ch'io mi scordi di te*, K.505) tended to fall into several sections (sometimes, though, no more than a recitative and aria), but it employed orchestra rather than keyboard, being essentially a dramatic episode – an offshoot of opera. The song cycle is not operatic; it is absolutely true to the burgeoning Lieder tradition.

In that sense, the song cycle came into existence not before time. In another sense, though, it seems it *was* before its time. *Die schöne Müllerin*, for example, although composed in 1823 was not performed in its entirety until 1856, for the simple reason that the public appetite was not ready for song cycles. Even in instrumental and orchestral concerts, it was not unusual for individual movements of symphonies or chamber works to be programmed, although complete works were the norm. The audience for songs was perhaps still more accustomed to and desirous of quick-change variety. The critic of the Munich *Allgemeine Musik Zeitung*, reviewing the publication of Part I of *Winterreise* by Haslinger (28 July 1928), put forward aesthetic objections to the very idea of a song cycle. German song, in his view, 'should unfold itself only in single flowers. To wind it into wreaths is infinitely difficult . . .' The critic proceeded to recommend to lovers of singing that the songs should be taken singly.[1]

The first of the cycles was *Die schöne Müllerin*. Here, Schubert boldly ignored Beethoven's model, by not linking his songs together to make one continuous piece. Instead, he wrote twenty separate songs, which are not bound by any explicit narrative but comprise a series of snapshots which together tell their tale. Each song can stand on its own, but all gain within their intended context. The origin of Müller's cycle of poems goes back to the period 1816–17 and to a *Liederspiel* performed by a circle of friends at a house in Berlin. The subject of this *Liederspiel* (a kind of party game in which members of the group were assigned parts) was a story about a miller maid and her suitors which had already enjoyed a long currency. In fact the title *Die schöne Müllerin* had already been used for German translations of a 1788 comic opera by Paisiello, *L'amor contrastato*, or *La bella molinara*. The young Müller was a member of this Berlin circle, and his text for Schubert's cycle was partly based on his own contributions to the *Liederspiel*. As Susan Youens has noted, however, biographical sub-currents seem to have been involved in the Berlin *Liederspiel*.[2] In particular, Müller's own love for one Luise Hensel is the subject of entries in Müller's diary in the years 1815–16. These entries ceased soon after a rival came upon the scene in late 1816 and proposed marriage. The final compilation may well be a rich amalgam of tradition and autobiography, though seen with a certain poetic detachment.

Schubert also had a hand in shaping the final poetic form, as he omitted the prologue and epilogue and three of the poems. The poems that remain have two characteristics which were important for Schubert's involvement. First, Müller wrote poetry to be set to music, favouring forms that would translate well into musical terms. Second, he preserved a folk flavour – proper to the subject matter – by giving emphasis to strophic form. A good half of Schubert's songs in this cycle are cast in strophic form, pure or modified. The miller is the first-person protagonist, and there are references to the maid, whose fickleness becomes apparent as the poetic sequence unfolds, and to the huntsman, to whom she transfers her attentions. The miller dies shortly before the end of the cycle.

The other character in this tale is the mill-stream, whose presence is felt in several of the songs, running through the piano texture in various manifestations. It first appears in the rolling sextuplets of the second song, *Wohin?* (Where To?), and finally takes centre stage in the last song, *Des*

Baches Wiegenlied (The Brook's Lullaby), a lullaby-lament for the miller in which Schubert makes the utmost simplicity on paper tell memorably in performance in context. To end a cycle by stripping away anything resembling complexity and allowing the plainest of materials to speak is daring in the extreme, whatever the poetic prompting. Schubert was to do it again with equally spellbinding effect in *Winterreise*. There cannot be many precedents for this in multi-movement works outside the realm of song, but one of them must be the E major Piano Sonata of Beethoven (Op. 109), where the finale's variations on a slow theme are crowned by a reprise of the theme itself in its unadorned pristine form.

Of all the songs, none is more straightforwardly strophic than the first, *Das Wandern* (Wandering), in which the miller fancies he goes aroving, to a chirpily gurgling accompaniment. But the second, *Wohin?*, which sounds for all the world as though it will be another plain strophic setting, turns out to be much more subtle, owing more to instrumental forms. The clue to its structure is the four–bar phrase with which Schubert closes the third of Müller's six stanzas, with its cadence to the dominant such as one would find at the end of the first section of a binary form or the exposition in sonata form. The fourth stanza is then treated as a short development section, moving to E minor and closing with that same four-bar phrase now transposed to E minor. The self-questioning couplet which begins the fourth stanza becomes a musical link, to the reprise which starts with that stanza's second couplet. The reprise, shortened by omitting the original bars 11–22, ends with the four-bar phrase, now varied, transposed back to the tonic (as it would usually be in binary form and in sonata form), followed by a short coda. There is nothing here that sounds contrived, perhaps because the brook ripples through it from beginning to end, and in any case there is no reason why formal principles developed in instrumental media should not be adaptable to song.

The cycle then moves still further from strophic regularity with a tautly-constructed, seamless *Halt!*, followed by the *Danksagung an den Bach* (Thanksgiving to the Brook), which offers a bewitching variety of phrase-lengths: while the piano prelude, which returns as postlude, provides an ordinary enough frame with its explicit four-bar phrase, once the voice has entered there is only one phrase in the whole song that has a four-bar span. *Am Feierabend* (After Work) recalls the clatter of the working mill and is notable for the way in which, after a reflective recitative-like middle section, Schubert re-activates the clattering figuration of the opening in an alien key and quickly modulates back to the home key when it is in full swing, for a varied repeat of the opening verse. For most of *Der Neugierige* (The Inquisitive One) all modulations except conventional ones are avoided: but when the miller confidingly asks the mill-stream whether his love is reciprocated – Yes or No? – the bright 'Yes' is followed,

precisely at the word 'No', by a subtle sidestep to G major, although the
tonal instability that follows (with immediate allusions to C major) and
the metrical instability caused by implications of a two-beat bar in conflict
with the prevailing three generate a profound disorientation which tells us
what a devastating effect a 'No' reply would have.

The 'impatience' of *Ungeduld* is heard before the voice enters. It is
present in the scrambling left-hand figure of the piano, in the impetuous
right-hand triplets, and in the unpredictable cadence habits of this 'prelude'
(the eight bars might be broken down as 3+3+1+1). The repetition of
the opening three bars a tone lower harks back to Beethoven's 'Waldstein'
opening – and forwards (dare one say) to 'Climb every mountain' in
Richard Rodgers's *The Sound of Music*. When the impassioned haste of the
voice is tellingly arrested at 'Dein ist mein Herz' (Yours is my heart) in a
nicely pointed long-note motive, the restlessness is transferred to the bass,
which resumes the scrambling figure of the prelude. And after the climactic
high A of the tenor, the singer's assertiveness is maintained by giving
him resolute duplets to create a new frisson with the triplets of the
accompaniment.

A charming three-bar refrain closes the strophe of *Des Müllers Blumen*
(The Miller's Flowers). For this garden of Eden, A major is aptly married
to 6/8 time – a combination prophetic of the initially idyllic next song,
Tränenregen (Shower of Tears), as of *Frühlingstraum* (Dream of Spring)
and *Täuschung* (Illusion) in *Winterreise*. Although *Tränenregen* carries distant
echoes of the second theme in the finale of Mozart's G minor String
Quintet, the prelude suggests rather a string trio, suited to the intimacy of
the miller's imagined encounter with the maid. When the last verse of the
seven-stanza poem turns love's idyll to disillusion, Schubert uses the tonic
minor, not just for its own colour but for the access to a new range of
related keys it affords.

Pause is a turning-point – a pause, in which the miller takes stock and
finds his love a burden. He has hung up his lute on the wall, and tied a
green ribbon to it. When the ribbon flutters in the breeze, catching the
strings to make a sighing sound, 'Ist es der Nachklang meiner Liebespein?'
(Is it the echo of my love's sorrow?) As the question is unanswered, the
suggestion of a remote C flat major goes unfulfilled, and by a classic
harmonic *double entendre* Schubert moves back to his home B flat major.
On this tonal guile hangs the climax of a remarkable song. The momentum
towards tragedy gathers pace, the rival huntsman appears (*Der Jäger*), the
miller looks for death, remembering his beloved's favourite colour (*Die
liebe Farbe*): only green turf must cover his grave. In sombre B minor, a
deathly F sharp tolls throughout, and the accented dissonances of the
prelude pull relentlessly downwards. The favourite colour becomes a hateful colour in the next song (*Die böse Farbe*). The miller would travel far

away, if there were not so much green in the woods and fields en route. Schubert has now moved from B minor to major: but it is neither a B major nor a 'Ziemlich geschwind' (Poco allegro) of joy – rather of resolve and stoicism. Here is a further prophecy of *Winterreise* – of its use of the 'ironic major', and, one might say, the 'ironic Ziemlich geschwind' of *Mut!* (Courage!). The cycle reaches its powerful climax (psychological and musical) in *Trockne Blumen* (Withered Flowers), whose atmosphere the subsequent variations for flute and piano (on the *Trockne Blumen* theme) neither sets out nor can hope to replicate.

Between *Die schöne Müllerin* in 1823 and *Winterreise* in 1827 came some fine individual songs, among them *Die junge Nonne*, the soliloquy of a nun who once experienced storms raging within her but now is all peace and tranquillity, nay death-longing. The most obvious observation to make about a piece written in Beethoven's adopted city and lifetime, involving the piano and beginning with a raging storm, and bearing the unusual combination of an F minor key-signature and a 12/8 time-signature is that it might just owe something to the 'Appassionata' Sonata. And so it does. The pianissimo opening (despite a stormy intent), the striding left-hand theme, the early shift to the Neapolitan key (minor in Schubert's case) – are all suggestive of the Beethoven source; Schubert's right-hand semiquaver-oscillation would then seem to originate in the half-dozen bars leading into Beethoven's recapitulation. What of the twofold dominant afterbeat in the second bar (Fig. 84)? Is it an echo from Beethoven's other sonata-form keyboard tempest, the Sonata in D minor, Op. 31, No. 2 (bars 220–4 of Beethoven's first movement)?

Fig. 84

Indeed one may equally hear Beethoven's entire four-bar configuration, with its treble response to the bass arpeggio, behind Schubert's two-bar one. One does not have to believe Ferdinand Ries's tale that the 'Appassionata' germinated in Beethoven's mind as the two walked in stormy weather, or even know that Beethoven's advice to would-be performers of Op. 31, No. 2, was 'Read Shakespeare's *Tempest*', to recognize that these models must have lurked deep in Schubert's subconscious as he set to work on the tale of the once-tormented nun who found ultimate serenity.

Craigher's poem conveys important structural invitations to its setter.

In mid-course the nun unconcernedly urges, 'Rage on, ye wild, violent storm! In my heart is peace and tranquillity.' This is the cue for Schubert to continue the right-hand semiquaver-oscillation, unifying the nun's two successive outlooks at a stroke. (Even the twofold dominant afterbeat is a permanent, multi-purpose fixture: it represents, if you fancy, the rattling house-timbers, the lightning flashes, the gently tolling bell, and perhaps the 'eternal heavens'. These devices are measures of the economy and expressive resource of a true tone-poet.)

The poet left another structural clue that did not go unheeded. There is a clear parallelism between lines 4 and 9 of the poem – 'und finster die Nacht, wie das Grab!' and 'und finster die Brust, wie das Grab!' (the night/ breast is dark on the grave). Closer inspection revealed to Schubert that line 5 could well be free-standing, while 6–9 as a group had certain correspondences with 1–4. Invited thus to impose a strophic form on a non–stanzaic poem, he duly recalled his musical strophe from 1–4 for use with 6–9, but tightened up the continuity in the process, by omitting and telescoping some short piano interludes. The result is a taut, unified design, impelled by a strong forward impetus and enriched with a liberal dash of modulatory colour.

The tuneful appeal of *Im Frühling* belies the subtlety with which its thematic material is uniquely deployed. The poet walks on the hillside, above the valley where he spent happy times with his loved one. He sees much that is the same; but much has changed. The piano leads off with a gently melodious tune (Fig. 85a), whose spell cannot be matched by the more functional word-carrying line with which the voice enters (Fig. 85b).

Fig. 85   a

Does this difference of theme have a programmatic purpose? Not necessarily, because Schubert sometimes takes his opening piano strain from the voice's last phrase at the cadence of the first stanza; in other words, it is a piano interlude, closely consequential upon the first stanza and leading to the second, which has been taken out to serve as prelude as well. But this is not Schubert's procedure here in *Im Frühling*: the piano tune returns duly after the first stanza, but that stanza comprises, to its last cadence, a wholly autonomous melody. But then, when the piano tune recommences as interlude, the voice adopts it at the earliest opportunity, and uses its own version of it for its entire second stanza. Schubert's scheme seems to be, then, that the piano tune represents the past, and the vocal theme the present. The piano prelude (Fig. 85a) anticipates the recall of past joy. The first stanza sets the scene, as the poet now sees it. As the first stanza ends – 'Where once . . . I was so happy' – the last note of Fig. 85b overlaps with the first note of theme a; and for the second stanza, which tells of walking by her side, the voice takes theme a.

The fact that the first two stanzas are musically independent of each other does not rule out the possibility of strophic treatment, and indeed as there are six stanzas and the present/past allusions alternate stanza by stanza throughout, Schubert takes the first two stanzas as his musical strophe, and lets it serve, with variation, for the rest of the six-stanza song, which therefore comes out in three musical strophes. With variation: from this point, the term which usually suffices to indicate some freedom in the treatment of the model strophe at later reappearances ('modified strophic') ceases to be precise enough, for these later strophes are variations in a palpable sense. While the voice alternates themes a and b for stanzas 3 and 4 (strophe 2) and again for stanzas 5 and 6 (strophe 3), the preludial theme a in the piano is varied in a decorative manner which recalls the B flat Impromptu (D.935, No. 3). The new texture is carried through both stanzas by the piano, so that strophe 2 sounds as variation 1. And a further new variation fills strophe 3 (variation 2). The song becomes a generic cross-breed, a variation-Lied.

This is no mere formal experiment on Schubert's part. For one thing, the treatment of two stanzas with different themes (e.g. stanzas 3 and 4, or 5 and 6), as a mono-textural variation helps to unite the pair, as the scenic locale unites the glimpses of two times, past and present. For another, the details of the scheme are worked out with expertise and aptness, notably when in stanza 5 Schubert replaces G major with G minor, to colour the references to strife and sorrow, introduces a spirited syncopated figure in lieu of the plain vamp in variation 2, and transmutes the move to the supertonic key (stanza 1) into a turn to the flattened supertonic (the Neapolitan).

If *Die schöne Müllerin* was slow to make its way in the world because the public was not ready for song cycles, the concentrated, desolate emotional climate of *Winterreise* must have compounded that problem. The only 'performance' of the cycle in Schubert's lifetime was a private recital for friends. 'We were quite dumbfounded by the gloomy mood of these songs,' wrote Schubert's friend Spaun.[3] The winter journey of the title is undertaken by a jilted lover, who sets out upon a long journey in the bleakness of winter, his hopes fixed on death. The poems do not form a continuous narrative, describing the journey, but present – in the first person – a series of episodes in a psychological soliloquy: a succession of winter scenes is married – often through the suggestive power of wayside symbols – to aspects of his despair. Any recollection of happier times, or of symbolically fairer seasons, is short-lived. As the cycle proceeds, the landscape may change (affording the minimal scope for musical variety which Schubert duly takes advantage of), but there is no escaping the unrelenting harshness of winter or of the traveller's inner torment.

On paper, *Winterreise* looks too gloomy, too monochrome, too doom-laden by half. In the best of performances a spell is cast and maintained through more than an hour of music, music which – however one responds to the unrelieved self-obsession of the poetry – achieves immense expressive power, as much by context and accumulation (*pace* the Munich critic) as by the potent yet simple inventiveness of each individual song. It has to be said here that, in many Schubert songs but in *Winterreise* in particular, downward transposition to bring the music within range of a particular singer's voice has an adverse effect. Below a certain depth on the keyboard, close harmonies become harder to distinguish the lower they are. Schubert has already placed some fairly close harmonies just about as low on the keyboard as they can reasonably go if their clarity is to be preserved (an instance being the end of the piano prelude in *Erstarrung* – Numbness – or the last chord before the reprise in *Der greise Kopf* – The Grey Head). One does not like to rob performers of music they may wish to call their own, but it has to be accepted that there is a palpable loss in effect which can also be regarded as a loss in authenticity if it is borne in mind that dense, low chords on Schubert's lighter-toned instruments were less muddy than on a modern piano.

The first song, *Gute Nacht* (Good Night), establishes a 'gehende Bewegung' as Schubert calls it (literally, a going motion) which returns, though not at always precisely the same pace, in the course of the cycle to implant a cyclic sense of weary plod in the listening ear. The key is D minor, but as soon as the traveller recalls the girl who jilted him – 'The girl spoke of love, Her mother even of marriage' – Schubert moves to the neighbouring major key of F. This begins the second stanza of the poem, which forms the second half of Schubert's strophe. At the fourth strophe, when the rejected lover passes the girl's house and resolves not to disturb her, the change to the tonic major has a special magic, because the vocal line begins with an upbeat on the high major third. Now that D major has superseded D minor, F major is no longer 'neighbouring', so Schubert takes advantage of the different range of closely related keys by moving to G major instead. Thus a profoundly refreshing variation of the strophe is achieved. When the G major phrase (Fig. 86a) is repeated in D major, Schubert avoids the obvious, strictly sequential contour (Fig. 86b), allowing the piano to take it over while the voice finds a lower path (Fig. 86c). He has pointedly postponed the high tenor A,

Fig. 86 a

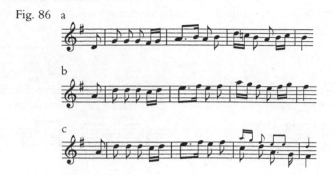

which must not appear so soon in the cycle: it is first used in *Wasserflut* (Flood), No. 6.

In the wonderfully inventive *Die Wetterfahne* (The Weather-vane), Schubert repeats the third stanza so as to develop it into an effective climax. He now makes the first developmental use of the trill which closed the piano prelude (the whistling wind, playing with the weather-vane and with hearts), and finally turns from A minor to A major with a touch of strident virtuosity. There is no grief in the girl's house, because their child has married money. Here, then, is another instance of the 'ironic major'. Winter imagery abounds in the following songs. *Gefrorne Tränen* (Frozen Tears) are depicted by a chill staccato alternating with icy, stratuesque single notes. In *Erstarrung*, numbness may be heard in the piano's right-hand broken chord figuration on fixed harmony, while the left hand's sinuous, serpentine melody seems to be searching for 'her footprints in the snow', that melody remaining piano property when the voice enters to sing a different melody to those words.

As the first two verses of Müller's *Der Lindenbaum* refer to the past while the third and fourth refer to the present, Schubert conceives a two-stanza strophe and varies it for the second pair of stanzas. This leaves two further stanzas of the six-verse poem. As the fifth brings less still weather conditions, it is treated individually. To make a full reprise of the strophe possible after that, Schubert needs to present the single verse 6 twice to make up the material for it. The rustling figure of the piano prelude is aptly transformed when the wind blows up in the fifth verse, and is brought back as final postlude with equal aptness, as the final couplet refers to the rustling still being heard.

The masterly harmonic strokes that abound in *Winterreise* are achieved not merely by vivid colouring but also by judicious timing. The first stanza of *Wasserflut* is set with the simplest of harmony, all tonic and dominant, but the last words of the stanza – 'heisse Weh' (burning grief) – occasion a pained, arching shape intensified by a shock chromatic chord (and the only forte in the song). According to a Baroque notational practice which persists into late Classical and indeed early Romantic scores, the dotted rhythms in Fig. 87 are modified in performance to match the prevailing triplets in the vocal part.

Fig. 87

dur - stig ein das hei - sse Weh,_____ dur - stig ein das hei - sse Weh.

An equally programmatic harmonic shock in the next song, *Auf dem Flusse* (On the River), occurs at the first mention of the river's being frozen: the first two lines are supported, again, by conventional tonic and dominant chords, but at 'Wie still bist du geworden' (How still you have become) the bass slips by a semitone, pointing the way to a remote key area, and the harmony 'freezes' for the duration of the line (Fig. 88).

Fig. 88

Der du so lu - stig rauschtest du hel - ler, wil - der Fluss, wie still bist du ge-

wor - den, giebst

At the emotional climax of the poem, in the fifth verse, the traveller recognizes in the stream the image of his heart – 'My heart, do you now recognize Your image in this brook? Is there not beneath its crust Likewise a seething torrent?' Schubert's inspired strategy here is to transfer the original vocal line (Fig. 88) to the piano bass, leaving the voice to counterpoint the words against this in an emotive recitative-like manner, thus distinguishing the two elements – stream and heart - that are being compared. The powerful remainder of this concluding section, with its further top A for the voice, completes one of the most imaginative and developed songs in the whole cycle.

The restlessness of Müller's *Rückblick* (Backward Glance) is conveyed not only by unflagging rhythm but by irregularities, or illusory irregularities, in the phrase-structure, touched off in particular by the 'stumbling' imagery of the second verse. *Irrlicht* (Will-o'-the-Wisp) presents a particular post-Baroque rhythmic problem at one point. The voice has the upper line of Fig. 89 while the piano has chords in the rhythm of the lower line in small notes. Should the dotted rhythm in the piano at the end of the bar be assimilated to the triplet in the voice? As there are no other triplets in view, some singers prefer to honour the piano rhythm and lengthen the voice's high F sharp − a strong solution.

Fig. 89

Frühlingstraum brings some strident harmonic representations of crowing cocks and cawing ravens, but perhaps the most remarkable aspect of this song is the bold policy of taking as many as three stanzas as the basis of a strophe, and assigning them three different tempi − each of which therefore comes round twice as there are six stanzas in all. There is no question of diffuseness, despite the risk. Richard Capell saw *Die Post* as an ill-fitting song in the context of *Winterreise* (its placing in the middle of the cycle rather than later was Schubert's decision, not Müller's, but that hardly affects Capell's reservations). The post-horn is heard, announcing the arrival of the mail from another town. Is there a letter for the traveller? No! That is the gist of the poem. Capell finds this out of character: the traveller has indulged in dreams, but never in false hopes.[4] What about the last hope he wilfully invests in the final leaf on the tree, in *Letzte Hoffnung*? And is not *Täuschung* all about happy self-delusion? The other problem raised by Capell is that while it is true that Schubert turns from E flat major to E flat minor when it is revealed that there is no letter, he persists with the jaunty rhythm of the trundling mail coach. This is merely a kind of musical irony, akin to the use of the major mode where minor might be expected − of which there are further examples in the next song, *Der greise Kopf*, as well as *Letzte Hoffnung*.

A crow has been the traveller's constant companion. So in *Die Krähe* the singer's line follows the left hand of the piano, just as the crow sticks to the traveller's path. The high tessitura is appropriate as the focus is on the bird in flight. In fact, the piano never drops below tenor F, until its postlude sinks to the depths of the keyboard, after the singer has asked if the crow − unlike the fickle girl who cast him off − will be faithful unto

the grave.[5] *Letzte Hoffnung* is a superb little tone-poem abounding in pictorial details such as the singer's suddenly singing long notes at 'Gedanken
stehn' (standing lost in thought) and so augmenting an eight-bar strain to
a nine-bar one. *Im Dorfe* (In the Village) continues the picturesqueness. If
the piano's opening gestures are the dogs barking or the chains rattling,
or both, the long silences between are as surely (how surely, the reader is
judge) the black stillness of night. *Der stürmische Morgen* (The Stormy Morning), comprising two surges of neo-Bachian unharmonized melody (but
for a few well-placed chords) in D minor framing a little four-bar march
in B flat major (that is the second verse), is possibly the shortest song
Schubert ever wrote, though its effect is hardly commensurate.

One of the most interesting of all song structures in Schubert is *Täuschung*. The poem is of ten lines, in rhyming couplets without stanzaic
division. The text and translation are shown in Fig. 90, with the vocal
melody to which each line is set. The first and second couplets become,
in Schubert's setting, a strophe, the second couplet being a varied repeat
of the first. The middle couplet substitutes minor for major, as the traveller
contemplates his own wretchedness. The reprise of the strophe then comes
not at the beginning of the next couplet, but halfway through it, so the
words 'helles, warmes Haus' (the bright, warm house of his lost beloved,
which he fancies he sees) coincide with the resumption of the A major
tune – a hushed homecoming marked piano after the preceding crescendo
over a dominant pedal. Although he thus splits the fourth couplet down
the middle, Schubert takes care not to disturb the rhyme of 'Graus' and
'Haus', which remain close together because he has made these two lines
– and only these two in the whole song – musically continuous. This
strategy leaves only three lines of text for the reprise of a strophe which
originally consumed four lines. Rather than repeat a line to make up the
four, Schubert this time imparts to the last line of the poem the function
of recapitulating, in abbreviated form, the music of both lines of the second
couplet. As the brackets over Fig. 90 indicate, the first two notes are those
that begin the first line of the second couplet, and the remainder are those
that end the second line of the second couplet. Thus, having responded
to the sense of the verse and located the beginning of his reprise accordingly,
Schubert makes a virtue of a necessity by compressing that reprise – a
policy often regarded as advantageous at this stage in a design, by whatever
means it is implemented.

Der Wegweiser is a song full of atmospheric and psychological detail.
The move back from the blameless G major of the second stanza to the
heavy-hearted G minor of the third is an astonishing wrench, as a chord
of B minor leads directly to one of G minor, but the effect is to intensify
the renewed resolve to shun the signposts pointing to towns and strike
out over secret paths. Schubert treats the fourth stanza as a coda, the singer's

Fig. 90

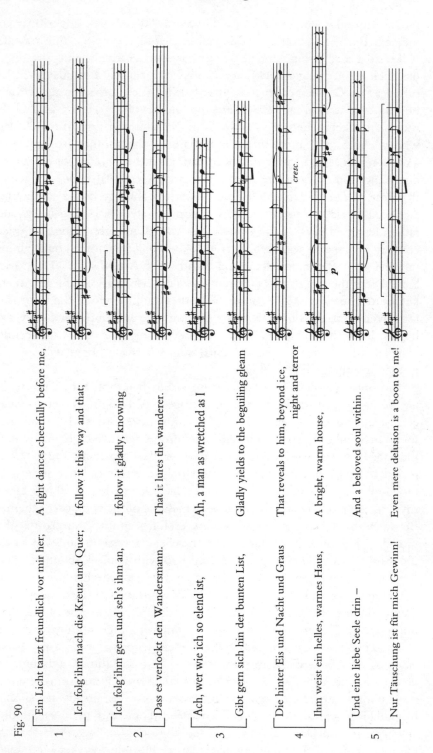

1 Ein Licht tanzt freundlich vor mir her;
A light dances cheerfully before me,

Ich folg'ihm nach die Kreuz und Quer;
I follow it this way and that;

2 Ich folg'ihm gern und seh's ihm an,
I follow it gladly, knowing

Dass es verlockt den Wandersmann.
That it lures the wanderer.

3 Ach, wer wie ich so elend ist,
Ah, a man as wretched as I

Gibt gern sich hin der bunten List,
Gladly yields to the beguiling gleam

4 Die hinter Eis und Nacht und Graus
That reveals to him, beyond ice, night and terror

Ihm weist ein helles, warmes Haus,
A bright, warm house,

5 Und eine liebe Seele drin –
And a beloved soul within.

Nur Täuschung ist für mich Gewinn!
Even mere delusion is a boon to me!

reiterated monotone prompted by the words 'Weiser . . . unverrückt vor meinem Blick' (signpost . . . immovable before my eyes). The traveller will tread a road 'From which no man has ever returned' (eine Strasse . . . die noch Keiner ging zurück), at which words the plod of quavers at last subsides for a G minor cadence of utter finality. He approaches a graveyard, but thinks of it as an inn (*Das Wirtshaus*, the next song), and asks if all the rooms are taken. The tempo is the Sehr langsam of a funeral march. But whoever heard of a funeral march in F major? Is this another 'ironic major', a warm response to the welcome of an inn? Or is the traveller (or composer) distancing himself from the poet's increasingly suicidal stance, of which the close of *Der Wegweiser* left little doubt? In any event, the sombreness sacrificed by eschewing a minor key is compensated for by the density and rather depressed pitch of the piano part. *Mut!* (Courage!) brings a musical contrast and the stoical resolve of a *marche militaire* (one could almost imagine an orchestration for wind band). *Die Nebensonnen* (The Mock Suns) keeps the pianist more extremely and persistently to the left of the keyboard than even *Das Wirtshaus*. Whether the first two of the three suns the traveller imagines he sees in the sky are love and hope, or the eyes of his lost love, they set to an eloquent descending line with decrescendo, completed in the piano; and the third sun, which he hopes will also set, is undoubtedly life itself.

The organ-grinder of *Der Leiermann* stands barefoot, tottering on the ice, doing his best to play with numb fingers. Although his plate remains empty and no one listens, his hurdy-gurdy never stops. Thus the first sound in Schubert's score is the left-hand drone, reactivated regularly until the end. Over this bare fifth the old man proffers a pathetic little scrap of melody, the sparse texture being filled only towards cadence-points. As his numb fingers struggle to articulate the second bar of this scrap, a rhythmic limp results, and this itself becomes one of the composer's themes. Between times, the singer sings his lines, each frozen into a similar two-bar mould. When, in the last stanza, the traveller addresses a question to the old man – 'Soll ich mit dir gehn?' (Shall I go with you?) – Schubert points the question by beginning it on the second beat of the bar, where every other utterance had been ponderously downbeat. The next question – 'Willst du meinen Liedern Deine Leier drehn?' (Will you grind your hurdy-gurdy To my songs?) – is left hanging on a high dominant. A later composer might have stopped at the penultimate bar, with a pause and fade-out. Schubert would not leap that far into the future, although the desolate texture of the song – to have its effect on the slow movement of a symphony he was to begin in his last weeks – is already far enough beyond his time. But his 'resolving' tonic chord does not, of course, resolve anything. In a spellbinding performance, the question lingers on through the tonic and into the pin-dropping silence. Has the traveller gone mad?

Does he die? Or does a modicum of human rapport (scarce commodity in *Winterreise*) with the organ-grinder, his association of himself with the old man's bereft plight, and his implied awareness of his resilience in the face of it, lead him to accept his lot with resignation and work out his allotted days in empathy with a fellow-sufferer? What, then, of the death-wish implicit in the bleak close of *Wegweiser* and *Nebensonnen*? That may still be genuine enough, if witnessing the old man and his hurdy-gurdy was the turning-point. And the defiance of *Mut!* ('Cheerfully out into the world!') should not be overlooked, any more than should the fact that *Das Wirtshaus* was major, not minor; 'Nun weiter denn, nur weiter, Mein treuer Wanderstab!' (On, then, press onwards, My trusty staff!)

There remains a small point in criticism of *Der Leiermann* which does, however, touch on the very nature and scope of Lieder. To Gerald Moore, the forte in the postlude was inadmissible: 'I cannot see how this miserable organ could be capable of loudening in this way'.[6] He is almost certainly correct that no contemporary hurdy-gurdy could produce this dynamic effect. But Schubert was writing for the pianoforte, not the hurdy-gurdy, and pianists (including Gerald Moore) employ infinitesimal gradations of tone in performing this song in a concert-hall acoustic that could not begin to be matched by the 'miserable organ' in the wintry great outdoors. Neither crowing cocks, nor cawing ravens, nor barking dogs, nor rattling chains, nor any other work of nature or of man is depicted with absolute verisimilitude in *Winterreise*, since literal mimicry is not the province of Lieder. There is no reason why the artistic licence of the creator should be denied on the last page of his greatest cyclic example of the genre.

Among the individual songs that followed *Winterreise*, two are worth comparing for their different approaches to the most ubiquitous of Romantic Lieder themes. *Heimliches Lieben* (Secret Love) seems to present love from a woman's standpoint: the poem was written by the mother of Wilhelmina von Chézy (of *Rosamunde* fame), the song was dedicated to Marie Pachler (Schubert's hostess at Graz in September 1827), and it is ideally performed by a soprano. *Des Fischers Liebesglück* (The Fisherman's Luck in Love) is the moonlit idyll of a lovestruck fisherman, calling for a tenor of some sensitivity. *Heimliches Lieben* is inclined to underplay the erotic sentiments behind the words, constrained as they are by the continuous use of a fairly ordinary piano figuration and by melodic lines of elegant beauty rather than unchained passion. Within the strophic setting – which pairs the verses so as to make two strophes out of four stanzas and treats the fifth as a coda – there are wonderful moments of localized expressive detail; but the undoubted ardour is a degree cooler than the hothouse desire that fills Karoline Louise von Klenke's lines. Perhaps the 'secret' of the title is a clue to Schubert's not altogether baring the lover's soul; and as Richard

Capell suggests, Schubert may have had an eye to the ethos of a Graz drawing-room, where the song was destined to be performed.[7] *Des Fischers Liebesglück*, on the other hand, gains erotic power through working in harness with certain idiosyncratic limitations built into the text, despite Capell's dismissal of it as 'charming', 'slighter', and 'for a light and ingratiating tenor'.[8] Leitner's poem, in which the fisherman and his sweetheart in a boat on the lake under the stars are transported to 'another shore', is characterized by very short lines, mostly of two words. Each stanza of seven lines therefore amounts to a not very long sentence, and there are eleven stanzas in all.

What Schubert daringly attempts is to respect this poetic quirk in his setting. Thus the vocal melody halts at each line-end, by the placing of a longer note there after shorter notes before it. This results in an attractive saraband-like stress on the second beat of each three-beat group (of which there are two in each 6/8 bar). A typical half-bar rhythm is Fig. 91. One might imagine this to be the rhythm of the oars: action on the first beat, the boat gliding through the water on the second and third. But, this being a strophic song, the rhythm persists long after the fisherman has abandoned rowing in favour of amatory pursuits; it acquires a hypnotic aura which suspends the tranquillity of the scene and the lovers' rapture in a seemingly timeless state. So spellbinding is the effect that at the pause which ends each strophe one imagines the motion of the boat, or the rippling of the waves, or the twinkling of the stars, continuing . . . There is still room for expressive detail. Schubert turns Leitner's eleven verses into twelve by repeating the tenth, then groups the twelve into four threes, and bases his strophic form on a musical verse of three poetic stanzas. As John Reed points out, he seems to take his cue from the end of the poem.[9] The octave leap (almost a yodel) finds its most apt purpose, at any rate, for the words of the last stanza 'Schon oben, Schon d'rüben zu sein' ([We think] we are already up above, On another shore') (Fig. 91).

Fig. 91

der Er - de, schon o - ben, schon drü - ben zu sein._____

Clearly this song, with its halting rhythm, has something in common with *Der Vater mit dem Kind*, Schubert's one and only setting of Bauernfeld, an underestimated song which paints a father-and-child picture sympathetically and with some enchanting harmonies and sonorities in apt pastel shades. (If not among his very greatest songs, it's a precious manifestation of his ripe art, none the less.) But *Des Fischers Liebesglück* is utterly compelling, as though the completion of *Winterreise* since *Der Vater* had made Schubert's assurance with this kind of musical material supreme. (One element of the appeal of Leitner's poem could have been that it is a technical *tour de force*, with its ultra–short lines – mostly of three syllables – and unusual rhyming scheme: Schubert too relished technical experiment, as in the *Die Zauberharfe* palindrome and the 'Tenth' Symphony.)

Another fine setting of Leitner is *Die Sterne*, a more conventional poem cast by Schubert in a strophic form with a yet novel twist. Leitner's imaginative eulogy of the stars and their many supposed functions for man prompts one of Schubert's tripping celebrations of the dactyl, a rhythm probably inherited from the slow movement of Beethoven's Seventh Symphony, which he admired, and well tried in such early works of Schubert's own as the Second Symphony (finale). The text clearly suggests a long-and-two-shorts rhythm. While, as John Reed points out, the crotchet-quaver-quaver pattern is present in every one of the song's 188 bars (except the last), the uniformity this suggests is relieved by the superimposition of different rhythms here and there – by, for instance, runs of four quavers in middle or outer parts (first heard in the course of the piano introduction), by long notes (at the end of vocal lines), by syncopations (in the fourth line of every verse), and by ornaments. Moreover, such is the attention to longer spans of directional melody that the dactyls recede into the background to become, as if were, the surface over which the invention glides. More fancifully, they may even symbolize the constant flickering to which the heaven-turned eye must accustom itself, or the immeasurable repetition of space between the galaxies and us.

The piano introduction typifies the larger contour to which the dactyls are subservient: over sixteen bars a single basic line rises from the third to the upper tonic, with just enough incidental decoration, deviation and dissonance to make exhilarating, satisfying music: a divine heavenward ascent indeed. In its superficial features the strophic form is transparent. The innovation lies in the deployment of keys. All four stanzas are of four equal lines each, and Schubert chooses the key of E flat major. All the verses are faithful to this key, except that the third line of each stanza is lifted bodily into another key, without the formalities of modulation. In the four verses the third-line keys are C major, C flat major, G major, and C major again (the third-relationships being pure Schubert). The reversion to C on the last occasion is offset by some added repetition and ornamentation. Through all the song, the first, second and fourth lines remain true to the strophic model, except that in verses 2 and 4 the vocal line reaches up to G instead of E flat in the penultimate bar. Two familiar tendencies are brought together here – the urge to diversify the pure strophic form, and the liking for shotgun migration from one key to another (which leaves its mark on the succession of strophes in *Der Musensohn*, for example, and occasions the unceremonious jump from D minor to B flat major for the second stanza of *Der stürmische Morgen*). There is, incidentally, no apparent textual reason for these quickfire tonal deviations: it was evidently a pure musical fancy on Schubert's part. *Die Sterne* is one of Schubert's most delightful songs, and surprisingly not among the best-known. The notes flow from his pen as naturally and joyously as in, for example, *Der Hirt auf dem Felsen* of the same year, his last.

During this last year Schubert continued work probably begun the previous year on the poetry of Rellstab and Heine. It is possible that some of the Rellstab poems had come to him from Beethoven's estate, which would add special point and poignancy to the homage to that composer found in the second of Schubert's Rellstab settings, *Auf dem Strom* (On the River). Rufus Hallmark has shown that the theme to which the second verse of the poem is set closely resembles that of the second movement of Beethoven's 'Eroica' Symphony.[10] If the melodic contour is not enough to clinch the affinity, there is unmistakable harmonic corroboration. Hallmark sees this lovely song, which has a horn obbligato, as a metaphorical depiction of death, thus explaining what could hardly have been a merely subconscious allusion to Beethoven's Funeral March. Seven of the Rellstab settings (excluding *Auf dem Strom*) appeared with all six of the Heine settings in the collection entitled *Schwanengesang*. Schubert had intended these Rellstab songs to be issued as a separate collection, however; and long-held views that the Heine songs were likewise destined by the composer for separate publication have been reinforced by a more recent diagnosis of cyclic tendencies therein.[11]

Of the Rellstab songs that appeared in *Schwanengesang*, the first, *Liebesbotschaft* (Love's Message), is a 'brook' song with a constantly rippling right hand and a left hand that adds a variety of subtle rhythmic, melodic, textural, imitative, and harmonic dimensions to the song. The strophic treatment has a refreshing nuance, in that the two-verse strophe ends out of key (in the subdominant) and even at the final reprise almost ends away from home, veering back to *terra firma* just in time. Another felicitous touch concerns the vocal rhythm. Schubert quickly establishes the pattern that every line of text will be set to the rhythm of Fig. 92 or a variant which does not disturb its overall length. But for the third verse he doubles this span for the first two lines (a kind of approximate augmentation) thus making possible a new left-hand pattern which induces some new and sublime modulations. Schubert alchemy at its best.

Fig. 92

The last of this Rellstab group, *Abschied*, re-invents a strophic scheme familiar from *Der Musensohn*, where successive stanzas appear in different keys. A rider bids farewell to the town, and to the sights on the way out, as the countryside and nightfall approach. There are six verses, set strophically. The odd-numbered ones repeat the strophe in the home key of E flat; verses 2 and 4 adapt the strophe (not much beyond what is minimally necessary) in A flat; and verse 6 sets off in C flat but veers back – like a horse checked by the bridle – through A flat to E flat again. As John Reed rightly observes, 'Schubert's motor images are analogues, not imitations';[12] one should not look for a metronomically apt 'trot' in the relentless staccato jog of this song. As often, the accompaniment, and the simple and rather square snatches of tune, take hold of the mind, however ordinary the ingredients may at first appear.

The six Heine songs, originally published as part of *Schwanengesang*, are all works of the first rank. Schubert imparts some of his most terse, individualistic ideas to poems which speak of alienation, each in a different but concentrated context. *Das Fischermädchen* (The Fishermaiden) apart, introversion predominates, the colours are primary with an emphasis on minor keys, and the designs are accomplished with bold strokes of the brush and a consistent avoidance of superfluities. *Der Atlas* combines a strong muscular rhythm with a depth of sonority that is entirely appropriate for the depiction of Atlas carrying a world of sorrows on his shoulders. This does not enable a singer with a titan voice to transpose it down and hope to retain its true impact. Schubert makes rich use of the lower half of the keyboard in several of his late songs (*In der Ferne* (In the Distance), *Am Meer* and *Der Doppelgänger* are examples in the *Schwanengesang*), but we can be sure he selects his key with care and precision when so doing. The G minor of *Der Atlas* permits gravitas without opacity. The ponderous theme in the bass is well calculated to suggest Atlas's burden, as the leading note in the second bar has tonic harmony above which tends to pull it back up to the tonic as though it has slipped under a heavy weight. It is the same harmony as that used by Brahms to identify the misanthrope at the beginning of his Alto Rhapsody. The choice of B major and a rollicking accompaniment for the lines which refer back to the protagonist's bold bid for happiness, as contrast to the 'unendlich elend' (infinitely wretched) G minor of the framing sections, is a powerful irony. The return to G minor from that distant key is done speedily and exactly in time to mirror the text's change of focus, within one line of verse, from the happiness of then back to the wretchedness of now. That return is Schubert's, not Heine's. The first verse is brought back to close the song, and the voice's final cadence is an extraordinary inversion, as it were, of the harmony in bar 2 described above. Against the G minor chord, the voice has not F sharp (the semitone below) but A flat, the semitone above. This flattened supertonic bears down on the keynote with all the oppression of the world on its back (Fig. 93). It is also one of the most unorthodox cadences

Fig. 93

gan -ze Welt der Schmer -zen muss ich tra - - gen.

in nineteenth-century music, teasing the analyst who would catalogue it
according to traditional cadence classifications. The last cadence of the
String Quintet may be a conscious echo of this one, although the harmony
is more classifiable.

Ihr Bild is one of those flawless miniatures in which every note has its
appointed place – and there are not many of them. For one thing, it has
a perfect formal balance, three short verses with the outer pair strophically
related and the central one following its own course (a common enough
plan in Schubert). For another, it finds expressive contrast by the simple
means of juxtaposing bare octaves, or other sparse textures, with eloquent
phrases in four-part or even richer homophony, and makes the graduations
between them with complete ease. There are clear analogies with both
the expressive climate and the note-content of the B flat Piano Sonata
(first movement) and the trio of the third movement of the String Quintet,
while the conversion to the minor – at the end of the song – of the
postlude to the first verse heartrendingly unites the twin veins of rapturous
nostalgia and aching loss which the poem so succinctly interweaves.

If we call *Das Fischermädchen* a barcarolle, we have to qualify the term
by noting that it is a singularly sprightly example of the genre, skimming
the very tops of the waves as it were, buoyed up and propelled by the joy
and hope of love. The tripping 6/8 motion favours the lightweight step
of the iamb, and when a note appears on the second or fifth quaver-
beat of a bar it is an adornment, or a deliciously throwaway resolution
of a suspension. This is a strophic song in A flat, with the middle of its
three verses set wholly in C flat; the intervening piano interludes effect
the modulations between these keys. One of the charms of the song
is the changes made to the melody in the C flat verse – all pressed upon
the composer by exigencies of vocal compass but some making a virtue

Fig. 94 a

b

of the necessity by finding a particularly inspired solution. Fig. 94b, for example, does more than merely replace the high A flat that would have resulted if Fig. 94a had been literally transposed.

Die Stadt, in which the protagonist observes a town from a boat, from twilight to dawn, remembering the love he lost there, is an impressionistic tone-poem before its time. There is no neater description of what transpires in the piano's introduction than John Reed's 'diminished sevenths . . . swirling',[13] unless it is 'diminished seventh . . . swirling'; for Schubert uses but one diminished seventh, repeatedly, and it holds sway – on and off – for about half of the song. What he never does here is explore the manifold routes of exit from the diminished seventh, a sort of Clapham Junction of harmony, from which many different destinations are instantly accessible, as nineteenth-century composers including Schubert liked to discover. He simply holds the chord suspended in a harmonic vacuum: it has a 'non-functional' value which antedates Debussy's non-functional use of harmony by over half a century.

But the most remarkable aspect of the song is that the middle verse of the three comprises nothing but that diminished seventh harmony from beginning to end: there is no change of chord throughout. Thus both the stillness and the mystery of night are suggested, all night long, from the twilit end of verse 1 ('in Abenddämmrung gehullt' – enshrouded in twilight) to the sunlit beginning of verse 3 ('Die Sonne hebt sich noch einmal' – the sun rises once more). Much is made of Wagner's long-stay parking on the E flat tonic chord at the start of *Das Rheingold*. Schubert's monochordal stanza, lasting not much less than a minute, is presumably a 'first' of its kind in the stretching of harmonic technique towards the expressive ends of Romanticism. It finds an odd successor in the third variation of Alkan's *Festin d'Ésope* (Aesop's Banquet), which to all intents and purposes consists of nothing but a German sixth. Schubert's last verse is a reprise of this first, but transformed to make an impressive musical climax, the only significant alteration being an arresting change in the timing and colour of a chord at one point.

The tremolando comes into its own in *Am Meer*. In keyboard terms, the tremolando is an oscillation which sets the player's hand(s) rocking at some speed from side to side. Schubert had recourse to the device often in his last decade, in works as diverse as the String Quartet in G major, the Octet, the melodramas, and several songs. It is, among its other virtues, a means of promoting sonority at a slow tempo, action without 'real' speed, excitement in an 'accompaniment' which can be combined with long full-toned notes in other instruments (or voice). The crescendo or diminuendo takes on a new vivid dimension with a tremolando, as the opening of the overture to *Fierabras* showed (see page 208). The song ends as did the duet 'Weit über Glanz und Erdenschimmer' in *Fierabras* (No. 9), with an evocative harmonic progression which in the present instance refers back to the opening of the piece (see page 206).

The last of the Heine songs, *Der Doppelgänger*, is perhaps the nearest Schubert came to athematicism, in his quest for atmosphere, drama, suspense, and epigrammatic terseness in the Lied. In one sense the voice is an accessory to the piano, spawning its own declamatory offshoots of notes picked out from the slow-moving keyboard chords, though it rises later to deliver more extended lines of immense sustained power. And the piano itself, apart from echoing a vocal cadence twice, confines itself to block chords in the lower half of the keyboard, with no figuration, no linear motives detaching themselves from this heavy, impenetrable thicket of sound. The only theme, if we may call it that, is the sum of the top notes of the four chords uttered by the piano before the voice enters. They are the notes from which Bach built a fugue subject, in Book 1, No. 4, of the 'Forty-eight'; they were also the springboard for the Allegro ma non troppo theme of Schubert's own *Fierabras* overture; but in *Der Doppelgänger* they undergo little of the development that would earn them the epithet 'theme', although they recur from time to time in pristine form and one often senses the piano part has an 'ostinato' quality – though this effect has a rhythmic more than melodic cause. At the end, however, in the piano postlude, comes a singular, stunning development: the supertonic, which is the fourth note of the 'theme' (Fig. 95a), is flattened so that its distance from the ensuing tonic is narrowed to a semitone (Fig. 95b). The mood of the whole song is encapsulated in this tragic single note, and the only parallel elsewhere in Schubert, where a supertonic in an opening theme is thus depressed in a final moment of almost unendurable *Angst*, is in the last slow movement he wrote, that of the 'Tenth' Symphony sketched in his final weeks.

Fig. 95 a

b

The Heine settings do not appear in *Schwanengesang* in the order decreed by the poet himself, and if Heine's order were to be restored the resulting sequence of songs would be: *Das Fischermädchen, Am Meer, Die Stadt, Der Doppelgänger, Ihr Bild, Der Atlas*. It is possible, in this order, to discern a narrative thread of sorts, and since Schubert was generally sensitive to a poet's intentions one may well ask whether the published order carries his authority. It is an established fact that it was the publisher, Tobias Haslinger, who lumped the Rellstab and Heine settings together and gave them their fancy overall title, although Schubert had been thinking of issuing two separate collections, one of Rellstab and one of Heine. It is not impossible that Haslinger stretched his licence to the extent of playing free with Schubert's order for the Heine settings.

Haslinger also included in *Schwanengesang*, for no obvious reason, the last of Schubert's Seidl settings, *Die Taubenpost*. Johann Seidl was a young Viennese poet who had come to Schubert's notice in 1826 and whose songworthy verse would surely have stimulated more songs from the composer if the collaboration had had time to blossom. *Die Taubenpost* itself is a simple love-song, Schubert's very last, a modified strophic setting in which we may fancy we hear, in the right hand of the piano from time to time, the flutter of wings as the carrier-pigeon bears away the poet's message. Seidl's poem is one of those that has a key word embedded in its last verse, of the sort which would normally receive special treatment by Schubert – as a climax, on a pregnant chord perhaps, or with a pause. In the present case, when the carrier–pigeon turns out to be 'die Sehnsucht' (longing), Schubert does not arrest the motion of the piano, but breaks up the vocal line to mark off 'die Sehnsucht' with rests on either side, and turns the supertonic chord major for a few moments, before changing to the minor form (four bars later) which is the expected and conventional route to the cadence. 'Sehnsucht' is a word of special resonance in Schubert's art, and indeed his previous setting of Seidl's *Sehnsucht*, demanding as it is on the technique and artistry of both performers, trips along with that perfectly judged momentum and abounds with those felicities of detail that characterize Schubert's music at its best.

After the bitter, introverted world of the Heine songs, *Der Hirt auf dem Felsen*, dated October 1828, the month before Schubert died, breathes the air of an alpine meadow. The text shows its triple origin – the two outer sections from two different Müller sources, the middle section probably from Wilhelmina von Chézy – yet neither that nor the sectional build of the music leaves a niggling sense of disunity in the listening ear, or detracts from the joyful affirmation of the brilliant close after the earlier expressions of love and grief. On the one hand, one may see this extended work with its concertante elements and tendency to use the piano in conventionally patterned support of the voice and obbligato clarinet as a throwback to a superseded phase of interest; on the other, it might be seen as the final testimony to a love–pain–joy syndrome which, reflected in many a creative endeavour, may be a characteristic of Schubert's innermost spiritual or religious outlook, and may then have come to the surface at times when he felt close to the next life.

The interplay of soprano and clarinet timbres had exerted a fascination over the composer since his early operas. There is a brilliance in the virtuoso vocal writing that recalls the Italian ingredient in some of the youthful exercises undertaken when Salieri was an influence. Then there is the unmistakable impact on the melodic lines of yodelling, a genre for which the clarinet – with its different 'voices' in different parts of its range – is the ideal instrumental exponent. The song also pays homage to Anna Milder, whom Schubert had admired since hearing her in Gluck's *Iphigenia in Tauris* in 1813. She had claimed that the public wanted 'only treats for the ear', and urged Schubert to write a song 'in a variety of measures, so that several emotions can be represented . . . [with] a brilliant ending.'[14] Those who examine Schubert's texts for clues that certain songs are suitable for male singers and others for female should note that the composer does not hesitate here to choose verses betokening a male persona ('sehn'ich mich so heiss nach ihr' – I long so ardently for her) for a song so specifically conceived for a soprano.

That Schubert could write this piece within a few months of the Heine songs (which were evidently begun in 1827) should surprise us no more than that the 'Wanderer' Fantasy could follow the 'Unfinished' Symphony by a month or the 'Trout' Quintet precede *Lazarus* by perhaps a year. 'The Shepherd on the Rock', although it shares with the 'Trout' Quintet and, for example, the Octet a certain easy-going manner that is reflected in extensive lyricism, brilliance, *joie de vivre*, and reliance on regular figurations and rhythms which tend to place some instruments in 'motor' roles, surpasses them in the refinement of its technique and the magnetism of its ideas. Everything, including some heart-rending modulations between remotely related keys, is carried through with the wisdom and practised command of the fully mature composer.

The opening bars, solemn and a touch portentous, are a prelude to something in G minor. But what follows turns out to be in B flat major. (G minor arrives later, for the central episode of the song.) It is the implicit non sequitur of keys at the start which allows the clarinet to pivot so ravishingly on its long-held opening D, which comes to us as a dominant and leaves us as a mediant anacrusis. The clarinet's melody undulates in long sinuous curves through the tonic arpeggio, anticipating certain boldly striding arpeggio themes of Brahms, and even some symphonic ones by Bruckner. But it is the continuation rather than the melodic opening that leaves its stamp on the work – the shorter phrases separated by rests, the serpentine cadence-shapes, the long notes which blossom into groups of shorter ones. Seen in isolation, the closing part of this clarinet exposition (Fig. 96) discloses a rhapsodic freedom of invention that is remarkable for its time. It is, as so often, a steady stepwise ascent in the bass that gives the passage its cogency and direction.

The soprano takes up the clarinet melody. Before the mention of echo ('Widerhall') the clarinet has already begun to echo the voice, once literally and once with a varied sequence – which in music is a satisfying alternative

Fig. 96

to a true echo. As soon as the word 'Widerhall' appears, Schubert responds with a delightfully varied 'echo'. Verisimilitude is not necessarily the same as musicality, where 'echoes' are concerned. Within this section there are three main key-changes, and in each case the new key is a major third below the old one: thus Schubert travels from B flat to G flat, from G flat to D, and from D to B flat again — a further symbol of distance (like the echo) in this scene of mountains and valleys.

The doleful G minor middle section begins with a theme reminiscent of the Arioso dolente ('Klagender Gesang') in the finale of Beethoven's Op. 110 Piano Sonata. An usual feature of the final Allegretto is that, after its central episode in D, the B flat theme is recapitulated with its first sub-phrase in retrograde — an enchanting twist which has all the more point because the shape it reverses is so extensively featured in this section. Something similar happens to the clarinet echoes eleven bars into the Piu mosso coda, adding a further dimension to the musical possibilities of 'echo'. If this is Schubert's last song (though at present there is an even chance that *Die Taubenpost* was), it closes the oeuvre not with a true Lied, but with a unique experiment (provided that 'experiment' does not deny artistic worth or integrity) that contains echoes of youth but at the same time points forward to what might have been. It points, perhaps, to the possibility that obbligato instruments (like the horn of *Auf dem Strom* or the clarinet here) might have become more frequent contributors to later songs; but also to the thought that the clarinet, in which Schubert had found not only an eloquent partner for the voice but a wonderfully expressive and pliant medium in its own right, might have been soon favoured with a sonata. Beethoven had done as much for the horn, and inaugurated a horn-and-piano repertory. Fig. 96 alone suggests that the time was ripe for the birth of a clarinet-and-piano medium, and that Schubert was ready to bring it into the world.

The Late Piano Sonatas

It is sometimes assumed that a pianist-composer writes his music at the piano, or at least conceives it there, through the fingers, before retiring elsewhere to put pen to paper. This was certainly the case with many composers. With Schubert a different pattern probably prevailed. Access to a piano was not always an easy matter for him. As a boy he had the use of a five-octave Konrad Graf instrument bought by his father at about the time of the first performance of the Mass in F, but his frequent changes of address thereafter often left him without a piano, and special arrangements were sometimes made for access to one. He certainly wrote many non-keyboard works away from the piano – including, one surmises, the symphonies and chamber music. There is no reason why he should not have composed songs or piano music without a keyboard to hand. Indeed his close friend Spaun tells us that 'his means were never sufficient for him to buy or to hire a pianoforte and he was restricted to composing his masterpieces at the writing-table.'[1] Spaun was perhaps unaware of instances when Schubert had access to pianos outside his lodgings. Even so, it is as likely as not that he worked for the most part out of immediate reach of a keyboard when he composed the sonatas and many other piano works of his later period. The late piano sonatas, incidentally, fill a compass of about five and a half octaves, reflecting the general availability of six-octave keyboards.

The earliest of the sonatas to keep a secure place in the repertoire dates from the summer of 1819, when Schubert enjoyed a two-month holiday at Steyr in Upper Austria. It was for the daughter of one of his hosts there that he composed his Sonata in A major, D.664, and if Schubert had not told us (in a letter to his brother Ferdinand back in Vienna) that Josefine was a pianist of some accomplishment, we would deduce as much from the sonata itself. 'Unimaginably lovely', wrote Schubert of the countryside around Steyr in the same letter to Ferdinand, and 'very pretty' of Josefine. Perhaps both delights are to be found celebrated in this music of wide-eyed youthful contentment. The shortest of his complete sonatas, it has moments of gravity, drama even, to leaven its prevailing serenity, lyricism and good humour; but that is no more than must be in a true sonata.

It matters little to the listener that the first movement defies two conventions of Classical sonata form, for it does this so nonchalantly and naturally that the ear simply finds the lyrical flow irresistible. Tradition has it that the first theme of such a movement should be terse, exhibit potential for development, and not be a fully formed melody. Schubert's leisurely tune contains a succession of perfectly balanced strains within its broad paragraph, and sounds more like an easy-going rondo tune than a subject for sonata form. In fact, one could almost imagine Schubert, after its first eight bars, continuing with the ninth bar of his Rondo in the same key for piano duet (D.951). The triplets which rise from the theme's last cadence lead to a second subject which begins in the same key, before moving off to the conventional second-subject key. That is the second denial of previously observed norms, except that Mozart had done the same, no less persuasively, in his String Quintet in G minor. A passionate outburst in the development section is the nearest this movement comes to bravura.

The following Andante is similarly unified in conception, its haunting second idea being a continuation of the first over a rocking left-hand figuration. Again, sonata form masquerades as an unbroken rhapsodic rumination. With its upbeat scale-descent to the first beat, the opening theme of the finale has a Haydnesque wit, married to a Mozartian limpidity of texture. After the short silence that follows the first group, another witticism enlivens the second theme, when a sudden long note perversely halts its progress. The jest is given a new slant when the theme shortly returns an octave higher: this time the accompaniment continues below the theme. The brilliant exertions and grand gestures that characterize the later progress of this movement always lead to a renewal of elegance or playfulness, the opening theme displaying new little twists even in the last bars.

Some four years elapsed before another sonata was completed – years in which the Quartettsatz and 'Unfinished' Symphony testify to a new capacity for self-discovery. The Sonata in A minor (D.784) too represents, in its own terms, a leap into the future. From the start, we are in a new landscape. Sibelius came to the mind of Gordon Jacob when he quoted a passage from this movement (bars 34–7).[2] We can never altogether explain a work's uniqueness, but there are a number of observations which might illuminate the particularity of Schubert's thinking in D.784. First, there is a marked absence of the conventional piano figurations on which he had to varying extents relied in his previous sonatas. By that measure, the first movement is not pianistic in an obvious way. Second, this music poses a bold new approach to the issue of timing – timing in a broad sense which embraces tempo, rhythm, motion and repose, and the wider aspects of architecture which depend on these. For this reason it is probably the hardest of his piano movements to interpret. Only if its progress is properly measured will the successive sections of the music coalesce into a meaningful whole. Third, the use of key colour is somewhat uncharacter-istically restrained.

The measured tread of the opening, enlivened by a few short dotted notes, owes something to the earlier F minor Sonata. The theme is given out in bare octaves, but the addition of harmony at the third bar implies that there is to be a fully harmonized cadence at the fourth bar. But Schubert seems to want to etch the line and rhythm of the melody firmly on the mind at this point, so withholds the obvious chord from the last two notes of the phrase, which, a thus naked C and A, are destined to be a mainspring of the movement – their rhythm being often more important than their exact melodic interval. That rhythm is indeed the starting point of the second subject, in the unusual key (for a minor-key movement) of the dominant major, which proceeds with gently swinging, hypnotic effect, challenged from time to time by a fortissimo interruption. There is such an illusion of space in the scarcely-varied somnambulistic tread of this second subject that Schubert curtails his second group earlier than is his habit.

The development is a broad dynamic arch, rising from *pp* to *ff* and falling back to *pp* so that the recapitulation can recreate the atmosphere of the beginning of the movement exactly. It is a singularly bold step, in the recapitulation, to clothe the second subject with triplets, which have had no place in the movement up to this point. The final climax of the coda is the delivery in four octaves of the fourth bar ('mainspring') idea in double augmentation. This dramatic happening sets the seal upon the importance of bar 4, whose rise to power adumbrates that of bar 3 in the first movement of the 'Great' C major Symphony; but it also isolates, for the last time, the texture of bare octaves which is a recurrent focus of this movement. (More than one fifth of the movement consists of a single line, presented in one, two, three or four octaves.) Also, in these final bars, the concern of this movement with elemental contrasts between *pp* and *ff* is played out to the last cadence.

This is a necessarily brief outline of a movement which, like some others in these sonatas, merits a chapter to itself. It is a vast movement, outlasting the other two movements of the sonata put together, yet so riveting is it in its elemental power that any question of long-windedness or diffuseness seems irrelevant.

The following Andante combines evanescence and elusiveness with poetic compression in a way which seems to anticipate some of Brahms's short free-standing piano pieces. To be sure, there is an obvious textural kinship, where the openings are concerned, with the Romance in F, Op. 118, No. 5 (the identity of key helps). But the initial deployment of material is more readily recalled by the Intermezzo in A minor, Op. 76, No. 7. Brahms's opening five-note strain picks out notes 3, 4, 5, 6 and 8 of

Schubert's, with octave-doubling as in Schubert: the ruminative parenthesis with which this overlaps is an oscillation on and below the dominant (where Schubert's oscillates above and below it) and this parenthesis becomes the foundation for an episode (but so extensive, in Brahms, as to become most of the piece).

In the finales of his piano sonatas, Schubert did not challenge Beethoven on his own ground: he attempted no fugue-within-a-fugue ('Hammerklavier'), no fusion of recitative, aria and fugue (Op. 110), no variation structures, whether circular (Op. 109) or heaven-bent (Op. 111). But the finale of D.784 has its own structural innovations, which Beethoven would surely have admired. A case could be argued for sonata form or sonata-rondo. Either way, it offers a bracing alternation of fire and lyricism, with the added dazzle of scurrying counterpoint and a brilliant virtuoso close which tests the player's agility in rapid octaves.

The unfinished Sonata in C (D.840) known as the 'Reliquie' offers a rare treat to Schubertians who know the finished works and wish to explore beyond. Dated April 1825, a few months before Schubert set out on the Gmunden–Gastein holiday which stimulated him to write another C major work, the 'Great' Symphony, it has something of that work's spaciousness but is far more wayward and unconventional in its tonal schemes – and at times in its harmonic progress from bar to bar. (The constraints placed upon the composer by the limited capabilities of brass instruments at this time would have prevented him from venturing in a symphony the degree of tonal adventure to be found in the 'Reliquie'.)

The first movement is not Schubert's longest. The impression of spaciousness is conveyed by the measured tempo, the focus on steady rhythms, and the leisurely deployment of a small amount of thematic material. Moreover, when a vast tonal distance is traversed in a short time, the ear may be fooled into equating distance with time, or at least may suffer temporal disorientation. It is in fact a unique tonal distance at which Schubert chooses to set his second subject: it is in the minor key on the leading note (B minor). (*Lebensstürme* for piano duet has its second subject in the major key on the leading note, in a minor-key work.) But in temporal terms, B minor need not be far. Schubert leaps to it from C in a matter of three bars, with an extraordinary accented dissonance on the way (Fig. 97). When the music cadences in B minor, the rhythm which

Fig. 97

has already been given prominence starts a new life as accompaniment to the second subject. Thus, however disorienting the shock modulation may have been, there is a compensating element of continuity and cohesion on the rhythmic front. The new subject itself takes its rhythm from the very first theme, but acquires a new breadth from its seamless flow in one four-bar phrase, specifically marked by Schubert 'ligato' (smoothly), and from its slow harmonic underpinning. Each chord lasts for two bars, and the first harmonic move is the unusual one from a tonic to the mediant, a type of progression notably lacking in dynamism, but mesmerizing in its somnambulistic effect.

There is more than a prophetic hint of Brahms at the heart of the development, where the first phrase of the first subject appears in cut-and-thrust, one-bar exchanges between left hand and right, with triplets ringing through whenever a hand can be spared for them. True, this has the look and feel of an orchestral set-to, making the most of timbral antiphonies; but between-the-hands antiphonies are hardly less exciting, when as neatly engineered as here. Another kind of engineering, of the broader structural sort, enables Schubert to fuse development to recapitulation so artfully that the point of junction is barely detectable. The coda, reviewing all the component ideas of the first subject, builds to a climax of Brucknerian breadth and power before fading to a soft close.

The Andante slow movement is in that form which might best be called 'abridged rondo', the C section of sonata-rondo being omitted to leave ABABA. In practice Schubert does not make the plan particularly easy to follow, because his impulse to diversify the surface of the music generates a richness of detail and waywardness of variation that puts local incident in sharper focus than broader architecture. The richness of detail has to do with a manner which is essentially epigrammatic. We hear two notes, a silence, three notes, another silence, eight short notes and more silence . . . The silences are short, and rhythmic, sufficing merely to dice the music into tiny blocks. Even when there is no silence, the invention still seems to articulate itself in bite-sized pieces. This character is not marked enough for us to be talking of the emergence of a new Schubert style, yet he does seem to be groping towards a new poetry in mosaic.

After his slow movement Schubert planned a minuet but failed to finish it, although he did return to it at some later date to add a complete trio. This minuet could be claimed to comprise one of the most daring technical experiments ever undertaken by Schubert, as audacious in its way as the palindrome in *Die Zauberharfe*. A minuet traditionally begins with a first section that is immediately repeated – the repeat being exact or slightly varied. Schubert here defies that convention, probably being the first to do so. In a minuet in A flat major, he repeats in A major. This is particularly daring. A second subject in the minor key on the leading note is one thing. But tinkering with minuet form is another, for no movement type found in multi-movement works is so hidebound by tradition as the minuet/scherzo. Strangely, Schubert later begins the reprise in A major, not A flat major, before laying down his pen. Equally strangely, at the beginning of the second section he writes 'accelerando', but there is no cancellation of this, nor any obvious place where cancellation would be appropriate. Did he mean 'accelerato' (faster)? Or did he intend the piece to accelerate right through to the end, or to the recapitulation? This minuet may have been an even more unorthodox conception than we thought.

There can be little doubt that Schubert would have ended his minuet in A flat major, leaving the trio in G sharp minor (which he completed) to follow on the same tonic. The return to A flat could have been simply effected, but perhaps he thought the resultant structure would not be viable. It is a matter for regret that, for whatever reason, this astonishing experiment was not taken to its conclusion. Whether the incompletion of the finale should occasion such regret is another matter. It has some characteristic ideas, but the life of each is over-extended, and the music sometimes lacks tonal direction. Incidentally, if he had gone on to complete what – as far as it goes – turns out to be a finale in sonata form, he would presumably have amended his initial 'rondo' heading.

Less than a month after abandoning the 'Reliquie' Schubert was at work on the superb Sonata in A minor (D.845). It begins with the sort of dramatic re-interpretation of sonata form that one might expect from Beethoven rather than Schubert. An opening phrase in octaves receives a hesitant harmonized response (Fig. 98a). A long crescendo builds to a new theme (Fig. 98b), again made of two terse contrasting blocks. This adds up to a volatile, highly charged opening paragraph for a sonata, looking forward to such later instances as the electrifying opening of Dvořák's Seventh Symphony in D minor. Everything pushes forward. The crescendo drives to the next idea; and the lack of self-fulfilment in the first theme

Fig. 98 a

leaves the ear expectant of later resumption and development. This cross-cutting technique is familiar in modern film, where a number of discrete scenes or episodes follow each other rapidly, to be drawn into a meaningful relationship later as the story unfolds.

It almost goes without saying that a movement based on such volatile ingredients will follow a course rich in contrasts, unexpected turns, and surprise shifts of key. When the drama is near its end, Schubert crowns it with one of his longest and most exciting coda 'excursions'. The excursion moves away towards the virgin key of B minor, so far untouched, and travels back through a succession of *double-entendre* harmonies, the right hand climbing steadily to distant heights. Once the tonic key is regained Schubert can hardly do other than adopt the Beethovenian device of multiple alternations of tonic and dominant harmony, to restore the balance after the footloose excursion. To close, a final derivative of the initial motive of Fig. 98a struggles, in heavy four-octave unison, to reach up to the minor third before falling back to the keynote, in much the same way as a more famous theme did three years earlier, to seal the tragic conclusion of the first movement of the 'Unfinished' Symphony.

The Andante con moto second movement brings an altogether lighter atmosphere, and the transparent structure of a set of variations. The theme is in C major, and the first two variations display that progressive efflorescence of short notes which characterizes so many Classical variation-sets. A remarkable transformation is brought about in the third variation. The switch to C minor at first occasions hushed rapture – but thereafter a marked rise in temperature, as dissonances are contrived on most beats of each bar. This single variation is as finely crafted a tone-poem as one will find among Schubert variation-sets, and is enough on its own to show that the frisson between his probing imagination and the formal constraints of the variation genre was a richly productive one. The third and fourth variations continue the trend begun in the first two.

The first idea of the scherzo, confined to the same mean ration of chords as Fig. 98b, cannot on this account be said to lack incident, thanks to variation in timing, chord-position, dynamics and articulation. In other words, it is true to the character stamped on the sonata from the start. The trio, in F major, marked Un poco piu lento, displays a harmonic sleight of hand that is all the more effective because it is applied in the context of a rustic trio with a tune of calculated diatonic simplicity, for the most part over a drone bass. The finale is a sonata-rondo, much of it conceived in two parts, a feature which calls to mind another A minor finale, by Mozart (K.310). Schubert does add to the texture in places, but manages to imbue the prevailing athleticism with due weight without thickening very often or very much. The second subject, as hard to distinguish from the first as in the first movement, culminates in the distinctive idea of four repeated whole-bar chords which evocatively anticipates the similar pattern in the same location (finale, second subject) in the 'Great' C major Symphony.

The Sonata in D was a product of the trip to Bad Gastein in the summer of 1825, and the amount of activity that the two hands are expected to encompass, or imply, in the first movement makes it sound at times like a piano sketch for a symphonic movement of such bustling energy as the finale of the 'Great' C major, begun on the same trip. But then this sonata, uniquely, was written for a professional pianist. Karl Maria von Bocklet was a member of the Schubert circle, and the composer exploited his virtuosity to forge a work of extravert abandon. Risks were taken in the process. This opening movement is characterized by a daring balance of rhythmic ingredients, in which the galloping triplets which first appear in the third bar dominate for long periods, yet never cause the initial thematic rhythm to lose influence or relevance; by a very full and active if not overloaded texture; and by a breathless haste, goaded by Schubert's use of the sign implying two beats rather than four in the bar. So impetuous is its racily pianistic progress that virtually all twelve keys are hurtled through in a not particularly long space of time.

But what is a passage marked Un poco piu lento e con cappriccio doing in the middle of a sonata exposition? It is all part of the extravert abandon; and it does come at the most relaxed moment of the exposition, immediately after a jaunty – and frankly rather facile – second subject has made its first appearance, in an easy-going, regular eight-bar strain. Its content even has non-sonata resonances, for it skips up and down huge intervals as a yodeller might do on the mountains Schubert described when writing about his Bad Gastein visit. To adopt the yodel in a keyboard dance, as Schubert sometimes did, is one thing; to admit it into a sonata is quite another, though it might gatecrash the trio of a minuet or scherzo without incongruity. The statuesque harmony – three bars of G major triad and three of C major, with little tail-echoes as though the mountains answer back – sustains the allusion to outdoor music, and almost allows those chords of G and C to acquire the meaning of two self-sufficient tonics. Perhaps Schubert had recalled Beethoven's easing of the tempo for a few bars at the equivalent point in another otherwise headlong movement, the first of his Op. 111 Sonata in C minor.

Some piano music offers its performer an acute pleasure of an almost tactile sort as the fingers trigger a stream of winsome sound. The luxuriant textures of the slow movement place it in this class, perhaps more surely than any other of Schubert's sonata movements. The form is 'abridged sonata-rondo', with a second subject but no central development or episode and thus represented as ABABA. Close study reveals a high degree of technical control and planning, but above this is music which pleases the ear and builds to a climax of sonorous power. Schubert reserves a triple forte marking for this climax, which caps the recapitulation of the second subject (the second B section) and makes use of the raw syncopated rhythm which has characterized the second subject from the start. Particularly effective, after the syncopated rhythm has been isolated in this way, is its carrying-forward into the restatement of the rondo theme, punctuating each tiny sub-phrase in a beautifully contrived manner.

Suddenly jerking into life with an extended upbeat-figure in dotted rhythm, the scherzo indulges its dance impulse in a variety of ways. At first, with its combination of thick middle-to-low chords and a thumping hemiola rhythm, it is an earthbound precursor of the Dvořákian furiant. But no sooner is its first strain complete than it trips airily in two-part counterpoint in the upper half of the keyboard. Both elements impress themselves on the ear with a rehearing. Then symphonic tensions darken the beginning of the second section, where the tonality is hoisted up to B flat, the music being impelled to its cadence in that key by a potent, energizing discord of Beethovenian toughness rather than Schubertian luxuriance (Fig. 99).

Fig. 99

Once in B flat, Terpsichore promptly shows a fourth face: this is an infectious Ländler, as jaunty in its sprightly pointed rhythms as any freestanding example of the genre Schubert wrote under that nomenclature. These are the four facets of Schubert's longest scherzo in all the sonatas; but one of them remains to be recast. When D major is restored for a reprise, the airy two-part counterpoint duly has its turn, but now becomes a stentorian utterance based on an illusory inversion of the original counterpoint. That is to say, the upper part in Fig. 100a becomes the bass (so that the counterpoint is inverted), but the melodic line is itself turned upside-down in the process (inverted in the other sense – melodic inversion), while the original bass line is padded out in chords by the right hand (Fig. 100b). What is particularly instructive here is that Schubert does not strive for exactitude, either in reproducing the shape of the left-hand line when it is transferred to the right hand, or in inverting the right-hand line when he wants it to act as bass. The ear will pick up the reference, if it's going to, without the need for more than an approximation. The trio, so close in bearing to that of the E major Sonata (D.157) as to borrow a snatch of melody or a chord progression from it here and there, is

Fig. 100

delightfully inexplicit in its phrase-structure. It builds to a climax through a fine modulating sequence, and the reprise within the second section is most imaginatively engineered.

Schubert himself designates his finale a rondo, and again it is of the older type, a double sandwich with two episodes interlaced between three statements of the rondo theme. The emphasis here is on lightness (even 'daintiness' is a term that fits, for all its pejorative overtones) and on good humour. This, at least, is the manner adopted by the rondo theme itself, and maintained throughout its returns too, none of which ever rises above a piano dynamic. Indeed, when the rondo theme makes its first return Schubert reminds the player what it is that is being recalled by adding a 'Con delicatezza' marking, followed by a further cautionary 'Leggiermente' at the second return. The two episodes both set off in a similarly restrained manner but rise to climaxes of some power and passion. In the first episode there is some stringent double counterpoint which calls to mind the abrasive linear conflicts of third-period Beethoven. The second episode, at a slightly slower tempo, evokes the sentiment of a heart-on-sleeve impromptu, Schubert even anticipating – in some of the long four-note gavotte upbeats – a tear-jerking Puccini touch by doubling the upper line an octave lower, with harmonic filling between (and only between). The stormier middle section of this ternary episode brings some startling key-juxtapositions, as when Schubert jumps from B minor to G minor within the one bar, or from D minor to F sharp minor in three bars. He likes to sharpen the colour of a key-relationship by causing the two keys to confront each other over as short a space as possible, and seems little daunted by the risk of incoherence.

Schubert began his G major Sonata of 1826 by doing two things he had never done before in the first movement of a sonata: he wrote a time-signature of 12/8 and a tempo indication of 'Molto moderato'. The only other sonata to share this tempo marking would be the last one of all, the still more expansive B flat, D.960. The combined effect of the 12/8 time and unhurried tempo is that the downbeats are that much further apart than usual. If that makes the rhythms sometimes appear lumbering on paper, they merely test the player's ability to make of them the compelling lyrical flow that was undoubtedly part of Schubert's conception.

As 'Cantabile' suggests, the invention is melody-driven, the songful urge scarcely being suppressed even when bursts of bravura not incongruously emerge. The spaciousness of the music tends to waywardness, but did the publisher who therefore called this movement a fantasy when he tried to sell the four movements off separately fail to observe the underlying defer-ence to sonata-form traditions? By Schubert's own standards, it is an unusual sonata form. The urge to explore distant keys, enjoying the colour of modulation, is for once channelled almost entirely into the development, except for an early touch of magic when the music slips without ceremony into B minor.

It is significant that Schubert's last string quartet, the G major, was written only three months before this sonata in the same key. In the quartet, as soon as the second subject has been first stated, Schubert repeats it in its entirety while the first violin soars aloft with a descant in shimmering short notes. Exactly the same procedure is followed in the sonata, with the pianist's right hand acting as violin and eventually reaching the same highest point (d'''', three octaves and a tone above middle C) as in the quartet. Soon, however, after the downward rushing scales, come moments of heart-stopping lyricism that are pure pianistic poetry, even if their finely judged economy of layout evokes the quartet medium. The development comes to grips with the serioso implications of the easy-going material, but at the end of the recapitulation Schubert is loth to disturb the serene calm which closed the exposition, so leaves it intact, merely adding varied repetitions – over stay-at-home harmony – of the movement's first motive, swelling and receding to a soft close.

One of Schubert's favourite schemes for a slow movement is represented in the Andante: gentle outer sections frame more dynamic inner spans.

These inner spans were an afterthought, yet so rich are they in both dramatic vehemence and haunting reflective sequels that one may easily regard them as the emotional core of the movement. In a sonata whose outer movements are only moderate in pace, Schubert resisted any temptation to insert a racy scherzo, preferring a more sedate dance genre to enhance the consistency of the work. The minuet and trio owe less to sonata-minuet conventions than to the keyboard dances, often of Ländler type, that Schubert had produced in sets throughout his career.

Did he have the finale of Beethoven's Op. 31, No. 1 in G at the back of his mind when he set about his own finale? It is an Allegretto, like Beethoven's, in the same key and time. Beethoven explicitly called his a rondo, while Schubert's implicitly is one. But he beats a path of his own, a more extended one than Beethoven's and one that includes the picturesque digressions we would expect from him. After the rondo theme – an informal succession of ideas – has completed its nonchalant course, a dance-like episode ensues, not without its tensions. The rondo section returns, with the first theme now sung by an inner 'tenor' voice. (Beethoven had given his rondo theme to the tenor voice earlier than this, when the theme was repeated within the first section of the movement, soon after its first statement.) The second, central episode is another dance of a kind, not unlike the first, but it quickly gives way to a simple song in the minor with an Alberti accompaniment, whose return in the major is one of Schubert's happiest inspirations. The second dance returns, to lead to the final reprise of the rondo section and an evanescent coda that almost brings the sonata full circle to where it began.

Schubert unknowingly uttered his last in the medium of the piano sonata with three works which all carry the date September 1828 but were probably worked on over several months. Like the three last symphonies Mozart completed in a shorter time, they have markedly individual characters. When Schubert allows Beethoven to stimulate his own invention by adopting a model from one of the older composer's works, he does not usually place the 'borrowed' material up front, nor leave it as thinly disguised as at the beginning of his Sonata in C minor. The risk is enormous, if a first theme is to leave its stamp on the entire movement it initiates. How can Schubert avoid writing a Beethovenian movement if its prime idea is so patently in Beethoven's debt? There are two answers to this question, one specific and one general. Specifically, if the structures of the movements concerned are generically different, the scope for diverging from the model will increase as the music unfolds. Schubert's model, for a movement in sonata form, is the theme of a set of variations – the Thirty-two Variations in C minor. More generally, the dominance of the model over the subsequent course of events will be resisted by sheer strength of personality.

The array of features which find their way from Beethoven's theme into Schubert's is pretty comprehensive: key, triple time, melodic outline, harmonic progression, tendency to equate first two beats of bar and lighten the third, forte, strong accentuation. He presents this theme, however, only twice more in his sonata movement, so that there are only two chances of his echoing Beethoven's theme again, or subsequent variations of it in Beethoven's set. Just once, twenty-one bars into the movement, he seems to forget himself for a few moments and write a variation. But this variation has nothing to do with Beethoven's set of thirty-two: rather, it has a fine impetus of its own, which is, if anything, more in the tradition of other C minor works by Beethoven, such as the C minor String Quartet, Op. 18, No. 4, and the Op. 13 Piano Sonata ('Pathétique'). In any case, it is characteristic of Schubert's late works that a first theme is presented twice, the second time in varied form, although usually the second statement is the more forceful one, which is not the case here.

Schubert is very much his own man in the second subject in E flat major, especially when it slips momentarily into D flat. And Beethoven is left a long way behind – as are Schubert's themes – when the time comes to prepare for the recapitulation. Here, at a *pp* dynamic, extended play on the rising semitone implicit in the first theme wriggles menacingly, deep in the bass, occasionally emerges in the treble, and through prolonged use comes to have almost the weight of a new theme, but for its nebulous character. Soon hushed chromatic semiquaver runs appear in the right hand, while this new 'theme' continues below, and as these serpentine lines writhe in eerie two-part counterpoint the tonality becomes nebulous too. The home dominant G is reached in both parts, the dynamic drops to *ppp*, and soon the rhythm of the first subject insinuates itself, as the bass pulls itself up chromatically from dominant to tonic for the recapitulation. This passage, which has been likened to passages in late Beethoven (as distinct from the early second-period Beethoven of the C minor Variations), reveals Schubert at his most original and daring. With many other details beyond the ordinary, it characterizes this opening movement as one of extreme individuality, for all the bold inheritance of its first bars. And it is this that stays in the mind as the movement closes, for its coda is solely concerned with this 'new theme', now more firmly anchored tonally but threatening metrical stability when a four-beat segment repeats itself at once in the context of the three-beat bars, so that it has a changed metrical meaning each time (Fig. 101).

Fig. 101

The slow movement is Schubert's only Adagio in the mature sonatas. In A flat major, its first theme, outwardly solemn and formal, speaks eloquently, with emotive touches of harmony. After its first eight-bar presentation, it repeats itself, but with an arrest at the fourth bar in the tonal area of D flat. This pause sows the seed of later excursions, for it is at this point in the theme's later appearances in the movement that opportunities for increasingly far-reaching modulatory excursions are taken. The final reprise of the first theme has a staccato bass reminiscent of that which underpins the theme of the D minor slow movement of Beethoven's 'Pastoral' Sonata, Op. 28.

The third movement is a hybrid. Schubert calls it a minuet. He marks it Allegro; but that does not make it a scherzo. Texturally it hovers between minuet and scherzo, while the trio is happy to assume it is the minuet trail that it should be picking up. There is, in the minuet itself, a play on phrase-structures, but this constitutes not so much a 'joke' as a serious probing of ambiguities. Even the sudden silences towards the end are a comment on these substantive issues rather than a Haydnesque frolic. The structure of the melody is elusive, but when its reprise at the end of the second section places a silent bar after every fourth bar Schubert seems to be assuring us that it is, and always has been, a 4+4+4 structure. A further, longer silence marks off the trio, a charming little A flat Ländler free of such metrical preoccupations.

No single movement by Schubert has been undervalued as much as the finale of this C minor Sonata. Philip Radcliffe was right, and perhaps unique, to recognize it as 'an astonishing achievement'.[3] He also correctly diagnosed a case of sonata form rather than rondo form. At a first hearing, however, the sheer quantity and eventfulness of the music that passes before the first theme is heard for a second time is disconcerting. Having thus covered 242 bars with his exposition, Schubert builds in no provision for its repeat. Thus 186 bars of development are added before (at bar 428) the first theme makes a comeback. The amazing fecundity of what passes between these points compounds the problem, as does the composer's disinclination to make it clear to the ear where exposition ends and development begins.

Any galloping 6/8 finale written after 1802 stands a chance of being indebted to the finale of Beethoven's E flat Sonata, Op. 31, No. 3, especially if it makes a special feature of quavers slurred across the bar (and the half-bar). But after the thematic similarity is noted, any comparison beyond that yields diminishing interest – except that while both first themes sound like rondo themes neither movement is a rondo. Schubert's finale is a movement to be enjoyed, reflected upon, and enjoyed all the more. Close familiarity can eventually bring one to an understanding of its complex form and an appreciation of the subtlety with which one theme is derived

from another. It is a tour de force of vitality, stamina (for the performer
as well as the composer) and colour.

The second of this final trilogy, the Sonata in A major (D.959), presents
a more brightly lit scenario. The forms are explicit, the themes outgoing,
the textures more conventionally lyrical, and at times dance-like. The first
theme is not altogether transparent, though. A majestic, solemn six-bar
strain, it conceals its essence between its initially static topmost and lowest
parts, in the middle strands which rise and fall in parallel thirds (Fig. 102a).
Its immediate sequel is a cascade of triplets falling through four octaves,
and two pointed chords on the second and third beats of the four-beat
bar. The opening strain now returns (Fig. 102b), but with the moving
thirds now exposed at the bottom of the texture, and a countermelody
added above which incorporates the pointed chord rhythm followed by
the triplet rhythm of the cascade. This fusing of different elements may
be unprecedented so early in a movement, but it typifies the strong developmental urge which may surface at any point in a late Schubert design.

Fig. 102

The 'theme' is then abandoned, and the triplets and chords take over,
being the subject of what – with its modulations to C major and A flat

major en route to the regular second-subject key of E major – is almost a premature development section standing for a transition. And a wonderful little 'development' it is too, with its marvellous pretence at double counterpoint, and its trenchant, forward-driving discords. It is sometimes suggested that Schubert errs in his appetite for development outside a development proper. But why should this not be a valid diversification of sonata form, if the 'out-of-turn development' is as vitally inventive as here and does not steal the real development's thunder? Like Beethoven, Schubert can justify an end-development (within a coda) too. In the present instance, he gives us another new version of the opening theme, extended into a long lyrical paragraph, before inversions of the triplet cascade dissolve the movement in a harp-like mist, the final cadence being that peculiarly rich one with which other products of Schubert's last three months bow out, the tonic chord being preceded by an augmented sixth on the flattened supertonic (the String Quintet, the slow movement of the 'Tenth' Symphony).

The Andantino in F sharp minor is, on the face of it, a barcarolle. One could imagine its theme in a Schubert song, suggesting the gentle motion of a boat on placid, twilit waters. To pursue the metaphor, the boat scarcely moves, in that the music clings doggedly to F sharp minor for nearly seventy bars. Even when the bass slips down to an E natural, while the opening of the melody is repeated at its original pitch as though in F sharp minor, the implication of A major (which is merely the relative major) is never fulfilled. A major remains a chimera, in the same way that A flat major did in the second bar of the F minor song *Erster Verlust* (D.226). This stay-at-home harmonic circling, together with the almost incessant rocking of the left hand, has its purpose: the pent-up emotional energy is to be released in a middle section which is probably the wildest outburst of fantasy Schubert ever committed to paper. It is not surprising that writers have seen its torrential scales, pulse-threatening rhythms, trills, shock harmonies, writhing chromaticism, fragments of recitative, dramatic silences, and stabbed chords as redolent of a *divertissement á l'hongroise*. The allusion is helpful, if it reminds us that this episode is not more out of place here than Brahms's rhapsody of Hungarianism in the middle of the slow movement of his Clarinet Quintet is unfitting. Whether such unexpected turbulence in the waters of a barcarolle reflect the spiritual state of Schubert himself or of his composing 'persona' is a matter for necessarily inconclusive debate. Listeners must judge for themselves, too, whether there is a disguised reminiscence of part of the G flat major Impromptu, D.899, No. 3, just before the barcarolle is resumed to complete the ternary design, and what significance that might have.

The brightly tripping scherzo uses the piano as percussionist and songster by turns. There is a moment of high drama when a downward-rushing

scale of C sharp minor interrupts a passage securely settled in C major.
The trio, especially marked Un poco piu lento, suggests Schubert in string
quintet mood (his String Quintet in C was possibly being worked on at
the same time). The three middle instruments carry the theme in close
harmony, while the first violin and cello alternate in a quick-fire exchange
of terse motives. The pianist's left hand acts out an adroit synthesis of the
violin and cello parts, skipping to right and left of the other hand.

The bald facts about Schubert's finale read like a recipe for third-rate
art. First, he borrows and adapts a theme from an earlier movement, the
slow movement of the A minor Sonata, D.537; second, he models the
plan of the movement on the finale of Beethoven's G major Sonata, Op. 31,
No. 1; and third, what results is a classic textbook case of sonata-rondo.
The musical impression is, on the contrary, of fresh-minted inspiration
carving out its own natural path as it goes. The external stimuli are completely absorbed and the gracious flow of the Allegretto theme (fleshing
out the skeleton of the D.537 theme into something new and individual)
infects the whole movement.

The schematic (not thematic) modelling on Beethoven has never been
more copiously explained and illustrated than by Charles Rosen.[4] To his
observations it may be added that both developments begin with the rondo
theme turned minor. In other respects, however, Schubert goes his own
way: his second group is three times as long as Beethoven's, its shapely
cantabile line shifting from treble to bass and exploring many a tonal corner
in a wholly engaging way; he begins his recapitulation in the bizarrely
unorthodox key of the submediant major (F sharp major), winning through
to the conventional A major ten bars later; and he refers back to the
opening of the sonata in its last bars – a particular kind of cyclic device
which is perhaps without precedent in the history of sonata composition
('sonata' here embracing quartet and symphony too).

If 'magisterial' is the epithet that comes to mind when one contemplates
Schubert's last work in this great final trilogy, the Sonata in B flat, that
may be because a first movement tends to be disproportionately formative
of a listener's response to the whole work of which it forms a part. But
then this particular first movement is one of Schubert's longest. And the
epithet is intended to be broad enough to encompass the sublime meditation of the slow movement, the mercurial elan of the scherzo, and both
the poetry and the passion of the finale.

'Molto moderato': the exhortation is not as ambiguous as it seems, in
that the music itself dictates a tempo on the spacious side of 'moderate'.
As first movements go, this one is gentle and restrained, lacking true
dynamism even in its development section. It is as though there was a
predetermined level of energy-expenditure above which Schubert, perhaps

in view of the nature of his opening theme, must not go. That theme seems to echo the noble solemnity of Beethoven's 'Archduke' Trio. Schubert had shown his acquaintance with Beethoven's theme more openly in the sketches for his opera *Adrast*. Now it is a more remote model, whose tendency to land heavily on the third beat (through a change of harmony) in its fifth and sixth bars affects Schubert's seventh bar. What happens at the end of Schubert's first strain is as archducal as his theme itself. For just as Beethoven reaches his cadence, arrests the flow, and creates a kind of interlude, before repeating his first strain, so does Schubert. Beethoven has trills and turns in the vicinity of the arrest: Schubert has a long trill in the bass – raising a profound question which, on the face of it directly answered when it returns at the end of the movement, yet resonates beyond that too-simple response of two cadence chords.

The silent pause after this first trill typifies an absence of haste that is endemic. A second trill leads comfortably into G flat major for a less stoical presentation of the theme over a suavely rocking accompaniment. It is the ultimate withdrawal from this key area that brings with it, at the return to B flat, the more forceful restatement of the theme that we might expect if we know the 'Death and the Maiden' Quartet, the String Quintet, and other mature works. With characteristic abruptness Schubert effects a transition, in four bars, to the second key of his three-key exposition, which is F sharp minor. The subject is unorthodox, like the key. If we take the over-simplistic view that a subject is a tune, we might have difficulty in identifying this particular tune (Fig. 103). That it is the 'tenor' that carries the leading line is demonstrated by the fact that this is what Schubert immediately pulls out for subsequent development. Schubert veers to the conventional dominant (F major) for a second theme in the second group, all dancing triplets above (and sometimes below) short chords. So far the music has been threaded by an almost constant flow of either quavers or triplets or semiquavers, Schubert moving easily between the three in paragraph-sized spans. The closing theme of the exposition,

Fig. 103

however, slows to a predominance of crotchets, and becomes fragmented as it proceeds, this fragmentation persisting in the bars leading back to a repeat of the exposition.

In view of the scale of events so far, it would not have been surprising if Schubert had decided to abandon the repeat, as Beethoven had done in such spacious movements as the first of the first 'Rasumovsky' Quartet. But he took pains to compose these special connecting bars, which are not often played. The development has received much attention at the hands of its commentators. An essential point not to be missed is that the 'dancing triplets' are developed by the addition of a new idea in the bass. This new idea becomes a theme in its own right, being presented as such in D flat major after a climax in that key, and later in D minor after a still stronger climax in that key. As the tonality oscillates between D minor and B flat, so this new theme gives way to the first theme, whose atmosphere is re–established well before B flat is unambivalently reached and the recapitulation begins. These are some of the features that contribute to the individuality of one of the greatest sonata movements of all time.

The slow movement has much in common with that of the String Quintet: the sense of time almost standing still, the harmonies slow to change, the theme in close harmony in the middle texture, the air of profound spiritual contemplation. The pianist's left hand is not so much a violin and cello combined, as it is in the similar trio of the D.959 Sonata: rather it provides a single part which gently sweeps upward across the right hand at each bar. The middle section of this ternary movement is based on more conventional tune-and-accompaniment textures, dispensing less ethereal, more heart-on-sleeve sentiments, and is in two sub-sections, the varied repeat of each bringing a more active accompaniment. When the first theme returns, a new murmuring bass figure links each bar to the next. Diversity is also achieved by a new tonal shift at the fourteenth bar, where the dominant chord of C sharp minor melts with breathtaking effect into a C major chord.

That Schubert gives the scherzo the (for him) unusual marking 'Con delicatezza' suggests that here is something of special character. Delicate it certainly is, with airy textures, clear distinctions between legato and staccato touch, and dynamic levels that rarely rise above piano. A forte entry would have been too much of a shock after the rapt quietude of the slow movement. The pianissimo start ensures a measure of continuity with that movement, the change of pace and key providing sensation enough. There is something populist about the tune itself, but this does not mean that it lacks sophistication. It swings from treble to bass to middle voice with kaleidoscopic effect; and the same could be said of its scurrying from one unlikely key to another. These are not the keys that would spring to a student's mind when set the task of writing a scherzo in B flat. The return to B flat in the second section is astonishing even for Schubert. A diminished triad, heard with reference to the foregoing A major, floats in limbo for a few bars before the B natural falls to B flat. With that minimal action the tonic is regained (Fig. 104). Was the merging of 'development' with recapitulation ever so smoothly accomplished? And if smoothness is the intention, what better additional cement than a four-bar melodic phrase which straddles the join, its third bar actually being the point at which recapitulation begins? In fact, the alchemy is still more subtle than that, for the three critical events fall in three successive bars: the phrase begins, the harmonic move follows a bar later, and the recapitulation comes a bar after that. In the tonic minor, the trio temporarily banishes the piercing sunlight, with its conflict between the syncopation of the right hand and the eccentric tread of the bass. The low dynamic level is retained, however, which makes the left-hand thumps all the more menacing.

Fig. 104

What the ear hears at the beginning of the finale is a held dominant of C minor followed by a theme in that key. Schubert is taking us for a ride, however: it quickly becomes clear that the key of the movement is the expected B flat. This oblique approach is, of course, a Beethovenian strategy, and the finale of the 'Eroica' presents the most useful analogy since there, as here, the composer is writing a finale in the same key as the previous movement and wishes to invest that key with an illusion of freshness. Even the momentary illusion of another key (G minor in the case of the E flat 'Eroica') washes the palate, as it were. The held dominant (G) is no mere curtain-raiser: it returns each time the theme returns, and as this is a rondo that is not infrequently. It is even 'resolved' near the close, where it slips to G flat, then to F, the true dominant. Also closely associated with the first theme is a carefree adjunct which, with its cheerfully stomping bass, seems the epitome of *joie de vivre*. One of the happiest moments in all Schubert occurs when this tune returns soon afterwards and at the fifth bar a single note in the melody is changed, this prompting Schubert to peer into the secret garden of A flat major for a few bars before rejoining the main path. No fewer than three further themes follow, comprising the 'second group' of this sonata-rondo in which the interest never flags for a moment and Schubert's skill as a tunesmith who knows that it's the harmony that makes the tune never deserts him. A Presto coda, short but wonderfully conclusive, culminates in a rapid ascent with crescendo to the final summit – crowning with pulse-quickening excitement the most distinguished nineteenth-century corpus of sonatas for piano after Beethoven.

Other Late Piano Works

It is tempting to dismiss Schubert's keyboard dances as lightweight music which holds little for the serious listener: they are part of the social fabric of his life but, in modern terms, more akin to commercial than to legitimate art. (There is no evidence that Schubert received fees for the provision of dance music, but he no doubt earned the respect and gratitude – and perhaps the odd 'consideration' – of a circle of 'society' admirers at little cost to himself.) The routine nature of much that he produced under this heading appears to support this judgement. He bequeathed dozens of miniatures in the most elementary binary form, some based on two chords only and many on no more than three or four, topped by tunes in some cases pretty enough to stay in the mind, and in many cases not.

No real composer, however, can produce reams of functional art without having his true musical instincts engaged from time to time. Schubert's dances do sometimes reveal the real Schubert, the creator of the tiny gem-like Lied or the *moment musical*. And sometimes a link with the grander musical forms emerges. One has to listen or sight-read patiently to unearth the treasure amid this bulky oeuvre, which in end-to-end performance would probably outlast six symphonies. An enlightened musicological survey of the field is overdue.

There is space here merely to lay some markers for the reader's exploration. The dances come in sets (of Ländler or Deutsche or Walzer for the most part, although the distinction is minimal), and the most rewarding set is the *Zwölf Deutsche*, D.790. But flashes of enterprise can be found in other sets. The ninth waltz of *Zwölf Walzer*, D.145, avoids anything like the ubiquitous oom-pah-pah accompaniment as a flowing line of quavers tumbles from the heights, down through the accompanying left hand, to emerge below it. The reprise (in the middle of the second section) inverts the scheme, the quaver line rising from a low bass note, through three and a half octaves, to a trill above the treble stave. Here, and in the penultimate dance of the *Sechzehn Deutsche*, D.783, where two sections of equal length both begin in F minor and gravitate to A flat major and both work out a melodic obsession with the note C, the dance has become the kind of forum for small-scale compositional sport which the bagatelle was to Beethoven.

The character of a scherzo touches D.783, No. 13, where a surprise accented upbeat chord punctuates at every fourth bar. In the *Zwölf Walzer* (published as 'Valses nobles'), D.969, the second section of No. 7 has the gravitas of a sonata movement, and could have come adrift from the minuet of the G major Sonata. Indeed the sixth dance of D.790, composed in 1823, actually became the kernel of the scherzo of the 'Death and the Maiden' String Quartet the following year. Like Mozart, who shortens the gap between 'social music' and 'chamber music' by making an arrangement of his Wind Serenade in C minor for string quintet, Schubert transcendentally raises background music to the highest artistic level. And if any dance attains to that level without the need for adaptation, it is the fifth piece of D.790. Written in the year after the 'Unfinished' Symphony and sharing its B minor key, it is an embryonic tone-poem of rare poignancy. The fact that Schubert sensed its special quality is perhaps indicated by his use of the triple piano marking (*ppp*) for the one and only time in his keyboard dances.

Most of these dances are written-down distillations of music improvised at private parties. There is abundant documentary evidence that the music was in fact danced to.[1] This is a matter of some importance to a consideration of the music. The physique of the biped – two feet normally employed in alternation – requires that in triple time (the metre of all Ländler, Deutsche and Walzer) the group of two bars (one foot leading in the first bar and the other in the second) should be the unit of construction. Why is it, then, that a few of Schubert's hundreds of dances have an odd number of bars? It is one thing to write an eleven-bar introduction, presumably played before the feet are set in motion (*Zwölf Wiener Deutsche*, D.128); quite another to add a choreographically compromising extra bar to the dance itself, as happens in No. 4 of this set. There are in fact two versions of this dance, one of 25 bars and one of 24. A study of the autograph leaves open the possibility that Schubert wrote the shorter version to create a 'dancing edition', having recognized the impracticality of the 25-bar version. But there are superfluous bars also in D.41, No. 15, and in D.335. In the first case, the first section is stretched to nine bars by a Mozartian extension: in the second, the reprise is postponed by a one-bar caesura, in Haydnesque fashion. These last two examples are both minuets. There had of course been some history of stylization in the minuet in the context of sonata and symphony; but it does appear that, even when dancing was the purpose, Schubert could get carried away by musical impulses which lost touch with the actual dance-floor, so that an idealized concept of dance results.

Between the sonatas and the dances comes a group of works which occupies a middle ground. The impromptus, *Moments Musicaux* and *Klavier-stücke* were well suited to performance by Schubert himself at social gatherings, whether they were musical evenings or artistic mixed-media soirées, but they sometimes touch the world of the sonata, just as they often embody the dance spirit. The *Moments Musicaux* comprise six short pieces, written between 1823 and 1828. No. 1 is a minuet and trio in form but has something of the enigmatic, quixotic air of some of the Beethoven bagatelles. No. 2, structured as ABABA, varies the A section at each return and contains some daring modulations, none more so than the direct jump from A flat major to F sharp minor for the second B section – one of the most astonishing tonal junctions in all Schubert. Originally published as *Air Russe*, the third piece, in F minor, is a perky little *pas seul* with latter-day counterparts in the ballet scores of Tchaikovsky and an elder sister in the *Rosamunde* music (Ballet Music No. 2 in G).

If the fourth piece is a dance, the stomping bass and two-part counterpoint of the framing sections carries a faint echo of the Baroque dance tradition, while the 'trio' has the flavour of a Bohemian national dance. No. 5 in F minor is a riot of galloping dactyls, hard-driven and single-minded from beginning to end. Like the first piece, the sixth has the build of a minuet and trio. There is an air of sorrow, deeply felt, softened by moments of consolation, but if one expects changes from minor to major and vice versa to coincide with the changes of mood in a predictable, formulaic manner, a hearing will be instructive as well as moving. When pacing this piece, the performer would do well to forget the title someone attached to the first edition – *Plaintes d'un Troubadour* – and think instead of the tempo of some of the minuets in Beethoven's early piano sonatas, which are also Allegretto.

It was not Schubert who gave the title Four Impromptus to his D.899 pieces but their publisher, Haslinger, perhaps in the hope of jumping aboard an 1820s bandwagon, in that the Bohemian composer Voříšek, for example, had used the term for his Op. 7 of 1822. The origins of the short, free-standing piano piece are, then, more to the point in this case than the title. Beethoven's first set of bagatelles (1802) may rightly claim the distinction of being first in this field, but the contribution of Voříšek's fellow countryman Tomášek (b. 1774) was perhaps more relevant. Even before Tomášek, Mozart's friend Joseph Mysliveček wrote some *Divertimenti per cembalo* which are one-movement divertimenti. Remaining unpublished, they probably acted as stimulus for the first published set of such short pieces, Tomášek's Six Eclogues, composed in 1807 and published in Prague in 1810. These are poetic miniatures in ternary form which are the true precursors of both Schubert's piano pieces and those of the later Romantic age. Tomášek's Eclogues arose from 'his objection to the vapid variation compositions of the time'.[2] The source of inspiration was poetry (another point of distinction from the Beethoven bagatelles). Tomášek explains in his preface that he wanted to apply the technique of poetry in the field of pure music.

Voříšek, Tomášek's pupil, followed with his Rhapsodies, a set of twelve pieces published in 1818. After his move to Vienna, Mechetti published there his Impromptus, Op. 7, in 1822. Back in Prague, Tomášek published his *Dithyramben* in 1823.³ The title 'Impromptu' which Schubert would use later, was Voříšek's invention. Schubert certainly knew Voříšek's pieces, and probably Tomášek's too; he probably knew Voříšek himself, who was active in Vienna and played in musical evenings at Sonnleithner's. His *Air russe* and *Plaintes*, whatever their debt to the Czech founders of the genre, are true Schubertian miniatures, the forerunners of some fine later examples. But it must be remembered that Schubert is also bound to have known Beethoven's bagatelles, the first of which appeared in 1802. Their influence is also felt in Schubert, notably in the first of the *Moments Musicaux* and the last of the Three Piano Pieces, D.946.

Schubert's first impromptu (D.899, No.1) alternates a march-like theme in C minor (with a rather formal cut) with a more expansive and fluid theme in A flat major. The second piece, in E flat major, sounds like an *étude*, with its *moto perpetuo* right-hand triplets running the gamut from feathery fleetness to stratospheric virtuoso dazzle, non-stop. Brahms turned it into an even more daunting '*étude*' by making an arrangement of it with the triplets in the left hand. The B minor episode, a heavy-footed dance of immense power and resonance, comes to dominate the piece, in that it eventually drives it to an unyielding minor-key close.

Nocturne or song without words, the third impromptu so embodies the intimate, poetic model of the Romantic piano miniature before its time that if it alone survived of all Schubert's works one would not hesitate to call him a Romantic composer. A mono-textural piece, it seems the natural successor to the first movement of Beethoven's so-called 'Moonlight' Sonata. The ternary form of the last impromptu accommodates orderly contrasts. While the middle 'trio' pulsates with dark passion in C sharp minor, the outer sections sparkle with coruscating arpeggios which are attractive enough on their own, when presented as the 'theme' at the start, but gain extra magic when later supplemented with a surging inner theme whose purposeful simplicity has no doubt helped to make this one of Schubert's most popular miniatures.

In the autograph, Schubert's Four Impromptus (D.935) are numbered five to eight, which suggests they were intended as a sequel to the four pieces of D.899 just discussed. Perhaps the length of the first piece lay behind the decision to issue this second set separately. It is an abridged sonata-rondo, but, having announced the second subject in his B section (of ABABA), Schubert adds another theme which takes binary form with repeats and lasts four times as long as the second subject proper. We should be thankful: whatever the effect on the proportions of the piece, this section distils the essence of Schubert the somnambulist, lost in a world of his own which knows no mundane measure of time.

The unassuming little Allegretto in A flat which begins the second impromptu has a simple chordal underlay to point the intimate, confiding tone of the melody. The 'trio' in D flat practises economy in another sense: it could almost be heard as an accompaniment to an absent melody, and one could readily 'do a Gounod' and spin a shapely lyrical line from first bar to last. But why? The pleasure is in picking up the implications of expressive linear movement – as they come and go – within the rolling triplet figuration itself. The third piece is a set of five variations on a theme already used for an entr'acte in *Rosamunde* (in B flat) and for the slow movement of the A minor String Quartet.

The last of these impromptus is one of Schubert's most interesting and unusual movements. One key to its character is the marking Allegro scherzando. It is in triple time, and the form is that of scherzo, trio, and scherzo reprise. But 'scherzo' (or even 'scherzando') implies more than metre and form. Schubert's humour is less obvious than Beethoven's, less ebullient; but it is present here even so, in the provocative suggestion of hemiola rhythm at the opening (Fig. 105a), its more open affirmation in octaves (Fig. 105b), and its riotous proclamation in convulsive oom-pahs (Fig. 105c); in the trilled dissonances that hover like predators in the sky; in the darting leaps, twirling runs and dashing scales that recall the *Divertissement à l'hongroise*; and perhaps even in the bizarre proportions of the sections (scherzo 86 bars, trio 237, scherzo 96, coda 106). It is partly because the material of the trio comes in four-bar waves that this section grows to such a size. Towards the end of the trio there are some scales, twisting down and up and down again, of extraordinary length and wildness. The Piu presto coda culminates in the longest scale of all, a straight sweep

Fig. 105

down through six octaves – an extravagant end to a movement of extreme wit and daring.

The three pieces known as *Drei Klavierstücke* (D.946) were untitled in the autograph and may have been intended as the starting point for another set of impromptus. They would be worthy of that designation, but they represent only a start in that two of the pieces exist only in draft, and the third only in a pencil sketch. In the first one Schubert crossed out the C section of an envisaged ABACA design, which is a pity because it has a beautiful second section and the innovative phrase-structure of the first section could surely have been made to work, with some adaptation. The A section is in the rare key of E flat minor. Only four of Schubert's songs are in this key, and they are all slow-moving songs of the graveside, of night, or of grief. This piece, by contrast, is a sprightly Allegro assai, which trips along on a bed of triplets until the sudden arrests of motion in the second section, where Schubert gives a new slant to 'Comfort ye' from Handel's *Messiah*, a work well known to him. The atmospheric runs and tremolando effects of the first episode (B) would have been especially effective on the Viennese instrument of Schubert's day.

The second piece is a pure ABACA rondo, its B episode a dramatic little tone-picture, ominous, excitable and quiescent by turns, its C episode finding Schubert in pensive mood and leisurely gait in A flat minor, making expansive use of simply crafted sequences to haunting effect. Schubert never came closer to the sonorities and thought-processes of a Beethoven bagatelle than in the mercurial third piece, an Allegro in C major. The syncopations, loud-soft oppositions, offbeat accents and bold but short-lived tonal sidesteps all conspire to bring Beethoven to mind in any case, but the central episode is pure somnambulistic Schubert. It is true that Schubert might have refined these pieces if he had prepared them for publication, but in their existing form they remain precious examples of an art-concealing miniaturism of which their composer was a master with few equals.

There remains one large-scale piano work to discuss, and a few shorter ones. There seems to have been an obsession with short piano pieces in 1817 and 1828, despite the larger works on the stocks, for in addition to the sets of four, four and three pieces already mentioned Schubert began two *Klavierstücke* (D.916B and C), the pencilled fragments of which were discovered in the 1970s. The first of these is of some interest as its opening theme resembles that of the 'Tenth' Symphony sketched the following year, while the second subject is essentially the same as the theme of the trio in the third movement of the Piano Trio in B flat. The two pieces were treated by Jorg Demus and Roland Solder as the outer movements of a sonata, completed by adding the Allegretto in C minor (D.900) between.[4] We therefore have the unlikely proposition of a late Schubert sonata in which all the movements share the same tonic.

As for the Allegretto in C minor itself, it displays wonderful originality but is sadly only a fragment. Walther Dürr finds at some places (bars 16 and 19) a layout which suggests this might be a sketch for an orchestral work, but stretches of a ninth are not all that unusual in Schubert's keyboard writing, and Dürr has presumably not claimed that the G major Sonata (see end of first movement, beginning of finale) is an orchestral work, while the scherzo of the F minor Sonata must trouble him even more.[5] The D.900 Allegretto should not be confused with another Allegretto in C minor (D.915) dated 1827, the embodiment of poetic thought of the highest order, matching economy and simplicity to brevity in a way that induces in an audience the rapt silence in which pins are heard to drop.

In contrast, the thick chords of the March in E echo the breeze-beating solidity of outdoor band scoring. The Hungarian Melody in B minor is simply a two-hand version of the stamping Magyar dance that was used to good effect in the *Divertissement à l'hongroise* for four hands. One must work hard to seek out a copy, never mind a performance, of the variation on a theme of Diabelli that was Schubert's contribution to the multi-author set Diabelli himself commissioned from fifty Austrian composers. But when one finds it, it is worth getting to know for its inspired, masterly treatment of the '*Schusterfleck*' (cobbler's patch) made famous through Beethoven's 'Diabelli' Variations. Only Beethoven could have written that mighty set, but only Schubert could have penned his one variation.

A fragment is all that exists of a Fantasy in C (D.605) written shortly before the 'Wanderer' Fantasy. All commentators so far have taken this fragment to be an excerpt from the middle of the piece, not the beginning, it being assumed that an outer double sheet of paper has been lost. The piece is written on six sides of paper.[6] On the last five sides, Schubert does not write in clefs at the beginning of the page. Nor does he write in clefs for new sections which have new key signatures, time signatures, and tempo indications. Why, then, are clefs present at the beginning of the fragment, at the top of its first (right-hand) page? Surely, because this is the beginning of the piece.

Two things are clear from the excerpt. First, a spread diminished seventh was used extensively as a linking device between sections. Perhaps the idea came from the 'Waldstein' Sonata of Beethoven, where this chord connects slow movement to finale. And second, the sections have a common bond in their use of the four-note motive to which Bernstein later set the words 'I feel pretty', though in different metre and rhythm. Despite the many references to and transformations of this idea in the opening section (for which no tempo is given), in an extensive Allegro moderato, and in an

Andantino in triple time, it is the spirit of fantasy that prevails, more so than in any of the fantasies Schubert completed in his maturity. It was only by checking the wilder extremes of this fantasy impulse and exerting a tighter structural control that the composer, now demanding more of himself than in the discursive youthful fantasies, would satisfy himself in such works as the 'Wanderer' Fantasy and the Fantasy in F minor for piano duet. That Brahms found the piece interesting is evident from the fact that he made his own copy of it.[7]

The 'Wanderer' Fantasy, which is then one of the principal culminations of a lifetime spent in creating valid personal realizations of the fantasy ideal, cannot be viewed as that alone, since it was coloured by external factors which affect it alone among the fantasies. First, it was finished two months after the B minor Symphony was left unfinished, at a time of personal upheaval, when progress on a potential symphonic masterpiece had come unstuck and Schubert possibly had some premonition of the onset of his disease. Second, it was written for an ex-pupil of Hummel's, who must have been a keyboard virtuoso as well as a wealthy landowner.

The effect of the first of these factors seems to have been, for one thing, that he would leave the world of the 'Unfinished' – with all its artistic and emotional associations – far, far behind, replacing introvert soul-searching with extravert assertiveness. And the second factor encouraged him to express this new-found assertiveness with carte blanche to use the resources of the keyboard unstintingly. The creative energy and fresh confidence that underlie the 'Wanderer' Fantasy are remarkable, and while to an extent the confidence may be genuine and hard-earned there may well be an element of defiance in it too.

As in the F minor Fantasy for piano duet of 1828, one can distinguish the four movements of a sonata, though they flow into each other without breaks and each is somewhat compressed. This compression leaves its mark on the outer movements more than the inner ones, so that in terms of relative length something nearer to equilibrium than is normal in a sonata is achieved. Yet Schubert finds time for expansive and idiomatic melodies in all movements except the last, which drives its fugal opening hard into a sequel of sheer pianistic grandeur that can only be capped by yet more grand pianism.

The work's title is derived from Schubert's own song *Der Wanderer* (1816). He bases his second movement on material from an episode in the song where Schmidt von Lübeck's text runs:

> Here the sun seems so cold,
> The blossom faded, life old;
> And men's words mere hollow noise:
> I am a stranger everywhere.

This is an Adagio, a genuinely slow movement such as is not normally found in Schubert's multi-movement works, and appears to be conditioned by the poetic atmosphere which the material originally served. These original strains are heard several times in a free variation form, in which they are adorned by an abundance of pianistic figuration, and sometimes separated by passages in which the figuration goes its own way. This is contemplative, inward-looking music, in marked contrast to the ebullient extraversion of the rest of the fantasy. Indeed, this Adagio also stands apart from its surrounding movements in that it does not share their unifying bond, rooted as they are in a common musical idea heard at the beginning of the work and suitably transformed for the purposes of the 'scherzo' third movement and the finale. The slow movement is brought into connection with these other movements only through the dactylic rhythm of the theme (which, however, yields a very different momentum at this slow pace), and, in its closing stages, the generation of a figuration (Fig. 106a) which can be transformed into the prime motive of the following scherzo (Fig. 106b).

Fig. 106 a   b

The bond that unites the other movements is of a very different sort. The whole first paragraph of the first movement is transformed, by a kind of Lisztian metamorphosis, into the first paragraph of the scherzo. (It is no wonder that Liszt's attention was caught by this work, although his attempt to make a piano concerto of it was misguided.) The finale uses part of this paragraph again, but cannot do so until the requirements of its fugal opening have been fulfilled. Fig. 107 shows the close of this paragraph, as it appears in the first (a), third (b) and fourth (c) movements.

Fig. 107

a

Fugal though the finale is, it is not a fugue. There are only five entries of the subject (derived from the theme of the first movement), one more than the statutory four of the fugal exposition alone. The texture is not consistently that of fugal counterpoint, either. This is in fact far less a fugue than is the finale of the A flat Piano Sonata (Op. 110) Beethoven had written in the previous year.

One other striking feature is that it does not 'go through the keys' as a fugue does, nor even as any instrumental movement by Schubert does. Why so? The reason is surely that the first movement, which is in sonata form, breaks off at the end of the development. The recapitulation is missing, as the slow movement follows at once. A characteristic of a recapitulation is that it is, in normal practice, entirely within the tonic key. Schubert's finale, by basing itself on the theme of the first movement and staying in the tonic, with little deviation, to this extent serves as a recapitulation. The work as a whole, then, has sonata elements, but is more compact than a sonata, with strong cyclic bonds, framed by a sort of sonata-form sandwich. If Schubert was trying to vanquish Hummel, the teacher of the dedicatee, on his own ground, that might help to explain why some who are susceptible to Schubert's familiar virtues hold this work in low esteem. For them it is the material, not the form, that is the problem. (The architectural sophistication was well beyond Hummel's reach.) However one responds to it as music, there is no doubting its importance in Schubert's creative development — and in his psychology, since it cleared the blockage which had hampered his progress for four years, and it therefore played a part in releasing the assured, mature masterpieces — among them fine string quartets and sonatas — of the years ahead.

The Late Chamber Music

The Allegro assai known as the 'Quartettsatz' (quartet movement) is the first work in which Schubert reached full maturity as an instrumental composer (in any medium), and the incompletion of the larger work to which it would have belonged is a tragedy comparable to the abandonment of the 'Unfinished' Symphony. It is at once intense, eventful and compact. Schubert enters a new emotional world, glimpsing many facets of anguish in a few pages of concentrated, tightly knit music. The agitated first theme gives way to more consolatory, lyrical ideas, but the initial momentum is never lost sight of, and the pithy return of the volatile opening at the end of the movement sets the seal on a compact, circular unity.

This was to be the first movement of a projected Quartet in C minor, and one may explain its pre-eminent position in the affections of modern string quartet ensembles by reference to its many fine details as much as its structural certainty. The hyperactive opening idea, unprecedented as a first subject in a sonata-type work, leads off like some intense, crepuscular scherzo, gathering the four players in turn on the way to its far-flung climax chord. The quixotic change from the intense, agitated first presentation to the slightly more contained unrest of the second presentation is quickly followed by a sideways move to A flat major for a more consolatory second subject (seldom do Schubert second subjects arrive so soon).

That second subject is pure Schubert. Or is it? There is no documentary evidence that Schubert knew the music of the French composer André Grétry, but the quartet from his opera *Lucile* of 1769 was reputed to be the best-known number in that work, and was apparently used as a royalist anthem by the Bourbons in the 1800s (Fig. 108a). Indeed it was the tune to which, with its words 'Où peut-on être mieux qu'au sein de sa famille?' (Where are things better than in the bosom of one's family?), Louis XVIII entered Paris in 1814, six years before the Quartettsatz. If Schubert did not have that theme at the back of his mind as he wrote his own (Fig. 108b), it is a curious coincidence that both settled for an unusual six-bar phrase-structure (twelve in Schubert's case, as his bars are half as long) at the same time as they opted for a similar melodic outline and harmonic path.[1]

Fig. 108

The exalted, stratospheric repeat of this second subject with the cello's bass line floating almost entirely above middle C typifies Schubert's growing concern for registral variety in his quartet writing. Schubert cunningly interpolates, here and there, some dramatic development of the volatile opening, as though building on the experience of Beethoven's F major Quartet, Op. 18, No. 1. A further theme combines melodic simplicity with harmonic poignancy so tellingly that he assigns his special triple piano marking to it (Fig. 109). This theme is in G major, completing the first example of a three-key exposition in the chamber music (C minor, A flat major, G major). Most of its chords are ordinary triads, but the way in which they are juxtaposed is uniquely colourful, and the arrival of the Neapolitan key (A flat, flattened supertonic of G) – remote yet accessible

– is nicely exaggerated, already illustrating the value of highly coloured harmony in Schubert's later style.

Fig. 109

Such are the riveting materials of this deeply felt, perfectly formed movement. What gives this music its impact is not just the force of crafts-manship and mature judgement, but the sheer quality of the material and the passion that impels it – and that lies largely beyond analysis. Schubert sustained something of this intensity into an Andante in A flat which was to have been the second movement of this C minor Quartet, but for reason unknown he broke off after about forty bars, by which time the quartet texture had opened up most promisingly.

When Schubert next ventured into quartet writing he had discovered that his health might be beyond repair. The observation that the A minor Quartet begins like a song may seem of little consequence. It perhaps gains significance, though, when one recalls the words of despair Schubert had written shortly before, in that spring of 1824. '"My peace is gone, my heart is sore, I shall find it never and nevermore," I may well sing every day now . . .' He was quoting from *Gretchen am Spinnrade*. The opening of the A minor Quartet could be called song-like because the lower instruments set off with an 'accompaniment', to which the first violin then adds a tune. The 'accompaniment' is harmonically static – an embellishment of the tonic chord. Now there are not many songs by Schubert which do actually begin like that, but *Gretchen* is one of them. The similarity does not end there. Etching in harmony which is fixedly tonic, the top part of the accompaniment (second violin in the quartet) takes the minor third and rotates around it, while a marked monotone rhythm appears below. Is the starting point of the A minor Quartet, then, a further recall of Gretchen's forlorn state? And is it perhaps a significant coincidence that the first violin's drooping theme falls through the very same three notes (same key, same rhythm) with which Verdi was to begin his *Requiem* fifty years later?

Those three notes seem to epitomize the pathos of the first movement as a whole. Clearly the emotional concentration – almost single-mindedness – has to do with thematic economy. There is only one theme in the first group, and only one in the second (which is in C major). The second, initially rising, is distinguished by the trill on its second note. That trill persists when the theme is re-characterized, and even when it is inverted in an unexpected A flat major. The development is undoubtedly the finest Schubert had yet conceived in a chamber medium, forging an emotional arch in which the first two segments build to an emphatic climax and the third segment carries the process of quiescence to heavenly lengths, with many a poetic sublimity and harmonic revelation on the way. The first segment leads the first theme from D minor to F minor, where a canon between cello and first violin extends the same line of lyrical thinking, building to a second segment in which the canon's initial two-note idea is subjected to tough neo-Baroque counterpoint that calls to mind a passage similarly located in the first of Beethoven's 'Rasumovsky' quartets.

The diminished seventh which is the climax of all this activity had not yet become a nineteenth-century cliché, and in any case Schubert's subtle transmutation of the chord as it throbs on softly in the rhythm with which the cello had underpinned the first theme at the outset gives the third segment what is perhaps the most inspired stroke of harmonic alchemy in the whole work. Later, the coda approaches with the same fragmented conversation between the players that began the development, so that one senses the music embarking on a new cycle of development. The succinctness of what follows is all the more effective, therefore. The recalled first theme quickly gets stuck in a groove, and thrice checked by a trenchant dissonance. Its resolution comes when the first three notes of the theme underpin the final cadence, driving the thematic argument right into the last bar of the movement, at the point where it is usual for themeless conclusive gestures to take over.

Some relaxation, solace even, comes with the Andante slow movement, whose theme Schubert later plundered for his hastily assembled incidental music to *Rosamunde* (unless musicology yet proves that it was vice versa). This is a tranquil eclogue in which every note – even in what is ostensibly 'passagework' – seems to spring from a melodic impulse. The form is as simple as the expression is pure (an ABABcoda in which the coda poetically mixes A and B elements). Once only the music rises to a climax forceful enough to threaten the prevailing tranquillity, and, as in the first movement, counterpoint plays a part in the tension-building process – counterpoint which for a few moments is as dynamic and abrasive as anything in Beethoven.

Seldom does a minuet absorb the emotional colour of the work to which it belongs as much as Schubert's does in this quartet. It is not simply

a matter of it taking the work's title key. Its opening bars are derived from
Schubert's own setting of Schiller's *Die Götter Griechenlands* (1819). 'Schöne
Welt, wo bist du?' (Fair world, where are you?) asked the singer: the
minuet poses the same question in its own terms, so becoming a microcosm
of the spiritual world inhabited by the A minor Quartet. The gently
swaying rhythms suggest a joyless dance, which reaches a desolate extreme
when the cello's deep prefatory sigh returns to sink the tonality to an
other-worldly C sharp minor. J. A. Westrup said of the major-key trio
that it 'seems to offer not consolation but rather a mere distraction from
grief'.[2] There is a clue to this in the fact that Schubert, at the end of the
minuet (and after its internal repeats have run their course), appends a few
bars which isolate its swaying rhythmic motif, then adds – before the trio
proper commences – a few bars in which this rhythm swings into the major.
Thus the minuet's most potent emotional symbol is carried pointedly over
into the trio.

   The ostensible rustic gaiety of the finale is similarly something of an
illusion. Constraints are foremost from the outset: 'Allegro moderato,'
warns Schubert, placing a little decoration on the first (short) note that
needs time if it is to register, and delaying the third bar by repeating the
second, as though in hesitation (whence the theme derives its five-bar
span: see Fig. 110).

Fig. 110

Soon a ritardando imposes a further check. This is not exactly the A major
of unbuttoned joy we know from Mozart's Symphony No. 29, Beethoven's
Seventh, Mendelssohn's 'Italian' Symphony, the *Carnaval Romain* Overture
of Berlioz, or the *Carnival* Overture of Dvořák. It owes more, in its
emotional cast and function, to the finales of such works of Mozart as the
K.464 String Quartet, the Clarinet Quintet and the Clarinet Concerto,
and, of Beethoven, the Op. 18, No. 5 String Quartet and Op. 69 Cello
Sonata. Even the second subject takes a minor key (the mediant), and,
although it veers to its relative major, jumps back at the last minute. When
the first theme returns (the first return in a rondo design that is pellucid
even if at the second return Schubert omits the first theme and heads into

the next theme of the first group), the way into it is through its second bar – which had been an object of hesitation from the start. It is now isolated, given an additional stalling sign (tenuto), and repeated fourfold so that the listener is not aware that the reprise has begun until the actual fourth bar of the theme follows (Fig. 111). The theme is to appear

Fig. 111

again without its first bar, and indeed the jettisoned first bar is never heard again after this halfway point in the movement. It is on the now regnant second bar that the final cadence of the movement stands, its presence *au fond* in viola and cello robbing the major-key cadence of some of its affirmative force by denying the possibility of two final chords being in root position.

Schubert had planned a set of three quartets. Although he completed a further two before his death, they were not in the end published under the same opus number as the A minor (Op. 29). The D minor followed soon, and was to acquire the nickname 'Death and the Maiden' because its slow movement makes use of material from Schubert's song of that title. It was not Schubert's name for it, and indeed the other three movements have no musical connection with the song. Those writers who have read into the work as a whole a 'hidden agenda' – a concern with death – perhaps overlooked the curious origin of the third movement, which tends to weaken the case for such an interpretation. Either way, the D minor is a work of immense power which is no less homogeneous than the A minor.

Fig. 112

It begins with a challenge, a terse thematic gesture whose strength is, if not steely, at least brassy: that is to say, while the inner instruments delineate the theme (Fig. 112) the first violin and cello are trumpets and drums, unable to offer the notes of the theme, so reiterating the keynote. It is a potent orchestral analogue, bringing the hollow ring of bare octaves, fourths or fifths on the main beats. After it, the softening is not only dynamic (*pp*) but harmonic, with full – though austere – chords. The constructive power

Schubert finds in the descending triplet motif is prodigious, and when a second statement of the opening is reached, with extra octaves added, such is the tense energy which has been accumulated that it seems inevitable that the silences between each gesture should themselves be filled with surging triplets. The second subject group similarly builds impressive size and weight from a nugget of material.

It is a measure of the searching, unsettled mood of this quartet that in the development the first and second subjects should confront each other at the closest possible quarters, by being simultaneously combined. The first theme as heard at bars 15–16 is compressed into three instruments while the first violin tops it with the second subject (Fig. 113). New developments are reserved for the coda, where the triplet figure is pursued inexorably towards strong repeated cadences, but motion is finally arrested in a plangent peroration, crowned by the aching grief of Neapolitan harmony turned minor, after which the cello's triplet descents to the keynote are the final sobs in a monumental tragedy.

Fig. 113

For the slow movement Schubert takes the piano part of the song *Der Tod und das Mädchen*, freely adapting the prelude and that part of the accompaniment that supports the voice of Death, to construct a new binary-form theme in G minor. 'Theme' is often a misleading word for the subject of variations, and especially here, since the harmony of Schubert's solemn, grief-choked 'model' – for which he might have borrowed from Beethoven's Op. 130 Quartet the expressive term 'beklemmt' (constricted, oppressed) – is more demonstrative than the melody. In its second section the anguish becomes intense, before the music sinks consolingly into B flat major. After a few moments locked in E flat major, the chromatic changes that lead back to G – now G major – are accomplished entirely in the lower parts, while the first violin continues its sombre dactyls on a monotone. This distinctive harmonic path is closely followed in the five variations, which are of the strictest construction. Indeed, the power of this movement, for all its inventive variety, lies in the self-imposed formal restriction from which no escape is permitted. In this it anticipates Brahms, whose variation slow movement in the B flat String Sextet is a self-evident successor.

Schubert's other self-borrowing in this work is a surprising one. The scherzo makes use of a German dance from the D.790 set (No. 6, see page 340), the adoption being almost note for note in the first few bars of both the two sections. It is remarkable to think that this powerful scherzo, with its tough sonorities, could have been spawned by one of Schubert's hundreds of keyboard dances. But then the scherzo genre was itself born of a dance genre, the minuet, and Schubert's D.790 set of *Zwölf Deutsche* transcends its Terpsichorean provenance more thinkingly than any other set, while the borrowed No. 6 is preceded there by an anguished B minor tone-poem (No. 5) which is almost a continuation of the 'Unfinished' Symphony in that same key, set aside a few months earlier. The more soothing D major trio, in binary form but with the repeats varied and so written out, picks up the dotted rhythm with which the scherzo ended in ringing octave–unison, and neatly incorporates it in the middle texture.

The finale is a breathless saltarello, large in scale but offering no easy resolution in the major. If its implied concern is still death, then this tireless Presto proves that the quick and the dead are not opposites after all. The first theme presents a fund of motives, entirely in octaves; these motives can be detached for development, and newly characterized by the addition of harmony. That process so occupies Schubert that much energy has been expended before the motion is arrested by a second subject distinguished by its chordal solidity ('con forza,' Schubert asks). When at last the first subject returns, the signal it seems to give is that this is to be a rondo, and that as this is only the first return, after more than three hundred bars of music, it is destined to be a rondo on a huge scale. In fact, the development that follows is relatively short, and Schubert omits the first subject from the recapitulation, which begins with the solid second subject in B flat major. Thus the finale is shorter than it led us to expect, although by the time its Prestissimo coda has reached its final quadruple quadruple-stop (sixteen notes) of D minor, there is no sense of important things having been left unsaid.

The G major Quartet stands among the heights of compositional endeavour a quarter of the way through the nineteenth century. It occupies a lone pinnacle, facing the ridge of Beethoven's late quartets on the opposite side of a valley. It does not meet those works on their own ground, in that Schubert eschews their radical transmogrification of the genre, in which the number and types of movement are diversified, and is less concerned than Beethoven with the twin third–period forces of fugal counterpoint and variation. The most radical step taken by Schubert is of a quite different kind: he elevates the opposition of major and minor to the status of a theme.

A held major triad flares up into a cataclysmic minor one, followed by convulsive aftershocks (Fig. 114a). That is the work's first theme: but its melodic elements take back seat to its major-minor altercation, and to its gestural shape – entailing rhythm, dynamics, scoring, texture and articulation more than melody. When this 'theme' returns at the recapitulation, the transmutation is reversed. Minor is supplanted by major – but peaceably: the physical energy is gone, the violent dynamics and jagged rhythm replaced by softened, smoothed-out features, the most aggressive event (at the moment of major-to-minor change) yielding to a piano pizzicato (Fig. 114b). As an example of the 'all is changed' scenario greeting the listener at the point of recapitulation, this is unprecedented.

Fig. 114

For decades after this, although the major-minor antithesis remained a vital ingredient of nineteenth-century musical thought, it was never expressed so nakedly until Mahler put the whole force of an orchestra behind it (Symphony No. 6). Schubert's gesture challenges the intimacy of the chamber-music medium, but does not infringe it, merely extending the scope of that intimacy a step further than Beethoven had. And the second idea that quickly follows, building fragments of the 'aftershock' into more melodious utterances over a hushed chordal tremolo in the lower instruments, sees Schubert evolving another kind of unfamiliar but still tensely dramatic atmosphere within the domestic framework of the quartet medium.

Schubert seems to be peering into the future again in his second subject – this time to Brahms. The second subject of Brahms's Piano Quartet, Op. 60, is notable for consisting almost entirely of a theme and varia-tions, in the strict sense. Schubert anticipates this scheme, presenting his thirteen-bar theme (A) in four successive versions, but interpolating an alternating twenty-bar segment, based on the same material, twice: the resulting pattern is AABABA. This is curtailed in the recapitulation to AABA. Thus we have in effect a large set of variations, split between the exposition and recapitulation, a feature which is again prophetic of the Brahms example.

In the slow movement Schubert maintains an atmosphere of heightened poetic eloquence throughout a free rondo design, initially exploiting the expressive potential of the cello above middle C, as he had in some of the second subject's variations in the first movement. After the theme has been heard twice, the cello continues at a lower pitch, against a harmonic stasis on the C major triad. The length of this triad implies that it is being proposed as a tonic, but the cello obstinately refuses to lower its Fs from sharp to natural, and a certain subtle tension is generated thereby. Similarly obstinate, in a vehement contrasting episode beginning in G minor, is the way in which a forceful little post–cadential tag (G to B flat, the tonic to the minor third) returns unamended after the ensuing quick modulations to remote C sharp minor and B flat minor, straining the listening ear's capacity to make harmonic sense of it. The ostinato is not a regular part of the Classical composer's vocabulary, but Schubert for a few moments here vividly and daringly calls to mind both the device and its etymological derivation (Italian: obstinate). The daredevil harmonic instincts underlying this passage may perhaps be traced to Beethoven (the sudden scale of A ending with a jump to D, near the end of the development in the F minor Quartet, Op. 95, and the alien A sharp in bar 17 of the Adagio ma non troppo e semplice variation in the fourth movement of the Op. 131 String Quartet), but the ostinato-like compounding of the dissonance is Schubert's.

There is an imaginative touch of scoring later in the movement when the first violin and cello unite on a throaty middle C while the other instruments fill out the harmony above and below. But the use of the medium is finely calculated throughout, and is at one with the unremitting inspiration of the musical ideas. Indeed, everything points to the fact that this movement was an important springboard from which, two years later, Schubert approached the sublime slow movement of his String Quintet.

The scherzo buzzes with Mendelssohnian lightness and élan, making something altogether more elfin of a rhythm which was to be put to weightier purpose in the scherzo of the 'Great' C major Symphony. At the point where the second section ends and its repeat is taken, there is an extraordinary lurch from B minor to B flat major. It is not an un-Schubertian move, but the shock is more considerable than usual in this context. The cello takes the lead again in the trio of this 'cello quartet', a Ländler in G which slips into B major for its central span with as little ceremony as the song *Der Musensohn* does for alternate verses.

The finale of the G major Quartet has much in common with that of the D minor. It is a fast movement, and a long one, in 6/8 time, is in sonata-rondo form with the first theme omitted at the recapitulation, and the first theme of the G major is a rough inversion of that of the D minor. Moreover, where the rapid motion of the D minor is checked by the more solid rhythm of the second subject, the rhythm and texture of that second subject is copied in the G major, not by the second subject itself but by the second theme in that group. The second theme of the first group could have come out of a Mozart string quintet, and when that theme returns at the very end to round the movement off it is preceded by a huge sequential build-up, with the first violin steadily climbing and the cello steadily falling, until the full panoply of post-Rasumovsky texture is attained and a Tchaikovskian head of steam has been generated. Such is the length and persistence of the diverging motion of first violin and cello that both instruments have to jump back by an octave (the violin three times) in order to keep the line within the instrumental compass.

It has already been suggested that in some way the G major Quartet prepared the way for the C major String Quintet. Charles Rosen, noting how the major-minor opening of the quartet is the source of energy for the whole first movement, rightly brackets this work and the Quintet and the C major Symphony together as evidence of a return to Classical principles, the forms being 'no longer imposed from without, but rather implied by the material'.[3] The Quintet entails the addition of a second cello to the quartet ensemble, and in some ways the G major Quartet was pointing to that outcome. It has sometimes been said that the latter is orchestrally conceived, but that is not so: it simply involves a new, expansive and demanding way of writing for the string quartet. Paul Griffiths, finding that the cello here alternates two roles, speaking sometimes with a tenor and sometimes with a deep bass voice, proposes that the 'string quartet is ceasing to be music expressly made for four individuals, and becoming instead music that four instruments are able to play'.[4] Griffiths is arguing that Schubert makes the quartet sound like a 'miniature orchestra', whereas, although that idea does not bear analysis, it is certainly the case that five instruments rather than four – an enlarged chamber ensemble but not an orchestral one – is a solution to which the three 'late' quartets have been pointing.

The issue cannot be more fully addressed here, but it is worth recalling that Schubert knew the Mozart string quintets and can hardly have failed to gain an understanding of how the medium became a unique and necessary tool in Mozart's hands. As for the distinction that Schubert chose an extra cello rather than Mozart's viola, compelling reasons for expansion in this particular direction are offered by Peter Gülke, one being Schubert's growing tendency to establish 'the tenor register as the fount of musical invention' and another being 'the luminous quality of [the cello's] top string'.[5] In this connection, the second subject of the Quintet's first movement will almost inevitably be the instance on which the Schubert-lover's memory will home in. Here the two cellos duet serenely, at first in parallel thirds or sixths (a peculiarly Viennese pattern), high above the viola's bass line. This has become the *locus classicus* of writing for string quintet with two cellos, and it is quintessentially a chamber-music texture. Boccherini, who died nearly a quarter of a century before Schubert wrote this quintet, had himself written string quintets employing a second cello. But Boccherini was a cellist, and tended to treat the first cello as a concertante prima donna. This was far from Schubert's approach, and even when Mozart in the slow movement of his C major Quintet treated the two violas somewhat as he did the violin and viola soloists in his Sinfonia Concertante, K.365, it was somehow done true to chamber-music scale and ethos. It is a less well-known fact, incidentally, that Boccherini also wrote some quintets with two violas, and some with double bass instead of the extra viola or cello.

Schubert's beloved Mozart G minor Quintet began with the upper trio taking the first paragraph, and the lower trio the second – the first viola doing double duty, of course. Schubert's begins with the upper quartet followed by the lower quartet, there being three players in common. The illusion of two ensembles is one of the strategies by which the 25 per cent increase in the workforce (over a string quartet) is in practice an addition of disproportionate value. But this beginning is daring in a way which has little to do with Mozart. The opening sounds lack the rhythmic terms of reference needed to define their measure. This enables Schubert to add in the missing rhythmic context when this opening theme very soon makes a more assertive return. This early return, which has its counterpart in the D minor Quartet and the A minor Piano Sonata, D.784, is an exhilarating first climax in a work not short of strenuous climaxes.

Long after the haunting cello duet which is the second subject (in remote

E flat, the second stop in a three-key exposition), and after a development in which the five players are set into tough contrapuntal conflict but make no less impact in the intervening softer, more lyrical spans, the first theme returns with yet different rhythmic accessories.

The slow movement, in the course of which divine peace confronts and dispels human *Angst*, is courageously slow, the theme in the middle three instruments so statuesque as to concede enormous expressive weight to the little first-violin interjections and the pulsations of the plucked cello. A final trill suddenly raises the level of activity and of tension, leading to a hyperactive and relentlessly burdened middle section in the Neapolitan minor key. Traces of this turbulence, as suppressed as the players choose to imagine, spill over into the reprise of the Elysian first theme; but by the coda serene stillness is restored – threatened but not banished by a cursory if powerful last turn to that Neapolitan minor key (complete with the original upbeat trill), which is Schubert's way of harking back to, and laying to rest, the dark currents of the middle section.

By adding a second cello Schubert was ostensibly defying the musical force of gravity (or inverse gravity, if you like) which obliges composers to leave more pitch-space between lower voices than between upper ones, in which sense a top-heavy texture is 'natural'. Thickness does sometimes characterize the Quintet, as in the third movement, where it helps to generate a stamping exuberance in the scherzo proper and an almost funereal introversion in the trio. Like most scherzi, this one is in fast triple time, but here the bars are grouped unmistakably in fours: one may count the bars as 1–2–3–4, 1–2–3–4, and so on. But there comes a point in the second section where Schubert resoundingly overthrows this pattern's dominance by bringing forward the next four-bar group so that it interrupts the previous one (1–2–3–4, 1–2–1–2–3–4). The subtleties of play with bar-groupings in Classical scores are a somewhat esoteric matter, but it is hard to think of an example which comes so near to lifting us, the listeners, out of our seats. The powerful upward-reaching coda subsumes, almost imperceptibly, the only other deviation from the 1–2–3–4 pattern.

The finale is a kind of idealized Viennese dance, in which the 'lilt' of the second subject is almost a tangible reality. The last in its procession of ideas is Fig. 115, in which the cellos duet above a viola bass just as they do in the second subject of the first movement. But the viola, between times, is part of the upper trio which accompanies this duet with waves of close-position triads. Soon, the cellos' theme drops out, leaving the 'waves' to be heard in antiphonal exchanges between the upper trio and the lower trio – a sensual, textural gesture of unforgettable beauty which attracts Schubert's only special triple piano marking in this finale. In the final throes of exaltation (Piu presto), a D flat weighs down upon the keynote C as a last reminder of earlier tensions.

Fig. 115

Part of a different tradition is the other chamber work for large ensemble without piano written in the 1820s. The Octet of 1824 falls decisively into the divertimento category. Its immediate model was clearly Beethoven's Septet. When Schubert adds a second violin to Beethoven's line-up of violin, viola, cello, double bass, clarinet, bassoon and horn, he is rounding off the ensemble to good effect by making the standard string quartet group its basis, to which the bass and the three winds are add-ons. The six movements of the Beethoven model are preserved, including variations and both minuet and scherzo. The Septet is strictly the work of an older composer than the Octet, yet, like the Octet, it had something of a preparatory function, being a means of approach to the writing of a first symphony. When Schubert wrote his Octet he was the still youthful veteran of eight symphonies and hundreds of songs. In spite of its derived scheme, the younger man's work betrays fewer signs of apprenticeship than the older man's. Indeed, little more than a year later Schubert was at work on his mature symphonic masterpiece. It was for that, the 'Great', that he was preparing, as he explained to Kupelwieser.[6] That is not to suggest that the

Octet is a quasi-orchestral exercise concerned with weighty issues. On the contrary, it is a cheerful piece of true chamber music, taking a hedonistic delight in manipulating rhythms, timing harmonic events, and sharing out favours among the players. If the clarinet seems to come off particularly well, this may be partly due to the fact that Count Troyer, who was to play clarinet in its first performance, also commissioned the work.[7] But the clarinet is, in any case, the obvious instrument to share the limelight with the first violin in a group thus constituted.

While Schubert is happy to display the individual voices, he is no less concerned to make an ensemble of them. The Adagio opening appears to present a small orchestra, setting wind and string bodies off against each other, while in the Allegro which follows we may be reminded of Rossini's second subjects when Schubert's (Fig. 116a) falls to different players in turn. This theme's obsession with certain notes of the tonic minor triad seems to derive from an idea in *Alfonso und Estrella* (Froila's aria, No. 2; Fig. 116b). The slow movement allots one of Schubert's most eloquent melodies to Troyer's clarinet, the subsequent entry of the first violin reminding us that the song composer knows how to mould an elegant countermelody. Yet the smoothly integrated sonorities of strings and wind are as likely to linger in the mind.

Fig. 116

There is enormous variety here, embracing the resounding *joie de vivre* of the scherzo, the courtly grace of the minuet and trio, and the almost concertante treatment of the first violin in the variations on a theme from *Die Freunde von Salamanka* which constitute the fourth movement. If much of this reflects a *gemütlich*, nostalgic frame of mind, the finale's slow introduction brings dark stirrings which belong unmistakably to the same Romantic decade as *Der Freischütz*, and the march-like tread of the final Allegro itself might strike us in hindsight as a limbering-up for the tireless athletics of the 'Great' C major Symphony.

The other principal chamber works of these last years involve the piano. Two of them are for violin and piano, exploring beyond the sonata format to which he had previously confined himself in this medium, and the first of them, the Rondo in B minor, is one of the best-kept secrets among connoisseurs of Schubert's mature oeuvre. The dedication to Slawjk is reflected in the virtuosity of the violin part (though the piano part is also demanding) and the stamina required in performance. It is a long piece, comprising an Andante introduction and an Allegro, together amounting to 713 bars. Not surprisingly, perhaps, it is little known because it is seldom played. But it is also undervalued: it scintillates, dances and sings, with a blend of infectious joy, tireless energy, rhythmic zip and – from time to time – heart-melting turns of melody and harmony. And, like some of the final rondos in Schubert's multi-movement works, it follows its own extended course with little heed for the traditional proportions of sonata-rondo design.

The Introduction is neatly bonded to the Allegro by becoming stuck on a discord which only the Allegro will resolve. Had Schubert heard the E flat Quartet which Beethoven composed in the previous year (Op. 127 of 1825)? Or did the two composers hit upon similar devices independently? Schubert's first episode (in sonata terms, his second subject) is a march-like tune in D major, but having asserted that key for 15 bars he travels to other keys for some 67 bars in what we would have to call a displaced development section, before returning for 77 further bars in D. Thus this amplified episode runs for 159 bars as against the rondo theme's 56 (and 4-bar transition). There is more daring disproportion to come; for after the expected return of the rondo theme, which the violin prepares for by recalling the gruppetto from the end of the Introduction, Schubert launches on a central episode – based on G major but enfolding its own development which deserts G major for more than a hundred bars – which totals 240 bars. After the next rondo return, the 'second subject', duly restored to B major, sparks off a brilliant Piu mosso coda. The proportions, then, are daring, but they are not ineffective; and the dimensions are not excessive for a stand-alone movement. It is a fine, exuberant piece, worthy of its 1826 vintage. 'Rondo brilliant' was Artaria's apt title for it when it was published in 1827.

The other work dedicated to Slawjk draws the violin-and-piano medium into the arena of Schubert's lifelong preoccupation with the fantasy principle. Perhaps one should say fantasy principles, for two broad types may be discerned, one of which might be called the 'fantasy-sonata' since it pays obeisance to the four-movement plan but partially dissolves or diversifies it at the composer's will. The Fantasy in C of 1827 is of the other type, represented by the first work in the Deutsch catalogue (the Fantasy in G for piano duet) and the *Grazer Fantasie*, for example: it follows its own multi-sectional scheme, with occasional thematic interconnections:

Andante molto	6/8	C
Allegretto	2/4	A minor, moving through E flat to
Andantino	3/4	A flat major
Tempo primo	6/8	C
Allegro vivace	𝄴	C
Allegretto	3/4	A flat
Presto	𝄵	C

There are two important inter-relationships: the opening Andante returns at 'Tempo primo' in a shortened reprise, and the Andantino is a set of variations, one of which is postponed and appears later as an interruption to the Allegro vivace (at 'Allegretto'), which then resumes in a Presto coda. In a performance of immense discretion and control, the piece has its attractions. Hungarian atmosphere is imparted to the opening Andante by the persistent tremolo effects, and to the ensuing Allegretto by the cut of its theme and rhythm.

Perhaps most notable is the theme taken as the subject for variations in the Andantino. This is derived from the 1822 song *Sei mir gegrüsst*, but is not simply a transcription of the theme of the song, nor even of its melody. The opening of the song is transformed into something closely resembling part of the first variation (bars 5–6) in the opening movement of Mozart's A major Piano Sonata, K.331. The second section of the little binary form Schubert creates from the song for the purpose of these variations is even more interesting. In each of the five stanzas of the song he had treated the last line ('Sei mir gegrüsst, sei mir geküsst!' – I greet you, I kiss you) as a musical refrain – a refrain which, with its distinctive harmony, he approached by different harmonic routes in each stanza. In the new version created for the Violin Fantasy, he finds yet another harmonic route of approach, and by this means – coupled with a richness of texture prophetic of Brahms – lifts the song material to a higher plane. Sadly, though, the variations that follow fall instantly and irretrievably from that plane, though they offer a thrill or two to those who like technical fireworks per se.

The two great piano trios display such a confident handling of, and fecund inventive response to, the violin–cello–piano medium that it is hard to believe Schubert had not written for this combination since he was fifteen, in 1812, when a mere single movement headed 'Sonata' appeared. In fact, this has to rank as one of the big mysteries of the Schubert oeuvre. True, his late friendship with Bocklet, Schuppanzigh and Linke could have provided an impetus for this sudden interest in the trio medium in 1827; but Schubert did not need friendship with performers, nor a promise of performance, as a stimulus for exercising himself in one medium rather than another. The two trios stand alone as twin peaks of the trio repertoire between Beethoven and Brahms, approached only by Mendelssohn. There can be little doubt that Schubert relished the exploration of a medium which suited his mature gifts ideally, and that if he had lived longer he would soon have returned to it.

The B flat Trio brings to mind the 'Trout' Quintet in certain peripheral ways: that is to say, it does so without the help of thematic reminiscence. It is in the first movement that the connection is particularly felt: after that, Schubert has worked his way into the chamber style and the trio medium more completely. When the opening theme, with its textural echoes of the song *An Silvia*, returns for its soft second presentation, it is given to the piano in octaves, with the violin maintaining the regular quavers and the cello punctuating with a plucked version of the piano's original bass line. This is the kind of airy piano-and-strings texture that Schubert had discovered in the 'Trout'.

Before this, the first theme exhibits an extravert and somewhat loose-jointed bonhomie that suggests the same source. When the cello puts a brake on proceedings to pave the way for an expansive second subject, there is still a vestige of divertimento style, redolent of the Octet as much as the 'Trout'. On the other hand, the initial stages of the recapitulation, which begins in the key of the flattened submediant, include some inspired variation of the pattern of events in the exposition, in a manner not typical of those other works. And in the coda Schubert is not averse to close argumentation involving the inversion of the first theme (twenty-two bars from the end of the movement) (**Fig. 117**).

Fig. 117

The slow movement lacks strong contrasts, being an almost unbroken stream of duetting by the violin and cello to a 'piano accompaniment', until the piano assumes the melodic lead in the central episode. The emphasis on melodic and harmonic simplicity in the early stages allows some surprise shifts of harmony and key later on to have all the more impact. If the delightful scherzo seems again to nod in the direction of the 'Trout' — this time its scherzo — perhaps it is because the one inverts the other (roughly, and with no pretence at exactitude). The continuations, beyond the four-bar theme in each case, bear comparison too. More tangible is the kinship of the trio with a piano piece (D.916b) probably written at about the same time, in the second half of 1827.

One of Schubert's most exhilarating finales crowns the work. It begins with youthful nonchalance, as though this is the finale of one of those early Schubert violin sonatas, although the dactyls recall the finale of the Second Symphony (Fig. 118a). (The placing of the cello's delayed first entrance is as felicitous as it is surprising.) But when a second theme in octave-unison enters the discussion (Fig. 118b), Schubert begins a display of unusual resource. This theme is put through a variety of hoops, but the most enterprising comes at the beginning of the development. (Not for the first time, Schubert announces 'Rondo' at the head of the movement and proceeds to write in sonata form.) The original accentuation of the theme (see Fig. 118b) is a cryptic clue to what happens here. Schubert accents the fourth bar but not the third – a pointed threat to the two-bar groupings that have prevailed so far. Now, in the development, the consequence of that accentuation is realized. The rabbit Schubert pulls out of his hat is a new, long three-beat bar, in which the original accented fourth bar becomes a new first beat, to which the original unaccented third bar becomes a light upbeat (Fig. 118c). The theme is in the cello, with the violin blithely rhapsodizing on the dactyls of the first theme. The static bass and repetitive circling of melody and harmony ('pipe and drum', as John Reed calls them[8]) ensures that what holds centre stage is the metrical

Fig. 118

jest. It is a moment one comes back to with joy at the nth hearing. Schubert sportingly repeats the witticism in the coda.

A single Adagio in E flat for piano trio, usually referred to as 'Notturno', could well have been a rejected slow movement for the B flat Trio, being in the same key as the existing slow movement, and of inferior quality. It is of special interest not so much for its hypothetical position in relation to the two piano trios proper, but for its bearing on the slow movement of the String Quintet in C still to be composed. In that later movement, also an Adagio, the three middle instruments sustain a very slow-moving melody and its close harmony, while cello and first violin provide foundation and embellishments: in the earlier one the violin and cello sustain similar middle parts, with the piano providing the outer parts. In both movements the central episode of the ternary design is in the Neapolitan key (major in the 'Nocturne', minor in the Quintet), and comprises much more strenuous music than the serene outer sections: and in both cases when the opening returns the outer instrumental parts are further elaborated while the inner melodic core remains unchanged. Both codas refer back to the main section and the episode. The prominent pizzicato in the main sections of the 'Nocturne' anticipates similar treatment in the later movement. All in all, one can clearly see Schubert in this 'Nocturne' moving towards what was to become perhaps his most famed and loved piece among Schubertians – the slow movement of the Quintet. If he had rejected the 'Nocturne' from one of the piano trios, he saw in it the seeds of something great, and found an early opportunity to let them germinate.

The E flat Trio, one of the great masterpieces of the trio repertoire, is also a work of unusual interest. The angular, triadic cut of its first theme would appear to announce a late flowering of Haydnesque Classicism. But that suggestion must be countered by some extraordinary statistics. The first theme spawns no more than one-eighth of the first movement. Is, then, the second subject (which comprises only one theme) that much more influential? In fact, it generates one-fifth of the movement. That leaves two-thirds of the movement to be based on an idea first introduced as an appendage to the first theme, at the sixteenth bar (Fig. 119a). This terse figure is the basis of most of the development, and most of the second group too. The second subject itself begins in remote B minor (the flat submediant minor) and winds its colourful way through other keys before settling in the orthodox dominant (B flat). It is now that this other figure takes over, destined to extend the second group to more than three times its length so far. It is shaped, fortuitously one supposes, into something like the BACH motive with which later composers paid homage to the Baroque giant (BABCH in fact, as Fig. 119b shows), before it seems to allude to the trio of the third movement of the B flat Trio (Fig. 119c). In the development it is stretched into a striking resemblance to that B flat

Fig. 119   a

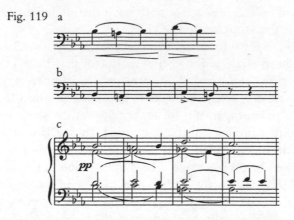

Trio's very first theme (which comes first for comparison in Fig. 120).
These allusions, or illusions, perhaps do no more than reflect the extreme
chronological closeness of the two works.

Fig. 120

The heart of the work is the Andante con moto – in the sense that it
combines poetry and power in a particularly memorable way, and it spreads
its influence into the finale and the first movement too. Oddly enough,
it is at the same time crucially indebted to Swedish material. A young
Swedish tenor called Isak Albert Berg visited Vienna in November 1827
and sang Swedish folksongs at the Fröhlichs' house. Schubert heard him,
and was affected by a song called *Se solen sjunker* (The sun has set), which
was given complete with a piano accompaniment, possibly by Berg himself.
From this song Schubert adopted the 'walking quaver chords' which begin
his slow movement, and the 'slide' (to use the technical name for the
ornament that consists of two notes ascending stepwise to a principal note).
More significantly, he appropriated three melodic/harmonic features which
are shown in Fig. 121 in the order in which they appear in the folksong.

Fig. 121   a   b

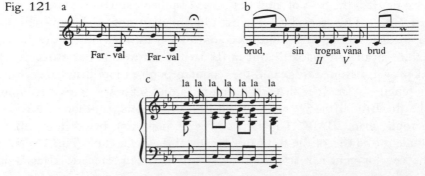

These appear in the order c, a, b, beginning at the ninth bar of Schubert's theme (Fig. 122). The falling octave (a) is then adapted to serve for Schubert's second theme, which at both its appearances (as B in a rondo structure ABABA) builds to a more imposing climax than had ever been attained in the piano trio medium. Schubert has made all this material his own with such conviction and skill that, although the ear may momentarily sense an alien turn of phrase in his theme, the compelling force of expression and all-of-a-piece construction leave one in awe of the artistic authority of what seems a wholehearted personal utterance.

Fig. 122

The scherzo is a superb example of listener-friendly canon. There are two canonic lines, imitating each other at the same pitch at one bar's (that is, three beats') distance. At first the imitation is exact, for a considerable period (which is what 'canon' implies), and only the two imitating 'voices' are heard. But to leaven the musical interest Schubert soon adds in other, non-canonic voices, and although canonic imitation is still audibly present, it becomes less exact (since the point of close linear dependence has been made). In the end all trace of canon is dismissed in light-hearted interplay between strings and piano. Lightness gives way to a somewhat galumphing heaviness in the trio – a well-judged contrast.

The finale begins like an unassuming 6/8 rondo, but soon changes time for a second subject initially in quadruple time but treated in sections of 6/8 too. This second theme, in fast repeated notes (at times to be expressed as single long notes), is one of Schubert's most captivating examples of instrumental scoring in chamber music. The development is prefaced by a surprise reprise of the theme of the slow movement, in its entirety but adapted to 6/8 time and allegro moderato tempo, with the result that it moves at the same speed as it did in its original context. The theme is in the cello, and the violin pretends to represent the original piano accompaniment. Later, at the corresponding place between recapitulation and coda, comes a further statement of this theme, though with its second segment omitted, and it is transmuted into the major to build a climactic coda which accordingly caps the finale with slow movement material. There is but a brief reference to the finale's first theme before the last cadence.

The cuts in the finale sanctioned by Schubert himself have already been referred to (page 267). The second of the two passages the composer was persuaded to omit is worth preserving in modern performance, as it is the only section in which he cunningly combines the theme of the slow movement with the second theme of the finale (the idea in fast repeated notes). This is no mere example of 'eye music': it appeals to the ear and adds a dimension to one's understanding of the principal characters of the musical plot. It also reflects Schubert's hitherto relatively unacknowledged concern with contrapuntal intricacies, and it repays close study with a score from that point of view.

Schubert has thus forged a novel cyclic structure – and in the process has created a finale which is protracted and diffuse to those who can resist it, heavenly in its length and diversity to those who cannot. The re-introduction of the theme of the slow movement naturally tends to amplify the customary finale proportions. But the influence of the Swedish theme goes even further than this. One passage in the second subject of the first movement (at bars 72–4, with repeat at 81–3) always seems somewhat alien to Classical practice in its melodic and, more particularly, harmonic style. It is in fact a transplant of 'c' from the Swedish folksong (see Fig. 121 above), melody and harmony intact. A study of the autograph of this movement at the Gesellschaft der Musikfreunde in Vienna reveals that this extension of the second subject, with the Swedish allusion, was not present in the first draft of the movement. It seems likely that Schubert added it after completing his slow movement, and perhaps the finale. It is improbable that he made the revision unaware that part of what he was adding originated in the Swedish source, since it is so distinctive, so 'un-Classical'. So the possibility arises that, having included a reprise of the folksong–based theme of the slow movement in his finale, he deliberately (but subtly) extended its cyclic influence by burying a fragment of it in the first movement too. Thus it seems that the climax of Schubert's piano-and-strings chamber music still has secrets to yield.

The Late Symphonies

Close upon the heels of the Sixth Symphony came the first of several unconsummated efforts to create its successor. Of the Symphony in D, D.615, the two surviving fragments are probably all that was ever written, since the finale was begun on the same page of piano score on which the first movement broke off. The fact that the first movement opens with a D minor Adagio that echoes the D minor Adagio of Haydn's Symphony No. 104 should not have deterred Schubert from seeing the work through, because the E flat which arrives when the opening gesture is repeated, leading to the distant key of A flat major, a tritone away, is a daring deviation which helps to keep this slow introduction on a level of inspiration commensurate, at the least, with Schubert's previous symphonic introductions (Fig. 123). All that is missing is the orchestration.

Fig. 123

If, however, the ensuing Allegro moderato which peters out at the end of its exposition raised doubts in the composer's mind, one can see why, for despite some promising ideas it runs out of wind before Schubert rests his pen. The finale is no less attractive, but perhaps Schubert in the end did not consider its prettiness and tendency to a loose balletic build as the right way forward for a maturing symphonist. The movement breaks off with the delightfully textured first return of the opening theme in what looks as if it was going to be the composer's first symphonic rondo finale.

The next attempt, also in D, after a gap of two years or so, must have come nearer to satisfying Schubert's current aspirations. He stayed with it long enough to commit substantial amounts of four movements to paper. The ideas, and their working out as far as it goes, are broadly the stuff of which he could have made a viable symphony, worthy of the 1820–1 winter, if he had seen no obstacle to doing so. The first movement, which has no introduction, has built into its early stages something of the ear-opening sense of wonder and excitement – and grandeur besides – proper to a slow introduction. Furthermore, it daringly adapts to the sonata-allegro a strategy previously evident in two slow introductions (those of the Fourth Symphony and D.615), a decisive move to the key a tritone away from home. Here, that move coincides with the arrival of a second theme, so that we have what is probably the first instance of a second subject in the tritone-distant key. (Reicha's use of the tritone-related key for the answer in the exposition of a fugue was a comparable example of such daring.[1]) The slow movement, of which – like the first movement – about one-third was sketched, contains some expressive lyrical counterpoint (alone worth salvaging in a posthumous orchestration of Schubert's piano score). Almost complete on two staves, and easily finishable, are both the scherzo and the trio. The scherzo is one of the most interesting and successful essays in counterpoint of these middle years, presenting its tripping first theme in fugal exposition, then combining it with a theme in longer notes, in a manner which anticipates the scherzo of the 'Great' C major. The heads of both themes (Figs. 124a and 124b) bear comparison with those of the later scherzo.

Fig. 124

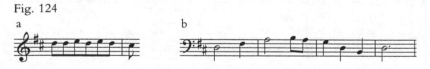

It is the finale which provides the clue to the likely obstacle that caused Schubert to stall. Shortly before he abandoned it he reached a point where two climactic chords of A flat major (fortissimo) and C sharp major (triple forte) seem to demand the force of the whole orchestra. Yet these chords, in a movement in D major, contain no notes which valveless horns or trumpets in D could play. If other reasons for aborting the symphony were present, such as the distraction of a tantalizing crop of alternative projects to fire his enthusiasm, that difficulty in the way of realizing his conception in orchestral score might have tipped the balance.

Schubert's next symphonic step, taken within a year, was a bold one. Instead of sketching in piano score, as he had done in the two recently abandoned symphonies, he began to compose one directly into orchestral score, as he had done with Nos. 1 to 6. To do that at this stage, when he was moving through a period of relatively fast stylistic development (the stylistic watershed of the Quartettsatz being some eight months past), was courageous, as was the choice of the rather unsymphonic key of E major. Yet the unfinished Seventh Symphony was to be the crucial link between the backward-glancing early symphonies and the visionary, forward-looking works that were to follow. It is in these pages that one can first glimpse the power of imagination that was to ennoble the 'Unfinished' B minor Symphony and the striding confidence that would impel the 'Great' C major.

Transitional and prophetic as the Symphony No. 7 in E is, it also shows Schubert working out formal experiments which were to have no sequel in the later symphonies. The E minor introduction brings new, unique sonorities. With trombones now added back in, having been excluded from Nos. 1 to 6 after not justifying their presence in the juvenile D.2B fragment, and two pairs of horns employed (as in Schubert's previous minor-key symphony, No. 4, and for the same reason), his symphonic orchestra reaches a size beyond what would be required for the 'Unfinished' or the 'Great'. There is a depth and solidity of sound in these opening pages that one will not find elsewhere in Schubert, except in an Overture in E minor/major composed in 1819 which was clearly important in helping Schubert find his feet with these resources in this key. That introduction is wholly Schubert's: it is only after some seventy-five bars of the following Allegro that his intentions have to be reconstructed if the symphony is to be performed. From that point to the end of the finale, only the leading melodic line is given (for two-thirds of the work in all), with other strands added at some places, especially when a change of texture was envisaged. As this was an orchestral sketch, every note that Schubert wrote was assigned to an instrument, and to that instrument's line in the score. As Schubert took full orchestral paper for every page, most of the staves lie empty.

The most radical experiment concerns the first movement, in which Schubert not only makes no provision for a repeat of the exposition but avoids altogether the explicit cadence that usually marks the end of the exposition, pushing through in seamless flow to remote C major, by which time development must be said to have begun. A similar truncation conceals the junction of development to recapitulation, with the result that when E major is regained the first theme is omitted and the recapitulation begins with the 'afterstatement'. Again, at the end of the recapitulation, before any transparent gesture has marked the termination the music has veered to F major and a coda has begun. Thus the movement, a long one despite procedures which tend to entail local contraction, appears as an attempt to forge a seamless sonata form. In no other work did Schubert venture such daredevil structural engineering. Of course, the omission of a first subject from a recapitulation was not revolutionary. It is the telescoping of a new section into the end of the previous section, elsewhere in the movement, that gives this particular experiment its distinction.

Oddly enough, a repeat of the exposition – jettisoned in the first movement – is a feature of the finale, where Schubert takes care to compose fully the 'first-time bars' which lead back to the beginning for this repeat. An exposition-repeat in a finale, common enough in the early Classical period, had become a rarity since the turn of the century. Later in his finale, Schubert again enters his recapitulation late, as it were, omitting the first subject and making a reprise instead from the sixth bar of the afterstatement.

In three of the movements of the Seventh Schubert enjoys the added freedom of tonal travel afforded by a three-key exposition. Although the three themes of the lovely slow movement all have common elements, Schubert highlights their differences, not only by presenting them in different keys (A major, D major, F sharp minor) but by making one an upper melody, one a bass melody, and one a beautiful lament by the two clarinets in thirds. As there is no development, and a short transition connects the F sharp minor theme to the reprise in the tonic A, there are five transitions in all (the three keys of the recapitulation being A major, F major, and A minor becoming major at a late stage) and the movement unfolds as an alternation of themes and transitions which exploits the composer's gifts as both melodist and bridge-builder in a concentrated and flavoursome form.

If it is in the transitions, of that Andante and of the other movements, that the Seventh most anticipates the 'Unfinished', while in the first themes of the outer fast movements Rossini's example can be discerned, it is in the scherzo as much as anywhere that a foreknowledge of the 'Great' will cause the listener to smile. It has to do with the weight of the scoring, with trombones at the ready to underpin the bigger gestures; but there is also the prophetic turn from C major (the key of the scherzo) to A major (that of the trio) by means of a pivotal E, which matches exactly the route from scherzo to trio in the later work.

One remaining distinction of the Seventh is the fact that it displays a stronger overall thematic unity than any other of his symphonies. The first themes of all the first three movements, at least, share a similar structure. Their opening phrases are all of five bars (or five half-bars, or five pairs of bars – it is the same thing to the ear), being essentially four-bar phrases expanded from within, as the second bar is followed by a repetition or sequence of itself (Fig. 125). This pattern is not unknown elsewhere in Schubert (the finale of the String Quartet in A minor begins with an example of it) but the concentration of three instances in one work is exceptional.

Fig. 125

There is a tendency to characterize multi-movement works like symphonies, and especially those of Classical times, by their first movements. Mention Beethoven's Fifth, the 'Jupiter', Haydn's No. 88 or Beethoven's 'Moonlight' Sonata, and as likely as not one will mentally hear its opening. It is usual for composers to maintain that the hardest part of composing is beginning a piece: as one gets further in, the options progressively narrow, but when the paper is blank anything is possible. One could believe that once Schubert had formulated the riveting first notes of his B minor Symphony, the continuation was to an extent a matter of realizing what was already predestined. When the unaccompanied cello-and-bass theme rises, falls and turns, bottoms out in idiosyncratic contour, and comes to rest, the shimmer of the violins over a gently reiterative rhythm below and the plangent fall of the wind melody then added above in the evocative and uncommon unison combination of oboe and clarinet seem inevitable sequels. Or does hindsight deceive us? Even the more vociferous, at times dramatic outbursts that follow later in the movement seem to grow causally from the ostensibly lyrical germ of the opening.

Yet, although this gently paced, melodious Allegro moderato seems all of a piece, whatever the variety of incident within it, we must take a cue from the sad fact that the B minor Symphony was another that went unfinished, and not assume that even a composer at the height of his powers who has successfully broken the initial silence will necessarily be able to fulfil his design. That this particular venture cost some effort, in any case, is confirmed by the existence of a piano sketch, which differs in some important details from the final version. Yet that effort is concealed, in the end, with supreme skill — a skill which leaves everything sounding spontaneous, inevitable, and like true Schubert rather than a Schubert diluted and distanced by an excess of working over and 'refining'.

Never did a formal transition sound less formal and more an indissoluble link in the expressive chain than the mere four bars which lead from the end of the first big B minor paragraph to the famous cello second subject in G major. When that tune has run its course, there is extended development of it, in and around G major. That comfortable key is not to be disturbed by any inclination to push on to the third staging post of a three-key exposition. A two-key exposition suffices to hold the matters of the moment, and the flavour of the ideas is arguably more concentrated thereby.

One may think that the formality of an exposition-repeat is alien to music which has this kind of rapturous continuity. Yet Schubert required it, and, as the previous symphony shows, he would not have hesitated to dispense with it if he had seen fit. One advantage is that the opening cello-and-bass theme is so implanted in the mind after two hearings that when, at the start of the development, it is freshly resolved downwards to the low tonic, and beyond by two further hushed steps, this deepening of the mystery gains in impact. The following lean, widely spaced texture is quite as venturesome as the un-Classical, futuristic opening-up of the orchestral weave to be found at places in the slow movement of the 'Eroica'.

If one wishes to invoke a structural model to explain the build of the exquisite slow movement, one may find here the ABABA of the equivalent movement of the Fifth Symphony, but with the final reprise of A replaced with a coda by no means solely concerned with A, and the first reprise of A preceded by a rather long (for Schubert) transition; or sonata form may be deduced, the transition being a development which begins imperceptibly (as in the first movement of the Seventh Symphony) and leads by a magical harmonic surprise into the recapitulated A. However that may be, the salient impression is of a heightened poetic feeling. The technical constructs that underlie this elevated, refined expressivity are, as always, essential to it, but the acute sentiments so dominate that one may well forget to enquire as to the provenance of the techniques that shape it. There is an abundance of finely crafted detail, not least in the second subject, which with hindsight might be seen as a prototype of Romantic rumination – the soft syncopated harmonies in the strings calling to mind Mendelssohn, the vulnerably exposed clarinet being only intermittently a prima donna since the long notes at the middle and end of its single long-drawn-out phrase allow the striking harmonic shifts below to hold centre stage. The final fade to triple piano for the ultimate resolution from minor to major reflects Schubert's growing exploitation of dynamic extremes as an orchestral resource. Another triple piano occurs in the coda, where a snatch of the opening theme is assigned to a wind quintet. Schubert would normally have mixed clarinet, horn and bassoon timbres here; but the key is remote A flat, and the valveless horns in E cannot provide the necessary notes. Schubert takes advantage of a trombone, which lacks the horn's limitations, to provide the bass line here. The narrow-bore trombone of Schubert's day would have made an excellent blend with the low woodwind, and Schubert availed himself of such opportunities again in the next symphony.

Only a piano sketch of the scherzo survives, apart from two pages of its orchestral realization. The scherzo itself is complete in structure though not in texture, but of the trio there is a melody line only, for the first section only. Of the finale there is no trace. The history of the manuscript and the reasons for the work's abandonment have been thoroughly explored elsewhere.[2] There is no definitive explanation as to why Schubert laid the work aside. One may select from the usual range of possibilities – lack of belief in the movement currently being worked on, compositional problems during its course, distractions – and mix a cocktail to one's taste. Two specific suggestions have been that Schubert was keenly aware of a debt to Beethoven in the scherzo,[3] and that he came to associate the symphony with the sexual act which caused his syphilis – something he wanted to forget.[4] (This proposition is only a possibility if the date of infection was earlier than current scholarly thinking has it.) Both suggestions are resistible: the debts to Beethoven in the scherzo are less pronounced than in other (finished) works and there is no evidence that Schubert was anxious to eliminate them, while art and reality were not necessarily so closely intertwined in his mind that he would forsake a project which he must have realized was of superfine quality on account of a worldly circumstance which did not prevent him from giving his time to other musical ventures of less dazzling promise. The enigma remains.

While attempts to complete the scherzo belong almost exclusively to the years after 1900, the tradition of playing the B minor Entr'acte from *Rosamunde* as the symphony's finale goes back well into the nineteenth century. Grove was among the first to endorse the idea. More recent scholarship has assembled arguments for believing that that entr'acte may indeed have been originally intended as the finale of the symphony. Central to the case are the following points: the entr'acte is a longer, more developed piece than seems to fit into the scheme of 'incidental music' for *Rosamunde*, being in a more ample sonata form than many an opera overture; it is in the same key as the symphony; it requires the same orchestral forces; it is in the form used by Schubert for nearly all his symphonic finales; and Schubert had little time to fulfil the *Rosamunde* commission, so appropriated material from some of his earlier works.[5] Maurice Brown repudiated the claimed connection between the two works, on the grounds that their scores were written on paper of different types with different watermarks.[6] A study of Schubert's sketching habits in other works suggests that he probably sketched all four movements of the 'Unfinished' before writing an orchestral score. When he stopped work on the scoring of the scherzo, he would have stored the finale sketch. When that sketch was brought out some fourteen months later, he would naturally have scored it on orchestral paper of the type in use towards the end of 1823 rather than that on which the 'Unfinished' was written in the autumn of 1822. It is possible, of course, that the sketch was incomplete, or that he made some changes to 'de-symphonize' it: could the pauses early in its course be adaptations for the theatrical purpose? As to the music itself, it contains some superb ideas of distinct originality, which could well have been products of the state of mind that spawned the rest of the 'Unfinished'. In debates on the issues raised here, it is important to keep two separate questions distinct: could Schubert have first intended the entr'acte as finale to the symphony? And, does it work as finale to the symphony?

Schubert's next symphony inhabits a quite different world from that of the 'Unfinished'. The 'Great' C major is a glorious last re-affirmation of the Classical principles of symphonic design, imbued with a Romantic spirit and impelled by an unflagging rhythmic verve which seems almost calculated to dispel any doubts that Schubert would never be able to finish a symphony again. It could be seen as evidence of Schubert having found in his Gmunden–Gastein summer a new life, disease-free, or the strength to face out the residual threat and attain a new, exalted creative plane. In its life-enhancing combination of richness and élan, it stands as a symbol of renewal, a beacon lit by the burning force of creativity and casting its light in turn over Schubert's last years as a referential backdrop to all the varied masterpieces yet to come.

Some may find an irony in the fact that Beethoven, no noted composer of Lieder, had recourse to the unsymphonic ingredients of voices and verbal text in his Ninth, while Schubert the prolific song-writer retained the instrumental purity of the symphonic strain to the last. He had reached the position – by virtue of commitment, practice and maturation – at which he was wholly at ease with the symphonic medium, its long-term architecture and its orchestral sound-world: he had used solo and choral voices often in conjunction with an orchestra (in his church music and operas), but even with a model by his idolized Beethoven to build from he resisted any inclination to let poetry, drama or the voice infiltrate the symphonic domain. He did, however, implicitly pay homage at a distance to the influence of the spoken word by allowing a clear reminiscence of the vocal 'joy' theme of the 'Choral' Symphony to lead him into the development of the finale of his own Ninth.[7]

The two symphonies by Beethoven and Schubert are almost contemporaneous, in the middle of the nineteenth century's third decade. At the end of the same decade came another notable symphony, the 'Fantastique' of

Berlioz. Schubert's looks conservative alongside the other two. Berlioz's two harps, swollen woodwind palette, extra percussion and cornets reflect a French tradition and programmatic purpose. Even Beethoven requires, in addition to his singers, four horns, a contrabassoon, piccolo and exotic percussion. Schubert's orchestra merely adds the three trombones to the Classical contingent of four woodwind pairs, two each of horns and trumpets, and two drums. Yet as his symphony unfolds, there is no lack of energy, no shortage of colour, nor any sense of a tired tradition. The last Classical symphony it may be, but its message is new-minted, its scope visionary, its momentum tireless.

Just as there was no truly fast music in the 'Unfinished' – or in the two finished movements at least – so there is nothing truly slow in the 'Great'. The 'slow' movement is a carefully marked Andante con moto, while the introduction to the first movement is an Andante whose time-signature has always been misrepresented in published scores (and even in one newly issued in the 1980s): the symbol Schubert uses is ¢, not C, so that Alla breve is suggested, with two beats to the bar. The intention was presumably that the same pulse should run through from this Andante into the Allegro ma non troppo, without the accelerando which is usually made but does not appear in Schubert's autograph score. This preference for livelier tempi, perhaps inherited from Beethoven's Seventh Symphony which Schubert so admired (although Beethoven's introduction does call for a more measured tread), goes hand in hand with a partiality for short rhythmic units which multiply to build the music's larger spans. The result might be likened to a vast mosaic, but only if one imagines a mosaic in which the grander designs are firmly planned and always held in sharp focus.

Is the introduction an introduction? It is, in that the sonata-form scheme begins with the Allegro, but the penetration of the introduction material into the sonata-allegro itself is so extensive that a radically new re-interpretation of first-movement form that out-Beethovens Beethoven is the outcome. Beethoven sometimes recalled a slow introduction in the course of its following Allegro: there are several such returns in the first movement of his String Quartet in B flat, Op. 130, and Haydn had done something similar in his 'Drum–Roll' Symphony, No. 103. Schubert, in his First Symphony, re-introduced his slow opening during the Allegro, in allegro tempo. These examples provide some of the context against which to appreciate what happens in the 'Great'. But the 'Pathétique' Sonata of Beethoven (Op. 13) is especially germane, as thematic material from the slow introduction is here *developed* within the Allegro's development section as though it were part of the Allegro's own stock of ideas. The 'Great' goes beyond this precedent, its Allegro redeploying material from the opening Andante theme – always in the current tempo – to build the last and principal climaxes of the exposition, development, recapitulation and coda. These passages amount to more than a quarter of the entire Allegro.

It is mainly the second bar of the Andante theme (Fig. 126) that is the topic for future use, just as it is strikingly developed within the Andante itself. At the very end of the movement, though, the entire eight-bar strain makes a powerfully conclusive comeback. So pervasive is this theme that the first theme of the Allegro does not exert quite the thematic dominance to be expected in a sonata scheme, functioning rather as a rhythmic power-house. (Schubert even changed its contour after he had finished the movement.)

Fig. 126

The coda of this movement, some of which Schubert added after the main period of composition, contains a dynamic double excursion – a descendant of that which drives the coda of the finale of the Third Symphony, in turn modelled on one in Beethoven's Second. The tonal vistas it opens up are awe-inspiring, and the second launch propels it on an even longer trajectory, attaining a peak of excitement which only the clamorous reinstatement of the Andante theme can sustain to a final cadence.

March-like as the second movement is, with its processional tread, its themes all beginning on downbeats, and the two accented notes of equal length which close the prefatory statement in the cellos and basses as well as the first phrase of the definitive oboe entry, it abounds in delicately precise colouring and intimate lyrical confidences alien to the functional outdoor genre. It is noteworthy in this connection that the Mozart work which Schubert seems to echo in the cantabile F major tune which sounds like an episode or second subject is music of the chamber, the Violin Sonata in E flat (K.481). Episode? Or second subject? One may hear the movement as an elongated sonata form without development, having three themes in its expanded first group which are repeated in the pattern 1–2–3–1–2–3–1–2, or as an amplified ternary form along the lines of that displayed by the slow movement of Beethoven's Seventh, to which Schubert's movement bears certain other resemblances too.

Among many treasured details are the soft trumpet counterpoint which adorns the first theme when it returns after the F major episode, almost staking a claim for that instrument as a candidate for chamber-music use; the transition back to A minor for that same reprise, where the bell-like reiterations of the horns are harmonically reinterpreted by the subtly shifting strings to make the homeward turn a magical event; and the later engulfing climax where a diminished seventh, strident with passion, breaks off to be confronted by a sudden, pin–dropping silence – looking forward across the decades to moments of high drama in Tchaikovsky. The hushed pizzicato that breaks the silence is no less Tchaikovskian, but the attempts of the cellos to lead off to B flat major (the Neapolitan key), along with the oboe's corrective tug back to A minor (and, the second time, to A major), are the mature Schubert's inimitable masterstrokes.

The vast scherzo, in which heavyweight scoring combines with super-charged rhythm to meet the demands of this particular symphonic context, springs to life with the force of all the strings in octave-unison. In fact more than half of the contribution of the strings to the scherzo has them all massed on a single line. The opening figure, from the unfinished scherzo of the Symphony in D, D.708A, later decorates the accompaniment to the second subject, a broader, waltz–like tune which subsequently can be heard sweeping down and up (later, up and down) in the whole string body united in one voice. In a soft lull in the strenuously active development (for this is a scherzo in full sonata form, like that of Beethoven's Ninth) comes the breathtaking moment when a songful strain in the flute in C flat major gives way to a repetition, suddenly a semitone higher, in violins and oboe (a telling mix, exuding warmth with a bit of edge, to which the mature Schubert was partial). When the trio swings into action – a full-throated chorus in the woodwind with a kick in the brass – the simple, homely tunefulness of the traditional trio is left far behind. There is something unvarying in the texture of this trio, from the perspective of a string or brass player, although the woodwind combinations are effectively diverse; and the doubling of the melody in Viennese thirds and sixths is pretty consistent too. This is all part of Schubert's purpose, and becomes the trio's strength; the long-reaching melodic spans, the ample sonority, the unyielding onward thrust, with its bouncy skips in the brass – these carry the listener along on waves of joyous sound, at that point in a symphony when some listeners might confess they are inclined to nod. And there are harmonic wonders besides.

It may be too fanciful to hear the opening convulsions of the finale, with their distant responses in the strings, as having alpine connotations. A symphonic pre-echo of the calls across the valley articulated by the soprano and clarinet in *Der Hirt auf dem Felsen*? These initial gestures, and their immediate sequels, are all upwards-aspiring, and it does no harm to recall that the inspiration for this symphony came to Schubert when he was surrounded by the great outdoors in terrain where the human gaze naturally rises to the skyline. Ascent, positivism, spiritual elation: they all seem to mingle in the affirmative outburst that sets the finale in motion.

By the time he reaches his second subject Schubert has already established the four-bar grouping as an almost invariable norm, the psychological effect of which is that the music now moves in long strides. Looked at in isolation, the first four notes of the second subject (Fig. 127) could equally well have been written as the four beats of one bar, but the appearance of those four notes as a four-bar spread underlines for the eye the aural impression of a long stride. These four repeated notes, which most clearly symbolize the four-bar grouping, assume greater importance later, since they become a topic for development on their own, and – at the end of the development – they form a continuing backdrop against which the recapitulated first theme is superimposed. Thus even that first theme is forced into allegiance, initially at least, to the four-bar grouping. Later, in the coda, the same four notes, in deep and forceful octave-unison, become the four hammer-blows that call the finale's accumulated hyperactivity to account, as it were – a decisive part of the process of conclusion, after which the final sprint to the finish is unleashed.

Fig. 127

The path to those hammer-blows in the coda is prepared by four large twenty-bar sequential blocks, each gathering itself to move into a new key to which, however, the interrupting next block denies access. Listen not to the Jeremiah who would have us all believe that Schubert is merely padding out an already long symphony by presenting the same twenty bars four times, merely transposed. Each of those twenty-bar blocks is slightly different, in harmonic construction and/or scoring and/or other textural detail, while the four of them together implement a carefully graded crescendo, in meticulously marked notches from the initial triple piano to the fortissimo of the hammer-blows themselves. It is, appropriately, a controlled, imaginative and grandly conceived approach to the crowning climax of Schubert's most ambitious symphony.

Schubert composed this Ninth Symphony directly into score, as the autograph with its various ink colours (representing additions and revisions made at different times) demonstrates. The sheer sweep of the invention is no doubt related to that circumstance. The revisions, in so far as they entailed the complete suppression of a significant first thought, were few. One cancelled idea was a projected second subject, which was replaced by the completely different second subject we now know. Schubert wrote only twelve bars of this original second subject, and they have been variously called fugal, canonic, or indeed 'a fugato'. There is in fact nothing fugal or canonic about them as they stand, although Schubert may later have given them contrapuntal treatment. But if he had stayed with them and worked them through they would have changed the face of this finale, for the four repeated notes which head the replacement second subject influence so much the thematic and indeed metrical character of the subsequent course of the movement.

Schubert's last attempted symphony was not composed into score: nor, on all the available evidence, was the scoring of it ever begun. It is likely that Schubert resorted to sketching symphonies in a two-stave particell (which we loosely call 'piano score') whenever he felt himself at a stylistic impasse or contemplated a work more ambitious or adventurous than its predecessor, which might therefore involve more trial and error in its composition. He returned to the piano–sketch method, for example, after the Sixth Symphony (for D.615 and D.708A), turned once more to direct composition into score for No. 7 in E, and when that could not be completed returned to the more cautious procedure for the 'Unfinished'. The long-planned 'Great', essentially a revitalization of Classical traditions, could be composed and scored in the one process. The Symphony in D major (D.936A) begun just a few weeks before the composer's death was, however, to be a singularly exploratory, experimental work, and Schubert duly worked tentatively on two staves.

This 'Tenth' Symphony came to light – and then was made accessible to the would-be listener – only in the last quarter of the twentieth century. At this time new dating techniques established beyond doubt that this was a work of the last year, not a transitional middle-period effort. (The manuscript had previously been bound with those of D.615 and D.708A, and it was supposed that all the fragments – of what we now know to have been three symphonies – were part of a workbook towards a single symphony.) A performing version of the symphony was subsequently made.[8]

This version was made on the assumption – based on deduction from internal indications – that Schubert had come close to the stage at which sketching was completed and scoring could begin when death intervened. The signs are that the symphony was ultimately to have taken a three-movement form, with a central slow movement and a third movement combining the functions of scherzo and finale. Having made the finale structurally complete, Schubert went back to the slow movement, added some material, and – possibly his last creative act – deleted the coda. It was clearly his intention to provide a revised coda, presumably in the light of the other change he had just made to the movement; but he did not live to do it. The structure of the sketched first movement is not easy to ascertain, but the fact that Schubert completed the structure of the finale and troubled to make minor revisions to the slow movement suggests that he had already mapped out the first movement in his head and the sketch was a substantial enough prompt to enable him to finish it.

The 'Tenth' Symphony is innovative on several fronts. There is no slow introduction, but the development of the first movement begins with a variant of the second subject in a slower tempo. The use of a slower tempo at this point, for a purpose other than the recall of a slow introduction, is probably unprecedented in a symphony, although it may be found in Spohr's *Faust* Overture, performed in Vienna in 1813 and published in 1823. Schubert indicates the use of trombones here, and it has been suggested that the passage bears a reference to the Equale No. 1 for four trombones by Beethoven, performed in a vocal transcription at Beethoven's funeral in Schubert's presence some eighteen months previously.[9] There is some difficulty with this proposition, for it is an inescapable fact that Schubert's trombone passage is based on the second subject presented earlier in the movement (Fig. 128b), which migrates from part to part in the trombone version (Fig. 128c); and that second subject was in turn derived from a theme in Schubert's own opera *Die Zwillingsbrüder* (chorus, No. 1) (Fig. 128a). At the same time, the melodic and harmonic affinity with the Beethoven piece is slender.[10]

Fig. 128

The deeply-felt second movement, closer in spirit to the 'Unfinished' than the 'Great', yet prophetic of Bruckner and even Mahler, displays at times a sparseness of texture comparable to that of *Der Leiermann*, the last song of *Winterreise*, but unprecedented in the orchestral repertoire. Sharing its B minor key and triple time with the first movement of the 'Unfinished', it begins with a theme which, like the opening of the 'Unfinished', climbs up to the minor third, then falls back (Fig. 129a). Far from there being any ultimate major-key resolution of this theme, the final reference to it actually flattens the second note, and falls back before even reaching the

Fig. 129

third. Fig. 129b shows this final residue as it appears in the sketch. The association of the flattened second of the scale with finality recalls the last bars of the String Quintet, completed only a few weeks earlier. Schubert returned to this bleak tone-poem after sketching his third movement and added a major-key melody of poignant beauty that enriches the emotional grain of the movement without bringing more than temporary consolation. It is a profoundly moving inspiration, and it was probably the last musical thought to issue from his pen, bringing tantalizingly close the completion of one of the most touchingly eloquent products of his creative life.

The first continuity draft of the third movement was headed 'Scherzo', but as work proceeded it became clear that Schubert's thinking was not to be confined by the implications of that term. This draft degenerated into a worksheet, as the outline of two themes was modified in order to make them compatible with each other in simultaneous combination. How this simultaneous combination would fit into the eventual structure of the movement was yet to be resolved, and Schubert took another sheet of paper to begin a new continuity draft. This time he omitted the 'Scherzo' title, and what took shape thereafter was a movement which has more characteristics of a finale than of a scherzo. In duple time, though with a proliferation of triplets now and then, it lacks the division into 'scherzo' and 'trio' sections, each with its own binary subdivisions, and prefers a through-composed rondo form, more usual for finales than scherzi. At the same time, it abounds in contrapuntal device, of kinds more likely to be found in finales (examples being Mozart's K.387 Quartet and 'Jupiter' Symphony). Schubert ventures double counterpoint, canon, augmentation and fugato, eventually bringing his two alternating themes together in contrapuntal combination (Fig. 130). The lower line here is the first theme of the movement – the rondo theme – and the upper one is the episode theme. Perhaps they were respectively the scherzo and trio themes of

Fig. 130

Schubert's original conception. At any rate, they do have contrasting characters that are more or less in line with traditional scherzo/trio contrast, and the scherzo-like nature of the rondo theme is particularly influential in the coda. It is appropriate, then, to regard the movement as a scherzo-finale.

A scherzo-finale may have been a new concept in symphonic music, although there are themes of scherzo character in some finales, such as that of Beethoven's Second Symphony. But an interesting precedent in the piano literature is the third movement of Beethoven's Sonata in G major, Op. 14, No. 2: it is the work's finale but is headed 'Scherzo' and is in a variety of rondo form. Schubert almost certainly knew the sonata and may have been conscious of it as he pioneered his own fusion of movement types. But the contrapuntal thrust of Schubert's scherzo-finale is more resistant to genealogical explanation. At one time it would have been thought contrary to his nature; but with our knowledge of his early efforts at fugal and canonic writing, his 'mirror' counterpoint in the 'Wanderer' Fantasy, his palindrome in *Die Zauberharfe*, his finely crafted contrapuntal sorties in such late works as the Fantasy in F minor for piano duet and *Lebensstürme*, and his decision to take lessons in counterpoint from Sechter while he was working on this symphony, we can regard his last projected symphonic finale as a development of existing technical interests and inclinations, which would surely have had consequences for any further symphonies he had survived to write. Idle as it may be to ask what kind of symphonies might have come from him if he had lived as long as Beethoven, the reflection that this would have enabled him to see in the year 1854 helps us to appreciate the historic role that was denied him. The thought of Schubert composing symphonies after Schumann had completed all four of his, likewise Mendelssohn and Berlioz, with Wagner's *Flying Dutchman*, *Tannhäuser* and *Lohengrin* already staged, Liszt at work on *Les Préludes* and Brahms on his D minor Piano Concerto, is intriguing in itself. But this hypothetical extrapolation of what would have been a reasonable lifespan, and the historical 'placing' that results, reminds us that Schubert, whom we refer to as a contemporary of Beethoven, was of a later generation, a generation nearer to Schumann, Chopin and Liszt. If he had lived, he would surely have fused Classical and Romantic elements in the symphony even more powerfully than he had in the 'Unfinished' and 'Great', looking ahead to the synthesis achieved by Brahms a generation later still.

~ 23 ~

Aspects of Technique

It is not the intention in this chapter to offer a portrait of Schubert's musical style, nor to explore with any attempt at comprehensiveness any single aspect of his technique, but rather to present some new analytical findings and to share some observations on technical aspects of his works in such a way, it is hoped, as to interest the lay reader who is already a seasoned Schubert listener. If references to harmony tend to dominate, no apology is called for. Harmony, seldom in Schubert separable from the considerations of tonality that govern it, arguably accounts for a good half of the content and effect of music of this period, and it is only because discussion of harmony requires a language, musicianly aural grasp and degree of conceptualization that would deter many an honest-to-goodness music-loving reader that it has formed so disproportionately tiny a part of writings about the great composers of the past. The capacity to respond to Schubert's harmony confers the power to enter his unique, charmed world. To respond is not to be able to expound in technical terms what happens in the music, or to be an expert reader of harmony textbooks. To take pleasure in this influential element of the Schubert spell, however, a measure of technical exposition is worth confronting.

Technique in musical composition may be acquired by training, by private study, or by a combination of both. Private study, involving the scrutiny of well-chosen models by ear and eye, has served composers well enough, Elgar among them. Schubert underwent early training, at the hands of Holzer and Salieri in particular, but there soon came a point when only independent study and experience of music could fulfil certain of his needs. It was customary at this time for composers to copy out works by others as one way of gaining inside knowledge. Some of the copies Schubert made of works by others have survived. It is significant that Mozart and Beethoven are chiefly represented: the young composer learned to be discriminating at an early age. Why, he asked in his early days at the Stadtkonvikt (according to Spaun), play Krommer when Haydn had written symphonies without number. Even a symphony by Koželuh was to be preferred: 'There is more rhyme and reason in this symphony than in the whole of Krommer.'[1] It was also normal for composers to take works by others as models for their own: Beethoven's Quintet for piano and wind, for example, is clearly indebted to Mozart's. Schubert's modelling – some of it referred to elsewhere in this study – was sometimes quite close. This modelling is not usually concerned with melodic detail, but homes in on fundamentals of construction – design in the short, medium or long term, and the harmonic structures that largely determine it.

There are suggestive internal indications that the finale of the G major Piano Sonata took the finale of Beethoven's G major Sonata, Op. 31, No. 1 as a model in certain respects. (Models are often in the same key as the work being composed, though not always.) The Rondo in A for piano duet is more obviously indebted to the finale of the Beethoven Sonata in E minor, Op. 90. Earlier in his career, Schubert's dependence on a Beethoven scheme was sometimes even more overt. At the age of eighteen he penned a Minuet in A major (D.334) whose opening strain (Fig. 131a) is unmistakably a by-product of the first strain of Beethoven's

Fig. 131

Sonata in D, Op. 10, No. 3 (Fig. 131b). At M1 both melodies move sequen-
tially, to cadence on the same two notes. Before that, both pieces move
off with the same bass line (B1). B2 is an imperfect cadence in both cases,
and B3 the same bass and perfect cadence. The last five notes of melody
are identical at M2. The harmonic colour introduced early in the second
phrase of the two examples yields to identical analysis. Whether such
modelling is consciously done is not a concern here: the mechanisms that
perform such tasks can be subconscious, but this does not make them of
no significance. Some of those instances where Schubert simply follows a
melodic outline in Beethoven (the *Prometheus* tune in the outer movements
of the First Symphony, or the 'Archduke' theme in *Adrast*) may likewise
be subconscious.

The technique of orchestration has attracted an extensive literature in the
nineteenth and twentieth centuries, and orchestral scoring can be studied in
educational institutions as a discrete discipline. Schubert may have had
some guidance in this art from Salieri, for what it was worth, but it is
unlikely that Holzer could have helped him. This did not stop Schubert
from taking an early interest in orchestral composition and learning by
studying the scores of his idols – Haydn, Mozart and Beethoven – and
eventually by having his own scores played. The fragmentary overture
(D.2A) and symphony (D.2B) of 1811 already betoken a game and competent orchestrator, but for a minor problem with the notation of trombone
parts. Even the teasing demands of writing for choir and orchestra seem
to inspire a sure response. A perusal of the Kyrie of the Mass in F soon
shows that at the age of seventeen he knew how, in a soft choral passage,
to avoid doubling the choral lines literally. Fig. 132 shows how the sopranos
(stems down) and first violins (stems up) have their moments of indepen-
dence although sharing the same essential outline. He knows how to add
a woodwind interjection by pulling out a middle part at some point and
descanting it at an upper octave, and to use the horns to touch in pivotal
notes in their own rhythm here and there. In one passage the doubling of
sopranos and basses by first violins and cellos while the second violins and
violas unite on a faster-moving independent inner strand is but one welcome alternative texture.

Fig. 132

Like orchestration, form could be learned by example. Schubert was
playing large-scale instrumental works with his family string quartet and
school orchestra from a tender age, and his acute ear and lively musical
mind will have enabled him to perceive (even when playing just one

part of the texture) how harmony, phrase-structure, repetition, variation, contrast and development were working together to promote coherent design. There were treatises on form, and he may have read some of them as part of his training, but his schoolboy compositions suggest he worked things out by trial and error – and there are indeed errors (by his own criteria, surely) in some of the early efforts. One need not look beyond the first four orchestral overtures that survive complete to identify one juvenile problem.

All four were written when he was fifteen. The overture to *Der Teufel als Hydraulicus* lasts 327 bars and never leaves the key of D major. The convention that, for one thing, in first-movement form the exposition should modulate to a second key area (usually the dominant) and present some of its thematic material there (normally a 'second subject') was duly expounded in current treatises, such as those of Koch and Portmann.[2] A knowledge of overtures by other composers should have told the youngster that an overture traditionally adopts first-movement form (what we call sonata form), and that the exposition does indeed move to a second key in mid-course. The Overture in D, D.12, again has its exposition entirely in D, yet in the recapitulation moves to the dominant for the 'second group' – which by well-documented tradition would be in the tonic key in the recapitulation. Also, Schubert is so obsessed with his first Allegro theme – which clearly evokes that of the first movement of Mozart's 'Prague' Symphony – that he delivers it no fewer than six times in its original form.

There is a move away from the tonic B flat major in the exposition of the overture to *Der Spiegelritter*, but after the second subject has been stated in G minor Schubert veers back to B flat, and only at the end of the exposition does he move to the conventional F, by way of C. The Overture in D, D.26, has its exposition wholly in D, but – like D.12 – modulates to the dominant in the recapitulation. Similar irregularities are found in some of the early string quartets. It is unlikely that these were, like some of Beethoven's mature strategies, 'convention-defying gestures' knowingly made, since when he discovered the norms, in the following overtures, he never reverted to his teenage practices.

In his middle and late works Schubert creates his own sonata-form conventions. One is the three-key exposition, in which the orthodox second key is preceded by a less closely related one, in which a second subject is announced. The ramifications of this practice have been abundantly reviewed by other writers.[3] Schubert did not exactly invent this more diversified scheme, but of no other composer did it become so characteristic. There were three-key tendencies in Haydn's Quartet in D, Op. 17, No. 6, and Beethoven's Piano Concerto No. 5, although Rosen rightly explains these as different in nature from Schubert's;

and Clementi's Piano Sonata, Op. 40, No. 2, is worth comparing too.

Another kind of diversification is the choice of keys other than the traditional dominant for the second subject proper. Here Schubert observes more freedom even than Beethoven. Among the unlikely keys he opts for are the key of the leading-note (major in the case of *Lebensstürme*, minor in the 'Reliquie' Sonata) and the key of the raised fourth, a tritone away from the home tonic (unfinished Symphony in D, D.708A). One reason for Schubert's partiality to the three-key exposition may well be that he takes pleasure (and usually gives it) in the process of modulation to more remotely related keys. This also helps to explain his preference for the short transition (the transition, that is, from the tonic to the second subject key).

Three broad categories of transition may be identified in Classical practice. The first, which becomes standard in the middle of the period, involves a carefully prepared modulation which enables the new key to be approached by way of its dominant. The modulation from tonic to dominant (the usual key for a second subject) in a sense defies musical gravity. A smooth, secure modulation requires reaching the new key through its dominant chord. If the starting key is C and new key is G, the modulation up a fifth to G will then be accomplished through the use of a major chord on D. That chord is somewhat remote from the tonic chord of C. If, however, the modulation were to be down a fifth, to F, the tonic chord of C is already F's dominant, so that the modulation is easily accomplished *with* the force of gravity. To acquire for themselves that gravity-advantage when modulating up to G, composers would often aim for the key a fifth higher than G (or at least go through the motions of doing so) so as to be able then to fall with gravitational ease into G. Making this pretence of going to the dominant of the dominant was a technique practised by Beethoven even in his first period, and was referred to by Tovey as 'enhancing the dominant'.

The second category of transition involves no transition at all in the strict tonal sense. The composer simply moves to the dominant chord of the home key . . . and continues as though it is a new tonic, trusting that formal cadence chords followed by a caesura will aid the illusion. This method was characteristic of the earlier part of the period, and is illustrated by Mozart's *Figaro* Overture. Even Schubert reverted to this type sometimes, especially in works of a generally early-Classical bearing. It is found in the Piano Sonata in E flat.

The third category, much favoured by Schubert, is the shortened transition. A four-bar transition is not uncommon. It is not clear whether the four-bar transition in the first movement of Beethoven's Ninth Symphony followed Beethoven's hearing of a work by Schubert which displayed this feature, or whether Beethoven arrived at his Schubertian solution independently. According to Ernest Newman, there was a school of thought that regarded the four-bar transition in the 'Unfinished' Symphony as 'an evasion of the symphonist's crucial problem of how to move convincingly from one main section of his structure to another'.[4] Others have held that the four-bar transition in the 'Great' C major Symphony is no such thing (because the following E minor theme is not the second subject but another part of the transition), and there can be no such thing as a four-bar transition. Obviously the latter instance is answered by the former. The whole world knows the G major theme in the 'Unfinished', rightly enough, as the second subject, and equally rightly refers to the E flat duetting of the two cellos in the String Quintet as the second subject. In both cases, there has been no more than four bars of transition from the main key.

These short transitions are a perfectly effective device, and in fact Schubert proves in *Lebensstürme* that one does not need a transition at all. In that work, the leading-note of A minor, sounded in the bass before the music has left its home key, is instantaneously converted into a tonic in the next bar, the second subject simultaneously materializing in this new key — which Schubert conveniently calls A flat major. This immediate juxtaposing of one key beside another, without any transition, is easily enough understood when it happens in the context of shorter structures. There are occasions in strophic songs, for example, where a strophe in one key is succeeded by a strophe in another key without mediation. In *Der Musensohn* strophes in G major and B major respectively skip by in direct succession and with enchanting effect. The same may happen in keyboard dances, where well-defined successive segments of the binary form may be wholly obeisant to different tonics. The Deutscher D.365, No. 32, has an eight-bar segment at the beginning of its second section in D flat, while the rest of the dance is in F; the Valse sentimentale D.779, No. 2, is in C major, with its 'middle eight' in E flat; the G major Ländler, D.734, No. 1, has its middle eight in E major. In all these cases there is no buffer between the succeeding keys. It is not necessary to conclude that Schubert's song practice has influenced his dances and symphonic writing, or his dance style has spilled over into songs and symphonies. Short or non-existent transitions are natural to him, and he probably enjoys them for the simple reason that the closer the two keys are brought together the more acutely the contrast between them will be felt. Where the junction between first and second subjects in sonata form is concerned, a remote key–relationship coupled with a minuscule transition is the ultimate ecstasy.

On several occasions Schubert begins a recapitulation in the subdominant key. Of the subdominant recapitulation in the Fifth Symphony, Tovey claims that Schubert chose this path 'in order that the second subject may come automatically into the tonic without needing an altered transition-passage'.[5] Tovey, like some other critics, implies that the subdominant

recapitulation is a labour-saving measure, for that reason. In the movement
he refers to, however, Schubert *does* change the transition, adding sixteen
bars of new invention. If one wishes to impute laziness (to a composer
who produced a thousand works in eighteen years?) one must choose one's
examples carefully. We could light upon the 'Trout' Quintet, for example,
where a subdominant recapitulation may be explained by the nature of
the work as a light-hearted *pièce d'occasion*. If there is no such justification
in, say, the Piano Sonata in C (D.279), we might allow the possibility that
the flow of invention simply took Schubert, without forethought on his
part, to the subdominant at the point where, for other reasons, recapitulation was due, and he saw no reason not to abandon the principle that
the restating of the first theme should coincide with the regaining of the
tonic.

Harmonic skill, in Classical times, entailed such matters as chord vocabulary, vertical distribution, timing (harmonic rhythm) and progression.
Schubert's harmonic vocabulary is wide, enriched by colourful chords some
of which were to become a stock–in–trade of Romanticism. Fig. 133 shows
four chords (all given here in C major) which have a special place in his
palette.

Fig. 133

The first is the Neapolitan sixth, the major triad on the flattened second
of the scale. Schubert inherits Mozart's partiality for this chord, and finds
expressive potential in two particular uses of it. First, he likes to use it as
a doorway into the Neapolitan key itself: the piano's opening nine-bar
strain in A minor in the 'Arpeggione' Sonata moves, in its sixth bar, to a
Neapolitan sixth (a B flat triad), swings for a moment or two between that
and the dominant seventh of B flat to imply partial entry into that key,
and pulls back to A minor for a cadence at the ninth bar. Such close, richly
expressive encounters between keys a semitone apart are found in many
scores, among them the slow movement of the 'Great' C major Symphony, where the dramatic main climax is followed by a pregnant silence,
from which soft plucked strings emerge to lead off into the Neapolitan
key. It is an unforgettable combination of events. Second, Schubert enlarges the scope of the Neapolitan-sixth concept by sometimes using the
minor version of the chord. The peculiarly oppressive atmosphere at
the close of the first movement of the D minor String Quartet stems from
this characteristically Schubertian allusion to the chord of (here) E flat
minor.

The second chord in Fig. 133 is the diminished seventh, consisting of
two interlocking tritones. Prized by later Romantics for its ambiguity and

therefore its value in pivoting between distantly related keys, it must have retained some of its virgin evocativeness for Schubert, who anticipated some favourite later uses of the chord. Any of the notes of the diminished seventh may be lowered by a semitone to create a dominant seventh, four alternative keys being opened up thereby. When, in the first movement of his A minor String Quartet, Schubert reaches the climax of his development, a powerful diminished seventh in the context of D minor, he repeats the chord in hushed, spotlit isolation and in due course changes just one note (viola, B natural to B flat) to lead off into E flat major (Fig. 134). Thus a breathtaking new vista is opened up.

Fig. 134

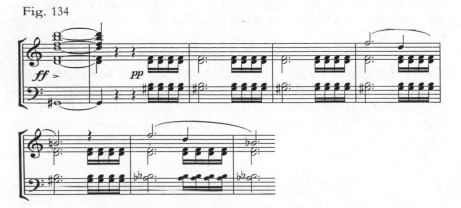

Another way of using this chord to move to a key a semitone above is by moving the upper three notes up by a semitone to create a new dominant seventh. This is done by Schubert in the manner illustrated in the development section of his overture to *Alfonso und Estrella* (Fig. 135). The dominant seventh of D is first clouded by the replacement of the A in the bass with a B flat, to produce a diminished seventh. The upper three notes then slide up in parallel semitones, and a dominant seventh of E flat results.

Fig. 135

Schubert repeats the process several times, and although the tonic of each new key is never reached, that key is clearly signposted by its dominant seventh. This is an exciting way of screwing up tension, particularly in a development, and it was one specific procedure which the Bohemian composers inherited from Schubert. It will be found in the *Bartered Bride* Overture of Smetana, and in many works by Dvořák including the Eighth

Symphony. A particularly poetic and almost non-functional use of the diminished seventh has already been noted in *Die Stadt*.[6]

The third chord in Fig. 133 is a German sixth, used increasingly during the Classical period but especially by Schubert. In its common form it is based on the flattened sixth of the scale. It or its siblings the Italian sixth and French sixth, both built around the A flat and F sharp and hence having the group name 'augmented sixths', may also be transposed down a fifth to stand on the flattened second of the scale – as the final cadence of Schubert's String Quintet demonstrates. More personal to Schubert is a version of the German sixth standing on the fourth of the scale (the fourth chord of Fig. 133). This chord, with a resolution to the tonic chord in first inversion (shown in parentheses in Fig. 133), is extensively used in the 'Great' C major Symphony and is one of the elements that subliminally unify that work.

Paul Badura-Skoda is right to state that this progression was one of Schubert's discoveries, but wrong to assert that there is 'no trace ... [of it] ... in his work before the end of 1826'.[7] He finds the progression in only one other work, the G major Piano Sonata (1826). It may be found also in the second act of *Alfonso und Estrella* (1821), near the end of the chorus and aria, 'Wo ist Sie' (Fig. 136).

Fig. 136

Still earlier, it appears in two songs of 1815, *Des Mädchens Klage* II (D.191), and *Nähe des Geliebten*. The piano's oblique approach to the key of E flat

Fig. 137

Langsam, feierlich mit Anmut

pp   cresc.

Ich

den - ke

f   decresc.

for the first entry of the voice in the latter song was discussed in Chapter 4. The piano begins as though the song is to be in E flat minor (Fig. 137). The progression we are concerned with is the one with which Schubert clinches his modulation to G flat major, the real tonic. This is, of course, a more subtle use, matched by only one of the instances in the 'Great', when in the trio of the scherzo the route back from a Neapolitan excursion is through these two chords. This German sixth on the subdominant also occurs in the A flat Piano Sonata of 1817, but with a different resolution (first movement, bar 34). Although the chord did not become a commonplace in the later nineteenth century, Berlioz used it in the *Shepherds' Chorus* of *The Childhood of Christ*.

Just as the instances of that chord in the 'Great' C major Symphony can be traced back to much earlier Schubert, it is interesting to find that an especially striking progression in the opening Andante section of the symphony (Fig. 138a) has its origin in the Gloria of the F major Mass of 1814 (Fig. 138b), where Schubert finds it convenient to call the D flat minor chord a C sharp minor chord for contextual reasons.

Fig. 138

There are other harmonic effects which become recognizable Schubertian fingerprints. One is the double appoggiatura in a dominant seventh chord, seen in Fig. 17b in Chapter 7. Other conspicuous examples are in the third bar of *Du liebst mich nicht* and at bar 403 in the first act of *Lazarus*. Schubert's stark use of secondary dominants deserves a mention, too. The treatment of G major harmony in the context of B flat major (where it is a dominant of the supertonic) in Fig. 67 in Chapter 14 is strangely prophetic of the close of the Dies Irae in Verdi's *Requiem*.

One further harmonic strategy of Schubert's must be taken into account here. There are in his works a few fascinating experiments in cyclic harmony. Beethoven, in his Ninth Symphony, began the development of his scherzo with a long and remarkable passage in which all the chords are triads but the bass of each triad is a third below its precursor. In his Divertissement on French Themes for piano duet Schubert similarly moves down by thirds in the bass, each note supporting a triad. A complete cycle from A to A results, as the harmonic precis in Fig. 139 shows. The reverse process is tried in the exotic *Divertissement à l'hongroise*: early in the finale, the successive bass notes D, F, A flat, C, E flat and G all support triads. A single move to a triad a third distant is not unusual; two successive moves of this type will sometimes be found; but a chain of such progressions is exceptional. The unfinished Allegretto in C minor (D.900) for piano has a startlingly original chain of third-related chords, in descent.

Fig. 139

The cycle of whole tones in the Piano Sonata in C major (D.279) is even more remarkable. Half of the cycle is shown in Fig. 140 (G sharp, F sharp, E and D in the bass). The appoggiatura on each first beat in the right hand adds to the sense of disorientation.

Fig. 140

The metrical aspect of Classical music receives relatively little attention, yet certain metrical assumptions are implicit (for composer and listener). One such assumption is that, just as beats are grouped in bars, so bars are often grouped in larger 'bars' or sets. Bar-groupings of two or four commonly subsist, especially in faster movements. The completely silent 'spare' bars found in the score of Schubert's 'Great', for example, at the ends of the first and last movements, ostensibly redundant, are there to complete bar-groups whose existence has been implied (though not indicated in the score by any visual sign such as a barline) either throughout the movement or during the later part of it. In the finale of the 'Great', four-bar grouping becomes increasingly felt, most noticeably so in the second subject and the lead-in to the recapitulation, where, accordingly, Schubert could have notated the music in the score in bars four times as long. The scherzo of the String Quintet is a similar case. Instead of counting – with the music – one–two–three in each bar, one may at a comfortable pace count the bars themselves, in fours. It is because we do this subconsciously in any case that when Schubert decides to wrong-foot us we rejoice in the effect. It is worth noting that when he brings forward a new four-bar group by two bars (see page 362), he does so with sudden fortissimo emphasis. It is a moment to treasure, and, when one knows the piece, to look forward to.

Schubert's counterpoint has often been denigrated, partly because due weight has not been given to the best examples of it. It is true that his was a naturally lyrical gift that shows itself readily in strongly melodic thought, and in attractive textures that subsume more or less fully realized harmonies. The tune-and-accompaniment ideal, put crudely, was one he found almost infinitely variable and congenial, while stark linear counterpoint – as would be appropriate to a conventional fugue – seemed to inhibit his penchant for Romantically inflected, harmony-driven texture. He did make efforts to work counterpoint into his vocabulary, early on in exercises for Salieri (perhaps dutifully done), by including fugal sections in some conventional places in his mass settings, by writing (little-known) free-standing canons for a variety of purposes, and by pursuing refresher studies with Sechter in his last weeks. The piano-duet works of his final year should be taken as one important measure of his contrapuntal prowess. The Fantasy in F minor and *Lebensstürme* contain superb spans of music in which tough linear writing, some of it fugal, carries its expressive function admirably and is convincingly integrated into musical arguments which involve a great deal of the more characteristically Schubertian textures.

He was but thirty-one when he composed these pieces. It is not an idle exercise, in this context, to stop and think of some examples of good counterpoint by Bach, then to see how many of them were written before 1716. Schubert knew some Bach, and some Handel. Sometimes his knowledge of particular Bach fugues shows through, as in the opening of a Kyrie fugue which is the furthest point reached in a fragmentary *Requiem* in C minor of 1816 (D.453). The finale of the 'Tenth' Symphony displays contrapuntal endeavours – in invertible counterpoint, canon, augmentation, and simultaneous combination of themes – that Bach would have found absorbing and Beethoven (no mean contrapuntist) would have wanted to stay on this earth a couple more years for. Looked at closely, a transitional passage in *Lebensstürme* reveals the secret that it is in quadruple counterpoint (bars 59–66). This could be presented in four different ways, with a different one of the strands as bass each time (one of the strands comprises two lines in parallel thirds): but Schubert makes use of only two of those possibilities. It is a passage of immense drive, ideal for its purpose.

It becomes clear on close enquiry that Schubert relished such intellectual challenges. The palindrome in *Die Zauberharfe* (see page 198) is a *ne plus ultra* of its type in the whole of eighteenth- and nineteenth-century music. In the 'Wanderer' Fantasy there is even an experiment with mirror forms. Fig. 141a shows a few bars of the first movement. If a mirror is held behind the printed copy, Fig. 141b is the result. A little later in the piece Schubert writes Fig. 141c. This last extract should be compared in minute detail with the mirror image. The effect of the mirror is both to invert the counterpoint, transferring bottom to top and so on, and to invert the melodic lines, so that they move in the opposite direction. Schubert is at pains to retain the exact quality of intervals (tone for tone, semitone for semitone) as far as the musicality of the result will allow.

Fig. 141

When, in 1814, the Emperor Franz I returned to Vienna from the Napoleonic Wars, Schubert's father placed a placard in view of passers-by, bearing a poem of welcome and the following Latin chronogram:

FRANCIsCo MAGNO, VICTORI REDEVNTI

A translation might be: Franz the Great, returning in victory! The larger capitals are Roman numerals whose sum is 1814. It is not unthinkable that a paternal taste for erudite mental games could be passed on to a child, through heredity or environment or both.[8] The father's literary–mathematical cogitations were entirely relevant to their purpose. The son's cerebrations would fit an artistic purpose, aiding and diversifying his musical expression. The three-part canonic Sanctus described in Chapter 9 will have required careful working out. No less intricate preparatory work was needed for a Canon in C in four parts over a free bass, in which all four upper parts are in strict canon, each entering a fifth lower than the previous one and at one bar's distance.[9] The meticulous preparation of the contra-puntal third movement of the 'Tenth' Symphony is laid out for all to see in the facsimile edition.[10] In the light of all these indications of mental and spiritual toil, of intellectual adroitness, and of commitment to extending the frontiers of musical expression, is it any longer possible to view Schubert as a passive vessel on whom ready-formed sounds were bountifully showered, requiring only that he should raise an arm to transmit them to the back of the nearest menu?

Schubert after 1828

Schubert was no self-publicist. Composing the next piece was more important than having the last one performed. The English musician and writer,
Edward Holmes, who visited Vienna in 1827 as part of a musical fact-
finding tour, made no mention of Schubert in his subsequent book. Sains-
bury's *Dictionary of Music*, published in London in the same year, 1827,
does refer to Franz Schubert – but only a Dresden violinist of that name.
When Kiesewetter published his *History of European–Occidental Music* in
1834, even he – a member of Schubert's circle – referred to the period
1800–32 as 'The Era of Beethoven and Rossini', and did not mention
Schubert at all. When Schubert's first biographer, Heinrich Kreissle von
Hellborn, wrote with greater knowledge and appreciation of the songs
than of Schubert's other works, it was not surprising. For one thing, the
Romantic age (Kreissle published in 1865) set greater store by 'interdisci-
plinarity' than the Classical; for another, the songs and dances had always
had wider currency than the rest of Schubert's music. When the verses
prompted by Schubert's death from his poet friends mentioned music, it
was usually the songs that were cited.

Reparation came slowly. There were two performances in Vienna of
the Sixth Symphony shortly after Schubert's death, in 1828 and 1829, then
nothing until the finale of the 'Great' was heard there in 1836.[1] Schumann's
initiative in securing a hearing for the 'Great' in Leipzig in 1839 is by
now legendary. Mendelssohn, who conducted the (incomplete) Leipzig
performance, also tried to arrange a performance in London in 1844. Yet
Schubert's music seems to have affected Mendelssohn's own less than it
affected Schumann's. Berlioz held the 'Great' in high esteem.[2] Bruckner
had a high regard for that work, and his general debt to Schubert is
recognized.[3] Liszt showed his affection by transcribing several songs for
the piano, orchestrating the 'Wanderer' Fantasy, and planning to transcribe
the 'Great' C major for piano. Dvořák was devoted to the Schubert symphonies, including the earlier ones.[4] Brahms, who played a critical part in
Schubert's posthumous fortunes, advised Richard Strauss to learn from
Schubert's dances,[5] and Strauss in his turn often spoke warmly of Schubert.
He conducted the 'Unfinished' and the 'Great', and orchestrated the song

Ganymed. Among twentieth-century composers, Britten's advocacy of Schubert is well known: in later life he distanced himself from Beethoven and came more and more to Mozart and Schubert, whose songs, cycles and piano duets he performed with great distinction. Those who have adopted musical ideas from Schubert in their own compositions include Berio and Crumb, whose *Black Angels* for electric string quartet makes overt reference to the slow movement of the D minor String Quartet.

The process of publishing the Schubert oeuvre and giving it exposure in public concerts occupied the whole nineteenth century and more. On Schubert's death his manuscripts were scattered in various places, many of them in the keeping of his friends. Ferdinand himself kept a substantial hoard, and was not averse to making use of ideas from them in his own works. But he did try to interest publishers in buying them. Diabelli acquired many works, but was slow to issue them. The Vienna libraries gradually amassed autographs and early editions, from such surviving friends and collectors as Dumba, Witteczek, Spaun and Stadler. Among important landmarks were the first hearings of the 'Unfinished' Symphony in Vienna in 1865, in Leipzig in 1866, and in London in 1867. Still the earlier symphonies were little known until August Manns gave them at the Crystal Palace in the 1860s and 1870s, and it was at this same venue that the same conductor directed the first cycle of all the symphonies in 1881. These events owed something to the efforts of George Grove, who spent time in Vienna unearthing what he could, of the symphonic repertoire in particular. With him was Arthur Sullivan, who absorbed much from Schubert into his own more populist style. The influence may be felt in many a turn of melody or harmony. A specific example is the 'excursion' just before the Act I finale in *The Pirates of Penzance*, where Sullivan lights up the Neapolitan key to crown his final tutti, in a manner clearly indebted to many an exciting Schubert eleventh-hour excursion.

Other works had reached England ahead of the symphonies. Several of the songs were given in London in the 1830s, including *Erlkönig, Der Wanderer, Die junge Nonne* and *Der Hirt auf dem Felsen*. The 1850s saw performances in England of the D minor String Quartet and both piano trios, and Charles Hallé played all the published piano works in one season in London, in 1868. A more methodical publication effort was required, however, before the greatest works of any type could penetrate the markets of music-loving nations in an enduring way. This effort duly came later in the nineteenth century, for in its last two decades Breitkopf & Härtel worked on the first critical edition of Schubert's works, the task taking them from 1884 to 1897. The Lieder were edited by Eusebius Mandyczewski and the symphonies by Brahms, who was also general editor. Brahms was an ardent admirer of Schubert's music, deriving from it certain elements of his own approach to harmony and tonality, but sometimes being indebted

more specifically, as in the Piano Quintet and the waltzes. The influence
on Brahms has come in for scholarly scrutiny, but the subject is by no
means exhausted.[6]

One of the best-kept secrets of the Schubert repertory is a German
Dance in C sharp minor composed in 1819 (Fig. 142). Brahms's enthusiasm
for Schubert's dances is not surprising in the light of this little Deutscher
(D.643), which could almost have been written by Brahms himself. The
accompaniment pattern of the left hand anticipates that of Brahms's D
minor Waltz, although the emphasis of the second beat at the expense of
the third is in any case a Brahmsian characteristic. The interesting mix of
different kinds of dissonant note in the right hand is perhaps Chopinesque,
where it is not Brahmsian. No passage sounds more like Brahms than the
fifth and sixth bars, where an enriching secondary voice is added in the
left hand, with an illusion of canon. Brahmsian as is the textural inversion
in the second section, with the 'accompaniment' now above the running
melodic part, Schubert now peers into the future even beyond Brahms.

Fig. 142

This section begins with a four-bar span, which makes for D major (or minor) but reaches an implied F major. It ends with a four-bar lead into a final cadence in the home key, now turned major. The point at which the first of these four-bar spans is welded to the second is one of the most happy-go-lucky bits of engineering one will find in nineteenth-century music. With a sudden piano, Schubert seems to turn a forbidden corner into a secret garden, linking the remotely related harmonies of bars 12 and 13 with a gratuitous *double entendre* when the first notes in C sharp major (A sharp above B sharp) may also be heard as a B flat and C within the superseded F major. If Brahms, who commended the dances to Strauss, knew this singular Deutscher he must have been captivated by it, for it enters an enchanted world of its own and accomplishes its probing design within a mere sixteen bars. Its history is revealing. The autograph bears an inscription to Josef Hüttenbrenner, and on the same paper appears a dance by Hüttenbrenner himself ('Tanz der Furien' – Dance of the Furies). Schubert's dance is presumably a riposte to Hüttenbrenner's piece, which is also in C sharp minor and in triple time and in almost the same form. Schubert's chromatic run (bars 11–12) is an inversion of Hüttenbrenner's. But Hüttenbrenner stays doggedly in C sharp minor throughout, while Schubert slips to E by the fourth bar and to F as substitute for D later. Hüttenbrenner's amateurish notation beside Schubert's professional, flowing script drives home the point: stimulated by a third-rate trifle, a first-rate composer creates a riveting miniature which makes a bridge to generations of composers to come.

With the advent of radio and the gramophone, wider and more intensive dissemination of Schubert's music became possible, yet until the middle of the twentieth century certain key works received the lion's share of representation (the Eighth and Ninth Symphonies, and to some extent the Third and Fifth; the 'Trout' Quintet; the last three string quartets; the late piano sonatas and impromptus; a relatively small proportion of the song output, and a few of the dances; the *Rosamunde* music; the Masses in G and E flat). A hundred years after his death, Schubert had already been made the subject of at least fifty novels.[7] When he became the subject of a musical in the 1920s, this could have been a positive development, if it had been sensitively done. But *Das Dreimäderlhaus* was put together with shamefully scant regard for truth or taste. Based on the novel *Schwammerl* by R. H. Bartsch which fabricated a tale of romanticized love,[8] and making use of a medley of Schubert tunes arranged by one Heinrich Berte, it enjoyed an eighteen-month run, several decades of touring and a number of revivals, crossing the English Channel as *Lilac Time* and the Atlantic as *Blossom Time*.[9] Unfortunately, fiction often being hardier than fact, this concoction had an enduring influence on the popular conception of Schubert as man and composer which has still not been eradicated. Among the cognoscenti, be they professional musicologists or lay Schubert enthusiasts, a gradual change of perception has been brought about in the second half of the twentieth century, largely as a result of the raising of Schubert's profile by a proliferation of Schubert scholarship, the issuing of new and revised basic research tools, and the establishment of Schubert societies in many countries. Yet there is no reason to suppose that, among those who cherish the world of fantasy-made–legend, the straightforward, *gemütlich* image of *Schwammerl* will not linger on into the twenty-first century. According to Ernst Krause, Richard Strauss used to say: 'As long as something like *Lilac Time* is possible no one can say that composers have any real protection.'[10] The damage has lasted more than twice as long as Strauss knew.

According to an ultra-puristic view, an arrangement of a composer's music for another medium may be as much of a distortion as a biographically revisionist musical. Schubert has come in for his share of transcriptions and arrangements. Most, like Liszt's transcriptions of the Lieder or Berlioz's orchestration of *Erlkönig*, tell us more about the arranger than about the original composer, but they can be diverting so long as they are in no way a replacement for the original. In fact, arrangements were rife in Schubert's day, and he was subject to them as Beethoven was. Some works would be issued in 'Walzer' versions, although they were not so conceived. There were many such versions for flute and guitar, among other combinations. The blessing of the composer was not sought for this treatment, any more than it was when a theme of his was appropriated for a set of variations. Czerny's Variations on a favourite Viennese Waltz, issued in 1821, were not the first to exploit the famous *Trauerwalzer* in this way – the 'Mourning Waltz' which a century later was to become an ingredient of *Lilac Time*. The *Rosamunde* music has always been fair game for arrangers, and if the 'Arpeggione' Sonata were to turn up in the repertory of the piccolo or euphonium little surprise would be expressed. In the latter case, the fact that the instrument is defunct but the music still has life justifies more serious attempts to provide it with a modern setting that suits it.

Since the Kreissle biography there had been a trickle of biographies during the nineteenth century, none of them able to or aiming to give more than a cursory account of the music. (The tradition of readable, sometimes pictorial biography concerned with life, legend and myth has continued through the twentieth century.) The foundation stone of enlightened modern research was undoubtedly laid by Deutsch with his *Documentary Biography* which appeared in Germany in 1914. The centenary of Schubert's death in 1928 stimulated a flurry of research which found its way into the special issues of musical periodicals. When Deutsch issued his Thematic Catalogue in 1951 an invaluable new aid was on the library shelf. Deutsch's other magnum opus, the *Memoirs*, first appeared in 1957 in the German edition (*Erinnerungen*). The Dover reprint of the complete edition in the 1960s served a useful temporary purpose, but not as temporary as might have been supposed, since the New Schubert Edition begun in 1968 has made slow progress and will take several times as long as the old edition to reach completion.

While much of the musicological research and musical analysis conducted in the last quarter of the twentieth century appears tangential to many lay Schubertians as well as to some professional ones, a good part of it is helping to round out our perception of an elusive composer – elusive because many aspects of his existence on earth were not well documented, and because the Schubert that matters most (the music) is so extensive and hard to track down that a proper perspective, impossible in his lifetime, is still only achieved with difficulty. Perhaps the most encouraging development associated with the bicentenary of Schubert's birth is the market growth in cyclic recordings. Apart from live performance, which remains the core desideratum in hopes for the future of the oeuvre, other media have had little to contribute. The potential of radio to do more than transmit recordings and performances remains, to be exploited when circumstances permit. Film and television have proved too preoccupied with commercial considerations and audience ratings to attempt the balance or depth which the subject demands. CD-Rom offers hope of fertile development if pure economics do not dictate the shape of things to come there too.

The new Schubert, whose music will be as relevant to the twenty-first century as it was to the nineteenth, both for its human values and as an inspirational source for future composers, is a creator of enduring works that take strength from their Classicism and colour from their Romanticism; the master of a 'lyric-epic sonata form' that has a valid existence alongside Beethoven's 'dramatic-dialect form';[11] an artist who – the first to live by compositions alone – received a considerable income from them in his final years;[12] a self-critic able to pinpoint weaknesses in a work and to revise it (although not always having the time to do so); and a highly skilled craftsman capable of producing several short songs of supreme finesse in one day but also of taking several years to fine-hone a major work, who could work laboriously at the contrapuntal complexities demanded by a piece, who opted to set himself technical challenges of a kind very few composers of the tonal period contemplated, and who ventured one technical tour de force which is unique of its type in the whole repertory of nineteenth-century music.

True as it is that 'Schubert is remarkable in the way in which he manages to elude his biographers'[13] – the uncertainty as to whether he was heterosexual or bisexual being but one small and newly uncovered aspect of our doubt – he has also eluded his musical commentators, a fact no less remark-

able in that most of his major works have been known for several generations: for one thing, his passing preoccupations with mirror forms, the
palindrome and the simultaneous combining of themes apparently went
unheeded until the last quarter of the twentieth century. Moreover, for
one who was at the leading edge of the expansion of harmonic vocabulary
and usage and of tonal relations as Classicism merged into Romanticism,
this aspect of his work has been somewhat underplayed. Could it be that,
while the world has tended to cling to the image of the man presented
by *Das Dreimäderlhaus*, so we have stuck too readily to an outmoded image
of the music, being reluctant to entertain the possibility of its being imbued
with a forward-looking, visionary energy?

Schubert's last musical legacy, sketched during the final weeks, was a
further symphony. This project was an appropriate sequel to a period of
intensive instrumental composition (the two piano trios, the Fantasy in F
minor for four hands, '*Lebensstürme*', the last three piano sonatas and the
String Quartet), just as the 'Great' C major Symphony was a sequel to the
two string quartets of 1824, the Octet and the Grand Duo. This last
symphony was to be quite unlike the 'Great' – less rooted in the conventions of Classical structure, more pioneering in content as well as design.
Death took the composer before he could finish it, but the sketch indicates
clearly enough that a three-movement scheme was ultimately envisaged.
No venture points forward beyond 19 November 1828 more suggestively
or tantalizingly than this forsaken symphony, the one work in progress
when death intervened.

The forlorn, post-*Winterreise*, Mahlerian lament of the slow movement
and the combination of scherzo lightness with unprecedented contrapuntal
experimentation in the finale set the 'Great' into perspective as not just a
climax to Schubert's symphonic career to date but a staging post on the
way to symphonic ventures ahead, the nature of which can only be guessed.
And what would have been the implications of these late innovations, and
the innovatory spirit behind them, for Schubert's string quartets of the
future, his sonatas, his songs? When Beethoven had lived as many years
as the Schubert of this 'Tenth' Symphony, he was about to set to work
on his Second Symphony. A quarter of a century and eight symphonies
later, he remained true to the four–movement tradition of the symphony,
despite one exception for special quasi-programmatic reasons in the Sixth.

If Schubert, who had already now abandoned that tradition, had been
given Beethoven's extra quarter of a century, what new symphonic ground
might he have covered, his composing career having been prolonged by
more than a hundred per cent? Would Beethoven, deserting the four-
movement scheme in his late quartets, have done so in later symphonies
had he lived to produce them? And would Schubert have gone on to
explore radical new designs – as well as new textures and challenging

contrapuntal strategies – in all kinds of instrumental work? Such 'what if' questions may lead us nowhere, yet they beg to be asked and they can inform our listening. They tantalize us more in Schubert's than in Beethoven's case, because the scope for artistic development if a working career is more than doubled – and if the productivity of one thousand works per eighteen years is maintained – is beyond imagination, especially when the composer's actual parting notes were poised so provocatively in a forward stance. Schubert can hardly be thought to have sold us short on his life's work. Rather, the sheer intensity with which his creative light burned in his last months, coupled with the ever-widening scope of his vision, encourages awestruck posterity's eager anticipation of what might have followed. There would be slighter cause for it were it not that the actual achievement – after less than thirty-two years of phenomenal clock-cheating creativity on earth – already leaves us with more than enough to celebrate.

Notes

Chapter 1: 1797–1813

1 Otto Erich Deutsch, *Schubert: A Documentary Biography* ('Doc'), trans. Eric Blom (London, 1946), p. xxvi; and Ernst Hilmar, *Franz Schubert in His Time*, trans. Reinhard G. Pauly (Portland, 1988), p. 16.

2 Edward Holmes, *A Ramble among the Musicians of Germany* (London, 1828; re-published New York, 1969), p. 115. Holmes's 56-page account of music in Vienna in Schubert's penultimate year makes no mention of the composer.

3 David Gramit, 'Schuberts "Bildender Umgang"', in *Schubert durch die Brille*, Mitteilungen 8 (January 1992), pp. 5, 19.

4 Otto Erich Deutsch, *Schubert: Memoirs by his Friends* ('Mem'), trans. Rosamund Ley and John Nowell (London, 1958), pp. 212–13.

5 Document in private hands in Switzerland. See Reinhard Van Hoorickx, 'Schubert: Further Discoveries since 1978', in *The Music Review*, Vol. 80 (1989), pp. 117–18.

6 Otto Erich Deutsch, 'Doc', p. 912.

7 ——, 'Mem', p. 62.

8 ——, 'Mem', p. 34.

9 ——, 'Doc', pp. 6–10.

10 ——, 'Mem', p. 126.

11 ——, 'Doc', p. 866.

12 Ibid., p. 866.

13 ——, 'Mem', p. 127.

14 ——, 'Doc', p. 15.

15 Ibid., p. 18.

16 Ibid., p. 28.

17 Ibid., p. 26.

18 ——, 'Mem', p. 129.

19 ——, 'Doc', p. 37.

20 ——, 'Mem', p. 13.

21 Ibid., pp. 81–2.

Chapter 2: First Steps in Composition

1 Otto Erich Deutsch, *Schubert: A Documentary Biography*, trans. Eric Blom (London, 1946), p. 866.

2 The fugues and fugal exercises are reprinted, and the canons 'realized', in NSA VIII/2, *Schuberts Studien* (Kassel, 1986).

Chapter 3: 1813–1815

1 Otto Erich Deutsch, *Schubert: A Documentary Biography*, trans. Eric Blom (London, 1946), p. 435.

2 Ibid., p. 597.

3 Elizabeth Norman McKay, *Franz Schubert: A Biography* (Oxford, 1996), p. 40.
4 Heinrich Kreissle von Hellborn, *The Life of Franz Schubert*, trans. A. D. Coleridge, 2 vols (London, 1869), I, p. 36.
5 Otto Erich Deutsch, *Schubert: Memoirs by his Friends* ('Mem'), trans. Rosamund Ley and John Nowell (London, 1958), pp. 60−1.
6 Ibid., page 182.
7 Rita Steblin, 'The Peacock's Tale: Schubert's Sexuality Reconsidered', in *19th-Century Music*, XVII/1 (Summer 1993), pp. 7−8, and Maynard Solomon, 'Schubert: Some Consequences of Nostalgia', in same, pp. 35−6.
8 Otto Erich Deutsch, 'Mem', p. 70.
9 See page 401.
10 Elizabeth Norman McKay, op. cit., p. 46.
11 See David Gramit, 'Schuberts "Bildender Umgang" ', in *Schubert durch die Brille*, Mitteilungen 8 (January 1992), p. 5.
12 These figures are an under-estimate, as they take no account of second or further versions of certain works (one song appeared in six different versions), and they make no allowance for works that were written but subsequently lost and never retrieved. (The second and third acts of *Claudine von Villa Bella*, understood to have been completed in August of this year, were inadvertently destroyed in the 1840s and have not been included in the present calculations. If they matched the first act in length, they would have run to some 2600 bars.) Notional figures were adduced for works whose composition straddled the year-end, such as the Second Symphony (10 December 1814−24 March 1815) and the Mass in B flat (11 November 1815−?). It was assumed that the Mass in B flat took as long to compose as the Second Symphony, per bar. In both cases, the average of bars per day for the Second Symphony was used to determine how much of the work was attributable to 1815.
13 The pieces listed comprise a roughly proportionate spread of genres − orchestral, choral/orchestral, keyboard, partsong, Lieder − since labour per bar varies according to the medium.
14 See Brian Newbould, 'Schubert: Symphony in E "1825" ', in *The Musical Times*, cxxxiv/1803 (May 1993), p. 280.

Chapter 4: The Composer of Lieder

1 See Leslie Orrey, 'Solo Song', in *New Oxford History of Music*, VIII (Oxford, 1982), pp. 540−2.
2 The two passages are juxtaposed in David Hoult, *Johann Friedrich Reichardt* (M.Phil. thesis, University of Lancaster, 1991), p. 44.
3 Otto Erich Deutsch, *Schubert: A Documentary Biography*, trans. Eric Blom (London, 1946), p. 677.
4 Ibid., p. 690.
5 See Ewan West, *Schubert's Lieder in Context: Aspects of Song Composition in Vienna, 1778−1828* (Ph.D. dissertation, University of Oxford, 1989).
6 Paul Nettl, 'Schubert's Czech Predecessors', in *Music & Letters*, Vol. XXIII (January 1942), pp. 61−8.
7 By Elly Ameling and Graham Johnson in the Hyperion Schubert Edition, No. 7 (CDJ33007).
8 Richard Capell, *Schubert's Songs* (London, 1928), p. 98.
9 John Reed, *The Schubert Song Companion* (Manchester, 1985), p. 123.
10 Walter Frisch (ed.), 'Schubert's *Nähe des Geliebten* (D.162): Transformation of the *Volkston*', *Schubert: Critical and Analytical Studies* (Nebraska, 1986), pp. 176−182.
11 The Hyperion Schubert Edition, No. 1, p. 8.
12 David P. Schroeder, 'Schubert the Singer', in *The Music Review*, Vol. 49 (1988), pp. 254−66.

13 Otto Erich Deutsch, *Schubert: Memoirs by his Friends*, trans. Rosamund Ley and John Nowell (London, 1958), p. 337.

Chapter 5: 1815–1818

1 Otto Erich Deutsch, *Schubert: A Documentary Biography* ('Doc'), trans. Eric Blom (London, 1946), p. 60.
2 Ibid., p. 64.
3 ——, *Schubert: Memoirs by his Friends* ('Mem'), trans. Rosamund Ley and John Nowell (London, 1958), p. 145.
4 ——, 'Doc', p. 58.
5 ——, 'Mem', p. 147.
6 ——, 'Doc', p. 68.
7 Elizabeth Norman McKay, *Franz Schubert: A Biography* (Oxford, 1996), p. 60.
8 Otto Erich Deutsch, 'Mem', p. 208.
9 Ibid., p. 130.
10 David Gramit, *Intellectual and Aesthetic Tenets of Franz Schubert's Circle* (Ph.D. dissertation, Duke University, 1987), p. 50.
11 Otto Erich Deutsch, 'Doc', pp. 488–9, 494.
12 ——, 'Mem', p. 13.
13 Ibid., p. 132.
14 ——, 'Doc', p. 119.
15 ——, 'Mem', pp. 178–9.
16 Other movements may belong to this work. See pages 103–4.
17 The Hyperion Schubert Edition, No. 21, p. 36.
18 See Brian Newbould, *Schubert and the Symphony: A New Perspective* (London, 1992), especially pp. 250–1.
19 See Zuzana Vitalova, 'Schubert in Zseliz', in *Schubert durch die Brille*, Mitteilungen 8 (January 1992), pp. 93–102.
20 Otto Erich Deutsch, 'Doc', p. 93.
21 Ibid., p. 100.
22 ——, 'Mem', p. 100.
23 ——, 'Doc', pp. 103–4.
24 ——, *Schubert: Die Dokumente seines Lebens*, revised and enlarged edition (Kassel, 1964), p. 71.
25 ——, 'Doc', p. 110.
26 Ibid., p. 99.
27 Ibid., p. 109.

Chapter 6: The Early Symphonies

1 Brian Newbould, *Schubert and the Symphony: A New Perspective* (London, 1992), p. 250.
2 Otto Erich Deutsch, *Schubert: A Documentary Biography*, trans. Eric Blom (London, 1946), p. 866; *Schubert: Memoirs by his Friends*, trans. Rosamund Ley and John Nowell (London, 1958), p. 126.
3 Brian Newbould, op. cit., pp. 66–7.
4 A detailed study appears in Brian Newbould, op. cit., pp. 70–4.
5 This matter is fully explained in Brian Newbould, op. cit., pp. 28–37.
6 Hans Gal, *Franz Schubert and the Essence of Melody*, trans. the author (London, 1974), p. 108.

Chapter 7: The Early Piano Music

1 Otto Erich Deutsch, *Schubert: Memoirs by his Friends*, trans. Rosamund Ley and John Nowell (London, 1958), p. 146.
2 Ibid., p. 176.
3 Ibid., p. 282.
4 Ibid., p. 180.
5 Ibid., p. 37.
6 Ibid., p. 330.
7 Maurice J. E. Brown, 'Schubert', in Grove's *Dictionary of Music and Musicians*, 5th edition (London, 1954), Vols 7, p. 562.
8 ——, *Schubert's Variations* (London, 1954), p. 31.
9 Walther Dürr, Neue Schubert-Ausgabe VII/2 Band 4, Klavierstücke I (Kassel, 1988), pp. xviii–xx.
10 Hummel and Weber were among Schubert's friends. Hummel and Anselm Hüttenbrenner were both, like Schubert, pupils of Salieri.
11 This passage is discussed in greater detail in Brian Newbould, 'Beethoven, Schubert, birds and scales', in *The Beethoven Newsletter*, Vol. 8/III and 9/I (Winter 1993–Spring 1994), pp. 110–11.
12 Howard Ferguson (ed.), Schubert: Complete Pianoforte Sonatas (London, 1978), Vol. 1, p. 151.
13 Maurice J. E. Brown, 'An Introduction to Schubert's Sonatas of 1817', in *The Music Review*, Vol. 12 (1951), see pp. 36–8.
14 Martin Chusid, 'A Suggested Redating for Schubert's Piano Sonata in E flat Op. 122', in Otto Brusatti (ed.), *Schubert-Kongress Wien 1978 Bericht*, pp. 37–44.
15 John Reed, *Schubert* (London, 1987), pp. 158–9.
16 See Brian Newbould, *Schubert and the Symphony: A New Perspective* (London, 1992), p. 121.

Chapter 8: The Early Chamber Music

1 Alfred Einstein, *Schubert* (London, 1951), p. 327.
2 Ibid., p. 42.
3 Heinrich Christoph Koch, Johann Gottlieb Portmann and August F. C. Kollmann.
4 See Heinrich Kreissle von Hellborn, *The Life of Franz Schubert*, trans. A. D. Coleridge, 2 vols (London, 1869), I, p. 35.

Chapter 9: The Early Church Music

1 Otto Erich Deutsch, *Schubert: A Documentary Biography*, trans. Eric Blom (London, 1946), p. 337.
2 Reinhard Van Hoorickx, 'Textänderungen in Schuberts Messen', in Otto Brusatti (ed.), *Schubert-Kongress Wien 1978 Bericht*, pp. 249–55.
3 Blom, Eric (ed.), *Mozart's Letters* (Harmondsworth, 1956), p. 33.
4 Frank Ruppert, *Schubert and the Spiritual Ascent* (unpublished).

Chapter 10: The Song-writer's Craft

1 Donald Francis Tovey, *Beethoven* (London, 1944), p. 125.
2 Otto Erich Deutsch, *Schubert: Memoirs by his Friends*, trans. Rosamund Ley and John Nowell (London, 1958), p. 127.

3 See John Reed, *The Schubert Song Companion* (Manchester, 1985), where songs are thus listed in Appendix II.
4 Otto Erich Deutsch, op. cit., p. 180.
5 The Hyperion Schubert Edition, No. 14, p. 14.
6 John Reed, op. cit., p. 254.

Chapter 11: 1818–1822

1 Otto Erich Deutsch, *Schubert: A Documentary Biography* ('Doc'), trans. Eric Blom (London, 1946), p. 117.
2 Ibid., p. 135.
3 Ibid., p. 124.
4 Ibid., p. 121.
5 ——, *Schubert: Memoirs by his Friends* ('Mem'), trans. Rosamund Ley and John Nowell (London, 1958), p. 855.
6 ——, 'Doc', p. 117.
7 Ernst Hilmar, *Verzeichnis der Schubert-Handschriften in der Musiksammlung der Wiener Stadt- und Landesbibliothek* (Catalogus Musicus VIII) (Kassel, 1978), pp. 21–3; and Elizabeth Norman McKay, *Schubert's Music for the Theatre* (Tutzing, 1991), p. 172.
8 Otto Erich Deutsch, 'Mem', p. 118.
9 John Reed, *Schubert* (London, 1987), p. 72.
10 See pages 198–9 and Fig. 55.
11 The Vienna *Allgemeine Musikalische Zeitung*. See Otto Erich Deutsch, 'Doc', p. 146.
12 The *Theaterzeitung*. See Otto Erich Deutsch, 'Doc', p. 145.
13 Otto Erich Deutsch, 'Mem', p. 63.
14 ——, 'Doc', p. 196.
15 ——, 'Mem', p. 208.
16 Ibid., pp. 23–4.
17 ——, 'Doc', p. 265.
18 Ibid., p. 162.
19 Ibid., p. 195.
20 Ibid., p. 248.
21 Ibid., p. 248.
22 Ibid., p. 226.
23 Otto Biba and Brian Newbould, 'Franz Schubert', in Michael Raeburn and Alan Kendall (eds), *Heritage of Music* (Oxford, 1989), p. 85.
24 Otto Erich Deutsch, 'Mem', p. 108.
25 Ibid., p. 109.
26 Ibid., p. 182.
27 Ibid., pp. 109–10.
28 ——, 'Doc', p. 71.
29 Quoting Kay Redfield Jamison, *Touched with Fire* (New York, 1993), p. 13.
30 Elizabeth Norman McKay, *Franz Schubert: A Biography* ('Schubert') (Oxford, 1996), pp. 138–39.
31 Otto Erich Deutsch, 'Doc', p. 231.
32 Ibid., p. 230.
33 Ibid., p. 212.
34 Maynard Solomon, 'Franz Schubert and the Peacocks of Benvenuto Cellini', in *19th-Century Music*, XII/3 (Spring 1989), pp. 193–206.
35 Rita Steblin, 'The Peacock's Tale: Schubert's Sexuality Reconsidered', in *19th-Century Music*, XVII/1 (Summer 1993), pp. 5–33.
36 Otto Erich Deutsch, 'Mem', pp. 85–6.
37 Rita Steblin, op. cit., p. 10.
38 Otto Erich Deutsch, 'Doc', p. 428.

39 Walpurga Litschauer, *Neue Dokumente zum Schubert-Kreis: Aus Briefen und Tagebuchern seiner Freunde* (Vienna, 1986), Vol. 1, p. 60.
40 Otto Erich Deutsch, 'Doc', p. 489.
41 For complete version, see Otto Erich Deutsch, 'Doc', pp. 226–8.
42 John Reed, op.cit., p. 94.
43 Elizabeth Norman McKay, 'Schubert', pp. 127–29.
44 Otto Erich Deutsch, 'Doc', pp. 246–7.
45 Ibid., pp. 247–9.
46 ——, 'Mem', p. 193.
47 ——, 'Doc', pp. 247–9.
48 John Reed, op. cit., pp. 104–5.
49 Otto Erich Deutsch, 'Doc', p. 740.
50 Brian Newbould, *Schubert and the Symphony: A New Perspective* (London, 1992), pp. 204–5.
51 Otto Erich Deutsch, 'Doc', p. 270.
52 Anthony Storr, *The Dynamics of Creation* (London, 1972), p. 83.
53 Elizabeth Norman McKay, 'Schubert', p. 149.

Chapter 12: Music for the Theatre

1 See Elizabeth Norman McKay, *Schubert's Music for the Theatre* ('Theatre') (Tutzing, 1991), pp. 39–52.
2 John Warrack, *Carl Maria von Weber*, 2nd edition (Cambridge, 1976), p. 255; and E. Pirchan, A. Witeschnik and O. Fritz, *300 Jahre Wiener Opemtheater* (Vienna, 1953), p. 158.
3 Elizabeth Norman McKay, *Franz Schubert: A Biography* (Oxford, 1996), pp. 41–8.
4 An attempted reconstruction of the plot is given in Elizabeth Norman McKay, 'Theatre', pp. 173–5.
5 In Brian Newbould, 'A Schubert Palindrome', in *19th-Century Music*, XV/3 (Spring 1992), pp. 207–14.
6 Ibid.
7 '[*Die Zauberharfe*] contains almost nothing of note. It is a depressing experience to turn the pages of this score . . .' – Maurice J. E. Brown, *Schubert: A Critical Biography* (London, 1958), p. 140.
8 Fritz Racek completed a version by interpolating extracts from several other operas, finished as well as unfinished.
9 Till Gerritt Waidelich, 'Einige Korrecturen zu *Alfonso und Estrella*', in *Schubert durch die Brille*, Mitteilungen 6 (June 1990), p. 31.
10 A too fast tempo is adopted in a recording by Suitner. Another recording by Ortner strangely omits this number.
11 Otto Erich Deutsch, *Schubert: A Documentary Biography*, trans. Eric Blom (London, 1946), p. 309.
12 Ibid., pp. 310–13.
13 Gerald Abraham and Maurice J. E. Brown, Preface dated 1969 to Eulenberg score No. 817.
14 The sketches are published in facsimile by Bärenreiter with commentary by Ernst Hilmar.

Chapter 13: 1822–1825

1 Eric Sams, 'Schubert's Illness Re-examined', in *The Musical Times*, cxxi/1643 (January 1980), pp. 15–22.
2 R. Scott (ed.), *Textbook of the Practice of Medicine* (Oxford, 1978), p. 99.

3 Otto Erich Deutsch, *Schubert: Die Dokumente seines Lebens*, revised and enlarged edition (Kassel, 1964), pp. 192–3.

4 ——, *Schubert: A Documentary Biography* ('Doc'), trans. Eric Blom (London, 1946), p. 279.

5 Eric Sams, op. cit., p. 15; and R. Scott (ed.), op. cit., p. 121.

6 John Reed, *Schubert* (London, 1987), p. 109.

7 Walpurga Litschauer, 'Unbekanntes zur Schubert-Ikonographie: Ein Kurzkrimi', in *Schubert durch die Brille*, Mitteilungen 6 (January 1991), pp. 56–65.

8 Otto Erich Deutsch, 'Doc', p. 278.

9 Ibid., p. 296.

10 Ibid., p. 288.

11 Ibid., p. 286.

12 Ibid., p. 295.

13 Ibid., p. 314.

14 Ibid., p. 300.

15 Elizabeth Norman McKay, *Schubert's Music for the Theatre* (Tutzing, 1991), p. 240.

16 'Fierabras' is historically correct, but both the librettist and the composer used 'Fierrabras'.

17 Otto Erich Deutsch, 'Doc', p. 301.

18 Elizabeth Norman McKay, op. cit., p. 271.

19 Eric Sams, op. cit., p. 15.

20 Otto Erich Deutsch, 'Doc', p. 374.

21 Ibid., p. 331.

22 Ibid., p. 339.

23 Ibid., p. 339.

24 ——, *Schubert: Memoirs by his Friends* ('Mem'), trans. Rosamund Ley and John Nowell (London, 1958), p. 100.

25 ——, 'Doc', p. 370.

26 Deutsch gives an instance in 'Doc', pp. 337–8.

27 Otto Erich Deutsch, 'Mem', p. 233.

28 ——, 'Doc', p. 895.

29 Gabriele Eder and Rita Steblin both claim a symbolic significance in the key of F minor as the vehicle of a work dedicated to a loved one. See Eder, 'Schubert und Caroline Esterhazy', and Steblin, 'Neue Forschungsaspekte zu Caroline Esterhazy', in *Schubert durch die Brille*, Mitteilungen 11 (June 1993), pp. 16, 29–33.

30 Eric Sams, op. cit., p. 17.

31 Doblhoff to Schober, 2 April 1824, in Otto Erich Deutsch, 'Doc', p. 342.

32 Ibid.

33 Otto Erich Deutsch, 'Doc', p. 339.

34 Ibid., p. 343.

35 ——, 'Mem', pp. 101–2.

36 ——, 'Doc', p. 336.

37 Ibid., pp. 336–7.

38 Ibid., p. 339.

39 Weekley and Arganbright, *Schubert's Music for Piano Four-hands* (New York, 1990), p. 48.

40 Otto Erich Deutsch, 'Mem', p. 102.

41 John Reed, op. cit., p. 133.

42 Otto Erich Deutsch, 'Doc', p. 429.

43 Ibid., p. 403.

44 Ibid., p. 403.

45 ——, 'Mem', p. 68.

46 Ibid., p. 221.

47 ——, 'Doc', p. 430.

48 Record booklet, CDC 7 49949-2 (EMI, rec. 1988).

49 Otto Erich Deutsch, 'Doc', p. 435.
50 Ibid., p. 434.
51 Ibid., p. 456.
52 Ibid., p. 458.
53 Ibid., pp. 456–7.
54 Ibid., p. 458.
55 Ibid., p. 465.
56 Ibid., p. 436.
57 Ibid., pp. 486–502.
58 Otto Biba, 'Schubert's Position in Viennese Musical Life', in *19th-Century Music*, III/2 (November 1979), p. 109.
59 Ibid., p. 107.
60 Ibid., p. 107.
61 Otto Erich Deutsch, 'Doc', p. 408.
62 Otto Biba, op. cit., p. 111.
63 Ibid., p. 109.
64 Otto Erich Deutsch, 'Mem', pp. 108–9. See also Chapter 11, page 175.

Chapter 14: Four Hands at One Piano

1 Donald Francis Tovey, *Essays in Musical Analysis* (London, 1935), Vol. I, p. 215.
2 Otto Erich Deutsch, *Schubert: Memoirs by his Friends*, trans. Rosamund Ley and John Nowell (London, 1958), p. 103.
3 Maurice J. E. Brown, 'Schubert and Some Folksongs', in *Music & Letters*, Vol. LIII (April 1972), pp. 173–4.

Chapter 15: 1826–1827

1 John Reed, *Schubert* (London, 1987), p. 154.
2 Where the date of a work is in contention, it seemed appropriate to accept Reed's dating. Texted music other than songs (partsongs, church music) is not included in the calculations, as it is not a part of the above argument, or of Reed's, and Schubert was not in the habit of borrowing material from songs to that category or vice versa.
3 Martin Chusid, 'A Suggested Redating for Schubert's Piano Sonata in E flat Op. 122', in Otto Brusatti (ed.), *Schubert-Kongress Wien 1978 Bericht*, pp. 37–44.
4 John Reed, op. cit., pp. 158–9.
5 Otto Erich Deutsch, *Schubert: A Documentary Biography* ('Doc'), trans. Eric Blom (London, 1946), p. 674.
6 Ibid., p. 559.
7 Otto Biba, 'Schubert's Position in Viennese Musical Life', in *19th-Century Music*, III/2 (November 1979), pp. 107–8.
8 Ibid., p. 108.
9 Otto Erich Deutsch, 'Doc', p. 599.
10 Ibid., pp. 538–9.
11 Elizabeth Norman McKay, *Schubert's Music for the Theatre* (Tutzing, 1991), p. 294.
12 Otto Erich Deutsch, 'Doc', pp. 538–9.
13 Ibid., p. 548.
14 For the Solomon–Steblin debate, see page 178.
15 Otto Erich Deutsch, 'Doc', p. 550.
16 Ibid., p. 571.
17 Ibid., p. 564.
18 Ibid., p. 510.
19 Denis Matthews, *Beethoven* (London, 1985), p. 74.

20 Otto Erich Deutsch, *Schubert: Memoirs by his Friends* ('Mem'), trans. Rosamund Ley and John Nowell (London, 1958), pp. 307–8.
21 Ibid., p. 366.
22 ——, 'Doc', p. 623.
23 ——,'Mem', pp. 283–4.
24 ——, 'Doc', p. 646.
25 Walpurga Litschauer, *Neue Dokumente zum Schubert-Kreis: Aus Briefen und Tagebuchern seiner Freunde* (Vienna, 1986), Vol. 1, p. 61.
26 Otto Erich Deutsch, 'Doc', p. 665.
27 Ibid., pp. 671–3.
28 Ibid., p. 671.
29 Ibid., p. 671.
30 Ibid., p. 679.
31 ——, 'Mem', p. 10.
32 ——, 'Doc', p. 669.
33 Ibid., p. 685.
34 Ibid., p. 681; and Otto Erich Deutsch, *Schubert: Die Dokumente seines Lebens*, revised and enlarged edition (Kassel, 1964), p. 458.
35 ——, 'Mem', p. 138.
36 Ibid., p. 138.
37 Denis Matthews, op. cit., p. 35.
38 The long-supposed date of the B flat Trio was reviewed and confirmed by Eva Badura-Skoda in 'The Chronology of Schubert's Piano Trios', in *Schubert Studies: Problems of Style and Chronology* (Cambridge, 1982), pp. 277–95.

Chapter 16: The Last Year: 1828

1 Otto Erich Deutsch, *Schubert: Die Dokumente seines Lebens* ('Dok'), revised and enlarged edition (Kassel, 1964), pp. 471–2.
2 ——, *Schubert: A Documentary Biography* ('Doc'), trans. Eric Blom (London, 1946), pp. 703–4.
3 ——, *Schubert: Memoirs by his Friends* ('Mem'), trans. Rosamund Ley and John Nowell (London, 1958), p. 138.
4 ——, 'Doc', p. 740.
5 ——, 'Dok', p. 495.
6 ——, 'Doc', p. 817.
7 Ibid., p. 774.
8 Einstein, Hutchings, Westrup, Gal and Reed make no mention of the cuts. Eva Badura-Skoda discusses the cuts without locating them, and without making it absolutely clear that the version usually heard in modern times is the cut version.
9 Otto Erich Deutsch, 'Mem', p. 115. Eva Badura-Skoda believes Sonnleithner is here referring to additional cuts which were sometimes tried ('The Chronology of Schubert's Piano Trios' in *Schubert Studies: Problems of Style and Chronology* (Cambridge, 1982), p. 294).
10 Otto Erich Deutsch, 'Doc', p. 771, and 'Dok', p. 114.
11 These cuts are discussed in more detail on page 372.
12 John Reed, *Schubert* (London, 1987), pp. 188–9.
13 Otto Erich Deutsch, 'Mem', p. 70.
14 Ibid., p. 114.
15 Ibid., p. 255.
16 Ibid., p. 180.
17 Ibid., p. 114.
18 Ibid., p. 180.
19 ——, 'Dok', p. 515.

20 ——, 'Mem', p. 228.
21 ——, 'Doc', p. 772.
22 ——, 'Mem', pp. 195–6.
23 ——, 'Doc', p. 780.
24 Ibid., pp. 781–3.
25 Ibid., p. 787.
26 ——, 'Mem', p. 361.
27 ——, 'Doc', p. 775.
28 Elaine Brody, 'Schubert and Sulzer revisited', in Eva Badura-Skoda and Peter Branscombe (eds), *Schubert Studies: Problems of Style and Chronology* (Cambridge, 1982), pp. 47–60.
29 Otto Erich Deutsch, 'Doc', p. 807.
30 Ibid., p. 811.
31 Frank Ruppert, *Franz Schubert and the Spiritual Ascent* (unpublished).
32 Otto Erich Deutsch, 'Mem', p. 238.
33 Ibid., p. 139.
34 Ibid., p. 106.
35 ——, 'Doc', pp. 819–20.
36 ——, 'Mem', p. 101.
37 ——, 'Doc', p. 820.
38 ——, 'Mem', p. 256.
39 ——, 'Doc', p. 822.
40 ——, 'Mem', p. 28.
41 The distinction was first made not later than 1837, when William Gerhard distinguished between *Typhus gravior* (true typhus) and *Typhus miteor* (typhoid). W. W. Gerhard, 'On the Typhus Fever . . .' *The American Journal of the Medical Sciences*, No. 38 (February 1837), p. 25.
42 Eric Sams, 'Schubert's Illness Re-examined', in *The Musical Times*, cxxi (January 1980), p. 21.
43 D. Kerner, 'Franz Schubert', in *Krankheiten grosser Musiker* (Stuttgart, 1963).
44 Eric Sams, op. cit., pp. 18–21.
45 Ibid., p. 21.
46 Robert Kurth, Lecture given at University of Kansas, March 1989.
47 Peter Gilroy Bevan, Lecture given at University of Hull, April 1995.
48 Anton Neumayr, *Music and Medicine*, Vol. 1 (Bloomington, 1994), pp. 403–11.
49 Anton Neumayr, op. cit., pp. 366 and 407.
50 Hans D. Kiemle, 'Woran starb Schubert eigentlich?', in *Schubert durch die Brille*, Mitteilungen 16/17 (January 1996), pp. 41–51.
51 Otto Erich Deutsch, 'Doc', p. 825.
52 Ibid., p. 829.

Chapter 17: The Late Church Music

1 Alfred Einstein, *Schubert* (London, 1951), p. 206.
2 Maurice J. E. Brown, 'Lazarus, or the Feast of Resurrection', in *Essays on Schubert* (London/New York, 1966), p. 107.
3 Alfred Einstein, op. cit., pp. 205–6.
4 Booklet accompanying recording of Schubert's Sacred Works, Vol. 2 (EMI Classics, 1983).
5 Artur Holde, *Jews in Music* (London, 1960), p. 17.
6 Elaine Brody, 'Schubert and Sulzer Revisited', in Eva Badura-Skoda and Peter Branscombe (eds), *Schubert Studies: Problems of Style and Chronology* (Cambridge, 1982), pp. 47–60.

Chapter 18: The Late Songs

1 Otto Erich Deutsch, *Schubert: A Documentary Biography* ('Doc'), trans. Eric Blom (London, 1946), p. 795.
2 Susan Youens, *Schubert: Die schöne Müllerin* (Cambridge, 1992), p. 5.
3 Otto Erich Deutsch, *Schubert: Memoirs by his Friends*, trans. Rosamund Ley and John Nowell (London, 1958), pp. 137–8.
4 Richard Capell, *Schubert's Songs* (London, 1928), p. 236.
5 The Lea Pocket Score mistranslates here.
6 Gerald Moore, *The Schubert Song Cycles* (London, 1975), p. 172.
7 Richard Capell, op. cit., pp. 244–5.
8 Ibid., p. 245.
9 John Reed, *The Schubert Song Companion* (Manchester, 1985), p. 144.
10 Rufus Hallmark, 'Auf dem Strom', in Eva Badura-Skoda and Peter Branscombe (eds), *Schubert Studies: Problems of Style and Chronology* (Cambridge, 1982), p. 41.
11 Richard Kramer, *Distant Cycles* (Chicago, 1994), pp. 125–47.
12 John Reed, op. cit., p. 365.
13 Ibid., p. 262.
14 Otto Erich Deutsch, 'Doc', p. 408.

Chapter 19: The Late Piano Sonatas

1 Otto Erich Deutsch, *Schubert: Memoirs by his Friends*, trans. Rosamund Ley and John Nowell (London, 1958), p. 355.
2 Gordon Jacob, *Orchestral Technique* (London, 1931), p. 87.
3 Philip Radcliffe, *Schubert Piano Sonatas* (London, 1967), p. 44.
4 Charles Rosen, *The Classical Style* (London, 1971), pp. 456–8.

Chapter 20: Other Late Piano Works

1 Otto Erich Deutsch, *Schubert: Memoirs by his Friends*, trans. Rosamund Ley and John Nowell (London, 1958), pp. 223, 265, 276, 281.
2 See Paul Nettl, 'Schubert's Czech Predecessors', in *Music & Letters*, Vol. XXIII (January 1942), p. 67.
3 Ibid.
4 Jorg Demus and Roland Solder, Schubert: 'Sonate oubliée' (Vienna, 1988).
5 Walther Dürr, Neue Schubert-Ausgabe VII/2, Band 5, Klavierstücke II (Kassel, 1984), Vorwort, pp. xiv–xv.
6 MH 149/c in the Stadt- und Landesbibliothek, Vienna.
7 A 133 in the Musikarchiv, Gesellschaft der Musikfreunde.

Chapter 21: The Late Chamber Music

1 The author is indebted to Anthony Goldstone, who noticed the Grétry–Schubert connection while exploring César Franck's *Deuxième duo sur le quatuor de Lucile de Grétry* for piano duet.
2 J. A. Westrup, *Schubert Chamber Music* (BBC Music Guide, London, 1969), p. 35.
3 Charles Rosen, *The Classical Style* (London, 1971), p. 459.
4 Paul Griffiths, *The String Quartet* (London, 1983), p. 105.
5 Peter Gülke, 'In what respect a Quintet?' in Eva Badura-Skoda and Peter Branscombe (eds), *Schubert Studies: Problems of Style and Chronology* (Cambridge, 1982), pp. 181, 177.

6 Letter of 31 March 1824; Otto Erich Deutsch, *Schubert: A Documentary Biography*, trans. Eric Blom (London, 1946), p. 339. See page 221.
7 Otto Erich Deutsch, 'Doc.', pp. 331–2, 341.
8 John Reed, *Schubert* (London, 1987), p. 180.

Chapter 22: The Late Symphonies

1 Fugue in A minor from Thirty-six Fugues for piano, Op. 36, first published in Vienna, c.1805.
2 Brian Newbould, *Schubert and the Symphony: A New Perspective* (London, 1992), pp. 179–84.
3 Martin Chusid, 'Beethoven and the Unfinished', in Martin Chusid (ed.), *Schubert: Symphony in B minor ('Unfinished')*, Norton Critical Score, revised edition (London, 1971), pp. 98–110.
4 Charles Osborne, *Schubert and his Vienna* (London, 1985), pp. 94–5.
5 A fuller discussion appears in Brian Newbould, op. cit., pp. 202–6.
6 Maurice J. E. Brown, *Schubert: A Critical Biography* (London, 1958), p. 123.
7 The appellation 'Symphony No. 9 in C' has been threatened by a double challenge. The numbering 'No. 7 in C', originating soon after Schubert's death in ignorance of the works left unfinished, still lingers on in some quarters although officially superseded long ago. More recently, the editors of the New Schubert Edition saw fit to exclude all unfinished works except the B minor Symphony from the numbered canon when they revised the Deutsch Catalogue in 1978, thus making the C major Symphony 'No. 8 in C'. The resultant confusion is unnecessary, and the suggested new numbering flies in the face of practicality, which is why it has been firmly resisted by most publishers, record companies and radio stations. It is to be hoped that when the late symphonies eventually appear in the New Schubert Edition the practical solution will prevail. See Brian Newbould, 'Zur Frage der Numerierung der Symphonien. Eine Entgegnung', in *Schubert durch die Brille*, Mitteilungen 13 (June 1994), pp. 103–5.
8 *Franz Schubert: Symphony No. 10 in D major, D.936A*, realization by Brian Newbould (London, 1995).
9 Daniel Jacobson with Andrew Glendening, 'Schuberts D.936A: Eine sinfonische Hommage an Beethoven?', in *Schubert durch die Brille*, Mitteilungen 15 (June 1995), pp. 113–26.
10 Brian Newbould, 'Schuberts D.936A: Eine sinfonische Hommage an sich selbst?', in *Schubert durch die Brille*, Mitteilungen 16/17 (January 1996), pp. 123–9.

Chapter 23: Aspects of Technique

1 Otto Erich Deutsch, *Schubert: Memoirs by his Friends*, trans. Rosamund Ley and John Nowell (London, 1958), p. 126.
2 Heinrich Christoph Koch, *Versuch einer Anleitung zur Composition* (Leipzig, 1782–93); Johann Gottlieb Portmann, *Leichtes Lehrbuch der Harmonie* (Darmstadt, 1789).
3 See Charles Rosen, *Sonata Forms* (New York, 1980), pp. 234f; James Webster, 'Schubert's Sonata Form and Brahms's First Maturity', in *19th-Century Music*, II/1 (July 1978), pp. 18–35; and Alan Rich, *Formal Practices in Schubert's Larger Instrumental Works* (MA dissertation, University of California, 1952).
4 Ernest Newman, 'Schubert: A Point in the "Unfinished"', in *The Sunday Times*, 2 February 1941; Felix Aprahamian (ed.), *Ernest Newman: More Essays from the World of Music* (London, 1958), p. 110.
5 Donald Francis Tovey, *Essays in Musical Analysis*, Vol. 1 (London, 1935), p. 203.
6 John Reed, *The Schubert Song Companion* (Manchester, 1985), p. 262.
7 Paul Badura-Skoda, 'The dating of the "Great" C major Symphony', in Eva

Badura-Skoda and Peter Branscombe (eds), *Schubert Studies: Problems of Style and Chronology* (Cambridge, 1982), p. 192.

8 Otto Erich Deutsch, *Schubert: A Documentary Biography*, trans. Eric Blom (London, 1946), p. 42.

9 D.deest. Included in NSA VIII/2, *Schuberts Studien* (Kassel, 1986), p. 161.

10 Ernst Hilmar (ed.), *Franz Schubert: Drei Symphonie-Fragmente* (Kassel, 1978). The implications of the preparatory sketch are studied in detail in Brian Newbould, 'A Working Sketch by Schubert (D.936A)', in *Current Musicology*, No. 43 (1987), pp. 22–32.

Chapter 24: Schubert after 1828

1 Otto Biba, 'Schubert's Position in Viennese Musical Life', in *19th-Century Music*, III/2 (November 1979), p. 108.

2 See *Journal des débats*, 27 November 1851, p. 2.

3 Franz Grasberger, 'Schubert and Bruckner', in Otto Brusatti (ed.), *Schubert-Kongress Wien 1978 Bericht*, pp. 215–28.

4 Antonin Dvořák and Henry T. Finck, 'Franz Schubert', in *The Century Magazine*, XLVIII (July 1894), pp. 341–48.

5 Ernst Krause, *Richard Strauss* (Leipzig, 1955), p. 154.

6 An important study is James Webster, 'Schubert's Sonata Form and Brahms's First Maturity', in *19th-Century Music*, II/1 (July 1978), pp. 18–35, and III/1 (July 1979), pp. 52–71.

7 Ernst Hilmar, *Schubert in his Time* (Oregon, 1988), p. 9.

8 R. H. Bartsch, *Schwammerl* (Leipzig, n.d.).

9 Kurt Ganzl, *The British Musical Theatre*, Vol. II (London, 1986), p. 189.

10 Ernst Krause, op. cit., p. 50.

11 Carl Dahlhaus, trans. Thilo Reinhard, 'Sonata Form in Schubert', in Walter Frisch (ed.), *Schubert: Critical and Analytical Studies* (Nebraska, 1986), p. 1.

12 Otto Biba, op. cit., pp. 107–12.

13 Ernst Hilmar, op. cit., p. 8.

List of Works

Works are listed chronologically in each category, except in the case of songs. The D. numbers are the standard means of identification, referring to the Deutsch Catalogue (1978 edition). In some instances opus (Op.) numbers are given also, where editions carrying them are still in use. (Op. numbers indicate the chronology of publication, which in Schubert's case has little bearing on date or order of composition.) The Deutsch Catalogue has a 'concordance' section which allows reconciliation of Op. to D. numbers. Dates given are of composition, as far as these are known. With a few exceptions, fragmentary works are not included.

1   ORCHESTRAL WORKS

D.no.   Title/date/other relevant information

Symphonies

2B	Symphony in D, (?)1811, fragment.
82	No. 1 in D, Oct. 1813.
125	No. 2 in B flat, 10 Dec. 1814–24 March 1815.
200	No. 3 in D, 24 May–19 July 1815.
417	No. 4 in C minor ('Tragic'), fin. 27 April 1816.
485	No. 5 in B flat, Sept.–3 Oct. 1816.
589	No. 6 in C, Oct. 1817–Feb. 1818.
615	Symphony in D, May 1818, fragments of 2 mts.
708A	Symphony in D, (?)spring 1821, fragments of 4 mts.
729	No. 7 in E, Aug. 1821, orchestral sketch.
759	No. 8 in B minor ('Unfinished'), Oct.–Nov. 1822.
849	No. 9 in C ('Great'), 1825–6.
936A	'No. 10' in D, summer/autumn 1828, 3 mts in piano score.

Overtures

2A	in D, (?)1811, fragment.
4	in D, for the comedy *Der Teufel als Hydraulicus*, (?)1812.
12	in D, (?)1812.
26	in D, fin. 26 June 1812.
470	in B flat, Sept. 1816.
556	in D, May 1817.
590	In D ('In the Italian style'), Nov. 1817.
591	in C ('In the Italian style'), Nov. 1817.
648	in E minor, Feb. 1819.

Opera overtures

11	*Der Spiegelritter* (B flat).
84	*Des Teufels Lustschloss* (F).
190	*Der vierjährige Posten* (D).

239	*Claudine von Villa Bella* (E).
326	*Die Freunde von Salamanka* (C).
647	*Die Zwillingsbrüder* (D).
644	*Die Zauberharfe* (C) (now known as the *Rosamunde* Overture).
732	*Alfonso und Estrella* (D).
796	*Fierabras* (F).

Solo instrument and orchestra

345	Concerto in D, 1816, vln and orch.
438	Rondo in A, June 1816, vln and str. orch.
580	Polonaise in B flat, Sept. 1817, vln and orch.

II CHAMBER MUSIC

D.no.   Title/date/(scoring)/other relevant information

String Quartets

2C	Quartet movement in D minor or F major, (?)1811, fragment.
3	Quartet movement in C, (?)1812, fragment.
18	Quartet in mixed keys, 1810 or 1811.
94	Quartet in D, 1811 or 1812.
32	Quartet in C, Sept.–Oct. 1812.
36	Quartet in B flat, 19 Nov. 1812–21 Feb. 1813.
46	Quartet in C, 3–7 March 1813.
68	Quartet in B flat, 8 June–18 Aug. 1813.
74	Quartet in D, 22 Aug.–Sept. 1813.
86	Minuet in D, (?)1813.
87	Quartet in E flat, Nov. 1813.
87A	(?)Quartet movement in C, Nov. 1813.
89	Five minuets and six trios, Nov. 1813.
90	Five Deutsche and seven trios, Nov. 1813.
103	Quartet movement in C minor, 23 April 1814.
112	Quartet in B flat, Sept. 1814.
173	Quartet in G minor, 25 March–1 April 1815.
353	Quartet in E, 1816.
703	Quartet movement in C minor ('Quartettsatz'), Dec. 1820, and fragment of Andante.
804	Quartet in A minor, Feb.–March 1824.
810	Quartet in D minor ('Death and the Maiden'), March 1824.
887	Quartet in G, fin. 20–30 June 1826.

Other works for strings

8	Overture in C minor for string quintet, 29 June 1811.
354	Four comic Ländler for two violins, Jan. 1816.
355	Eight Ländler for solo violin, Jan. 1816.
370	Nine Ländler in D for (?)violin, Jan 1816.
374	Eleven Ländler for solo violin, Feb. 1816.
471	String Trio in B flat, Sept. 1816, incomplete.
581	String Trio in B flat, Sept. 1817.
956	String Quintet in C, Sept.–Oct. 1828.

Piano and strings

28	Piano Trio in B flat, 27 July–28 Aug. 1812, one mt.
487	Adagio and Rondo concertante in F, Oct. 1816 (piano quartet).
667	Piano Quintet in A (the 'Trout'), autumn 1819 (pf, vln, vla, vcl, db).
897	Piano Trio movement in E flat ('Notturno'), (?)Oct. 1827.

| 898 | Piano Trio in B flat, (?)Sept.–Oct. 1827. |
| 929 | Piano Trio in E flat, Nov. 1827. |

Piano and one other instrument

384	Sonata in D, March 1816 (vln, pf).
385	Sonata in A minor, March 1816 (vln, pf).
408	Sonata in G minor, April 1816 (vln, pf).
574	Sonata in A, Aug. 1817 (vln, pf).
802	Introduction and Variations on *Trockne Blumen*, Jan. 1824 (fl, pf).
821	Sonata in A minor ('Arpeggione'), Nov. 1824 (arpeggione, pf).
895	Rondo brillant in B minor, Oct. 1826 (vln, pf).
934	Fantasy in C, Dec. 1827 (vln, pf).

Works including wind instruments

2D	Six Minuets, 1811 (2 ob, 2 cl, 2 bn, 2 hn, trbn).
72	Wind Octet in F, fin. 18 Aug. 1813 (2 ob, 2 cl, 2 bn, 2 hn).
79	Wind Nonet in E flat minor ('*Eine kleine Trauermusik*'), Sept. 1813 (2 cl, 2 bn, dbn, 2 hn, 2 trbn).
96	Arrangement of W. Matiegka's Notturno, 26 Feb. 1814 (fl, vla, vlc, guitar).
803	Octet, Feb.–1 March 1824 (cl, hn, bn, 2 vln, vla, vcl, db).

III PIANO MUSIC

Sonatas

347	Allegro moderato in C, (?)1813.
157	Sonata in E, Feb. 1815.
178	Adagio in G, 8 April 1815.
279	Sonata in C, Sept. 1815.
346	Allegretto in C, (?)1815, fragment.
348/349	Andantino and Adagio in C, (?)summer 1817, fragments.
459	Sonata in E, Aug. 1816.
459A	Adagio, Allegro and Allegro patetico, (?)1816.
537	Sonata in A minor, March 1817.
557	Sonata in A flat, May 1817.
566	Sonata in E minor, June 1817.
567	Sonata in D flat, June 1817.
570	Scherzo in D and Allegro in F sharp minor, (?)July 1817, fragments.
571	Allegro moderato in F sharp minor, July 1817, fragment.
604	Andante in A, (?)summer 1817.
575	Sonata in B, Aug. 1817.
593	Scherzi in B flat and D flat, Nov. 1817.
612	Adagio in E, April 1818.
613	Sonata in C, April 1818, two fragments.
625	Sonata in F minor, Sept. 1818, 1 mt complete and two fragments.
505	Adagio in D flat, (?)Sept. 1818.
655	Sonata movement in C sharp minor, April 1819, fragment.
664	Sonata in A, (?)summer 1819.
769A	Sonata movement in E minor, (?)1823.
784	Sonata in A minor, Feb. 1823.
900	Allegretto in C minor, (?)1823, fragment.
840	Sonata in C ('Reliquie'), spring 1825, unfin.
845	Sonata in A minor, spring 1825.
850	Sonata in D, Aug. 1825.
568	Sonata in E flat, (?)summer 1826 (revised version of D.567).

894	Sonata in G, Oct. 1826.
916B	Piano piece in C, (?)summer 1827, fragment.
916C	Piano piece in C minor, (?)summer 1827, fragment.
958	Sonata in C minor, fin. Sept. 1828.
959	Sonata in A, fin. Sept. 1828.
960	Sonata in B flat, fin. Sept. 1828.

Miscellaneous

2E	Fantasy in C minor, (?)1811.
156	Ten Variations in F, Feb. 1815.
576	Thirteen Variations on a theme by Anselm Hüttenbrenner, Aug. 1817.
606	March in E with Trio, (?)1818.
605A	Fantasy in C ('Grazer Fantasy'), (?)1818.
718	Variation on a waltz by Diabelli, March 1821.
605	Fantasy in C, (?)summer 1822, fragment.
760	Fantasy in C (the 'Wanderer'), Nov. 1822.
780	Six *Momens musicals* (sic)
	No. 3 (*'Air russe'*), 1823.
	No. 6 (*'Plaintes d'un Troubadour'*), 1824.
	Nos. 1, 2, 4 and 5, (?)summer 1827.
817	'Hungarian Melody' in B minor, 2 Sept. 1824.
844	'Albumblatt': Waltz in G, 16 April 1825.
899	Four Impromptus, (?)summer 1827 (Op. 90).
915	Allegretto in C minor, 26 April 1827.
935	Four Impromptus, Dec. 1827 (Op. posth. 142).
946	Three Piano Pieces, in E flat minor, E flat and C, May 1828.

Dances (A selective shortlist)

128	12 Viennese Deutsche, (?)1812.
41	20 Minuets with Trios, 1813.
299	12 Ecossaises, autumn 1815.
145	12 Waltzes, 17 Ländler and 9 Ecossaises, 1815–July 1821.
681	8 Ländler, c.1815.
146	20 Waltzes, 1815 (nos. 1, 3–11) and Feb. 1823 (nos. 2, 12–20).
365	36 Original Dances, 1816–July 1821.
378	8 Ländler in B flat, 13 Feb. 1816.
380	3 Minuets each with 2 Trios, 22 Feb. 1816.
420	12 Deutsche, 1816.
421	6 Ecossaises, May 1816.
529	8 Ecossaises, Feb. 1817.
697	6 Ecossaises, May 1820.
734	16 Ländler and 2 Ecossaises ('Wiener Damen-Ländler'), c.1822.
781	12 Ecossaises, Jan. 1823.
779	34 Valses Sentimentales, c.1823.
783	16 Deutsche and 2 Ecossaises, Jan. 1823–July 1824.
790	12 Deutsche, May 1823.
820	6 Deutsche Tanze, Oct. 1824.
977	8 Ecossaises, (?)1825.
969	12 Walzer ('Valses Nobles'), (?)1826.
924	12 Grazer Walzer, (?)Oct. 1827.

Works for four hands

1	Fantasy in G, 8 April–1 May 1810.
9	Fantasy in G minor, Sept. 1811.
48	Fantasy in C minor ('Grande sonate'), April–June 1813.
592	Arrangement of the Overture in D (D.590), Dec. 1817.

597	Arrangement of the Overture in C (D.591), late 1817.
599	Four Polonaises, July 1818.
602	*Trois Marches Héroiques*, (?)summer/autumn 1818.
603	Variations in B flat on an Original Theme, (?)1818 or 1824.
968	Allegro moderato in C and Andante in A minor ('Sonatine'), (?)1818.
608	Rondo in D ('*Notre amitié est invariable*'), Jan. 1818.
617	Sonata in B flat, summer/autumn 1818.
618	Deutsche in G with 2 Trios and 2 Ländler, summer/autumn 1818.
618A	Polonaise in B flat, July 1818.
624	Variations in E minor on a French Song, Sept. 1818.
733	Three *Marches Militaires*, summer/autumn 1818.
668	Overture in G minor, Oct. 1819.
675	Overture in F, (?)Nov. 1819.
773	Arrangement of overture to *Alfonso und Estrella*, 1823.
798	Arrangement of overture to *Fierabras*, late 1823.
812	Sonata in C ('Grand Duo'), June 1824.
813	Variations in A flat on an Original Theme, June/July 1824.
814	Four Ländler, summer 1824.
818	*Divertissement à l'hongroise* in G minor, (?)autumn 1824.
819	Six *Grandes Marches*, summer/autumn 1824.
823	Divertissement on French Themes, in E minor, (?)autumn 1825.
824	Six Polonaises, early 1826.
859	*Grande Marche funèbre* in C minor, Dec. 1825.
885	*Grande Marche Héroique* (for coronation of Nicholas I of Russia), Sept. 1826.
886	Two Characteristic Marches in C, (?)1825–6.
908	Variations in C on a theme from Hérold's 'Marie', Feb. 1827.
928	*Kindermarsch* in G, 12 Oct. 1827.
940	Fantasy in F minor, Jan.–April 1828.
947	Allegro in A minor ('*Lebensstürme*'), May 1828.
951	Rondo in A, June 1828.
952	Fugue in E minor, 3 June 1828 (for piano or organ).

IV STAGE WORKS

11	*Der Spiegelritter*, Dec. 1811–1812, Singspiel (incomplete).
84	*Des Teufels Lustschloss*, Oct. 1813–Oct. 1814.
190	*Der vierjährige Posten*, May 1815, Singspiel.
220	*Fernando*, June/July 1815, Singspiel.
239	*Claudine von Villa Bella*, begun 26 July 1815, Singspiel (Acts II and III lost).
326	*Die Freunde von Salamanka*, Nov./Dec. 1815, Singspiel.
435	*Die Bürgschaft*, begun 2 May 1816 (Act III incomplete).
647	*Die Zwillingsbrüder*, fin. Jan 1819, Singspiel.
137	*Adrast*, (?)autumn 1819, fragment.
644	*Die Zauberharfe*, summer 1820, melodrama.
701	*Sakuntala*, Oct. 1820, incomplete.
723	*Das Zauberglöckchen*, spring 1821, two additional nos.
732	*Alfonso und Estrella*, Sept. 1821–Feb. 1822, grand opera.
787	*Die Verschworenen* (alias *Der häusliche Krieg*), March/April 1823, Singspiel.
791	*Rüdiger*, May 1823, sketches.
796	*Fierabras*, May–Oct. 1823, grand opera.
797	*Rosamunde*, Nov./Dec. 1823, incidental music.
918	*Der Graf von Gleichen*, June/July 1827, sketches.

V   CHURCH MUSIC

24E	Mass in F, (?)summer 1812, fragment.
27	*Salve Regina* in F, 28 June 1812.
31	Kyrie in D minor, 25 Sept. 1812 (soloists, SATB, orch.).
45	Kyrie in B flat, 1 March 1813 (SATB).
49	Kyrie in D minor, fin. 15 April 1813 (soloists, SATB, orch.).
56	Sanctus, 21 April 1813 (canon for 3 voices).
66	Kyrie in F, May 1813 (SATB, orch., organ).
71A	Alleluja in F, (?)July 1813 (canon for 3 voices).
105	Mass in F, May–July 1814 (soloists, SATB, orch., organ).
106	*Salve Regina* in B flat, 28 June–1 July 1814 (tenor, orch.).
739	*Tantum ergo* in C, 1814 (SATB, orch.).
136	Offertory: *Totus in corde*, (?)1815 (tenor or sop., orch.).
167	Mass in G, March 1815 (soloists, SATB, orch., organ).
175	*Stabat mater* in G minor, April 1815 (SATB, orch.).
181	Offertory: *Tres sunt* (A minor), April 1815 (SATB, orch., organ).
184	Gradual: *Benedictus es, Domine*, April 1815 (SATB, orch., organ).
185	Dona nobis pacem, April 1815 (alternative version for D.105).
223	*Salve Regina* in F, 5 July 1815 (sop., orch., organ).
324	Mass in B flat, begun Nov. 1815 (soloists, SATB, orch., organ).
379	*Salve Regina*, 21 Feb. 1816 (SATB, organ).
383	*Stabat mater* in F, begun 28 Feb. 1816 (soloists, SATB, orch.).
386	*Salve Regina* in B flat, early 1816 (SATB).
452	Mass in C, June–July 1816 (soloists, SATB, orch., organ).
453	*Requiem* in C minor, July 1816, fragment.
460	*Tantum ergo* in C, Aug. 1816 (sop., SATB, orch.).
461	*Tantum ergo* in C, Aug. 1816 (soloists, SATB, orch.).
486	*Magnificat*, (?)Sept. 1815, or 1816 (soloists, SATB, orch.).
488	*Auguste jam coelestium*, Oct. 1816 (sop., tenor, orch.).
621	*German Requiem (Trauermesse)*, Aug. 1818 (soloists, SATB, orch.).
676	*Salve Regina* in A, Nov. 1819 (sop., str. orch.).
678	Mass in A flat, Nov. 1819–Sept. 1822 (revised 1826).
689	*Lazarus*, Feb. 1820 (soloists, SATB, orch.).
696	Six Antiphons for Palm Sunday, March 1820 (SATB).
730	*Tantum ergo* in B flat, 16 Aug. 1821 (soloists, SATB, orch.).
750	*Tantum ergo* in D, 20 March 1822 (SATB, orch., organ).
755	Kyrie in A minor, May 1822, fragment.
811	*Salve Regina* in C, April 1824 (TTBB).
872	*Deutsche Messe*, autumn 1827 (SATB, organ. Second version with orch.).
948	*Hymnus an den heiligen Geist*, May 1828 (TTBB soloists, TTBB choir).
950	Mass in E flat, June–July 1828.
953	92nd Psalm, July 1828 (soloists, SATB).
954	*Glaube, Hoffnung und Liebe*, Aug. 1828 (soloists, SATB, piano or wind instruments).
961	Benedictus in A minor, Oct. 1828 (soloists, SATB, orch. Alternative version for D.452).
962	*Tantum ergo* in E flat, Oct. 1828 (soloists, SATB, orch.).
963	Offertory: *Intende voci*, Oct. 1828 (tenor, SATB, orch.).

VI CANTATAS, PARTSONGS AND CHORUSES

Voice-setting exercises done for Salieri in 1812 and 1813 have been omitted.

For mixed or unspecified voices

642	*Vieltausend Sterne prangen*, (?)1812 (quartet SATB, pf).
168	*Begräbnislied*, 9 March 1815 (choir SATB, pf).
168A	*Osterlied*, 9 March 1815 (choir SATB, pf).
169	*Trinklied vor der Schlacht*, 12 March 1815 (double choir, pf).
170	*Schwertlied*, 12 March 1815 (soloist, unison choir, pf).
183	*Trinklied*, 12 April 1815 (soloist, unison choir, pf).
189	*An die Freude*, May 1815 (soloist, unison choir, pf).
199	*Mailied*, 24 May 1815 (duet for voices or hns).
202	*Mailied* (*Der Schnee zerrinnt*), 26 May 1815 (duet for voices or hns).
203	*Der Morgenstern*, 26 May 1815 (duet for voices or hns).
204	*Jägerlied*, 26 May 1815 (duet for voices or hns).
205	*Lützows wilde Jagd*, 26 May 1815 (duet for voices or hns).
232	*Hymne an den Unendlichen*, 11 July 1815 (quartet SATB, pf).
244	*Willkommen, lieber schöner Mai*, (?)Aug. 1815 (canon for 3 voices).
253	*Punschlied: im Norden zu singen*, 18 Aug. 1815 (duet).
294	*Namensfeier*, 27 Sept. 1815 (trio STB, orch.).
330	*Das Grab* (2), 28 Dec. 1815 (choir SATB, pf).
357	*Gold'ner Schein*, May 1816 (canon for 3 voices).
442	*Das grosse Halleluja*, June 1816 (trio or 3-part choir, pf).
443	*Schlachtlied*, June 1816 (choir, pf).
439	*An die Sonne*, June 1816 (quartet SATB, pf).
440	*Chor der Engel*, June 1816 (choir SATB).
451	*Prometheus*, June 1816, lost.
472	*Kantate zu Ehren von Josef Spendou*, Sept. 1816 (soloists, choir SATB, orch.).
521	*Jagdlied*, Jan. 1817 (unison choir, pf).
609	*Die Geselligheit*, Jan. 1818 (quartet SATB, pf).
643A	*Das Grab* (5), 1819 (quartet SATB).
666	*Kantate zum Geburtstag Michael Vogl*, 10 Aug. 1819 (trio SATB, pf).
748	*Am Geburtstag des Kaisers*, Jan. 1822 (soloists, choir SATB, orch.).
763	*Des Tages Weihe*, 22 Nov. 1822 (quartet SATB, pf).
815	*Gebet*, Sept. 1824 (quartet SATB, pf).
875A	*Die Allmacht*, Jan. 1826 (choir SATB, pf), incomplete.
985	*Gott im Ungewitter*, (?)1827 (choir, SATB, pf).
986	*Gott der Weltschöpfer*, (?)1827 (SATB, pf).
930	*Der Hochzeitsbraten*, Nov. 1827 (trio STB, pf).
936	*Kantate für Irene Kiesewetter*, 26 Dec. 1827 (soloists, choir SATB, pf 4 hands).
826	*Der Tanz*, early 1828 (quartet SATB, pf).
942	*Mirjams Siegesgesang*, March 1828 (sop., choir SATB, pf).

For women's voices

269	*Das Leben ist ein Traum*, 25 Aug. 1815 (trio SSA).
706	23rd Psalm, Dec. 1820 (quartet SSAA).
757	*Gott in der Natur*, Aug. 1822 (quartet SSAA).
836	*Coronach*, 1825 (choir SSA).
920	*Ständchen*, July 1827 (alto, choir SSAA, pf).

For men's voices

37	*Die Advokaten*, 25–27 Dec. 1812 (trio TTB, pf).
38	*Totengräberlied*, (?)1813 (trio TTB).
51	*Unendliche Freude* (1), 15 April 1813 (trio TTB).
53	*Vorüber die stöhnende Klage*, 18 April 1813 (trio TTB).

54	*Unendliche Freude* (2), 19 April 1813 (trio TTB or BBB).	
55	*Selig durch die Liebe*, 21 April 1813 (trio TTB).	
57	*Hier strecket der wallende Pilger*, 29 April 1813 (trio TTB).	
58	*Dessen Fahne Donnerstürme wallte*, May 1813 (trio TTB).	
62	*Thronend auf erhabnem Sitz*, 9 May 1813 (trio TTB).	
63	*Wer die steile Sternenbahn*, 10 May 1813 (trio TTB).	
64	*Majestätsche Sonnenrosse*, 10 May 1813 (trio TTB).	
67	*Frisch atmet des Morgens lebendiger Hauch*, 15 May 1813 (trio TTB).	
43	*Dreifach ist der Schritt* (1), 8 July 1813 (trio TTB).	
70	*Dreifach ist der Schritt der Zeit* (2), 8 July 1813 (trio TTB).	
71	*Die zwei Tugendwege*, 15 July 1813 (trio TTB).	
75	*Trinklied*, 29 Aug. 1813 (bass, choir TTB, pf).	
80	*Zur Namensfeier meines Vaters*, 27 Sept. 1813 (trio TTB, guitar).	
60	*Hier umarmen sich getreue Gatten*, 3 Oct. 1813 (trio TTB).	
88	*Verschwunden sind die Schmerzen*, 15 Nov. 1813 (trio TTB).	
110	*Wer ist gross?*, 24–25 July 1814 (bass, choir TTBB, orch.).	
129	*Mailied*, c.1815 (trio TTB).	
140	*Klage um Ali Bey*, 1815 (trio TTB).	
148	*Trinklied*, Feb. 1815 (tenor, choir TTB, pf).	
236	*Das Abendrot*, 20 July 1815 (trio TTB, pf).	
242	*Trinklied im Winter*, (?)Aug. 1815 (trio TTB).	
243	*Frühlingslied*, (?)Aug. 1815 (trio TTB).	
267	*Trinklied*, 25 Aug. 1815 (quartet TTBB, pf).	
268	*Bergknappenlied*, 25 Aug. 1815 (quartet TTBB, pf).	
269	*Das Leben ist ein Traum*, Aug. 1815 (trio TTB, pf).	
277	*Punschlied*, 29 Aug. 1815 (trio TTB, pf).	
147	*Bardengesang*, 20 Jan. 1816 (trio TTB).	
331	*Der Entfernten* (1), c.1816 (quartet TTBB).	
337	*Die Einsiedelei* (1), c.1816 (quartet TTBB).	
338	*An den Frühling* (2), c.1816 (quartet TTBB).	
364	*Fischerlied* (2), 1816–17 (quartet TTBB).	
377	*Das Grab* (3), 11 Feb. 1816 (quartet TTBB, pf).	
407	For Salieri's 50th anniversary celebration, early June 1816 (tenor, quartet TTBB, pf).	
423	*Andenken*, May 1816 (trio TTB).	
424	*Erinnerung*, May 1816 (trio TTB).	
427	*Trinklied im Mai*, May 1816 (trio TTB).	
428	*Widerhall*, May 1816 (trio TTB).	
494	*Des Geistertanz* (4), Nov. 1816 (quintet TTBBB).	
513	*La Pastorella al Prato*, (?)1817 (quartet TTBB, pf).	
538	*Gesang der Geister über den Wassern* (2), March 1817 (quartet TTBB).	
569	*Das Grab* (4), June 1817 (unison choir).	
572	*Lied im Freien*, July 1817 (quartet TTBB).	
598	*Das Dörfchen*, Dec. 1817 (quartet TTBB, pf).	
635	*Leise, leise, lasst uns singen*, c.1819 (quartet TTBB).	
656	*Sehnsucht* (*Nur wer die Sehnsucht kennt*) (4), April 1819 (quintet TTBBB).	
657	*Ruhe, schönstes Glück der Erde*, April 1819 (quartet TTBB).	
714	*Gesang der Geister über den Wassern* (3) and (4), Dec. 1820–Feb. 1821 (octet 4T 4B, strings).	
724	*Die Nachtigall*, spring 1821 (quartet TTBB, pf).	
422	*Naturgenuss*, (?)summer 1822 (quartet TTBB, pf).	
740	*Frühlingsgesang*, early 1822 (quartet TTBB, pf).	
710	*Im Gegenwärtigen Vergangenes*, (?)March 1821 (quartet TTBB, pf).	
747	*Geist der Liebe* (2), Jan. 1822 (quartet TTBB, pf).	
983	*Jünglingswonne*, (?)1822 (quartet TTBB).	

983A	*Liebe*, (?)1822 (quartet TTBB).
983B	*Zum Rundetanz*, (?)1822 (quartet TTBB).
983C	*Die Nacht*, (?)1822 (quartet TTBB).
809	*Gondelfahrer* (2), March 1824 (quartet TTBB, pf).
822	*Lied eines Kriegers*, 31 Dec. 1824 (bass, unison choir, pf).
825B	*Flucht*, early 1825 (quartet TTBB).
835	*Bootgesang*, 1825 (quartet TTBB, pf).
847	*Trinklied aus dem 16. Jahrhundert*, July 1825 (quartet TTBB).
848	*Nachtmusik*, July 1825 (quartet TTBB).
825	*Wehmut*, (?)1825 (quartet TTBB).
825A	*Ewige Liebe*, (?)1825 (quartet TTBB).
865	*Widerspruch*, (?)1826 (quartet TTBB).
875	*Mondenschein*, Jan. 1826 (quintet TTBBB, pf).
892	*Nachthelle*, Sept. 1826 (tenor, quartet TTBB, pf).
893	*Grab und Mond*, Sept. 1826 (quartet TTBB).
901	*Wein und Liebe*, spring 1827 (quartet TTBB).
903	*Zur guten Nacht*, Jan. 1827 (bar., choir TTBB, pf).
912	*Schlachtlied* (2), 28 Feb. 1827 (double choir TTBB).
913	*Nachtgesang im Walde*, April 1827 (quartet TTBB, 4 hns).
914	*Frühlingslied*, April 1827 (quartet TTBB).
984	*Der Wintertag*, (?)after 1820 (quartet TTBB, pf).

VII SONGS

Songs are listed alphabetically by title. Individual songs within cycles are listed under title of cycle.

D.no.   Title/(author)/date

650	*Abendbilder* (Silbert), Feb. 1819.
382	*Abendlied (Sanft glänzt)* (Anon.), 24 Feb. 1816.
499	*Abendlied (Der Mond)* (Claudius), Nov. 1816.
276	*Abendlied (Gross und rotentflammet)* (Stolbert), 28 Aug. 1815.
495	*Abendlied der Fürstin* (Mayrhofer), (?)Nov. 1816.
856	*Abendlied für die Entfernte* (A. W. v. Schlegel), Sept. 1825.
690	*Abendröte* (F. v. Schlegel), (?)1820–March 1823.
235	*Abends unter der Linde* (1) (Kosegarten), 24 July 1815.
237	*Abends unter der Linde* (2) (Kosegarten), 25 July 1815.
265	*Abendständchen: an Lina* (Baumberg), 23 Aug. 1815.
806	*Abendstern* (Mayrhofer), March 1824.
475	*Abschied: nach einer Wallfahrtsarie* (Mayrhofer), Sept. 1816.
829	*Abschied von der Erde* (Pratobevera), Feb. 1826, melodrama.
406	*Abschied von der Harfe* (Salis-Seewis), March 1816.
578	*Abschied von einem Freunde* (F. Schubert), 24 Aug. 1817.
95	*Adelaide* (Matthisson), 1814.
211	*Adelwold und Emma* (Bertrand), June 1815.
904	*Alinde* (Rochlitz), Jan. 1827.
241	*Alles um Liebe* (Kosegarten), 27 July 1815.
153	*Als ich sie erröten sah* (Erlich), 10 Feb. 1815.
477	*Alte Liebe röstet nie* (Mayrhofer), Sept. 1816.
361	*Am Bach im Frühling* (Schober), (?)1816.
344	*Am ersten Maimorgen* (Claudius), (?)1816.
878	*Am Fenster* (Seidl), March 1826.
160	*Am Flusse* (1) (Goethe), 27 Feb. 1815.
766	*Am Flusse* (2) (Goethe), Dec. 1822.

504	*Am Grabe Anselmos* (Claudius), 4 Nov. 1816.
746	*Am See (In des Sees)* (Bruchmann), (?)1822
124	*Am See (Sitz ich im Gras)* (Mayrhofer), 7 Dec. 1814.
539	*Am Strome* (Mayrhofer), March 1817.
195	*Amalia* (Schiller), 19 May 1815.
122	*Ammenlied* (Lubi), Dec. 1814.
166	*Amphiaraos* (Körner), 1 March 1815.
462	*An Chloen (Bei der Liebe reinsten Flammen)* (Jacobi), Aug. 1816.
283	*An den Frühling* (1) (Schiller), 6 Sept. 1815.
587	*An den Frühling* (2) (Schiller), Oct. 1817.
259	*An den Mond* (1) *(Füllest wieder Busch und Tal)* (Goethe), 19 Aug. 1815.
296	*An den Mond* (2) (Goethe), (?)autumn 1819.
193	*An den Mond (Geuss lieber Mond)* (Hölty), 17 May 1815.
468	*An den Mond (Was schauest)* (Hölty), 7 Aug. 1816.
614	*An den Mond in einer Herbsnacht* (Schreiber), April 1818.
447	*An den Schlaf* (Anon.), June 1816.
518	*An den Tod* (Schubart), 1817.
197	*An die Apfelbäume wo ich Julien erblickte* (Hölty), 22 May 1815.
765	*An die Entfernte* (Goethe), Dec. 1822.
189	*An die Freude* (Schiller), 1815.
654	*An die Freunde* (Mayrhofer), March 1819.
303	*An die Geliebte* (Stoll), 15 Oct. 1815.
394	*An die Harmonie* (Salis-Seewis), March 1816.
905	*An die Laute* (Rochlitz), Jan. 1827.
737	*An die Leyer* (Bruchmann), (?)1822−23.
547	*An die Musik* (Schober), March 1817.
497	*An die Nachtigall (Er liegt und schläft)* (Claudius), Nov. 1816.
196	*An die Nachtigall (Geuss nicht so laut)* (Hölty), 22 May 1815.
372	*An die Natur* (Stolberg), 15 Jan. 1816.
270	*An die Sonne (Sinke, liebe Sonne)* (Baumberg), (?)Aug. 1815.
272	*An die Sonne (Königliche Morgensonne)* (Tiedge), 25 Aug. 1815.
478(3)	*An die Türen will ich schleichen* (Goethe), Sept. 1816.
457	*An die untergehende Sonne* (Kosegarten), July 1816−May 1817.
530	*An eine Quelle* (Claudius), Feb. 1817.
113	*An Emma* (Schiller), 17 Sept. 1814.
115	*An Laura* (Matthisson), 2−7 Oct. 1814.
860	*An mein Herz* (Schulze), Dec. 1825.
342	*An mein Klavier* (Schubart), c.1816.
161	*An Mignon* (Goethe), 27 Feb. 1815.
315	*An Rosa (Warum bist du nicht hier)* (Kosegarten), 19 Oct. 1815.
316	*An Rosa (Rosa, denkst du an mich?)* (Kosegarten), 19 Oct. 1815.
369	*An Schwager Kronos* (Goethe), (?)1816.
288	*An Sie* (Klopstock), 14 Sept. 1815.
891	*An Silvia* (Shakespeare), July 1826.
99	*Andenken* (Matthisson), April 1814.
542	*Antigone und Oedip* (Mayrhofer), March 1817.
585	*Atys* (Mayrhofer), Sept. 1817.
543	*Auf dem See* (Goethe), (?)March 1817.
943	*Auf dem Strom* (Rellstab), March 1818 (pf and hn acc.).
774	*Auf dem Wasser zu singen* (Stolberg), 1823.
81	*Auf den Sieg der Deutschen* ((?)Schubert), autumn 1813.
201	*Auf den Tod einer Nachtigall* (1) (Hölty), 25 May 1815.
399	*Auf den Tod einer Nachtigall* (2) (Hölty), 13 May 1816.
853	*Auf der Brücke* (Schulze), (?)March 1825.
553	*Auf der Donau* (Mayrhofer), April 1817.

611	*Auf der Riesenkoppe* (Körner), March 1818.
151	*Auf einen Kirchhoff* (Schlechta), 2 Feb. 1815.
807	*Auflösung* (Mayrhofer), March 1824.
297	*Augenlied* (Mayrhofer), (?)early 1817.
458	*Aus 'Diego Manazares'* (*Ilmerine*) (Schlechta), 30 July 1816.
753	*Aus 'Heliopolis'* (*Im kalten*) (Mayrhofer), April 1822.
754	*Aus 'Heliopolis'* (*Fels auf Felsen*) (Mayrhofer), April 1822.
134	*Ballade* (Kenner), (?)early 1815.
866(2)	*Bei dir allein* (Seidl), (?)summer 1828.
669	*Beim Winde* (Mayrhofer), Oct. 1819.
653	*Bertas Lied in der Nacht* (Grillparzer), Feb. 1819.
631	*Blanka* (F. v. Schlegel), Dec. 1818.
626	*Blondel zu Marien* (Anon.), Sept. 1818.
431	*Blumenlied* (Hölty), May 1816.
258	*Bundeslied* (Goethe), Aug. 1815.
263	*Cora an die Sonne* (Baumberg), 22 Aug. 1816.
282	*Cronnan* (Ossian), 5 Sept. 1815.
411	*Daphne am Bach* (Stolberg), April 1816.
627	*Das Abendrot* (Schrieber), Nov. 1818.
155	*Das Bild* (Anon.), 11 Feb. 1815.
868	*Das Echo* (Castelli), (?)1826–27.
219	*Das Finden* (Kosegarten), 25 June 1815.
250	*Das Geheimnis* (1) (Schiller), 7 Aug. 1815.
793	*Das Geheimnis* (2) (Schiller), May 1823.
309	*Das gestörte Glück* (Körner), 15 Oct. 1815.
442	*Das grosse Halleluja* (Klopstock), June 1816.
456	*Das Heimweh* (Hell), July 1816.
917	*Das Lied im Grünen* (Reil), June 1827.
532	*Das Lied von Reifen* (Claudius), Feb. 1817.
652	*Das Mädchen* (*Wie so innig*) (F. v. Schlegel), Feb. 1819.
117	*Das Mädchen aus der Fremde* (1) (Schiller), 16 Oct. 1814.
252	*Das Mädchen aus der Fremde* (2) (Schiller), 12 Aug. 1815.
281	*Das Mädchen von Inistore* (Ossian), Sept. 1815.
623	*Das Marienbild* (Schreiber), Aug. 1818.
280	*Das Rosenband* (Klopstock), Sept. 1815.
231	*Das Sehnen* (Kosegarten), 8 July 1815.
174	*Das war ich* (1) (Körner), 26 March 1815.
926	*Das Weinen* (Leitner), autumn 1827.
871	*Das Zügenglöcklein* (Seidl), (?)March 1826.
775	*Dass sie hier gewesen* (Rückert), (?)1822/23.
857(1)	*Delphine* (Schütz), Sept. 1825.
291	*Dem Unendlichen* (Klopstock), 15 Sept. 1815.
221	*Der Abend* (*Der Abend blüht*) (Kosegarten), 15 July 1815.
108	*Der Abend* (*Purpur malt*) (Matthisson), July 1814.
524	*Der Alpenjäger* (*Auf hohem Bergesrücken*) (Mayrhofer), Jan. 1817.
588	*Der Alpenjäger* (*Willst du nicht das Lämmlein hüten*) (Schiller), Oct. 1817.
833	*Der blinde Knabe* (Cibber/Craigher), early 1825.
731	*Der Blumen Schmerz* (Majláth), Sept. 1821.
622	*Der Blumenbrief* (Schreiber), Aug. 1818.
800	*Der Einsame* (Lappe), (?)Jan. 1825.
350	*Der Entfernten* (Salis-Seewis), (?)spring 1816.
699	*Der entsühnte Orest* (Mayrhofer), (?)March 1817.
225	*Der Fischer* (Goethe), 5 July 1815.
402	*Der Flüchtling* (Schiller), 18 March 1816.
515	*Der Flug der Zeit* (Széchényi), (?)1821.

693	*Der Fluss* (F. v. Schlegel), March 1820.
116	*Der Geistertanz* (3) (Matthisson), 14 Oct. 1814.
560	*Der Goldschmiedsgesell* (Goethe), May 1817.
254	*Der Gott und die Bajadere* (Goethe), 18 Aug. 1815.
405	*Der Herbstabend* (Salis-Seewis), March 1816.
490	*Der Hirt* (Mayrhofer), 8 Oct. 1816.
965	*Der Hirt auf dem Felsen* (Müller/v. Chézy), October 1828 (pf and clarinet acc.).
30	*Der Jüngling am Bache* (1) (Schiller), 24 Sept. 1812.
192	*Der Jüngling am Bache* (2) (Schiller), 15 May 1815.
638	*Der Jüngling am Bache* (3) (Schiller), April 1819.
300	*Der Jüngling an der Quelle* (Salis-Seewis), (?)1821.
385	*Der Jüngling auf dem Hügel* (H. Hüttenbrenner), Nov. 1820.
545	*Der Jüngling und der Tod* (Josef v. Spaun), March 1817.
594	*Der Kampf* (Schiller), Nov. 1817.
692	*Der Knabe* (F. v. Schlegel), March 1820.
579	*Der Knabe in der Wiege* (Ottenwalt), Sept. 1817.
367	*Der König in Thule* (Goethe), early 1816.
932	*Der Kreuzzug* (Leitner), Nov. 1827.
432	*Der Leidende* (Anon.), May 1816.
207	*Der Liebende* (Hölty), 29 May 1815.
861	*Der liebliche Stern* (Schulze), Dec. 1825.
209	*Der Liedler* (Kenner), (?)Jan. 1815.
141	*Der Mondabend* (Kumpf), 1815.
264	*Der Morgenkuss* (Baumberg), 22 Aug. 1815.
172	*Der Morgenstern* (Körner), 12 March 1815.
764	*Der Musensohn* (Goethe), Dec. 1822.
794	*Der Pilgrim* (Schiller), May 1823.
663	*Der 13. Psalm* (M. Mendelssohn), June 1819.
255	*Der Rattenfänger* (Goethe), 19 Aug. 1815.
149	*Der Sänger* (Goethe), Feb. 1815.
482	*Der Sänger am Felsen* (Pichler), Sept. 1816.
517	*Der Schäfer und der Reiter* (Fouqué), April 1817.
256	*Der Schatzgräber* (Goethe), 19 Aug. 1815.
536	*Der Schiffer* (*Im Winde, im Sturme*) (Mayrhofer), (?)1817.
694	*Der Schiffer* (*Friedlich lieg ich*) (F. v. Schlegel), March 1820.
633	*Der Schmetterling* (F. v. Schlegel), (?)March 1820.
805	*Der Sieg* (Mayrhofer), March 1824.
565	*Der Strom* (Anon.), (?)autumn 1817.
77	*Der Taucher* (Schiller), Sept. 1813–late 1814.
375	*Der Tod Oscars* (Ossian), Feb. 1816.
531	*Der Tod und das Mädchen* (Claudius), Feb. 1817.
213	*Der Traum* (Hölty), 17 June 1815.
713	*Der Unglückliche* (Pichler), Jan. 1821.
906	*Der Vater mit dem Kind* (Bauernfeld), Jan. 1827.
10	*Der Vatermörder* (Pfeffel), 26 Dec. 1811.
742	*Der Wachtelschlag* (Sauter), (?)1822.
931	*Der Wallensteiner Lanzknecht beim Trunk* (Leitner), Nov. 1827.
489	*Der Wanderer* (*Ich komme vom Gebirge her*) (Schmidt), Oct. 1816.
649	*Der Wanderer* (*Wie deutlich das Mondes Licht*) (F. v. Schlegel), (?)Feb. 1819.
870	*Der Wanderer an den Mond* (Seidl), (?)March 1826.
271	*Der Weiberfreund* (Cowley/Ratschky), 25 Aug. 1815.
938	*Der Winterabend* (Leitner), Jan. 1828.
320	*Der Zufriedene* (Reissig), 23 Oct. 1815.
785	*Der zürnende Barde* (Bruchmann), Feb. 1823.
707	*Der zürnenden Diana* (Mayrhofer), Dec. 1820.

771 *Der Zwerg* (M. v. Collin), (?)Nov. 1822.
933 *Des Fischers Liebesglück* (Leitner), Nov. 1827.
6 *Des Mädchens Klage* (1) (Schiller), (?)1811.
191 *Des Mädchens Klage* (2) (Schiller), 15 May 1815.
389 *Des Mädchens Klage* (3) (Schiller), March 1816.
832 *Des Sängers Habe* (Schlechta), Feb. 1825.
510 *Didone Abbandonata* (Metastasio), Dec. 1816.
514 *Die abgeblühte Linde* (Széchényi), (?)1821.
852 *Die Allmacht* (Pyrker), Aug. 1825.
104 *Die Beifreier Europas in Paris* (Mikan), 16 May 1814.
634 *Die Berge* (F. v. Schlegel), (?)March 1820.
102 *Die Betende* (Matthisson), autumn 1814.
519 *Die Blumensprache* ((?)Platner), (?)Oct. 1817.
246 *Die Bürgschaft* (Schiller), Aug. 1815.
329 *Die drei Sänger* (Bobrik), 23 Dec. 1815.
393 *Die Einsiedelei* (1) (Salis-Seewis), (?)March 1816.
563 *Die Einsiedelei* (2) (Salis-Seewis), May 1817.
390 *Die Entzückung an Laura* (Schiller), March 1816.
989 *Die Erde* (Matthisson), autumn 1817.
229 *Die Erscheinung* (Kosegarten), 7 July 1815.
182 *Die erste Liebe* (Fellinger), 12 April 1815.
159 *Die Erwartung* (Schiller), May 1816.
550 *Die Forelle* (Schubart), (?)early 1817.
262 *Die Fröhlichkeit* (Prandstetter), 22 Aug. 1815.
430 *Die frühe Liebe* (Hölty), May 1816.
290 *Die frühen Gräber* (Klopstock), 14 Sept. 1815.
646 *Die Gebüsche* (F. v. Schlegel), Jan. 1819.
712 *Die gefangenen Sänger* (A. W. v. Schlegel), Jan. 1821.
444 *Die Gestirne* (Klopstock), June 1816.
677 *Die Götter Griechenlands* (*Schöne Welt, wo bist du?*) (Schiller), Nov. 1819.
404 *Die Herbsnacht* (Salis-Seewis), March 1816.
828 *Die junge Nonne* (Craigher), 1824/early 1825.
400 *Die Knabenzeit* (Hölty), 13 May 1816.
214 *Die Laube* (Hölty), 17 June 1815.
210 *Die Liebe* (*Freudvoll und leidvoll*) (Goethe), 3 June 1815.
522 *Die Liebe* (*Wo weht der Liebe hoher Geist?*) (Leon), Jan. 1817.
751 *Die Liebe hat gelogen* (Platen), spring 1822.
673 *Die Liebende schreibt* (Goethe), Oct. 1819.
446 *Die Liebesgötter* (Uz), June 1816.
308 *Die Macht der Liebe* (Kalchberg), 15 Oct. 1815.
194 *Die Mainacht* (Hölty), 17 May 1815.
866(3) *Die Männer sind méchant* (Seidl), (?)summer 1828.
238 *Die Mondnacht* (Kosegarten), 25 July 1815.
788 *Die Mutter erde* (*Des Lebens Tag ist schwer*) (Stolberg), April 1823.
534 *Die Nacht* (*Die Nacht ist dumpfig*) (Ossian), Feb. 1817.
358 *Die Nacht* (*Du verstörst uns nicht*) (Uz), (?)June 1816.
208 *Die Nonne* (Hölty), 28 May–16 June 1815.
466 *Die Perle* (Jacobi), Aug. 1816.
745 *Die Rose* (F. v. Schlegel), (?)March 1820.
50 *Die Schatten* (Matthisson), 12 April 1813.
795 *Die schöne Müllerin* (song-cycle) (W. Müller), summer/autumn 1823.
  Das Wandern
  Wohin?
  Halt!
  Danksagung an den Bach

Am Feierabend
Der Neugierige
Ungeduld
Morgengruss
Des Müllers Blumen
Tränenregen
Mein
Pause
Mit dem grünen Lautenbande
Der Jäger
Eifersucht und Stolz
Die liebe Farbe
Die böse Farbe
Trockne Blumen
Der Müller und der Bach
Des Baches Wiegenlied

289   *Die Sommernacht* (Klopstock), 14 Sept. 1815.
247   *Die Spinnerin* (Goethe), Aug. 1815.
186   *Die Sterbende* (Matthisson), (?)May 1815.
176   *Die Sterne (Was funkelt)* (Fellinger), 6 April 1815.
313   *Die Sterne (Wie wohl)* (Kosegarten), 19 Oct. 1815.
939   *Die Sterne (Wie blitzen)* (Leitner), Jan. 1828.
684   *Die Sterne (Du staunest)* (F. v. Schlegel), (?)1819–20.
670   *Die Sternennächte* (Mayrhofer), Oct. 1819.
307   *Die Sternenwelten* (Fellinger), 15 Oct. 1815.
965A   *Die Taubenpost* (Seidl), Oct. 1828.
230   *Die Täuschung* (Kosegarten), 7 July 1815.
866(1)   *Die Unterscheidung* (Seidl), (?)summer 1828.
409   *Die verfehlte Stunde* (A. W. v. Schlegel), April 1816.
391   *Die vier Weltalter* (Schiller), (?)March 1816.
691   *Die Vögel* (F. v. Schlegel), March 1820.
778A   *Die Wallfahrt* (Rückert), (?)1822/23.
801   *Dithyrambe* (Schiller), (?)1824.
 93(1)   *Don Gayseros I (Don Gayseros)* (Fouqué), (?)end of 1815.
 93(2)   *Don Gayseros II (Nächtens)* (Fouqué), (?)end of 1815.
 93(3)   *Don Gayseros III (An den jungen Morgenhimmel)* (Fouqué), (?)end of 1815.
770   *Drang in die Ferne* (Leitner), (?)end of 1822.
776   *Du bist die Ruh* (Rückert), (?)1823.
756   *Du liebst mich nicht* (Platen), 1822.
445   *Edone* (Klopstock), June 1816.
923   *Eine altschottische Ballade* (trans. Herder), Sept. 1827.
620   *Einsamkeit* (Mayrhofer), July 1818.
837   *Ellens Gesang I (Raste, Krieger)* (Scott/Storck), spring 1825.
838   *Ellens Gesang II (Jäger, ruhe von der Jagd)* (Scott/Storck), spring 1825.
839   *Ellens Gesang III (Ave Maria)* (Scott/Storck), April 1825.
584   *Elysium* (Schiller), Sept. 1817.
 33(1)   *Entra l'uomo allor che nasce* (Metastasio), autumn 1823.
413   *Enzückung* (Matthisson), April 1816.
749   *Epistel: Musikalischer Schwank* (M. v. Collin), Jan. 1822.
 98   *Erinnerung* (Matthisson), Sept. 1814.
586   *Erlafsee* (Mayrhofer), Sept. 1817.
328   *Erlkönig* (Goethe), Oct. 1815.
434   *Erntelied* (Hölty), May 1816.
226   *Erster Verlust* (Goethe), 5 July 1815.
607   *Evangelium Johannis* (Pericope for the Mass), spring 1818.

526	*Fahrt zum Hades* (Mayrhofer), Jan. 1817.
351	*Fischerlied* (1) (Salis-Seewis), (?)1816.
562	*Fischerlied* (2) (Salis-Seewis), May 1817.
881	*Fischerweise* (Schlechta), (?)March 1826.
857(1)	*Florio* (Schütz), Sept. 1825.
450	*Fragment aus dem Aeschylus* (Mayrhofer), June 1816.
700	*Freiwilliges Versinken* (Mayrhofer), (?)1817.
455	*Freude der Kindejahre* (Köpken), July 1816.
520	*Frohsinn* (Castelli), Jan. 1817.
686	*Frühlingsglaube* (Uhland), Sept. 1820.
398	*Frühlingslied* (*Die Luft ist blau*) (Hölty), 13 May 1816.
919	*Frühlingslied* (*Geöffnet sind des Winters Riegel*) (Pollak), (?)spring 1827.
854	*Fülle der Liebe* (F. v. Schlegel), Aug. 1825.
285	*Furcht der Geliebten* (Klopstock), 12 Sept. 1815.
544	*Ganymed* (Goethe), March 1817.
171	*Gebet während der Schlacht* (Körner), March 1815.
719	*Geheimes* (Goethe), March 1821.
491	*Geheimnis* (Mayrhofer), October 1816.
233	*Geist der Liebe* (*Wer bist du, Geist der Liebe*) (Kosegarten), 15 July 1815.
414	*Geist der Liebe* (*Der Abend schleiert Flur und Hain*) (Matthisson), April 1816.
100	*Geisternähe* (Matthisson), April 1814.
142	*Geistesgruss* (Goethe), (?)1815.
143	*Genugsamkeit* (Schober), (?)1815.
831	*Gesang der Norna* (Scott/Spiker), early 1825.
955	*Glaube, Hoffnung und Liebe* (Kuffner), Aug. 1828.
808	*Gondelfahrer* (Mayrhofer), March 1824.
448	*Gott im Frühlinge* (Uz), June 1816.
218	*Grablied* (Kenner), 24 June 1815.
454	*Grablied auf einen Soldaten* (Schubart), July 1816.
616	*Grablied für die Mutter* (Anon.), June 1816.
778	*Greisengesang* (Rückert), (?)autumn 1822.
716	*Grenzen der Menschheit* (Goethe), March 1821.
118	*Gretchen am Spinnrade* (Goethe), 19 Oct. 1814.
583	*Gruppe aus dem Tartarus* (Schiller), Sept. 1817.
5	*Hagars Klage* (Schücking), March 1811.
552	*Hänflings Liebeswerbung* (Kind), April 1817.
257	*Heidenröslein* (Goethe), 19 Aug. 1815.
922	*Heimliches Lieben* (Klenke), Sept. 1827.
726	*Heiss mich nicht reden* (1) (Goethe), April 1821.
822(2)	*Heiss mich nicht reden* (2) (Goethe), (?)Jan. 1826.
312	*Hektors Abschied* (Schiller), 19 Oct. 1815.
945	*Herbst* (Rellstab), April 1828.
502	*Herbstlied* (Salis-Seewis), Nov. 1816.
322	*Hermann und Thusnelda* (Klopstock), 27 Oct. 1815.
651	*Himmelsfunken* (Silbert), Feb. 1819.
890	*Hippolits Lied* (Gerstenberger), July 1826.
463	*Hochzeitlied* (Jacobi), Aug. 1816.
295	*Hoffnung* (*Schaff, das Tagwerk meiner Hände*) (Goethe), (?)Oct. 1819.
251	*Hoffnung* (1) (*Es reden und träumen*) (Schiller), 7 Aug. 1815.
637	*Hoffnung* (2) (Schiller), (?)1817.
240	*Huldigung* (Kosegarten), 27 July 1815.
659	*Hymne I* (*Wenige wissen das Geheimnis*) (Novalis), May 1819.
660	*Hymne II* (*Wenn ich ihn nur habe*) (Novalis), May 1819.
661	*Hymne III* (*Wenn all untreu werden*) (Novalis), May 1819.
662	*Hymne IV* (*Ich sag es jedem*) (Novalis), May 1819.

227   *Idens Nachtgesang* (Kosegarten), 7 July 1815.
317   *Idens Schwanenlied* (Kosegarten), 19 Oct. 1815.
736   *Ihr Grab* (Engelhardt), (?)end of 1822.
902(3)   *Il modo di prender moglie* (Anon.), 1827.
902(2)   *Il traditor deluso* (Metastasio), 1827.
799   *Im Abendrot* (Lappe), (?)Jan. 1825.
880   *Im Freien* (Seidl), March 1826.
882   *Im Frühling* (Schulze), March 1826.
738   *Im Haine* (Bruchmann), (?)1822.
708   *Im Walde* (*Windes Rauschen*) (F. v. Schlegel), Dec. 1820.
834   *Im Walde* (*Ich wandre über Berg*) (Schulze), (?)March 1825.
464   *In der Mitternacht* (Jacobi), Aug. 1816.
403   *Ins stille Land* (Salis-Seewis), March 1816.
573   *Iphigenia* (Mayrhofer), July 1817.
866(4)   *Irdisches Glück* (Seidl), (?)summer 1828.
521   *Jagdlied* (Werner), Jan. 1817.
215   *Jägers Abendlied* (1) (Goethe), 20 June 1815.
368   *Jägers Abendlied* (2) (Goethe), early 1816.
909   *Jägers Liebeslied* (Schober), Feb. 1827.
419   *Julius an Theone* (Matthisson), 30 April 1816.
990A   *Kaiser Maximilian* (H. v. Collin), (?)1818.
321   *Kennst du das Land* (Goethe), 23 Oct. 1815.
415   *Klage* (*Die Sonne steigt*) (Matthisson), April 1816.
512   *Klage* (*Nimmer trag' ich länger*) (Anon.), (?)1817.
371   *Klage* (*Trauer umfliesst mein Leben*) (Anon.), (?)Jan. 1816.
436   *Klage an den Mond* (Hölty), 12 May 1826.
323/991 *Klage der Ceres* (Schiller), Nov. 1815–June 1816.
496A   *Klage um Ali Bey* (Claudius), (?)1815 or 1816.
23   *Klaglied* (Rochlitz), 1812.
217   *Kolmas Klage* (Ossian), 22 June 1815.
528   *La Pastorella al Prato* (Goldoni), Jan. 1817.
302   *Labetrank der Liebe* (Stoll), 15 Oct. 1815.
777   *Lachen und Weinen* (Rückert), (?)1822–23.
301   *Lambertine* (Stoll), 12 Oct. 1815.
388   *Laura am Klavier* (Schiller), March 1816.
508   *Lebenslied* (Matthisson), Dec. 1816.
395   *Lebensmelodien* (A. W. v. Schlegel), March 1816.
937   *Lebensmut* (*Fröhlicher Lebensmut*) (Rellstab), (?)1827.
883   *Lebensmut* (*O wie dringt das junge Leben*) (Schulze), March 1826.
7   *Leichenfantasie* (Schiller), 1811.
509   *Leiden der Trennung* (H. v. Collin), Dec. 1816.
298   *Liane* (Mayrhofer), Oct. 1815.
352   *Licht und Liebe* (M. v. Collin), (?)1822 (duet).
222   *Lieb Minna* (Stadler), 2 July 1815.
698   *Liebeslauschen* (Schlechta), Sept. 1820.
164   *Liebesrausch* (1) (Körner), March 1815.
179   *Liebesrausch* (2) (Körner), 8 April 1815.
206   *Liebeständelei* (Körner), 26 May 1815.
558   *Liebhaber in allen Gestalten* (Goethe), May 1817.
535   *Lied* (*Brüder, schrecklich brennt die Träne*) (Anon.), Feb. 1817.
284   *Lied* (*Es ist so angenehm*) ((?)Schiller), 6 Sept. 1815.
483   *Lied* (*Ferne von der grossen Stadt*) (Pichler), Sept. 1816.
373   *Lied* (*Mutter geht durch ihre Kammern*) (Fouqué), 15 Jan. 1816.
107   *Lied aus der Ferne* (Matthisson), July 1814.
830   *Lied der Anne Lyle* (Scott), (?)early 1825.

109	*Lied der Liebe* (Matthisson), July 1814.
843	*Lied des gefangenen Jägers* (Scott/Storck), April 1825.
474	*Lied des Orpheus* (Jacobi), Sept. 1816.
596	*Lied eines Kindes* (Anon.), Nov. 1817.
822	*Lied eines Kriegers* (Anon.), 31 Dec. 1824.
360	*Lied eines Schiffers an die Dioskuren* (Mayrhofer), (?)1822.
416	*Lied in der Abwesenheit* (Stolberg), April 1816.
473	*Liedesend* (Mayrhofer), Sept. 1816.
273	*Lilla an die Morgenröthe* (Anon.), 25 Aug. 1815.
902(1)	*L'Incanto degli occhi* (Metastasio), 1827.
343	*Litanei auf das Fest aller Seelen* (Jacobi), Aug. 1816.
711	*Lob der Tränen* (A. W. v. Schlegel), (?)1818.
248	*Lob des Tokayers* (Baumberg), Aug. 1815.
150	*Lodas Gespenst* (Ossian), 17 Jan. 1816.
319	*Luisens Antwort* (Kosegarten), 19 Oct. 1815.
503	*Mailied* (Hölty), Nov. 1816.
658	*Marie* (Novalis), (?)May 1819.
215A	*Meeres Stille* (1) (Goethe), 20 June 1815.
216	*Meeres Stille* (2) (Goethe), 21 June 1815.
305	*Mein Gruss an den Mai* (Kumpf), 15 Oct. 1815.
541	*Memnon* (Mayrhofer), March 1815.
429	*Minnelied* (Hölty), May 1816.
152	*Minona* (Bertrand), 8 Feb. 1815.
42	*Misero pargoletto* (Metastasio), (?)1813.
381	*Morgenlied* (*Die frohe neubelebte Flur*) (Anon.), 24 Feb. 1816.
266	*Morgenlied* (*Willkommen rotes Morgenlicht*) (Stolberg), 24 Aug. 1815.
685	*Morgenlied* (*Eh die Sonne früh aufersteht*) (Werner), 1820.
561	*Nach einem Gewitter* (Mayrhofer), May 1817.
827	*Nacht und Träume* (M. v. Collin), (?)1822.
119	*Nachtgesang* (*O gib vom weichen Pfühle*) (Goethe), 30 Nov. 1814.
314	*Nachtgesang* (*Tiefer Feier schauert*) (Kosegarten), 19 Oct. 1815.
687	*Nachthymne* (Novalis), Jan. 1820.
672	*Nachtstück* (Mayrhofer), Oct. 1819.
752	*Nachtviolen* (Mayrhofer), April 1822.
162	*Nähe des Geliebten* (Goethe), 27 Feb. 1815.
695	*Namenstaglied* (Stadler), March 1820.
188	*Naturgenuss* (Matthisson), (?)May 1815.
846	*Normans Gesang* (Scott/Storck), April 1825.
513A	*Nur wer die Liebe kennt* (Werner), (?)1817.
310	*Nur wer die Sehnsucht kennt* (1) (Goethe), 18 Oct. 1815.
359	*Nur wer die Sehnsucht kennt* (2) (Goethe), 1816.
481	*Nur wer die Sehnsucht kennt* (3) (Goethe), Sept. 1816.
877(4)	*Nur wer die Sehnsucht kennt* (4) (Goethe), Jan. 1826.
877(1)	*Nur wer die Sehnsucht kennt* (5) (Goethe), Jan. 1826 (duet).
874	*O Quell, was strömst du rasch und wild* (Schulze), (?)March 1826.
548	*Orest auf Tauris* (Mayrhofer), March 1817.
278	*Ossians Lied nach dem Falle Nathos* (Ossian), (?)Sept. 1815.
551	*Pax Vobiscum* (Schober), April 1817.
76	*Pensa, che questo istante* (Metastasio), Sept. 1813.
467	*Pflicht und Liebe* (Gotter), Aug. 1816.
392	*Pflügerlied* (Salis-Seewis), March 1816.
500	*Phidile* (Claudius), Nov. 1816.
540	*Philoktet* (Mayrhofer), March 1817.
789	*Pilgerweise* (Schober), April 1823.
674	*Prometheus* (Goethe), Oct. 1819.

253	*Punschlied: im Norden zu singen* (Schiller), 18 Aug. 1815.
17(1)	*Quell' innocente figlio* (Metastasio), (?)autumn 1812.
138	*Rastlose Liebe* (Goethe), 19 May 1815.
397	*Ritter Toggenburg* (Schiller), 13 March 1816.
114	*Romanze (Ein Fräulein klagt' im finstern Turm)* (Matthisson), Sept. 1814.
907	*Romanze des Richard Löwenherz* (Scott/Müller), (?)March 1826.
476	*Rückweg* (Mayrhofer), Sept. 1816.
163	*Sängers Morgenlied* (1) (Körner), 27 Feb. 1815.
165	*Sängers Morgenlied* (2) (Körner), 1 March 1815.
121	*Schäfers Klagelied* (Goethe), 30 Nov. 1814.
761	*Schatzgräbers Begehr* (Schober), Nov. 1822.
910	*Schiffers Scheidelied* (Schober), Feb. 1827.
443	*Schlachtgesang* (Klopstock), June 1816.
527	*Schlaflied* (Mayrhofer), Jan. 1817.
318	*Schwanengesang (Endlich stehn die Pforten offen)* (Kosegarten), 19 Oct. 1815.
744	*Schwanengesang (Wie klag ich's aus)* (Senn), (?)autumn 1822.
957	*Schwanengesang* (song-cycle), fin. Aug. 1828.
	Liebesbotschaft (Rellstab)
	Kriegers Ahnung (Rellstab)
	Frühlingssehnsucht (Rellstab)
	Ständchen (Rellstab)
	Aufenthalt (Rellstab)
	In der Ferne (Rellstab)
	Abschied (Rellstab)
	Der Atlas (Heine)
	Ihr Bild (Heine)
	Das Fischermädchen (Heine)
	Die Stadt (Heine)
	Am Meer (Heine)
	Der Doppelgänger (Heine)
	(see also *Die Taubenpost*)
559	*Schweizerlied* (Goethe), May 1817.
170	*Schwertlied* (Körner), 12 March 1815.
762	*Schwestergruss* (Bruchmann), Nov. 1822.
123	*Sehnsucht (Was zieht mir das Herz so)* (Goethe), 3 Dec. 1814.
516	*Sehnsucht (Der Lerche)* (Mayrhofer), (?)spring 1817.
52	*Sehnsucht (Ach, aus dieses Tales Gründen)* (1) (Schiller), 15–17 April 1813.
636	*Sehnsucht* (2) (Schiller), (?)early 1821.
879	*Sehnsucht (Die Scheibe friert, der Wind ist rauh)* (Seidl), March 1826.
180	*Sehnsucht der Liebe* (Körner), 8 April 1815.
741	*Sei mir gegrüsst* (Rückert), 1822.
743	*Selige Welt* (Senn), (?)autumn 1822.
433	*Seligkeit* (Hölty), May 1816.
286	*Selma und Selmar* (Klopstock), 14 Sept. 1815.
35(1)	*Serbate, O dei custodi* (Metastasio), Dec. 1812.
198	*Seufzer* (Hölty), 22 May 1815.
293	*Shilrik und Vinvela* (Ossian), 20 Sept. 1815.
896A	*Sie in jedem Liede* (Leitner), autumn 1827.
306	*Skolie (Lasst im Morgenstrahl des Mai'n)* (Deinhardstein), 15 Oct. 1815.
507	*Skolie (Mädchen entsiegelten die Flaschen)* (Matthisson), Dec. 1816.
469	*So lasst mich scheinen* (1) and (2) (Goethe), Sept. 1816 (fragment).
727	*So lasst mich scheinen* (3) (Goethe), April 1821.
877(3)	*So lasst mich scheinen* (4) (Goethe), Jan. 1826.
78	*Son fra l'onde* (Metastasio), 13 Sept. 1813.
628	*Sonnett I* (A. W. v. Schlegel), Nov. 1818.

629	*Sonnett II* (A. W. v. Schlegel), Nov. 1818.
630	*Sonnett III* (Gries), Dec. 1818.
410	*Sprache der Liebe* (A. W. v. Schlegel), April 1816.
889	*Ständchen* ('*Hark, hark, the lark*') (Shakespeare), July 1826.
187	*Stimme der Liebe* (1) (*Abendgewölke schweben hell*) (Matthisson), (?)May 1815.
418	*Stimme der Liebe* (2) (Matthisson), 29 April 1816.
412	*Stimme der Liebe (Meine Selinde!)* (Stolberg), April 1816.
720	*Suleika I* (*Was bedeutet die Bewegung*) (M. v. Willemer), March 1821.
717	*Suleika II* (*Ach um deine feuchten Schwingen*) (M. v. Willemer), (?)late 1824.
126	*Szene aus 'Faust'* (Goethe), Dec. 1814.
533	*Täglich zu singen* (Claudius), Feb. 1817.
73	*Thekla: eine Geisterstimme* (1) (Schiller), 22–23 Aug. 1813.
595	*Thekla: eine Geisterstimme* (2) (Schiller), Nov. 1817.
876	*Tiefes Leid* (Schulze), Dec. 1825 or March 1826.
274	*Tischlerlied* (Anon.), 25 Aug. 1815.
234	*Tischlied* (Goethe), 15 July 1815.
758	*Todesmusik* (Schober), Sept. 1822.
101	*Todtenopfer* (Matthisson), April 1814.
44	*Totengräberlied* (Hölty), 19 Jan. 1813.
842	*Totengräbers Heimweh* (Craigher), April 1825.
869	*Totengräber-Weise* (Schlechta), 1826.
275	*Totenkranz für ein Kind* (Matthisson), 25 Aug. 1815.
465	*Trauer der Liebe* (Jacobi), Aug. 1816.
888	*Trinklied* (*Bacchus*) (Shakespeare), July 1826.
183	*Trinklied* (*Ihr Freunde*) (Zettler), 12 April 1815.
523	*Trost* (*Nimmer*) (Anon.), Jan. 1817.
671	*Trost* (*Hörnerklänge*) (Mayrhofer), Oct. 1819.
97	*Trost, an Elisa* (Matthisson), 1814.
546	*Trost im Liede* (Schober), March 1817.
120	*Trost in Tränen* (Goethe), 30 Nov. 1814.
682	*Über allen Zauber* (Mayrhofer), (?)autumn 1819.
884	*Über Wildemann* (Schulze), March 1826.
862	*Um Mitternacht* (Schulze), Dec. 1825.
554	*Uraniens Flucht* (Mayrhofer), April 1817.
287	*Vaterlandslied* (Klopstock), 14 Sept. 1815.
177	*Vergebliche Liebe* (Bernard), 6 April 1815.
792	*Vergissmeinnicht* (Schober), May 1823.
59	*Verklärung* (Pope/Heder), 4 May 1813.
715	*Versunken* (Goethe), Feb. 1821.
688	*Vier Canzonen*, Jan. 1820.
	(1) *Non t'accostare all'urna* (Vittorelli)
	(2) *Guarda, che bianca lunca* (Vittorelli)
	(3) *Da quel sembiante appresi* (Metastasio)
	(4) *Mio ben ricordati* (Metastasio)
786	*Viola* (Schober), March 1823.
989	*Vollendung* (Matthisson), autumn 1817.
632	*Vom Mitleiden Mariä* (F. v. Schlegel), Dec. 1818.
228	*Von Ida* (Kosegarten), 7 July 1815.
927	*Vor meiner Wiege* (Leitner), autumn 1827.
224	*Wandrers Nachtlied I* (*Der du von dem Himmel bist*) (Goethe), 5 July 1815.
768	*Wandrers Nachtlied II* (*Über allen Gipfeln ist Ruh*) (Goethe), (?)Dec. 1822.
772	*Wehmut* (M. v. Collin), (?)Nov. 1822.
261	*Wer kauft Liebesgötter* (Goethe), 21 Aug. 1815.
480(1)	*Wer nie sein Brot mit Tränen ass* (1) (Goethe), Sept. 1816.
480(2)	*Wer nie sein Brot* (2) (Goethe), Sept. 1816.

480(3)	*Wer nie sein Brot* (3) (Goethe), autumn 1822.
325	*Wer sich der Einsamkeit ergibt* (1) (Goethe), 13 Nov. 1815.
478	*Wer sich der Einsamkeit ergibt* (2) (Goethe), Sept. 1816.
639	*Widerschein* (Schlechta), 1819 or 1820.
525	*Wie Ulfru fischt* (Mayrhofer), Jan. 1817.
855	*Wiedersehn* (A. W. v. Schlegel), Sept. 1825.
498	*Wiegenlied* (*Schlafe, schlafe, holder, süsser Knabe*) (Anon.), Nov. 1816.
304	*Wiegenlied* (*Schlummer sanft!*) (Körner), 15 Oct. 1815.
867	*Wiegenlied* (*Wie sich der Äuglein kindlicher Himmel*) (Seidl), (?)1826.
767	*Willkommen und Abschied* (Goethe), Dec. 1822.
401	*Winterlied* (Hölty), 13 May 1816.
911	*Winterreise* (song-cycle) (Müller), Feb.–Oct. 1827.

        Gute Nacht
        Die Wetterfahne
        Gefrorne Tränen
        Erstarrung
        Der Lindenbaum
        Wasserflut
        Auf dem Fluss
        Rückblick
        Irrlicht
        Rast
        Frühlingstraum
        Einsamkeit
        Die Post
        Der greise Kopf
        Die Krähe
        Letzte Hoffnung
        Im Dorfe
        Der stürmische Morgen
        Täuschung
        Der Wegweiser
        Das Wirtshaus
        Mut
        Die Nebensonnen
        Der Leiermann

260	*Wonne der Wehmut* (Goethe), 20 Aug. 1815.
362	*Zufriedenheit* (1) (Claudius), (?)April 1816.
501	*Zufriedenheit* (2) (Claudius), Nov. 1816.
492	*Zum Punsche* (Mayrhofer), Oct. 1816.
83	*Zur Namensfeier des Herrn Andreas Siller* (Anon.), 28 Oct.–4 Nov. 1813.

Glossary

Brief definitions of some technical terms used in this book. Italics indicate cross-references to other entries in the Glossary.

anacrusis An upbeat figure: a note or group of notes initiating a melodic idea in advance of a downbeat.

appoggiatura A note alien to the prevailing harmony, resolving by step to a note of the harmony.

binary form A two-section form, each section being repeated. The first normally moves away to a second key (dominant, or relative minor), and the second makes its way back to the *tonic*.

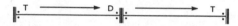

bravura section Authentically, the bravura section occurs late in the *exposition* of a concerto's first movement, and is characterized by an accumulation of shorter note-values, virtuoso scale and arpeggio matter, and 'stretched' harmonies leading to a big end-of-exposition cadence. The same tendency may be found in many sonata-form movements outside the concerto (sonata, quartet, symphony).

caesura A moment or two of complete silence, usually following an intermediate cadence and heralding an event of importance. A caesura often precedes a *second subject*.

canon Exact *imitation*. A second 'voice' copies a first with near-exactitude, entering after only a short delay and continuing for sufficient time to produce an appreciable 'overlap' in which both lines play simultaneously.

chromatic Entailing semitonal inflection of the notes of the diatonic scale, whole-tone steps being filled in with semitone half-steps.

closing theme A short final theme at the end of an *exposition* in *sonata form*.

coda A section added at the end of a movement, after the *recapitulation* in *sonata form* or *rondo*; in other forms, after the characteristic segments of the form have been completed.

codetta In *sonata form* a retrospective closing section at the end of an *exposition*, typically referring back to the first subject.

dactyl A rhythmic pattern of one long followed by two shorts (♩♪♪) Several terms are borrowed from poetic prosody for use in music, other examples being iamb (♪♩), trochee (♩♪), spondee (♩♩) and anapaest (♪♪♩).

descant An upper part which appears, even if only momentarily, above what is recognizably the leading melodic line.

development The central segment of *sonata form*, characterized by travel through a relatively wide range of keys, with new treatments of thematic material.

diminished seventh A four-note chord whose constituent notes are a minor third (three semitones) equidistant from each other.

dominant See *tonic*.

dominant pedal The fifth of the scale sustained in the bass (or, less usually, in some other part) as a means of (a) postponing and raising expectation of the *tonic*, and (b) generating harmonic conflicts in the process.

dominant preparation Preparation for a new key, or the return of an old key, by prolonged emphasis on its *dominant* (which is the most direct route of entry to a key).

dominant seventh A four-note chord on the *dominant* comprising that note with its third, fifth and seventh.

episode (1) In *rondo* and any other form except fugue, a contrasting section presenting its own theme in its own key. (2) In fugue, a connecting passage, itself containing no complete entry of the subject, modulating from the key of the previous set of subject entries to that of the next.

exposition The expository first section of *sonata form*, in which themes are announced in two keys (or three in the case of a three-key exposition). The exposition is normally repeated.

feminine cadence A cadence is a harmonic as much as melodic event, articulated by two chords, one of which (at least) is the tonic or dominant. The two chords commonly fall on a weak followed by a strong beat ('masculine cadence'). 'Feminine cadence' traditionally denotes the reverse strong-to-weak pattern.

fermata A pause, signified by the sign ⌒, during which a note or chord is held for an unmeasured length of time.

German sixth A chromatic chord containing two notes an augmented sixth apart, the flattened sixth (usually in the bass) and sharpened fourth of the scale, these two notes resolving by contrary motion to a (therefore doubled) *dominant*. There is a family of chords of this type (called 'augmented sixths'). The German sixth contains additionally the *tonic* and minor third of the scale. The chord is frequently used as a cadence-approach.

harmonic series The natural series of overtones generated by a fundamental note. The valveless brass instruments, up to and including Schubert's time, could obtain only the notes of this harmonic series (a scale but with many gaps in it), except (in the case of horns, not trumpets) if the hand was manoeuvred in the bell of the instrument to coax additional notes between the natural notes, though these extra notes were of inferior timbre and Schubert preferred to avoid them.

hemiola In triple time, the temporary illusion of a three-beat bar occupying twice the length of a single bar. The effect may be achieved by means of rhythm, the timing of chord-change, accentuation, syncopation, or a combination of any of these. Handel was partial to the device at cadences, and the Czech furiant makes a feature of it – as an opening gambit in the case of Smetana's furiant in *The Bartered Bride* and Dvořák's Slavonic Dance in G major/minor.

homophonic Of block-chordal texture, with all 'voices' moving predominantly in the same rhythm.

imitation Any approximate copying of one 'voice' by another, such that the melodic idea is recognized as being essentially the same.

melisma In vocal music, the allotting of more than one note of melody to a syllable of text. The term is sometimes used by analogy in non-vocal music.

Neapolitan sixth The major triad on the flattened second of the scale, in first inversion. This is a chromatically altered supertonic chord, often used – like the supertonic chord itself – as a means of approach to a cadence. The 'Neapolitan key' is the key a semitone above the *tonic* (e.g. D flat major in relation to C major).

ostinato A short melodic figure, in any part, that repeats itself obstinately at the same pitch.

palindrome A piece or section of music comprising a statement followed by its retrograde (presentation backwards).

passing notes Notes which are alien to the prevailing harmony and are 'justified' by being approached and quitted by step (major or minor second).

recapitulation In *sonata form*, the restatement – after the development – of the exposition material, varied at least to the extent of restoring to the tonic key those elements which in the exposition appeared outside the tonic (the second subject or second group).

rondo A 'rounded' form, whose first theme returns like a refrain, always in the tonic key, after intervening *episodes*. The old rondo form (ABACADA – though the number of alternating episodes and returns varies) is much less common in Schubert's time than the sonata-rondo (ABACABA), in which a *second subject* returns, as in *sonata form*, and C may be a *development*.

root position A chord whose root is in the bass is said to be 'in root position'.

second subject In the *exposition* of a movement in *sonata form*, material presented in the second main key (in Schubert, sometimes second and third keys). The second subject, or second group of themes, is therefore identified as much by its being in a key other than the tonic as by its melodic content.

sequence The immediate repetition of a melodic line and/or harmonic progression at a higher or lower pitch. There may be any number of successive sequences of a 'model'. (Adjective: sequential.)

sonata form The principal form of the Classical period, found in nearly all first movements, many finales, and often in slow movements too. Although modern terminology identifies three main sections (*exposition*, *development* and *recapitulation*), the form is in fact an expansion of *binary form*, diversified by the exploration of more keys and enriched by the addition of more themes. In slow movements there is a tendency to omit the development and the repeat of the exposition ('abridged sonata form'). The repeat of the second section (development-cum-recapitulation) is rare after Haydn and Mozart. The diagram below shows the location of some component features, defined separately in this Glossary, within the overall scheme. Those enclosed in brackets are not always present.

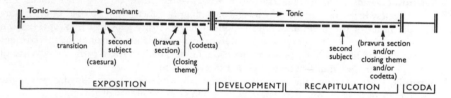

strophic A song is strophic if the same music is repeated for each stanza of a poem.

ternary form A three-section form, ABA, in which the second A is a reprise (perhaps varied) of the first.

tessitura The pitch range within which a part is 'placed', usually in relation to the compass of the voice or instrument concerned.

through-composed Any music not based on *strophic* repetition can be referred to as through-composed.

tonality Observance of the key system as a basis of musical organization; or, the key system itself. ('Tonal music' is music based on keys.)

tonic The keynote. The other notes of the diatonic scale are, in ascending order: supertonic, mediant (a major third in the major, minor third in the minor), subdominant, *dominant* (the 'opposite pole' to the tonic in the tonal system), submediant and leading-note (having a marked tendency to rise to the tonic).

transition In *sonata form*, the passage which effects the modulation away from the tonic key to the second main key, in preparation for the *second subject*.

triad A three-note chord built by superimposing a third and fifth upon a 'root'. A triadic theme is one which expresses a triad in melodic form.

Select Bibliography

Source Collections

F. *Schuberts Werke: kritisch durchgesehene Gesamtausgabe* (Leipzig, 1884–97), 41 vols in 21 series. Reprinted in 19 vols (Dover, New York, 1965–9).

W. Dürr, A. Feil, C. Landon and others (eds), *F. Schubert: Neue Ausgabe sämtlicher Werke* (Bärenreiter, Kassel, 1968–). New revised edition of the complete works in eight series, in course of production.

Otto Erich Deutsch, *Schubert: Thematic Catalogue of all his works in chronological order* (London, 1951).

——, *Franz Schubert: Thematisches Verzeichnis seiner Werke in chronologischer Folge*. New, revised, and enlarged edition of the Thematic Catalogue in German issued as part of the *Neue Schubert Ausgabe* (Bärenreiter, Kassel, 1978).

——, *Schubert: A Documentary Biography*, trans. Eric Blom (London, 1946).

——, *Schubert: Die Dokumente seines Lebens*, revised and enlarged edition (Kassel, 1964).

—— (collected and ed.), *Schubert: Memoirs by his Friends*, trans. Rosamund Ley and John Nowell (London, 1958).

——, *Schubert: Die Erinnerungen seiner Freunde*, original German edition of the above (Leipzig, 1957).

Historical, Biographical, Iconographical

Gerald Abraham (ed.), *Schubert: A Symposium* (London, 1946).

Otto Biba, 'Schubert's Position in Viennese Musical Life', in *19th-Century Music*, III/2 (November 1979), pp. 106–13.

—— and Brian Newbould, 'Franz Schubert', in Michael Raeburn and Alan Kendall (eds), *Heritage of Music* (Oxford, 1989), pp. 75–93.

Maurice J. E. Brown, *Schubert: A Critical Biography* (London, 1958).

Alfred Einstein, *Schubert* (London, 1951).

Hans Gal, *The Golden Age of Vienna* (London/New York, 1948).

David Gramit, *Intellectual and Aesthetic Tenets of Franz Schubert's Circle*, Ph.D. dissertation (Duke University, 1987).

Alice M. Hanson, *Musical Life in Biedermeyer Vienna* (Cambridge, 1985).

Ernst Hilmar, *Franz Schubert in His Time*, trans. Reinhard G. Pauly (Portland, 1988).

—— and Otto Brusatti (eds), *Franz Schubert: Illustrated Catalogue of the 1978 Schubert Exhibition* (Vienna, 1978).

Heinrich Kreissle von Hellborn, *The Life of Franz Schubert*, trans. A. D. Coleridge, 2 vols (London, 1869).

D. Kerner, 'Franz Schubert', in *Krankheiten grosser Musiker* (Stuttgart, 1963).

Walpurga Litschauer, *Neue Dokumente zum Schubert-Kreis: Aus Briefen und Tagebuchern seiner Freunde* (Vienna, 1986).

——, 'Unbekanntes zur Schubert-Ikonographie: Ein Kurzkrimi', in *Schubert durch die Brille*, Mitteilungen 6 (January 1991), pp. 56–65.

Elizabeth Norman McKay, *Franz Schubert: A Biography* (Oxford, 1996).

Alfred Orel, *F. Schubert 1797–1828, sein Lebem in Bildern* (Leipzig, 1939).

Charles Osborne, *Schubert and his Vienna* (London, 1985).

John Reed, *Schubert* (London, 1987).

——, *Schubert: The Final Years* (London, 1972).

Eric Sams, 'Schubert's Illness Re-examined', in *The Musical Times*, cxxi/1643 (January 1980), pp. 15–22.

Maynard Solomon, 'Franz Schubert and the Peacocks of Benvenuto Cellini', in *19th-Century Music*, XII/3 (Spring 1989), pp. 193–206.

Rita Steblin, 'The Peacock's Tale: Schubert's Sexuality Reconsidered', in *19th-Century Music*, XVII/1 (Summer 1993), pp. 5–33.

Zuzana Vitalova, 'Schubert in Zseliz', in *Schubert durch die Brille*, Mitteilungen 8 (January 1992), pp. 93–102.

Repertoire, Genre and Style

Eva Badura-Skoda and Peter Branscombe (eds), *Schubert Studies: Problems of Style and Chronology* (Cambridge, 1982).

Eva Badura-Skoda, 'The Chronology of Schubert's Piano Trios', in *Schubert Studies: Problems of Style and Chronology* (Cambridge, 1982), pp. 277–95.

Alfred Brendel, 'Schubert's Piano Sonatas 1822–28', in *Musical Thoughts and Afterthoughts* (London, 1976), pp. 57–74.

Maurice J. E. Brown, *Essays on Schubert* (London/New York, 1966).

Richard Capell, *Schubert's Songs* (London, 1928).

Martin Chusid, 'A Suggested Redating for Schubert's Piano Sonata in E flat Op. 122', in Otto Brusatti (ed.), *Schubert-Kongress Wien 1978 Bericht*, pp. 37–44.

Walter Frisch (ed.), *Schubert: Critical and Analytical Studies* (Nebraska, 1986).

Hans Gal, *Franz Schubert and the Essence of Melody* (Frankfurt, 1970; trans. the author, London, 1974).

David Gramit, 'Schuberts "Bildender Umgang" ', in *Schubert durch die Brille*, Mitteilungen 8 (January 1992), pp. 5–21.

Ernst Hilmar (ed.), *Franz Schubert: Drei Symphonie-Fragmente* (Kassel, 1978).

Ernst Hilmar, *Verzeichnis der Schubert-Handschriften in der Musiksammlung der Wiener Stadt- und Landesbibliothek* (Catalogus Musicus VIII) (Kassel, 1978).

Reinhard Van Hoorickx, 'Textänderungen in Schuberts Messen', in Otto Brusatti (ed.), *Schubert-Kongress 1978 Bericht*, pp. 249–55.

Richard Kramer, *Distant Cycles* (Chicago, 1994).

Elizabeth Norman McKay, *Schubert's Music for the Theatre* (Tutzing, 1991).

Gerald Moore, *The Schubert Song Cycles* (London, 1975).

Brian Newbould, 'A Schubert Palindrome', in *19th-Century Music*, XV/3 (Spring 1992), pp. 207–14.

——, 'A Working Sketch by Schubert (D.936A)', in *Current Musicology*, No. 43 (1987), pp. 22–32.

——, *Franz Schubert: Symphony No. 10 in D major, D.936A*, realization by Brian Newbould (London, 1995).

——, *Schubert and the Symphony: A New Perspective* (London, 1992).

——, 'Schubert's Last Symphony', in *The Musical Times*, cxxvi/1707 (May 1985), pp. 272–5.

——, 'Schubert's Other Unfinished', in *The Musical Times*, cxix/1625 (July 1978), pp. 587–9.

E. G. Porter, *Schubert's Song Technique* (London, 1961).

Philip Radcliffe, *Schubert Piano Sonatas* (London, 1967), p. 44.

John Reed, 'How the "Great" C major was written', in *Music & Letters*, Vol. LVI (January 1975), pp. 18–25.

——, *The Schubert Song Companion* (Manchester, 1985).

David P. Schroeder, 'Schubert the Singer', in *The Music Review*, Vol. 49 (1988), pp. 254–66.

Dallas Weekley and Nancy Arganbright, *Schubert's Music for Piano Four-hands* (New York, 1990).

James Webster, 'Schubert's Sonata Form and Brahms's First Maturity', in *19th-Century Music*, II/1 (July 1978), pp. 18–35, and III/1 (July 1979), pp. 52–71.

Ewan West, *Schubert's Lieder in Context: Aspects of Song Composition in Vienna, 1778–1828* (Ph.D. dissertation, University of Oxford, 1989).

Jack Westrup, *Schubert Chamber Music* (BBC Music Guide, London, 1969).

Richard Wigmore (trans.), *Schubert: The Complete Song Texts* (London, 1988).

Index of Works

The principal references are indicated in bold type.

Orchestral and Instrumental (including stage works)

Church and Choral

Solo songs

General Index